Dear Student:

You have chosen to begin a career as a business p
discipline. If your experience is anything like mine, you will
Working in business leads to fulfilling and enjoyable experiences and relations.
with interesting, quality people. Working in a company you admire that sells products
or services in which you believe will enable you to feel positive about yourself, your
contributions, and your professional life.

The overall purpose of this book is to help you prepare for success in your business
career. In writing the book, I kept in mind three goals:

- To explain how you can use information systems to solve problems
  and make better decisions in business
- To show you how to improve your problem solving skills
- To describe, in the context of management information systems
  (MIS), how you can become a better business professional

Notice the emphasis is on *you*. It's up to you to prepare yourself. No particular book, no
course, no professor, no TA can do it for you. However, many people have worked hard
to structure this book so that you can maximize the benefit from your study time.

To help you achieve your goals, we have included boxed inserts, which we call ***Guides***.
Perhaps you've formed the habit of ignoring such boxes in texts. Do not ignore them
here; in many ways they contain the most important material for your future success. If
possible, discuss the questions in these guides with other students. Such discussions
will give you a chance to practice your listening skills and to learn to assert your own
opinions in an effective manner.

Like all worthwhile endeavors, this course is work. That's just the way it is. No one
succeeds in business without sustained focus, attention, desire, motivation, and hard
work. It won't always be easy, it won't always be fun. On the other hand, you will learn
concepts, skills, and behaviors that will serve you well throughout your business career.

I wish you, as an emerging business professional, the very best success!

Sincerely,

David Kroenke

Seattle, Washington

THE GUIDES

Each chapter includes five *unique* guides that focus on current issues in information systems. In business, you'll deal with similar issues, and you may be asked to recommend solutions to these problems. The content of each guide is designed to stimulate thought, discussion, and active participation to help YOU develop your problem solving skills and become a better business professional.

A description for each category of guide is provided below, along with a page reference for its location in the chapter.

ETHICS GUIDES

Ethical issues abound in business. As recent news stories indicate, some businesspeople are better than others at sorting through ethical conflicts. The **Ethics Guides** stimulate debate on how ethics apply to information systems issues. These guides will help you respond to future ethical dilemmas authentically and in a way that is consistent with your own values.

SECURITY GUIDES

We live in an information age, and securing information is critical for businesses. The **Security Guides** highlight appropriate security skills and behaviors to protect valuable assets, both yours and those of your company.

ProblemSolving
GUIDES

Improving the quality of your thinking will improve any information system that you use, and your ability to use MIS in your career. The **Problem Solving Guides** present ideas from cognitive science and apply them to MIS. Not only will you learn to use technology more wisely to attain your business goals, you'll learn methods of how to better analyze and solve many other problems that life throws at you.

OpposingForces
GUIDES

In almost any situation, you will find one or more people with opinions contrary to the generally accepted wisdom. The **Opposing Forces Guides** introduce you to someone who disagrees with one of the main ideas or methods in the chapter. (All of the people whose opinions are included in these guides actually exist.) More likely than not, you will encounter one or more such "contrarians" during your career. These guides help you learn to manage their opinions and respond effectively.

Reflections
GUIDES

In business, people will differ in their opinions and then "agree to disagree," meaning they will back off, reflect, and sometimes alter their viewpoints. In the **Reflections Guides**, I state some strong personal opinions. Every editorial expresses a justifiable opinion, but you should approach them with skepticism and a critical eye. Your task in reading them will be to respond to these opinions and discuss their merit.

LEARNING AIDS FOR STUDENTS

We have structured this book so you can maximize the benefit from the time you spend reading it. As shown in the table below, each chapter includes a series of learning aids to help you succeed in this course.

RESOURCE	DESCRIPTION	BENEFIT	EXAMPLE
Guides	Each chapter includes five guides that focus on current issues in information systems.	Stimulates thought and discussion. Helps develop your problem solving skills.	Pages 33a, 205a, 215a, 251a, and 325a. Also, see pages ii-iii for a list of all guides.
Chapter Opening and Closing Scenarios	Each chapter (except for Chapter 1) opens with a compelling business problem employees may encounter on the job. At the end of the chapter we revisit the same scenario and offer solutions or responses.	Shows you how to apply knowledge gained from the chapter to solve real business problems.	"Is $80,000 Enough?" pp. 47, 64
MIS in Use Cases	Each chapter includes two *MIS in Use* case studies. These cases describe how experiences of current companies relate to the chapter. In some chapters, an MIS in Use case continues in a Case Study in the homework material.	Provides you with an inside look at real companies in action and how they are embracing information technology.	MIS in Use 5-1, p. 127
Application Exercises	These exercises ask you to solve situations using spreadsheet (Excel) or database (Access) applications.	Helps develop your computer skills.	Question 21, p. 222
Career Assignments	These exercises require you to do online research for information about career opportunities. You will analyze what knowledge you need and what real-world experiences (such as internships) might be beneficial.	Provides strategies and tactics for finding the right job, for YOU!	Questions 30–32, pp. 40, 41
Case Studies	Two case studies close each chapter. You will reflect on the use in real organizations of the technology or systems presented in the chapter, and recommend solutions to business problems.	Requires you to apply newly acquired knowledge to real situations.	Case Study 8-1, Getty Images, pp. 258, 259

RESOURCE	DESCRIPTION	BENEFIT	EXAMPLE
Summary	Each chapter concludes with a summary section to reinforce key ideas in the chapter.	Offers a quick review of important points in what you have just read.	p. 220
Key Terms List	Highlights the major terms and concepts with their appropriate page reference.	Provides a summary of key terms for review before exams.	p. 104
Review Questions	These questions ask you to recall definitions and reason from the chapter discussions.	Tests your understanding of the concepts presented in the chapter.	p. 298
Applying Your Knowledge	These exercises ask you to take your new knowledge one step further and apply it to a practice problem.	Tests your critical thinking skills.	Question 31, p. 184
Glossary	At the end of the text, a comprehensive list includes definitions of the key terms.	Provides one place for your quick review.	p. 369
Companion Web site	Includes Self-Study Quizzes for each chapter, plus PowerPoint presentations and a Glossary. You will receive automatic feedback upon submitting each quiz.	Helps you cement your understanding of the material in the text.	www.prenhall.com/kroenke
Student CD	To bring concepts to life, the optional Student CD includes video clips of the author sharing strategies for how to tackle the chapter material, answering questions about difficult concepts, and providing key tips to help you with your studies. An icon in the margin of the book indicates related video clips.	Relates chapter material and helps you develop better study skills.	Check with your instructor.

Using MIS

Using MIS

David M. Kroenke

University of Washington

PEARSON
Prentice
Hall

Upper Saddle River, New Jersey

Library of Congress Cataloging-in-Publication Data

Kroenke, David.
    Using MIS / David M. Kroenke.
        p. cm.
    Includes index.
    ISBN 0-13-143372-5
    1. Management information systems.   I. Title.

    HD30.213.K76 2007
    658.4′038011--dc22   2005054966

Executive Editor: Bob Horan
Editorial Director: Jeff Shelstad
Director, Market Development: Annie Todd
Market Development Manager: Kathleen McLellan
Developmental Editor: Ann Torbert
Director of Development: Steve Deitmer
Editorial Assistant: Ana Cordero
Media Product Development Manager: Nancy Welcher
Executive Marketing Manager: Debbie Clare
Marketing Assistant: Joanna Sabella
Associate Director, Production Editorial: Judy Leale
Production Editor: Michael Reynolds
Permissions Supervisor: Charles Morris
Manufacturing Buyer: Michelle Klein
Creative Director: Maria Lange
Art Director: Pat Smythe
Interior Design: Judy Allan and Liz Kril
Cover Design: Anthony Gemmellaro
Cover Illustration: Amanda Duffy
Illustrator (Interior): Amanda Duffy
Line Art: Techbooks/GTS
Director, Image Resource Center: Melinda Reo
Manager, Rights and Permissions: Zina Arabia
Manager, Visual Research: Beth Brenzel
Manager, Cover Visual Research & Permissions: Karen Sanatar
Image Permission Coordinator: Richard Rodrigues
Photo Researcher: Rachel Lucas
Manager, Print Production: Christy Mahon
Formatter: Suzanne Duda
Composition/Full-Service Project Management: Bookmasters
Printer/Binder: Quebecor
Cover Printer: Phoenix Color
Typeface: 10/12 Utopia

Credits and acknowledgments borrowed from other sources and reproduced, with permission, in this textbook appear on appropriate page within text.

Pearson Education LTD.
Pearson Education Singapore, Pte. Ltd
Pearson Education, Canada, Ltd
Pearson Education–Japan

Pearson Education Australia PTY, Limited
Pearson Education North Asia Ltd
Pearson Educación de Mexico, S.A. de C.V.
Pearson Education Malaysia, Pte. Ltd

10 9 8 7 6 5 4 3 2 1
ISBN 0131433733

*Dedicated to my students over many years,
with whom I've woven the fabric for this book*

Brief Contents

Defines MIS, describes how MIS relates to students as future business professionals, and explains what students should learn in the course.

Describes reasons why organizations create and use information systems: to gain competitive advantage, solve problems, and support decisions.

Focus on key components of IT.

Discusses IS within organizations, including functional and cross-functional systems.

Discusses IS among organizations.

Describes business intelligence and knowledge management, including reporting systems, data mining, and knowledge management systems.

Describes the role, structure, and function of the IS department; the role of the CIO and CTO; outsourcing; and related topics.

Describes organizational response to information security: security threats, policy, and safeguards.

Contents

The MIS class can be tough to teach. The course tends to be five miles wide and one inch deep; I just get to the meat of one topic and it's time to rush to the next one. The course can seem like "death by coverage," as one of my colleagues says.

At the same time, the students are so varied in their hopes and expectations for the class, and their experiences are so different, I feel I teach in a one-room school-house. At the University of Washington, we sometimes teach the class to 125 students in a large lecture hall, twice per week in sessions about 1.5 hours long. At least a third of the class is foreign students, many with weak English skills, and most with a cultural heritage that says they should be respectful, which means silent. Getting some of those students to speak up, let alone engage in debate, is a challenge.

Yet the class can be a pure joy to teach: There are so many opportunities to impart important skills like problem solving and critical thinking, and many opportunities to discuss ethics, all in the context of the core MIS topics. I find the students are willing to work, sometimes work hard, if they see the relevance of what they're doing. Accordingly, over the years, I've added more and more problems and small-group exercises to my classes. These experiences have improved my classes and, I believe, have also added more to students' long-term memory of the course. As described in the next section, the hallmark feature of this book is the boxed "Guides" in every chapter, which are the problem and small-group exercises I use in class. I hope that they will add interest and excitement to your classroom.

One more macro point before I describe the guides in more detail: If this class ever had a reason to be a glossary of MIS concepts, Google, *www.whatis.com*, and other sites have taken away that reason. Students can readily find definitions on their own, allowing us to show how they can apply those terms for organizational benefit.

Therefore, rather than seeking to be a glossary of terms, this book aims to teach students *how to use* the principles they learn in this class. Throughout the book, we maintain a focus on how students will *use* MIS in their business careers. Indeed, many of the concepts presented in the book will turn out to apply not just to careers, but to lives as well.

This book is full of practical applications and stories of people I have met and experiences I have had with them. The stories here are real, though sometimes I have changed names and industries, and sometimes I have omitted major sections of the story for brevity or to suit the pedagogical goal at hand. Whether you enjoy the stories and scenarios, agree, disagree, endorse, or reject them, I hope they will help you teach your classes the way you want and will help make this subject enjoyable to teach.

Chapter Content and Boxed Guides

Each chapter presents core material for the topic, and that core is surrounded by five essays and related questions, presented as boxed inserts titled "Guides." These inserts are intended to force the students to grapple with the core material, to think about its relevance to them and their future needs, and to discuss that material in small groups or as a class.

The same five guides appear in every chapter. They are:
- Security Guide
- Ethics Guide

■ Problem Solving Guide
■ Opposing Forces Guide
■ Reflections Guide

Descriptions, purposes, and listing of the five types of guides appear in the first few pages inside the front cover. (See also "Introduction to the Teaching Guidelines," on page xxxii, for further discussion about how I use each type of guide in class.)

Some people have asked why I have chosen to include ethics and security material in every chapter, rather than place each of these topics in its own chapter. There are two reasons: One, there is something to say about security and about ethics for the core material of every chapter. Two, by including those topics in every chapter, we discuss these very important topics *every week*. Note, by the way, that there is a separate chapter (Chapter 11) that also addresses security, but it does so from an organizational managerial perspective.

Each guide ends with a handful of discussion questions. I use these questions in class in two ways: one planned, and one in desperation. In the planned situation, I use them to reinforced a lecture point. For example, when discussing Chapter 7, I describe the interdependencies of departments when using integrated IS, but I'm not sure the students know what I mean. To drive the point home, I ask them to read the ethics guide (page 205a) in class and to answer the questions. This activity not only lets me address business ethics, but it also illustrates firsthand the dynamics of integrated IS.

For the desperate situation, I use the discussion questions in class when I'm unable to connect with the class. Maybe I'm tired, or maybe my students spent all night cramming for an exam in finance, but what I want to happen is simply not happening. Rather than drone on, *covering* the material, I stop and use a guide to get things going. (The Opposing Forces Guides often work well for this purpose.) With that boost, I can then go back to where I was.

Guideline answers for the guides' discussion questions are included in the Teaching Guidelines in the Annotated Instructor's Edition and also in the Supplementary Materials for Instructors section of the text's Web site. For more on the Teaching Guidelines, see the description on page xxxii of this preface.

■ The Core Material and the Book's Organization

I believe there is consensus on the basic topics that belong in this class, and the book's outline reflects that consensus.

Part One introduces MIS, sets basic definitions, and explains the rationale for MIS. Chapter 1 defines MIS and describes how MIS relates to students as future business professionals. Chapter 2 describes the fundamental reasons that organizations create and use MIS applications.

Parts Two and Three distinguish between information technology and information systems. Part Two addresses key components of IT: hardware and software (Chapter 3), database processing (Chapter 4), data communications and Internet technology (Chapter 5), and systems development (Chapter 6).

Part Three discusses IS. Chapter 7 considers IS *within* organizations, and Chapter 8 looks at IS *among* organizations, specifically e-commerce and supply chain systems. Chapter 9 describes business intelligence and knowledge management systems including reporting and data mining systems and data warehouses and data marts.

Finally, Part Four addresses management of IS resources. Chapter 10 presents the essential ideas and concepts for IS management, and Chapter 11 concludes the book with a description of the organizational response to information security.

Other Features

The guides described above form a critical part of the book. In addition, various other features are in place to help guide student learning. See the grid titled "Learning Aids for Students" in the first few pages after the front cover for a list of these features and their benefits to student learning.

Supplements

For Students

The book's **Companion Web site** (*www.prenhall.com/kroenke*) offers various materials to help students cement their understanding of the material in the text. The Companion Web site includes Self-Study Quizzes for each chapter, plus PowerPoint presentations and a Glossary. Self-Study Quizzes include multiple-choice, true/false, and essay questions, plus hints for students. Students receive automatic feedback upon submitting each quiz.

In addition, the Student CD in each book includes video clips of the author sharing strategies for how to tackle the chapter material, answering questions about difficult concepts, and providing key tips. Icons in the page margins indicate related video clips.

For Instructors

The following supplements are available to ease and improve your experience teaching the course:

- **Instructor's Resource Center Online and CD-ROM.** Both the online resource center (accessible through *www.prenhall.com/kroenke*) and CD-ROM include all the supplements: Instructor's Manual, Test Item File, TestGen, TestGen conversions in WebCT and Blackboard-ready files, PowerPoint Presentations, and Image Library (text art). Through either medium, you have easy access to the entire supplement package.

- **Instructor's Manual.** Prepared by Roberta Roth of the University of Northern Iowa, the manual includes answers to all review and discussion questions, exercises, and case questions, plus teaching tips and lecture notes. It is a convenient source of answers as well as material to enhance lectures and classroom teaching.

- **Test Item File, TestGen, and TestGen Conversions.** Prepared by William Wagner of Villanova University, the test items include a large selection of true/false, fill-in, multiple-choice, and essay questions for each chapter. The test file is a convenient source of questions for class quizzes and exams, delivered in MS Word as well as in the form of TestGen and the TestGen conversions for WebCT, Blackboard, and Course Compass.

- **PowerPoint Presentations.** Prepared by Lou Thompson of the University of Texas at Dallas, the PowerPoints highlight text learning objectives and key topics. An excellent aid for classroom presentations and lectures, they are also available on the Web at *www.prenhall.com/kroenke*.

- **Image Library.** This collection of the figures and tables from the text offers another aid for classroom presentations and PowerPoint slides.

- **OneKey Online Courses.** Available in WebCT, Blackboard, and CourseCompass formats. Because all instructor resources are in one place to maximize effectiveness and minimize time and effort, OneKey is all that you need to plan and administer the course. OneKey is also all that students need for anywhere-anytime access to your course materials conveniently organized by text chapter.

- **OneKey: WebCT (www.prenhall.com/webct).** Gold Level customer support, available exclusively to adopters of Prentice Hall courses. An excellent course management tool provided free of charge on adoption; provides priority assistance, training discounts, and dedicated technical support.
- **OneKey: Blackboard (www.prenhall.com/blackboard).** Abundant online content, combined with Blackboard's popular tools and interface. Robust Web-based courses are easy to implement, manage, and use, promoting student interaction and learning.
- **OneKey: CourseCompass (www.prenhall.com/coursecompass).** A dynamic, interactive online course management tool powered exclusively for Pearson Education by Blackboard. It enables you to teach market-leading Pearson Education content in an easy-to-use customizable format.

■ **Prentice Hall MIS Videos, Volumes I and II.** The PH MIS videos can be used to enhance class discussion and projects. *Volume I* includes custom clips created exclusively for Prentice Hall featuring real companies. *Volume II* clips highlight real-world organizations and illustrate key concepts found in the text.

■ **Using MIS Tutorial Videos.** These videos feature author David Kroenke giving chapter overviews and motivational insights for understanding key topics. They provide an out-of-class supplement to instructor lectures as well as a visual study tool.

■ Acknowledgments

First, I wish to acknowledge and thank the many instructors from colleges and universities around the country who contributed their time, energy, and thought to helping us develop and craft this book. I am grateful for the efforts of all those whose names are listed on pages xxx and xxxi.

In addition, Professor Ray Panko of the University of Hawaii graciously reviewed at least 10 versions of Chapter 5, maybe even 15, and was incredibly patient with the slow pace of growth in my knowledge of data communications technology. Whatever merit that chapter has is due to Ray's unflagging willingness to say, "Well, almost, but . . . " Ray is truly a gentleman and scholar. I also thank David Auer of Western Washington University for his patient assistance with that same chapter.

Rich Mathieu of James Madison University provided insights and helpful commentary on the nature and needs of the MIS class, from the earliest stages of this book. At the University of Washington, I'm thankful to Doug MacLachlan for his assistance with the data mining portions of Chapter 9, and also Mark McKay, who is now at Trinity Western University, for his assistance with the supply chain management section of Chapter 8. Don Nilson at the Microsoft Corporation helped me with XML Web services in Chapter 8, and Don Gray, independent consultant, provided insight into the realities of offshore outsourcing for Chapter 10. Thanks especially to my friend and colleague of many years, Chuck Yoos, of Fort Lewis College, for many interesting thoughts, perspectives, and extended email conversations on the Problem Solving and Ethics Guides.

I'm grateful for insights given me by my MIS-teaching teammates Jim Smith, Russ Fish, Eileen Sikkema, Anjana Susarla, and Al Maimon. Jim, Russ, and I are still apologizing for the noise and fun we had when once we shared an office. Of course, I would never have had the opportunity to teach the MIS class without the support of my departmental chairmen, Bruce Faaland and Deb Dey.

What a pleasure it has been to work with Bob Horan, acquisitions editor at Prentice Hall. Bob has the rare ability to inspire, encourage, guide, motivate, and, when necessary, put the project back on track, all simultaneously and graciously. Without Bob's enthusiastic support, I would never have finished this project—nor wanted to.

Prentice Hall has given me unparalleled support in the form of the numerous talented people it brought to the book. Thanks to Theresa O'Dell for managing the review process and for organizing dozens of review responses for easy use and ready understanding. I thank Ann Torbert, development editor, for her patience and wisdom helping me to interpret and respond to reviewers' comments and also for shaping this book into its final form. Ann is an untiring professional, in every best sense of those words. Thanks as well to Pat Smythe and Maria Lange for the book's design and wonderful art, especially the art that supports the guides. Thanks, too, to Mike Reynolds, production editor, who kept the process organized and moving along, no small task with so many hands in such a complicated pie. Thanks to Charles Morris for his unflagging patience in unraveling and tracking down permissions requests. Thanks to Sharon Anderson at BookMasters, who guided the book production.

Thanks also to Deb Clare, who so enthusiastically helped me to understand the needs and requirements for communicating the features of this book to faculty and students, everywhere. I am also grateful to Jeff Shelstad, Business Publishing editorial director, for his active involvement and support of this project.

Finally, I thank my wife, Lynda, for her love, support, and understanding through the trials and tribulations of this, my longest book project ever.

David Kroenke
Seattle, Washington

■ Thanks to Our Reviewers

The following people deserve special recognition for their careful reading, thoughtful and insightful comments, sensitive criticism, and for their willingness to follow up with email conversations, many lengthy, when necessary.

Hans-Joachim Adler, *University of Texas, Dallas*

Michael Bartolacci, *Penn State Lehigh Valley*

Ozden Bayazit, *Central Washington University*

Jack Becker, *University of North Texas*

James Borden, *Villanova University*

Siew Chan, *University of Massachusetts, Boston*

Andrea Chandler, *independent consultant*

Jimmy Clark, *Austin Community College*

Tricia Clark, *Penn State University, Capital Campus*

Stephen Crandell, *Myers University*

Mel Damodaran, *University of Houston, Victoria*

Carol DesJardins, *St. Claire Community College*

Chuck Downing, *University of Northern Illinois*

Patrick Fan, *Virginia Polytechnic Institute and State University*

Jonathan Frank, *Suffolk University*

Linda Fried, *University of Colorado, Denver*

William H. Friedman, *University of Central Arkansas*

Donald Gray, *independent consultant*

George Griffin, *Regis University*

Randy Guthrie, *California Polytechnic State University, Pomona*

Richard Herschel, *St. Joseph's University*

Richard Holowczak, *Baruch College*

Walter Horn, *Webster University*

Dennis Howard, *University of Alaska, Anchorage*

Mark Hwang, *Central Michigan University*

Brian Kovar, *Kansas State University*

Yvonne Lederer-Antonucci, *Widener University*

Diane Lending, *James Madison University*

David Lewis, *University of Massachusetts, Lowell*

Purnendu Mandal, *Marshall University*

Richard Mathieu, *James Madison University*

Sathasivam Mathiyalakan, *University of Massachusetts, Boston*

Patricia McQuaid, *California Polytechnic State University, San Luis Obispo*

Adriene Nawrocki, *John F. Kennedy University*

Margaret O'Hara, *East Carolina University*

Richard Peschke, *Minnesota State University, Mankato*

Eric Santanen, *Bucknell University*

David Scanlan, *California State University, Sacramento*

Ken Sears, *University of Texas, Arlington*

Tom Seymour, *Minot State University*

Geanesan Shankar, *Boston University*

Glenn Smith, *James Madison University*

Stephen Solosky, *Nassau Community College*

Howard Sparks, *University of Alaska, Fairbanks*

Arta Szathmary, *Bucks County Community College*

Robert Szymanski, *University of Central Florida*

Asela Thomason, *California State University, Long Beach*

Lou Thompson, *University of Texas, Dallas*

Anthony Townsend, *Iowa State University*

Goran Trajkovski, *Towson University*

Betty Tucker, *Weber State University*

Therese Viscelli, *Georgia State University*

Don Yates, *Louisiana State University*

Thanks, too, to the following reviewers whose reviews of chapters helped us understand the needs of the market and whose ideas helped shape the direction of the project and its message.

Dennis Adams, *University of Houston, Main*

Mark Alexander, *Indiana Wesleyan University*

Cynthia Barnes, *Lamar University*

Jack Becker, *University of North Texas*

Paula Bell, *Lock Haven University*

Doug Bickerstaff, *Eastern Washington University*

Hossein Bidgoli, *California State University, Bakersfield*

Mari Buche, *Michigan Technological University*

Jeff Corcoran, *Lasell College*

Michael Cummins, *Georgia Institute of Technology*

Charles Davis, *University of St. Thomas*

Roy Dejoie, *Purdue University*

Dawna Dewire, *Babson College*

Michael Doherty, *Marian College of Fond du Lac*

Mike Doherty, *University of Wyoming*

Charlene Dykman, *University of St. Thomas*

William Eddins, *York College*

Lauren Eder, *Rider University*

Badie Farah, *Eastern Michigan University*

Bryan Foltz, *East Carolina University*

Sharyn Gallagher, *University of Massachusetts, Lowell*

Randy Guthrie, *Cal Poly, Pomona*

Bogdan Hoanca, *University of Alaska, Anchorage*

James Hu, *Santa Clara University*

Adam Huarng, *California State University, Los Angeles*

Brent Hussin, *University of Wisconsin*

James Isaak, *Southern New Hampshire University*

Wade Jackson, *University of Memphis*

Chuck Johnston, *Midwestern State University*

Iris Junglas, *University of Houston, Main*

Andreas Knoefels, *Santa Clara University*

Brian Kovar, *Kansas State University*

Subodha Kumar, *University of Washington*

Keith Lindsey, *Trinity University*

Stephen Loy, *Eastern Kentucky University*

Steven Lunce, *Midwestern State University*

Ron McFarland, *Western New Mexico University*

Irina Neuman, *McKendree College*

Ravi Paul, *East Carolina University*

Leonard Presby, *William Paterson University of New Jersey*

Harry Reif, *James Madison University*

Ramesh Sankanarayanan, *University of Connecticut*

Charles Saxon, *Eastern Michigan University*

Atul Saxena, *Mercer University*

Sherri Shade, *Kennesaw State University*

David Smith, *Cameron University*

George Strouse, *York College*

Albert Tay, *Idaho State University*

Kim Troboy, *Arkansas Technical University*

Jonathan Trower, *Baylor University*

William Tucker, *Austin Community College*

David VanOver, *Sam Houston State University*

Linda Volonino, *Canisius University*

William Wagner, *Villanova University*

Rick Weible, *Marshall University*

Elaine Winston, *Hofstra University*

Joe Wood, *Webster University*

Michael Workman, *Florida State University*

Kathie Wright, *Salisbury University*

James Yao, *Montclair State University*

The textbook you have in your hands is an annotated instructor's version of *Using MIS*. It differs from the student version in that it contains teaching guidelines for elements of the text. Specifically, it provides teaching guidelines for the introductory and closing scenarios and for each of the five guides in the chapter (Ethics, Problem Solving, Security, Opposing Forces, and Reflections).

For every chapter, each set of teaching guidelines, titled "You Be The Guide," contains the following:

- Goals of the scenario or guide
- Background and presentation strategies
- Ways to stimulate student involvement with the scenarios and ideas for responding to the challenge set in the scenario
- Suggested responses to the discussion questions in each guide and suggestions for using the discussion questions
- A wrap-up

The material in this instructor's edition is fodder for the class, to be used in any way you see fit. You may decide to use the annotations as-is, or you might marry them with your own stories, or adapt them to companies in your local area, or use them as examples with which you disagree. Or, if this material doesn't fit your teaching style, just throw it out. The text was designed to work without any of it.

I wrote these annotations in the hope that they might save you time, facilitate the students' learning, and possibly make the class more fun to teach. If you see ways to make the annotations better, please drop me an email either at *DavidKroenke@gmail.com* or via the blog *teachingmis.com* (more below).

How to Use the Scenarios

In my classes, I use the chapter-opening scenarios to get the students involved. I want them to mentally place themselves in the situation of a new manager or other junior business professional and to ask themselves, "What would I do if that happened to me?" The scenario on the $80,000 question in Chapter 3 (page 47) provides a typical example.

In the first lecture, I ask my students to email me their goals for the course. I'll often get responses like "get the highest grade possible." I send such responses back as unacceptable and again ask, "What do you, as a future businessperson, want to know about information systems? How will you use them in your career? How will you use them to facilitate your success?"

I remind students they've chosen to become business students, which must mean that they want to become business professionals. I tell them that I believe that is a laudable goal, and I will help them all I can. I will be their coach, their mentor, their facilitator. The point of each opening scenario is to reinforce the idea that as they become business professionals, they will be asked to work with information systems. I tell them to note the title of the book: ***Using*** MIS.

The scenarios set up the chapter's material. For example, Chapter 9, which examines business intelligence (BI) systems, describes the owner of a small business who has lost a customer and doesn't know it. The owner can use a business intelligence technique (RFM analysis) to learn about lost customers, but the students don't know that at the beginning. So, I ask them as they read the material to think about the owner's problem as they learn about each type of BI system and to ask themselves if systems of that type can solve the problem.

If the students are sincere about becoming business professionals, it's hard for them to justify, within themselves, not reading or studying the material. The chapter-opening scenario provides an obvious example of why the material is relevant. If the students don't read or get involved, they will have internal conflict: "If I want to be a business professional, I should know this. If I'm not reading this, then, well what? Am I insincere about being a businessperson? Lazy? What?"

These internal queries are, in my experience, the very best motivators. It's no longer me telling them, like an angry parent, that they should study the material. Rather, it's me putting evidence before them that if they are sincere about being business professionals, they should get involved and learn the material. Pedagogically, I use these scenarios to move the responsibility for learning the material from *me* to the *student*. The conflict is no longer between me and the students, but is instead within the students' own minds.

Later in the chapter (usually at the end), we return to the situation set up in the opening scenario. As the book progresses, I attempt to give less hand-holding to these solutions, letting students take on increasing responsibility for finding solutions to the scenarios. By the time students get to Chapter 10, most of the work of addressing the scenario is up to them.

With one exception, every chapter has a different scenario. The exception is that the scenario in Chapter 7 carries over into Chapter 8. This was done because the material in Chapter 7 was insufficient to solve the problem.

How to Use the Guides

The guides are fun. I use them primarily in class as group exercises. I try to break up my lecture and, in an 80-minute period, usually use two and sometimes three of them. I ask the students to work in groups of three, and I ask them to work with different people each time. Often I have them pick their group number out of a hat, before class starts.

For each group exercise, I ask the students to introduce themselves to one another, to review (or read) the guide, and then to answer the questions. This annotated edition contains specific ideas for using each guide, bound just after the guide to which it refers.

A few brief comments about the use of each type of guide:

Ethics Guides: These describe ethical dilemmas regarding the use of IS. They normally produce an active discussion, and students have lots of opinions. There normally is no single answer, unless the behaviors described are illegal. I recommend sometimes having two (or more) groups of students debate one another.

Security Guides: These tend to be a bit more cut-and-dried than the other guides. Each Security Guide presents security in the context of the chapter's content. Chapter 11, however, considers security broadly, from the standpoint of the organization and its response. I like to bring up security in every chapter because it's so important—if I leave it to one chapter, it is too easily dismissed. Sometimes I assign these guides as homework.

Problem Solving Guides: Chapter 1 defines the five components of information systems as hardware, software, data, procedures, and people, and stresses the people component. Because people are a component, we can tell students, "You are an important, maybe the *most important* component, of every information system you use. Hence, improving the quality of your thinking improves the quality of your information systems." Accordingly, each of these guides addresses some way in which students can improve their problem-solving and critical-thinking skills. See the Problem Solving Guide in Chapter 1 for more information. I suggest using these guides both in-class and for homework.

Opposing Forces Guides: These present views that oppose some part of the chapter's contents. Their purpose is to motivate the students' thinking and to foster classroom discussion. These guides work best as in-class exercises, I think, because the small group discussion provides a chance for the students to share their own opposing views.

Reflection Guides: These are basically editorials. In them, I reflect on future directions, consequences, and what I think the trends of the chapter might mean for students. Although I believe the statements I make in these editorials, they by no means reflect a consensus opinion in our industry. Students will benefit, I think, if it turns out that you disagree.

TeachingMIS.com

Nearly 2,000 people teach this class in the United States alone, and yet we seldom have a chance to talk with one another and compare notes. I've set up a blog, at *www.teachingMIS.com*, which is intended to help reduce this sense of isolation. It addresses contemporary issues for teaching the MIS class. The goal with the blog is to provide a place where our community of MIS teachers can openly discuss challenges and opportunities for teaching this class. You can leave comments at the blog, send an email to *Ideas@TeachingMIS.com*, or email me there at *Kroenke@TeachingMIS.com*.

Notation

The teaching guidelines have two types of information: information for you, and also information for you to give to your students. Thus, we needed to introduce some notation to separate one category from the other. Comments and questions *for you to address to students* are typeset in boldface tye and appear as follows:

➤ **What are some of the major limitations of data mining?**

➤ **If you are interested in learning more about these techniques and maybe specializing in one of them, you should take the department's database processing class. Drop me an email if you want to know more.**

Because these statements are intended for the instructor's use, the *me* in the above statement refers to you, the professor (and not me, the author).

General statements and conceptual points from me, as author, *addressed to you*, the instructor, are set in regular type, as follows:

I like to start the class even before the class begins. I arrive around 5 minutes early and talk with the students. I ask the students their names, where they are from, what their majors are, what they know about computers, and so on, as a way of breaking the ice.

I hope at least some of this will be useful to you. Have fun!

David Kroenke

PART I

Introduction to MIS

We begin this text with two introductory chapters. Chapter 1 defines MIS and describes how MIS relates to your future career as a business professional. Chapter 2 then describes the fundamental reasons that organizations create and use MIS applications.

Before proceeding, reflect on the title of this text: *Using MIS*. Our goal is to help you learn to *use* information systems to accomplish your personal goals as a business professional and to accomplish the goals of the organizations in which you work. As you read, keep in mind that it is not enough just to learn the meanings of the terms presented in this text; you also need to learn how to successfully apply them to situations that will arise in your professional career.

MIS and You

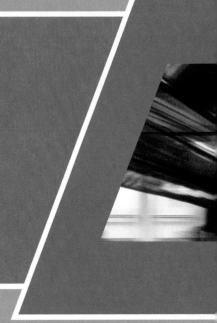

Learning Objectives

* Know how MIS is defined.
* Understand the goals of this class.
* Recognize the utility of the five-component framework.
* Know the characteristics of information.
* Understand the relationship between information technology (IT) and information systems (IS).
* Prepare to enjoy (yes!) this class.

Guides

SECURITY GUIDE
Passwords and Password Etiquette

PROBLEM SOLVING GUIDE
Understanding Perspectives
and Points of View

ETHICS GUIDE
Ethics of Misdirected Information Use

OPPOSING FORCES GUIDE
"I Don't Need This Class"

REFLECTIONS GUIDE
Duller Than Dirt?

Chapter Preview

If you are like most students, you have no clear idea of what your MIS class will be about. If someone were to ask you, "What do you study in that class?" you might respond that the class has something to do with computers and maybe computer programming. Beyond that, you might be hard-pressed to say more. You might add, "Well, it has something to do with computers in business," or maybe, "We are going to learn to solve business problems with computers using spreadsheets and programs like that."

None of these answers is more than partially correct. So, a good place for us to begin this course—and this book—is to answer the following two questions: What is MIS? And what should you expect to learn in this class?

What Is MIS?

MIS stands for **management information systems**, which we define as *the development and use of information systems that help businesses achieve their goals and objectives*. This definition has three key elements: *development and use, information systems*, and *business goals and objectives*. Let's consider each, starting first with information systems and their components.

Components of an Information System

A **system** is a group of components that interact to achieve some purpose. As you might guess, an **information system (IS)** is a group of components that interact to produce information. That sentence, although true, raises another question: What are these components that interact to produce information?

Figure 1-1 shows the **five component framework**—the five fundamental components of an information system: **computer hardware**, **software**,[1] **data**, **procedures**, and **people**. These five components are present in every information system, from the simplest to the most complex. For example, when you use a computer to write a class report, you are using hardware (the computer, storage disk, keyboard, and monitor), software (Word, WordPerfect, or some other word-processing program), data (the words, sentences, and paragraphs in your report), procedures (the methods you use to start the program, enter your report, print it, and save and back up your file), and people (you).

Consider a more complex example, say an airline reservation system. It, too, consists of these five components, even though each one is far more complicated. The hardware consists of dozens or more computers linked together by telecommunications hardware. Further, hundreds of different programs coordinate communications among the computers, and still other programs perform the reservations and related services. Additionally, the system must store millions upon millions of characters of data about flights, customers, reservations, and other facts. Hundreds of different procedures are followed by airline personnel, travel agents, and customers. Finally, the information system includes people, not only the users of the system, but also those who operate and service the computers, those who maintain the data, and those who support the networks of computers.

The important point here is that the five components in Figure 1-1 are common to all information systems, from the smallest to the largest. As you think about an information system, learn to look for each of these five components. Realize, too, that an information system is not just a computer and a program, but rather an assembly of computers, programs, data, procedures, and people.

As we will discuss later in this chapter, these five components also mean that many different skills are required besides those of hardware technicians or computer programmers when building or using an information system. People are needed who can design the databases that hold the data and who can develop procedures for people to follow. Managers are needed to train and staff the personnel for using and operating the system. We will return to this five-component framework later in this chapter, as well as many other times throughout this text.

Figure 1-1
Five Components of an
Information System

Hardware	Software	Data	Procedures	People

---

[1]In the past, the term *software* was used to refer to computer components that were not hardware (e.g., programs, procedures, user manuals, etc.). Today, the term *software* is used more specifically to refer only to programs, and that is how we use the term throughout this book.

You Be the Guide

Unlike all of the other chapters in this text, Chapter 1 does not have an opening scenario. I thought too much else would be going on in this first lecture for it to be effective.

In place of the opening scenario, I usually spend time asking the students about their goals and how they think those goals relate to this class. I also try to ensure that they understand that they, not I, have the responsibility for learning this material. I use the Opposing Forces and Reflections Guides for both of these purposes.

GOALS FOR THE OPENING CLASS

* Place the responsibility for learning the class material on the student.

* Establish myself as a coach, a trainer, a mentor, who can help.

* Start the students thinking about how this class relates to their goal to become business professionals.

WAYS TO STIMULATE STUDENT INVOLVEMENT

I like to start the class even before the class begins. I arrive around 5 minutes early and talk with the students. I ask the students their names, where they are from, what their majors are, what they know about computers, and so on, as a way of breaking the ice.

Often I begin the session with the question:

➤ **Why are you here?**

The students are usually startled at that question and stammer something like, "Because I have to be," "Because it's a required course," or "Because I needed an elective, and this seemed like an easy one."

I follow up with:

➤ **OK. Right now the water temperature in the Sea of Cortez is 80 degrees, the water's clear, and the sailing, kayaking, and scuba diving are terrific (or something else depending on the season). So, why are you here rather than there? (The same example is used in the Reflections Guide, page 15a.)**

This leads to some comments like, "I can't afford it," "I have to get a degree," and so on.

➤ **Really? You know, you could support yourself as a clerk in a dive shop in Mexico. Why not do that instead of take this class?**

Eventually, they'll say they're taking the class because they're business majors and it's a required class.

From that point, I try to lead them into the realization that *they* have *chosen* to be business majors. Nobody else chose that for them. (Aside: Some of the students are majoring in business to please their parents or family. They're coming to realize it may not be *their* goal. See the Reflections Guide for more on this issue.) This class is a direct result of the decision they made to be a business major. They could be diving in the Sea of Cortez, instead.

➤ **Why do you want to major in business?**

They'll give reasons for that. Then I ask:

➤ **OK, you want to be a businessperson. Great. That's a wonderful goal. Now, how do you think this class can help you?**

They often respond with: "I don't know. I don't know what this class is about." Sometimes at this point I use the Opposing Forces Guide as a group exercise. Or, I continue on . . .

➤ **Well, suppose you manage a local bank. What do you need to know?**

➤ **As bank manager, suppose someone asks you for your opinion about how to improve the bank's CRM?**

➤ **That could happen, you know. First, you need to know the following:**

➤ **What's a CRM?**

➤ **What does a CRM do?**

➤ **What makes a good CRM?**

➤ **Suppose your boss asks you if you want to be one of the user representatives on the new CRM system. Is that a good thing to do or a waste of your time?**

About here, I transition to the lecture that begins by defining MIS and go on from there.

Yet another approach is to start with the students' current IS experiences. They probably have an instant messaging buddy list, an MP3 play list, or an account with Yahoo!, Google, or MSN. As such, they are already using an information system—the one that provides the services they are using. There is a profit-making business behind those services; those information systems need to support those businesses.

➤ **What IS must exist to support the IM, etc.?**

➤ **What knowledge about IS would students need to have in order to work for one of those businesses?**

WRAP UP

Sometime before the end of the first lecture, either as part of this exercise, as part of the Opposing Forces or the Reflections Guides, or just at the end of the hour, I like to leave with statements like these:

➤ So, you've chosen to be a business major because you want to be a business professional. That's a worthy goal and I'll help.

➤ The College of Business has required this class in order to get a business degree.

➤ They weren't wrong. You will need the knowledge from this class to be a successful business professional—especially in the twenty-first century.

➤ So, if you're serious about your goal, you need to learn this material.

➤ I'll help; I'll be your coach. But you have to do the work—you have to do the reading, the thinking, the exercises. I'm just here to point the way and help when you get stuck.

Before we move forward, note that we have defined an information system to include a computer. Some people would say that such a system is a **computer-based information system**. They would note that there are information systems that do not include computers, such as a calendar hanging on the wall outside of a conference room that is used to schedule the room's use. Such systems have been used by businesses for centuries. Although this point is true, in this book we focus on computer-based information systems. To simplify and shorten the book, we will use the term *information system* as a synonym for *computer-based information system*.

Development and Use of Information Systems

The next key element in our definition of MIS is the *development and use* of information systems. This course in particular, and MIS in general, are concerned with development because information systems do not pop up like mushrooms after a hard rain; they must be constructed. You may be saying, "Wait a minute, I'm a finance (or accounting, or management) major, not an information-systems major. I don't need to know how to build information systems."

If you are saying that, you are like a lamb headed for fleecing. Throughout your career, in whatever field you choose, information systems will be built for your use. To have an information system that meets your needs, you need to take an *active role* in that system's development. Even if you are not a programmer or a database designer or some other IS professional, you must take an active role in specifying the system's requirements and in helping manage the development project. Without active involvement on your part, it will only be good luck that causes the new system to meet your needs.

To that end, throughout this text we will discuss your role in the development of information systems. In addition, we devote all of Chapter 6 to this important topic. As you read this text and think about information systems, you should begin to ask yourself questions like, "I wonder how that system was constructed?" and "I wonder what roles the users played during its development?" If you start asking yourself these questions now, you will be better prepared to answer them once you start work, when financial, career, and other consequences will depend on your answers.

In addition to development tasks, you will also have important roles to play in the *use* of information systems. Of course, you will need to learn how to employ the system to accomplish your goals. But you will also have important ancillary functions as well. For example, when using an information system, you will have responsibilities for protecting the security of the system and its data. You may also have tasks for backing up data. When the system fails (most do, at some point), you will have tasks to perform while the system is down as well as tasks to accomplish to help recover the system correctly and quickly. The *Security Guide* on page 5a discusses one aspect of systems use, passwords and password etiquette.

Achieving Business Goals and Objectives

The last part of the definition of MIS is that information systems exist to help businesses achieve their *goals and objectives*. First, realize that this statement hides an important fact: Businesses themselves do not "do" anything. A business is not alive, and it cannot act. It is the people within a business who sell, buy, design, produce, finance, market, account, and manage. So, information systems exist to help people who work in a business to achieve the goals and objectives of that business.

Information systems are not created for the sheer joy of exploring technology. They are not created so that the company can be "modern" or so that the company can claim to be a "new-economy company." They are not created because the information systems department thinks it needs to be created or because the company is "falling behind the technology curve."

This point may seem so obvious that you wonder why we mention it. Every day, however, some business somewhere is developing an information system for the wrong

In this text, every chapter includes essays called Guides containing ideas that will help you become a better business professional. Every chapter has one Guide on each of the following key topics: security, ethics, problem solving, dealing with opposing forces, and reflections on the future.

Security Guides highlight skills and behaviors to protect valuable IS assets, both yours and those of your company.

Passwords and Password Etiquette

All forms of computer security involve passwords. Most likely, you have a university account that you access with a user name and password. When you set up that account, you were probably advised to use a "strong password." That's good advice, but what is a strong password? Probably not "sesame," but what then? Microsoft, a company that has many reasons to promote effective security, provides a definition that is commonly used. Microsoft defines a **strong password** as one with the following characteristics:

» Has seven or more characters

» Does not contain your user name, real name, or company name

» Does not contain a complete dictionary word, in any language

» Is different from previous passwords you have used

» Contains both upper- and lowercase letters, numbers, and special characters (such as ~ ! @; # $ % ^ &; * ( ) _ +; - =; { } | [ ] \ : " ; ' <; >; ? , . /)

Examples of good passwords are:

Enter Username:

DonaldT

Enter Password:

✳✳✳✳✳✳✳✳

LOG IN

» Qw37^T1bb?at

» 3B47qq<3>5!7b

The problem with such passwords is that they are nearly impossible to remember. And the last thing you want to do is write your password on a piece of paper and keep it near the workstation where you use it. Never do that!

One technique for creating memorable, strong passwords is to base them on the first letter of the words in a phrase. The phrase could be the title of a song or the first line of a poem or one based on some fact about your life. For example, you might take the phrase, "I was born in Rome, New York, before 1990." Using the first letters from that phrase and substituting the character < for the word *before*, you create the password IwbiR,NY<1990. That's an acceptable password, but it would be better if all of the numbers were not placed on the end. So, you might try the phrase, "I was born at 3:00 A.M in Rome, New York." That phrase yields the password Iwba3:00AMiR,NY which is a strong password that is easily remembered.

Once you have created a strong password, you need to protect it with proper behavior. Proper password etiquette is one of the marks of a business professional. Never write down your password, and do not share it with others. Never ask someone else for his password, and never give your password to someone else.

But, what if you need someone else's password? Suppose, for example, you ask someone to help you with a problem on your computer. You sign on to an information system, and for some reason, you need to enter that other person's password. In this case, say to the other person, "We need your password," and then get out of your chair, offer your keyboard to the other person, and look away while she enters the password. Among professionals working in organizations that take security seriously, this little "do-si-do" move—one person getting out of the way so that another person can enter her password—is common and accepted.

If someone asks for your password, do not give it out. Instead, get up, go over to that person's machine, and enter your own password, yourself. Stay present while your password is in use, and ensure that your account is logged out at the end of the activity. No one should mind or be offended in any way when you do this. It is the mark of a professional.

DISCUSSION QUESTIONS

1. Here is the first line of a famous poem by T. S. Eliot, "Let us go then, you and I, while the evening is spread out against the sky." Explain how to use this line to create a password. How could you add numbers and special characters to the password in a way that you will be able to remember?

2. List two different phrases that you can use to create a strong password. Show the password created by each.

3. One of the problems of life in the cyber-world is that we all are required to have multiple passwords—one for work or school, one for bank accounts, another for eBay or other auction sites, and so forth. Of course, it is better to use different passwords for each. But in that case you have to remember three or four different passwords. Think of different phrases you can use to create a memorable, strong password for each of these different accounts. Relate the phrase to the purpose of the account. Show the passwords for each.

4. Explain proper behavior when you are using your computer and you need to enter, for some valid reason, another person's password.

5. Explain proper behavior when someone else is using her computer and that person needs to enter, for some valid reason, your password.

reasons. Right now, somewhere in the world, a company is deciding to create a Web site for the sole reason that "every other business has one." This company is not asking questions like, "What is the purpose of the Web site?" "What is it going to do for us?" or "Are the costs of the Web site sufficiently offset by the benefits?"—but it should be!

Even more serious, somewhere right now is an IS manager who has been convinced by some vendor's sales team or by an article in a business magazine that her company must upgrade to the latest, greatest high-tech Gizmo Version 3.0.[2] This IS manager is attempting to convince her manager that this expensive upgrade is a good idea. We hope that someone somewhere in the company is asking questions like, "What business goal or objective will be served by the investment in Gizmo 3.0?"

Most chapters contain two MIS in Use cases, which discuss a relevant issue encountered by an actual company or organization. These cases link the chapter topic to its application in real-world organizations.

Throughout this text, we will consider many different information system types and underlying technologies. We will show the benefits of those systems and technologies and will illustrate successful implementations of them. *MIS in Use* cases, such as the one about the Internal Revenue Service in *MIS in Use 1-1*, discuss IS implementations in specific real-world organizations. As a future business professional, you need to learn to look at information systems and technologies only through the lens of *business need*. Learn to ask, "All of this technology may be great, in and of itself, but what will it do for us? What will it do for our business and our particular goals?"

Again, MIS is the development and use of information systems that help businesses achieve their goals and objectives. Already you should be realizing that there is much more to this class than buying a computer, writing a program, or working with a spreadsheet.

What Should You Learn from This Class?

As a business professional in the twenty-first century, you need sufficient MIS knowledge to be an informed and effective consumer of information technology products and services. In particular, you need to be able to ask pertinent questions, you need to be able to correctly interpret the responses to your questions, and you need to have the knowledge to make wise decisions and to manage effectively.

For example, suppose you are an accounts payable manager and someone in the IS department is proposing the Gizmo 3.0 upgrade to you. You need to understand basic terminology and concepts so as to be able to ask effective questions. Assume that you have that knowledge and you ask a question like, "Wait a minute. If we convert to version 3.0, won't we have to upgrade all of our telecommunications facilities as well?"

Now, suppose that, in fact, your company will have to upgrade its telecommunications facilities. Further, suppose that no one else had thought of that. You have asked a great question—one that will result in a better decision, and one that demonstrates to the IS professionals that you know what you are doing. Your credibility with all of the techies in the meeting will have increased immeasurably.

On the other hand, suppose Gizmo 3.0 has absolutely nothing to do with telecommunications, and that they are completely separate technologies. You have just asked an irrelevant question, one that demonstrates your ignorance of IS and causes the IS professionals to groan inwardly and wonder why they work for such a poorly managed organization.

Or, suppose you are not sure whether Gizmo 3.0 relates to telecommunications. Rather than risk asking an irrelevant question, you do nothing. At this point you have put yourself and your company at risk of a serious problem, only because of your ignorance about information systems.

---

[2]Gizmo 3.0 is a fictitious name. During your career, you will be confronted with many variations of "Gizmo 3.0." It may be the latest version of Windows. Or it may be a new kind of mobile communications technology; a new industry standard, like XML Web Services; or something else. These various gizmos may be just the solution for your situation, or they may be a complete waste of money. Learning how to discriminate one from the other is one of the major goals of this class.

You Be the Guide

Using the Security Guide
(page 5a)

GOALS

* Teach the students an easy way to create and remember strong passwords.

* Teach the students proper password etiquette.

* Underline the importance of passwords and password protection.

BACKGROUND AND PRESENTATION STRATEGIES

The first Security Guide concerns passwords, because students need to start practicing good password techniques, now. Universities are, unfortunately, common targets of security attacks. We start this class by teaching very important self-protection strategies.

Using the initial letters of a line of poetry or a phrase is a very easy way to remember strong passwords. In order to create and remember different passwords for different accounts (one for the university, one for Amazon.com, one for the student's ISP, etc.), it's useful to employ a phrase that's relevant to the account. "Last year, 2005, I spent more than 700 dollars on books" yields, Ly2005Is>700dob, which is an easily remembered strong password. See Discussion Question 3.

The only reason any of us should ever type a password is for authentication. **There is no other valid reason to type it.** I tell my students if they find themselves typing their password for any other reason, stop! Whatever they're doing is wrong. Don't type it in an email, don't type it on a piece of paper to remember, don't type it in response to some phisher's query. (Phishing is described in detail in Chapter 11.)

I think we need to teach that among IS professionals it is rude not to look away when someone is typing a password. In June 2005, I was giving a demo to a very senior database manager at Microsoft and I needed to enter my password. Even though he and I have known each other for years and have become personal friends, as soon as he saw what I was doing, he quite pointedly looked out the window.

➤ **Brush your teeth twice a day, don't talk with your mouth full, and look out the window when someone is typing their password.**

The same comment applies to never asking someone for their password. It is rude. Ask the person to come to your computer and enter his or her password.

➤ **If someone asks for your password, don't tell them they're rude. Just smile, get up, go to their keyboard, and enter it yourself. Then be sure to stay around until they log off.**

All of these behaviors simply indicate that the person takes security seriously and is a thoughtful and professional business person.

Students may not know this, but for many networks, when they log in using their password, they gain access not only to the network to which they're connecting, but also to other networks. One network (the business school) may authenticate them to a second network (the library), which will authenticate them to a third (the state library system), and so on. Thus, loss of a password may cause much more damage than just to the local network. We'll briefly mention Kerberos in Chapter 11, but the point for now is that one password may authenticate the student to many networks, networks the student may not even know about. Protect those passwords!

 ### SUGGESTED RESPONSES FOR DISCUSSION QUESTIONS

These questions require straightforward application of the material in the guide and of the points just made. I use them not to create a discussion, but to be certain that the students understand the techniques.

1. This phrase is the first line of "The Lovesong of J. Alfred Prufrock" by T. S. Eliot. Without the commas, it is: LugtyaIwteisoats. That's a little long. Maybe put in the comma and shorten it to Lugt,yaI. Or, how about, "Let us go then, you and I, before 6 PM," which results in the password Lugt,yaI<6PM.

2. A practice exercise to make sure the students understand the principle. Answers depend on the students.

3. Make the phrase be related to the purpose or nature of the account. Examples:

Account	Phrase	Password
Work	"Back in the saddle at 8:00 AM."	Bitsa8:00AM
School	"I take IS300 before Sarah."	ItIS300<S
eBay	"I want to sell more than 1,000 dollars of goods."	Iwts>1000dog or Iwts>$1000og
Bank	"Is University Savings before 3rd Street?"	IUS<3rdS?

4. Tell the other person what you are doing and why you need their password. Ask them to log on to your computer. Get out of your chair and let them sit at your keyboard and enter the password. Look away. Use their account to do what you need to do and log off (or offer to let them log off). Thank the person and tell them that you have logged off.

➤ **These are professional manners in a cyber world!**

5. Get up, go over to their computer, and ask to log in. Stay in the neighborhood while they're using your account. Sign out or be certain that they sign out. It's not bad manners, by the way, to inquire, politely, why they need your password.

WRAP UP

Some statements I make in summary:

➤ **Passwords are important. As a professional, you have a responsibility to take your passwords seriously and to protect them.**

➤ **Throughout the course, we'll show how passwords are used to provide organizational security. In Chapter 4, for example, you'll learn how passwords are used to provide privileges for database access.**

➤ **Later in the course, you'll learn to periodically change your password. For now, if you haven't changed your university password in some time, go home and do it!**

MIS in Use 1-1

Requirements Creep at the IRS

The United States Internal Revenue Service (IRS) serves more people in the United States than any other public or private institution. Each year it processes over 200 million tax returns from more than 180 million individuals and more than 45 million businesses. The IRS itself employs more than 100,000 people in over 1,000 different sites. In a typical year, it adapts to more than 200 tax law changes and services more than 23 million telephone calls.

Amazingly, the IRS accomplishes this work using information systems that were designed and developed in the 1960s. In fact, some of the computer programs that process tax returns were first written in 1962. In the mid-1990s, the IRS set out on a Business System Modernization (BSM) project that would replace this antiquated system with modern technology and capabilities. However, by 2003 it was clear that this project was a disaster. Billions of dollars had been spent on the project, and all major components of the new system were months or years behind schedule.

In 2003, newly appointed IRS commissioner Mark W. Everson called for an independent review of all BSM projects. Systems development experts from the Software Engineering Institute at Carnegie Mellon University and the Mitre Corporation and managers from the IRS examined the project and made a list of factors that contributed to the failure and recommendations for solutions. In their report, the first two causes of failure cited were:

- "There was inadequate business unit ownership and sponsorship of projects. This resulted in unrealistic business cases and continuous project scope 'creep' (gradual expansion of the original scope of the project)."
- "The much desired environment of trust, confidence, and teamwork between the IRS business units, the BSM organization [the team of IRS employees established to manage the BSM project], the Information Technology Services (ITS) [the internal IRS organization that operates and maintains the current information systems], and the Prime [the prime contractor, Computer Sciences Corporation] did not exist. In fact, the opposite was true, resulting in an inefficient working environment and, at times, finger pointing when problems arose."

The BSM team developed the new system in a vacuum. The team did not have the acceptance, understanding, or support for the new system from either the existing IRS business units (the future users of the system) or from the existing ITS staff. Consequently, the BSM team poorly understood the system needs, and that misunderstanding resulted in continual changes in project requirements, changes that occurred after systems components had been designed and developed. Such requirements creep is a sure sign of a mismanaged project and always results in schedule delays and wasted money. In this case, the delays were measured in years and the waste in billions of dollars. The bottom line: Users must be involved in both the *development* and *use* of information systems.

Sources: "Independent Analysis of IRS Business Systems Modernization, Special Report," IRS Oversight Board, 2003, www.treas.gov/irsob/index.html; "For the IRS, There's No EZ Fix," *CIO Magazine*, April 1, 2004.

Therefore, you need to understand more than just the meaning of basic terms. Figure 1-2 (page 8) lists categories of knowledge you should gain and shows examples of each. As you can see from this figure, you need to know why, what, and how: *Why* information systems are necessary; *what* are the fundamental terms, essential technologies, and basic information system types; and *how* information systems are to be managed and developed.

Most importantly, because IS technology changes so fast, you also need to learn how to find out about new technology. As you will see in the next section, the frameworks shown in the bottom row of Figure 1-2 will help you to do this.

One final point: To get the most from this class, you need to do more than just memorize the terms and ideas and then give them back on an exam. Instead, you need to digest this material, making it part of the fabric of your business thinking and processes. To do that, you need to work the questions and problems in the Guides and at the end of each chapter. Educational research shows that working with the material

	Knowledge Category	Examples	Where in Text
Why	Need for information systems	• Competitive advantage • Problem solving • Decision making	Chapters 1, 2, 7, and 8
What	Fundamental terms	• CPU • DBMS • IP address	Chapters 3, 4, and 5
	Essential technologies	• Relational data model • LANs, WANs, and the Internet • HTML and XML	Chapters 4, 5, and 8
	Information systems types	• Customer Relationship Management (CRM) • Enterprise Resource Planning (ERP) • Decision Support Systems (DSS)	Chapters 7, 8, and 9
How	Methodologies	• Data modeling • Systems development processes and techniques • Management of MIS • Security management	Chapters 5, 6, 10, and 11
	Technology frameworks	• Five components of an IS • TCP/IP-OSI architecture • Systems development lifecycle	Chapters 1, 4, 5, and 6

Figure 1-2
Summary of MIS Course
Content

to answer questions and to solve problems is the best way to incorporate knowledge into your long-term memory.

Using the Five-Component Framework

The five-component framework in Figure 1-1 can help guide your learning and thinking about IS, both now and in the future. To understand this framework better, first note in Figure 1-3 that these five components are symmetrical. The outermost components, hardware and people, are both actors; they can take actions. The software and procedure components are both sets of instructions: Software is instructions for hardware, and procedures are instructions for people. Finally, data is the bridge between the computer side on the left and the human side on the right.

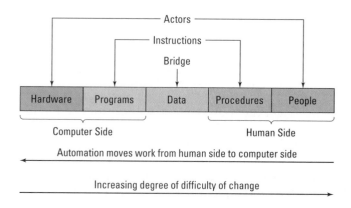

Figure 1-3
Characteristics of the Five
Components

Now, when we automate a business process, we take work that people are doing by following procedures and move it so that computers will do that work, following instructions in the software. Thus, the process of automation is a process of moving work from the right side of Figure 1-3 to the left.

The Most Important Component—YOU

You are part of every information system that you use. When you consider the five components of an information system, the last component, *people*, includes you. Your mind and your thinking are not merely *a* component of the information systems you use, they are *the most important* component.

Consider an example. Suppose you have the perfect information system, one that can predict the future. No such information system exists, but assume that it does for this example. Now suppose that on December 14, 1966, your perfect information system tells you that the next day, Walt Disney will die. Say you have $50,000 to invest; you can either buy Disney stock or you can short it (an investment technique that will net you a positive return if the stock value decreases). Given your perfect information system, how do you invest?

Before you read on, think about this question. If Walt Disney is going to die the next day, will the stock go up or down? Most students assume that the stock will go down, so they short it, on the theory that the loss of the founder will mean a dramatic drop in the share price.

In fact, the next day, the value of Disney stock increased substantially. Why? The market viewed Walt Disney as an artist; once he died, he would no longer be able to create more art. Thus, the value of the existing art would increase because of scarcity, and the value of the corporation that owned that art would increase as well.

Here's the point: Even if you have the perfect information system, if you do not know what to do with the information that it produces, you are wasting your time and money. The *quality of your thinking* is a large part of the quality of the information system. Substantial cognitive research has shown that although you cannot increase your basic IQ, you can dramatically increase the quality of your thinking. You cannot change the computer in your brain, so to speak, but you can change the way you have programmed your brain to work. The first *Problem Solving Guide,* on page 9a, asks you to think about perspectives and points of view.

Each of the chapters in this text contains a Problem Solving Guide that presents ideas from cognitive science and applies them to business situations. We discuss thinking skills in an MIS book because improving your thinking improves the quality of every information system that you use.

High-Tech Versus Low-Tech Information Systems

Information systems differ in the amount of work that is moved from the human side (people and procedures) to the computer side (hardware and programs). For example, consider two different versions of a customer support information system: A system that consists only of a file of email addresses and an email program is a very low-tech system. Only a small amount of work has been moved from the human side to the computer side. Considerable human work is required to determine when to send which emails to which customers.

In contrast, a customer support system that keeps track of the equipment that customers have and the maintenance schedules for that equipment and then automatically generates email reminders to customers is a higher-tech system. This simply means that more work has been moved from the human side to the computer side. The computer is providing more services on behalf of the humans.

Often, when considering different information systems alternatives, it will be helpful to consider the low-tech versus high-tech alternatives in light of the amount of work that is being moved from people to computers.

Understanding New Information Systems

The five-component framework can also be used when learning about new systems. When in the future some vendor pitches the need for the new Gizmo 3.0 to you, think

Understanding Perspectives and Points of View

Every human being speaks and acts from the perspective of a personal point of view. Everything we say or do is based on—or equivalently, is biased by—that point of view.

Thus, everything you read in any textbook, including this one, is biased by the author's point of view. The author may think that he is writing an unbiased account of neutral subject material. But no one can write an unbiased account of anything, because we all write from a perspective.

Similarly, your professors speak to you from their points of view. They have experience, goals, objectives, hopes, and fears, and, like all of us, those elements provide a framework from which they think and speak.

Examine the statements in the *Opposing Forces Guide* in this chapter. Now examine the statements in the *Reflections Guide* later this chapter. Both of those guides contain what is obviously editorial, opinion-oriented material. When you read them, it is easy to recognize that they are written from a strongly held point of view and therefore contain personal biases.

But consider statements that are less apparently opinions. For example, consider the following definition of information: "Information is a difference that makes a difference." By this definition, there are many differences, but only those that make a difference qualify as information.

This definition is not obviously an opinion, but it nevertheless was written from a biased perspective. The perspective is just less evident because the statement appears as a definition, not an opinion. But, in fact, it is the definition of information in the opinion of the well-known psychologist Gregory Bateson.

I find his definition informative and useful. It is imprecise, but it is a good guideline, and I have used it to advantage when designing reports and queries for end users. I ask myself, "Does this report show someone a difference that makes a difference to them?" So, I find it a useful and helpful definition.

My colleagues who specialize in quantitative methods, however, find Bateson's definition vapid and useless. They ask, "What does it say?" "How could I possibly use that definition to formalize anything?" or "A difference that makes a difference to what or whom?" or they say, "I couldn't quantify anything about that definition; it's a waste of time."

And they are right, but so am I, and so was Gregory Bateson. The difference is a matter of perspective, and surprisingly, conflicting perspectives can all be true at the same time.

One last point: Whether it is apparent or not, authors write and professors teach not only from personal perspectives, but also with personal goals. I write this textbook in the hope that you will find the material useful and important and tell your professor that it is a great book so that he will use it again. Whether you (or I) are aware of that fact, it and my other hopes and goals bias every sentence in this book.

Similarly, your professors have hopes and goals that influence what and how they teach. Your professors may want to see light bulbs of recognition on your face, they may want to win the Professor of the Year award, or they may want to gain tenure status in order to be able to do some advanced research in the field. Whatever the case, they, too, have hopes and goals that bias everything they say.

So, as you read this book and as you listen to your professor, ask yourself, "What is her perspective?" and "What are her goals?" Then compare their perspectives and goals to yours. Learn to do this not just with your textbooks and your professors, but with your colleagues as well. When you enter the business world, being able to discern and adapt to the perspectives and goals of those with whom you work will make you much more effective.

DISCUSSION QUESTIONS

1. Consider the following statement: "The quality of your thinking is the most important component of an information system." Do you agree with this statement? Do you think it is even possible to say that one component is the most important one?

2. This text claims that although it is not possible to increase your IQ, it is possible to improve the quality of your thinking. Do you agree? Whether or not you agree, give three examples that illustrate differences in quality of thinking. They can be all from one person or they can be examples from three different people.

3. Though it does not appear to be so, the statement "There are five components of an information system: hardware, software, data, procedures, and people" is an opinion based on a perspective. Suppose you stated this opinion to a computer engineer who said, "Rubbish. That's not true at all. The only components that count are hardware and maybe software." Contrast the perspective of the engineer with that of your MIS professor. How do those perspectives influence their opinions about the five-component framework? Which is correct?

4. Consider Bateson's definition: "Information is a difference that makes a difference." How can this definition be used to advantage when designing a Web page? Explain why someone who specializes in quantitative methods might consider this definition to be useless. How can the same definition be both useful and useless?

5. Some students hate open-ended questions. They want questions that have one correct answer, like 7.3 miles per hour. When given a question like that in question 4, a question that has multiple, equally valid answers, some students get angry or frustrated. They want the book or the professor to give them the answer. How do you feel about this matter?

6. Do you think someone can improve the quality of their thinking by learning to hold multiple, contradictory ideas in their mind at the same time? Or, do you think that doing so just leads to indecisive and ineffective thinking? Discuss this question with some of your friends. What do they think? What are their perspectives?

about the five components. What new hardware will you need? What programs will you need to license? What databases and other data must you create? What procedures will need to be developed for both use and administration of the information system? And finally, what will be the impact of Gizmo 3.0 on people? Which jobs will change? Who will need training? How will the new Gizmo affect morale? Will you need to hire new people? Will you need to reorganize?

Components Ordered by Difficulty and Disruption

Finally, as you consider the five components keep in mind that Figure 1-3 shows them in order of ease of change and the amount of organizational disruption. It is usually a simple matter to order new hardware and install it. Obtaining or developing new programs is more difficult. Creating new databases or changing the structure of existing databases is still more difficult. Changing procedures, requiring people to work in new ways, is even more difficult. Finally, changing personnel responsibilities and reporting relationships and hiring and terminating employees are both very difficult and very disruptive to the organization.

The *Ethics Guide* on page 11a considers the ethics of using information that is not intended for you.

The Ethics Guide in each chapter of this book considers the ethics of informations systems use. These guides challenge you to think deeply about ethical standards, and they provide for some interesting discussions with classmates.

▮ Information Characteristics

Using the discussions in the last two sections, we can now define an information system as an assembly of hardware, software, data, procedures, and people that interact to produce information. The only term left undefined in that definition is *information*, and we turn to it next.

What Is Information?

Information is one of those fundamental terms that we use every day but that turns out to be surprisingly difficult to define. Defining information is like defining words such as *alive* and *truth*. We know what those words mean, we use them with each other without confusion, but nonetheless, they are difficult to define.

In this text, we will avoid the technical issues of defining information and will use common, intuitive definitions instead. Probably the most common definition is that **information** is knowledge derived from data, where *data* is defined as recorded facts or figures. Thus, the facts that employee James Smith earns $17.50 per hour and that Mary Jones earns $25.00 per hour are *data*. The statement that the average hourly wage of all employees in the Garden Department is $22.37 per hour is *information*. Average wage is knowledge that is derived from the data of individual wages.

Another common definition is that *information is data presented in a meaningful context*. The fact that Jeff Parks earns $10.00 per hour is data.[3] The statement that Jeff Parks earns less than half the average hourly wage of the Garden Department, however, is information. It is data presented in a meaningful context.

Another definition of information that you will hear is that *information is processed data*, or sometimes, *information is data processed by summing, ordering, averaging, grouping, comparing, or other similar operations*. The fundamental idea of this definition is that we do something to data to produce information.

---

[3]Actually the word *data* is plural; to be correct we should use the singular form *datum* and say "The fact that Jeff Parks earns $10 per hour is a datum." The word *datum*, however, sounds pedantic and fussy, and we will avoid it in this text.

You Be the Guide

Using the Problem Solving Guide (page 9a)

GOALS

* Reinforce the text's statement that, although none of us can change our IQ, we can improve the way we think, and thus improve our effective "smarts."

* Teach the importance of perspective in thinking and communication—everyone interprets the world in the context of their perspective.

* Encourage the students to think critically about the text, about your presentations, and about comments made by their fellow students.

BACKGROUND AND PRESENTATION STRATEGIES

I begin the discussion of this guide with the text's story about Walt Disney's death and the impact it had on Disney's stock price. (By the way, this story was told to me many years ago by an investor whose girlfriend worked at the hospital where they admitted Walt Disney. She told him she doubted that Disney would live through the night. He shorted Disney for the next day and lost his shirt. He told me, "That was the last time I traded on insider information. Not only is it illegal, it seldom works.")

Considerable academic research supports the notion that one can improve the quality of one's thinking. If the students Google "critical-thinking skills" or "problem-solving skills," they will find hundreds of references.

If the students learn nothing else from this class except how to improve their thinking skills, even a little bit, it will be worth hundreds of hours of labor and thousands of dollars. (And, they're going to learn a lot more than that!)

Here's an example of perspective:

➤ **If I say that our MIS class is more important than Intro to Accounting and if your accounting professor says that Intro to Accounting is more important than MIS, is either of us wrong?**

➤ **Is one of us lying? Is one of us being insincere?**

➤ **Is it possible to prove that one of us is right and one of us is wrong?**

➤ **In fact, each of us is right. So, here's the million-dollar question:**

➤ **What do you, as a student, do about that? Whom do you believe?**

➤ **How does the concept of perspective—mine and the accounting prof's—relate to this?**

No one can make any statement except from a perspective. Just as one must have a physical location (one has to be standing, sitting, or reclining somewhere), so, too, one's statements arise from a mental location, from a perspective. We cannot speak about anything except from some perspective. Usually, when two people disagree strongly, it is because they have different perspectives. Which leads to:

➤ **If I have a different perspective from someone, and if we're arguing about something, will any discussion about the facts of the matter have any impact on the outcome?**

(No. We have to come to the same perspective.)

➤ **How likely is it that the other person will change his or her perspective?**

(Not very.)

➤ **So what can I do?**

(Understand what's going on and adapt.)

It's very difficult for people to change their perspective. Most people will resist, and strongly. However, successful business people seem to have mastered the skill, or at least are better at it than most people.

There's a story about Bill Gates in the early days of the computer profession, when he was meeting with another company, and the meeting was going nowhere. Finally, Gates is supposed to have said, "Wait. I see the problem. We think we're the customer, and you think you're the customer. Actually, you're right—you are the customer. We need to go back and rethink our position. We'll get back to you in a couple of weeks." There are so many apocryphal stories about Bill Gates, but I think this one is true. It was told to me by someone who was in the meeting.

A key skill: Being able to perceive that difference in perspective is the root of a problem, and being able to alter one's perspective to achieve a solution, or to at least be able to communicate about a solution.

➤ **The key difference between animals and humans isn't that humans can think. Animals can think. The key difference is that humans can think about thinking. We can examine how we think, evaluate how our techniques are working for us, and choose to change how we think. Try it!**

❓ SUGGESTED RESPONSES FOR DISCUSSION QUESTIONS

1. I wrote that statement based on my perspective. I wrote it because I've watched end users misuse the outputs of well-designed information systems or not use them at all. But, another author, one with a different perspective, might say something else.

   The students don't have enough experience to know if they agree or not. They might decide provisionally to believe that statement until they know more. At this stage, the biggest impact on what they believe is you, their professor!

   From one perspective: If a system is like a chain, then every link is equally important. The third link is not more important than the fifth one. So all five components are the same. From a different perspective: How one thinks about the information people receive has the greatest impact on what they will do with that information. So, from that perspective, the statement is true.

2. There's a lot of research to back it up. Usually the students will agree, too, or at least they'll **want** to believe that it's true.

   The point of this question is to compel the students to think about different kinds and quality of thinking. Here are three examples of three different qualities:

   "I'm taking this class because it's required."

   "I'm not sure about this class. In fact, I'm not sure I'm in the right major. I always thought I'd be a business major, but that was because my Dad so loved accounting. I'm starting to wonder about my goals."

   "My expectations are modest. If I can get three or four useful skills or ideas out of a class, and if it's more or less interesting and enjoyable, then I'm content. I hope this will be one of those classes."

   More statements about the class appear in the Opposing Forces Guide in this chapter.

3. The engineer will have spent his or her career thinking about computer design. All of the "interesting" problems will lie there. The MIS professor will have spent his or her career thinking about information systems; that is, what they are, how they are built, and how they do or do not facilitate the goals of organizations. The "important" problems arise when groups of people try to work together to accomplish something.

   Both are correct, from their own perspectives.

4. Design the Web page so that the critical information, the differences that are important to that person, are obvious and easily perceived. But, in quantitative methods, where's the equation? What can I compute? That definition is given from a perspective—it's useful for problems that are within the scope of its perspective.

5. Most classes have students who are at different levels of thinking. Some students will feel most comfortable when the answer is concrete. Others will have advanced to understand that thinking occurs within a particular context. I like to address this issue head on. Often students with higher cognitive skills can help those with less-developed skills. This exercise works well in groups—especially if the students have varying ages and life experiences. William Perry wrote several articles on this topic that had a profound impact on my teaching.[1]

6. The discussion, especially involving students of different levels of cognitive maturity, is the critical part of this exercise. Multifaceted thinking can seem (and be) indecisive. However, it can be wise. There is no answer. It depends. Some students will be squirming at this point, and that's OK. I just want to keep them talking about why they're squirming.

WRAP UP

➤ **The quality of your thinking can be improved.**

➤ **One way to improve your thinking is to consider perspectives—yours and others.**

➤ **Suppose you ask two people how far it is to the business school library. Suppose one of them is sitting next to you in class and the other is sitting at the nearest airport.**

➤ **Will they give different answers to the same question? Of course! Is either wrong? No. Are you surprised?**

➤ **Suppose you ask two people if college tuition is too high. Suppose one works two jobs to pay for school and the other is dying of cancer. Will they give different answers?**

➤ **Bottom line: Consider perspectives when understanding yourself and anyone else!**

[1]William A. Perry, "Different Worlds in the Same Classroom," *On Teaching and Learning,* Harvard Danforth Center (May 1985), pp. 1–17; and William A. Perry, "Cognitive and Ethical Growth," in Arthur W. Chickering (Ed.), *The Modern American College* (San Francisco: Jossey-Bass, 1981), pp. 76–115. The first is available at *bokcenter.harvard.edu/docs/perry.html.*

There is yet a fourth definition of information, which was presented in the *Problem Solving Guide* on page 9a. There, information was defined as *a difference that makes a difference*.

For the purposes of this text, any of these definitions of information will do. Choose the definition of information that makes sense to you. The important point is that you discriminate between data and information. You also may find that different definitions work better in different situations.

Information Is Subjective

Consider the definition that information is data presented in a meaningful context. What exactly is a *meaningful context*? Clearly, context varies from person to person. If I manage the Garden Department and you are the CEO, our contexts differ. To me, the average hourly wage of the Garden Department is information. To you, it is a data point—the average hourly wage of employees in one of your departments. To you, as CEO, information would be the average hourly wage of all employees in all departments, a list of all departmental averages presented in ascending order, or some other arrangement of the average wages in the context of the entire company.

Sometimes you will hear this same idea expressed as, "One person's information is another person's data." This statement simply means that information in one person's context is just a data point in another person's context. All of us have experienced this phenomenon one time or another when we excitedly report something to another person, only to have them suppress a yawn and say, "Yeah, so what?"

Context changes occur in information systems when the output of one system feeds a second system. For example, suppose an information system in the manufacturing department produces a summary of the day's activity as its information. That summary is input to the general ledger system in the accounting department, where the summary is just another data point. The general ledger system takes inputs from manufacturing, sales, accounts receivable, accounts payable, and so forth and transforms those data into the information that it produces, such as the monthly balance sheet and income statement. Those financial statements go to investors, where they become data points in the portfolios of the investors. This process is illustrated in Figure 1-4.

The bottom line is that information is always understood in a context, and that context varies from one user to another. Therefore, information is always subjective.

Characteristics of Good Information

All information is not equal: Some information is better than other information. Figure 1-5 (on page 12) lists the characteristics of good information.

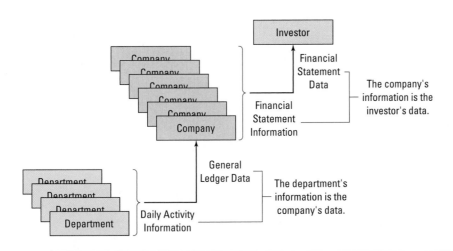

Figure 1-4
One User's Information Is
Another User's Data

Ethics of Misdirected Information Use

Consider the following situations:

Situation A: Suppose you are buying a condo and you know that at least one other party is bidding against you. While agonizing over your best strategy, you stop at a local Starbucks. As you sip your latte, you overhear a conversation at the table next to yours. Three people are talking loudly enough that it is difficult to ignore them, and you soon realize that they are the real estate agent and the couple who is competing for the condo you want. They are preparing their offer. Should you listen to their conversation? If you do, do you use the information you hear to your advantage?

Situation B: Consider the same situation from a different perspective—instead of overhearing the conversation, suppose you receive that same information in an email. Perhaps an administrative assistant at the agent's office confuses you and the other customer and mistakenly sends you the terms of the other party's offer. Do you read that email? If so, do you use the information that you read to your advantage?

Situation C: Suppose that you sell computer software. In the midst of a sensitive price negotiation, your customer accidentally sends you an internal email that contains the maximum amount that the customer can pay for your software. Do you read that email? Do you use that information to guide your negotiating strategy? If your customer discovers that the email may have reached you and asks, "Did you read my email?" how do you answer?

Situation D: Suppose a friend mistakenly sends you an email that contains sensitive personal medical data. Further, suppose you read the email before you know what you're reading and you're embarrassed to learn something very personal that truly is none of your business. Your friend asks you, "Did you read that email?" How do you respond?

Situation E: Finally, suppose that you work as a network administrator and your position allows you unrestricted access to the mailing lists for your company. Assume that you have the skill to insert your email address into any company mailing list without anyone knowing about it. You insert your address into several lists and, consequently, begin to receive confidential email that no one intended for you to see. One of those emails indicates that your best friend's department is about to be eliminated and all of its personnel fired. Do you forewarn your friend?

DISCUSSION QUESTIONS

1. Answer the questions in situations A and B. Do your answers differ? Does the medium by which the information is obtained make a difference? Is it easier to avoid reading an email than it is to avoid hearing a conversation? If so, does that difference matter?

2. Answer the questions in situations B and C. Do your answers differ? In situation B, the information is for your personal gain; in C, the information is for both your personal and your organization's gain. Does this difference matter? How do you respond when asked if you have read the email?

3. Answer the questions in situations C and D. Do your answers differ? Would you lie in one case and not in the other? Why or why not?

4. Answer the questions in situation E. What is the essential difference between situations A through D and situation E? Suppose you had to justify your behavior in situation E. How would you argue? Do you believe your own argument?

5. In situations A through D, if you access the information you have done nothing illegal. You were the passive recipient. Even for item E, although you undoubtedly violated your company's employment policies, you most likely did not violate the law. So, for this discussion, assume that all of these actions are legal.

   a. What is the difference between legal and ethical? Look up each term in a dictionary and explain how they differ.

   b. Make the argument that business is competitive, and that if something is legal, then it is acceptable to do if it helps to further your goals.

   c. Make the argument that it is never appropriate to do something unethical.

6. Summarize your beliefs about proper conduct when you receive misdirected information.

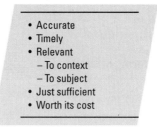

Figure 1-5
Characteristics of Good
Information

Accurate

First, good information is **accurate**. Good information is based on correct and complete data, and it has been processed correctly as expected. Accuracy is crucial; managers must be able to rely on the results of their information systems. The IS function can develop a bad reputation in the organization if a system is known to produce inaccurate information. In such a case, the information system becomes a waste of time and money as users develop work-arounds to avoid the inaccurate data.

A corollary to this discussion is that you, a future user of information systems, ought not to rely on information just because it appears in the context of a Web page, a well-formatted report, or a fancy query. It is sometimes hard to be skeptical of information delivered with beautiful, active graphics. Do not be misled. When you begin to use an information system, be skeptical. Cross-check the information you are receiving. After weeks or months of using a system, you may relax. Begin, however, with skepticism.

Timely

Good information is **timely**—produced in time for its intended use. A monthly report that arrives 6 weeks late is most likely useless. The information arrives long after the decisions have been made that needed that information. An information system that tells you not to extend credit to a customer after you have shipped the goods is unhelpful and frustrating. Notice that timeliness can be measured against a calendar (6 weeks late) or against events (before we ship).

When you participate in the development of an IS, timeliness will be part of the requirements you will ask for. You need to give appropriate and realistic timeliness needs. In some cases, developing systems that provide information in near real time is much more difficult and expensive than producing information a few hours later. If you can get by with information that is a few hours old, say so during the requirements specification phase.

Consider an example. Suppose you work in marketing and you need to be able to assess the effectiveness of new online ad programs. Your want an information system that will not only deliver ads over the Web, but that also will enable you to determine how frequently customers click on those ads. Determining click ratios in near real time will be very expensive; saving the data in a batch and processing it some hours later will be much easier and cheaper. If you can live with information that is a day or two old, the system will be easier and cheaper to implement.

Relevant

Information should be **relevant** both to the context and to the subject. Considering context, you, the CEO, need information that is summarized to an appropriate level for your job. A list of the hourly wage of every employee in the company is unlikely to be useful. More likely, you need average wage information by department or division. A list of all employee wages is irrelevant in your context.

Information should also be relevant to the subject at hand. If you want information about short-term interest rates for a possible line of credit, then a report that shows 15-year mortgage interest rates is irrelevant. Similarly, a report that buries the information you need in pages and pages of results is also irrelevant to your purposes.

You Be the Guide

Using the Ethics Guide (page 11a)

GOALS

* Teach students about the problem of unintentionally revealing sensitive information in public places.

* Explore ethical issues concerning the use of misdirected information.

* Differentiate between *unethical* and *illegal*.

BACKGROUND AND PRESENTATION STRATEGIES

I begin by asking the students what are the only two questions that a business professional can ask in an elevator. Usually someone will have worked in a law or CPA office and they'll know. The standard answer is:

➤ **What floor?**

➤ **How is the weather?**

That's it. *No other question is allowed in an elevator.* Airplanes and public places, like Starbucks in this story, are other places to avoid conversations about sensitive matters.

The first scenario happened to me. Fortunately, I was relieved of my ethical dilemma when a third party purchased the property from underneath all of us.

The people were loud and boorish. I wasn't sneaking around picking up newspapers by their table. I was passively sitting while they talked, very loudly. They were speaking loudly on cell phones to their inspector and their bank! I suppose I'm confounding my dislike for loud, public, cell phone users with my ethical principles. What difference does it make, ethically, if they were rude?

Did I have a responsibility to move to another table where I couldn't hear them? Or to warn them that I could hear them and that I was bidding on the same property? Or, did fate just drop something in my lap, like winning the lottery? I asked our agent about it, and she said by all means use the information. But do I want the realtor to be the guardian of my ethical principles? If so, I am avoiding my personal responsibility.

Usually, my students say they would use the information and never look back. I don't think I agree.

When evaluating behavior in business, we can consider three sets of criteria: *ethics, corporate policy,* and *laws.* Behaviors concerning the latter two categories are easy

to define: Is the behavior against a law or corporate policy?

Ethical behavior is harder to define. Microsoft Encarta defines ethical as *"conforming to accepted standards"* or *"consistent with agreed principles of correct moral conduct"* and ethics as *"a system of moral principles governing the appropriate conduct for an individual or group."*

So, the question becomes, *"What system of moral principles governs conduct for business professionals?"* This is the core of the matter that we will address in all of the Ethics Guides in the text.

The legal community makes this issue clear, at least among lawyers and in the courts. Use of any misdirected information is unethical, and court judgments can be lost by a party that uses such information. Legal ethics state that if a lawyer mistakenly receives a document intended for the other side, the lawyer is forbidden to use the contents of that document and is supposed to direct the document to its proper source, or at least return it to the sender with an appropriate notice. Often, law firms place a notice reminding the receiver of that obligation at the bottom of every email or other correspondence. (You also will find it at the bottom of some corporate emails.)

➤ **If we apply the lawyer's criteria to the scenarios in A–D, they are all unethical.**

➤ **Should professional business people have a lower standard than lawyers?**

 SUGGESTED RESPONSES FOR DISCUSSION QUESTIONS

1. I don't think the medium should make a difference. Using the lawyer's criteria mentioned earlier, the use of information in either case is unethical. Also, there's a difference in that the email server at the real estate office has a record that it sent that email to you. In scenario A, no one could prove you heard. That difference doesn't change the ethics—it just changes the chance that you might be discovered.

   Also, in scenario B there is another possibility: If you received the terms of their offer, there's a good chance the addresses were switched and they received the terms of your offer. From a practical perspective, setting aside the ethical issues, it's probably best to let your agent know what happened.

2. Scenario C is more complicated. For one, what if the customer wants you to have that information? Or,

what if that information is false, the real number is higher, but the customer wants you to think that's their top number? This could be a mistake or a negotiating ploy. I think notifying the customer is not only ethical, it's also smart.

➤ **Nothing is more serviceable than the truth. Maybe it's not the most convenient, but it's the easiest in the long run.**

➤ **I don't think whether the information gives you or your company an advantage is relevant. By the way, your company may have a written ethical policy that governs your behavior here. You could lose your job by not following those guidelines.**

3. I think a person could make an argument that it is more ethical to lie to your friend about having received the email. The purpose of your lie would be to save your friend from embarrassment. However, lying to friends is not a great way to build relationships. It might be better to tell your friend that you did receive the email; that you're available to talk about it if he or she wants; and that, as a good friend, you can also forget all about it.

4. I think the actions of the person in scenario E are most unethical and undoubtedly against corporate policy. This is *"You're fired!"* territory. Were I that person's employer, I would not provide a reference. I don't think the person should have received the email, and I don't think the person should notify his or her friend. Anyone who abused his job authorities in this way is unlikely to care about the ethical principles of telling his or her friend, however. They'd probably tell. To me, the whole scenario stinks!

➤ **By the way, we'll talk about this in Chapters 5 and 11, but corporate email is not secure. Even if someone has not invaded the corporate system, as this person did, emails you send at work are not private.**

5. **a.** For definitions, see Background and Presentations Strategies.

b. I suppose one could argue that business is competitive; it's dog eat dog, and you'll take any advantage that falls in your lap. (Of course, there is the possibility that the emails are setups, and you could be playing into someone's plan.) Or, it might be that in some industries, such behaviors are normal. If they are truly normal, if everyone accepts them, then according to the definition of ethical, these behaviors are ethical.

c. One argument, a pragmatic one, centers on the idea that "nothing is more serviceable than the truth." Once you start taking advantage of information under the table, you've placed yourself in a spot to be manipulated (if, for example, the top number in scenario C is not really the top number). Another argument is a personal one: "I strive to act ethically, and I know I won't be happy engaging in unethical behavior. I want to work around people and industries in which ethical behavior is expected." A third argument takes the moral high ground. It doesn't matter if ethical behavior is pragmatic or personally preferred, unethical behavior is just wrong.

6. Answer is up to the students. See the Wrap Up.

WRAP UP

Some questions to summarize the discussion:

➤ **How do you define the difference between legal and ethical?**

➤ **Can something be against corporate policy and still be legal?**

➤ **What is your personal policy about dealing with information that is misdirected to you?**

➤ **Did your thoughts about this matter change as a result of this discussion? If so, how?**

Just Barely Sufficient

Information needs to be **sufficient** for the purpose for which it is generated, but **just barely so**. We live in an information age; one of the critical decisions that each of us has to make each day is what information to ignore. The higher you rise into management, the more information you will be given, and because there is only so much time, the more information you will need to ignore. So, information should be sufficient, but just barely.

Worth Its Cost

Information is not free. There are costs for developing an information system, costs of operating and maintaining that system, and costs of your time and salary for reading and processing the information the system produces. For information to be **worth its cost**, there must be an appropriate relationship between the cost of information and its value.

Consider an example. What is the value of a daily report of the names of the occupants of a full graveyard? Zero, unless grave robbery is a problem for the cemetery. The report is not worth the time required to read it. It is easy to see the importance of information economics for this silly example. It will be more difficult, however, when someone proposes the Gizmo 3.0 to you. You need to be ready to ask, "What's the value of the information?" "What is the cost?" "Is there an appropriate relationship between value and cost?" Information systems should be subject to the same financial analyses to which other assets are subjected.

Speaking of "worth its cost," what about this course? You are paying for this experience, so a good question to ask is, "Is it worth it?" Check the *Opposing Forces Guide* on page 13a to read statements that student contrarians have voiced about the MIS class.

Throughout this book, Opposing Forces Guides present a set of thoughts and ideas that run counter to the theme of each chapter. The purpose of these comments is to spur discussion and motivate your thinking.

■ Information Technology Versus Information Systems

Information technology and information systems are two closely related terms, but they are different. **Information technology (IT)** refers to the products, methods, inventions, and standards that are used for the purpose of producing information. As stated in the previous section, an *information system (IS)* is an assembly of hardware, software, data, procedures, and people that produces information.

Information technology drives the development of new information systems. Advances in information technology have taken the computer industry from the days of punched cards to the Internet, and such advances will continue to take the industry to the next stages and beyond.

Moore's Law

Gordon Moore is the cofounder of Intel Corporation, the world's leading manufacturer of computer chips and other computer-related components. In 1965, he said that because of technology improvements in electronic chip design and manufacturing, "The number of transistors per square inch on an integrated chip doubles every 18 months." This observation is known as **Moore's Law**. Moore's prediction has proved generally accurate in the 40 years since it was made.

The density of transistors on a computer chip relates to the speed of the chip, and so you will sometimes hear Moore's Law expressed as, "The speed of a computer chip doubles every 18 months." This is not exactly what Moore said, but it comes close to the essence of his idea.

"I Don't Need This Class"

Over the years, student-contrarians in my classes have voiced the following opinions:

» "I already know how to use Excel and Word. I can build a Web site with FrontPage. OK, it's a simple Web site, but I can do it. And when I need to learn more, I can. So let me out of this class!"

» "We're going to learn how to work with information systems? That's like practicing the stomach flu. If and when the time comes, I'll know how to do it."

» "I'm terrified of computers. I'm a people-person, and I don't do well with engineering-like things. I've put this class off until the last quarter of my senior year. I hope it's not as bad as I fear; I just wish they didn't make me take it."

» "There's really no content in this class. I mean, I've been programming since high school, I can write in C++, though PERL is my favorite language. I know computer technology. This class is just a bunch of management-babble mixed up with some computer terms. At least it's an easy class, though."

» "Well, I'm sure there is some merit to this class, but consider the opportunity cost. I really need to be taking more microeconomics and international business. The time that I spend on this class could be better spent on those subjects."

» "The only thing I need to know is how to surf the Web and how to use email. I know how to do those, so I just don't need this class."

» "What, you mean this class is not about learning Excel and FrontPage? That's what I thought we were going to learn. That's what I need to know. Why all this information systems stuff? How do I make a Web site? That's what I need to know."

There you have it, some contrarians' positions. You may have had one or two of these thoughts yourself—certainly, you've heard them from other students. Do those positions have merit?

DISCUSSION QUESTIONS

1. According to this chapter, what is the purpose of this class?

2. Look at this book's table of contents and thumb through the chapters. Notice that the text is broken down into four parts: two chapters in an introduction, four chapters on information technology, three chapters of information systems, and two chapters on IS management. Summarize what the book's organization tells you about the nature of this class.

3. List what you think are the five most important information technology topics. Because you've just started this class, you probably don't have much knowledge to guide you, but make the best judgments you can, given your current knowledge.

4. Given what you know now, list the five most important information systems topics.

5. Use Word or WordPerfect to write a memo to a senior manager of a major corporation, say a high-level executive in your major field of study (e.g., CFO if you are in accounting). Your memo can have one of two themes:

   a. It can claim that this course is a waste of time and that the executive should use her influence with the university to have this class removed from the curriculum. Use your answers to questions 3 and 4 as evidence for your position by saying that these topics, which are the most important ones in the class, just do not justify the time required.

   b. It can state that the students who graduate from your university are particularly well suited for employment at the executive's company because they have taken this class. Use your answers to questions 3 and 4 as evidence for your position by explaining how these topics will help you be more effective as a business professional.

Price Performance Ratio of Intel Processors

Year	Cost per 100,000 Transistors (2005 dollars)
1983	$3,923.00
1985	$902.95
1988	$314.50
1997	$17.45
2002	$0.97
2005	$0.05

Figure 1-6
Computer Price/Performance Ratio Decreases

Dramatic Reduction in Price/Performance Ratio

As a result of Moore's Law, the price/performance ratio of computers has fallen dramatically for years (see Figure 1-6). The result has been that computers have shrunk from multimillion dollar, room-filling machines in 1968 to $300 small desktop devices in 2005. Along the way, the availability of increased computing power has enabled developments such as laser printers, graphical user interfaces like Windows, high-speed communications, cell phones, PDAs, email, and the Internet.

In March 2003, Moore stated that he expects Moore's Law to hold for at least another 10 years. This means that computers will continue to become faster and cheaper through at least the early years of your career.

No one has been good at predicting what this means. The rapid rise of the Internet surprised even Microsoft co-founder Bill Gates. All we can say is that, because of the decreasing price/performance ratio, information technology will continue to change and improve, information systems will become even more powerful and effective, and businesses will find new ways of using these systems. The result should be further increases in worker productivity.

All of this means that information systems will increase in importance throughout your career. The knowledge you gain here will benefit you for many, many years to come. For example, read *MIS in Use 1-2* to learn about the successful use of information systems in the recovery from Hurricane Katrina in 2005.

◼ Enjoying This Class

One measure of whether you enjoy this class will be whether you learn things from it that seem relevant to you and that help you think more deeply about the subject matter. There is almost no better way to foster independent thought than to confront the opinions of others. The Opposing Forces Guides and the Problem Solving Guides will help you do that. In addition, each chapter concludes with an editorial, called a *Reflections Guide,* in which I express my personal ideas about material in the chapter. You may or

Using the Opposing Forces Guide (page 13a)

GOALS

* Teach the purpose of the MIS class.
* Expose fallacies in students' preconceived ideas about the class.

BACKGROUND AND PRESENTATION STRATEGIES

Most students will have little idea of what this class is about. If your class includes a software lab component, students will view this class as "the computer class." If it does not, then many students will be confused and view the class as having something to do with management and computers.

If you have time, this guide makes a good in-class, group exercise, because the students can compare notes about the nature of the class. Some questions to ask are:

➤ **Do these statements seem familiar to any of you? Has anyone thought one of these thoughts or heard rumors around campus like one of these?**

➤ **Which one?**

➤ **How many of you think this is the computer class?**

➤ **If this class isn't a computer class, or at least not primarily a computer class, then what do you think it's about?**

Another way to proceed is to put the students into some real-life situations in which they will apply what they will learn in this class.

➤ **Let's consider a real business. Suppose you are a departmental manager, say a manager of customer service at a local car dealership. Suppose your dealership is installing a new customer tracking system. You've been asked to meet with a team that is selecting the system.**

➤ **With regards to this situation, what would it be useful to know?**

Some of the students may have some idea of systems development, requirements specification, understanding what features and functions a "customer tracking system" should have, and what a CRM is. But, not many.

➤ **Looks like you're not real sure what you should know. So, would it be useful to learn in this class what you should know? Or, is that like practicing the flu?**

➤ Let's suppose that you do learn in this class what you should know, that you do your homework, that you are well prepared to be a team member, and that you play a major role in selecting an appropriate system.

➤ How does your dealership benefit?

➤ How do you benefit?

➤ How does this place your dealership at a competitive advantage vis-à-vis the competition where the manager of customer service hasn't a clue?

Another tactic is to introduce some terminology and technology that will be discussed in class, but do so in the context of a business manager.

➤ Consider another situation. Suppose you manage a traveling sales force. Your salespeople are frustrated that they can't readily log on to the company network while on the road. One of them tells you, "Hey, when I was with ABC corporation [your competitor], we used a VPN [virtual private network]. Why don't we have one?"

➤ Now, suppose you have no idea of what a VPN is or does. How do you respond? Avoid the issue? Say, "I don't know." Or take it to management? But what if it's a silly idea, one having nothing to do with remote access. How will you look when the experts tell your boss that you don't know what you're talking about?

➤ Now, as you'll learn in Chapter 5, it turns out that a VPN could be a great solution for a problem like this one. But, what if someone who doesn't know what he's talking about says that a VPN is a stupid idea? Given your ignorance, you back down. How does that feel? You were defeated by your own ignorance.

➤ There's a wonderful thing about ignorance. It's curable! All it takes is time and effort.

➤ As I said earlier, I'll point the way. It's up to you to take the opportunity to learn what you need to learn!

 SUGGESTED RESPONSES FOR DISCUSSION QUESTIONS

1. There is no sentence in Chapter 1 that says "The purpose of the class is." But, page 6 provides a set of guidelines:

   As a business professional in the twenty-first century, you need sufficient MIS knowledge to be an *informed and effective consumer* of information technology products and services. In particular, you need to be able to *ask pertinent questions*, you need to be able to *correctly interpret the responses* to your questions, and you need to have the *knowledge to make wise decisions and to manage effectively.*

Also see Figure 1-2. From this statement and figure, the students should be able to determine the purpose of the course.

2. Set aside the introductory chapters. The text has four chapters on technology—no, let's say three and a half, because systems development is as much management as it is technology—and it has five and a half chapters on business systems and management. So, the course is 3.5/5.5, or 38 percent, technology and 62 percent business systems and management. How's that for a *real* answer—not one of those squishy opinion-oriented ones!

3. Some possibilities:

   Appropriate uses of spreadsheets and databases

   Database technology

   Communications technology

   Systems development methodologies

   Security technology

4. Some possibilities:

   Understand fundamental intraorganization information system types and their purposes, characteristics, features, and functions.

   Understand fundamental interorganization information system types and their purposes, characteristics, features, and functions.

   Learn the relationship between information systems and organizational competitive strategy.

   Learn applications of business intelligence systems.

   Understand the key elements of IS management.

   Learn components of an organizational security plan.

   and others . . .

5. **a.** This is a difficult answer for me to write. I don't believe it at all. Were I forced to write such a memo, I supposed I'd focus on opportunity cost; saying something like, "Students need more accounting or finance or marketing instead of this class." It's all I can do, however, *to force myself to write those words.* I don't believe any of them.

   b. I believe a key characteristic for all successful managers today is to be able to find/manage/understand/support innovative applications of information technology and information systems. I'd base my memo around that characteristic.

WRAP UP

One way to conclude is to go back to the business settings.

➤ **Let's conclude with one other business situation. Suppose you manage telesales and all of your activities depend on data in the customer database. You work at a small company that does not have a permanent IS staff. One day, your boss says to you, "Do you think we're doing enough to protect our database?" How do you respond?**

➤ **We will consider this very case when we come to Chapter 11. Stay tuned!**

Using IS in Hurricane Katrina Recovery

Information systems played a vital role for rescue and recovery operations following Hurricane Katrina. During rescue operations, normal street addresses had little meaning to helicopter pilots flying over flooded streets and neighborhoods. To help pilots locate those in need, the U.S. Geological Survey provided computer-based information and maps that converted street addresses to GPS (latitude and longitude) coordinates.

Many U.S. businesses used information systems to provide support for disaster victims. For example, the hurricane displaced more than 34,000 Wal-Mart employees, severely damaged 17 of its stores and distribution centers, and damaged a total of 89 Wal-Mart facilities. Despite these disruptions, Wal-Mart responded rapidly by leveraging sophisticated information systems that support its supply chain, one of the world's most efficient. Using these information systems, Wal-Mart located and shipped needed items from distribution centers, warehouses, and suppliers across the United States. The company was able to ship to hurricane victims 1,900 truckloads of merchandise and food for 100,000 meals. Even before the hurricane made landfall, Wal-Mart had stocked 45 trucks with goods specific to the needs of survivors.

Other companies also provided assistance using information systems. IBM and Lenovo donated 1,500 laptop computers for use by agencies tracking air and water quality tests and by relief agencies registering evacuees for food stamps, Medicaid, and other social services. The donations included database management software (see Chapter 4), which is especially useful for tracking purposes.

After the hurricane, businesses faced the huge challenge of recovering from the disaster and resuming operations. Northrop

Grumman, a $30 billion shipbuilder and defense contractor, employs thousands of people in facilities at New Orleans and at Gulfport and Pascagoula, Mississippi. Northrop used its Web site to inform employees of policies and directives during the hurricane recovery. Immediately after the hurricane, it published contact phone numbers for employees to use and disseminated information about employee payment policy. In the following weeks, Northrop used the Web to inform employees where and when they should report to work. This use of the Web saved days and weeks of administrative chaos for both the company and its employees.

Larger companies like Wal-Mart and Northrop Grumman had established backup and recovery facilities for their information systems in sites well away from the hurricane's damage. Such companies were able to quickly resume information systems operations in those remote sites.

Some medium- and many small-sized organizations were less fortunate. For them, restoring their customer, sales, human resources, and accounting systems was time consuming and difficult. To help these small businesses, the Louisiana Technology Park in Baton Rouge offered free use of office space, computers, and Internet connections to New Orleans businesses having 25 or fewer employees. Such facilities enabled businesses to reconnect with their employees, customers, and suppliers, and to plan for restarting their businesses.

Sources: Michael Barbaro and Justin Gillis, "Wal-Mart at Forefront of Hurricane Relief," *Washington Post*, September 6, 2005, p. D01; IBM, "IBM Response Gains Ground in Aftermath of Katrina," *www.ibm.com* (accessed September 2005); Joseph F. Kovar, "Technology Park Open for New Orleans Small Businesses," CRN, September 6, 2005, *www.crn.com* (accessed September 2005); *www.northropgrumman.com/katrina/index.html* (accessed September 2005); and U.S. Geological Survey Web site, *www.usgs.gov/katrina/* (accessd September 2005).

---

may not agree with these ideas. But the activity of critically reading and considering them will help you marshall your thoughts and opinions about the chapter material.

Beyond such critical reading and thinking, the key to enjoying the class is to apply what you are learning to situations and organizations of interest to you. For example, think about the information systems around you. Consider your university's class enrollment system and ask as many questions as you can think of: What hardware, software, data, procedures, and people are involved? Who are the users? What procedures do they follow? How are those people trained? How do you suppose your class enrollment system was developed? Was it constructed just for your university? Was the software written in-house by university employees or was it purchased from vendors? Do other universities use this same system?

What information does the university gain from this system? Of course, the system schedules classes, but what other information does it produce? What can the university

Each chapter of this book concludes with an editorial, called the Reflections Guide. These editorials express my personal ideas about material in the chapter. These ideas are just my opinions; you, the student next to you, and your professor may all disagree with them. The goal of the Reflections Guide is to stimulate your thinking about the chapter's contents.

Duller Than Dirt?

Yes, you read that title correctly: This subject can seem duller than dirt. Take the phrase, "development and use of IS in organizations." Read just that phrase, and you start to yawn, wondering, "How am I going to absorb 400+ pages of this?"

Stop and think: Why are you reading this book? Right now in the Sea of Cortez the water is clear and warm, and the swimming and diving are wonderful. You could be kayaking to Isla San Francisco this minute. Or, somewhere in the world, people are skiing. Whether in Aspen, Colorado, or Portillo, Chile, people are blasting through the powder somewhere. You could be one of them, living in a small house with a group of friends, having good times at night. Or, whatever it is that you like to do, you could be doing it right now. So, why are you here, where you are, reading this book? Why aren't you there?

Waking up should be one of your goals while in college. I mean waking up to your life. Ceasing to live according to someone else's plan and beginning to live your own plan. Doing that requires you to become conscious of the choices you make and the consequences they have.

Suppose you take an hour to read your assignment in this book tonight. For a typical person, that is 4,320 heartbeats (72 beats times 60 minutes) that you have used to read this book—heartbeats that you will never have again. Despite the evidence of your current budget, the critical resource for humans is not money,

it is time. No matter what we do, we cannot get more of it. Was your reading today worth those 4,320 heartbeats?

For some reason, you chose to major in business. For some reason, you are taking this class, and for some reason, you have been instructed to read this textbook. Now, given that you made a good decision to major in business (and not to kayak in Baja), and given that someone is requiring you to read this text, the question then becomes, "How can you maximize the return on the 4,320 heartbeats you are investing per hour?"

The secret is to personalize the material. At every page, learn to ask yourself, "How does this pertain to me?" "How can I use this material to further my goals?" If you find some topic irrelevant, ask your professor or your classmates what they think. What's this topic for? Why are we reading this? What I am going to do with it later in my career? Why is this worth 1,000 (or whatever) heartbeats?

MIS is all-encompassing. To me that's one of its beauties. Consider the components: hardware, software, data, procedures, and people. Do you want to be an engineer? Then work the hardware component. Do you want to be programmer? Write software. Do you want to be a practicing philosopher, an applied epistemologist? Learn data modeling. Do you like social systems and sociology? Learn how to design effective group and organizational procedures. Do you like people? Become an IS trainer or a computer systems salesperson. Do you enjoy management? Learn how to bring all of those disparate elements together.

I've worked in this industry for almost 40 years. The breadth of MIS and the rapid change of technology have kept me fascinated for every one of those years. Further, the beauty of working with intellectual property is that it doesn't weigh very much; you don't wear yourself out moving symbols around. And you do it indoors in a temperature-controlled office. They may even put your name on the door.

So, wake up. Why are you reading this? How can you make it relevant? Jump onto Google and search for MIS careers or some other phrase from this chapter and see what you get. Challenge yourself to find something that is important to you personally, in every chapter.

You just invested 780 heartbeats in reading this editorial. Was it worth it? Keep asking!

DISCUSSION QUESTIONS

1. Explain what it means to "wake up to your life."

2. Are you awake to your life? How do you know? What can you do once a week to ensure that you are awake to your life?

3. What are your professional goals? Are they yours, or are they someone else's? How do you know?

4. How does this class pertain to your professional goals?

5. How are you going to make the material in in this class interesting?

learn about trends in education? About trends in student goals and objectives? What information can it extract from this system to facilitate planning and budgeting?

Every day you touch dozens of information systems. Begin to ask yourself about the nature of those systems and how they impact you. What, besides the obvious, do they do? At the grocery store, is the information system that interprets the UPC codes on the items that you buy connected to the information system that processes your credit card? If so, could the credit card company refuse to allow you to buy certain items? Would they? Would it be legal if they did? Who owns the data about your grocery store purchases? What keeps the credit card company from selling the fact that you buy lots of ice cream to the Association of Dairy Farmers of America? Could your insurance company raise the premium on your health insurance because you buy lots of calorie-laden foods?

Less controversial, consider the information systems you encounter in the context of your major field of study. For example, if you are studying marketing, how could the marketing department of the grocery store use the purchase data to plan sales? Or how can management use the effectiveness of sales promotions? How can the grocery store use its information systems to control theft?

As you proceed through this class, learn to be curious about the information systems around you. Ask the employees of stores and restaurants what they think about the systems they use. How long have they had their information system? What did they do before it? How well do they like it? The more you apply the knowledge you gain in this class to your life, the more interesting it will be, and the more you will enjoy this class.

SUMMARY

- MIS stands for *management information systems.* The term is defined as the development and use of information systems that help businesses achieve their goals and objectives. The three major elements of this definition are: *development and use, information systems*, and *business goals and objectives.*

- An information system is a group of components that interact to produce information. The five components of an information system are: hardware, software, data, procedures, and people. These components are common to all information systems, from the smallest to the largest. Because information systems include people and procedures, they involve more than just a computer. Also, a variety of skills besides those of computer technicians and programmers are required to develop and use information systems.

- Non-IS majors need to know about IS development because, as future users, they will provide requirements for new systems and facilitate the management of new IS projects. Business professionals also need to know how to use information systems and how to assist in managing an IS for better security and reliability.

- Businesses are inanimate; they do not do anything. *People* provide the energy that activates businesses.

The purpose of information systems is to help people accomplish the goals and objectives of the business or organization at which they work. As a future business professional, you need to look at information systems through the lens of business need. Learn to ask the question, "It may be wonderful technology, but what will it do for our goals and objectives?"

- As a business professional, you need sufficient MIS knowledge to be an informed and effective consumer of information technology products and services. You need to be able to ask relevant questions and interpret the responses correctly, to make wise IS decisions, and to manage your IS responsibilities effectively. You need to know more than basic terminology; you also need to know why information systems are needed, what the essential technologies and systems are, and how information systems are to be managed and developed. Finally, and most importantly, you need to learn how to learn about IS technology.

- The five-component framework can guide your learning. When we automate some process, we take work from the human side of these five components and move it to the computer side, as shown in Figure 1-3. Low-tech information systems do not move as much work from one side to the other as do

You Be the Guide

Using the Reflections Guide
(page 15a)

GOALS

* Share our excitement about MIS with our students.

* Establish the fact that this class is work. Some topics take time and effort to learn. That's OK.

* Discuss strategies for making the subject interesting.

* Introduce students to the idea of "waking up to your life."

BACKGROUND AND PRESENTATION STRATEGIES

See the annotation for the start of this chapter. You might choose to use some of that material with this guide at the end of your presentation.

I use the "waking up to your life" theme as a wrap up for this lecture. See the Wrap Up.

I take the students' goal of being a business professional very seriously—occasionally more seriously than some of them do. Given that goal, I'm here to help those who want to learn how to use IS and related topics to help them strengthen their personal competitiveness.

I love this field, and you probably do too. Tell the students why! They will be very interested to know why you picked this discipline, what you like about it, what the challenges are, what you find interesting. Few students will want to be professors, but they will want to know what aspects of your interests will apply to them.

This class can be *fun and incredibly interesting.* Especially if students learn to *personalize the topics;* that is, to constantly to ask themselves, how can I use this knowledge to get a job? To get a better job? To gain a competitive advantage? To be a better professional? Examples:

➤ **How will I, as a future public relations agent, use this material? What do I need to know to get a public relations job in technology? How can I use data communications technology to make me more productive?**

➤ **What do I, as a future general manager, need to know about this subject? What do I need to know about developing information systems? What do I need to know about using IT to advance corporate strategy?**

➤ **Should I think about an IS career? Although hardware and software jobs exist, not every IS professional writes computer programs or installs network gear. It's all about the innovative application of IT and IS for the solution of business problems. That could be interesting!**

Having said all of that, at times this topic is duller than dirt. No getting around it. So, sometimes a person just has to buckle down and do the work. *Ignorance is curable, but it doesn't cure itself.* Not every topic will be exciting and interesting to every student all the time. That doesn't mean the topics aren't important.

Depending on the students' age and maturity, sometimes I leave it at that. But, if they are young and need coaching, I'll go on with something like:

➤ **Like any challenging course, you cannot succeed by channel surfing. You can't switch channels when the going gets hard. You have to stay with it.**

➤ **If you're a CFO and the financial statements have to be filed, they have to be filed, and you make that happen. It's all part of being a business professional.**

➤ **If you're a manager, and the computer budget needs to be submitted, you do what you have to do. If you don't know what something is or does, you find out. It doesn't matter how tired you are, how many other things you have to do, you just keep working; it must be done. At least, you do that *if you're a professional.***

➤ **So, learn not to quit when the going gets rough. Learn that behavior now, before you start your career!**

Students are students, and undergraduates are undergraduates. Many are young. They get busy with other classes; they get distracted with their friends; they get involved in campus activities that consume their study time. As the class proceeds, I have to keep stoking the fires of their interest by showing them my excitement about the material. Ultimately, however, *it's not my excitement about the class that motivates them; it's their excitement.* Mine just gets them going.

Every lecture, I need to do something to build that excitement. If I can do that, this class is a joy to teach. When I don't do that, it's like dragging a 500-pound sack of potatoes across campus. Again, it's the excitement of the students that moves the class along.

SUGGESTED RESPONSES FOR DISCUSSION QUESTIONS

1. To realize that every morning I'm a day older. That my life is going by and whether or not I'm aware of it, decisions I make each day impact the quality of my life. Here's a question that is sometimes revealing to students:

   ➤ **Have you ever heard the statement, "You need to take responsibility for your life"?**

   ➤ **I'm curious, how can any of us *not* take responsibility for our lives?**

   If we choose not to think about our lives, that's taking responsibility by default. It's taking responsibility by not taking responsibility. In fact, we cannot avoid taking responsibility for our lives. We're condemned to it.

2. You might ask the class the following questions:

   ➤ **Do you think about your goals? About how well you're accomplishing your goals? Do you think about what you want to accomplish in "this awkward time between birth and death"?**

   ➤ **Write a note to remind yourself that you cannot avoid responsibility for your life. Make goals; see how you're doing. Once a week may be too often. How about once a month?**

3. The purpose of this question is to ask the students to ask themselves whether they're living their lives by someone else's criteria. I think that's such an important task for undergraduates—especially for the traditional 20-year-old junior. Why do they attend college? Why are they business majors? What to they want to do? Are these their goals or their parents' goals? Are they an interpretation of what it means to be successful?

   If the answers to these questions indicate they chose these goals for themselves, then the students can rededicate themselves to the goals. But if not, now's the time to find out. If you'd rather be a painter, an engineer, or a biochemist, now's the time to figure that out.

4. Because it will help you learn to use IS to solve problems, make better decisions, and become a more complete business professional.

5. The text suggests personalizing it—making the material relevant to the students' goals.

WRAP UP

Sometimes I wrap up the first lecture with the following:

➤ **You and I, all of us, have just invested 3,600 heartbeats in the last 50 minutes. That's 3,600 heartbeats we'll never have again. Was it worth it? If not, what can *we* (that is *all of us—you and me*) do to make it worth it next time?**

➤ **Over the years, I've come to view a class like a woven tapestry. Each of us contributes one string of yarn, one string of the warp or one of the weft. We weave this experience together. I bring my excitement for the topic, my knowledge, my experiences, and I frame the experience. What happens, next, however, is up to you. Did you do the homework? Did you read the assignment? Are you surfing the Web or sending emails or are you listening? Are you relating this material to your goals?**

➤ **We make this experience together. I hope we will weave a beautiful tapestry, and to that end, I will do all I can. I hope you will, too. See you next time!**

high-tech systems. Also, when you learn about a new IS, look for all five components; remember the impact of IS on procedures and people, the components to which you, as a manager, will be closest. Finally, remember that the components are listed in Figure 1-3 from left to right in increasing order of difficulty of change and disruption to the organization.

■ The term *information* is easy to use yet difficult to define. Four definitions are given in this chapter: Information is (a) knowledge derived from data; (b) data presented in a meaningful context; (c) data processed by summing, ordering, averaging, grouping, comparing, or other similar operations; and (d) a difference that makes a difference.

■ Information is subjective; one person's data is another person's information. As shown in Figure 1-5, good information is accurate, timely, relevant to context and subject, just barely sufficient, and worth its cost.

■ The terms *information technology* and *information systems* differ. Information technology (IT) refers to products, inventions, methods, and standards used for the purpose of producing information. An information system (IS) refers to the assembly of hardware, software, data, procedures, and people that produces information.

■ Moore's Law states that the number of transistors per square inch on an integrated chip doubles every 18 months. Sometimes this statement is taken to mean that the speed of a computer processor doubles every 18 months; this latter statement is not what Moore said, but it is close and it has the gist of the idea. Because of this phenomenon, the price/performance ratio of computers has fallen exponentially. Moore expects his law to hold for at least another 10 years, so you will see dramatic changes in the use of IT during at least the early years of your career.

■ To enjoy this class, you need to make the material personal. You need to apply what you are learning to situations and organizations that hold your interest. The more you apply this material to situations in your life, the more you will enjoy it.

KEY TERMS AND CONCEPTS

Accurate information **12**
Computer hardware **4**
Computer-based information system **5**
Data **4**
Five-component framework **4**
Information **10**
Information system (IS) **4**

Information technology **13**
Just-barely-sufficient information **13**
Management information systems (MIS) **4**
Moore's Law **13**
People **4**

Procedures **4**
Relevant information **12**
Software **4**
Strong password **5a**
System **4**
Timely information **12**
Worth-its-cost information **13**

ASSIGNMENT MATERIAL

Review Questions

1. Why do business professionals need to be involved with the development of information systems?

2. Explain some of the roles business professionals need to play in the use of information systems.

3. Explain the statement, "Businesses don't do anything."

4. Give an example of each of the five components of the system you use to register for classes.

5. What is a computer-based information system? In this text, what is the difference between an information system and a computer-based information system?

6. List three invalid reasons for creating an information system.

7. List three characteristics of MIS knowledge you need to have to be an effective business professional in the twenty-first century.

8. Summarize the "why" component of this class.

9. Summarize the "what" component of this class.

10. Summarize the "how" component of this class.

11. Because IS technology changes so fast, what else do you need to learn about MIS?

12. Explain the symmetry in the five-component framework.

13. How can you use the five-component framework to guide your learning about a new information system?

14. Explain in your own words why changing the procedure and people components of an information system is difficult.

15. Give four different definitions of information.

16. Which of the four definitions of information do you like best? Explain your choice.

17. Explain why information is subjective.

18. Explain the difference between information technology and information systems.

19. State Moore's Law.

Applying Your Knowledge

20. Using your own knowledge and opinions, as well as those listed in the *Opposing Forces Guide* (pages 13a and 13b), describe three misconceptions of the purpose of this class. In your own words, describe what you think the purpose of this class is.

21. Describe three to five personal goals for this class. None of these goals should include anything about your GPA. Be as specific as possible and make the goals personal to your major, interests, and career aspirations. Assume that you are going to evaluate yourself on these goals at the end of the quarter or semester. The more specific you make these goals, the easier it will be to perform the evaluation. Use Figure 1-2 for guidance.

22. Consider costs of a system in light of the five components: costs to buy and maintain the hardware; costs to develop or acquire licenses to the software programs and costs to maintain them; costs to design databases and fill them with data; costs of developing procedures and keeping them current; and finally, human costs both to develop and use the system.

    a. Over the lifetime of a system, many experts believe that the single most expensive component is people. Does this belief seem logical to you? Explain why you agree or disagree.

    b. Consider a poorly developed system that does not meet its defined requirements. The needs of the business do not go away, but they do not conform themselves to the characteristics of the poorly built system. Therefore, something must give. Which component picks up the slack when the hardware and software programs do not work correctly? What does this say about the cost of a poorly designed system? Consider both direct money costs as well as intangible personnel costs.

    c. What implications do you, as a future business manager, take from questions (a) and (b)? What does this say about the need for your involvement in requirements and other aspects of systems development? Who eventually will pay the costs of a poorly developed system? Against which budget will those costs accrue?

23. Consider the four definitions of information presented in this chapter. The problem with the first definition, "knowledge derived from data," is that it merely substitutes one word we don't know the meaning of (*information*) for a second word we don't know the meaning of (*knowledge*). The problem with the second definition, "data presented in a meaningful context," is that it is too subjective. Whose context? What makes a context meaningful? The third definition, "data processed by summing, ordering, averaging, etc.," is too mechanical. It tells us what to do, but it doesn't tell us what information is. The fourth definition, "a difference that makes a difference," is vague and unhelpful.

    Also, none of these definitions helps us to quantify the amount of information we receive. What is the information content of the statement that every human being has a navel? Zero—you already know that. On the other hand, the statement that someone has just deposited $50,000 into your checking account is chock-full of information. So, good information has an element of surprise.

    Considering all of these points, answer the following questions:

    a. What is information made of?

    b. If you have more information, do you weigh more? Why or why not?

    c. If you give a copy of your transcript to a prospective employer, is that information? If you show that same transcript to your dog, is it still information? Where is the information?

    d. Give your own best definition of information.

    e. Explain how you think it is possible that we have an industry called the *information technology industry*, but we have great difficulty defining the word *information*.

24. The text states that information should be worth its cost. Both cost and value can be broken into tangible and intangible factors. *Tangible* factors can be directly measured; *intangible* ones arise indirectly and are difficult to measure. For example, a tangible cost is the cost of a computer monitor; an intangible cost is the lost productivity of a poorly trained employee.

   Give five important tangible and five important intangible costs of an information system. Give five important tangible and five important intangible measures of the value of an information system. If it helps to focus your thinking, use the example of the class scheduling system at your university or some other university information system. When determining whether an information system is worth its cost, how do you think the tangible and intangible factors should be considered?

Application Exercises

25. Suppose that you are seeking employment and you want to keep track of companies and the contacts you've had with those companies.

   a. Create a spreadsheet with the following headings: CompanyName, WebSite, City, State, ContactDate, PersonContacted, EmailAddress, Phone, ContactRemarks.

   b. Place sample data into your spreadsheet. Your data should have multiple companies and multiple contacts per company.

   c. Describe the five components of an information system for using the spreadsheet to obtain a job.

   d. Suppose you share this spreadsheet with a group of other students—perhaps roommates or classmates or members of a student club. Describe the five components of an information system for how your group would use this spreadsheet.

   e. How does your answer differ between questions c and d above? What general conclusions can you draw from this example?

26. Suppose that you are seeking employment and you want to keep track of companies and the contacts you've had with those companies.

   a. Create an Access database with two tables: COMPANY having the columns CompanyName, WebSite, City, State and CONTACT having the columns ContactDate, PersonContacted, EmailAddress, Phone, ContactRemarks, and CompanyName. Assume that CompanyName in CONTACT relates to CompanyName in COMPANY.

   b. Place sample data into both tables. Your data should have multiple companies and multiple contacts per company.

   c. Create a data entry form for both tables. The type of form you create depends on your knowledge of Access. If you are a novice, just open the tables and add the data.

   d. Create a simple report that lists companies and the contacts you've made with those companies. Use the Access Report wizard. (*Hint:* First define the relationship between COMPANY and CONTACT. In Access, click on Tools/Relationships. Right click in the design space and select Show Table. Add tables COMPANY and CONTACT. In the design space, drag CompanyName from COMPANY and drop on CompanyName in CONTACT. Click Create. Close the design space and save your changes. Now run the Report Wizard to create your report.)

   e. Describe the five components of an information system for using this database to obtain a job.

   f. Suppose you share this database with a group of other students—perhaps roommates or classmates, or members of a student club. Describe the five components of an information system for how your group would use this database.

   g. How does your answer differ between questions e and f above? What general conclusions can you draw from this example?

Career Assignments

27. Using Google (*google.com*) or your favorite Web search tool, search for job opportunities that relate to information systems. Some terms that you might use in your search are:

   - Information systems job opportunities
   - Computer sales job opportunities
   - Computer support job opportunities
   - Computer training job opportunities
   - Systems analyst job opportunities
   - Business computer programmer job opportunities
   - Software testing job opportunities
   - Computer software product manager job opportunities
   - Computer-based marketing job opportunities

   If you can imagine or know of other job possibilities, search for them as well. If you think that pure IT is too technical for you, concentrate your search on jobs that involve the human side of information systems, such as sales, support, marketing, training, consulting, and systems analysis.

28. From the results of your searches, identify five different job opportunities related to information systems. Try to find as wide a range of job types as you can. Some will be technical, like computer engineer; others will be less technical, like computer sales or computer support. Identify job types that involve the use of computers and IT in the business environment.

29. Select two of the job types in your answer to question 28 in which you might be interested. From the descriptions, describe the general educational requirements of these two jobs. Describe the general experience requirements of these two jobs.

30. For each of your two job types in your answer to question 28, search the Web for internship possibilities. For example, if you might be interested in software testing, search for "software testing internship jobs." Identify two or three different possibilities.

31. Summarize actions you can take to prepare for these two jobs. Consider not just what courses you should take, but also part-time work, internships, volunteer work, and other activities.

Case Study 1-1

Computerizing the Ministry of Foreign Affairs

In 1994, the Ministry of Foreign Affairs of a West African country embarked on an ambitious program to computerize its internal services and communications. The project began slowly, with limited funding, and it relied on donated hardware and software. In 1999, the goals of the project were revised to include the development of Web-based applications, and at that point the project received internal budget allocations. Between 1999 and 2002, a total of $650,000 was allocated.

The system's purpose was to make the organization dynamic and modern via the use of information technology. For example, the United Nations provides data and documents electronically, and the Foreign Affairs Ministry wanted to participate in the use of this new technology.

Another project goal was to facilitate communication between the Ministry of Foreign Affairs home office and its diplomatic missions abroad. In particular, the new system would use an external Web site and email to distribute information and facilitate discussions and decision making between geographically separated participants. A specific objective was to reduce travel costs by half.

Unfortunately, by 2002 the project had delivered few benefits. Data continued to be stored on paper, a local computer network within the Ministry was inoperative, and the diplomatic correspondence bag remained the primary means of exchanging paper-based information. Diplomats continued to travel, and travel expenses were not reduced by the new system. In short, the project was a failure.

In his case study of this application, Kenhago Olivier identified three factors behind the failure of this system:

1. Vendor contracts were awarded not on the basis of competence, but rather on personal relations between Ministry officials and vendor personnel.
2. The major application threatened the perquisites ("perks") of diplomats. Travel is an important source of revenue for headquarters personnel; they compensate for their low salaries by travel compensation and by the opportunity to trade goods.

3. The computing infrastructure was limited; there were a maximum of two personal computers per department at headquarters and only 35 computers in a building housing more than 300 officials.

Source: K. T. Olivier, "Problems in Computerising the Ministry of Foreign Affairs," Success/Failure Case Study No. 23, eGovernment for Development, *www.egov4dev.org/mofa.htm* (accessed October 2004).

Questions

1. The purpose of this system was for the Ministry of Foreign Affairs "to become a more dynamic, modern organization via the use of information technology." What are the dangers of stating the purpose of a system in this way? How could this statement be improved?

2. Why was the goal of reducing travel costs not achieved? What steps would need to be taken before this goal could ever be achieved? What is the likely outcome in any system in which the goals of the system conflict with the interests of important users? Which is stronger—the momentum of the new system or the resistance of the users?

3. When the features of new information systems conflict with the needs and desires of important user groups, what should be done? Should system development be stopped? If not, should the features be changed? What can be done to reduce the users' resistance? Who is in a position to resolve the conflict—the development team? The business users? Someone else?

4. This case description implies that the project was severely underfunded. Attempting to modernize a department with donated equipment sounds desperate, and trying to change communication patterns using email when 300 officials share 35 personal computers is probably impossible. The desire to use the U.N.'s computer-based systems to reduce travel and to enable email communication are appropriate goals for a governmental organization today. But, the limited funding is a reality. If you were placed in charge of a project that was underfunded like this one, what would you do?

5. In most cases, the costs of an information system are not known at the beginning of a project. It is only after specifying requirements and identifying alternative solutions that costs can be approximated. Knowing this, how would you proceed if you were given the responsibility for managing a new development project? What would you do if you found that the funding available is not nearly enough? What would you do if you found that the funding is 10 to 20 percent too low? What would you do if the funding appeared to be adequate, but you sensed that the cost estimates were optimistically low? In each of these cases, what is the best strategy for your organization? For your career?

Case Study 1-2

IRS Requirements Creep, Revisited

Reread the "Requirements Creep at the IRS" case on page 7 In response to the problems that it identified, the IRS Oversight Board recommended the following two actions:[4]

Video

[4]The report identified more than two problems and made more than two recommendations. See the "Independent Analysis of IRS Business Systems Modernization Special Report" at *www.irsoversightboard.treas.gov.*

- "The IRS business units must take direct leadership and ownership of the Modernization program and each of its projects. In particular, this must include defining the scope of each project, preparing realistic and attainable business cases, and controlling scope changes throughout each project's life cycle..."
- "Create an environment of trust, confidence, and teamwork between the business units, the BSM and ITS organizations, and the Prime...."

Questions

1. Why did the Oversight Board place leadership and ownership of the Modernization program on the business units? Why did it not place these responsibilities on the ITS organization?

2. Why did the Oversight Board place the responsibility for controlling scope changes on the business units? Why was this responsibility not given to the BSM? To ITS? To Computer Sciences Corporation?

3. The second recommendation is a difficult assignment, especially considering the size of the IRS and the complexity of the project. How does one go about creating "an environment of trust, confidence, and teamwork?"

   To make this recommendation more comprehensible, translate it to your local university. Suppose, for example, that your College of Business embarked on a program to modernize its computing facilities, including computer labs, and the computer network facilities used for teaching, including Internet-based distance learning. Suppose that the Business School dean created a committee like the BSM that hired a vendor to create the new computing facilities for the college. Suppose further that the committee proceeded without any involvement of the faculty, staff, students, or the existing computer support department. Finally, suppose that the project was one year late, had spent $400,000, was not nearly finished, and that the vendor complained that the requirements kept changing.

   Now, assume that you have been given the responsibility of creating "an environment of trust, confidence, and teamwork" among the faculty, staff, other users, the computer support department, and the vendor. How would you proceed?

4. The problem in question 3 involves at most a few hundred people and a few sites. The IRS problem involves 100,000 people and over 1,000 sites. How would you modify your answer to question 3 for a project as large as the IRS's?

5. If the existing system works (which apparently it does), why is the BSM needed? Why fix a system that works?

Purposes of Information Systems

Learning Objectives

- Know the eight principles of competitive advantage.
- Understand how information systems create competitive advantage.
- Define *problem*.
- Recognize that different information systems are needed to solve different problem definitions.
- Know the characteristics of decision making.
- Understand how information systems facilitate decision making.

Guides

SECURITY GUIDE
Security as Competitive Advantage

ETHICS GUIDE
Limiting Access to Those Who Have Access

OPPOSING FORCES GUIDE
G. Robinson Old Prints and Maps

PROBLEM SOLVING GUIDE
Egocentric vs. Empathetic Thinking

REFLECTIONS GUIDE
Your Personal Competitive Advantage

Chapter Preview

Recall from Chapter 1 that MIS is the development and use of information systems that help organizations achieve their goals and objectives. Here in Chapter 2 we address the last part of this definition: achieving organizational goals and objectives. In particular, this chapter explains three purposes of information systems:

- *To gain competitive advantage*
- *To solve problems*
- *To assist in decision making*

These purposes sometimes overlap. A particular information system may help achieve competitive advantage, it may help to solve problems, and it may assist decision making. Despite this overlap, we will consider each of these purposes independently.

This chapter introduces several information system examples. These examples by no means represent all possible information systems. Instead, they are just samples that we use to show some of the ways information systems help organizations accomplish their goals and objectives. A comprehensive description of information system types is presented in Chapters 7, 8, and 9.

We begin this and all of the following chapters in this book with a business situation that you could encounter early in your career. These situations include a problem whose solution requires the ideas and concepts presented in the chapter. As you read each chapter, think about how to apply what you're reading to this introductory problem. At the end of each chapter, we discuss the use of the chapter contents for solving the problem. In some cases, you will have an opportunity to apply the concepts in end of chapter exercises as well.

Not Worth It?

Advance the clock a couple of years. You've landed the job you always wanted at Amalgamated Industries (or some company), and you like it. You're doing well, and as a sign of confidence, your boss nominated you to a temporary project team investigating the development of a Web-based customer support application. You worked on the team part time over several weeks and helped to create a presentation that was delivered to your division's group manager. As the most junior member of the team, you had no speaking role at the presentation, but because of your active team involvement, the team leader asked you to prepare many of the presentation slides.

Several nights after the presentation, you happen to run into the division's group manager on your way to your car in the parking lot. He waves at you and says something, so you walk over to say hello. You exchange pleasantries for a minute or two, and then he says, "I don't think it's worth it."

"You mean the new project?" you ask, surprised at the abrupt change in the conversation.

"Yes, exactly. I don't think it's worth it. It won't generate any revenue, so why proceed?"

"But," you stammer, "it's a good idea, anyway. With it we could...."

And at this point, you realize you're talking one-on-one with your boss's boss's boss. You get nervous and start to stammer, "Well, well, we could, I mean I know, uh, that...."

"Go on," he says, "tell me why we should build it. Since it won't generate any revenue, what will it do? "

Scenarios like one this happen every day. Such accidental meetings offer an opportunity to build your network and your reputation in the company. When an opportunity like this falls into your lap, you need to take advantage of it. In this situation, you need a framework of the purposes of information systems in order to organize your answer. You will learn such a framework in this chapter.

Information Systems for Competitive Advantage

Video

Businesses continually seek to establish *competitive advantage* in the marketplace as a way to gain an edge over other businesses that are seeking the same customers. Figure 2-1 lists eight **principles** by which businesses can create **competitive advantage**.[1] The first three principles concern products. Organizations gain a competitive advantage by creating *new* products or services, by *enhancing* existing products or services, and by *differentiating* their products and services from those of their competitors. As you think about these three principles, realize that an information system can be part of a product or it can provide support for a product.

Consider, for example, a car rental agency like Hertz or Avis. An information system that produces information about the car's location and provides driving instructions to destinations is part of the car rental and thus is part of the product itself (see Figure 2-2a). In contrast, an information system that schedules car maintenance is not part of the product, but instead supports the product (Figure 2-2b). Either way, information systems

1. Create a new product or service
2. Enhance products or services
3. Differentiate products or services
4. Lock in customers and buyers
5. Lock in suppliers
6. Raise barriers to market entry
7. Establish alliances
8. Reduce costs

Figure 2-1
Principles of Competitive Advantage

[1]The discussion here is based on the work of Michael Porter. We will investigate his work in more detail in Chapters 7 (pages 206–209) and 8 (pages 230–231).

Not Worth It? (page 26)

GOALS

* Motivate the need for a framework regarding the organizational uses of information systems.

* Illustrate one way that non-IS professionals can use knowledge of MIS to advance their careers.

WAYS TO STIMULATE STUDENT INVOLVEMENT

The protagonist of this story is not an IS person, yet he or she is using knowledge of MIS to advance his or her career. The content of this class is vital background knowledge that *every* business professional today must know.

➤ **You cannot effectively participate as the member of a management team without knowledge of IS. If you try to do so without this knowledge, you'll be at a serious disadvantage.**

The senior manager does not want to know about technology. He wants to know about the business justification for the system. He asks, "Why should we build it?" This vignette encapsulates the nature of this MIS class: How can we use technology to serve a business need? It's not about computers and software and databases, it's about business needs and applications of those components to the solution of those needs.

Conversations like the one in the parking lot happen all the time. It's a great way for people to communicate without the restrictions of a formal meeting with all the baggage that impedes communication when multiple layers of management meet.

Ask the students to consider this scenario from the standpoint of the senior manager. Why would the manager encourage the conversation?

• It's a great way to get to know junior employees. Senior managers can find out how junior employees think and learn their strengths and weaknesses. Managers can also build rapport with new people.

• Senior managers know that their organization is only as good as the people who work in it. They also are concerned that the right people with the right skills are in the right jobs. The senior manager might be considering this person for an opportunity that's coming up.

• However, the senior manager could be just chatting because he or she has 10 minutes to spare before a dinner engagement. In such meetings, you just don't know, but you need to present yourself well in any case.

• Then, too, the senior manager may truly want to talk about the proposed system. The manager may have misgivings and want to discuss them with someone on the team. The manager might prefer to discuss them with the junior person, because that person might be less likely to shape remarks in terms of organizational politics.

➤ **The bottom line: You don't know why you're having this conversation, but whatever the reason, you'd like to do well.**

➤ **This chapter provides three different frameworks for the ways in which organizations use information systems:**

  • **To achieve competitive advantage**

  • **To solve problems**

  • **To improve decision making**

➤ **Frameworks are essential for organizing one's thinking. When someone proposes the Gizmo 3.0 system to you, use these frameworks to understand the benefits of the system:**

  • **Will it give competitive advantage?**

  • **Does it solve an important problem?**

  • **Will it help people make better decisions?**

WRAP UP

➤ **The purpose of this chapter is to help you give a quality answer to the question, "Why do organizations use IS?" Or, more specifically, for this scenario, the question, "Since it won't generate revenue, what will it do?" We will consider the various ways that information systems help organizations achieve their goals and objectives.**

When we're done, you'll know how to respond to this senior manager.

➤ **These frameworks, by the way, will also help you organize the material you learn in this class. As we talk about IT and IS in the weeks to come, keep asking yourself, how does this material contribute to one of the three purposes you learned here?**

a. Information System as Part of a Car Rental Product

Daily Service Schedule -- November 17, 2005

StationID   22
StationName   Lubrication

ServiceDate	ServiceTime	VehicleID	Make	Model	Mileage	ServiceDescription
11/17/2005	12:00 AM	155890	Ford	Explorer	2244	Std. Lube
11/17/2005	11:00 AM	12448	Toyota	Tacoma	7558	Std. Lube

StationID   26
StationName   Alignment

ServiceDate	ServiceTime	VehicleID	Make	Model	Mileage	ServiceDescription
11/17/2005	9:00 AM	12448	Toyota	Tacoma	7558	Front end alignment inspect

StationID   28
StationName   Transmission

ServiceDate	ServiceTime	VehicleID	Make	Model	Mileage	ServiceDescription
11/17/2005	11:00 AM	155890	Ford	Explorer	2244	Transmission oil change

b. Information System that Supports a Car Rental Product

Figure 2-2
Two Roles for Information
Systems Regarding Products

can achieve the first three objectives in Figure 2-1. The *Security Guide* on page 27a discusses ways to use security for competitive advantage.

The next three principles of competitive advantage shown in Figure 2-1 concern the creation of barriers. It seems obvious that businesses might want to establish barriers to keep out competitors. Less obvious, perhaps, is that those businesses also want to establish barriers to lock in their customers and suppliers. Organizations can *lock in customers* by making it difficult or expensive for customers to switch to another product. This strategy is sometimes called establishing high **switching costs**. Organizations can *lock in suppliers* by making it difficult to switch to another organization, or, stated positively, by making it easy to connect to and work with the organization. Finally, competitive advantage can be gained by *creating entry barriers* that make it difficult and expensive for new competition to enter the market.

Another means to gain competitive advantage is to *establish alliances* with other organizations. Such alliances establish standards, promote product awareness and needs, develop market size, reduce purchasing costs, and provide other benefits. Finally, organizations can gain competitive advantage by *reducing costs*. Such reductions enable the organization to reduce prices and/or to increase profitability. Increased profitability means not just greater shareholder value, but also more cash, which can fund further infrastructure development for even greater competitive advantage.

All of these principles of competitive advantage make sense, but the question you may be asking is, "How do information systems help to create competitive advantage?" To answer that question, consider a sample information system.

Information System that Creates a Competitive Advantage

ABC, Inc.[2] is a worldwide shipper with sales well in excess of a billion dollars. From its inception, ABC invested heavily in information technology and led the shipping industry

---

[2]The information system described here is used by a major transportation company, but unfortunately, that company refused to allow Prentice Hall to print its name or logo. That decision is difficult to understand because this case places the company in a very favorable light. In spite of their request for anonymity, we can still learn important principles from their example.

Security as Competitive Advantage

The two news items shown in Figures 1 and 2 describe two different security problems. These items include terms that we will not define until Chapters 3 through 5, so for now, just read these two items to get the gist of the situation.

The Slammer worm was a computer program that infected computers that were operating a Microsoft program called SQL Server. The worm was so effective that it even infected computers at Microsoft's headquarters. The worm did nothing harmful; it just consumed so many computer resources that serious traffic jams occurred over the Internet. Microsoft had posted a fix to plug the hole used by this worm on its Web site, but many, possibly most, SQL Server users had not installed that fix.

The second problem occurred in software from the PeopleSoft division of Oracle Corporation. This particular problem allowed hackers to exploit PeopleSoft software to install unauthorized programs on the computers of PeopleSoft's customers. The

Figure 1

cnet NEWS.COM
TECH NEWS FIRST

Front Page | Enterprise | E-Business | Communications | Media

Week in review: Worm's wrath

By Steven Musil
Staff Writer, CNET News.com
February 7, 2003, 10:00 AM PT

A week after Slammer disrupted Net traffic and caused chaos on some corporate networks, the tech world managed to catch its breath and assess the damage caused by the lightning-fast worm.

The worm infected more than 90 percent of vulnerable computers within 10 minutes, opening a new era of fast-spreading viruses on the Internet. The SQL Slammer worm--also known as Sapphire--doubled in size every 8.5 seconds when it first appeared, and reached the full rate at which it was scanning for vulnerable computers--a rate of more than 55 million scans per second--after about three minutes.

This puts Slammer into the realm of what some researchers call a "Warhol" worm because it could infect the entire Internet within 15 minutes. Slammer's spread was two orders of magnitude faster than Code Red, which infected 359,000 computers in the summer of 2001, and doubled in size about every 37 minutes.

The worm caused between $950 million and $1.2 billion in lost productivity in its first five days worldwide, making it the No. 9 most-costly malicious code, behind the likes of the Code Red worm, with its average of $2.6 billion in productivity loss; the LoveLetter virus, with $8.8 billion; and the Klez virus, with $9 billion.

Figure 2

unauthorized software could then gain unauthorized access to customer programs and data.

One can imagine that Microsoft's and Oracle's competitors used these news reports to gain advantage in sales situations over the ensuing weeks. However, no software is known to be completely secure; there is always the chance that a hole will be found in any company's software. Thus, using another vendor's security problems to gain a sales advantage is a strategy that can backfire if you later develop your own security problems.

Suppose that you work for a software company like PeopleSoft/Oracle, and your management decides to embark on an initiative to help your customers improve their computer security when using your software. Part of this initiative is to examine your products and attempt to find and eliminate any security holes in them. Another part of the initiative is to train your customers on secure ways of using your software through employee training and other nonsoftware solutions. Additionally, your company plans to work with third-party companies that have expertise in this area, even if that means working with competitors.

DISCUSSION QUESTIONS

1. Review the first three items in Figure 2-1. Describe, in general terms, how to use product security to gain competitive advantage.

2. Describe ways in which the security initiative will lock in customers and buyers. Are there ways that it can lock in suppliers as well?

3. In what ways can the new security initiative raise barriers to market entry?

4. Describe potential alliances that your new security initiative might foster. Some alliances might be among your customers; others might be with your competitors; still others might be with independent organizations.

5. How could this new security initiative reduce your costs? How might it reduce costs to your customers? How could you document these cost savings?

6. Do you think that attempting to use the new security initiative to gain competitive advantage is a good idea? How likely is it to be effective? What dangers exist in this plan? Would you recommend such a plan?

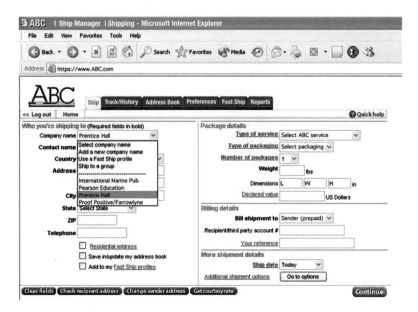

Figure 2-3
ABC, Inc. Web Page to Select
a Recipient from the
Customer's Records

in the application of information systems for competitive advantage. Here we consider one example of an information system that illustrates how ABC successfully uses information technology to gain competitive advantage.

ABC maintains customer account data that includes not only the customer's name, address, and billing information, but also data about the identity and locations to which the customer ships. Figure 2-3 shows a Web form that an ABC customer is using to schedule a shipment. When the ABC system creates the form, it fills the Company name drop-down list with the names of companies that the customer has shipped to in the past. Here, the user is selecting Prentice Hall.

When the user clicks on the Company name, the underlying ABC information system reads the customer's contact data from a database. The data consist of names, addresses, and phone numbers of recipients from past shipments. The user then selects a Contact name, and the system inserts that contact's address and other data into the form using data from the database, as shown in Figure 2-4. Thus the system saves the customer from having to reenter data for people to whom they have shipped in the past. Providing the data in this way also reduces data-entry errors.

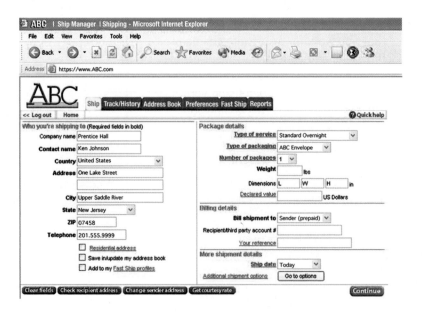

Figure 2-4
ABC, Inc. Web Page to Select
a Contact from the
Customer's Records

Using the Security Guide
(page 27a)

GOALS

* Use security to increase students' understanding of the elements of competitive advantage in Figure 2-1.

* Sensitize students to the cost of computer viruses and worms.

* Illustrate that computer software is not just something that people buy and use, it is also something that vendors create, market, and sell.

* Motivate students to consider jobs in the software industry.

BACKGROUND AND PRESENTATION STRATEGIES

This guide opens the door for the security discussions throughout this text. Every chapter addresses security; in particular, we'll discuss viruses and worms in more detail in Chapter 3, after we discuss hardware and software. We'll discuss encryption in Chapter 5, and in Chapter 11, we'll discuss spyware, adware, and problems like the one PeopleSoft reported. We'll also look at problems like the ChoicePoint data loss in Chapter 11. You might want to scan Chapter 11 and possibly pull up the ChoicePoint discussion to here.

Meanwhile, the students should think of these problems as having been caused by harmful programs developed by malicious people.

The Slammer worm cost around $1 billion. Think about that! For what? Nothing. In a world that has as many problems as ours does, why does anyone need to create something as expensive, malicious, and purposeless as a computer virus?

Ironically, the Slammer worm caused substantial problems with SQL Server installations *inside Microsoft*. I'm told that Microsoft has since hardened its servers, but it is ironic that they hadn't followed their own advice and installed their own security patches!

Subsequent to this article, PeopleSoft was acquired by Oracle. In fact, the sequence was that J.D. Edwards, a vendor of manufacturing software, was acquired by PeopleSoft, and PeopleSoft was in turn acquired by Oracle in a hostile takeover. Depending on the background and experience of your students, you might discuss why companies make such acquisitions. For the revenue? For the products? For the customers?

(As an aside, considering competitive advantage and customer product lock-in, Larry Ellison did a curious thing during the PeopleSoft acquisition. When announcing the acquisition, Ellison indicated that Oracle would be transitioning PeopleSoft customers to Oracle's products, thus eliminating any product lock-in advantage PeopleSoft enjoyed. Imagine how the PeopleSoft customers responded to that announcement. Think of the five components: Hardware and software are the easy parts. If your databases are not Oracle databases, you'll have to switch them. Then you'll need to change procedures to work with the Oracle products' interfaces and train all of your people. This is a potentially huge and expensive task. I doubt Oracle was as successful transitioning the customers as they thought they might be. Ellison has always been controversial, but successful, too!)

The questions in this guide ask students to think like marketing people for a software company. How can security be used to position and sell a product? As an aside, you might point out that there are very interesting and high-paying positions in software marketing.

 SUGGESTED RESPONSES FOR DISCUSSION QUESTIONS

1. This calls for the straightforward application of items in Figure 2-1: create a new (security) product that complements your existing products; enhance your existing products with new security features; add security features and functions beyond those of your competitors.

2. If the new or enhanced security products have features that are either unavailable from the competition or that would require lots of work to obtain from the competitor's products, customers will be locked in. The term *buyer* in this context is the same as customer. Locking in suppliers is not too important here—the suppliers aren't key elements of the software company's value chain. (Value chains are covered in Chapter 7.)

3. By creating the perception in the customers' minds that security is critical, any new product entry will have to have similar security features. That raises the cost, difficulty, and time-to-market for any new entrant.

4. Everyone is concerned about improving security. The billion-dollar loss hit the industry, not just one

company. The following are good questions for the class in answering this question:

➤ **Suppose your company has 5,000 customers. How many of those customers are concerned about security?**

➤ **How could you use the security concern to start a security alliance among your customers?**

➤ **What value would accrue to your company by starting such an alliance?**

➤ **Suppose there is an industry-wide security alliance that includes your customers, your competitors' customers, and your competitors. Should you participate?**

➤ **Can you afford not to participate?**

➤ **How could you turn such an alliance into a competitive advantage?**

5. Developing a new security product or feature in an existing product will increase your costs (unless you can use that product yourself to protect your company from security problems). The real cost advantage will accrue to your customers. If your new product or enhancement can prevent just one security problem, you will have saved your customer thousands, maybe hundreds of thousands, of dollars in wasted labor hours alone. You could produce a "white paper" that documents the cost savings of preventing just one security problem.

6. The following are interesting questions to ask the class:

➤ **Do you think that attempting to use the new security initiative to gain competitive advantage is a good idea?**

The issue is whether you can pull it off: You would need to find a great product or enhancement concept that involves security. You would need to make sure that it will work. And you would need to do this ahead of the competition.

➤ **How likely is it to be effective?**

This depends on how strong the product or enhancement is, how well it is marketed, and how the customers respond. If done well, it could be great.

➤ **What dangers exist in this plan?**

The biggest danger is that it backfires: You raise your customers' awareness and expectations and then don't deliver. Another danger is that even if you do deliver, after raising your customers' awareness and expectations, your competition delivers a better product.

➤ **Would you recommend such a plan?**

Maybe. It would depend on the strength of the product concept or enhancement.

WRAP UP

➤ **Security problems are expensive—both in terms of dollars and in terms of loss of reputation. For example, consider the impact of loss of customer data by a financial institution.**

➤ **Factors that are important to customers, such as security, are areas to examine when considering competitive advantage.**

➤ **We'll keep talking about security—once in every chapter and again in the last chapter!**

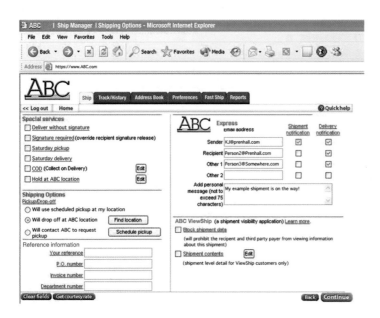

Figure 2-5
Using the ABC, Inc. System
to Specify Email Notification

Figure 2-5 shows another feature of this system. On the right-hand side of this form, the customer can request that ABC send email messages to the sender (the customer), the recipient, and others as well. The customer can choose for ABC to send an email when the shipment is created and when it has been delivered. In Figure 2-5, the user has provided three email addresses. The customer wants all three addresses to receive delivery notification, but only the sender to receive shipment notification. The customer can add a personal message as well. By adding this capability to the shipment scheduling system, ABC has extended its product from a package-delivery service to a package- *and* information-delivery service.

Figure 2-6 shows one other capability of this information system. It has generated a shipping label, complete with bar code, for the user to print. By doing this, the company not only reduces errors in the preparation of shipping labels, but it also causes the customer to provide the paper and ink for document printing! Millions of such documents are printed every day, resulting in a considerable savings to the company.

Note that only customers who have access to the Internet can use this shipping system. Do organizations have an ethical obligation to provide equivalent services to those who do not have access? The *Ethics Guide* on page 29a explores this question.

Figure 2-6
Using the ABC, Inc. System
to Print a Shipping Label

Limiting Access to Those Who Have Access

An adage of investing is that it's easier for the rich to get richer. Someone who has $10 million invested at 5 percent earns $500,000 per year. Another investor with $10,000 invested at that same 5 percent earns $500 per year. Every year the disparity increases as the first investor pulls farther and farther ahead of the second.

This same adage applies to intellectual wealth as well. It's easier for those with considerable knowledge and expertise to gain even more knowledge and expertise. Someone who knows how to search the Internet can learn more readily than someone who does not. And every year, the person with greater knowledge pulls farther and farther ahead. Intellectual capital grows in just the same way that financial capital grows.

Searching the Internet is not just a matter of knowledge, however. It's also a matter of access. The increasing reliance on the Web for information and commerce has created a digital divide between those who have Internet access and those who do not. This divide continues to deepen as those who are connected pull farther ahead of those who are not.

Various groups have addressed this problem by making Internet access available in public places such as libraries, community centers, and retirement homes. The Bill and Melinda Gates Foundation has given more than $262 million to public libraries for the purchase of personal computers and Internet access for them. Such gifts help, but not everyone can be served this way,

and even with such access, there's a big convenience difference between going to the library and walking across your bedroom to access the Internet, and you don't have to stand in line.

The advantages accrue to everyone with access, every day. Do you want directions to your friend's house? Want to know when a movie is playing at a local theater? Want to buy music, books, or tools? Want convenient access to your checking account? Want to decide whether to refinance your condo? Want to know what TCP/IP means? Use the Internet.

All of this intellectual capital resides on the Internet because businesses benefit by putting it there. It's much cheaper to provide product support information over the Internet than on printed documents. The savings include not only the costs of printing, but also the costs of warehousing and mailing. Further, when product specifications change, the organization just changes the Web site. There is no obsolete material to dispose of and no costs for printing and distributing the revised material. Those who have Internet access gain current information faster than those who do not.

What happens to those who do not have Internet access? They fall farther and farther behind. The digital divide segregates the haves from the have-nots, creating new class structures. Such segregation is subtle, but it is segregation, nonetheless.

Do organizations have a responsibility to address this matter? If 98 percent of our market has Internet access, do we have a responsibility to provide non-

1. Do you see evidence of a digital divide on your campus? In your hometown? Among your relatives? Describe personal experiences you've had regarding the digital divide.

2. Do organizations have a legal responsibility to provide the same information for nonconnected customers that they do for connected customers? If not, should laws be passed requiring organizations to do so?

3. Even if there is no current legal requirement for organizations to provide equal information to nonconnected customers, do they have an ethical responsibility to do so?

4. Are your answers to questions 2 and 3 different for government agencies than they are for commercial organizations?

5. Because it may be impossible to provide equal information, another approach for reducing the digital divide is for the government to enable nonconnected citizens to acquire Internet access via subsidies and tax incentives. Do you favor such a program? Why or why not?

6. Suppose that nothing is done to reduce the digital divide and that it is allowed to grow wider and wider. What are the consequences? How will society change? Are these consequences acceptable?

Internet materials to that other 2 percent? On what basis does that responsibility lie? Does a government agency have a responsibility to provide equal information to those who have Internet access and those who do not? When those who are connected can obtain information nearly instantaneously, 24/7, is it even possible to provide equal information to the connected and the unconnected?

It's a worldwide problem. Connected societies and countries pull farther and farther ahead. How can any economy that relies on traditional mail compete with an Internet-based economy?

If you're taking MIS, you're already connected; you're already one of the haves, and you're already pulling ahead of the have-nots. The more you learn about information systems and their use in commerce, the faster you'll pull ahead. The digital divide increases.

How This System Creates a Competitive Advantage

Now consider the ABC shipping information system in light of the competitive advantage factors in Figure 2-1. This information system *enhances* an existing product because it eases the effort of creating a shipment to the customer while reducing errors. The information system also helps to *differentiate* the ABC package delivery product from competitors that do not have a similar system. Further, the generation of email messages when ABC picks up and delivers a package could be considered to be a *new* product.

Because this information system captures and stores data about recipients, it reduces the amount of customer work when scheduling a shipment. Customers will be *locked in* by this system: If a customer wants to change to a different shipper, he or she will need to rekey recipient data for that new shipper. The disadvantage of rekeying data may well outweigh any advantage of switching to another shipper.

This system achieves a competitive advantage in two other ways as well: First, it raises the barriers to market entry. If another company wants to develop a shipping service, it will not only have to be able to ship packages, it will also need to have a similar information system. In addition, the system reduces costs. It reduces errors in shipping documents, and it saves ABC paper, ink, and printing costs. (Of course, to determine if this system delivers a *net savings* in costs, the cost of developing and operating the information system will need to be offset against the gains in reduced errors and paper, ink, and printing costs. It may be that the system costs more than the savings. Even still, it may be a sound investment if the value of intangible benefits, such as locking in customers and raising entry barriers, exceeds the net cost.)

Before continuing, review Figure 2-1. Make sure that you understand each of the principles of competitive advantage and how information systems can help achieve them. In fact, the list in Figure 2-1 probably is important enough to memorize, because you can also use it for non-IS applications. You can consider any business project or initiative in light of competitive advantage.

▮ Information Systems for Problem Solving

Competitive advantage is just one perspective on the reasons for having an information system. Another perspective is that information systems can be used to solve problems. In the following sections, we will consider an example problem and three different information systems for solving that problem. Again, these systems are just examples; other types of information systems could be used to solve the problem as well.

A Laptop Problem

Suppose you buy a new laptop computer and within a few days it fails. It locks up, and neither the mouse nor the keyboard will function until you turn the power off and then on. You call the manufacturer's customer support hotline, and the support representative leads you through a procedure to fix the problem by installing software from the manufacturer's Web site. After you follow the instructions, the laptop seems to work fine.

A day or so later, however, your computer locks up again. You call back to the support center, and this time you speak to a different representative, one who has no record of your prior call. She instructs you to repeat all the actions you performed before. This procedure takes time, but after you do it, the computer works again—for a while. Sure enough, several days later your laptop fails again.

Clearly, there is some problem here. Is it one that might be solved with an information system? Before we can determine whether an information system can help, we need to create a clear description of what the problem is.

You Be the Guide

Using the Ethics Guide
(page 29a)

GOALS

* Teach students that knowledge grows exponentially—just like capital.

* Sensitize students to the social problem of the digital divide.

* Explore the responsibilities for business and government with respect to the digital divide.

BACKGROUND AND PRESENTATION STRATEGIES

The more money you have, the easier it is to make more money. **And the more knowledge you have, the easier it is to acquire more knowledge.** Knowledge and capital both grow exponentially.

Thus, learning *strategies for learning* is critical. Learning how to learn efficiently using the Web and other contemporary resources should be one of the students' primary goals while in college.

Being connected, by the way, means being able to send emails, use ftp, engage in instant messaging and texting, etc. All of these are also important ways of learning. (IM as a tool for learning? It could be.)

But what about those who are on the nonconnected side of the digital divide? What happens to them? They fall farther and farther behind. Actually, they stay right where they are, and the rest of the world moves farther and farther ahead, accelerating. The gap grows exponentially.

The Gates Foundation donated over $262 million for libraries to buy computers to provide Internet access for the public. See www.gatesfoundation.org/ libraries for more information about the Foundation's library program, including a state map that describes library donations.

To the surprise of many (including, I believe, the Gates Foundation), the most popular activity on those library computers was finding a job!

The Gates' donation was a generous and appropriate action for the world's richest couple. But what about businesses? What about government?

➤ **Today, in the United States, what groups of people are not connected to the Internet? (Examples include those living in poverty, the elderly, the poorly**

educated, and those who've stuck their heads in the sand.)

➤ **Does it make sense for benefactors or government agencies to provide access to those in poverty?**

➤ **What keeps the elderly from accessing the Internet?**

➤ **Should the government help the elderly?**

➤ **What could be done to provide Internet access for the poorly educated? Does government have a role?**

Most MIS classes have a number of foreign students. If yours does, you might want to consider this guide from a world perspective.

➤ **Some of you are from outside the United States. What is the connectivity situation in your country?**

➤ **Is there a digital divide?**

➤ **Are some countries more behind the connectivity trend than others?**

➤ **What does this mean for those countries' ability to compete? For the citizens of those countries?**

Today, two trends are underway that complicate the situation: ubiquitous high-speed data communications and the merger of computers and entertainment devices.

➤ **How do these changes alter the situation for the nonconnected?**

I think these questions lead to an optimistic note. Once televisions are merged with Internet access devices, then anyone who can afford and operate a TV will have some kind of computer. And, with cheaper and cheaper data communications, they will have at least some access to the Internet.

⑦ SUGGESTED RESPONSES FOR DISCUSSION QUESTIONS

1. Answers will depend on students' experiences. Are there students on campus who are disadvantaged by a lack of computer equipment? How do they cope? Do they have access at home or through relatives?

   What about foreign students? Is their situation different from students in the United States? See comments in the Background section above about bringing in the perspective of different countries.

2. No, there is no law that requires organizations to provide equal access to the nonconnected. *Should there be?*

Laws imply enforcement, and enforcement implies lawsuits. This all gets very expensive for society. Some would say it would be better to focus resources on programs like the Gates' library donation.

Another argument uses the Declaration of Independence. Citizens have an equal right to life, liberty, and the pursuit of happiness. If being nonconnected threatens any of these, then laws should be passed to protect the disconnected.

But, is going to a movie one aspect of the pursuit of happiness? So, if movie theaters have a Web site, do they have a responsibility to provide access for the nonconnected? This seems silly.

3. Whether organizations have an ethical obligation to provide equal access depends on the organization. A religious organization would seem to have an ethical responsibility to ensure equal access to information for its members. What about a yacht club? What about an athletic league?

4. I think most would agree that government agencies have greater responsibilities than do commercial entities. Public health information, for example, should be equally available to the connected and the nonconnected. But, how is this possible? With instantaneous 24/7 connectivity, there is no way that a nonconnected person can have the same access to late-breaking disease information as the connected person. However, what government will buy computers for its citizens just for that reason?

5. What groups are nonconnected? Would those groups be helped by subsidies or tax incentives? Is the answer in education? Or, is the problem of Internet access so low on the list of priorities of these groups that any available tax dollars should be spent on other programs? Obviously, there is no clear answer.

6. The following are several questions to explore this:

➤ **Is the gap between the connected and the nonconnected the same gap as that between the educated and the noneducated?**

➤ **In the future, will there be just three kinds of employees: techies, flunkies, and managers?**

➤ **What sort of world will that be? Will it be stable?**

➤ **Those of us on an academic campus will have opportunities that those on the wrong side of the digital divide will not have. What responsibilities do we have to help those nonconnected people?**

WRAP UP

➤ **Knowledge grows exponentially. Those with more knowledge will be able to obtain new knowledge at a faster rate. Not being connected reduces the rate at which people can obtain knowledge.**

➤ **In school, it is important to focus on ways to use the Web and other resources to learn, and to do so efficiently.**

➤ **People who are not connected are at a serious disadvantage. It's not an easy disadvantage to fix. Equal access through traditional means is impossible. A brochure cannot provide the latest information, 24/7.**

➤ **Possibly the best hope, the great equalizer, will be the blending of televisions and Internet devices. Then, everyone with a TV (almost every person) can have Internet access. Cheap data communications will make it easy to connect as well.**

Problem Definition

A **problem** is a *perceived difference between what is and what ought to be.* Notice that a problem is a *perception*; it is the view of a situation held by an individual or a group. Because a problem is a perception, different people or groups may have different problem definitions. For example, in the laptop computer example, you may define the problem as, "The fix they gave me didn't work." The customer support representative, however, may define the problem as, "I have no record of the customer's prior contact with our company."

A good problem definition defines the difference between what is and what ought to be by describing both the current situation and the desired situation. Suppose you say, "I spent 10 minutes on hold and then another 15 minutes following the instructions the support rep gave me. After almost a half hour of my time, my computer still wasn't fixed. I want to spend less than five minutes altogether, and I want the fix to work." However, the support representative may define the problem as, "I had no data about the prior call. I wanted to know the customer's prior history with our company: the products he owns, previous problems reported, and contact data including the dates, the names of our representatives, and a summary of the situation for each prior call."

A third person, someone in manufacturing, might define the problem as, "We are shipping too many faulty computers. We need to reduce our new computer failure rate to less than one-half percent."

All of these problem definitions are valid. None of them makes the others wrong. They are different perceptions of the same situation.

Information systems, however, solve particular problems. Thus, different problem definitions require the development of different information systems. Before constructing an information system, all personnel in the organization must have a clear understanding of *which definition of the problem* the information system will address.

If the organization focuses on the need to have data about prior customer contacts, it will build a customer relationship management system. (See *MIS in Use 2-1*, page 32, for an example of a customer service system.) Alternatively, if the organization focuses on the unhelpful remedy, it will build a knowledge management system. Or, if the organization focuses on the fact that your computer ought not to have broken in the first place, it will construct a manufacturing quality-control information system.

In the following sections, we will consider each of these popular types of information systems. Again, these systems are just examples of the many types of information system that could be used.

A Customer Relationship Management System

A **customer relationship management (CRM) system** is an information system that maintains data about customers and all of their interactions with the organization. We will study CRM in detail in Chapter 7, but for now, consider Figure 2-8 (page 32). As shown, the CRM database includes data from all aspects of customer contact—sales activity, purchases, returns, training, support calls, and service and repair.

CRM systems vary in their size and complexity. A simple system stores customer contacts; others store customer support calls; still others store customer purchases and returns. A large and complex system stores all of the data shown in this figure.

To return to the example of your laptop computer, if the support representative had access to a CRM system, then the representative would have had data about your prior call. The support representative would know not to repeat the procedure you did before and would suggest other remedies. To you, the customer, it would feel as if you were dealing with one person, even though you spoke with two different support representatives. The system would save both you and the laptop manufacturer time and money.

As the story in the *Opposing Forces Guide* on page 31a demonstrates, not every business, however, sees the need for a CRM system. Indeed, in almost any organization, whether small or large, there will be someone who prefers existing ways of doing business.

G.Robinson Old Prints and Maps

George Robinson buys and sells old prints and maps out of his retail store in Taos, New Mexico. George has been in business for 25 years, and as he puts it, "I just don't need a computer in my business—in fact, you won't find one in the store. I'm not computer-illiterate, I just don't need a computer here.

George, a one-time hippie from California, left the crazy scene of Haight-Ashbury in 1967 and moved his young family to Mexico. He lived a year in San Miguel Allende and then migrated back to the United States and settled in Taos. He worked odd jobs for several years until he opened his shop with a partner. "I loved it. I was good at it, and never knew I could enjoy something so much. It agrees with me." Within a year he bought out his partner and has been successfully selling maps and prints ever since. "I don't make a lot of money, but I make enough. And I enjoy every minute of it.

George keeps a list of customers to whom he sends a newsletter two to four times a year. "I cull my list very carefully. I try to keep it to around a thousand or so of the best customers. More than that and I'm just wasting money on printing and postage.

"No, I don't use a computer for my customer list. I type the names and addresses on little sticky labels and paste them on an 8-1/2 x 11 piece of paper. When I want to send out a newsletter, I go to the copy center, copy my list onto sheets of mailing labels that I buy there, and then paste the labels on the newsletters. To delete a customer, I just pull that person's sticky off my list—making a hole for somebody else."

Apparently, his approach works. He sells 90 to 95 percent of the items in his catalog within a month.

"When a map or print comes in, I know who would be interested in it. I call them and sell it to them over the phone. Of course, I take any of my items back if the customer isn't happy, but in 25 years, I think I've had 9 or 10 items returned. That's all.

"I enjoy speaking with people; I like the personal contact, and I think that contact is important to my sales. I suppose I could use email to sell, but that just isn't me. I don't operate that way.

"We have a computer at home, and if someone insists, they can send me email there. The problem is, I don't check my email more than once a week, if that, so I'd rather people just call me here.

"The biggest challenge I have is finding new inventory. There just isn't much out there these days. I do find some items on eBay, but pricing is weird there. People pay way too much for some things, and others are stolen at ridiculously low prices. Not often, though.

"Inventory control? Well, when I buy an item, I make an entry in a ledger book and record the date and how much I paid. Then, when I sell it, I note the date sold, and how much it sold for on the item's entry in the book. I suppose I could go through and compute the gross margin on all the items, but I don't do that. I'm satisfied with what I make in this business.

"I've developed my customer list myself. I never bought any lists from anybody. Early on, I ran a few ads here and there, but mostly, I've developed my clientele myself, gradually over the years. No, I don't have a Web site. People find me without it.

"Could I use customer relationship management software? I doubt it. Like I said, when something comes in, I usually know who to sell it to. It may take me a day or two to remember—and if I don't remember, well, I just sell it to someone else. Maybe if I were just starting out I'd get a computer, but my current system works just fine.

"You're from Seattle, are you? You know, I've got a beautiful map of the North Pacific, printed in 1810, wonderfully colored, near perfect condition. You really should take a look at it. I can send it to you; send it back if you don't like it...."

DISCUSSION QUESTIONS

1. Given the nature of his product, can you see reasons why George would prefer not to have a computer in his store? What image does he project?

2. What is George's biggest problem? In what ways could he use a computer-based information system to solve that problem?

3. Using Figure 2-1 as a guide, describe potential information systems that George could use to gain competitive advantage.

4. List what you believe are the five most important decisions that George must make. Describe computer-based information systems that could help George to make those decisions.

5. By not using computer-based information systems, George saves money and has greater physical control over his data. In light of your answers to questions 2 through 4, do you think it would be worthwhile for George to start using computer-based systems? Why or why not?

6. Suppose George hired you as an intern to assess the desirability of investing in computer-based information systems. How would you proceed?

MIS in Use 2-1

Horizon Healthcare Services

Horizon Healthcare Services is New Jersey's largest health insurer, providing coverage to more than 2.9 million people throughout the state. Although Horizon employs 1,200 people in its customer service call center, service quality suffered because the service representatives were hampered by cumbersome and difficult-to-use information systems. In fact, Horizon used five separate customer and claim systems, and the service representatives had no unified record of customer interactions. Customers had to call multiple phone numbers, were frequently transferred from one representative to another, and often had to re-explain their needs several times.

To solve this problem, Horizon launched a new IT strategy to integrate the information from these disparate systems into a single display that provided a comprehensive view of the customer. To implement this strategy, Horizon licensed a call center application from Siebel Systems, a division of the Oracle Corporation, a San Mateo, California, enterprise software vendor. The new system reduced customer service times by 20 percent and increased customer service productivity by 15 percent. Additionally, the new system reduced the training time for new customer service hires from 20 weeks to 4 weeks. Also, it allowed Horizon to balance workload and handle call overflow by moving people between service teams. Horizon experienced a $2.1 million reduction in expenses in the first year; it expects to save a total of $21 million in the first 5 years of use.

Knowledge Management System

A **knowledge management system (KMS)** is an information system for storing and retrieving organizational knowledge, whether that knowledge is in the form of data, documents, or employee know-how. The goal of a KMS is to make the organization's knowledge available to employees, vendors, customers, investors, the press, and any other person who needs it.

With regard to the laptop-failure example, someone in the organization may have documented a procedure for diagnosing such problems. Or, someone in the organization may have documented a repair procedure. Or, someone may have written an article about laptop design that would enable the support representative to solve the problem. Or, there may be in-house experts on such problems whom the support representative can call. The goal of a KMS is to make any and all such organizational knowledge available to the support representative.

Figure 2-9 shows some of the knowledge resources in a KMS for customer support. As shown, these resources are stored in databases, which, as you will learn in Chapter 4, are collections of related data. Here, the databases contain prior problem descriptions

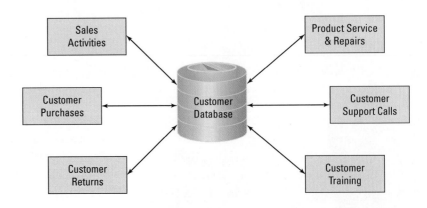

Figure 2-8
Example of Customer Relationship Management (CRM) System

Using the Opposing Forces Guide (page 31a)

GOALS

* Evaluate the need for a computer-based CRM for a small business by discussing the statements of someone who claims that he doesn't need one.

* Apply the principles of competitive advantage to customer-tracking requirements.

* Introduce the need for knowledge about systems development.

BACKGROUND AND PRESENTATION STRATEGIES

George is a happy person. He's the embodiment of the expression, "Find your passion and develop your career around it." He loves to talk, he loves people, he loves maps and old books, and he wanted to live in Taos, New Mexico. He found this business and turned it into a success.

George operates a small-scale operation, and he knows it. Key to his success is managing expenses. He would carefully scrutinize the costs of any kind of computer system before he would buy. The guide does not bring this out, but George's competitive strategy is to be the cost leader. He sells his maps and books at what he calls a "very fair price." This strategy conditions some of the answers to the questions, but I find it's better to let the students answer question 3 without that knowledge. (See continuation of this point in question 3.)

George himself is a key part of his business. He projects his low-key personality in his store. Having a visible computer system is not part of the image that George wants to project.

Some questions for discussion:

➤ **Does George have a CRM?**

(Yes, it's just not a computer-based CRM.)

➤ **What is George's CRM?**

(His customer list, his memory.)

➤ **George has been in business a long time. Would it be possible today to start a business like George's without computer-based systems? Would it be desirable?**

George was adamant that he did not want to sell via email. He is convinced that his product is so unique that he needs to talk directly with the customer. He knows that some of his competitors are selling via email and over the Web, but he said it just isn't him. He thought he'd fail if he tried. All of this poses some interesting questions:

➤ **George believes that his personality and friendly manner are key parts of his competitive advantage. To what extent do computer-based systems eliminate that competitive advantage?**

They might eliminate it. George's business model may be doomed. Many of us today far prefer email to voice mail and would rather buy from one of his competitors online.

Also, there are ways of combining conversation with information systems:

➤ **How could George use instant messaging, texting, or other non-email forms of computer-supported communication?**

If George ever did have a Web site, he could enable a voice over IP system like Click to Chat on that site. Possibly, George isn't thinking broadly enough about his use of IS.

➤ **What are other examples of new computer-based systems eliminating someone's personal competitive advantage?**

Two examples:

• People whose expertise is replaced by databases. A purchasing manager, for example, whose competitive advantage is his knowledge, accumulated over the years, of vendors, product inventory, product quality, the company's terms, and so forth.

• People whose style of work has been replaced by technology. For example, a traveling salesperson in an industry where e-commerce has replaced direct sales.

➤ **What can a person do when this happens?**

• First, don't let it be a surprise. Watch technology, see the change coming, and change style or jobs before it arrives.

• Modernize, adapt, innovate. Find new ways of disseminating one's expertise.

➤ **Suppose you're managing a department in a company that is installing a new information system. Suppose one or more of your employees' skills will be threatened by that new system. How do you expect that your employees will react?**

They won't like it! Morale may suffer. Resistance will likely occur.

➤ **What can you do about that reaction?**

Help them find a new role, a new skill, a new job, or retire.

We'll talk more about managing change when we get to Chapter 7.

George was fun. All the while I was interviewing him he was trying to sell me books and maps. He was very good at it, and sure enough, I left the store with the 1810 map mentioned at the end of the guide! I like the map, but it wasn't what I came to his store to do. An excellent salesperson!

 ## SUGGESTED RESPONSES FOR DISCUSSION QUESTIONS

1. He's selling *old maps* in *Taos, New Mexico,* neither of which sounds high tech. A highly visible computer does not fit his image. He projects easy conversation, low key, low tech, life is good. Even if he does have a computer in his store, he'd be wise to keep it under wraps—at least as long as he wants to portray that image.

2. In the guide he says, "The biggest challenge I have is finding new inventory." He admits that he finds some items on eBay (which means he's doing more with his computer at home than he admits). George was very wary when I asked him about his product sources. I asked him several times, and though he made general comments about building relationships with map sellers, he wouldn't answer the question. I suspect that George believed his product sources were a big part of his competitive advantage.

   Supposing that to be true, the question then becomes:

   ➤ **How could George use computer-based systems to build his network of sources and suppliers (worldwide)?**

3. The answers are a direct application of Figure 2-1. The students should have many ideas. The guide does not point this out, but George wants to be a cost leader. This means that many of the ideas that the students originate when they work through Figure 2-1 will be infeasible. I don't tell students this at the onset, because I want them to be creative in their answers. However, this question gives me a good chance to talk about competitive strategy and how it relates to information systems. This also sets up that discussion in Chapter 7.

4. Many questions are possible, but I'd guess these would be high on the list:

   • Where can I get more product?

   • Should I buy this map at this price?

   • To which of my customers should I sell this product?

   • A customer offered me a price below my asking price. Should I take it?

   • What products should I feature in my catalog?

   • How much money am I making?

   • Have I lost any good customers?

5. George plans to sell his business and retire. I sensed that he knows he needs to change the way he runs his business, but he doesn't want to do it. It wouldn't be him. The new owners will need to decide their competitive strategy. If it's to continue as a cost leader, they need to be careful about the costs of new information systems. If their chief problem is finding product to sell, then I'd think about building simple, cheap information systems to find sources. I'm not sure, though, that the cost would be worth it. If the owners have the skill and interest to use a small customer-tracking product like Goldmine, they might do that, or they could build an Access customer database, if they know how. Or, maybe they could use Outlook or another email program to keep track of customer data. If I were the new owners, I'd do exactly what George was doing until I understood the economics of the business.

6. The purpose of this question is to set up the need for knowledge of systems development in Chapter 6. Right now, the students will probably flounder a bit, and that's OK. I explain that there are established methods of developing new information systems and those methods include techniques for assessing feasibility. In short, the intern needs to define the problem the new information system will solve and then assess cost, organizational, schedule, and technical feasibility.

WRAP UP

➤ **George has run his business successfully for many years without a computer-based information system. It has worked for him, but in truth, his era is passing. Anyone starting that business today would want at least a computer-based list of customers, purchases, and interests. Further, it would be impossible to compete for product without a connection to the Internet.**

➤ **When we consider the particular features and functions of an information system, the competitive advantage criteria in Figure 2-1 can help us determine the goals and objectives that we want to accomplish. But, we also need to think about the competitive strategy of the business. George wants to offer low prices; that strategy restricts the kinds of information systems he will consider. Other businesses have other strategies, as you will learn in Chapter 7.**

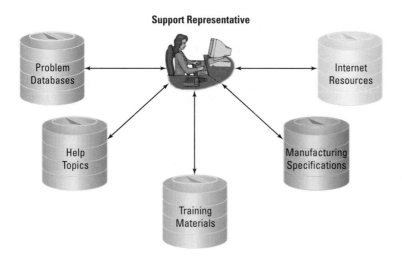

Figure 2-9
Customer Support Knowledge
Management System

and solutions, help topics, training materials, manufacturing specifications and other manufacturing data, and Internet resources. The support representative can use all of these sources to solve your problem.

Notice, however, that these sources are just resources to the support representative. Some organizations provide knowledge resources to their customers as well. This alternative assumes that customers will have access to computers and the Internet, which may not be the case.

A Manufacturing Quality-Control Information System

Many organizations believe that the optimal way to provide customer service is to eliminate the need for it. If the customer never needs to call, the cost of the service is zero. If your laptop never fails, you will have enjoyed perfect customer service.

One way to provide such service is to improve manufacturing quality. To that end, the manufacturer of your laptop may develop a system that identifies product failures before they leave manufacturing. Such a system can also pinpoint the causes of failures to prevent the manufacture of defective products in the future. **Manufacturing information systems** focus on various aspects of the manufacturing process, from quality control to planning to scheduling. We will discuss manufacturing systems in Chapter 7. For now, just realize that another way to solve your laptop problem is not to produce the defect. Or, as the machinists say, "The very best way to solve a problem is not to have it."

In summary, the type of system to develop depends on the way the organization defines the problem. Before developing a system, the organization must have a complete, accurate, and agreed-upon problem definition. If not, it runs the risk of solving the wrong problem or of solving only part of the problem.

The *Problem Solving Guide* on page 33a explains a skill that will help you develop better problem definitions.

▌ Information Systems for Decision Making

In addition to gaining competitive advantage and solving problems, a third reason for developing information systems is to facilitate decision making. Decision making in organizations is varied and complex, and so before discussing the role of information systems in support of decision making, we need to investigate the characteristics and dimensions of decision making itself.

Video

PROBLEMSOLVING
GUIDE

Egocentric vs. Empathetic Thinking

As stated earlier, a problem is a perceived difference between what is and what ought to be. When developing information systems, it is critical for the development team to have a common definition and understanding of the problem. This common understanding can be difficult to achieve, however.

Cognitive scientists distinguish between egocentric and empathetic thinking. Egocentric thinking centers on the self; someone who engages in egocentric thinking considers his or her view as "the real view" or "what really is." In contrast, those who engage in empathetic thinking consider their view as one possible interpretation of the situation and actively work to learn what other people are thinking.

Different experts recommend empathetic thinking for different reasons. Religious leaders say that such thinking is morally superior; psychologists say that empathetic thinking leads to richer, more fulfilling relationships. In business, empathetic thinking is recommended because it's smart. Business is a social endeavor, and those who can understand others' points of view are always more

effective. Even if you do not agree with others' perspectives, you will be much better able to work with them if you understand their views.

Consider an example. Suppose you say to your MIS professor, "Professor Jones, I couldn't come to class last Monday. Did we do anything important?" Such a statement is a prime example of egocentric thinking. It takes no account of your professor's point of view and implies that your professor talked about nothing important. As a professor, it's tempting to say, "No, when I noticed you weren't there, I took out all the important material."

To engage in empathetic thinking, consider this situation from the professor's point of view. Students who do not come to class cause extra work for their professors. It doesn't matter how valid your reason for not coming to class; you may actually have been contagious with a fever of 102. But, no matter what, your not coming to class is more work for your professor. He or she must do something extra to help you recover from the lost class time.

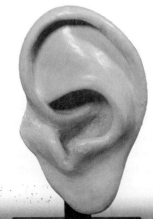

Using empathetic thinking, you would do all you can to minimize the impact of your absence on your professor. For example, you could say, "I couldn't come to class, but I got the class notes from Mary. I read through them, and I have a question about establishing alliances as competitive advantage.... Oh, by the way, I'm sorry to trouble you with my problem."

Before we go on, let's consider a corollary to this scenario: Never, ever, send an email to your boss that says, "I couldn't come to the staff meeting on Wednesday. Did we do anything important?" Avoid this for the same reasons as those for missing class. Instead, find a way to minimize the impact of your absence on your boss.

Now, what does all of this have to do with MIS? Consider the problem you had with your laptop. In that scenario, there are three different views of the problem: (1) Customer support representatives do not have data about prior customer contacts; (2) the customer support representative recommended a solution that did not work; and (3) the company is shipping too many defective laptops. The solution to each of these different problem definitions requires a different information system.

Now imagine yourself in a meeting about this situation and suppose that different people in the meeting hold the three problem views. If everyone engages in egocentric thinking, what will happen? The meeting will be argumentative and acrimonious and likely will end with nothing accomplished.

Suppose, instead, that the attendees think empathetically. In this case, people will make a concerted effort to understand the different points of view, and the outcome will be much more positive—possibly a definition of all three problems ranked in order of priority. In both scenarios, the attendees have the same information; the difference in outcomes results from the thinking style of the attendees.

Empathetic thinking is an important skill in all business activities. Skilled negotiators always know what the other side wants; effective salespeople understand their customers' needs. Buyers who understand the problems of their vendors get better service. And students who understand the perspective of their professors get better....

DISCUSSION QUESTIONS

1. In your own words, explain the difference between egocentric and empathetic thinking.

2. Suppose you miss a staff meeting. Using empathetic thinking, explain how you can get needed information about what took place in the meeting.

3. How does empathetic thinking relate to problem definition?

4. Suppose you and another person differ substantially on a problem definition. Suppose she says to you, "No, the real problem is that..." followed by her definition of the problem. How do you respond?

5. Again, suppose you and another person differ substantially on a problem definition. Assume you understand his definition. How can you make that fact clear?

6. Explain the statement, "In business, empathetic thinking is smart." Do you agree?

Decision Level

Figure 2-10
Decision-Making Dimensions

As shown in Figure 2-10, decisions occur at three levels in organizations: *operational*, *managerial*, and *strategic*. The types of decisions vary depending on the level. **Operational decisions** concern day-to-day activities. Typical operational decisions are: How many widgets should we order from vendor A? Should we extend credit to vendor B? Which invoices should we pay today? Information systems that support operational decision making are called **transaction processing systems (TPS)**.

Managerial decisions concern the allocation and utilization of resources. Typical managerial decisions are: How much should we budget for computer hardware and programs for department A next year? How many engineers should we assign to project B? How many square feet of warehouse space do we need for the coming year? Information systems that support managerial decision making are called **management information systems (MIS)**. (Notice that the term *MIS* can be used in two ways: broadly, to mean the subjects in this entire book, and narrowly, to mean information systems that support managerial-level decision making. Context will make the meaning of the term clear.)

Strategic decisions concern broader-scope, organizational issues. Typical decisions at the strategic level are: Should we start a new product line? Should we open a centralized warehouse in Tennessee? Should we acquire company A? Information systems that support strategic decision making are called **executive information systems (EIS)**.

Notice that, in general, the decision timeframe increases as we move from operational to managerial to strategic decisions. Operational decisions normally involve actions in the short term. What should we do today or this week? Managerial decisions involve longer timeframes. What is appropriate for the next quarter or year? Strategic decisions involve the long term; their consequences are not realized for years.

On a personal level, career planning can be an example of strategic planning. This is an activity to which you can apply the competitive advantage model, as discussed in the *Reflections Guide* on page 35a.

The Decision Process

Figure 2-11 shows levels of information systems with two decision processes: *structured* and *unstructured*. These terms refer to the method by which the decision is to be made, not to the nature of the underlying problem. A **structured decision** is one for which there is an understood and accepted method for making the decision. A formula for computing the reorder quantity of an item in inventory is an example of a structured decision process. A standard method for allocating furniture and equipment to employees is another structured decision process.

An **unstructured decision** process is one for which there is no agreed-on decision-making method. Predicting the future direction of the economy or the stock market is a famous example. The prediction method varies from person to person; it is neither stan-

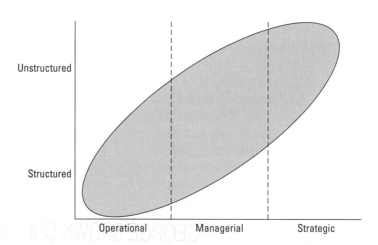

Figure 2-11
Relationship of Decision
Level and Decision Type

You Be the Guide

Using the Problem Solving Guide (page 33a)

GOALS

* Raise the level of professionalism in the class.

* Explore empathetic thinking and discuss why it's smart.

* Discuss two applications of empathetic thinking.

* Emphasize that a problem is a perception and that perceptions differ among people. Different problem perceptions require different information systems.

BACKGROUND AND PRESENTATION STRATEGIES

How many times have we all been asked, "I couldn't come to class. Did we do anything important?" I'm always tempted to say, "No, when I saw you weren't here, I took all the important material out." Another rejoinder, more mature on my part is, "Well, first tell me what you think important material is." If they say, "Is it going to be on the test . . . ?" then we have some talking to do.

You might want to underline the corollary about not asking your boss, when you've missed a meeting, "Did we do anything important?"

Part of the reason for this guide is to raise the level of professionalism in the class. I find students' maturity rises to meet expectations. By asking them to engage in empathetic thinking with regard to not coming to class, I'm also asking them to step up in their maturity:

➤ **If you choose not to come to class, that's your choice. But, realize there's a cost to me and our teaching assistants, and do what you can to minimize that cost.**

Empathetic thinking does result in better relationships, but this guide says that business people should engage in it because it's smart. Negotiators, for example, need to know what the other side wants, what's important to it, what issues they can give on, and what ones are nonnegotiable.

Here's a simple example:

➤ **Suppose you have an employee who wants more recognition in the group. You know the employee is doing a good job, and you want to reward her. Not engaging in empathic thinking, you give her a pay raise. What have you done?**

➤ **How could empathetic thinking have helped you in this situation?**

So, using this example, just what is empathetic thinking?

• Understanding the other person's perspective (See the Problem Solving Guide in Chapter 1)

• Realizing that people who hold a perspective different from yours are not necessarily WRONG (but you don't have to be wrong, either)

• Not attempting to convince the other person that his or her perspective should be changed to match yours

• Adapting your behavior in accordance with the other person's perspective

➤ **Does thinking empathically mean that you change your way of thinking to match the other person's?**

(No.)

➤ **Does it mean always giving the other person what he or she wants?**

(No.)

➤ **What are different ways you could adapt your behavior in accordance with another person's perspective?**

All of us have been in meetings that are going nowhere. Whenever we find ourselves in such a meeting, is the problem due to different perspectives? If so, one can sometimes find the root cause by engaging in empathetic thinking.

The scenario at the end of the guide is right on point. If three factions hold three different problem definitions, and if they don't realize they hold those different definitions, then the meeting will go nowhere. And it doesn't matter what the "facts" are. The facts aren't the problem; the different problem definitions are.

 SUGGESTED RESPONSES FOR DISCUSSION QUESTIONS

1. Considering the other person's perspective.

   ➤ **What are some examples of egocentric thinking?**

   ➤ **What are some examples of empathetic thinking?**

2. Read the minutes, if any. Ask others who were at the meeting. Prior to the meeting, ask someone else to take notes or make a recording. If possible, let your boss know ahead of time that you'll be absent, and

why. Otherwise, apologize for your absence, explain why, and say that you have the information. Minimize the burden on your boss!

3. A problem is a perception. Different people perceive in different ways. So, different people can have different problems, *even though they may give the same name to the problem.*

4. First, based on her words, the *real problem* is that you know she is not engaged in empathetic thinking. Notice that you are in a much stronger position than she is. You know that there are two (yours and hers), and possibly more, different problem definitions. Unlike her, your thinking is broad and flexible enough to understand that multiple perceptions, and hence multiple problem definitions, can exist at the same time.

   You have at least four different strategies: (1) Change your definition to match hers. (2) Try to teach her about empathetic thinking. (3) Without saying anything about her thinking skills, and without needlessly repeating your understanding of the problem, use your understanding of her and her definition to arrive at a solution that is mutually acceptable. (4) Say something polite and close the conversation because you're just wasting your time.

   ➤ **Under what circumstances would you use each of these strategies?**

5. Restate his position to him. "You perceive the problem as . . . ," and do the best possible job of restating his position. This does not mean you agree with his position, but it will let him know that you understand his words. He'll know, if you continue to disagree with him, that it's not because you don't understand him.

   Having convinced him that you understand his position, you should attempt to express your view of the problem. His knowing that you understand his position may allow him to be able to understand yours. However, he may not be able to, in which case there may be no possibility of good communication with him on this issue.

6. It comes down to power. You are in a much more powerful position if you understand other people's perceptions and your own, but they understand only their own. You can imagine solutions and possibilities that they cannot. Also, as countless books on negotiating skills imply, understanding someone else's point of view enables you to manipulate them, if you are so inclined.

   Finally, empathetic thinking results in better relationships, and in the final analysis, business is nothing but relationships. Businesses themselves do nothing. Business is people working together in relationships. Better relationships equate to better business.

WRAP UP

Sometimes I end with a little practice:

➤ **Anybody learn anything today? What?**

➤ **All right, let's practice. Using empathetic thinking, tell me why you think I included this exercise in today's presentation.**

dardized nor broadly accepted. (As one wit put it, "If you laid all the economists in the world end to end, they still would not reach a conclusion.") Another example of an unstructured decision process is assessing how well suited an employee is for performing a particular job. Managers vary in the manner in which they make such assessments.

Again, keep in mind that the terms *structured* and *unstructured* refer to the decision process, not the underlying subject. Weather forecasting is a structured decision because the process used to make the decision is standardized among forecasters. Weather itself, however, is an unstructured phenomenon, as tornadoes and hurricanes demonstrate every year.

The Relationship Between the Decision Type and the Decision Process

The decision type and decision process are loosely related. As shown in Figure 2-11, decisions at the operational level tend to be structured, and decisions at the strategic level tend to be unstructured. Managerial decisions tend to be both structured and unstructured.

We use the words *tend to be* because there are exceptions to the relationship illustrated in Figure 2-11. Some operational decisions are unstructured (e.g., "How many taxicab drivers do we need on the night before the homecoming game?"), and some strategic decisions can be structured (e.g., "How should we assign sales quotas for a new product?"). In general, however, the relationship shown in Figure 2-11 holds.

Different Types of Information Systems for Different Types of Decisions

Figure 2-12 contrasts two types of information system. **Automated information systems** are those in which the hardware and program components do most of the work. An information system that computes the quantity of items to order for inventory is an example of an automated system. Humans start the programs and use the results, but hardware and programs do most of the work.

Augmentation information systems are those in which humans do the bulk of the work. The information system exists to augment, support, or supplement the work done by people. An information system that uses email, instant messaging, and videoconferencing to assist the decision of whether to buy a competing company is an augmentation system. Unlike the order-quantity computation system, the users look for support rather than answers.

Figure 2-13 (page 36) shows the relationship between the decision type and the IS type. In general, structured decisions can be supported by automated information systems, and they are generally applied at the operational and managerial levels of decision making. In contrast, unstructured decisions are supported by augmentation information systems, and they are generally applied at the managerial and strategic levels.

At this point, you may be wondering, "Why does all this matter?" One of the goals of this class is to help you become a better consumer of information systems and information technology. When you think about a new information system, you will be a better IT consumer if you ask yourself, "What is the nature of the underlying decision process?" If you can identify the type of process, you will know what type of information system may be helpful. Additionally, you will know not to invest in automated information systems for unstructured problems or in augmentation information systems for

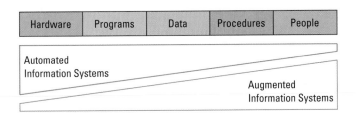

Figure 2-12
Automated vs. Augmented
Information Systems

Your Personal Competitive Advantage

onsider the following possibility: You work hard, earning your degree in business and graduating, only to discover that you cannot find a job in your area of study. You look for 6 weeks or so, but then you run out of money. In desperation, you take a job waiting tables at a local restaurant. Two years go by, the economy picks up, and the jobs you had been looking for become available. Unfortunately, your degree is now 2 years old; you are competing with students who have just graduated with fresh degrees (and fresh knowledge). Two years of waiting tables, good as you are at it, does not appear to be good experience for the job you want. You're stuck in a nightmare—one that will be hard to get out of, and one that you cannot allow to happen.

Examine Figure 2-1 again, but this time consider those elements of competitive advantage as they apply to you personally. As an employee, the skills and abilities you offer are your personal product. Examine the first three items in the list and ask yourself, "How can I use my time in school, and in this MIS class in particular, to create new skills, to enhance those I already have, and to differentiate my skills from the competition?" (By the way, you will enter a national/international market. Your competition is not just the students in your class, it's students in classes in Ohio, California, British Columbia, Florida, New York, and every place else they're teaching MIS today.)

Suppose you are interested in a sales job. Perhaps, for example, you want to sell in the pharmaceutical industry. What skills can you learn from your MIS class that will make you more competitive as a future salesperson? Ask yourself, "How does the pharmaceutical industry use MIS to gain competitive advantage?" Get on the Internet and find examples of the use of information systems in the pharmaceutical industry. How does Parke-Davis, for example, use a CRM system to sell to doctors? How can your knowledge of CRM differentiate you from your competition for a job there? How does Parke-Davis use a knowledge management system? How does the firm keep track of drugs that have an adverse effect on each other?

The fourth and fifth items in Figure 2-1 concern locking in customers, buyers, and suppliers. How can you interpret those elements in terms of your personal competitive advantage? Well, to lock in, you first have to have a relationship to lock in. So, do you have an internship? If not, can you get one? And, once you have an internship, how can you use your knowledge of MIS to lock in your job so that you get a job offer? Does the company you are interning for have a CRM system (or any other information system that is important to the company)? If users are happy with the system, what characteristics make it worthwhile? Can you lock in a job by becoming an expert user of this system? Becoming an expert user not only locks you into your job, it also raises barriers to entry for others who might be competing for the job. Also, can you suggest ways to improve the system, thus using your knowledge of the company and the system to lock in an extension of your job?

Human resources personnel say that networking is one of the most effective ways of finding a job. How can you use this class to establish alliances with other students? Does your class have a Web site? Is there an email list server for the students in your class? How can you use those facilities to develop job-seeking alliances with other students? Who in your class already has a job or an internship? Can any of those people provide hints or opportunities for finding a job?

Don't restrict your job search to your local area. Are there regions of your country where jobs are more plentiful? How can you find out about student organizations in those regions? Search the Web for MIS classes in other cities and make contact with students there. Find out what the hot opportunities are in other cities.

Finally, as you study MIS, think about how the knowledge you gain can help you save costs for your employers. Even more, see if you can build a case that an employer would actually save money by hiring you. The line of reasoning might be that because of your knowledge of IS, you will be able to facilitate cost savings that more than compensate for your salary.

In truth, few of the ideas that you generate for a potential employer will be feasible or pragmatically useful. The fact that you are thinking creatively, however, will indicate to a potential employer that you have initiative and are grappling with the problems that real businesses have. As this course progresses, keeping thinking about competitive advantage and strive to understand how the topics you study can help you to accomplish, personally, one or more of the principles in Figure 2-1.

DISCUSSION QUESTIONS

1. Summarize the efforts you have taken thus far to build an employment record that will lead to job offers after graduation.

2. Considering the first three principles in Figure 2-1, describe one way in which you have a competitive advantage over your classmates. If you do not have such competitive advantage, describe actions you can take to obtain one.

3. In order to build your network, you can use your status as a student to approach business professionals. Namely, you can contact them for help with an assignment or for career guidance. For example, suppose you want to work in banking and you know that your local bank has a CRM system. You could call the manager of that bank and ask her how the CRM system creates a competitive advantage for the bank. You also could ask to interview other employees, and go armed with the list in Figure 2-1. Describe two specific ways in which you can use your status as a student and the list in Figure 2-1 to build your network in this way.

4. Describe two ways that you can use student alliances to obtain a job. How can you use information systems to build, maintain, and operate such alliances?

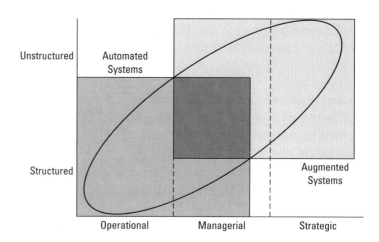

Figure 2-13
How Decision Level,
Decision Type, and IS Type
Are Related

structured problems. This point may seem obvious, but organizations have wasted millions of dollars by not understanding the basic relationships shown in Figure 2-13.

Information Systems and Decision Steps

Another way to examine the relationship between information systems and decision making is to consider how an information system is used during the steps of the decision-making process. The first two columns of Figure 2-14 show the typical steps in the decision-making process: intelligence gathering, formulation of alternatives, choice, implementation, and review. During *intelligence gathering,* the decision makers determine what is to be decided, what the criteria for the decision will be, and what data are available. Alternatives formulation is the stage in which decision makers lay out various alternatives. They analyze the alternatives during the choice step, and then implement the decision. Finally, the organization reviews the results of the decision. The review step may lead to another decision and another iteration through the decision process.

As summarized in the right column of Figure 2-14, each of these decision-making steps needs a different type of information system. During intelligence gathering, email and videoconferencing facilitate communication among the decision makers. Also, during the first phase, decision makers use query and reporting and other types of data analysis applications to obtain relevant data. Decision makers use email and videoconferencing systems for communication during the alternatives-formulation step. During the choice step, analysis applications such as spreadsheets and financial and other modeling applications help decision makers to analyze alternatives. The

Decision Step	Description	Examples of Possible Information Systems
Intelligence gathering	• What is to be decided? • What are the decision criteria? • Obtain relevant data	• Communications applications (email, video conferencing, word processing, presentation) • Query and reporting systems • Data analysis applications
Alternative formulation	• What are the choices?	• Communications applications
Choice	• Analyze choices against criteria using data • Select alternative	• Spreadsheets • Financial modeling • Other modeling
Implementation	• Make it so!	• Communications applications
Review	• Evaluate results of decision; if necessary, repeat process to correct and adapt	• Communications • Query and reporting • Spreadsheets and other analysis

Figure 2-14
Decision-Making Steps

You Be the Guide

Using the Reflections Guide
(page 35a)

GOALS

* Raise students' awareness that they should be engaged in job planning/searching right now.

* Show the application of the principles of competitive advantage to career planning.

* Suggest innovative tasks for job searching.

BACKGROUND AND PRESENTATION STRATEGIES

Students seldom understand how their status as students gives them access to business people that they will lose after they graduate. Ask the students if they understand the difference in the response they will receive to the following two statements:

➤ **Hi, my name is XXX, and I'm a student at YYY University. We're studying information systems and competitive advantage. I see that your company, ZZZ, is using a CRM application. I'm wondering if you would have a few minutes to talk with me about how your CRM system gives ZZZ a competitive advantage.**

➤ **Hi, my name is XXX, and I'm looking for a job. I see that your company, ZZZ, is using a CRM application. I'm wondering if you would have a few minutes to talk with me about how your CRM system gives you a competitive advantage.**

What will be the difference in response? Huge. In the first, the person will feel like they're helping along some bright, ambitious person. Most will say, sure, and maybe offer to buy the student a cup of coffee. In the second, the person will feel like they're being manipulated to find a job. Most will say, "Contact our HR department."

Why should students talk with business people, and now? To build their networks.

➤ **Have the conversation. Make a list of great questions to ask; be appreciative that the business person took the time. Then, toward the end of the interview, ask if the person has any advice for finding a job in that industry.** Not, *do they have a job,* but rather, *do they have any advice for finding a job.* **If they have a job, they'll tell you. If not, they may give you some good advice. Even if you get no good advice, you have another point in your network. Take**

Figure 2-1 along and ask the person how you can use it to gain a competitive advantage.

See question 3.

Why do students not use their special student status in this way? I don't know, but I try to ensure that they at least know about these strategies.

Some students may be too shy. If this is the case, sometimes I make it an assignment, possibly an extra credit assignment.

Similarly, students should be availing themselves of every resource the university provides for outreach to business people.

➤ **If there is a mentor program, get a mentor. If there is a chance to visit a business, go visit the business. If someone from industry speaks on a topic of interest, by all means go. Talk to the speaker afterwards, make one or two positive comments, and ask a good question. Ask for the person's business card. In a day or two, send them an email thanking them. See if you can get an interview to discuss some topic of mutual interest.**

Sometimes I lead them carefully through the disaster scenario. I tell them I had this horrible dream last night. And my dream was that they graduated, couldn't get a job, took a dead-end job for 2 years, and then couldn't get out of that track. To avoid this nightmare, they have to start thinking about their jobs, now! (I'm assuming mostly junior-level students.)

By the way, every chapter in the text has a section of questions called Career Assignment that will ask them to look for information about jobs in the IS field. I ask my students to answer these questions in at least two of the chapters sometime during the class.

SUGGESTED RESPONSES FOR DISCUSSION QUESTIONS

1. Answer depends on the student. Sometimes I say, "If your list is short, tell me what you plan to do in the next quarter."

2. Again, the answer depends on the student. I also encourage them to realize that they aren't competing just with the students they see on our campus. They're competing with students all over the world. (More on this topic in Chapter 3.)

3. There are many ways to build networks. Here are two types of answers:

   • Read trade magazines, relevant Web sites (e.g., *www.cio.com*), and other sources. Find an article on a topic of interest and think of ways the ideas in that article apply to you and one or more items in the list in Figure 2-1. Contact the author of the article. Make a few complimentary comments; ask questions that pertain to the article, you, and the list.

- Approach business people working in your major field of study and ask them how you can use knowledge of information systems to gain a competitive advantage in that field. Tell them of your interest in both your major and in IS. Use this situation to generate further introductions, perhaps to specialists in your field.

4. Get active. Join clubs. Meet with lots of students. Participate in campus life both in and beyond the business school. As we'll discuss in the Reflections Guide in Chapter 5, you add more connections to your network by meeting students that are outside of your major or even outside of the business school. As you meet people, tell them of your career interests. Ask if they know anyone working in that field. Ask if they know someone you could meet with, as described in question 3.

Join a business-specific club, for example, the Accounting Club or the Marketing Club. Get involved, especially with activities that engage local business people. Arrange for speakers and host speakers on campus. As you meet business people on campus, query them about their careers. How did they get where they are?

Use an IS to keep track of the people whom you've met. Put contacts in a spreadsheet or database. Keep track of contacts you've had, emails you've sent, meetings you've attended. At an interview, when appropriate, show off your database. Use the Web and email to contact people who are doing interesting things.

WRAP UP

➤ You don't want to find just any job. You want to find a *great* job! You want to find one with appropriate responsibilities, with a growing company, with job growth potential, and where you work with interesting people. You also want one that pays well.

➤ Finding that great job may not be easy. Start now! Start thinking about what kind of job you want, and start preparing yourself to find that job. The last semester of your senior year will be too late.

➤ If you're not an IS major, combining IS knowledge with your other major can make for a great combination. Think about taking some more IS classes.

implementation stage again involves use of communications applications, and all types of information systems can be used during review.

Not Worth It? (continued)

At the beginning of this chapter, we left you stammering in the parking lot, talking with your boss's boss's boss. You were trying to respond to his "Not worth it" statement.

Having read this chapter, you now know that organizations create information systems to gain a competitive advantage, to solve problems, and to improve decision making. You can use this framework to formulate your response, something like, "Well, in theory there are three reasons to build an IS," and name the three. You can elaborate, "But in our case, not all of them pertain. For example, ...," and you're off and running.

SUMMARY

- Organizations develop and use information systems to gain competitive advantage, to solve problems, and to assist in decision making. Some information systems accomplish two or more of these goals.

- Figure 2-1 lists eight principles of competitive advantage. Some of these pertain to products, some pertain to barriers established by creating switching costs, and others concern alliances and cost savings. Information systems can help achieve all eight of these principles. Some information systems are part of the product, whereas others exist to support the product.

- Some organizations develop information systems to solve problems. A problem is a perceived difference between what is and what ought to be. Because a problem is a perception, different people can have different problem definitions. When using an information system to solve a problem, it is critical that the organization have a single, agreed-on definition of the problem.

- For the laptop problem described in this chapter, we defined three problems and three different solutions. One solution is a customer relationship management (CRM) system, one is a knowledge management system (KMS), and the third is a manufacturing quality-control system.

- A third purpose of information systems is to facilitate decision making. Decisions can be made at the operational (TPS), managerial (MIS), and strategic levels (EIS). The decision timeframe increases as we move from operational to managerial to strategic decisions. Decisions also vary according to whether a structured or unstructured process is used to make them. A structured process involves an understood and accepted method; an unstructured process has no agreed-on decision-making method. Remember that the terms *structured* and *unstructured* refer to the process for making the decision, not to the underlying subject matter. The loose relationship between the decision type and the decision process is illustrated in Figure 2-11.

- Automated information systems are those in which the computer and program side of the five components do most of the work. Augmentation information systems are those in which humans do the bulk of the work, with the computer and program components being used to assist the humans as they make decisions. Figure 2-13 shows the relationship between the decision type and the IS type.

- Another way to consider information systems and decision making is to consider the steps of the decision process: intelligence gathering, formulation of alternatives, decision choice, implementation, and review. Different types of information systems are used for different steps of the decision process, as summarized in Figure 2-14.

KEY TERMS AND CONCEPTS

Augmentation information systems   35
Automated information systems   35
Customer relationship management (CRM)   31
Executive information systems (EIS)   34
Knowledge management system (KMS)   32

Management information systems (MIS)   34
Managerial decision   34
Manufacturing information systems   33
Operational decision   34
Principles of competitive advantage   26
Problem   31

Strategic decision   34
Structured decision   34
Switching costs   27
Transaction processing systems (TPS)   34
Unstructured decision   34

ASSIGNMENT MATERIAL

Review Questions

1. Name three purposes for information systems in organizations.
2. List three principles of competitive advantage that pertain to products.
3. List three principles of competitive advantage that pertain to barriers.
4. List principles of competitive advantage not listed in your answers to questions 2 and 3.
5. Explain the difference between using an information system as part of a product and using one to support a product.
6. Explain how the ABC example achieves the principles of competitive advantage that you provided in your answer to question 2.
7. Does the ABC information system achieve the principles of competitive advantage that you provided in your answer to question 3? Why or why not?
8. Does the ABC information system achieve the principles of competitive advantage that you provided in your answer to question 4? Why or why not?
9. Why is it important that a problem is a perception?
10. How does the definition of a problem relate to the information system created to solve that problem?
11. What is the purpose of a customer relationship management (CRM) system?
12. What is the purpose of a knowledge management system (KMS)?
13. What is the purpose of a manufacturing quality-control information system?

14. Identify the three levels of decision making defined in this chapter.
15. Describe the nature of operational decision making.
16. Describe the nature of managerial decision making.
17. Describe the nature of strategic decision making.
18. Is the process of choosing a major structured or unstructured? Is the process of choosing classes structured or unstructured? Explain your answers.
19. Explain the nature of an automated information system. Use the five components in your answer.
20. Explain the nature of an augmentation information system. Use the five components in your answer.
21. List the five steps of the decision-making process and describe the types of information systems useful for each.

Applying Your Knowledge

22. Suppose you work for the company that manufactured the problematic laptop used as an example in this chapter. Company managers have defined three different problems, each with a different IS solution. Suppose the company has the resources to create only one of these systems. How should the company go about deciding which one to build?
23. Suppose you are an adviser to one of the sports teams at your university, say the intercollegiate soccer team. (Or, pick another sport in which you have experience or interest.)

    a. Explain how the principles of competitive advantage in Figure 2-1 pertain to this team.

You Be the Guide

Not Worth It (continued)
(page 37)

The goal of this vignette was to motivate students to learn the principal ways that businesses use information systems. According to the chapter, they are competitive advantage, problem solving, and improved decision making.

RESPONDING TO THE CHALLENGE

➤ **OK, let's assume you're talking with your boss's boss's boss. He's said that the new information system is not worth it because it won't generate any revenue. You've said, "But that's not the only reason to have an information system."**

"Go on" he says, "Tell me why we should build it. Since it won't generate any revenue, what *will* it do?"

➤ **Summarize the reasons for using IS for competitive advantages in a few sentences. (Remember, you're standing in the parking lot.)**

➤ **What would you say about problem solving?**

➤ **What would you say about improved decision making?**

➤ **Suppose he says, "Wait, those categories overlap with one another." How do you respond?**

➤ **Suppose he asks, "How much do you think this system will cost?"**

Unlike the previous questions, this one is not obvious from the chapter material. I raise it here because it would be a natural one for a manager who is fishing for information (and many do).

I think you have to say you don't know. Or you say whatever your team said in its presentation. Note, too, he could be asking this question just to see how you handle it. It could be a test of your maturity or of whether you know to say you don't know when you don't know.

➤ **Suppose he asks, "How long will it take to build this system?"**

I think you say don't know or whatever the team said, for the same reasons as stated earlier regarding costs.

➤ **After you have this encounter, do you have a professional responsibility to tell anyone about it? If so, whom would you tell and what would you say?**

WRAP UP

I sometimes conclude this section with an assignment, as follows:

➤ **Informal, ad-hoc meetings like this one are common and important. If you don't know how to already, you need to learn how to express yourself clearly and confidently at such times.**

➤ **I have an assignment for you. It won't be graded, but I want you to prepare it anyway. Go home tonight and, knowing what you know now, practice an answer. It should be a minute or two long, at most.**

➤ **Next lecture, I'm going to call on two or three of you and ask you to present your response to the class. Again, it's not graded, it's just a chance to use our class for practice. See you then!**

b. Describe how an information system could be used to achieve or help to achieve three of the principles of competitive advantage in your answer to part a.

24. Suppose you are an adviser to an investment club at your university.

   a. Explain how the principles of competitive advantage in Figure 2-1 pertain to this club.
   b. Describe how an information system could be used to achieve or help to achieve three of the principles of competitive advantage in your answer to part a.

25. Samantha Green owns and operates Twigs Tree Trimming Service. Samantha graduated from the forestry program of a nearby university and worked for a large landscape design firm performing tree trimming and removal. After several years of experience, she bought her own truck, stump grinder, and other equipment and opened her own business in St. Louis, Missouri.

   Although many of her jobs are one-time operations to remove a tree or stump, others are recurring, such as trimming a tree or groups of trees every year or every other year. When business is slow, she calls former clients to remind them of her service and of the need to trim their trees on a regular basis.

   a. Explain how the principles of competitive advantage in Figure 2-1 pertain to Twigs Tree Trimming.
   b. Describe how an information system could be used to achieve or help to achieve three of the principles of competitive advantage in your answer to part a.
   c. Suppose that Samantha says that she has a problem keeping track of her customers and their needs. This statement is vague and could mean many different things. To demonstrate this to her, write two different, but possible, problem definitions that one could infer from the words "a problem keeping track of her customers and their needs."
   d. Give an example of:
      i. An operational decision that Samantha makes.
      ii. A managerial decision that she makes.
      iii. A strategic decision that she makes.
   e. Give three examples of information systems that could help Samantha to make the decisions in part d.

26. FiredUp, Inc., is a small business owned by Curt and Julie Robards. Based in Brisbane, Australia, FiredUp manufactures and sells a lightweight camping stove called the FiredNow. Curt, who previously worked as an aerospace engineer, invented a patented burning nozzle that enables the stove to stay lit in very high winds—up to 90 miles per hour. Julie, an industrial designer by training, developed an elegant folding design that is small, lightweight, easy to set up, and very stable. Curt and Julie manufacture the stove in their garage, and they sell it directly to their customers over the Internet, via fax, and via postal mail.

   a. Explain how the principles of competitive advantage in Figure 2-1 pertain to FiredUp.
   b. Describe how an information system could be used to achieve or help to achieve three of the principles of competitive advantage in your answer to part a.
   c. Suppose Curt and Julie say they have a problem keeping track of their customers and their stoves. This statement is vague and could mean many different things. To demonstrate this to FiredUp's owners, write two different, but possible, problem definitions that one could infer from the words "a problem keeping track of their customers and their stoves."
   d. Give an example of:
      i. An operational decision that Curt and Julie make.
      ii. A managerial decision that they make.
      iii. A strategic decision that they make.
   e. Give three examples of information systems that Curt and Julie could use to make the decisions in part d.

27. Singing Valley Resort is a top-end (rooms cost from $400 to $2,500 per night), 50-unit resort located high in the mountains of Colorado. Singing Valley prides itself on its beautiful location, its relaxing setting, and its superb service. The resort's restaurant is highly regarded and has an extensive list of exceptional wines. The well-heeled clientele are accustomed to the highest levels of service.

   a. Explain how the principles of competitive advantage in Figure 2-1 pertain to Singing Valley.
   b. Describe how an information system could be used to achieve or help to achieve three of the principles of competitive advantage in your answer to part a.
   c. Suppose Singing Valley says that it has a problem keeping track of its customers and their needs. This statement is vague and could mean many different things. To demonstrate this to Singing Valley, write two different, but possible, problem

definitions that one could infer from the words "a problem keeping track of its customers and their needs."

d. Give an example of:
   i. An operational decision that Singing Valley makes.
   ii. A managerial decision that Singing Valley makes.
   iii. A strategic decision that Singing Valley makes.

e. Give three examples of information systems that Singing Valley could use to make the decisions in part d.

Application Exercises

28. Suppose you work for a small electronics retailer who sells expensive, high-quality home entertainment equipment. When customers call about problems with their equipment, you want to record data about the customer, the equipment, and the problem the customer is having, and the resolution you have given for this problem.

   a. Create a spreadsheet with the following columns: *CustomerName*, *Phone*, *Email*, *EquipmentMake*, *EquipmentModel*, *Date*, *ProblemDescription*, *ProblemResolution*. Enter sample data into this spreadsheet.

   b. Suppose you have used your spreadsheet for several months and have entered data for, say, 1,000 problems. Explain how you would use your spreadsheet to find all of the problems for a particular customer.

   c. Suppose you have used your spreadsheet for several months and have entered data for, say, 1,000 problems. Explain how you would use your spreadsheet to find all of the problems for a particular item of equipment.

   d. Suppose you have used your spreadsheet for several months and have entered data for, say, 1,000 problems. Suppose that some customers have called multiple times. Explain what you need to do when a customer changes his or her phone or email address.

   e. Explain how this spreadsheet gives your organization a competitive advantage.

   f. Explain how this spreadsheet improves decision making.

   g. Assess the desirability of using a spreadsheet for this application. What are the advantages of using a spreadsheet? What are the disadvantages? How would your answer change if your organization needed to keep data for 10,000 problems?

29. Suppose you work for a small electronics retailer who sells expensive, high-quality home entertainment equipment. When customers call about problems with their equipment, you want to record data about the customer, the equipment, and the problem the customer is having, and the resolution you have given for this problem.

   a. Create an Access database with three tables: CUSTOMER, EQUIPMENT, and PROBLEM. The CUSTOMER table should have *CustomerName*, *Phone*, and *Email* columns. The EQUIPMENT table should have *ItemNumber*, *EquipmentMake*, and *EquipmentModel* columns. The PROBLEM table should have *Phone* (which matches *Phone* in CUSTOMER), *ItemNumber* (which matches *ItemNumber* in EQUIPMENT), *Date*, *ProblemDescription*, and *ProblemResolution*. Select appropriate data types for each column.

   b. Enter sample data into your database. Explain how each row in problem is related to the customer and the equipment involved.

   c. Suppose you have used your database for several months and have entered data for, say, 1,000 problems. Explain how you would find all of the problems for a customer, given the customer's phone number.

   d. Suppose you have used your database for several months and have entered data for, say, 1,000 problems. Explain how you would find all of the problems for a particular customer, given the customer's name. (*Hint*: Use a query to answer this question. Also, how will you deal with the situation if two customers have the same name?)

   e. Suppose you have used your database for several months and have entered data for, say, 1,000 problems. Suppose that some customers have called multiple times. Explain what you need to do when a customer changes his or her phone or email address.

   f. Explain how this database gives your organization a competitive advantage.

   g. Explain how this database improves decision making.

   h. Assess the desirability of using a database for this application. What are the advantages of using a database? What are the disadvantages? How would your answer change if your organization needed to keep data for 10,000 problems?

Career Assignments

30. Using Google.com or your favorite other Web search tool, query the Internet for "customer support job opportunities."

   a. Locate and describe three jobs in which you might be interested.

b. Summarize the qualifications necessary for these jobs.

c. Explain how you can use the principles of competitive advantage in Figure 2-1 to prepare yourself to obtain a job like one of these.

d. Name two concepts, ideas, processes, or frameworks that you can learn in your MIS class that will help you obtain one of these jobs.

31. Same as question 30, except query for "knowledge management job opportunities."

32. Same as question 30, except query for "quality assurance manager." Look for jobs that require a business rather than engineering background (unless, of course, you are majoring in engineering).

Case Study 2-1

Customer Support and Knowledge Management at Microsoft

Many companies believe that "the best customer service is no service at all." In other words, the product works, the customer never calls, and there's never a need for service. The next best customer service is that which someone else pays for. One such example occurs when users support one another. To this end, Microsoft and other software vendors create and administer "user communities" featuring newsgroups, user groups, and most valuable professionals (MVPs). See *microsoft.com/communities* for more examples.

In a *newsgroup*, users post questions about errors, problems, and product use. Other customers who have experience and expertise with the relevant product answer the posted questions. Microsoft employees can also post answers to questions. A side benefit to Microsoft is that it learns about product and documentation problems from the questions that are posted to the newsgroups.

A *user group* consists of product users who meet periodically in a particular geographic location. For example, a Microsoft Office user group in Washington D.C. meets periodically to discuss best practices, new developments, problems, and other issues related to the use of Microsoft Office. User groups not only save Microsoft support dollars, but they also promulgate Microsoft products in a more intimate, local setting. Microsoft employees attend user groups as speakers, advisers, and observers.

Microsoft designates 1,900 individuals from its millions of users worldwide as MVPs, or Most Valuable Professionals. These people possess expert-level knowledge of Microsoft products that they share with peers and other Microsoft product users. Microsoft selects these people "for their outstanding efforts to help people around the world do amazing things with technology." These people, who are not Microsoft employees, serve as Microsoft product and technology ambassadors. Microsoft hosts them in an annual MVP Conference at which they meet senior executives like Bill Gates and Steve Ballmer.

Source: Microsoft, *microsoft.com* (accessed May 2005).

Questions

1. Explain why the best customer support is none at all.

2. List the benefits and costs to Microsoft of supporting newsgroups.

3. Why do users bother to answer other users' questions? What's in it for them? Suppose you manage a group of technical personnel. How much time do you want them to spend each day solving other peoples' problems? How can you control such activities?

4. What are the dangers to Microsoft in supporting a newsgroup? How can a newsgroup backfire on Microsoft? Do you think Microsoft edits or censors the newsgroup postings? Should it be able to do so?

5. List the benefits and costs to Microsoft of supporting user groups. Consider both customer support and marketing benefits.

6. What are the dangers to Microsoft in supporting a user group? How can a user group backfire on Microsoft? What control can Microsoft exert over such groups?

7. How does an individual benefit from joining a user group?

8. List the benefits and costs to Microsoft in supporting the MVP program. Consider both support and marketing benefits.

9. Why, besides the chance to meet Bill Gates, would someone want to become an MVP? What benefits accrue with that status?

10. Summarize the information systems that Microsoft uses to support these programs.

11. Using the list in Figure 2-1, summarize how these programs give Microsoft a competitive advantage.

Case Study 2-2

Bosu Balance Trainer

Video

The Bosu balance trainer is a device for developing balance, strength, and aerobic conditioning. Invented in 1999, Bosu has become popular in leading health clubs, in athletic departments, and in homes. Bosu stands for "both sides up," because either side of the equipment can be used for training.

Bosu is not only a new training device, but it also reflects a new philosophy in athletic conditioning that focuses on balance. According to the Bosu inventor, David Weck, "The Bosu Balance Trainer was born of passion to improve my balance. In my life-long pursuit of enhanced athleticism, I have come to understand that balance is the foundation on which all other performance components are built." Bosu devices are sold by Bosu.com.

Bosu devices have been successful enough that copycat products are undoubtedly on the way. For Bosu to be successful over the long term, it must transform its early market lead into a sustainable and durable market share. This means that Bosu must be used and recommended by coaches, personal trainers, and other significant purchase influencers. Bosu must develop a reputation among these market leaders as delivering significant benefits without risk of injury.

Bosu Balance Trainer

Source: Bosu, *bosu.com* (accessed May 2005).

Questions

1. Review the principles of competitive advantage in Figure 2-1. What information systems can Bosu create to enhance or differentiate its product from existing and emerging competition?

2. What information systems can Bosu develop to create barriers to entry to the competition and to lock in customers?

3. What information systems can Bosu develop to establish alliances?

4. Read the Microsoft Customer Support and Knowledge Management case on page 41. (You need not answer the questions in this case; just understand how Microsoft uses newsgroups, focus groups, and MVPs.)

5. How can Bosu develop programs similar to those used by Microsoft to provide customers support and create a competitive advantage?

6. What information systems will Bosu need to develop to support the programs identified in your answer to question 5?

PART II

Information Technology

The next four chapters address the information technology that underlies information systems. Chapter 3 discusses hardware and software and defines basic terms and fundamental computing principles.

Chapter 4 addresses the data component by describing database processing. Here you will learn essential database terminology and be introduced to techniques for processing databases. We will also introduce data modeling, because you may be required to evaluate data models for databases that others develop for you.

Chapter 5 continues the discussion of computing devices begun in Chapter 3 and describes data communications and Internet technologies.

Finally, Chapter 6 addresses the development of information systems. It describes the methods and procedures by which people construct new information systems and modify existing ones. Here you will also learn the roles and responsibilities that you will have as a user of an information system.

The purpose of these four chapters is to teach you technology sufficient for you to be an effective IT consumer. You will learn basic terms, fundamental ideas, and useful frameworks so that you will have the knowledge to ask good questions and make appropriate requests of the information systems professionals who will serve you.

Hardware and Software

Learning Objectives

* Learn the terminology necessary to be an intelligent consumer of hardware products.

* Know the functions and basic features of common hardware devices.

* Understand the essentials of the representation of computer instructions and data.

* Know the purpose of the CPU and main memory, and understand their interaction.

* Learn about viruses, Trojan horses, and worms and how to prevent them.

* Understand the key factors that affect computer performance.

* Learn basic characteristics of the four most popular operating systems.

* Know the sources and types of application software.

Guides

PROBLEM SOLVING GUIDE
Questioning Your Questions

SECURITY GUIDE
Viruses, Trojan Horses, and Worms

OPPOSING FORCES GUIDE
Churn and Burn

ETHICS GUIDE
Using Hardware to Enforce Licenses

REFLECTIONS GUIDE
Keeping Up to Speed

Chapter Preview

This chapter presents basic computer hardware and software terms and concepts. The goal here is not to start you on a career as a computer engineer or software developer. Rather, our goal is to help you develop the knowledge you need to be an effective consumer of computing devices. To understand the need for this goal, consider the following scenario.

Is $80,000 Enough?

Suppose that you manage the accounts payable department at a company that generates $100 million in sales—say, a manufacturer of fireplaces and related equipment. Assume that you just started the job and that at the end of your second day your boss sticks her head in your office and announces, "I'm in a rush and have to go, but I wanted to let you know that I put $80,000 in the budget for computers for your department next year. Is that OK? Unfortunately, I've got to know by the day after tomorrow. Thanks."

How do you respond? You have two days to decide. If you agree to $80,000 and it turns out to be insufficient, then sometime next year your department will lack computing resources and you'll have a management problem. If that happens, you may have to spend over your budget. You know that effective cost control is important to your new company, so you dread overspending. However, if you ask for more than $80,000, you will need to justify why you need it. How do you proceed?

The goal of this chapter is to prepare you to ask the right questions so you can respond effectively to your boss's question. As a start, read the *Problem Solving Guide* on page 49a about learning how to ask the right questions. We will return to this budget scenario at the end of the chapter.

▮ Essential Hardware Terminology

Computing devices consist of computer *hardware* and *software*. **Hardware** is electronic components and related gadgetry that input, process, output, and store data according to instructions encoded in computer programs or software.

Your personal computer and other computers like it are **general-purpose computers**. They can run different programs to perform different functions. For example, you can run Microsoft Excel on your computer to do a financial analysis, and your roommate can run Adobe Acrobat on the same computer to generate formatted documents. You and your roommate are using the same hardware; you are just using that hardware to run two different software programs.

Some computers are **special-purpose computers**. The programs they run are fixed in memory. The computer in your cell phone is a special-purpose computer, and so is the computer in your car that meters fuel to your car's engine. The principles and fundamental components of general-purpose and special-purpose computers are the same; the sole difference is whether the computer can process a variety of different programs.

With regard to information systems, when we refer to computer hardware, we mean a general-purpose computer, one that can run a variety of programs. Special-purpose computers hide within the devices that use them and normally are not even noticed. When you use your cell phone, for example, you normally don't even think that you are also using a computer.

Input, Processing, Output, and Storage Hardware

To answer a question like whether $80,000 is enough for your computer budget, you need a way of categorizing the hundreds of different computing devices that exist. One easy way to categorize hardware is by its primary function—whether it is input hardware, processing hardware, output hardware, storage hardware, or communication hardware. We will address the first four categories in this chapter. Communications hardware—devices that send and receive data over communications lines—is discussed in Chapter 5.

As shown in Figure 3-1, typical **input hardware** devices are the keyboard, mouse, document scanners, and bar-code (Universal Product Code) scanners like those used in grocery stores. Microphones also are input devices; with tablet PCs, human handwriting can be input as well. Older input devices include magnetic ink readers (used for reading the ink on the bottom of checks) and scanners like the Scantron test scanner shown in Figure 3-2.

Processing devices include the **central processing unit (CPU)**, which is sometimes called "the brain" of the computer. Although the design of the CPU has nothing in common with the anatomy of animal brains, this description is helpful because the CPU does have the "smarts" of the machine. The CPU selects instructions, processes them, performs arithmetic and logical comparisons, and stores results of operations in memory.

CPUs vary in speed, function, and cost. Hardware vendors such as Intel, Advanced Micro Devices, and National Semiconductor continually improve CPU speed and capabilities while reducing CPU costs (as discussed under Moore's Law in Chapter 1). Whether you or your department needs the latest, greatest CPU depends on the nature of your work.

You Be the Guide

The $80,000 Question
(page 47)

GOALS

* Motivate students to learn about hardware and software. Many think they will leave these decisions to someone else in their companies.

* Show students that *learning about hardware and software*, in sufficient depth to answer this question, is a *skill* they will need in their business careers.

WAYS TO STIMULATE STUDENT INVOLVEMENT

Like all of the technology chapters, the goal for the students should be to learn enough to be effective consumers of IT products and services. This means *learning key terms,* and it also means *learning key concepts.* An example of key concepts in this chapter are the roles of processor speed and main memory. A user who needs numerous programs in memory at once and whose computer is constrained by memory will waste money on a faster CPU. He or she should buy memory, instead.

One way to develop this idea is to ask following questions:

➤ **Is the "$80,000 question" a credible problem?**

➤ **Does it seem like a question that a departmental manager will get?**

➤ **Is this situation something that could happen to you?**

➤ **Can you see yourself in this situation in the future?**

Next, ask:

➤ **What happens if you answer the $80,000 question incorrectly?**

➤ **If you say, "Sure, $80,000 is enough," and it's only two-thirds of what you need, what will happen?**

➤ **Or, if you say, "No, I need $120,000," what will happen? How will you justify your request?**

➤ **What if you stumble while justifying the need for more money? What reputation will you be creating for yourself?**

Once the students agree that this question is (1) realistic, (2) likely, and (3) important, they're hooked on learning the material in this chapter. If they're serious about being business professionals, then they need to know how to answer this question. If they don't learn this material, they are setting themselves up for failure.

By the way, this might be a good time to ask the students:

➤ **Whom do you think you are competing against?**

Other students are studying this chapter and learning how to answer this question. Who and where are they? Looking around, it's other students in this class, for sure.

➤ **But who else?**

Other students who are taking this class at this university? Other students who took this class last term or who will take it next term? What about other students in the university across the city? Across the state? In the South, the North, the West? Literally thousands of other students are learning this material in preparation for their careers; if the students choose not to learn it, they're falling behind.

WRAP UP

This may be a good time to remind the students that **learning this material is the students' choice.** If they want to be effective consumers of information technology products and services, we're here to help them gain that competitive advantage. The motivation, however, must come from the students.

Having established the credibility and importance of the $80,000 question, you might recommend that as the students read and study the chapter that they list questions they must ask to be able to answer the $80,000 question.

Note: The Problem Solving Guide on page 49a is a useful additional exercise for preparing the students to answer the $80,000 question.

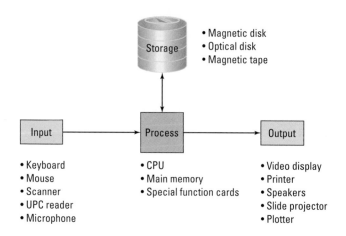

• Magnetic disk
• Optical disk
• Magnetic tape

Storage

Input → Process → Output

• Keyboard
• Mouse
• Scanner
• UPC reader
• Microphone

• CPU
• Main memory
• Special function cards

• Video display
• Printer
• Speakers
• Slide projector
• Plotter

Figure 3-1
Input, Process, Output, and
Storage Hardware

The CPU works in conjunction with **main memory**. The CPU reads data and instructions from memory, and it stores results of computations in main memory. We will describe the relationship between the CPU and main memory in the next section.

Finally, computers also can have **special function cards** (see Figure 3-3) that can be added to the computer to augment the computer's basic capabilities. A common example is a card that provides enhanced clarity and refresh speed for the computer's video display.

Output hardware consists of video displays, printers, audio speakers, overhead projectors, and other special-purpose devices, such as large flatbed plotters.

Storage hardware saves data and programs. Magnetic disk is by far the most common storage device, although optical disks such as CDs and DVDs also are popular. In large corporate data centers, data are sometimes stored on magnetic tape.

MIS in Use 3-1 (page 50) describes the business model used by one particular company to sell computer hardware to business customers.

Representing Computer Instructions and Data

Before we can further describe hardware, we need to define several important terms. We begin with binary digits.

Binary Digits

Computers represent data using **binary digits**, called **bits**. A bit is either a zero or a one. Bits are used for computer data because they are easy to represent physically,

Figure 3-2
Scantron Scanner

Figure 3-3
Special Function Card

Questioning Your Questions

Many school experiences mislead you to believe that answering a question is the important part of learning. In fact, answering a question is the easy part. For most problems in the business world, the difficult and creative acts are generating the questions—and formulating a strategy for getting the answers. Once the questions and strategy are set, the rest is simply legwork.

As a future consumer of information technology and services, you will benefit from being able to ask good questions and effectively obtain answers to them. It is probably the single most important behavior you can learn. Because of the rapid change of technology, you will constantly be required to learn about new IS alternatives and how you can apply them in your business.

Perhaps you've heard that "there is no such thing as a bad question." This statement is nonsense. There are billions of bad questions, and you will be better off if you learn not to ask them.

"It is not possible to become a good thinker and be a poor questioner. Thinking is not driven by answers, but rather, by questions."*

Questions can be bad in three ways: They can be irrelevant, dead, or asked of the wrong source. Consider the first way. If you know the subject and if you're paying attention, you can avoid asking irrelevant questions. One of the goals of this text is to teach you about IT and IS so that you can avoid asking irrelevant technology questions.

A dead question is one that leads to nowhere—it provides no insight into the subject. Here's an example of a dead question: "Is the material on How a Computer Works going to be on the test?" The answer will tell you whether or not you need to study that topic for the exam, but it won't tell you why. The answer will help you in school, but it won't help you use MIS on the job.

Instead, ask questions like, "What is the purpose of the section on how a computer works?" "Why are we studying it?" or "How will it help me use MIS in my career?" These are good questions because they go somewhere. Your professor may respond, "From that discussion you'll learn how to save money because you'll know whether to buy your staff more memory or a faster CPU." Possibly, you won't understand that answer; in that case, you can ask more questions that will lead you to understand how it pertains to your use of MIS.

*Richard Paul and Linda Elder, *Critical Thinking* (Upper Saddle River, NJ: Prentice Hall, 2001), p. 113.

Or, your professor may say, "Well, I think that section is a waste of time, and I told the author that in a recent email." From there, you can ask your professor why she thinks it's a waste of time, and you can wonder why the author would write something that is a waste of time. Maybe the author and your professor have different points of view. Such musings are excellent because they lead you to more learning.

The third way questions can be bad is that they are asked of the wrong source. Information technology questions fall into three types: "What is it?" "How can I use it?" and "Is it the best choice?" The first type asks for a simple definition. You can easily look up the answers to such questions in a book or at Internet sites like *whatis.com*. You ought not to ask "What is it?" questions of valuable or expensive sources; you are wasting your money and their time if you do. Also, when you ask such a question, you appear unprepared because you didn't take the time to find the easy answer.

The next type of question, "How can I use it?" is harder. Answering that question requires knowledge of both technology and your business. Although you can research that question over the Internet, you need knowledge to relate it to your present circumstance. In a few years, this is the sort of question that you will be expected to answer for your organization. It's also the type of question you might ask an expert.

Finally, the most difficult type of question is "Is it the best choice?" Answering this type of question requires the ability to judge among alternatives according to appropriate criteria. These are the kinds of questions you probably do want to ask an expensive source.

Notice, too, that only "What is it?" questions have a verifiably correct answer. The next two types are questions of judgment. No answer can be shown to be correct, but some answers are better than others. As you progress in your educational career, you should be learning how to discern the quality of judgment and evaluative answers. Learn to question your questions.

DISCUSSION QUESTIONS

1. Using your own words, distinguish between a good question and a bad one.

2. What types of questions waste time?

3. What types of questions are appropriate to ask your professor?

4. Under what circumstances would you ask a question to which you already know the answer?

5. Suppose you have 15 minutes with your boss's boss's boss. What kinds of questions are appropriate in such an interview? Even though you don't pay money to meet with this person, explain how this is an expensive source.

6. How do you know when you have a good answer to a question? Consider the three types of questions described here in your answer.

7. Evaluate the quality of questions 1 through 5. Which are the best questions? What makes one better than the other? If you can, think of better ways of asking these questions, or even better questions.

CDW, Inc.: A New Model for Buying Hardware

CDW, Inc. provides computer hardware products and services to business, government, and education. It describes itself as a **B2B**, or **business-to-business**, company, which means that its primary market is businesses. Although individuals can purchase from CDW, it's services and support are directed toward the business customer.

CDW was founded in 1984 and today has more than 400,000 customers. Based in Vernon Hills, Illinois, CDW generated $4.6 billion in sales in 2003. It was voted number 11 in *Fortune* magazine's poll of the Best 100 Places to Work in America.

CDW buys products from **OEMs (original equipment manufacturers**, such as Hewlett-Packard and IBM) as well as from distributors, such as Tech Data and Ingram Micro. It then resells those products to business users.

CDW's primary competitor is Dell, with whom the company competes on the basis of choice. According to John Edwardson, CDW's CEO, "We acknowledge that Dell offers customers the best Dell solution. We say that CDW can offer customers the best industry solution. Choice is really the Number 1 way we compete."

Traditionally, the hardware needs of small businesses have been supplied by **VARs (value-added resellers)**—generally small, local companies that analyze customer needs, determine computer requirements, buy the hardware, and set up and maintain the systems. This model requires the VAR to purchase the equipment before reselling, and often the VAR must extend its customers credit.

The traditional VAR model worked well when margins on computer hardware were higher than they are today. There was sufficient profit to enable the VAR to manage the risk of customer debt and still make money. Margins today do not support that model.

Consequently, in late 2004, CDW announced a new program, the Agent Program, in which CDW will partner with existing VARs. CDW will sell the hardware to the customer (according to Edwardson, CDW ships 90 percent of its orders on the day they are received), extend credit as necessary, and manage the credit risk. The VAR will continue to provide setup and support services and will bill the customer for those services. Additionally, CDW will pay a commission to the VAR based on customer orders.

The Agent Program is controversial; it requires transforming what had been small CDW competitors into allies. CDW believes the new model will work, especially given the continuing low margins on computer hardware. In theory, this program will allow CDW to specialize in what it does best and will allow the local VAR to specialize in what it does best.

Sources: Craig Zarley, "CDW's Edwardson Outlines Agent Strategy," CRN, *crn.com* (accessed January 2005); Craig Zarley, "Peace Offering," CRN, *crn.com* (accessed January 2005).

as illustrated in Figure 3-4. A switch can be either closed or open. A computer can be designed so that an open switch represents zero and a closed switch represents one. Or, the orientation of a magnetic field can represent a bit; magnetism in one direction represents a zero, magnetism in the opposite direction represents a one. Or, for optical media, small pits are burned onto the surface of the disk so that they will reflect light. In a given spot, a reflection means a one; no reflection means a zero.

Computer Instructions

Computers use bits for two purposes: instructions and data. Consider the first. A given instruction, say to add two numbers together, is represented by a string of bits. This string might appear something like 0111100010001110. When the CPU reads such an instruction from main memory, it adds the numbers or takes whatever action the instruction specifies. The collection of instructions that a computer can process is called the computer's **instruction set**.

You Be the Guide

Using the Problem Solving Guide *(page 49a)*

GOALS

* Teach the difference between formulating questions and answering questions.

* Emphasize the importance of question formulation.

* Describe and illustrate questions of varying quality.

BACKGROUND AND PRESENTATION STRATEGIES

Eleanore Baxendale, a seasoned and successful business commerce trial attorney, gave me the idea for this Problem Solving Guide. She told me that she'd learned over the years that the key to winning judgments lay in *determining what questions to ask.* Once she had the right list of questions, she could delegate to others the task of obtaining the answers. Her role, and a major reason for her success, was being able to think of the right questions to ask. "The rest is just legwork," she said.

The Paul and Elder quote at the start of this guide provides another perspective. *Questions guide thinking.* As the students sit in the class, the questions they are asking themselves are guiding their thoughts. If they're asking themselves, "When is the class going to be over?" that leads them down one path. If they're asking, "How does this knowledge relate to the $80,000 question?" that leads them down another. Which path do they want to be on? On which path are the students against whom they're competing?

Students may be threatened by all of this discussion regarding bad questions. They may feel inhibited about asking questions in class. My goal here is to *challenge the students to do their best work*—to endeavor not to ask irrelevant or dead questions—but *to do so in a nonthreatening way.* I let them know that although I expect good questions, bad questions will not be disastrous for them.

Every question requires taking a calculated risk. And *this class can help them* to ask effective questions of IT and IS professionals.

Very important: *Only simple, unimportant questions have a single, demonstrably correct answer.* Every other kind of question depends on perspective and can have multiple, correct answers. Depending on their cognitive development, some students will not be comfortable with the idea of multiple correct answers.

Some students are so grounded in the "Professor, you are the font of all knowledge, just give me the answer" mind-set that they will resist this notion. In fact, some feel angry because they *don't want to deal with the anxiety* of a world in which there are multiple correct answers. Some will say that I'm an incompetent teacher, or that I don't prepare for classes, or that I'm not as good a professor as Dr. ABC who always gives good answers.

I think I have a professional responsibility to stand up to that criticism. To me, a major purpose of college education is to help those students advance themselves past this immature way of viewing the world. And this advancement in thinking is especially important in business. Consider, for example, questions like, "Should IBM have sold its personal computer business?" There is no single, demonstrably correct answer.

(By the way, I'm easily trapped by my own ego into the students' expectations. There's a part of me that *wants to be the font* of all knowledge. It makes me feel powerful. Alas, it's all illusion.)

A great source on this phenomenon, by the way, is the work of William Perry, referenced in the annotations to the Problem Solving Guide in Chapter 1 (following page).

 SUGGESTED RESPONSES FOR DISCUSSION QUESTIONS

Note: The questions in this guide vary in quality. Some, like number 2, are intentionally not as good as others, in order to set up question number 7.

1. According to the guide, bad questions fall into three types: *irrelevant, dead,* or *asked of the wrong source.* Good questions are *questions that lead somewhere* and that are *asked of an appropriate source.* Good questions are also those beyond "What is it?" questions, such as "How can I use it?" and "Is it the best choice?"

➤ **What are examples of irrelevant, dead, and asked-of-the-wrong source questions?**

➤ **Using the $80,000 question, give examples of good questions.**

➤ **Do you agree with the definition of bad question in the guide?**

➤ **Are there other kinds of bad questions?**

➤ **Have you ever been embarrassed by a question you or someone else has asked? What was it? Why were you embarrassed?**

➤ **Are you intimidated by this discussion? Does it make you reluctant to ask a question?**

(If so, what's to be done? See comments in the Background and Presentation Strategies.)

Application: It is very common for a naïve and inexperienced manager to ask technical people a question that is so irrelevant that it is embarrassing. When that happens, the techies lose respect for that manager. This is never desirable, but it may be OK if the manager has little interaction with the techies. However, if he or she is managing the techies, it's a start toward a miserable existence. *This class can help avoid that situation!*

2. This question, as stated, isn't a very good question. It's almost a dead question. The following are questions that waste time: bad questions (see previous discussion); questions that aren't really questions (i.e., I want to show off my ability to ask a question); questions that were just asked; questions that we all know the answer to.

   ➤ **What do you think of this question?**

   ➤ **How could this question be made stronger?**

   (Change it to also ask, "What can we learn from this?")

3. A professor is an expensive source of information, so don't ask "What is it?" questions. Instead ask questions like, "How can I use it?" "Is it the best choice?" and other questions that lead somewhere. Like all such sources, think about the questions you ask. You only get so many.

   ➤ **When have you been in a position of authority? As a camp counselor, maybe? As a manager in an office or factory? In some other setting?**

   ➤ **What did you think when you were asked bad questions? What were the consequences?**

4. You might ask a question to which you already know the answer when you want to test another person's knowledge. It's been reported that former U.S. president Franklin Roosevelt seldom asked a question for which he did not already know the answer. He was always testing the person. Keep this in mind.

   ➤ **Your boss may already know the answer and may just be testing your knowledge. It could be dangerous to blather on.**

5. This person is an expensive source. Given this, this is a dead question, because it's nothing more than a thinly veiled attempt at making the same point as question 3.

   ➤ **How good is this question?**

   ➤ **How could this question be made better?**

   ➤ **Given question 3, should this question even be in this list?**

6. Answers to "What is it?" questions are verifiably correct. Answers to "How can I use it?" and "Is it the best choice?" questions are very difficult to assess. Consider the reputation of the answerer as well as the process that person used. Probably apply more weight to the latter. Stress the difference between an answer process and an answer. Practice by assessing answers to the following questions:

   ➤ **Should I sell my Microsoft stock and use the proceeds to purchase Google stock?**

   ➤ **My employees say we need $122,000 for the computer budget. How do I evaluate that answer?**

7. I think 2, 3, and 5 are questionable for the reasons stated. The best questions, to me, are 6 and 7. Question 1 is OK because it asks the students to think rather than regurgitate.

WRAP UP

➤ **What did you learn? Did you change your perspective about questions?**

➤ **If so, how? If not, why not?**

➤ **How would you apply this knowledge to the $80,000 question?**

➤ **How can you apply this knowledge to this course? Other courses? Your life?**

➤ **By the way, asking bad questions does happen. When it does, what should one do?**

➤ **Everyone, usually because of inadequate meeting preparation, does ask a stupid question from time to time (but, one hopes, only rarely). Here's what to do: Make a very brief apology, shut up, and sit down. Don't make the situation worse by attempting to justify the question. You'll just be digging the hole deeper and deeper. Change the subject and move on.**

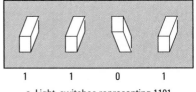

a. Light switches representing 1101

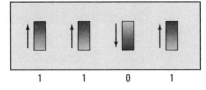

b. Direction of magnetism representing 1101

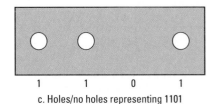

c. Holes/no holes representing 1101

Figure 3-4
Bits Are Easy to Represent
Physically

All of the personal computers that run Microsoft Windows are based on an instruction set developed by Intel Corporation that is called the **Intel instruction set**. Until 2006, all Macintosh computers used a different instruction set, the **PowerPC instruction set**, designed for PowerPC processors. In 2006, Apple began offering Macintosh computers with a choice of either Intel or PowerPC processors.

You cannot run a program designed for one instruction set on a computer having a different instruction set. Thus, you cannot run Windows on a Macintosh that uses the PowerPC instruction set. In the future, you may be able to run Windows on a Macintosh that uses the Intel instruction set, though the particulars of that are currently (early 2006) uncertain. In the case of the $80,000 question, if your company is committed to Windows, you cannot buy Macintosh computers that have the PowerPC processor. They won't run Windows.

The bottom line is this: When you pick a family of computers, that run a particular instruction set (Intel or PowerPC, for example), you pick not only the hardware, but also the sets of programs that can run on that family of computers.

Computer Data

All computer data are represented by bits. The data can be numbers, characters, currency amounts, photos, recordings, or whatever. All are simply a string of bits.

For reasons that interest many, but are irrelevant for answering the $80,000 question, bits are grouped into 8-bit chunks called **bytes**. (To learn more, see "Data Representation" on the book's Web site at *prenhall.com/ kroenke*.) For character data, such as the letters in a person's name, one character will fit into one byte. Thus, when you read a specification that a computing device has 100 million bytes of memory, you know that the device could hold up to 100 million characters.

Bytes are used to measure sizes of noncharacter data as well. Someone might say, for example, that a given picture is 100,000 bytes in size. This statement means the length of the bit string that represents the picture is 100,000 bytes or 800,000 bits (because there are 8 bits per byte). The specifications for the size of main memory, disk, and other computer devices are expressed in bytes. Figure 3-5 (page 52) shows the set of abbreviations that are used to represent data-storage capacity. A **kilobyte**, abbreviated **K**, is a collection of 1,024 bytes. A **megabyte**, or **MB**, is 1,024K bytes. A **gigabyte**, or **GB**, is 1,024MB bytes, and a **terabyte**, or **TB**, is 1,024GB.

Sometimes you will see these definitions simplified as 1K equals 1,000 bytes and 1MB equals 1,000K. Such simplifications are incorrect, but they do ease the math. Also, disk and computer manufacturers have an incentive to propagate this misconception. If a disk maker defines 1MB to be 1 million bytes, and not the correct 1,024K, the manufacturer can use its own definition of MB when specifying drive capacities. A buyer may think that a disk advertised as 100MB has space for 100 × 1,024K bytes, but

Term	Definition	Abbreviation
Byte	Number of bits to represent one character	
Kilobyte	1,024 bytes	K
Megabyte	1,024 K = 1,048,576 bytes	MB
Gigabyte	1,024 MB = 1,073,741,824 bytes	GB
Terabyte	1,024 GB = 1,099,511,627,776 bytes	TB

Figure 3-5
Important Storage-Capacity
Terminology

in truth the drive will have space for only 100 × 1,000,000 bytes. Normally, the distinction is not too important, but be aware of the two possible interpretations of these abbreviations. If you wonder why K is 1,024 and not 1,000, see the Data Representation reference, cited earlier, at the book's Web site.

Ambiguity of Binary Data

Before we leave the topic of computer data representation, you need to understand one additional point: It is not possible to determine the type of computer data just by looking at the data. The bit string 0100 0001 can be interpreted as the decimal number 65, as the character A, or as part of a picture or a sound file. Further, it could be part of a computer instruction. You cannot tell what a bit string is just by looking at it.

The CPU determines how to interpret a bit string from the context in which it encounters it. If the string occurs in the context of reading instructions, it will be interpreted as a computer instruction. If it occurs while processing a character string, say in the middle of a name, it will be interpreted as the character A. If it occurs during arithmetic operations, it will be interpreted as the decimal number 65.

This ambiguity is more than a curiosity; virus authors and other cyber-criminals use it to their advantage. Sequences of computer instructions, say instructions to send the system password to the hacker, can be stored in memory as if they were simply characters of data. Then the CPU can be infiltrated and directed to execute the instructions that were previously disguised as data. In this way, the hacker can gain control over the CPU. For more discussion on how different types of computer viruses work and what you can do to prevent them, read the *Security Guide* on page 53a.

■ Knowledge for the Informed Professional

Given the background discussions in the previous sections, we will now present knowledge that you will need to be an effective consumer of computer hardware and software as a business professional. The question is broader than, "What personal computer should I buy?" After all, you can ask your techie friends that question. The focus of the discussion here is to prepare you to answer the $80,000 question at the start of this chapter.

For example, considering the $80,000 question, say that you will need to buy at least five computers for new employees in your department. Suppose that your IS department states that you can buy three different computer configurations for three different prices. The computers are described by expressions like the following:

- Intel Pentium 4 Processor at 2.8 GHz with 533MHz Data Bus and 512K cache. 256MB RAM.
- Intel Pentium 4 Processor at 2.8 GHz with 533MHz Data Bus and 512K cache. 512MB RAM.
- Intel Pentium 4 Processor at 3.6 GHz with 533MHz Data Bus and 1MB cache. 256MB RAM.

Now, you, like many business managers, can roll your eyes and say, "I'm not a computer geek," and tell the people in the IS department to specify what they think is best. Or, with a little bit of knowledge on your part, you can work with that department to ask intelligent questions about the relationship of these computers to the kind of work your department does. The purpose of the next several pages is to prepare you to be able to ask those intelligent questions.

CPU and Memory Usage

Let's suppose that you are using your computer with three different software programs. Suppose you are processing a spreadsheet with Excel, examining a picture with Paint Shop Pro, and creating a brochure with Adobe Acrobat. If we were to open the lid of your computer, and if we could see the inner workings of the circuitry (which we cannot), we would see something like the situation shown in Figure 3-6.

In this figure, the **motherboard** is a circuit board upon which the processing components are mounted and/or connected. The *central processing unit (CPU)* reads instructions and data from main memory, and it writes data to main memory via a **data channel**, or **bus**. Main memory consists of a set of cells, each of which holds a byte of data or instruction. Each cell has an address, and the CPU uses the addresses to identify particular data items.

Main memory is also called **RAM memory**, or just **RAM**. RAM stands for *random access memory*. The term *random* is used to indicate that the computer does not need to access memory cells in sequence; rather, they can be referenced in any order.

To store data or instructions, main memory or RAM must have electrical power. When power is shut off, the contents of main memory are lost. The term **volatile** is used to indicate that data will be lost when the computer is not powered. Thus, main memory is volatile.

Magnetic and optical disks are shown on the left hand side of Figure 3-6. Both of these types of devices maintain their contents without power and serve as storage devices. You can turn the computer off and back on, and the contents of both magnetic and optical disks will be unchanged. Magnetic and optical disks are therefore **nonvolatile**. (*Warning:* This is true only as long as the devices operate correctly. Although the reliability of such devices is very high, they [especially magnetic disks] do fail occasionally. Therefore, you should periodically back up your files. We will discuss backup further in Chapter 4.)

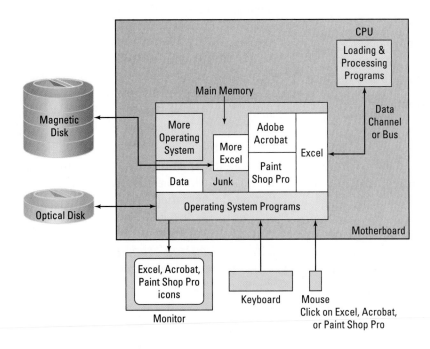

Figure 3-6
Computer with Applications Loaded

Viruses, Trojan Horses, and Worms

A **virus** is a computer program that replicates itself. Unchecked replication is like computer cancer; ultimately, the virus consumes the computer's resources. Furthermore, many viruses also take unwanted and harmful actions.

The program code that causes unwanted activity is called the **payload.** The payload can delete programs or data, or, even worse, modify data in undetected ways. Imagine the impact of a virus that changed the credit rating of all customers. Some viruses publish data in harmful ways; for example, sending out files of credit card data to unauthorized sites.

There are many different virus types. **Trojan horses** are viruses that masquerade as useful programs or files. The name refers to the gigantic mock-up of a horse that was filled with soldiers and moved into Troy during the Peloponnesian Wars. A typical Trojan horse appears to be a computer game, an MP3 music file, or some other useful, innocuous program.

Macro viruses attach themselves Word, Excel, or other type of document. When the infected document is opened, the virus places itself in the startup files of the application. After that, the virus infects every file that the application creates or processes.

A **worm** is a virus that propagates using the Internet or other computer network. Worms spread faster than other virus types because they are specifically programmed to spread. Unlike nonworm

viruses which must wait for the user to share a file with a second computer, worms actively use the network to spread. Sometimes, worms so choke a network that it becomes unusable.

In 2003, the Slammer worm clogged the Internet and caused Bank of America ATM machines and the information systems of hundreds of other organizations to fail. Slammer operated so fast that 90 percent of the vulnerable machines were infected within 10 minutes.

You can take several measures to prevent viruses. First, most viruses take advantage of security holes in computer programs. As vendors find these holes, they create program modifications, called **patches,** that fix the problem. To keep from getting a virus, check Microsoft and other vendors sites for patches and apply them immediately. A patch for the Slammer worm was available from Microsoft several months before Slammer occurred. The worm did not infect any site that had applied the patch.

When you think about it, it is not surprising that the problem occurred some time after the patch appeared. As soon as a vendor publishes the problem and the patch, every computer criminal in the world can learn about the hole. Virus developers can then write code to exploit the hole, and any machine that does not apply the patch is then doubly vulnerable. Therefore, the first rule in preventing viruses is to find and apply patches to the operating system and to applications.

Other prevention steps are:
» Never download files, programs, or attachments from unknown Web sites.

» Do not open attachments to emails from strangers.

» Do not open unexpected attachments to emails, even from known sources.

» Do not rely on file extensions. A file marked MyPicture.jpg is normally a picture (because of the jpg file extension). For a variety of reasons, however, this file may be something else—a virus.

» Companies such as Symantec, Sophos, McAfee, Norton, and others license products that detect and possibly eliminate viruses. They can operate in proactive mode by checking attachments as you receive them. They can also operate retroactively by checking memory and disk drives for the presence of viral code. You should run a retroactive antivirus program at regular intervals, at least once a week.

Such **antivirus programs** search the computer's memory and disk for known viruses. Obviously, if a virus is unknown to the antivirus software, then that virus will remain undetected. Consequently, you should periodically obtain updates for the latest virus patterns from the vendor who produces the antivirus product. Additionally, realize that even though you use antivirus software, you are still vulnerable to viruses that are unknown to the virus detection company.

Now for the ugly news: What do you do if you have a virus? Most antivirus products include programs for removing viruses. If you have a virus, you can follow the instructions provided by that software to remove it. However, it is possible that the virus may have mutated into a different form. If so, then the antivirus product will not see the mutated version, and it will remain on your computer.

Unfortunately, the only sure way to eliminate a virus is to delete everything on your magnetic disk by reformatting it. Then you must reinstall the operating system and all applications from known, clean sources (e.g., the original CD from the vendor). Finally, one by one, you must reload data files that you know are free of the virus. This is a laborious and time-consuming process, and it assumes that you have all of your data files backed up. Because of the time and expense involved, few organizations go through this process. However, reformatting the disk is the only sure way of removing a virus.

Viruses are expensive. C/Net estimated that the Slammer worm caused between $950 million and $1.2 billion in lost productivity during the first 5 days of its existence. To protect your organization, you should ensure that procedures exist to install patches as soon as possible. Also, every computer should have and use a copy of an antivirus program. You and your organization cannot afford not to take these precautions. We will discuss other problematic programs such as spyware in more detail in Chapter 11.

DISCUSSION QUESTIONS

1. Define virus and explain the term payload.

2. What damage do viruses cause?

3. List and briefly describe three kinds of viruses.

4. What is a patch? Why are patches important?

5. Describe actions you can take to prevent a virus.

6. What are the two ways that antivirus software can work? Why is it important to update the antivirus software patterns?

7. What steps must be taken to eradicate a virus from a computer?

The monitor, keyboard, and mouse are shown along the bottom of Figure 3-6. In the diagram, these devices, plus the disks, connect directly to main memory. This is not strictly true, but for our purposes, we will make this assumption. Even though steps are missing, ultimately keystrokes do go into memory for processing, and the image on your monitor is taken from the contents of main memory.

The Contents of Memory

If we could look directly into memory, we would see that it is being used for three purposes: It holds instructions of the operating system; it holds instructions for application programs, such as Excel or Acrobat; and it holds data.

Considering the first, the **operating system (OS)** is a computer program that controls all of the computer's resources: It manages the contents of main memory, it processes keystrokes and mouse movements, it sends signals to the display monitor, it reads and writes disk files, and it controls the processing of other programs. We will discuss specific operating systems, like Windows, later in the chapter.

Figure 3-6 also shows sections of memory that contain instructions for Excel, Paint Shop Pro, and Adobe Acrobat. Finally, a section of memory contains data that are being used by the programs in memory. Notice that operating system instructions occupy two different sections of memory. Excel also is loaded into two different sections. This happens because some parts of programs are not loaded until they are needed.

Figure 3-6 shows one section of memory used to store data. In truth, there will be many such sections, because programs frequently request the operating system to allocate memory to them. For example, Paint Shop Pro will obtain memory space every time you open a new picture file.

Memory Swapping

Now suppose that you are busy with tasks using the three application programs when you decide to open another picture file. When you click *Open* in Paint Shop Pro, that program will ask the operating system to allocate memory for the picture. But, suppose there is insufficient memory—the picture won't fit in the available, unused space in memory. What happens then?

In that case, the operating system will have to remove something to make space. The operating system follows sophisticated logic to determine what to remove. Suppose in our case that the section labeled "More Excel" programs is removed. If that section contains data that have been changed since they were read from disk, then the data will need to be rewritten to the disk. Otherwise, the memory will simply be taken from Excel, and space for the new picture will be allocated in its place, as shown in Figure 3-7.

As you continue to work, the OS will continue this **memory swapping**: It will swap programs and data in and out of memory. If immediately after looking at the picture file that caused Excel to be removed from memory you return to Excel, the operating system may have to bring back the code that it just removed. Such swapping of data and programs in and out of memory can degrade system performance.

If your computer has a very large main memory, if you use only one or a few programs at a time, or if you only use small files, then little swapping will occur. If, however, your computer has a small memory capacity or if you need to use many programs or process many large data files, then you may have a serious swapping (and performance) problem. In this latter case, adding more main memory will substantially improve your computer's performance.

Work at the CPU

The CPU reads instructions and data from memory via the data bus. The maximum speed at which it transfers data is determined by the speed of main memory and the speed and width of the data bus. A bus that is 16 bits wide can carry 16 bits at a time; one that is 64 bits wide can carry 64 bits at a time. The wider the bus, the more data it can carry in a given interval of time. To understand this, think of a metro bus. The

Using the Security Guide

(page 53a)

GOALS

* Introduce basic terminology about computer viruses and related terms.

* Increase students' awareness of the business costs of viruses and worms and other such attacks.

BACKGROUND AND PRESENTATION STRATEGIES

Before proceeding, note that Chapter 11 considers this topic in much greater detail. The reason for introducing it here is to *encourage the students to begin using antivirus software now,* if they do not already do so. If we wait until the last chapter to bring up this topic, we leave the student vulnerable to attack throughout the course, which seems irresponsible.

This discussion does not include *adware* and *spyware,* nor does it use the term *malware.* These terms are addressed in Chapter 11, starting on page 350. The discussion here addresses the most dangerous malware. But, *you might wish to address all types of malware at this time.*

The economist Steven Landsburg performed an economic analysis that concluded, *"On a pure cost-benefit basis, we should be quicker to execute a vermiscripter (virus writer) than a murderer"* (*slate.msn.com/id/2101297*).

❓ SUGGESTED RESPONSES FOR DISCUSSION QUESTIONS

You might point out to the students that these discussion questions are nothing more than a sequence of "What is it?" questions. Consequently, in terms of the Problem Solving Guide, these are not good questions., (They are here to *emphasize the students' need to know* the meaning of all bold terms in the guide.)

1. A *virus* is a computer program that replicates itself. Some viruses take unwanted and harmful actions. The *payload* is the code that takes such actions.

   ➤ **Do all viruses have a payload?**

   (No, some just cause problems by choking systems and networks with junk.)

2. Viruses delete or change programs and data, perform nuisance actions by interfering with the operating system, and steal data.

Amplifying question:

➤ **How much do viruses cost?**

Viruses and related attacks are expensive, and all of the money spent to fix them is loss. It is a drag on every company's bottom line, and, in fact, a drag on the world economy. *It's all waste!*

One way to drive that point home is to *consider local consequences at your university.* Recently, the business school at the University of Washington, where I teach, suffered an attack on its servers. To recover, the system administrators removed the domain that faculty used. One consequence was that when I went to class, I was unable to sign on to the classroom computer, and hence could not connect to the server that stored my lecture materials. It took me 15 minutes to find a solution. Luckily, this occurred in an MBA class that had only 20 students, but still that 15 minutes meant five lost student-labor hours (plus mine). Had it occurred in the intro MIS class, where I sometimes teach 125 students, the loss would have been more than 30 labor hours.

Multiply those 30 labor hours for every class taught last spring, and *our business school lost hundreds of, perhaps more than a thousand, labor hours.* That's not including the cost of the administrators to fix the problem.

When Bank of America's cash machines failed during the Slammer attack, *how many labor hours were lost?* Consider not just the labor hours to fix the problem or the labor hours lost to employees who could not work or who could not handle customers' problems, but also the lost time of customers who had to find another ATM.

Again, viruses and worms are *acts of criminals* that cause a drain on the world's economy. Given all the important problems to be solved throughout the world, such crimes are, to my mind, inexcusable. The victims of such crimes are innocent and unknown to the virus authors. Inexcusable!

3. Three kinds of viruses are Trojan horses (hidden in "safe" code), macro viruses (attachments to Office and other documents), and worms (written to be very infectious).

4. Patches are fixes to problems in software. They are often used to fix security holes, but they may be used to fix other problems, too.

   ➤ **What do you suppose happens when Microsoft or another vendor announces a patch to fix a security problem?**

By announcing the patch, the vendor causes the undesirable side-effect of alerting every virus writer and other computer criminal (for that's what they are) to the security hole. That hole becomes general knowledge. Anyone who does not install the patch leaves him or herself vulnerable to a threat that everyone now knows about.

5. To protect yourself from a virus, install antivirus software. Frequently update the software's virus definitions. Run antivirus software at least once a week.

➤ **How many of you know if you have antivirus software?**

➤ **How many of you have antivirus software?**

➤ **How do you update the virus patterns?**

➤ **How often do you run a virus check?**

6. Antivirus software works proactively or retroactively. Proactively is better! Update definitions frequently, because new viruses are coming out all of the time.

7. The only sure way to eliminate a virus is to wipe the disk clean and reinstall all software from known clean sources. Then install only files that you know to be clean.

➤ **Is this possible?**

(Almost never.)

So, most people use the antivirus software to remove the virus. Most of the time that works. But, you never know for sure. So, at bottom, don't get a virus!!!

WRAP UP

There's an important life lesson buried in this guide:

➤ **What is the best way to solve a virus problem?**

Don't have it. *The very best way to solve a virus problem is not to have it in the first place!* Be vigilant in installing patches and antivirus software to minimize the chances of catching the virus.

In general, what is *the very most efficient and effective way of solving a problem?* Don't have it!

I ask the students some related "life-lesson" questions:

➤ **What is the best way to deal with a DUI (driving under the influence of alcohol) charge? Don't have it.**

➤ **What is the best way of dealing with a mountain of credit card debt and a personal bankruptcy? Don't have it.**

➤ **What is the best way to recover from a failed course? Don't fail it.**

Learning such lessons is all part of growing up, and *choosing* to have a quality life.

(These kinds of extensions are not strictly "part of the MIS course." I highly recommend them, anyway. We are in the business of educating students, and educating them in the broadest possible sense. Additionally, most students appreciate such extensions because they make students feel like people instead of "just students." These extensions wake up the students and keep them listening. At least, that's been my experience.)

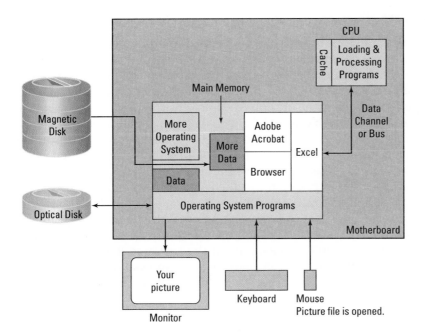

Figure 3-7
Picture File Overlays Memory
Previously Used by Excel

number of passengers delivered depends both on the speed of the bus and the number of seats across the bus.

Because the data transfer rate depends on both the speed and width of the data bus and the speed of main memory, another way to speed up the computer is to obtain faster memory. There are practical limits to this—very fast memory is expensive.

It turns out, however, that some data are accessed more frequently than other data. Because of this, computer engineers found they could speed up the overall throughput of the CPU by creating a small amount of very fast memory, called **cache memory**. The most frequently used data are placed in the cache. Typically, the CPU stores intermediate results and the most frequently used computer instructions in the cache. Cache can be thought of as a local, dedicated memory for the CPU and as "elbow room" for processing.

In some cases, there are two or three levels of cache memory. In 2005, a typical desktop computer could have 8K of very fast and very expensive cache, another 512K of fast and expensive cache, and perhaps 512MB of regular main memory. In accordance with Moore's Law, these sizes will be larger by the time you read this statement, of course.

Each CPU has a **clock speed** that is measured in cycles per second, or hertz. A fast modern computer has a clock speed of 3.0 gigahertz (abbreviated GHz), or 3 billion cycles per second. By the time you read this, CPU speeds will be greater. Clock speed determines the rate computations are accomplished, but in a complex way that is beyond the scope of this text. In general, the faster the clock speed, the faster work will be done.

However, the clock speed of the CPU is not the only important factor in computer performance. As stated, the speed of memory, the number and type of data caches, and the speed and width of the data bus are all factors. In a quality computer, the designers match the components appropriately. Only a bad designer would equip a 3.0 GHz CPU with slow memory.

▮ Factors that Affect Computer Performance

At this point, we are finished with hardware definitions. We will now *apply* what you just learned to discuss the factors that influence computer performance. Knowing these factors will help you ask intelligent questions of your IS department and will help you formulate answers to questions like the $80,000 one.

The CPU and Memory

Figure 3-8 summarizes factors that influence computer performance. Each row in this table concerns a different computer component. The first row shows the characteristics of the CPU and data bus that most influence performance. They are processor speed, amount and type of cache memory, data bus speed, and data bus width. These terms were explained in the previous section.

According to this table, a fast CPU and data bus are most useful when processing data that already reside in main memory. Once you download a large spreadsheet, for example, a fast CPU will rapidly perform complicated, formula-based what-if analyses. A fast CPU also is useful for processing large graphics files. If, for example, you are manipulating the brightness of the elements of a large picture, a fast CPU will enable that manipulation to proceed quickly.

If the applications that you or your employees use do not involve millions of calculations or manipulations on data in main memory, then buying the fastest CPU is probably not worthwhile. In fact, a lot of the excitement about CPU speed is just industry "hype." Speed is an easily marketed and understood idea, but for most business processing, having a very fast CPU is often not as important as other factors, such as main memory.

Figure 3-8
Hardware Components and Computer Performance

Component	Performance Factors	Beneficial for:	Example Application
CPU and data bus	• CPU speed • Cache memory • Data bus speed • Data bus width	• Fast processing of data once the data reside in main memory	• Repetitive calculations of formulas in a complicated spreadsheet • Manipulation of large picture images
Main memory	• Size • Speed	• Holding multiple programs at one time • Processing very large amounts of data	• Running Excel, Word, Paint Shop Pro, Adobe Acrobat, several Web sites, and email while processing large files in memory and viewing video clips • 3D games
Magnetic disk	• Size • Channel type and speed • Rotational speed • Seek time	• Storing many large programs • Storing many large files • Swapping files in and out of memory	• Store detailed maps of counties in the United States • Large data downloads from organizational servers • Fix computer with too little memory
Optical disk—CD	• Up to 700 MB • CD-ROM • CD-R (recordable) • CD-RW (rewritable)	• Reading CDs • Writable media can be used to back up files	• Install new programs • Play and record music • CD being replaced by DVD • Backup data
Optical disk—DVD	• Up to 4.7 GB • DVD-ROM • DVD-R (recordable) • DVD-RW (rewritable)	• Process both DVDs and CDs • Writable media can be used to back up files	• Install new programs • Play and record music • Play and record movies • Backup data
Monitor—CRT	• Viewing size • Dot pitch • Optimal resolution • Special memory?	• Small budgets	• Nongraphic applications, such as word processing • Less used computers
Monitor—LCD	• Viewing size • Pixel pitch • Optimal resolution • Special memory?	• Crowded workspaces • When brighter, sharper images are needed	• More than one monitor in use • Lots of graphics to be processed • Continual use

Main Memory

According to the second row of Figure 3-8, the two key performance factors for main memory are speed and size. Normally, a particular computer make and model is designed to use a given memory type, and the speed for that type is fixed. Once you buy the computer, there is nothing you can do to increase memory *speed*.

You can, however, increase the *amount* of main memory, up to the maximum size of memory that your computer brand and model can hold. In 2005, the maximum amount of memory for new personal computers ranged from 1.5 to 2.0GB.

By the way, if budget is a consideration, you can sometimes buy memory from third parties more economically than from the computer manufacturer. However, you must make sure that you buy the correct memory type. Installing more memory is easy; low-skill technicians can perform that task, or if no vendor support is available, someone in your IS department can do it.

As shown in Figure 3-8, installing more memory is beneficial for situations in which you run many different applications at the same time or if you process many large files (several megabytes or more, each). If your computer is constantly swapping files, installing more memory will dramatically improve performance. In truth, memory is cheap and is often the best way to get more performance out of a computer.

Your operating system has tools and utilities that measure main memory utilization and file swapping. A computer technician can use these tools to determine, quite easily, whether more memory would be helpful. Of course, one could ask why we need so much memory, a question addressed in the *Opposing Forces Guide* on page 57a.

Magnetic Disks

As stated earlier, magnetic and optical disks provide long-term, nonvolatile data storage. The types and sizes of such storage devices will affect computer performance. First, understand that data are recorded on magnetic disks in concentric circles (Figure 3-9). The disks spin inside the disk unit, and as they spin magnetic spots on the disk are read or written by the *read/write head*.

The time required to read data from a disk depends on two measures: The first measure, called the **rotational delay**, is the time it takes the data to rotate under the read/write head. The second, called **seek time**, is the time it takes the read/write arm to position the head over the correct circle. The faster the disk spins, the shorter the rotational delay. Seek time is determined by the make and model of the disk device.

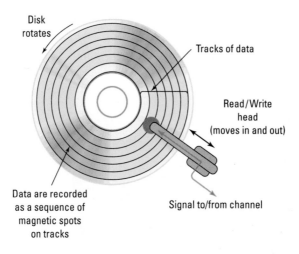

Figure 3-9
Magnetic Disk Components

Churn and Burn

An anonymous source, whom we'll call Mark, made the following statements about computing devices:

"I never upgrade my system. At least, I try not to. Look, I don't do anything at work but write memos and access email. I use Microsoft Word, but I don't use any features that weren't available in Word 3.0, 10 years ago. This whole industry is based on "churn and burn": They churn their products so we'll burn our cash.

"All this hype about 3.0GHz processors and 120GB disks. Who needs them? I'm sure I don't. And if Microsoft hadn't put so much junk into Windows, we could all be happy on an Intel 486 processor like the one I had in 1993. We're suckers for falling into the 'you gotta have this' trap.

"Frankly, I think there's a conspiracy between hardware and software vendors. They both want to sell new products, so the hardware people come up with these incredibly fast and huge computers. Then, given all that power, the software types develop monster products bloated with features and functions that nobody uses. It would take me months to learn all the features in Word, only to find out that I don't need those features.

"To see what I mean, open Microsoft Word, click on View, then select Toolbars. In my version of Word, there are 19 toolbars to select, plus one more to customize my own

toolbar. Now, what in the world do I need with 19 tool-bars? I write all the time, and I have two selected: Standard and Formatting. Two out of 19! Could I pay Microsoft 2/19 of the price of Word, because that's all I want or use?

"Here's how they get you, though. Because we live in a connected world, they don't have to get all of us to use those 19 toolbars, just one of us. Take Bridgette, over in legal, for example. Bridgette likes to use the redlining features, and she likes me to use them when I change draft contracts she sends me. So, if I want to work on her documents, I have to turn on the Reviewing toolbar. You get the idea; just get someone to use a feature and, because it is a connected world, then all of us have to have that feature.

"Viruses are one of their best ploys. They say you better buy the latest and greatest in software, and then apply all the patches that follow so that you'll be protected from the latest zinger from the computer 'bad guys.' Think about that for a minute. If vendors had built the products correctly the first time, then there would be no holes for the baddies to find, would there? So, they have a defect in their products that they turn to a sales advantage. You see, they get us to focus on the virus and not on the hole in their product. In truth, they should be saying, 'Buy our latest product to protect yourself from the defective junk we sold you last year.' But truth in advertising hasn't come that far.

"Besides that, users are their own worst enemies as far as viruses are concerned. If I'm down on 17th Street at 4 in the morning, half drunk and with a bundle of cash hanging out of my pocket, what's likely to happen to me? I'm gonna get mugged. So, if I'm out in some weirdo chat room—you know, out where you get pictures of weird sex acts and whatnot—and I download and run a file, then of course I'm gonna get a virus. Viruses are brought on by user stupidity, that's all.

"One of these days, users are going to rise up and say, 'That's enough. I don't need any more. I'll stay with what I have, thank you very much.' In fact, maybe that's happening right now. Maybe that's why software sales aren't growing like they were. Maybe people have finally said, 'No more toolbars!'"

DISCUSSION QUESTIONS

1. Summarize Mark's view of the computer industry. Is there merit to his argument? Why or why not?

2. What holes do you see in the logic of his argument?

3. Someone could take the position that these statements are just empty rantings—that Mark can say all he wants, but the computer industry is going to keep on doing as it has been. Is there any point in Mark sharing his criticisms?

4. Suppose you are conducting a staff meeting to assess the $80,000 hardware budget question at the start of this chapter, and one of the employees in your department makes statements similar to Mark's. How would you respond?

5. Sometimes people say that there's nothing in TV network news because the content is lowered to the "lowest common denominator," meaning the lowest IQ of all people watching TV. According to Mark's statements, though, software is just the opposite. In a connected world, if one person uses a feature, then everyone must have it. So, software is raised to the "highest common denominator." Do you believe that? What would that imply about the marketing of all software products?

6. Read the *Security Guide* (page 53a) if you have not done so already. Comment on Mark's statement, "Viruses are brought on by user stupidity, that's all."

7. Do you see any evidence of users rising up and saying, "That's enough"? Put on your marketing hat: If there were evidence of such a movement, what should the computer industry do?

Once the read/write head is positioned over the correct spot on the disk, data can flow over the channel to or from main memory. Like the data bus, the rate of data transfer depends on the width and speed of the channel. There are a number of different standards for channel characteristics. As of 2005, a common standard is the **ATA-100** (Advanced Technology Attachment) standard. The number 100 indicates that the maximum transfer rate is 100MB per second.

When you buy a computer, you generally have just a few disk type choices. You may be able to choose one or two different channel standards (e.g., ATA-66 or ATA-100), and you may be able to choose disks with different rotational speeds.

You will always, however, be offered a number of choices in disk size. For most business users, 30GB is more than enough disk space. Large disks are cheap to manufacture, however, and you will be offered disks much larger than this (200GB or more). If you need to store a detailed map of every county in the United States or if you need to store huge downloads from your organization's server computers, then you may need such a large disk. Otherwise, don't fall prey to the hype; buy your employees better monitors or something else, instead.

As stated in Figure 3-8, you can use a fast disk to compensate, to some extent, for too little memory. Recall that if you have too little memory, your computer will be swapping files in and out; a fast disk will speed this process. You might attempt to compensate with a fast disk if you have installed the maximum memory your computer can take and you still have a swapping problem. In that case, however, you would probably also benefit from a faster processor, and you might just as well buy a new computer.

Optical Disks

There are two kinds of optical disks: CDs (compact disks) and DVDs (digital versatile disks). Both are made of plastic and are coated with a photosensitive material. As stated earlier, bits are recorded by burning a pit into the photosensitive material using a low-power laser. The presence of a pit causes light to reflect and signifies a one; the absence of reflection signifies a zero. Like magnetic disks, optical disks are non-volatile; they maintain their contents even when not powered.

The major difference between CDs and DVDs is how they store data; that difference is unimportant to this discussion, however. The *practical* differences between CDs and DVDs are capacity and speed. A typical CD has a maximum capacity of 700MB, whereas a DVD disk can store up to 4.7GB. Additionally, DVD transfer rates are about 10 times faster than those for CDs.

As shown in Figure 3-8, some optical disks are *read only*; they cannot record data. These disks are abbreviated as **CD-ROM** and **DVD-ROM**. (*ROM* stands for *read-only memory*.) Other optical disks, denoted **CD-R** and **DVD-R**, can record data once. (The *R* stands for *recordable*.) A third group, denoted **CD-RW** and **DVD-RW**, can write data hundreds of times. (The *RW* stands for *rewritable*.)

CDs and DVDs see their greatest use in the entertainment industry for playing music and videos. CDs are used widely in commerce for distributing programs and other large files. Operating systems and programs, such as Windows and Microsoft Office, are distributed and installed from CD, for example. Also, writable media can be used to back up magnetic disk files.

Today, every computer should have at least a CD-ROM for installing programs. Most computers should also have some version of a writable optical disk for backing up data. Beyond those purposes, the major reason for having a CD or DVD is entertainment, and that reason may not be the best use of your organization's resources.

Video Displays

There are two types of video display monitors: CRTs and LCDs. **CRT monitors** use *cathode ray tubes*, the same devices used in traditional TV screens. Because they use a large tube, CRTs are big and bulky, about as deep as they are wide. **LCD monitors** use

Using the Opposing Forces Guide (page 57a)

GOALS

* Think critically about software products.

* Assess the responsibilities of users and software vendors.

* Be a better consumer of software products by learning when to hold software vendors accountable.

* Consider ways of managing an employee like Mark.

BACKGROUND AND PRESENTATION STRATEGIES

You can use this guide not only to engage the students via the opinions of the contrarian, but also to extend the discussion beyond basic definitions to consider software as a product, the nature of the software industry, and the financial needs of software vendors. Questions 5 and 7 work well for this purpose.

Products like Microsoft Office are developed from market feedback. Microsoft and others convene hundreds of focus groups that tell them what features to add. They invite groups of typical users, show them various possibilities, and ask for opinions. They also ask typical users what else they want. The favorite feature of every one of these focus groups gets put "into the pot," for possible inclusion in the product. This is feature design by committee—and it leads to bloated products with little conceptual integrity.

Taking items out of the pot is the job of product managers. But it's difficult for product managers to say, "No, that's just too much, we won't add that feature." The design strategy has been to hide the extra complexity behind not-visible toolbars. As long as the semiconductor industry keeps churning out faster computers with bigger memories, this strategy will probably continue to work.

Software vendors should be *held accountable for security holes* in their products. They allowed the problem to be there in the first place, and they should bear some consequences. In some ways, computer users are too polite; they should object more to security holes than they do.

To avoid continuing PR problems, vendors like Microsoft and Adobe are making it easier and easier to obtain and install updates to their products. This easy installation *hides the fact that they are fixing glitches* in their products. Microsoft is now making such installations automatic, as AOL has done for years.

I particularly recommend question 4, which asks the students what they would do if they had to manage someone like Mark. See the comments interspersed in the answer to that question.

 SUGGESTED RESPONSES FOR DISCUSSION QUESTIONS

These questions are all open-ended and subject to judgment and interpretation. Thus, this section provides questions to ask the students to stimulate the conversation.

1. One way to answer this question is to ask:

   ➤ **What can we learn from Mark's contrarian position? Describe some of the points he makes.**

   Write the list on the board and then ask the class to rank the items in order of importance. At each point, ask the class if they agree with point, and how important it is. You might also ask them what the software vendors could do differently to eliminate the problem.

   ➤ **Do you agree with Mark's point about software patches and security holes?**

Vendors want to manage this patch process so as to make it as invisible as possible and avoid close scrutiny and the attendant bad PR. In truth, the vendors did leave the holes in the product in the first place, and they did leave their customers vulnerable to attack. They should be accountable in some way. However, read the license agreements—according to the agreements, the vendors are liable for the cost of the CD, at most $1.50. They may not be liable even for that much, if the product was shipped electronically.

   Another line of questions relates to the analogy of being mugged in a bad neighborhood. You might ask:

   ➤ **Are viruses brought on by user stupidity?**

   ➤ **Is the analogy of being mugged in a bad neighborhood a good one?**

   ➤ **How can a student find out which cyber-neighborhoods are bad?**

2. You may have answered this question if you asked the students to prioritize the list in question 1. If not, here are some questions to ask to stimulate the discussion:

   ➤ **Are software products bloated?**

➤ Isn't it an advantage to have features that you don't need now, but might need in the future?

➤ Would Mark really be happy with his old computer? It might take him hours just to read his email.

➤ What is the relationship between hardware and software vendors? How do they depend on one another? What will happen to software if Moore's Law stops?

3. This is a fun question that we ask for many of the contrarians.

➤ Is there any point in Mark sharing his opinions?

➤ Does it do any good for him to say what he says?

➤ Is there a way that Mark could change his questions and behavior to accomplish more good?

These questions lead to the next one.

4. Time is of the essence. Mark is using up valuable staff time to answer the $80,000 question. What should the manager do?

Ask the class to make two lists based on the following two questions:

➤ How is Mark helping himself to answer the $80,000 question?

➤ How is Mark hindering his ability to answer to the question?

Now, given those lists, what actions can the class, as future managers, take to obtain the benefits of the first list and avoid the problems of the second?

➤ Has anyone ever managed someone like Mark? At work? In a student club? On a committee? On a student project? What did you do?

➤ What are the consequences of getting frustrated and just telling Mark to shut up?

➤ There are no easy answers here. Just start thinking about it because someday you may have to manage someone like Mark.

5. One way to answer this question is to consider the process software vendors use to create products. Explain the use of focus groups. Some useful follow-up questions are:

➤ If you were the product manager for Word, would you behave any differently in responding to focus groups?

➤ How would you go about deciding what features to put in and which to take out?

➤ How does the idea of "highest common denominator" help you as a product manager for products like Word?

➤ Suppose you are in charge of cash management at Microsoft or Adobe. What happens if you don't bring out a new version of the company's products every year or every other year? How might these factors influence you as a product manager at Microsoft?

6. Some viruses are brought on by user stupidity, but not all.

➤ What are instances of viruses that are not caused by user stupidity?

7. If there were a "That's enough!" movement, marketing personnel at major software companies would rise up and meet the need. Or, is that answer too naïve? Consider the following series of questions:

➤ Because no such alternative products are available, does that mean that this need does not exist? Or does it mean that product managers aren't doing their jobs?

➤ Microsoft Office has almost no competition. Does Microsoft have any incentive to develop other, simpler products?

➤ Is Microsoft just a "fat cat" sitting on its monopoly? If it had competition, would there be a better choice of products?

➤ Does the complexity of Office frustrate you? Would you buy a simpler product if you found one?

WRAP UP

Most students will agree that people like Mark do exist. I tell the class:

➤ Contrarians are like hot-pepper flakes: They make a great contribution to the stew, but too much ruins the dinner. The question is how to manage someone like Mark without letting him ruin the group.

Chances are there's a Mark in the class. It's very interesting to see how such students respond to these Opposing Forces Guides. Often, their responses are insightful.

a different technology called *liquid crystal display*. With LCD monitors, no tube is required, so they are much slimmer, around 2 inches or so deep.

Both types of monitors display images by illuminating small spots on the screen called **pixels**. Pixels are arranged in a rectangular grid. An inexpensive monitor might display an image 800 pixels wide and 600 pixels high. A higher quality monitor would display a grid of 1,024 × 768 pixels, and some display as many as 1,600 × 1,200 pixels.

The number of pixels displayed depends not only on the size of the monitor, but also on the design of the mechanism that creates the image. For a CRT monitor, the **dot pitch** of the monitor is the distance between pixels. The smaller the dot pitch, the sharper and brighter the screen image will be. For an LCD monitor, the **pixel pitch** is the distance between pixels on the screen. As with CRT monitors, the smaller the pixel pitch, the sharper and brighter the image will be.

Each monitor has an **optimal resolution**, which is the size of the pixel grid (e.g., 1,024 × 768) that will give the best sharpness and clarity. This optimal resolution depends on the size of the screen, the dot or pixel pitch, and other factors. More expensive monitors have higher optimal resolution than others.

Each pixel on the monitor is represented in main memory. If the resolution of the monitor is 1,024 × 768, then there will be a table in memory with 1,024 rows and 768 columns. Each cell of this table has a numeric value that represents the color of the pixel that it represents. Programs change the display on the monitor by instructing the operating system to change values in this image table.

The amount of memory used for each cell in the pixel grid depends on the number of colors that each pixel is to display. For a black and white image, the cells can consist of a single bit: zero for white and one for black. To represent 16 colors, each pixel is represented by four bits. (Four bits can hold the numbers from 0 to 15—each number signifies a particular color.) Today, most monitors use a large color palette that necessitates 32 bits for each pixel and allows for 8,589,934,591 colors.

Substantial main memory is needed for this large palette. To represent an image in 1,024 × 768 resolution, a total of 3,145,728 bytes of memory (1,024 × 768 × 4 bytes) is needed. For reasons beyond the scope of this text, sometimes several versions of this pixel table are in memory.

Because these tables occupy a large amount of memory, some computers dedicate a separate memory cache just to the video display. The design of such memory is optimized for video use as well. Such special-purpose video memory is particularly important for multimedia applications where large images change rapidly. It is also important for 3D video in computer games.

For monitors of equivalent quality, the initial cost of CRT monitors is less than that for LCD monitors. LCD monitors have a longer life, however, so they may actually cost less over time. In truth, though, because of the speed at which technology improvements take place, most people upgrade to a better computer before they ever wear out their monitor, so this extra life may not matter.

The big advantage of LCD monitors is, of course, their smaller footprint, which means they take up less desk space. They are especially desirable when work requires viewing more than one monitor at a time. Stock traders on Wall Street, for example, need three or four monitors, and these monitors are always LCDs.

MIS in Use 3-2 (page 60) describes a visual display created by MCSi Corporation for use by U.S. Army Tactical Operations Centers (TOC). You should be able to interpret this description using the definitions and concepts in this chapter.

A Survey of Software

Computing devices consist of both hardware and software programs. As discussed in conjunction with Figure 3-6, there are two major types of software: operating systems and application programs. In this section, we will survey common operating systems

Visual Display for the U.S. Army

"MCSi [MCSi Corporation] was charged with developing a new mobile command post that would perform flawlessly under extreme conditions with optimum image quality," says Betsy Mayer, senior account executive for MCSi and civilian manager for the project. "This new TOC [U.S. Army Tactical Operations Centers] had to meet portability requirements of the infantry command and integrate numerous live battlefield images into a centralized observation and command center."

"Previous command centers tracked the battlefield theater in an outdated manner. Personnel used 6-foot by 6-foot maps and stuck

pins with labels in them. They also used old computer systems to track data, which had to be printed and placed on the map because the information could not be fed into any type of display device. Our mission was to evolve this primitive system to a far more efficient and effective battlefield communication center."

"To maximize situation awareness for the command personnel, we needed a display system that could show multiple images from a variety of inputs on one screen. Additionally, the equipment had to withstand the harsh conditions out in the desert. This was a custom design, which came down to quality and reliability. MCSi's [prior] experience with RGB Spectrum's QuadView display processor made the choice simple. The QuadView offers field-proven dependability, supports the myriad of battlefield input signals required, and displays four images simultaneously in real time on a single display with excellent quality."

The QuadView processors receive computer and video inputs. Computer inputs come from a group of 12 PCs with images consisting of maps, force tracking, and resources databases, satellite down-linked broadcasts and surveillance, intelligence reports, weapons control, enemy target acquisition, Internet pages, and PowerPoint briefings, RGB Spectrum officials say. Video sources include DVD players, VCRs, and surveillance video cameras. User-selectable output settings go as high as a 1,600-by-1,200 resolution. With some formats, a pure digital signal path runs from source to display for optimal image quality, company officials say. The QuadView XLRT automatically determines the output display's characteristics and optimizes its output signal for that device.

Source: John McHale, "Army Tactical Operations Centers in Iraq Use RGB Spectrum's Display Technology," *Military and Aerospace Electronics* (September 2004). Used with permission of Military and Space Electronics.

and describe sources and categories of application programs. We will address software again when we describe the process of program development in Chapter 6.

Operating Systems

The four major operating systems listed in Figure 3-10 are very important. We describe them in the following sections.

Windows

For business users, the most important operating system is Microsoft Windows. Some version of Windows resides on more than 85 percent of the world's desktops, and considering just business users, the figure is more than 95 percent. There are many different versions of Windows; some versions run on user computers and some support

Name	Principal Use	Principal Proponent	Instruction Set
Windows	Business users Servers	Microsoft	Intel
Macintosh	Graphic artists Arts community	Apple	Power PC (as of 2006, also Intel)
Unix	Scientists Engineers	Sun Microsystems and others	Many
Linux	Servers Scientists Engineers	IBM	Many

Figure 3-10
Contemporary Operating Systems

server computers for Web sites, email, and other processes (discussed in Chapter 5). Windows runs the Intel instruction set.[2]

Mac OS

Apple Computer, Inc. developed its own operating system for the Macintosh, **Mac OS**. The current version is Mac OS X. Macintosh computers are used primarily by graphic artists and workers in the arts community. Mac OS was designed originally to run the line of CPU processors from Motorola. In 1994, it switched to the PowerPC processor line from IBM. As of 2006, Macintosh computers will be available for both PowerPC and Intel CPUs. A Macintosh with an Intel processor is able to run both Windows and the MAC OS.

Most people would agree that Apple has led the way in developing easy-to-use interfaces. Certainly, many innovative ideas have first appeared in a Macintosh and then later been added, in one form or another, to Windows.

Unix

Unix is an operating system that was developed at Bell Labs in the 1970s. It has been the workhorse of the scientific and engineering communities since then. Unix is generally regarded as being more difficult to use than either Windows or the Macintosh. Many Unix users know and employ an arcane language for manipulating files and data. However, once they surmount the rather steep learning curve, most Unix users swear by it. Sun Microsystems and other vendors of computers for scientific and engineering applications are the major proponents of Unix. In general, Unix is not for the business user.

Linux

Linux is a version of Unix that was developed by the **open-source community**. The community is a loosely coupled group of programmers who mostly volunteer their time to contribute code to develop and maintain Linux. The open source community owns Linux, and there is no fee to use it. Linux is a popular operating system for Web servers.

IBM is the primary proponent of Linux. Although IBM does not own Linux, IBM has developed many business systems solutions that use Linux. By using Linux, IBM does not have to pay a license fee to Microsoft or another vendor.

Own Versus License

When you buy a Windows or Macintosh or some other program, you are not actually buying that program. Instead, you are buying a *license* to use that program. For example, when you buy Windows, Microsoft is selling you the right to use Windows. Microsoft continues to own the Windows program.

Some vendors are considering using hardware to enforce licenses, a possibility that has frightening implications as discussed in the *Ethics Guide* on page 61a.

---

[2]There are versions of Windows for other instruction sets, but they are unimportant for our purposes here.

Using Hardware to Enforce Licenses

Every commercial software program, whether an operating system or an application, is sold under the restrictions of a **license agreement**, which stipulates how the program can be used. Normally, the license agreement specifies the number of computers on which the program can be installed and, sometimes, the number of users that can connect to and use the program remotely. Such agreements also stipulate limitations on the liability of the software vendor for the consequences of errors in the software.

Software piracy occurs when programs are used in violation of the license agreement. Piracy occurs on a large scale when a company illegally copies a program and sells it on the black market. But piracy also occurs on a small scale when one user allows another user to load the program on her computer in violation of the license agreement.

Over the years, vendors have applied many different techniques to prevent software piracy. The most effective strategies involve a combination of hardware and program identity. Today, Microsoft, Intel, and other companies have been working together on a project called **TCG/NGSCB** to control the copying of files and programs. TCG stands for Trusted Computing Group and refers to an organization of computer and software vendors created to develop standards for the

project. NGSCB stands for Next Generation Secure Computing Base; it consists of a new architecture and code in Microsoft Windows for implementing the TCG standards. No products yet implement this work, but product designs are underway.

According to the TCG standard, future computers will include a hardware component that emits passwords and other security data that uniquely identify that particular computer. Because these identifiers are created by the hardware, they cannot be hacked without ruining the hardware. The new Windows NGSCB components use the emitted identifying data to control the programs and files that can be run. The bottom line is that software companies will be able to license programs to a particular computer.

Once the TCG/NGSCB has been implemented, it can be used to enforce not only program licenses, but content licenses as well. Entertainment companies and other content vendors will be able to license music, video, and similar content to a particular computer. With the TCG/NGSCB components in place, no other computer will be able to play copies of that music, video, or file.

The consequences go still further. Microsoft and other software vendors will license software to a particular computer, possibly for a particular time period. The license will automatically expire at the end of that period. Any attempt to run unlicensed software will fail and could result in the sending of a report to the vendor that such an attempt was made.

Files, too, can be made usable only by licensed software on specific computers. Software vendors can make files unusable after licenses expire. Governments can ensure that sensitive government documents are readable only on certain machines. Whistleblowers would be unable to produce documents for external reviewing authorities.

The industry groups justify this program as providing a "secure computing environment" and attempt to spin this initiative as something that will benefit the consumer. TCG (*www.trustedcomputinggroup.org*) says that the new initiative will provide more secure local storage and lower risk of identity theft. Other stated benefits are that organizations can deploy more secure information systems and products.

Hundreds of independent observers disagree with these stated objectives and believe the real object is to prevent unauthorized copying of software and files. They believe this program invades privacy and potentially can be used for totalitarian control. In fact, TCG/NGSCB is the second name for this program. The original name TCGP/Palladium was dropped. Some say they changed the names to avoid the baggage of Palladium's bad reputation.

DISCUSSION QUESTIONS

1. You buy a new computer that has a copy of Microsoft Office already installed. The vendor includes a CD that has a backup copy of the Office programs. You plan never to use the backup copy, so you give it to your friend. Do you think you have cheated Microsoft? Why or why not?

2. At present, vendors have every right to implement the TCG/NGSCB initiative. Do you think laws should be passed to make this program and similar programs illegal? Do you think government agencies will be helped by the TCB/NGSCB program? Will government agencies have a conflict of interest when addressing this issue?

3. If documents can be made unreadable except on the computer that created them and on other computers authorized by the creator, organized crime, terrorist groups, and rogue states will be able to protect their documents. The FBI, CIA, and other government agencies will then ask for a "trap door" that they can use to circumvent these measures. Should such a trap door be developed?

4. Every security program has both costs and benefits. The costs include not only the costs of developing and implementing the security program, but also societal costs, such as inconvenience, loss of privacy, and increased government control. If TCB/NGSCB is implemented, do you think the benefits will justify the costs? In your answer, construct a list of benefits and another list of costs.

In the case of Linux, no company can sell you a license to use it. It is owned by the open source community, which states that Linux has no license fee (with certain reasonable restrictions). Companies like IBM and smaller companies like RedHat can make money by supporting Linux, but no company makes money selling Linux licenses.

Application Software

Application software consists of programs that perform a business function. Some application programs are general purpose, such as Excel or Word. Other application programs are specific. QuickBooks, for example, is an application program that provides general ledger and other accounting functions. We begin by describing sources for application programs and then move on to categories of application programs.

Sources

You can acquire application software in exactly the same ways that you can buy a new suit. The quickest and least risky option is to buy your suit off-the-rack. With this method, you get your suit immediately, and you know exactly what it will cost. You may not, however, get a good fit. Alternately, you can buy your suit off-the-rack and have it altered. This will take more time, it may cost more, and there's some possibility that the alteration will result in a poor fit. Most likely, however, an altered suit will fit better than an off-the-rack one.

Finally, you can hire a tailor to make a custom suit. In this case, you'll have to describe what you want, be available for multiple fittings, and be willing to pay considerably more. Although there is an excellent chance of a great fit, there is also the possibility of a disaster. Still, if you want a yellow and orange polka dot silk suit with a hissing rattlesnake on the back, tailor-made is the only way to go.

You can buy computer software in exactly the same ways: **off-the-shelf**, off-the-shelf with alterations, or tailor-made. Tailor-made software is called **custom software**. As with suits, you can hire someone else to perform the alterations or construct the custom programs or your company can do it "in house."

In the following sections, we consider types of software that typically are obtained in these three ways.

Horizontal-Market Application Software

Horizontal-market application software provides capabilities common across all organizations and industries. Word processors, graphics programs, spreadsheets, and presentation programs are all horizontal-market application software.

Examples of such software are Microsoft Word, Excel, and PowerPoint. Examples from other vendors are Adobe Acrobat, Photoshop, and PageMaker and Jasc Corporation's Paint Shop Pro. These applications are used in a wide variety of businesses, across all industries. They are purchased off-the-shelf, and little customization of features is necessary (or possible).

Vertical-Market Application Software

Vertical-market application software serves the needs of a specific industry. Examples of such programs are those used by dental offices to schedule appointments and bill patients, those used by auto mechanics to keep track of customer data and customers' automobile repairs, and those used by parts warehouses to track inventory, purchases, and sales.

Vertical applications usually can be altered or customized. Typically, the company that sold the application software will provide such services or offer referrals to qualified consultants who can provide this service.

You Be the Guide

Using the Ethics Guide

(page 61a)

GOALS

* Teach students the difference between owning and licensing software.

* Sensitize students to the criminal nature of illegal copying.

* Create awareness of threats to privacy by exploring the trade-off between security and social cost.

BACKGROUND AND PRESENTATION STRATEGIES

The TCG/NGSCB movement is changing rapidly. Be sure to Google the topic prior to discussing this guide so that you have the latest information. Or, have the students Google it prior to class.

Before I get into the ethics of this case, I explain that when we buy a copy of Microsoft Office, we are in fact buying a license to *use* Office under certain terms and conditions. In fact, the correct wording is to say, "We *buy a license to use Word.*" Microsoft never "sells Word." It *sells a license to use Word.*

The license we buy has restrictions on how we can use the product. Those restrictions are legally binding; if we use the product, we agree to follow the restrictions. If we do not follow them, Microsoft will prevail if they choose to sue us. Violating license agreements is not only unethical, it is illegal.

Having said that, and understanding that all software vendors have a right to revenue for the products they produce, I also have to say that the *TCB/NGSCB movement frightens me.* I see too much potential for abusive privacy intrusions and organizational control of individuals' behavior. Usually the students have opinions on this matter:

➤ **What would you think if suddenly your copy of Microsoft Word stopped working because your license had expired? (This assumes that Microsoft begins to sell time limited licenses.)**

➤ **Would Microsoft have a right to do this?**

➤ **When you use Google mail, it examines the content of your emails and displays advertising related to that content. It would be a simple extension of that capability using TCB/NGSCB for the email program to examine what you are writing and cease working if you're writing on some Google-forbidden topic. That**

system would enable organizations or governments to control what you can email. Do you see this as a threat?

The appropriateness of the TCB/NGSCB movement *depends on one's perspective.* If I view it as someone who is concerned about personal privacy and overreaching governmental control, I find the TCB/NGSCB to be frightening. If I view it from the standpoint of a software vendor, maybe an upcoming startup that needs its fair revenue to survive, I view it as a help— or maybe as a *necessary evil that needs strong control against abuse.*

SUGGESTED RESPONSES FOR DISCUSSION QUESTIONS

1. In this case, you have cheated Microsoft and your action is illegal. Were Microsoft to sue you, they would prevail. Microsoft may be large, rich, bloated, overbearing, politically incorrect, or anything else, but they are entitled to their license fees according to the legal contracts that they ship with their products. Your actions are illegal.

2. The answer to this question depends on one's perspective. One way to drive home the idea of different perspectives is to make lists of *benefits* and *costs* to different constituencies. Divide the class into five groups and ask each group to list the benefits and costs for one of the following:

   ➤ **Software vendors**

   ➤ **Hardware vendors**

   ➤ **Individuals who use software/content**

   ➤ **Corporations that use software**

   ➤ **The federal government**

   Now, ask the class to argue for their group. Use this exercise to drive home the notion that *multiple correct answers do exist.*

   In my experience, if I don't get some resistance to this concept from someone, then the students are not paying attention. Some students will HATE the notion of multiple correct answers. If you don't get the resistance, raise it yourself:

   ➤ **Wait a minute, how can there be multiple correct answers?**

   Once you get that theme going, ask:

   ➤ **What do we do in a world of multiple correct answers? How do we make decisions?**

These queries will raise anxiety and many questions, like this one, asked with a snarl, "So Dr. Kroenke, if that's true, how can you grade our exams? Aren't all answers equally good?"

See also the annotations for the Problem Solving Guide as well as the Perry references in Problem Solving, Chapter 1 (page 9a).

The answer depends on how one perceives the role of government and the rights of law enforcement personnel. Democrats, Republicans, Libertarians, and people of other political persuasions will answer this question differently, much as they differ in their views of the Homeland Security Act.

If you addressed the problems of multiple correct answers in question 2, you can build on that discussion with the following query:

➤ **We just discussed how there can be multiple correct answers. But in this case, either there is a trap door or there isn't. What do you do with multiple correct answers in this case?**

One response is that in a democracy you can vote. Or, in our representative democracy, you can elect people who will vote on your behalf. There are still multiple correct answers, but we take the one the majority prefers.

Or, in recognition of the different, correct answers, we can restrict the trap door so as to give only limited capability to a limited number of people. But, that's a slippery slope: If it exists, chances are it will be abused. Perhaps that's an acceptable social cost, or perhaps not.

3. Here are some ideas to prime the pump:

Benefits	Social Costs
Dramatically reduced piracy (software, entertainment, data).	Computers and software will be harder to set up and hence more difficult to use.
Stronger software and entertainment industries because of greater protection of their revenue stream.	Without trap door, criminals, terrorists, and others will have greater security to protect their illegal activities.
Reduced costs to legitimate users, because illegal users will have to pay (unless vendors keep all that revenue to themselves, in which case costs will not be lower, but profits will be higher).	With trap door abuse, legitimate users can be spied upon. Privacy will be reduced.
Better security for confidential and proprietary data and documents of organizations.	Potential for abuse by governmental agencies.
	Greater control to totalitarian states.

The students may suggest other costs and benefits as well.

➤ **Given these lists, should TCB/NGSCB be implemented?**

How to decide? By vote? By professor fiat?

WRAP UP

➤ **In brief, what is TCB/NGSCB?**

➤ **What impacts will TCB/NGSCB have on the software industry?**

➤ **What impacts will TCB/NGSCB have on the entertainment industry?**

➤ **What posture should a concerned citizen take with regard to TCB/NGSCB?**

Some application software does not neatly fit into the horizontal or vertical category. For example, CRM software is a horizontal application because every business has customers. But, it usually needs to be customized to the requirements of businesses in a particular industry, and so it is also akin to vertical market software.

You will learn about other examples of such dual-category software in Chapter 7 when we discuss materials requirements planning (MRP), enterprise resource planning (ERP), and other such applications. In this text, we will consider such applications to be vertical market applications, even though they do not fit perfectly into this category.

Custom-Developed Software

Sometimes organizations develop custom application software. They develop such programs themselves or hire a development vendor. Like buying the yellow and orange polka dot suit, such development is done in situations in which the needs of the organization are so unique that no horizontal or vertical applications are available. By developing custom software, the organization can tailor its application to fit its requirements.

Custom development is difficult and risky. Staffing and managing teams of software developers is challenging. Managing software projects can be daunting. Many organizations have embarked on application development projects only to find that the projects take twice as long, or longer, to finish as planned. Cost overruns of 200 and 300 percent are not uncommon.

In addition, every application program needs to be adapted to changing needs and changing technologies. The adaptation costs of horizontal and vertical software are amortized over all of the users of that software, perhaps thousands or millions of customers. For custom software developed in-house, however, the developing company must pay all of the adaptation costs itself. Over time, this can be a heavy burden.

Because of the risk and expense, in-house development is the last-choice alternative and is used only when there is no other option. Figure 3-11 summarizes software sources and types.

Over the course of your career, application software, firmware, and hardware will change, sometimes rapidly. The *Reflections Guide* on page 63a challenges you to *choose* a strategy for keeping up (or not).

Firmware

Firmware is computer software that is installed into devices like printers, print servers, and various types of communication devices. The software is coded just like other software, but it is installed into special, read-only memory of the printer or other device. In this way, the program becomes part of the device's memory; it is as if the program's logic is designed into the device's circuitry. Users do not need to load firmware into the device's memory.

Software Type	Software Source		
	Off-the-shelf	Off-the-shelf and then customized	Tailor-made
Horizontal applications	▓		
Vertical applications	▓	▓	
Custom applications			▓

Figure 3-11
Software Sources and Types

Keeping Up to Speed

Have you ever been to a cafeteria where you put your lunch tray on a conveyor belt that carries the dirty dishes into the kitchen? That conveyor belt reminds me of technology. Like the conveyor, technology just moves along, and all of us run on top of the technology conveyor, trying to keep up. We hope to keep up with the relentless change of technology for an entire career without ending up in the techno-trash.

Technology change is a fact, and the only appropriate question is, "What am I going to do about it?" One strategy you can take is to bury your head in the sand: "Look, I'm not a technology person. I'll leave it to the pros. As long as I can send email and use the Internet, I'm happy. If I have a problem, I'll call someone to fix it."

That strategy is fine, as far as it goes, and many business people use it. Following that strategy won't give you a competitive advantage over anyone, and it will give someone else a competitive advantage over you, but as long as you develop your advantage elsewhere, you'll be OK—at least for yourself.

What about your department, though? What about the $80,000 question at the start of this chapter? Are you going to relegate knowledge about how to answer that question to someone else? If the expert says, "Every computer needs a 120GB disk," are you going to nod your head and say, "Great. Sell 'em to me!" Or, are you going to know enough to realize that's a big disk (by 2006 standards, anyway) and ask why

everyone needs such a large amount of storage? Maybe then you'll be told, "Well, it's only another $150 per machine from the 30GB disk." At that point you can make a decision, using your own decision-making skills, and not rely solely on the IS "expert." The prudent business professional in the twenty-first century has a number of reasons not to bury his head in the technology sand.

At the other end of the spectrum are those who love technology. You'll find them everywhere—they may be accountants, marketing professionals, or production-line supervisors who not only know their field, but also enjoy information technology. Maybe they were IS majors or had double majors that combined IS with another area of expertise (e.g., IS with accounting). These people read CNET News and ZDNet most days, and they can tell you the latest on IPv6 addresses (Chapter 5—just wait!). Those people are sprinting along the technology conveyor belt; they will never end up in the techno-trash, and they will use their knowledge of IT to gain competitive advantage throughout their careers.

Many business professionals are in between these extremes. They don't want to bury their heads, but they don't have the desire or interest to become "technophiles" (lovers of technology), either. What to do? There are a couple of strategies. For one, don't allow yourself to ignore technology. When you see a technology article in the *Wall Street Journal*, read it. Don't just skip it because it's about technology. Read the technology ads, too. Many vendors invest heavily in ads that instruct without seeming to. Another option is to take a seminar or pay attention to professional events that combine your specialty with technology. For example, when you go to the banker's convention, attend a session or two on "Technology Trends for Bankers." There are always sessions like that, and you might make a contact in another company with similar problems and concerns.

Probably the best option, if you have the time for it, is to get involved as a user representative in technology committees in your organization. If your company is doing a review of its CRM system, for instance, see if you can get on the review committee. When there's a need for a representative from your department to discuss needs for the next-generation help-line system, sign up. Or, later in your career, become a member of the business practice technology committee, or whatever they call it at your organization.

Just working with such groups will add to your knowledge of technology. Presentations made to such groups, discussions about uses of technology, and ideas about using IT for competitive advantage will all add to your IT knowledge. You'll gain important contacts and exposure to leaders in your organization as well.

It's up to you. You get to choose how you relate to technology. But be sure you choose; don't let your head fall into the sand without thinking about it.

DISCUSSION QUESTIONS

1. Do you agree that the change of technology is relentless? What do you think that means to most business professionals? To most organizations?

2. Think about the three postures toward technology presented here. Which camp will you join? Why?

3. Write a two-paragraph memo to yourself justifying your choice in question 2. If you chose to ignore technology, explain how you will compensate for the loss of competitive advantage. If you're going to join one of the other two groups, explain why and describe how you're going to accomplish it.

4. Given your answer to question 2, assume that you're in a job interview and the interviewer asks about your knowledge of technology. Write a three-sentence response to the interviewer's question.

Firmware can be changed or upgraded, but this is normally a task for IS professionals. The task is easy, but it requires knowledge of special programs and techniques that most business users choose not to learn.

Is $80,000 Enough? (continued)

With this chapter as background, we can now return to the question of the $80,000 budget for computers. You need to respond by the end of the next day, and you had scheduled other work that you cannot just drop. So, you must figure out how to respond quickly in the limited time you have.

First, you need to know what the $80,000 is supposed to cover. Is it just for hardware? Is it for both hardware and software? Is it for the PCs that your employees use, or is it for those PCs and also for departmental servers, networks, and other overhead expenses? For our purposes, suppose the $80,000 is for hardware and software for your employees; it does not include servers, networks, or other computing infrastructure. We will address those issues in the Chapter 5.

Next, you need to consider the work that employees in your department perform. Do all of them do the same work and hence need the same computing resources? If not, can you categorize the work according to the computing resources required by each type of job? Maybe one group of employees needs computers just for email and word processing, whereas another group performs those functions as well as using corporate vertical applications. Given categories of computer need, you can then assess the hardware and program requirements for each category.

Next, you need to decide if the existing equipment is sufficient for the anticipated workloads. If not, what new hardware is needed? Perhaps more memory or more disk? Or, are new computers with new processors needed?

Because the employees in your department will bear the conse-quences of these decisions, you may decide to involve them in these determinations. You can ask one or two key employees to specify the computer resources they believe are necessary for each category of work. (They can be doing this while you do the other tasks you had planned for tomorrow.)

Once you have determined what hardware and software your existing employees need, you add the requirements for new employees. Again, categorize the new hires according to the work they will do and plan accordingly.

Finally, you need to determine software costs. You will need to obtain software licenses for all new machines, and you may need to upgrade licenses of some software on existing machines.

When addressing this question, you might obtain assistance from the IS or accounting departments. It is possible that either of these departments has already performed hardware/software needs analyses that you can adapt to your situation.

Throughout all of this, you will be asking questions and carefully evaluating answers. Why do we need a new processor for that type of work? Why isn't more main memory sufficient? How do you know? Why do we need such big disks? Do we have the right video monitors? Given the background of this chapter, you should be able to understand the answers to these questions and to generate more questions on your own.

Knowing how to approach the "$80,000 question" will stand you in good stead throughout your business career.

Using the Reflections Guide
(page 63a)

GOALS

* Raise students' awareness of the unrelenting change of technology.

* Encourage students to take a stand about how they will react to technological change—in the words of the guide, to "choose a posture."

* Emphasize that this issue is inescapable in modern business. If students ignore it, they are unknowingly and by default choosing a personal competitive *disadvantage*.

* Teach the students the benefits of this class and of IS education, in general.

BACKGROUND AND DISCUSSION STRATEGIES

Technological change is a factor in every businessperson's life. Many of the hardware facts described in this chapter are susceptible to change. It's *perishable content:* Just like produce at the market, it has a short shelf life.

So what's a professional to do? One response is to recognize the problem and to *choose a response.* Business professionals must decide how to respond. They may choose to stick their heads in the sand, but if so, they'd better find other ways to gain a competitive advantage over their peers.

I tell my students:

➤ **Please, after taking the MIS class, don't let random happenstance determine your technology posture. Instead, consciously choose a posture.**

Students who don't want to stick their heads in the sand and ignore technology need to learn coping strategies. First, *they need to learn how to learn about technology,* and they need to learn *how to learn it efficiently.*

The best strategy, I think, is to combine learning about technology with some other activity. This essay recommends volunteering to sit on technology review committees, volunteering to work with systems development professionals as user representatives, going to conferences, and sitting in on at least one or two technology sessions.

The advantage of such a strategy is that it's a "three-fer":

1. As a business professional, you are serving the business, while at the same time making a deposit in your knowledge bank.

2. You also are networking, so the next time you need an answer to a difficult technology question, you'll know whom to ask. (Note: In terms of the "Question Your Questions" guide, networking allows the student to obtain the opinion of an expensive source for a cheap price.)

3. It's also a way of being noticed in a positive way while learning and extending—a great way to obtain a competitive advantage.

Encourage students who are currently employed to *volunteer for projects* now, even as interns. I had a student who, as an intern, volunteered to sit on a CRM review committee to provide end-user feedback. He made his section of the report, and the manager of the review committee was impressed and asked him why he volunteered for the committee. He said he learned about it in his MIS class. The manager said, "Be sure our company picks up the cost of that class."

All of this is just creating strategies to turn a problem—the rapid change of technology—into a *competitive advantage.* If you are comfortable confronting your class, ask them to look around and see who is bored and not paying attention and who isn't. Those who are actively participating are creating a competitive advantage. I ask my students just to think about it. This is also a good time to promote additional IS classes—maybe a database class or a systems development class—for the non-IS major.

Another perspective concerns the *off-shore outsourcing* of jobs (discussed in detail in Chapter 10, pp. 321–322). According to a recent RAND study, jobs that are unlikely to be off-shored are those that involve creative ways of applying new technology to solve business problems in innovative ways.

Example: In spite of Wal-Mart's pronouncement that every vendor must supply *RFID tags* on their goods, nobody (not even Wal-Mart) has quite figured out how best to use RFID in retailing. But you can bet that the person who does won't find his or her job off-shored to the Far East.

Taken to the next step, rapidly changing technology creates opportunities for *entrepreneurship.* When technology stagnates, products become commodities, and opportunities for new products are rare. With rapidly changing technology, opportunities for new products and companies abound.

SUGGESTED RESPONSES FOR DISCUSSION QUESTIONS

1. Technology change is a good news/bad news situation.

    ➤ **How does technology change impact you in positive ways?**

    - It continuously creates new opportunities.

    - You'll never get bored; there will always be something new to learn and do.

    - Technology change will relevel the playing field frequently. People who have dominant expertise in some technology domain will lose that expertise—creating an opportunity for you.

    ➤ **How does technology change impact you in negative ways?**

    - You constantly need to learn.

    - Your expertise is perishable. Without renewal or without knowledge of new technology, you'll fall behind.

    ➤ **How does technology change impact organizations in positive ways?**

    - It continuously creates new opportunities for competitive advantage.

    - It will relevel the playing field frequently. Organizations that have dominant expertise in some technology domain will lose that expertise—creating an opportunity for your organization.

    ➤ **How does technology change impact organizations in negative ways?**

    - The cost of adapting to new technology can be high.

    - Competitive advantages may not be sustainable.

2. The three choices are:

    - Head-in-the-sand

    - Technophile

    - Technology-informed professional

    Ask sample students:

    ➤ **Which posture do you choose? Why?**

If students choose head-in-the-sand, they'd better develop a competitive advantage in another field or discipline.

➤ **Does choosing technophile or technology-informed mean writing computer programs or designing electronic circuits?**

No, definitely not! It means knowing about *technology and how to use it* to solve business problems in innovative ways.

3. The purpose of this question is to *compel* the students to choose a posture. They must not kid themselves—which posture will they choose and why?

    You might ask the students to read their memos to the class.

4. This is another question to *compel* the students to choose a posture. There can be good reasons for the head-in-the-sand posture, but again, does the student truly want to choose that posture? But rather than focus on that posture, I like to ask:

    ➤ **For those of you who have chosen to be IS technology-informed professionals, how do you respond?**

    Then I help them hone and improve their answers. I know, all of this discussion is advertising for IS education, but, hey, this is an IS class!

WRAP UP

➤ **Wake up to the opportunities that the conveyor belt of technology change offers.**

➤ **Because you cannot ignore this issue, choose a strategy. Otherwise, fate will choose a strategy for you.**

➤ **Learning about IS does not mean, necessarily, becoming a computer programmer or a communications technician. It means helping businesses to use information technology and information systems to accomplish their goals and objectives. (This is the definition of MIS given in Chapter 1.)**

➤ **If you want to know about other IS classes we offer that you should be taking, drop me an email or come by my office.**

You Be the Guide

The $80,000 Question (continued) (page 64)

In this section of the text, I've written a sequence of questions that students can use to work out the problem of the $80,000 budget. I fear that I may have given too much away, too much spoon-feeding, but I didn't want the students to flounder and become discouraged early in the class.

The questions in the wrap up omit one important issue: system maintenance costs. Does the $80,000 include the cost of hardware maintenance? Does it include the cost of software upgrades? Will the MIS department be requiring upgrades that are to be included in this $80,000?

RESPONDING TO THE CHALLENGE

You might use the sequence of questions on page 64 as a straw man to evaluate. Before they do anything else, students should carefully read this section. Then ask:

➤ **Is this list complete?**

➤ **Is it correct?**

➤ **Are there issues unaddressed?**

➤ **Are there better questions to obtain needed information?**

Students have been trained that the correct answer to any business problem is to do another study. So, when I assign this problem for written work, I often get back proposals for lengthy projects to study the problem—and this usually from the "better" students.

Remind the students what the point is: *You have to answer the question tomorrow night, and you've already scheduled a day full of meetings that you cannot just drop.* You don't have lots of time to research the question, and you must decide by tomorrow, when the budget is due. What to do? The key here, I think, is *delegation.*

Therefore, ask the class:

➤ **If $80,000 is not enough, who will bear the consequences?**

The answer, of course, is that the employees in the department will do so. Realizing that, suggest to students that now would be a good time to convene a quick ad-hoc committee to address the question. Point out that you could get the number-two person in the department to assemble a small team of employees to address the question. (Of course, those employees, too, will have work they have to drop, but it can be justified on the importance of the query.) You could meet with this team late in the afternoon to find out what they think and then adjust the numbers before giving the answer to the boss.

This is also a good time to bring up the *importance of networking.* Point out that you've had your job only two days, but had you been there longer, you might know someone in accounting who can help you. You could ask an acquaintance in accounting questions on an informal basis: How important are these budget projections? How strict is the adherence to budgets in this company? Will it be difficult to find more dollars later in the year, if need be? What is the "real strategy" that other managers use?

Another problem of being new is that you don't yet know your boss. Should you put conditional language in your budget request like, "I made these projections with only two days' experience on the job. They may need to be adjusted later"? Or, will such language be off-putting to your boss?

Point out to students that, all in all, this exercise is a *good test:*

➤ **It's a good test of how you respond to unexpected questions with short fuses.**

➤ **It's a good test of how you manage your employees.**

➤ **It's a good test of how you will communicate with your boss.**

It's possible that your boss already has a good answer to the $80,000 question, but wants to see how you respond to it. The *process* you use may be far more important to your boss than your answer.

SUMMARY

- Computing devices consists of hardware and software. General-purpose computers can run multiple programs; special-purpose computers, like those in cell phones, run only one program that is fixed in memory.

- Hardware can be categorized according to its primary function: input, processing, output, and storage. Input hardware includes devices such as keyboards and mice. Processing hardware includes the CPU and main memory. Output devices are video displays, printers, and the like. Storage devices include magnetic and optical disks. Chapter 5 will consider communications hardware as well.

- Computers use bits to represent data. A bit, or binary digit, has a value of zero or one. Bits are used to represent computer instructions and data.

- It is not possible to determine the type of data just by looking at the data; this fact is used to advantage by virus authors and other cyber-criminals.

- As you use applications, the initial portions of them are read into memory. During processing, additional portions of the operating system or applications are read into memory as well. Data also are added. In time, main memory fills up, and data or programs must be moved out to make room for new data and program instructions. This operation can cause memory swapping and result in performance problems.

- Figure 3-8 summarizes how hardware characteristics affect performance. The critical features to select are the speed of the CPU, the size of main memory, the size of the magnetic disk, the type of optical disk, and the type and optimal resolution of the video monitor.

- Four popular operating systems are Windows, Mac OS, Unix, and Linux.

- Computer software consists of the operating system and application software. Software can be purchased off-the-rack, purchased off-the-rack and then altered, or tailor-made. Types of software include horizontal, vertical, and custom. Firmware is program code installed in read-only memory of printers or communications devices. The relationship between types and sources is summarized in Figure 3-11.

KEY TERMS AND CONCEPTS

Antivirus programs   **53b**
Application software   **62**
ATA-100   **58**
Binary digit   **49**
Bit   **49**
B2B (business-to-business)   **50**
Bus   **53**
Byte   **51**
Cache memory   **55**
CD-R   **58**
CD-ROM   **58**
CD-RW   **58**
CRT monitor   **58**
Central processing unit
   (CPU)   **48**
Clock speed   **55**
Custom software   **62**
Data channel   **53**
Dot pitch   **58**
DVD-R   **58**
DVD-ROM   **58**

DVD-RW   **58**
Firmware   **63**
General-purpose
   computer   **48**
Gigabyte (GB)   **51**
Hardware   **48**
Horizontal-market
   application   **62**
Input hardware   **48**
Intel instruction set   **51**
Instruction set   **50**
Kilobyte (K)   **51**
LCD monitor   **58**
License agreement   **61a**
Linux   **61**
Mac OS   **61**
Macro virus   **53a**
Main memory   **49**
Megabyte (MB)   **51**
Memory swapping   **54**
Motherboard   **53**

Nonvolatile   **53**
OEM (original equipment
   manufacturer)   **50**
Off-the-shelf software   **62**
Open-source community   **61**
Operating system (OS)   **54**
Optimal resolution   **59**
Output hardware   **48**
Patch   **53a**
Payload   **53a**
Pixel   **58**
Pixel pitch   **59**
Power PC instruction set   **51**
RAM memory   **53**
Rotational delay   **57**
Seek time   **57**
Software piracy   **61a**
Special function cards   **49**
Special-purpose computer   **48**
Storage hardware   **48**
TCG/NGSCB   **61a**

ASSIGNMENT MATERIAL

Review Questions

1. Explain the difference between general-purpose and special-purpose computers.

2. Comment on the statement, "The CPU is the brain of the computer."

3. Give an example of each of the following types of hardware: input, output, processing, and storage. What is a special function card?

4. Why are bits used for computers?

5. How are computer instructions represented?

6. Define the correct meaning for byte, K, MB, GB, and TB.

7. Give the simplified meaning for K, MB, GB, and TB.

8. Explain why computer manufacturers have an incentive to state capacities using the simplified meaning for K, MB, etc.

9. Explain why the interpretation of binary data is ambiguous.

10. How do virus writers use the ambiguity in the interpretation of binary data?

11. How does Moore's Law influence the way that you should learn about computer hardware?

12. Explain the difference between volatile and nonvolatile memory. Which memory devices have which type of memory?

13. What is the purpose of the operating system?

14. Can you rely on the contents of main memory when the computer is started?

15. Explain why memory swapping is necessary.

16. Under what conditions can memory swapping cause serious performance degradation? How can you fix this problem?

17. Using Figure 3-8 as a guide, under what conditions do you need a faster CPU?

18. Using Figure 3-8 as a guide, under what conditions do you need more main memory?

19. Using Figure 3-8 as a guide, under what conditions do you need a larger magnetic disk?

20. What does 1,024 × 768 refer to with regard to video displays?

21. What is the key factor in determining what computer hardware you need?

22. Explain the relationship between application software sources and types.

23. Explain why CRM does not fit neatly into the software types defined in the text.

Applying Your Knowledge

24. Figure 3-12 shows a portion of a 2003 ad for Dell desktop computers. The three computers are presented in decreasing order of cost from left to right. Interpret this ad to answer the following questions:

    a. What is the difference in processor capabilities for the three computers? (Note: A "front side bus" is a data bus that is proprietary to Dell. "L2" refers to a level-2 cache. Apparently, there is a first-level cache that is not mentioned in the ad.)

    b. What is the difference in main memory capabilities for the three computers? (RDRAM and SDRAM are two types of RAM.)

    c. Explain the specifications shown for the magnetic disk (called "hard drive" in the ad).

    d. What is the difference between the two monitors? What additional information do you need before choosing between these monitors?

    e. The "graphics card" refers to a special function card that drives the computer monitor. Interpret the specifications shown for this card.

    f. Explain the different optical disks offered with these systems. The expression 4x means that the DVD is 4 times faster than a baseline speed for DVDs. The expression 48x means that the CD is 48 times faster than a baseline speed for CDs.

    g. What are the principal differences in these three computers?

    h. Describe characteristics of applications that would cause you to choose the "Advanced system" computer.

    i. Describe characteristics of applications that would cause you to choose the "Picture perfect" computer.

8250
Cutting-edge Technology

Advanced system	Digital filmmaker
processor • Intel® Pentium® 4 Processor at 2.80GHz with 533MHz Front Side Bus and 512K L2 Cache	• Intel Pentium 4 Processor at 2.66GHz with 533MHz Front Side Bus and 512K L2 Cache
memory • 256MB PC1066 RDRAM	• 256MB PC1066 RDRAM
hard drive • 60GB Ultra ATA/100 Hard Drive (7200 RPM)	• 60GB Ultra ATA/100 Hard Drive (7200 RPM)
monitor • 19" (18.0" v.i.s., .24dp) M992 Monitor	• 17" (16.0" v.i.s., .25dp) M782 Monitor
AGP graphics card • New 128MB DDR ATI® RADEON™ 9700 Pro Graphics Card with TV-Out and DVI	• New 128MB DDR ATI RADEON 9700 TX Graphics Card with TV-Out and DVI
optical drives • New 4x DVD+RW/+R Drive* with CD-RW including Roxio's Easy CD Creator® and Sonic™ MyDVD™	• New 4x DVD+RW/+R Drive* with CD-RW including Roxio's Easy CD Creator and Sonic MyDVD

4550
Superior Performance, Smart Value

Picture perfect

• Intel Pentium 4 Processor at 2.66GHz with 533MHz Front Side Bus and 512K L2 Cache

• 256MB DDR SDRAM at 333MHz

• 60GB Ultra ATA/100 Hard Drive (7200 RPM)

• 19" (18.0" v.i.s., .24dp) M992 Monitor

• New 128MB DDR ATI RADEON 9700 TX Graphics Card with TV-Out and DVI

• New 48x/24x/48x CD-RW Drive with Roxio's Easy CD Creator

Figure 3-12
2003 Ad for Dell Desktop Computers

Source: © 2005 Dell Inc. All Rights Reserved.

25. Figure 3-12 shows three computer systems from 2003. Visit *dell.com, hewlett-packard.com,* and *lenovo.com.* On each site, find desktop computers that cost around $2,000, the 2003 cost of the Dell 8250.

  a. Compare the capabilities of the computers you find with the computers specified in Figure 3-12. Consider the CPU, memory, magnetic disk, optical disks, and monitor.
  b. What buying strategy does your answer to part a suggest?
  c. Some organizations have a policy for replacing or upgrading computers based on a 2- to 5-year cycle. What buying strategy would you use if your company used a 2-year cycle? What strategy would you use if your company used a 5-year cycle?

26. Reread the sections on the $80,000 question at the start and end of this chapter. Also read the *Problem Solving Guide* on pages 49a–49b. Answer the following questions. Be as specific as you can, given the data available. Make appropriate assumptions if necessary and justify your assumptions.

  a. List the questions you need to answer about workload.
  b. Given your busy schedule and the short timeframe available, how you will get answers to the questions in part a? How will you judge the quality of the answers?
  c. List the questions you need to answer about existing computer hardware.
  d. Given your busy schedule and the short timeframe available, how you will get answers to the questions in part c? How will you judge the quality of the answers?

  e. List the questions you need to have answered about the need for new hardware.
  f. Given your busy schedule and the short timeframe available, how you will get answers to the questions in part e? How will you judge the quality of the answers?
  g. List the questions you need to answer to determine if $80,000 is sufficient for your department.
  h. Given your busy schedule and the short timeframe available, how you will get answers to the questions in part g? How will you judge the quality of the answers?

27. Assume that you have been asked to prepare a computer hardware budget. Your company has identified three classes of computer user. Class-A employees use the computer for email, Web browsing, Internet connectivity, and limited document writing. Class-B employees use the computer for all of the activities of class A, plus they need to be able to read and create complicated documents. They also need to be able to create and process large spreadsheets and process small graphics files. Class-C employees are data analysts who perform all of the tasks that class-A and class-B employees do; they also analyze data using programs that make extensive computations and produce large and complicated graphics.

  a. Using the Internet, determine two appropriate alternatives for each class of employee. Search *dell.com, lenovo.com, hewlett-packard.com,* and any other sites you think appropriate.
  b. Justify each of the selections in your answer to part a.

c. Specify the cost of each of the selections in part a.

Application Exercises

28. Based on your answer to question 27, create a budgetary spreadsheet that computes the total hardware cost for each of your alternatives. Assume that the number of employees of each class is to be input by the spreadsheet user. Create your spreadsheet so that the cost of each alternative need be entered only once. Submit your spreadsheet in accordance with your professor's instructions.

29. Create a database application to keep track of your organization's computer equipment. Your database should have the following two tables:

    EMPLOYEE (EmpNumber, FirstName, LastName, Email)

    EQUIPMENT (ItemNumber, Make, Model, Type, Cost, EmpNumber)

    EmpNumber should be a unique identifier for employees, and ItemNumber is a unique identifier for computer equipment. Example values of Type are "Monitor," "CPU," "Printer," "Notebook," and the like. The EmpNumber in EQUIPMENT has the number of the employee that has been assigned that equipment. If the equipment is unassigned, EmpNumber is null.

    a. Open Microsoft Access, create a new database, and then create the two tables. Use your own judgment to determine the data type for each column.
    b. Open the Tools/Relationship window and create a one-to-many relationship between EMPLOYEE and EQUIPMENT. Do not select "Enforce Referential Integrity."
    c. Fill your tables with data. Enter values for equipment that is both assigned and not assigned to employees.
    d. Open the Employee data in data sheet view and click the plus sign under each employee.
    e. Use the Microsoft Access wizard to create a report that shows all of the data from both the EMPLOYEE and EQUIPMENT tables. Your report should list assigned equipment under each employee. Adjust the appearance of your report so that it has a professional appearance.
    f. Use the Microsoft Access wizard to create a form that has all data from both the EMPLOYEE and EQUIPMENT tables. Use your form to enter a new item of equipment for an existing employee. Additionally, use your form to enter a new employee with several new items of equipment.
    g. Submit your results in accordance with your professor's instructions.

Career Assignments

30. Every department, not just accounts payable, needs to assess its hardware and software budget. Suppose you decide that you want to become an in-house consultant who will help people assess their computer and software needs.

    a. Would it be essential to have a strong business background to perform such a service? Why or why not?
    b. Would it be essential to have a strong technical background to perform such a service? Why or why not?
    c. For this job, which is more important, business knowledge or technical skills? Explain your answer.
    d. What courses and other activities could you engage in while you are in college to prepare for this job?
    e. Even if you do not perform such a job full time, explain how having the skills to perform such a job would increase your desirability to a departmental manager. How could you use such a skill in a job interview?

31. Go to the Occupational Outlook Handbook at *bls.gov/oco/home.htm*.

    a. Summarize the job outlook for jobs of this type.
    b. Describe the educational requirements necessary for this job.
    c. What courses and other activities could you engage in while you are in college to prepare you for this job?
    d. Answer part c, but suppose your goal is to be or to become a *manager* of computer support specialists.

32. Sometimes you will see employee ads that state, "No computer skills required." Instead of searching for such jobs, suppose you attain some degree of proficiency using computers and information systems. Query your favorite Web search engine for the phrase "job opportunities with computer skills." Visit three of the links that seem interesting.

    a. You will not find any consistent definition of the term "computer skill." Summarize several of the definitions (possibly implied rather than stated) that you do find.
    b. Considering your answer to part a, how can you improve your job prospects by taking more IS classes in combination with your major (assuming you are not an IS major)?
    c. Describe two jobs that involve significant computer skills, but that are not strictly in the computer industry. What can you do while you are in college to prepare for one of those jobs?

Case Study 3-1

Wall Data IS Support

In 1993, Wall Data was an up-and-coming company that developed and licensed computer communications software to large organizations. During that year, its sales increased from $35 million to nearly $80 million, and the number of employees grew from 90 to 160. Also, management was busy preparing for an initial public stock offering that was to occur at the end of that year.

The company employed in-house personnel to manage the organization's computer resources. This group acquired new computers, installed initial software, and provided service and support when problems occurred. To simplify computer management, the company defined three types of employee and specified a standard computer equipment configuration for each type. The types were (1) clerical/administrative, (2) professional office (e.g., accountants and marketing personnel), and (3) professional software developers and computer support personnel. The professional software developers received the fastest and most elaborate computers.

Over time, a number of problems developed. For one, the service and support workload was too high for the available personnel, and problem resolution was unacceptably slow. Another problem was that the company found it difficult to keep track of software licenses. The software developers, in particular, would install software on their own machines, but it was not always certain that every employee had an appropriate license for the software on her computer. As a software vendor, senior management was strongly opposed to software piracy and wanted a legitimate license for every computer program on every machine. Finally, turnover was high in the computer support group, and the level of support service decreased dramatically when personnel departed. Managing and staffing the support function and dealing with related problems began to consume more and more management attention.

Unfortunately, this was a critical time for senior management; they needed to focus on the upcoming public offering rather than on solving the in-house computer support problem. Accordingly, management eliminated the in-house computer support group and hired an outside vendor to manage its hardware and software assets. The outside vendor agreed to provide specified equipment at negotiated prices, to test the new equipment and install software, to manage software licenses, and to provide customer support and service. To ensure that only appropriately licensed software was in use, no employee was allowed to install software on his own machine. Only the outside vendor was allowed to acquire software and install it.

As you might imagine, this new rule became very unpopular among the software developers: "Are you telling me that I can't install software on my own machine? I've never heard of such a thing!" In fact, the policy was so different from standard practice among software development professionals that development managers could not bring themselves to enforce it. Soon developers began acquiring software under bogus accounting entries like "Miscellaneous departmental expense, meals." The computer license situation became even worse.

Furthermore, the price-to-performance ratio for computer hardware was decreasing exponentially. In a matter of months, the market offered newer, more powerful computers than those that were specified in the outsourcing agreement, and these new computers sold for considerably less than the ones specified in the contract. Developers follow computer technology like cats watch mice, and soon every developer was saying, "Please don't give me the standard computer. Let me buy my own computer. I can get twice the computer for half the price from Gateway."

No software development company can allow its developers to be distracted by anything for very long. Software developers are expensive, but the true expense of developer unrest is not direct labor costs; the true expense is in opportunity costs. Delaying the shipment of a new product by as little as a month can cost an organization millions of dollars in marketing expense and lost revenue. Something had to be done, but what?

Questions

1. Summarize the problems that led Wall Data to the outsourcing agreement. Remember the definition from Chapter 2 that a *problem* is a "perceived difference between what is and what ought to be."

2. Describe two solutions, in addition to the one that was chosen by Wall Data, to solve the problems in your answer to question 1.

3. Summarize the problems the company had with the outsourcing agreement. Use the definition of *problem* from Chapter 2.

4. Describe three solutions to the problems you listed in your answer to question 3.

5. What effect did the upcoming initial public offering have on the company's senior management?

6. This case occurred in 1993, prior to the widespread use of the Internet. What Internet-based solutions to these problems are available today that were not available in 1993?

7. Is it still a problem today to ensure that every computer program has a legitimate license? How do organizations solve this problem?

8. Invite the manager of your college's computer lab to class. How does the computer lab manager control computer software licenses?

9. Search *dell.com*, *cdw.com*, and *hewlett-packard.com* to see what license-control products or services these companies offer to organizations that purchase their hardware.

Case Study 3-2

Dell Leverages the Internet, Directly

When Michael Dell started Dell Computer in 1984, personal computers were sold only in retail stores. Manufacturers shipped to wholesalers, who shipped to retail stores, which sold to end users. Companies maintained expensive inventories at each stage of this supply chain. Dell thought that if he could eliminate the retail channel by selling computers directly to consumers he could dramatically reduce their price. In 2004, while speaking to a group of students in New York City he recalled,

> I was inspired by how I saw computers being sold. It seemed to me that it was very expensive and it was inefficient. A computer cost at the time about $3,000 but there were only about $600 worth of parts inside the computer. And so I figured, hey, what if you sold the computer for $800? You don't need to sell it for $3,000. And so we changed the whole way computers were being sold by lowering the cost of distribution and sales and taking out this extra cost that was inefficient.

Now, what I didn't know was that the Internet would come along and now people can go on the Internet and they can go to Dell.com and buy a computer and that makes it a lot easier.

I'd say the most important thing we did was listen very carefully to our customers. We asked, what do they want, what do they need and how can we meet their needs and provide something that's really valuable to them? Because if we could take care of our customers, they'll want to buy more products from us, and they have.[3]

Indeed they have. In 2004, Dell's revenue topped $45 billion, representing over 18 percent of the computer hardware market. Dell employs over 50,000 people, worldwide, and its investors have benefited as well. A share of Dell purchased for $8.50 in the initial public offering would be worth over $3,500 in 2004 (allowing for multiple stock splits over the years).

Eliminating retail stores not only reduced costs, it also brought Dell closer to the customer, enabling it to listen better than the competition. It also eliminated sales channel inventories, which allowed Dell to rapidly bring new computers with new technology to the customer. This eliminates the need to recycle or sell off existing pipeline inventory whenever a new model is announced. In fact, today Dell builds every computer system to customer order. Every computer in Dell's finished goods inventory has already been sold!

Additionally, Dell focused on its suppliers and has one of the most efficient supply chains in the industry. Dell pays close attention to its suppliers and shares information with them on product quality, inventory, and related subjects via its secure Web site *valuechain.dell.com*. According to its Web site, the first two qualities Dell looks for in suppliers are (1) cost competitiveness and (2) an understanding of Dell's business. Dell listens to its customers, and it expects its suppliers to do the same in return.

In addition to computer hardware, Dell provides a variety of services. It provides basic technical support with every computer, and customers can upgrade this basic support by purchasing one of four higher levels of support. Additionally, Dell offers deployment services to organizations to configure and deploy Dell systems, both hardware and preinstalled software, into customers' user environments. Dell offers additional services to maintain and manage Dell systems once they have been deployed.

Questions

1. Explain how selling direct has given Dell a competitive advantage. Use the factors listed in Figure 2-1 (page 26) in your answer.

2. What information systems does Dell need to have to sell directly to the consumer? Visit *dell.com* for inspiration and ideas.

3. Besides selling direct, what other programs has Dell created that give it a competitive advantage?

4. Hewlett-Packard, Toshiba, Sony, and other computer manufacturers sell both directly and through Internet stores. Visit *www.cnet.com* and search for the term *notebook*. The site will return laptop computers from several manufacturers. If you look at notebooks from Hewlett-Packard, Toshiba, or Sony, you will see that they must be purchased from Internet vendors. (Click "Check Prices" to see vendor sources.) In contrast, Dell computers can be purchased only from Dell, as you will see when you check for prices for one of its computers.

---

[3]Michael Dell, speech before the Miami Springs Middle School, September 1, 2004. Retrieved from *dell.com*, under Michael/Speeches (accessed January 2005).

In order to use an intermediary, Hewlett-Packard and others must sell their computers to the supplier at a price below the consumer's price; otherwise the supplier has no incentive to sell the product. But, those vendors cannot offer the supplier's price to the public without losing its suppliers. Does this situation mean that Dell computers will be cheaper than Hewlett-Packard and other computers? Why or why not?

5. Assume that, because of the need to sell through a channel, Hewlett-Packard's computers will always be more expensive than Dell's. How can Hewlett-Packard successfully compete with Dell?

6. What information systems can Hewlett-Packard set up that will better enable it to compete with Dell? Visit *hp.com* for inspiration and ideas.

7. Do you think Dell would have been successful if the Internet had not been invented? Why or why not?

Source: © 2005 Dell Inc. All rights reserved.

Database Processing

Learning Objectives

* Know the purpose of database processing.
* List the components of a database system.
* Understand important database terms.
* Know the elements of the entity-relationship model.
* Know how to interpret and validate an entity-relationship model.
* Understand the general nature of database design.
* Recognize the need for and know the basic tasks of database administration.

Guides

ETHICS GUIDE
Nobody Said I Shouldn't

SECURITY GUIDE
Database Security

PROBLEM SOLVING GUIDE
Immanuel Kant, Data Modeler

OPPOSING FORCES GUIDE
No, Thanks, I'll Use a Spreadsheet

REFLECTIONS GUIDE
Requirements Creep

Chapter Preview

Businesses of every size organize data records into collections called databases.
*At one extreme, small businesses use databases to keep track of customers; at
the other extreme, huge corporations like* Dell *and* Amazon *use databases to
support complex sales, marketing, and operations activities.*

*This chapter discusses the why, what, and how of database processing. We
begin by describing the purpose of databases and then explain the important
components of database systems. We then overview the process of creating a
database system and summarize the role for you, a future user.*

*Users have a crucial role during the development of database applications.
Specifically, the structure and content of the database depends entirely on how
users view their business activity. To build the database, the developers will
create a model of that view using a tool called the* entity-relationship model. *You
need to understand how to interpret such models, because the development
team may ask you to validate the correctness of such a model when building a
system for your use. Finally, we describe tasks for* database administration.

*This chapter focuses on database technology. Here we consider the basic
components of a database and its applications and the features and functions of
those components. You will learn about the use of databases for reporting and
data mining in* Chapter 9.

Thanks for Volunteering

Suppose you are the manager of fund-raising for a local public television station. Twice a year you conduct fund drives during which the station runs commercials that ask viewers to donate. These drives are important; they provide nearly 40 percent of the station's operating budget.

One of your job functions is to find volunteers to staff the phones during these drives. You need 10 volunteers per night for 6 nights, or 60 people, twice per year. The volunteers' job is exhausting, and normally a volunteer will work only one night during a drive.

Finding volunteers for each drive is a perpetual headache. Two months before a drive begins, you and your staff start calling to find volunteers. You first call volunteers from prior drives, using a roster that your administrative assistant prepares for each drive. Some volunteers have been helping for years; you'd like to know that information before you call them so that you can tell them how much you appreciate their continuing support. Unfortunately, the roster does not have that data.

Additionally, some volunteers are more effective than others. Some have a particular knack for increasing the callers' donations. Although those data are available, the information is not in a format that you can use when calling for volunteers. You think you could better staff the fundraising drives if you had that missing information.

You know that you can use a computer database to keep better track of prior volunteers' service and performance, but you are not sure how to proceed. By the end of this chapter, when we return to this fundraising situation, you will know what to do.

▊ Purpose of a Database

The purpose of a database is to keep track of things. When most students learn that, they wonder why we need a special technology for such a simple task. Why not just use a list? If the list is long, put it into a spreadsheet.

In fact, many professionals do keep track of things using spreadsheets. If the structure of the list is simple enough, there is no need to use database technology. The list of student grades in Figure 4-1, for example, works perfectly well in a spreadsheet.

Suppose, however, that the professor wants to track more than just grades. Say that the professor wants to record email messages as well. Or, perhaps the professor wants to record both email messages and office visits. There is no place in Figure 4-1 to record that additional data. Of course, the professor could set up a separate spreadsheet for email messages and another one for office visits, but that awkward solution would be difficult to use because it does not provide all of the data in one place.

Instead, the professor wants a form like that in Figure 4-2. With it, the professor can record student grades, emails, and office visits all in one place. A form like the one in Figure 4-2 is difficult, if not impossible, to produce from a spreadsheet. Such a form is easily produced, however, from a database.

The key distinction between Figures 4-1 and 4-2 is that the list in Figure 4-1 is about a single theme or concept. It is about student grades only. The list in Figure 4-2

You Be the Guide

Thanks for Volunteering
(page 76)

GOALS

* Motivate students on why, as future business professionals, they will need to know database technology.

* Teach sufficient database development for students to become effective consumers of database developers' services.

WAYS TO STIMULATE STUDENT INVOLVEMENT

The goal of this chapter is not to teach the students how to build a database, but rather to teach students how to become *effective consumers of database developers' services.* Also, it should teach future managers *their responsibilities when they are part of a database construction project.*

➤ **Suppose you work for the TV station. How do you proceed? It's not like you can search the Yellow Pages or advertise in Craig's List for the term "database contractor."**

➤ **Suppose someone volunteers to build a database for you. How do you decide if that person knows what he or she is doing? How do you know you won't waste a lot of your and your staff's time, and then get nothing?**

➤ **In short, as a manager, what do you need to do to be a good consumer of a database team or a consultant's services?**

Some students will find that they enjoy this topic. Be sure to describe and recommend your database class. Another thought: Invite the professor who teaches that class to give a 5-minute presentation, including a description of the class, at some point while you're discussing database technology.

A common mistake by professionals is to use a spreadsheet for a database problem. Several characteristics of this vignette make a spreadsheet inappropriate: the need to store multiple phone numbers, multiple contacts, and multiple records of past service.

➤ **You can use a spreadsheet to keep track of things, but watch out! If you need data beyond the simplest list, you'll soon regret it.**

➤ **Look at Figure 4-30. This form shows the data that the volunteer manager needs. It is nearly impossible,**

and very wasteful, to try to produce a data format like that from a spreadsheet.

➤ **Using a spreadsheet to track anything other than the simplest list is using the wrong tool—like trying to open a can of tuna with a screwdriver.**

➤ **People use spreadsheets because they know how to use them and because they don't know anything about database technology. A little database knowledge will make your life a lot easier and give you a competitive edge as well!**

I introduce the idea of themes to drive home the differences between spreadsheets and databases. If you want to keep track of a single topic or theme, then you can use a spreadsheet. If you want to keep track of multiple topics or themes, then you should use a database. For example, if you want to keep track of movie stars, their stage name, real name, date of birth, number of Oscars, then you have a single theme and can use a spreadsheet. However, if you want to keep track of movie stars' data and data about the movies they've been in, then you have two themes and should use a database.

A commercial example of this same idea concerns computers. If you just want to track computers, their serial number, their disk capacity, their CPU type, and that's all, then you have a single theme, *computer*. A spreadsheet will work. But, if you want to keep track of computers, the software licenses they have, and the employee to whom those computers are assigned, then you have not one theme, but three: *computer, software,* and *employee.*

Bottom line:

➤ **If I have *one* theme, then I can *use a spreadsheet.***

➤ **If I have (or think I will soon have) *more than one theme,* then I *should use a database.***

WRAP UP

➤ **The purpose of this chapter is to teach you what you need to know to become an effective consumer of the services of professional database developers.**

➤ **As you will learn, users have a vital role: Only users know what the database needs to contain. The development team is dependent on you to tell them the data and relationships you need. You will get much better service from them if you know how to interpret a data model and have other knowledge, which we will now discuss.**

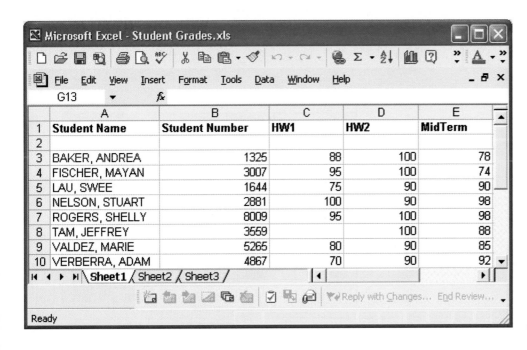

Figure 4-1
A List of Student Grades

has multiple themes; it shows student grades, student emails, and student office visits. We can make a general rule from these examples: Lists that involve a single theme can be stored in a spreadsheet; lists that involve multiple themes require a database. We will say more about this general rule as this chapter proceeds.

To summarize, the purpose of a database is to keep track of things that involve more than one theme.

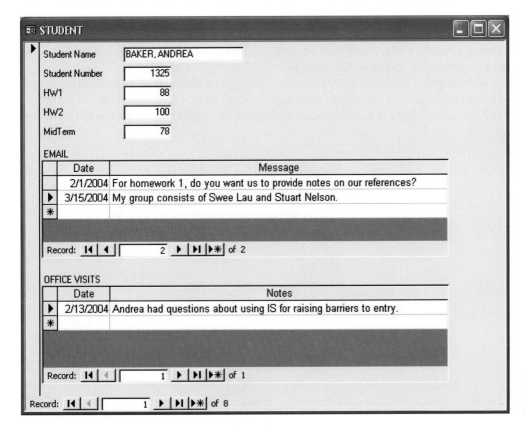

Figure 4-2
Student Data Shown in Form from Database

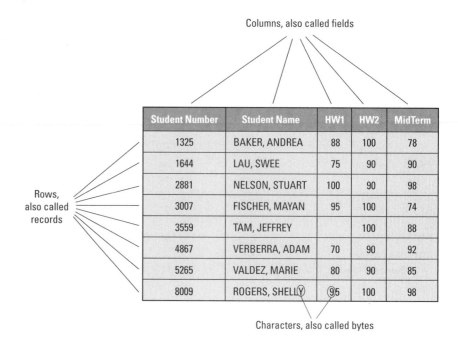

Columns, also called fields

Student Number	Student Name	HW1	HW2	MidTerm
1325	BAKER, ANDREA	88	100	78
1644	LAU, SWEE	75	90	90
2881	NELSON, STUART	100	90	98
3007	FISCHER, MAYAN	95	100	74
3559	TAM, JEFFREY		100	88
4867	VERBERRA, ADAM	70	90	92
5265	VALDEZ, MARIE	80	90	85
8009	ROGERS, SHELLY	95	100	98

Rows, also called records

Characters, also called bytes

Figure 4-3
Student Table (also called File)

What Is a Database?

A **database** is a self-describing collection of integrated records. To understand this definition, you first need to understand the terms illustrated in Figure 4-3. As you learned in Chapter 3, a **byte** is a character of data. Bytes are grouped into **columns**, such as *Student Number* and *Student Name*. Columns are also called **fields**. Columns or fields, in turn, are grouped into **rows**, which are also called **records**. In Figure 4-3, the collection of data for all columns (*Student Name, Student Number, HW1, HW2,* and *MidTerm*) is called a row or a record. Finally, a group of similar rows or records is called a **table** or a **file**. From these definitions, you can see that there is a hierarchy of data elements, as shown in Figure 4-4.

It is tempting to continue this grouping process by saying that a database is a group of tables or files. This statement, although true, does not go far enough. As shown in Figure 4-5, a database is a collection of tables *plus* relationships among the rows in those

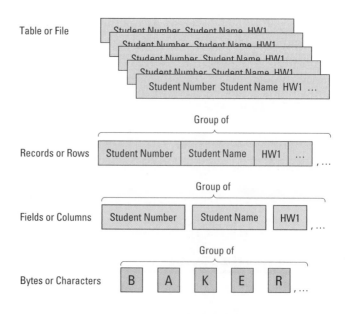

Table or File

Student Number Student Name HW1

Group of

Records or Rows | Student Number | Student Name | HW1 | ... | , ...

Group of

Fields or Columns | Student Number | Student Name | HW1 | , ...

Group of

Bytes or Characters   B   A   K   E   R   , ...

Figure 4-4
Hierarchy of Data Elements

tables, *plus* special data, called *metadata*, that describes the structure of the database. By the way, the cylindrical symbol ▊ represents a computer disk drive. It is used in diagrams like that in Figure 4-5 because databases are normally stored on magnetic disks.

Relationships Among Records

Consider the terms on the left-hand side of Figure 4-5. You know what tables are. To understand what is meant by *relationships among rows in tables*, examine Figure 4-6. It shows sample data from the three tables *Email*, *Student*, and *Office_Visit*. Notice the column named *Student Number* in the *Email* table. That column indicates the row in *Student* to which a row of *Email* is connected. In the first row of *Email*, the *Student Number* value is 1325. This indicates that this particular email was received from the student whose *Student Number* is 1325. If you examine the *Student* table, you will see that the row for Andrea Baker has this value. Thus, the first row of the *Email* table is related to Andrea Baker.

Now consider the last row of the *Office_Visit* table at the bottom of the figure. The value of *Student Number* in that row is 4867. This value indicates that the last row in *Office_Visit* belongs to Adam Verberra.

From these examples, you can see that values in one table relate rows of that table to rows in a second table. Several special terms are used to express these ideas. A **key** is a column or group of columns that identifies a unique row in a table. *Student Number* is the key of the *Student* table. Given a value of *Student Number*, you can determine one and only one row in *Student*. Only one student has the number 1325, for example.

Tables or Files
+
Relationships among Rows in Tables
+
Metadata
= Database

Figure 4-5
Components of a Database

Email Table

EmailNum	Date	Message	Student Number
1	2/1/2004	For homework 1, do you want us to provide notes on our references?	1325
2	3/15/2004	My group consists of Swee Lau and Stuart Nelson.	1325
3	3/15/2004	Could you please assign me to a group?	1644

Student Table

Student Number	Student Name	HW1	HW2	MidTerm
1325	BAKER, ANDREA	88	100	78
1644	LAU, SWEE	75	90	90
2881	NELSON, STUART	100	90	98
3007	FISCHER, MAYAN	95	100	74
3559	TAM, JEFFREY		100	88
4867	VERBERRA, ADAM	70	90	92
5265	VALDEZ, MARIE	80	90	85
8009	ROGERS, SHELLY	95	100	98

Office_Visit Table

VisitID	Date	Notes	Student Number
2	2/13/2004	Andrea had questions about using IS for raising barriers to entry.	1325
3	2/17/2004	Jeffrey is considering an IS major. Wanted to talk about career opportunities.	3559
4	2/17/2004	Will miss class Friday due to job conflict.	4867

Figure 4-6
Example of Relationships Among Rows

Every table must have a key. The key of the *Email* table is *EmailNum,* and the key of the *Student_Visit* table is *VisitID.* Sometimes more than one column is needed to form a unique identifier. In a table called *City,* for example, the key would consist of the combination of columns (*City, State*), because a given city name can appear in more than one state.

Student Number is not the key of the *Email* or the *Office_Visit* tables. We know that about *Email* because there are two rows in *Email* that have the *Student Number* value 1325. The value 1325 does not identify a unique row, therefore *Student Number* is not the key of *Email.*

Nor is *Student Number* a key of *Office_Visit,* although you cannot tell that from the data in Figure 4-6. If you think about it, however, there is nothing to prevent a student from visiting a professor more than once. If that were to happen, there would be two rows in *Office_Visit* with the same value of *Student Number.* It just happens that no student has visited twice in the limited data in Figure 4-6.

Columns that fulfill a role like that of *Student Number* in the *Email* and *Office_Visit* tables are called **foreign keys**. This term is used because such columns are keys, but they are keys of a different (foreign) table than the one in which they reside.

Before we go on, databases that carry their data in the form of tables and that represent relationships using foreign keys are called **relational databases**. (The term *relational* is used because another, more formal name for a table is **relation**.) In the past, there were databases that were not relational in format, but such databases have nearly disappeared. Chances are you will never encounter one, and we will not consider them further.[1]

Metadata

Recall the definition of database again: A database is a self-describing collection of integrated records. The records are integrated because, as you just learned, relationships among rows are represented in the database. But what does *self-describing* mean?

It means that a database contains, within itself, a description of its contents. Think of a library. A library is a self-describing collection of books and other materials. It is self-describing because the library contains a catalog that describes the library's contents. The same idea also pertains to a database. Databases are self-describing because they contain not only data, but also data about the data in the database.

Metadata are data that describe data. Figure 4-7 shows metadata for the *Email* table. The format of metadata depends on the software product that is processing the database. Figure 4-7 shows the metadata as they appear in Microsoft Access. Each row of the top part of this form describes a column of the *Email* table. The columns of these descriptions are *Field Name, Data Type,* and *Description. Field Name* contains the name of the column, *Data Type* shows the type of data the column may hold, and *Description* contains notes that explain the source or use of the column. As you can see, there is one row of metadata for each of the four columns of the *Email* table: *EmailNum, Date, Message,* and *Student Number.*

The bottom part of this form provides more metadata, which Access calls *Field Properties,* for each column. In Figure 4-7, the focus is on the *Date* column (note the filled-in right-face pointer next to its name, like the one shown here ▶). Because the focus is on *Date* in the top pane, the details in the bottom pane pertain to the *Date* column. The Field Properties describe formats, a default value for Access to supply when a new row is created, and the constraint that a value is required for this column. It is not important for you to remember these details. Instead, just understand that metadata are data about data and that such metadata are always a part of a database.

The presence of metadata makes databases much more useful. Because of metadata, no one needs to guess, remember, or even record what is in the database. To find

---

[1]Another type of database, the **object-relational database**, is rarely used in commercial applications. Search the Web if you are interested in learning more about object-relational databases. In this book, we will describe only relational databases.

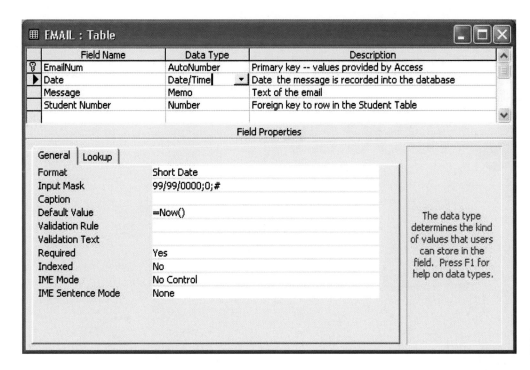

Figure 4-7
Example Metadata (in Access)

out what a database contains, we just look at the metadata inside the database. Metadata make databases easy to use—for both authorized and unauthorized purposes, as described in the *Ethics Guide* on page 81a.

Components of a Database Application System

A database, all by itself, is not very useful. The tables in Figure 4-6 have all of the data the professor wants, but the format is unwieldy. The professor wants to see the data in a form like that in Figure 4-2 and also as a formatted report. Pure database data are correct, but in raw form they are not pertinent or useful.

Figure 4-8 shows the components of a **database application system**. Such applications make database data more accessible and useful. Users employ a database application that consists of forms (like that in Figure 4-2), formatted reports, queries, and application programs. Each of these, in turn, calls on the database management system (DBMS) to process the database tables. We will first describe DBMSs and then discuss database application components.

The Database Management System

A **database management system (DBMS)** is a program used to create, process, and administer a database. As with operating systems, almost no organization develops its own DBMS. Instead, companies license DBMS products from vendors like IBM,

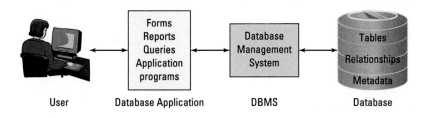

Figure 4-8
Components of a Database Application System

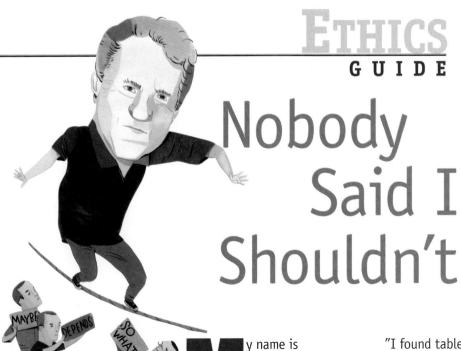

Nobody Said I Shouldn't

My name is Kelly and I do systems support for our group. I configure the new computers, set up the network, make sure the servers are operating, and so forth. I also do all of the database backups. I've always liked computers. After high school, I worked odd jobs to make some money, then I got an associate degree in information technology from our local community college.

"Anyway, as I said, I make backup copies of our databases. One weekend, I didn't have much going on, so I copied one of the database backups to a CD and took it home. I had taken a class on database processing as part of my associate degree, and we used SQL Server (our database management system) in my class. In fact, I suppose that's part of the reason I got the job. Anyway, it was easy to restore the database on my computer at home, and I did.

"Of course, as they'll tell you in your database class, one of the big advantages of database processing is that databases have metadata, or data that describe the content of the database. So, although I didn't know what tables were in our database, I did know how to access the SQL Server metadata. I just queried a table called sysTables to learn the names of our tables. From there it was easy to find out what columns each table had.

"I found tables with data about orders, customers, salespeople, and so forth, and, just to amuse myself, and to see how much of the query language SQL that I could remember, I started playing around with the data. I was curious to know which order entry clerk was the best, so I started querying each clerk's order data, the total number of orders, total order amounts, things like that. It was easy to do and fun.

"I know one of the order entry clerks, Jason, pretty well, so I started looking at the data for his orders. I was just curious, and it was very simple SQL. I was just playing around with the data when I noticed something odd. All of his biggest orders were with one company, Valley Appliances, and even stranger, every one of its orders had a huge discount. I thought, well, maybe that's typical. Out of curiosity, I started looking at data for the other clerks, and very few of them had an order with Valley Appliances. But, when they did, Valley didn't get a big discount. Then I looked at the rest of Jason's orders, and none of them had much in the way of discounts, either.

"The next Friday, a bunch of us went out for a beer after work. I happened to see Jason, so I asked him about Valley Appliances and made a joke about the discounts. He asked me what I meant, and then I told him that I'd been looking at the data for fun and that I saw this odd pattern. He just laughed, said he just 'did his job,' and then changed the subject.

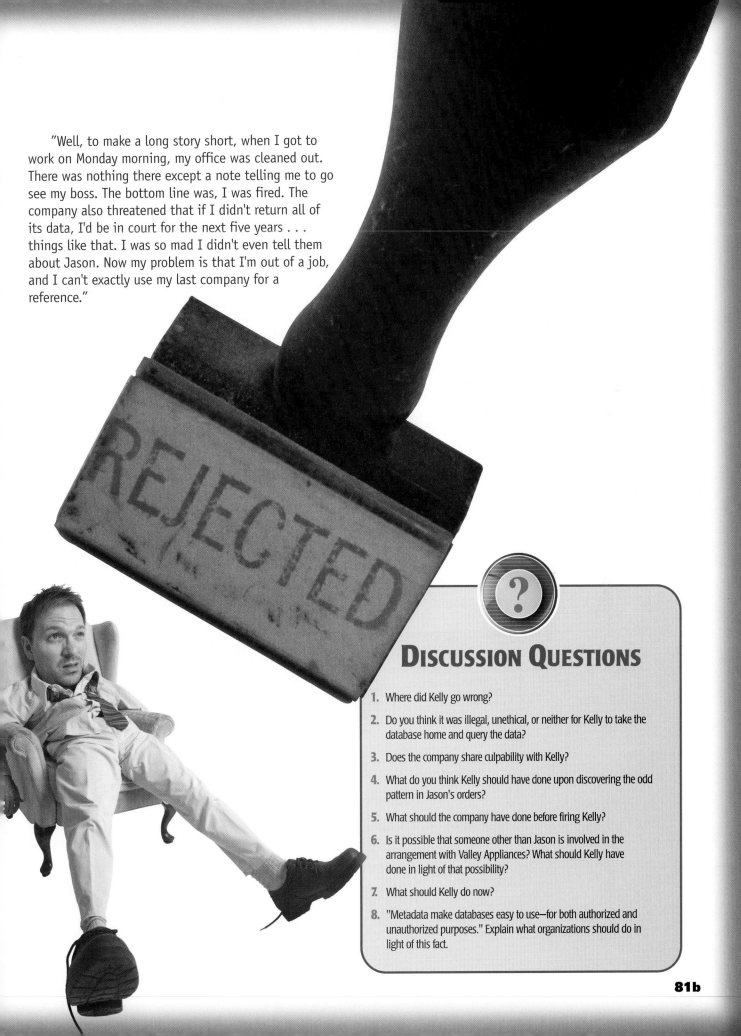

"Well, to make a long story short, when I got to work on Monday morning, my office was cleaned out. There was nothing there except a note telling me to go see my boss. The bottom line was, I was fired. The company also threatened that if I didn't return all of its data, I'd be in court for the next five years . . . things like that. I was so mad I didn't even tell them about Jason. Now my problem is that I'm out of a job, and I can't exactly use my last company for a reference."

DISCUSSION QUESTIONS

1. Where did Kelly go wrong?

2. Do you think it was illegal, unethical, or neither for Kelly to take the database home and query the data?

3. Does the company share culpability with Kelly?

4. What do you think Kelly should have done upon discovering the odd pattern in Jason's orders?

5. What should the company have done before firing Kelly?

6. Is it possible that someone other than Jason is involved in the arrangement with Valley Appliances? What should Kelly have done in light of that possibility?

7. What should Kelly do now?

8. "Metadata make databases easy to use—for both authorized and unauthorized purposes." Explain what organizations should do in light of this fact.

Microsoft, Oracle, and others. Popular DBMS products are **DB2** from IBM, **Access** and **SQL Server** from Microsoft, and **Oracle** from the Oracle Corporation. Another popular DBMS is **MySQL**, an open-source DBMS product that is free for most applications. Other DBMS products are available, but these five process the great bulk of databases today.

Note that a DBMS and a database are two different things. For some reason, the trade press and even some books confuse the two. A DBMS is a software program; a database is a collection of tables, relationships, and metadata. The two are very different concepts. See *MIS in Use 4-1* for a description of an interesting database consisting of high-resolution photos and topographic maps of the United States. The DBMS that runs it is Microsoft's SQL Server.

Creating the Database and Its Structures

Database developers use the DBMS to create tables, relationships, and other structures in the database. The form in Figure 4-7 can be used to define a new table or to modify an existing one. To create a new table, the developer just fills out a new form like the one in Figure 4-7.

To modify an existing table—say, to add a new column—the developer opens the metadata form for that table and adds a new row of metadata. For example, in Figure 4-9 the developer has added a new column called *Response?*. This new column has the data type *Yes/No*, which means that the column can contain only one of the values—Yes or No. The professor will use this column to indicate whether he has responded to the student's email. Other database structures are defined in similar ways.

Processing the Database

The second function of the DBMS is to process the database. Applications use the DBMS for four operations: to *read, insert, modify,* or *delete* data. The applications call upon the DBMS in different ways. From a form, when the user enters new or changed data, a computer program behind the form calls the DBMS to make the necessary database changes. From an application program, the program calls the DBMS directly to make the change.

Structured Query Language (SQL) is an international standard language for processing a database. All five of the DBMS products mentioned earlier accept and

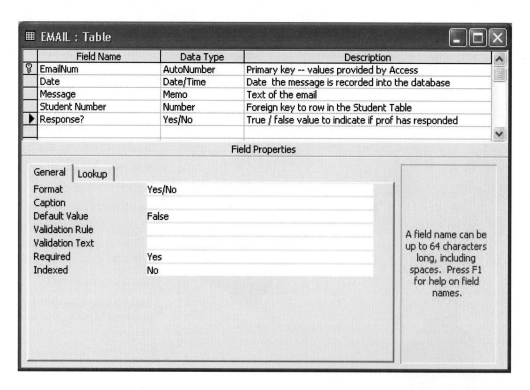

Figure 4-9
Adding a New Column to a Table (in Access)

You Be the Guide

Using the Ethics Guide
(page 81a)

GOALS

* Illustrate the utility of metadata and SQL, even for nonauthorized purposes.

* Discuss the ethics of unauthorized data access.

* Consider the need for organizational data policies.

BACKGROUND AND PRESENTATION STRATEGIES

SQL was designed to be powerful and easy to use. Here's a SQL statement Kelly used to display the average order total and average discount for each combination of company and salesperson:

```
SELECT    AVG(Total), AVG(Discount),
          CompanyName, SPName
FROM      SALES_ORDER
GROUP BY  CompanyName, SPName;
```

That's all Kelly needed! No programs, no special interfaces, just those few lines of SQL entered into the DBMS. It could be done in 5 minutes or less.

➤ As a future business manager or owner, what does the ease with which this can be done tell you?

In order for Kelly to write the SQL statement above, he needed to know the names of the tables and columns to query. The names were easy for him to obtain because every database contains metadata that describes its content. Kelly used the DBMS to query the metadata to learn there was a table named Sales_Order that contained the columns *Total*, *Discount*, *CompanyName*, and *SPName*.

Nothing that Kelly did was illegal; it's even questionable that what he did was unethical. Suppose he stumbled upon an internal criminal conspiracy, one unknown to the company's management or ownership. By discovering it, he would be a hero, if the discovery was reported to someone not involved in the conspiracy.

If the company has a policy that no employee is to remove company data from the company premises, then he violated that policy. Can any company enforce such a policy today? If a sales manager sends an email with proprietary company product information to a salesperson working at a customer site, that action would be a violation the policy not to remove data from company premises. But if the salesperson needs the data to support a crucial sale, who would want to

prohibit that data access? Still, removing an entire database is on a different scale from sending an attachment in an email.

Data is an asset. Data is just as much an asset as buildings, trucks, and equipment. It has value and needs to be protected.

➤ What is a reasonable policy for an organization to have regarding employees taking data home?

This question is not easy to answer. The policy needs to be loose enough to allow employees to do their work, while providing appropriate protection to data assets. Most employment contracts use statements like "protect the company's data assets as directed by management" or other general language.

Bottom line: Companies need to have policies with regard to the data asset. We'll discuss this further when we discuss security management in Chapter 11.

We could view Kelly as the victim of bad luck: His curiosity, knowledge of database technology, ambition, and friendships caused him to lose his job.

Kelly probably should hire an attorney who might advise him to contact law enforcement as well. He may not get his job back, he may not want his job back, but he's probably entitled to some compensation. He also deserves a decent job referral—assuming he was otherwise a desirable employee.

 ### SUGGESTED RESPONSES FOR DISCUSSION QUESTIONS

1. Kelly went wrong by taking the data home. Had he processed the data at work, it would be hard to fault him.

   ### ➤ Was he in error about mentioning to his friend what he'd found?

   ### ➤ Once he saw the odd pattern, what should he have done?

   This is a tough one. Either forget about it or do a careful analysis and then take the results to the most senior manager he can meet. But what if this is an innocuous coincidence? Then he'll look like he betrayed his friend. Maybe Kelly hasn't done anything wrong, yet. *Maybe the story isn't over.* One possible continuation of the story is that he goes to an attorney who advises him to contact senior management and law enforcement.

2. It was not illegal. Taking the data home may have been against corporate policy. He may have been

overly curious, but is that unethical? I think taking the data home might be construed as poor judgment on the part of a smart and ambitious employee, but I wouldn't say it was unethical. Recall Encarta's definition of ethical: "Consistent with agreed principles of correct moral conduct."

➤ **Do his intentions matter? If he had gone home with the intention of using the customer data to sell his own home-care products, would your answer be different?**

➤ **If he had gone home with the hope of gathering dirt on fellow employees, would your answer be different?**

➤ **Why should his intentions matter?**

It goes back to "agreed principles." Most would find it hard to fault improving one's job skills, even if there is an element of unbridled curiosity.

3. Culpability for what? For allowing him to take home the data? If there is no clear company policy, if he had not been instructed not to remove data, then the company probably does share culpability. If he violated a clearly stated company policy of which he had been made aware, then probably not. Culpability for firing him? It depends on how high up the organization the conspiracy reaches. If it goes all the way to the top, then they do. If not, then firing him was the protective action of guilty employees. Company culpability depends on what happens next.

4. First, I ask the class to vote:

➤ **How many of you think that Kelly should:**

- **Ignore the whole thing?**
- **Confirm his analysis, gather even stronger evidence, if possible, and then take the information he has to the CFO?**
- **Never have learned SQL? (This is a joke!)**
- **Done what he did, and now go see an attorney?**

Now ask the students why they voted the way they did.

My vote: probably go to the CFO. If he then is fired, definitely go to the attorney.

5. If there is no criminal conspiracy, then I believe the company's actions were precipitous. He ought not to be fired for his ambition and knowledge, even if he did show poor judgment in taking the data home.

First, the company should determine if the information he has uncovers employee wrongdoing. If not, then he should be instructed not to take data home, or maybe put on probation, but firing him seems overly harsh. This also depends on whether he violated a clear corporate policy on which he had been trained.

If there is a criminal conspiracy, then the company has major problems. They need to consult their attorneys and law enforcement. They also possibly should hire investigators to identify members of the conspiracy and then clean up the organization.

6. I think there's little doubt that someone else is involved. Jason is not in a position to force Kelly's firing. In that case, he should have not spoken with Jason. He should have gone as high in the organization as he could. But, see question 4.

7. Say nothing to anyone. Hire an attorney with expertise in labor law.

➤ **Do you think he should "sue the pants off" this company?**

8. Understand their vulnerability. Treat organizational data as an important asset. Establish data policies and train employees on those policies. (More on this in the next chapter and in Chapter 11.)

WRAP UP

➤ **This is a rather weird case. Should we conclude:**

- **A little knowledge is a dangerous thing?**
- **Curiosity got the cat?**
- **Don't stick your nose in other people's business?**
- **Don't socialize with fellow employees after work?**

➤ **Two sure conclusions:**

- **Data is an important asset that needs to be protected.**
- **Metadata and SQL are powerful.**

➤ **We're in the middle of the story. What happened next? Did he hire an attorney? Or, did he slink off and take an entry-level job in another industry?**

➤ **Assume he hired an attorney, and you finish the story. Think about it tonight and next class, after which two or three of you can tell us how the story ends.**

Free, Public Access to U.S. Aerial Photos

TerraServer is an Internet-accessible database of high-resolution photos and topographic maps of the United States. At *terraserver.microsoft.com*, you can enter the name of a famous place, an address, or the latitude and longitude of a location, and your browser will display a photo and map of that location. You can zoom in and out and scroll to adjacent locations. The photo in Figure 1 resulted from a search for "Golden Gate Bridge." Figure 2 is a topographic map of the same location.

TerraServer is the result of a Microsoft marketing promotion. In the mid-1990s, Microsoft redesigned SQL Server, partly in response to industry criticism that SQL Server performed slowly on large databases. To demonstrate the capabilities of the new version, Microsoft decided to publish a database application that used SQL Server to process a very large database. To accomplish the marketing objectives, the database had to be both free and interesting.

Microsoft wanted a database with at least a terabyte of data, and finding a suitable database was difficult. Most large databases are either private or boring. Eventually, Microsoft discovered the library of aerial photos accumulated over the years by the United States Geological Survey (USGS). This library of photos met all of Microsoft's need: The digital files of the photos are huge and are public, and most people are interested in at least a photo of their house or business.

Settling on that database, Microsoft next partnered with a number of other organizations. Compaq provided computers, ADIC and Veritas provided backup hardware and software, and Extreme Networks provided a backbone of private networks. One of the early partners, Aerial Images of Raleigh, North Carolina, split off from the team and now runs a commercial version of the project at *terraserver.com*. Although Microsoft Research developed and supported the original TerraServer, the project is now supported and paid for by Microsoft Home Service.

Because the original USGS photo files are far too large to be transmitted over the Internet, each photo is cut into sections. These sections are then stored as images in the TerraServer database. The database also includes metadata that facilitate image searching as well as smaller amounts of data for administration.

Altogether, the TerraServer database has more than 30 tables. The primary table that stores image data requires 3 terabytes of storage. Because of its size, the database is divided into thirds and is processed by three separate computers. The partitioning of the database is, of course, invisible to the users.

According to Tom Barclay, program manager at Microsoft's Bay Area Research Group, "The largest mistake we made on TerraServer was underestimating its popularity. We initially planned for approximately 1 million hits per day." In fact, the site averages three times that, and as of February 2003 TerraServer had been used by more than 67 million unique users and had processed more than 7.5 billion database queries.

Source: terraserver.microsoft.com (accessed February 2005).

Figure 1   Aerial Photo of the Golden Gate Bridge

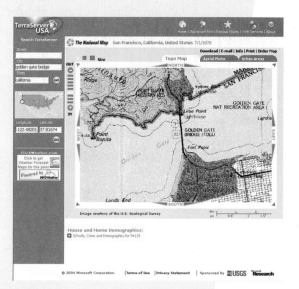

Figure 2   Topographic Map of the Golden Gate Bridge

process SQL (pronounced "see-quell") statements. As an example, the following SQL statement inserts a new row into the *Student* table:

```
INSERT INTO Student
    ([Student Number], [Student Name], HW1, HW2, MidTerm)
    VALUES
    (1000, 'Franklin, Benjamin', 90, 95, 100)
```

Statements like this one are issued "behind the scenes" by programs that process forms. Alternatively, they can also be issued directly to the DBMS by an application program.

You do not need to understand or remember SQL language syntax right now. Instead, just realize that SQL is an international standard for processing a database. Also, SQL can be used to create databases and database structures. You will learn more about SQL if you take a database management class.

Administering the Database

A third DBMS function is to provide tools to assist in the administration of the database. Database administration involves a wide variety of activities. For example, the DBMS can be used to set up a security system involving user accounts, passwords, permissions, and limits for processing the database. To provide database security, a user must sign on using a valid user account before she can process the database. For additional discussion of database security, see the *Security Guide* on page 85a.

Permissions can be limited in very specific ways. In the Student database example, it is possible to limit a particular user to reading only *Student Name* from the *Student* table. A different user could be given permission to read all of the *Student* table, but limited to update only the *HW1*, *HW2*, and *MidTerm* columns. Other users can be given still other permissions.

In addition to security, DBMS administrative functions include backing up database data, adding structures to improve the performance of database applications, removing data that are no longer wanted or needed, and similar tasks. We will discuss these administrative functions further, starting on page 97.

Database Applications

A **database application** is a collection of forms, reports, queries, and application programs that process a database. A database may have one or more applications, and each application may have one or more users. Figure 4-10 shows three applications; the top two have multiple users. These applications have different purposes, features, and functions, but they all process the same inventory data stored in a common database.

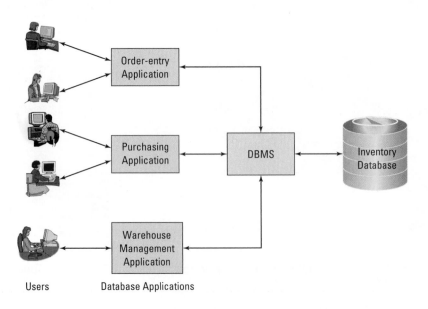

Figure 4-10
Use of Multiple Database
Applications

Forms, Reports, and Queries

Figure 4-2 (page 77) shows a typical database application data entry **form**, and Figure 4-11 shows a typical **report**. Data entry forms are used to read, insert, modify, and delete data. Reports show data in a structured context.

Some reports, like the one in Figure 4-11, also compute values as they present the data. An example is the computation of *Total weighted points* in Figure 4-11. Recall from Chapter 1 that one of the definitions of information is "data presented in a meaningful context." The structure of this report creates information because it shows the student data in a context that will be meaningful to the professor.

DBMS programs provide comprehensive and robust features for querying database data. For example, suppose the professor who uses the Student database remembers that one of the students referred to the topic *barriers to entry* in an office visit, but cannot remember which student or when. If there are hundreds of students and visits recorded in the database, it will take some effort and time for the professor to search through all office visit records to find that event. The DBMS, however, can find any such record quickly. Figure 4-12(a) (page 86) shows a **query** form

Student Report with Emails

Student Name	BAKER, ANDREA		HW1	88	
			HW2	100	
Student Number	1325		MidTerm	78	(= 3 homeworks)
		Total weighted points:		422	

Emails Received

Date	Message
2/1/2004	For homework 1, do you want us to provide notes on our references?
3/15/2004	My group consists of Swee Lau and Stuart Nelson.

Student Name	LAU, SWEE		HW1	75	
			HW2	90	
Student Number	1644		MidTerm	90	(= 3 homeworks)
		Total weighted points:		435	

Emails Received

Date	Message
3/15/2004	Could you please assign me to a group?

Figure 4-11
Example Student Report

SECURITY
GUIDE

Database Security

Databases are repositories of critical, often proprietary, data. Protecting them with appropriate security is therefore vital. The computer that runs the DBMS should always be protected by a **firewall**. The firewall, a computing device located between a firm's internal network and external networks, prevents unauthorized access to the internal network. If the database is not processed over the Internet, the firewall should allow no Internet traffic whatsoever to reach the DBMS computer. If the database is processed over the Internet, the firewall should provide limited access through packet filtering and other techniques. (For more on firewalls, see Chapter 11.)

For the best security, the DBMS computer should be protected by a firewall, and then all other security measures should be designed as if the firewall has been breached. In particular, all operating system and DBMS patches should be installed as soon as they become available. In the spring of 2003, the Slammer worm infected computers running SQL Server. Months before, Microsoft had published a patch that prevented access by this worm. Only computers that did not have patch were infected.

To prevent unauthorized access, no one other than authorized operations personnel should be able to directly access the computer that runs the DBMS. Instead, all access should be via authorized application programs. The computer running the DBMS should be secured behind locked doors, and visits to that room should be recorded in a log.

All major DBMS products have extensive, built-in security features. These features allow for the definition of **user accounts** and **user roles**. Each user account belongs to a specific person. A role is a generic employee function, such as payroll clerk or field salesperson. Each user account and user role is assigned specific actions for specific tables and for columns in those tables. For example, an account can be defined to allow access for a specific person, say Garret Rogers, and a password is defined to protect that account. Some DBMS products, such as Oracle, will disallow the definition of not-strong passwords. (See page 5a for a description of strong passwords.) Accounts that are not protected by strong passwords are locked from use.

Once an account is defined, it can be assigned specific permissions, and it can also be assigned particular roles. When assigned a role, the user will inherit all permissions for that role. The means by which this is done varies from DBMS to DBMS. The nearby figure shows how permissions are assigned to the *Fund_manager* role for the Volunteer database that could be developed for the fundraising situation described at the beginning of the chapter (see page 76).

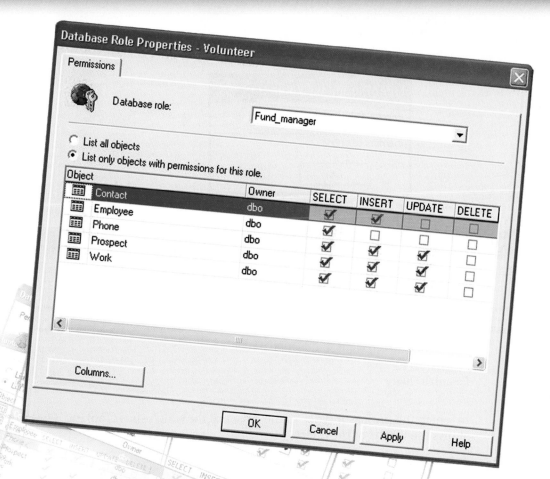

Database Role Properties - Volunteer

Permissions

Database role:

Fund_manager

○ List all objects
● List only objects with permissions for this role.

Object	Owner	SELECT	INSERT	UPDATE	DELETE
Contact	dbo	✔	✔	☐	☐
Employee	dbo	✔	☐	☐	☐
Phone	dbo	✔	✔	✔	☐
Prospect	dbo	✔	✔	✔	☐
Work	dbo	✔	✔	✔	☐

Columns...

OK   Cancel   Apply   Help

The *Fund_manager* role is assigned specific permissions for each of the tables in the Volunteer database. If Garret Rogers is assigned the *Fund_manager* role, then he can, for example, read (select) and insert rows into the Contact table. He may not, however, update or delete any row in Contact. Other permissions for the other tables are as shown. It is also possible to further restrict actions to particular columns of each table.

Most DBMS products log failed attempts to sign on and produce other usage reports as well. The database administrator (DBA) should periodically monitor such logs and reports for suspicious activity.

Finally, it is important to have a plan of action for security emergencies. The steps to take vary from database to database. If the database contains little confidential data, this plan may just have steps to report the security problem and to take corrective action to prevent such problems in the future. However, if the database contains sensitive and confidential data, then the plan should include procedures for preventing further loss and for contacting the corporate legal staff and law enforcement agencies.

DISCUSSION QUESTIONS

1. Summarize the steps that can be taken to protect the DBMS and its databases.

2. Explain why it is important to apply security patches to the operating system and the DBMS as soon as possible.

3. What is the difference between a user account and a user role?

4. In the figure, what actions can accounts having the Plan_manager role take on the Employee table? Why do you think the permission is defined this way?

5. Should managers always have the highest levels of permission? Why or why not?

6. Suppose that a database having valuable proprietary data has been breached. What steps will need to be taken?

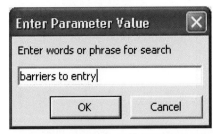

a. Form used to enter phrase for search

Office Visits Keyword Query : Select Query		
Student Name	Date	Notes
▶ BAKER, ANDREA	2/13/2004	Andrea had questions about using IS for raising barriers to entry.
*		

Record: ◄◄ ◄   1   ▶ ▶◄ ▶* of 1

b. Results of query operation

Figure 4-12
Example Query

in which the professor types in the keyword for which she is looking. Figure 4-12(b) shows the results of the query.

Database Application Programs

Forms, reports, and queries work well for standard functions. However, most applications have unique requirements that a simple form, report, or query cannot meet. For example, in the order entry application in Figure 4-10, what should be done if only a portion of a customer's request can be met? If someone wants 10 widgets and we only have three in stock, should a backorder for seven more be generated automatically? Or, should some other action be taken?

Application programs process logic that is specific to a given business need. In the Student database, an example application is one that assigns grades at the end of the term. If the professor grades on a curve, the application reads the breakpoints for each grade from a form, and then processes each row in the *Student* table, allocating a grade based on the break points and the total number of points earned.

Another important use of application programs is to enable database processing over the Internet. For this use, the application program serves as an intermediary between the Web server and the database. The application program responds to events, such as when a user presses a submit button; it also reads, inserts, modifies, and deletes database data.

Figure 4-13 shows four different database application programs running on a Web server computer. Users with browsers connect to the Web server via the Internet. The Web server directs user requests to the appropriate application program. Each program then processes the database as necessary. You will learn more about Web-enabled databases in the discussion of e-commerce in Chapter 8.

Multi-User Processing

Figures 4-10 and 4-13 show multiple users processing the database. Such **multi-user processing** is common, but it does pose unique problems that you, as a future manager, should know about. To understand the nature of those problems, consider the following scenario.

Two users, Andrea and Jeffrey, are clerks using the order entry application in Figure 4-10. Andrea is on the phone with her customer, who wants to purchase five widgets. At the same time, Jeffrey is talking with his customer, who wants to purchase three widgets. Andrea reads the database to determine how many widgets are in

Using the Security Guide
(page 85a)

GOALS

✱ Teach the fundamentals of database security.

✱ Help future users and managers of users understand the relationship of accounts, roles, and permissions.

BACKGROUND AND PRESENTATION STRATEGIES

This guide is a straightforward explanation of database security principles. As such, it is not as suitable for class discussion as other guides. I use it as homework.

As discussed in the Ethics Guide, databases are valuable organizational assets that companies need to protect. This guide presents some safeguards for protecting the database.

We will describe more safeguards and present more information on recovery planning in Chapter 11. We also describe firewalls in that chapter.

Both future users and managers need to understand how administrators assign permissions, user accounts, and roles (or groups of users). With this understanding, they will be better able to help database administrators establish an appropriate security scheme for their departments.

 SUGGESTED RESPONSES FOR DISCUSSION QUESTIONS

1. Straightforward answers from the text:

   Run the DBMS behind a firewall.

   However, DBMS security should be designed as if the firewall has been breached.

   Install operating system and DBMS patches.

   Limit access to the DBMS. (Kelly, in the Ethics Guide, had direct access to the DBMS—the one he was running at home!)

   Secure the DBMS and database in a locked facility and log visits.

   Set up appropriate user accounts, roles, and permissions.

   Review processing and error logs.

   Plan for security breaches and other incidents.

   There are other important security measures, like running the DBMS in an account with as low-level permissions as possible, removing unused stored procedures and triggers, removing access from unused communications protocols, designing applications to prevent SQL injection attacks, and so forth. These are beyond the scope of this text, but it's probably worth mentioning to the students that the items in this guide are not all that should be done. The guide does not address all important security measures—just those that general business professionals should know.

2. The company should apply security patches as soon as possible, because, as we said in Chapter 3, the announcement of the patch is also an announcement of the hole!

   Note, however, that sometimes organizations are using licensed software that will not run if the new version of the DBMS is installed. This situation can create a security problem, so when considering new licensed software, this is a good query to make of the vendors. Will their software prohibit your organization from installing DBMS patches promptly? Also ask that question of other users of that vendor's software.

3. An account belongs to a person. A role belongs to a group of people.

4. The *Plan_manager* role is read only. It is defined this way to protect employee records. People who are given the *Plan_manager* role are likely to be employees. They shouldn't be able to update their own accounts. Also, *Plan_managers* don't need to insert, update, or delete employee data to do their jobs.

5. No. Employees should have the permissions necessary to do their jobs, and no more. This policy, by the way, not only protects the organization, it protects the manager. If a security breach does occur, the manager is out of suspicion. Also, no one can ask the manager to do something that the manager cannot do.

   When I worked as a software development manager, I never wanted (nor had) permission to check in code. Nor did I have the administrator passwords for the systems involved. Not having those passwords, I could never cause a problem. And, late at night, if a programmer hadn't followed procedures to check in code, if he or she asked me to do it, I couldn't; this forced the employee to follow procedures. I did ensure that the system administration and other high-level passwords were escrowed (like key escrow, see Chapter 11), so that if something happened to the people who knew the passwords, we weren't locked out by our own security.

6. The steps to be taken depend on the content of the database and the severity of the breach. In the case of identity information (Social Security number, driver's license number) and credit data (credit card, credit records), state and federal laws require the loss to be reported to a government agency and to the individuals whose identity or other data has been compromised. This is a serious problem, and truly, *the very best way to solve it is not to have it.*

WRAP UP

➤ **Database security is important. As a future manager, help your database administrator set up appropriate user accounts and roles. Take security seriously. Communicate its seriousness to your employees. Protect your passwords, and ensure your employees protect theirs as well.**

➤ **In most cases, as a manager, you should be trained on your responsibilities when a security breach has occurred. If not, ask your manager or contact in the IS department. As a manager, you have a data security responsibility, even if no one tells you that you do.**

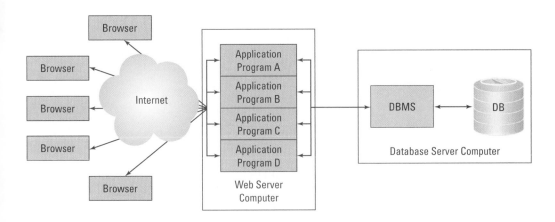

Figure 4-13
Four Application
Programs on Web
Server Computer

inventory. (She unknowingly invokes the order entry application when she types in her data entry form.) The DBMS returns a row showing 10 widgets in inventory.

Meanwhile, just after Andrea accesses the database, Jeffrey's customer says she wants widgets, and so he also reads the database (via the order entry application program) to determine how many widgets are in inventory. The DBMS returns the same row to him, indicating that 10 widgets are available.

Andrea's customer now says that he'll take five units, and Andrea records this fact in her form. The application rewrites the widget row back to the database, indicating that there are five widgets in inventory.

Meanwhile, Jeffrey's customer says that he'll take three units. Jeffrey records this fact in his form, and the application rewrites the widget row back to the database. However, Jeffrey's application knows nothing about Andrea's work and subtracts 3 from the original count of 10, thus storing an incorrect count of 7 widgets in inventory.

Clearly, there is a problem. We began with 10 widgets, Andrea took 5 and Jeffrey took 3, but the database says there are 7 widgets in inventory. It should show 2, not 7.

This problem, known as the **lost-update problem**, exemplifies one of the special characteristics of multi-user database processing. To prevent this problem, some type of locking must be used to coordinate the activities of users who know nothing about one another. Locking brings its own set of problems, however, and those problems must be addressed as well. We will not delve further into this topic here, however.

Realize from this example that converting a single-user database to a multi-user database requires more than simply connecting another computer. The logic of the underlying application processing needs to be adjusted as well.

Be aware of possible data conflicts when you manage business activities that involve multi-user processing. If you find inaccurate results that seem not to have a cause, you may be experiencing multi-user data conflicts. Contact your MIS department for assistance.

Enterprise DBMS Versus Personal DBMS

DBMS products fall into two broad categories. **Enterprise DBMS** products process large organizational and workgroup databases. These products support many users, perhaps thousands, of users and many different database applications. Such DBMS products support 24/7 operations and can manage databases that span dozens of different magnetic disks with hundreds of gigabytes or more of data. IBM's DB2, Microsoft's SQL Server, and Oracle's Oracle are examples of enterprise DBMS products.

Personal DBMS products are designed for smaller, simpler database applications. Such products are used for personal or small workgroup applications that involve fewer than a 100 users, and normally fewer than 15. In fact, the great bulk of databases in this category have only a single user. The professor's Student database is an example of a database that is processed by a personal DBMS product.

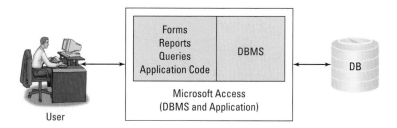

Figure 4-14
Personal Database System

In the past, there were many personal DBMS products—Paradox, dBase, R:base, and FoxPro. Microsoft put these products out of business when they developed Access and included it in the Microsoft Office suite. Today, the only remaining personal DBMS is Microsoft Access.

To avoid one point of confusion for you in the future, the separation of application programs and the DBMS shown in Figure 4-10 is true only for enterprise DBMS products. Microsoft Access includes features and functions for application processing along with the DBMS itself. For example, Access has a form generator and a report generator. Thus, as shown in Figure 4-14, Access is both a DBMS *and* an application development product.

Developing a Database Application System

In Chapter 6, we will describe application development in detail. However, business professionals and other users have such a critical role in the development of database systems that in this chapter we need to introduce two topics—data modeling and database design.

The reason that user involvement is so important for database development is that the database design depends entirely on how users view their business environment. Think about the Student database. What data should it contain? Possibilities are: *Students, Classes, Grades, Emails, Office_Visits, Majors, Advisers, Student_Organizations*—the list could go on and on. Further, how much detail should be included in each? Should the database include campus addresses? Home addresses? Billing addresses?

In fact, there are several possibilities, and the database developers do not and cannot know what to include. They do know, however, that a database must include all the data necessary for the users to perform their jobs. Ideally, it contains that amount of data and no more. So, during database development, the developers must rely on the users to tell them what to include in the database.

Database structures can be complex, in some cases, very complex. So, before building the database, the developers construct a logical representation of database data called a **data model**. It describes the data and relationships that will be stored in the database. It is akin to a blueprint. Just as building architects create a blueprint before they start building, so, too, database developers create a data model before they start designing the database. To understand the basis of the problem, see the *Problem Solving Guide* on page 89a.

The database development process is summarized in Figure 4-15. Interviews with users lead to database requirements, which are summarized in a data model. Once the users have approved (validated) the data model, it is transformed into a database design. That design is then implemented into database structures. We will consider data modeling and database design briefly in the next two sections. Again, your goal should be to learn the process so that you can be an effective user representative for a development effort.

The Entity-Relationship Data Model

Video

The most popular technique for creating a data model is the **entity-relationship (E-R) data model**. With it, developers describe the content of a database by defining the things (*entities*), that will be stored in the database, and the *relationships* among those

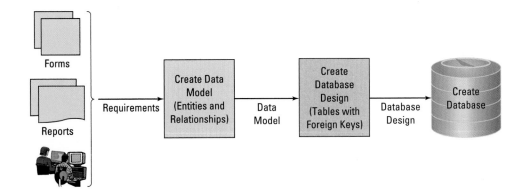

Figure 4-15
Database Development
Process

entities. A second, less popular tool for data modeling is the **Unified Modeling Language (UML)**. We will not describe that tool here. However, if you learn how to interpret E-R models, with a bit of study, you will be able to understand UML models as well.

Entities

An **entity** is some thing that the users want to track. Examples of entities are *Order*, *Customer*, *Salesperson*, and *Item*. Some entities represent a physical object, such as *Item* or *Salesperson;* others represent a logical construct or transaction, such as *Order* or *Contract*. For reasons beyond this discussion, entity names are always singular. We use *Order* not *Orders; Salesperson* not *Salespersons*.

Entities have **attributes** that describe characteristics of the entity. Example attributes of *Order* are *OrderNumber, OrderDate, SubTotal, Tax, Total,* and so forth. Example attributes of *Salesperson* are *SalespersonName, Email, Phone,* and so forth.

Entities have an **identifier**, which is an attribute (or group of attributes) whose value is associated with one and only one entity instance. For example, *OrderNumber* is an identifier of *Order,* because only one *Order* instance has a given value of *OrderNumber*. For the same reason, *CustomerNumber* is an identifier of *Customer*. If each member of the sales staff has a unique name, then *SalespersonName* is an identifier of *Salesperson*.

Before we continue, consider that last sentence. Is the salesperson's name unique among the sales staff? Both now and in the future? Who decides the answer to such a question? Only the users know whether this is true; the database developers cannot know. This example underlines why it is important for you to be able to interpret data models, because only users like yourself will know for sure.

Figure 4-16 shows examples of entities for the Student database. Each entity is shown in a rectangle. The name of the entity is just above the rectangle, and the identifier is shown in a section at the top of the entity. Entity attributes are shown in the

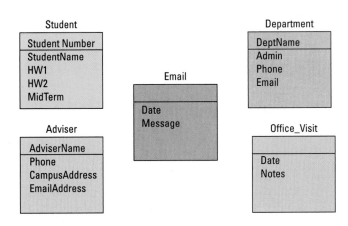

Figure 4-16
Student Data Model Entities

Immanuel Kant, Data Modeler

Only the users can say whether a data model accurately reflects their business environment. What happens when the users disagree among themselves? What if one user says orders have a single salesperson but another says that sales teams produce some orders? Who is correct?

It's tempting to say, "The correct model is the one that better represents the real world." The problem with this statement is that data models do not model "the real world." A data model is simply a model of what the data modeler perceives. This very important point can be difficult to understand; but if you do understand it, you will save many hours in data model validation meetings and be a much better data modeling team member.

The German philosopher Immanuel Kant reasoned that what we perceive as reality is based on our perceptive apparatus. That which we perceive he called phenomena. Our perceptions, such as of light and sound, are processed by our brains and made meaningful. But we do not and cannot know whether the images we create from the perceptions have anything to do with what might or might not really be.

Kant used the term noumenal world to refer to the essence of "things in themselves"—to whatever it is out there that gives rise to our perceptions and images. He used the term phenomenal world to refer to what we humans perceive and construct.

It is easy to confuse the noumenal world with the phenomenal world, because we share the phenomenal world with other humans. All of us have the same mental apparatus, and we all make the same constructions. If you ask your roommate to hand you the toothpaste, she hands you the toothpaste, not a hairbrush. But the fact that we share this mutual view does not mean that the mutual view describes in any way what is truly out there. Dogs construct a world based on smells, and orca whales construct a world based on sounds. What the "real world" is to a dog, a whale, and a human are completely different. All of this means that we cannot ever justify a data model as a "better representation of the real world." Nothing that humans can do represents the real, noumenal world. A data model, therefore, is a model of a human's model of what appears to be "out there." For example, a model of a salesperson is a model of the model that humans make of salespeople.

To return to the question that we started with, what do we do when people disagree about what should be in a data model? First, realize that anyone

attempting to justify her data model as a better representation of the real world is saying, quite arrogantly, "The way I think of the world is the way that counts." Second, in times of disagreement we must ask the question, "How well does the data model fit the mental models of the people who are going to use the system?" The person who is constructing the data model may think the model under construction is a weird way of viewing the world, but that is not the point. The only valid point is whether it reflects how the users view their world. Will it enable the users to do their jobs?

DISCUSSION QUESTIONS

1. What does a data model represent?

2. Explain why it is easy for humans to confuse the phenomenal world with the noumenal world.

3. If someone were to say to you, "My model is a better model of the real world," how would you respond?

4. In your own words, how should you proceed when two people disagree on what is to be included in a data model?

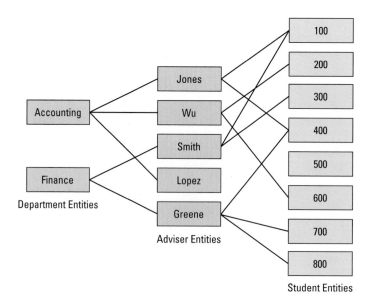

Figure 4-17
Example of Department,
Adviser, and Student Entities
and Relationships

remainder of the rectangle. In Figure 4-16, the *Adviser* entity has an identifier called *AdviserName* and the attributes *Phone*, *CampusAddress*, and *EmailAddress*.

Observe that the entities *Email* and *Office_Visit* do not have an identifier. Unlike *Student* or *Adviser*, the users do not have an attribute that identifies a particular email. We could make one up. For example, we could say that the identifier of *Email* is *EmailNumber*, but if we do so we are not modeling how the users view their world. Instead, we are forcing something onto the users. Be aware of this possibility when you review data models about your business. Do not allow the database developers to create something that is not part of your business world.

Relationships

Entities have **relationships** to each other. An *Order*, for example, has a relationship to a *Customer* entity and also to a *Salesperson* entity. In the Student database, a *Student* has a relationship to an *Adviser*, and an *Adviser* has a relationship to a *Department*.

Figure 4-17 shows sample *Department*, *Adviser*, and *Student* entities and their relationships. For simplicity, this figure shows just the identifier of the entities and not the other attributes. For this sample data, *Accounting* has three professors, Jones, Wu, and Lopez, and *Finance* has two professors, Smith and Greene.

The relationship between *Advisers* and *Students* is a bit more complicated, because in this example an adviser is allowed to advise many students, and a student is allowed to have many advisers. Perhaps this happens because students can have multiple majors. In any case, note that Professor Jones advises students 100 and 400 and that student 100 is advised by both Professors Jones and Smith.

Diagrams like the one in Figure 4-17 are too cumbersome for use in database design discussions. Instead, database designers use diagrams called **entity-relationship (E-R) diagrams**. Figure 4-18 shows an E-R diagram for the data in Figure 4-17. In this figure, all of the entities of one type are represented by a single rectangle. Thus, there are rectangles for the *Department*, *Adviser*, and *Student* entities. Attributes are shown as before in Figure 4-16.

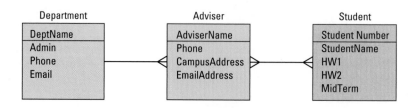

Figure 4-18
Example Relationships—
Version 1

Using the Problem Solving Guide (page 89a)

GOALS

* Understand why the statement, "My data model is a better model of reality than your data model" is nonsense—and arrogant!

* Realize that a data model is a model of users' mental models, *not* a model of reality.

* Stimulate students' curiosity about the philosophical foundations of information systems.

BACKGROUND AND PRESENTATION STRATEGIES

This guide presents two points: one practical and pragmatic, the other deep and philosophical. I have fun with this material; students are surprised to be discussing Immanuel Kant in this class.

This guide works best as a class discussion. I recommend either assigning it as reading ahead of time or having the students read it in class. I ask the students to discuss it among themselves, but if they're going nowhere, I lead the discussion along the following lines:

Humans have a brain, an instruction set. That brain has a built-in mental apparatus, or set of instincts if you will. That instruction set or instinctive structure enables us to process our perceptions and create what we refer to as "the real world." We think that world is real because we share the same mental apparatus with other humans. All of our interactions with other people reinforce the idea of the "real world," but it's a shared mutual hallucination. We have no idea of the nature of the correspondence between what we think and what is "out there." All we can say is that so far, our mental apparatus has enabled the human species to survive and flourish.

For background on the science of our mental apparatus, see Steven Pinker, *The Blank Slate* (Viking Adult, 2002).

For Kant, the *noumenal world* is that which exists—that which is "out there." He and others who followed (Karl Popper for one) believed that humans can know absolutely nothing about that world. We can know only what we can perceive, process, and construct. That world, the one we perceive and construct, is the *phenomenal world*.

For some students, understanding this difference leads to a fundamental existential awareness, one that can be uncomfortable: What we've always thought is "out there" is really "in here," inside my brain. The reality I know is in my head; I'm trapped by my perceptions and my mental apparatus. That's all I can ever know.

Now, why talk about this in an MIS class? In particular, why talk about it in the database lecture? A data model (and later, a database) is a model of the phenomenal world, not of the noumenal world. *It is not a model of reality because we cannot know what reality is.* Instead, it is a *model of users' models* of reality. It is a model of human models.

"What's the bottom line?" some students will ask. It is this: *No one can ever say, sensibly, "My model is a better model of the real world than your model."* The only accurate statement is "My model is a better model of the users' model than your model is."

I have wasted literally hundreds of hours of my life in meetings in which someone said that his or her model was a better model of reality. Then, everyone argues that, no, their model is a better model of reality. Those statements are arrogant: In essence, they are saying, "The way I see the world is the one that counts."

A data model is a model of how the users construct their world. Period. No more and no less. *If you want to know whose model is better, ask the users.*

This is where our students come in. *As future business people, only they can determine which data model fits their world.* Hence, students need to learn how to interpret a data model. This is why I have included the material in this chapter on the entity-relationship model.

I hope you have as much fun with this guide as I do!

 SUGGESTED RESPONSES FOR DISCUSSION QUESTIONS

1. A data model is a representation of the users' world. To illustrate this point, construct an E-R model in class about some aspect of the students' lives. Maybe one involving the entities: STUDENT, AUTO, PARKING_PERMIT, VIOLATION, and PAYMENT.

   ➤ **What is the relationship between STUDENT and AUTO?**

   ➤ **How many AUTOs does a STUDENT relate to? How many STUDENTs does an AUTO relate to?**

   ➤ **I think one can justify that the relationship is 1:1. In this case, university policy dictates that a student may have a permit for one auto only. The university parking department doesn't care that the** student has an auto collection at home. Also, that auto is owned by one student.

➤ **Equally possible, I think one could say the relationship is 1:N. In this case, a student is allowed permits for each auto he or she owns. But each auto is owned by at most one student.**

➤ **Equally possible, I think one could say the relationship is N:1. In this case, the university allows a permit for only one auto per student, but it allows multiple students to be affiliated with an auto, say, for a group parking permit.**

➤ **Equally possible, I think one could say the relationship is N:M. In this case, the university allows multiple autos per permit, and it recognizes multiple students to be affiliated with a particular auto for a group parking permit.**

➤ **Pick one (it doesn't matter which),** *and say, "My model is a better model of reality than your model."*

Have fun. And, this is just one relationship! We've got several more to go.

Now consider a business data model that has 100 entities. How long will it take to build the data model? And who pays for the data modeling meetings? Ugh.

2. Humans confuse the two worlds because we share a mutual hallucination that the phenomenal world is real. When I say (to a student), please pass me your book, the student passes me the book and not her purse.

3. You could respond with a lecture about Immanuel Kant and his epistemological theories.

Or, and probably far preferable, you could tailor your response to who is making the statement. If it was made by a data modeler (shame on them!), you could say, "Well, that might be. But we're building this information system for the users, so let's ask them." If the person making this statement is a user, and if that person speaks for all the other users, then you say, "Thanks for the correction," and you change the data model to that view. If that person is just one user, then you say, "Great. Let's see how your model works for the other users."

4. The answer is really the same as question 3, but let the students respond. Let them paraphrase what you've said and summarize what they've learned.

WRAP UP

Some possible concluding remarks:

➤ **I'll bet you never thought you'd be hearing about Immanuel Kant in this class! We've just seen one of the reasons why this field is so interesting: The study of the human uses of information systems takes you to so many interesting fields!**

➤ **The bottom line: A data model is a model of the users' world.**

➤ **Thus, and this is very important, the only people who can verify that the data model is accurate is** *you,* **the future users!**

➤ **Hence,** *learn how to interpret a data model.* **It's not that hard, and it will be a useful skill. You can also use data modeling skills to clarify your own thinking (e.g., to clarify your thinking about organizational relationships in a supply chain).**

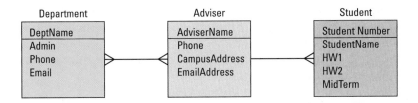

Figure 4-19
Example Relationships—
Version 2

Additionally, a line is used to represent a relationship between two entities. Notice the line between *Department* and *Adviser*, for example. The forked lines on the right side of that line signify that a department may have more than one adviser. The little lines, which are referred to as a **crow's foot**, are shorthand for the multiple lines between *Department* and *Adviser* in Figure 4-17. Relationships like this one are called **1:N**, or **one-to-many**, relationships because one department can have many advisers.

Now examine the line between *Adviser* and *Student*. Here, a crow's foot appears at each end of the line. This notation signifies that an adviser can be related to many students and that a student can be related to many advisers, which is the situation in Figure 4-17. Relationships like this one are called **N:M**, or **many-to-many**, relationships because one adviser can have many students and one student can have many advisers.

Students sometimes find the notation N:M confusing. Interpret the *N* and *M* to mean that a variable number, greater than one, is allowed on each side of the relationship. Such a relationship is not written *N:N*, because that notation would imply that there are the same number of entities on each side of the relationship, which is not necessarily true. *N:M* means that more than one entity is allowed on each side of the relationship and that the number of entities on each side can be different.

Figure 4-18 is an example of an entity-relationship diagram. Unfortunately, there are several different styles of entity-relationship diagrams. This one is called, not surprisingly, a **crow's-foot diagram version**. You may learn other versions if you take a database management class.

Figure 4-19 shows the same entities with different assumptions. Here, advisers may advise in more than one department, but a student may have only one adviser, representing a policy that students may not have multiple majors.

Which, if either, of these versions is correct? Only the users know. These alternatives illustrate the kinds of questions you will need to answer when a database designer asks you to check a data model for correctness.

The crow's-foot notation shows the maximum number of entities that can be involved in a relationship. Accordingly, they are called the relationship's **maximum cardinality**. Common examples of maximum cardinality are 1:N, N:M, and 1:1 (not shown).

Another important question is, "What is the minimum number of entities required in the relationship?" Must an adviser have a student to advise, and must a student have an adviser? Constraints on minimum requirements are called **minimum cardinalities**.

Figure 4-20 presents a third version of this E-R diagram that shows both maximum and minimum cardinalities. The vertical bar on a line means that at least one entity of that type is required. The small oval means that the entity is optional; the relationship *need not* have an entity of that type.

Thus, in Figure 4-20 a department is not required to have a relationship to any adviser, but an adviser is required to belong to a department. Similarly, an adviser is

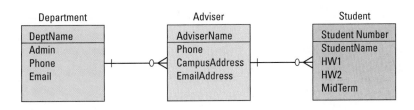

Figure 4-20
Example Relationships
Showing Minimum
Cardinalities

not required to have a relationship to a student, but a student is required to have a relationship to an adviser. Note, also, that the maximum cardinalities in Figure 4-20 have been changed so that both are 1:N.

Is the model in Figure 4-20 a good one? It depends on the rules of the university. Again, only the users know for sure.

Database Design

Database design is the process of converting a data model into tables, relationships, and data constraints. The database design team transforms entities into tables and expresses relationships by defining foreign keys. Database design is a complicated subject; as with data modeling, it occupies weeks in a database management class. In this section, however, we will introduce two important database design concepts: normalization and the representation of two kinds of relationships. The first concept is a foundation of database design, and the second will help you understand key considerations made during design.

Normalization

Normalization is the process of converting poorly structured tables into two or more well-structured tables. A table is such a simple construct that you may wonder how one could possibly be poorly structured. In truth, there are many ways that tables can be malformed—so many, in fact, that researchers have published hundreds of papers on this topic alone.

Consider the *Employee* table in Figure 4-21(a). It lists employee names, hire dates, email addresses, and the name and number of the department in which the employee works. This table seems innocent enough. But consider what happens when the Accounting department changes its name to Accounting and Finance. Because department names are duplicated in this table, every row that has a value of "Accounting" must be changed to "Accounting and Finance."

Data Integrity Problems.   Suppose the Accounting name change is correctly made in two rows, but not in the third. The result is shown in Figure 4-21(b). This table has what is called a **data integrity problem**: Some rows indicate that the name of Department 100 is "Accounting and Finance," and another row indicates that the name of Department 100 is "Accounting."

Employee

Name	HireDate	Email	DeptNo	DeptName
Jones	Feb 1, 2002	Jones@ourcompany.com	100	Accounting
Smith	Dec 3, 2004	Smith@ourcompany.com	200	Marketing
Chau	March 7, 2004	Chau@ourcompany.com	100	Accounting
Greene	July 17, 2003	Greene@ourcompany.com	100	Accounting

a. Table before Update

Employee

Name	HireDate	Email	DeptNo	DeptName
Jones	Feb 1, 2002	Jones@ourcompany.com	100	Finance and Accounting
Smith	Dec 3, 2004	Smith@ourcompany.com	200	Marketing
Chau	March 7, 2004	Chau@ourcompany.com	100	Finance and Accounting
Greene	July 17, 2003	Greene@ourcompany.com	100	Accounting

b. Table with Incomplete Update

Figure 4-21
A Poorly Designed Employee Table

This problem is easy to spot in this small table. But consider a table like the *Image* table in the TerraServer database that has over 300 million rows. Once a table that large develops serious data integrity problems, months of labor will be required to remove them.

Data integrity problems are serious. A table that has data integrity problems will produce incorrect and inconsistent information. Users will lose confidence in the information, and the system will develop a poor reputation. Information systems with poor reputations become serious burdens to the organizations that use them.

Normalizing for Data Integrity.   The data integrity problem can occur only if data are duplicated. Because of this, one easy way to eliminate the problem is to eliminate the duplicated data. We can do this by transforming the table in Figure 4-21 into two tables, as shown in Figure 4-22. Here, the name of the department is stored just once, therefore no data inconsistencies can occur.

Of course, to produce an employee report that includes the department name, the two tables in Figure 4-22 will need to be joined back together. Because such joining of tables is common, DBMS products have been programmed to perform it efficiently, but it still requires work. From this example, you can see a trade-off in database design: Normalized tables eliminate data duplication, but they can be slower to process. Dealing with such trade-offs is an important consideration in database design.

The general goal of normalization is to construct tables such that every table has a *single* topic or theme. In good writing, every paragraph should have a single theme. This is true of databases as well; every table should have a single theme. The problem with the table in Figure 4-21 is that it has two independent themes: employees and departments. The way to correct the problem is to split the table into two tables, each with its own theme. In this case, we create an *Employee* table and a *Department* table, as shown in Figure 4-22.

As mentioned, there are dozens of ways that tables can be poorly formed. Database practitioners classify tables into various **normal forms** according to the kinds of problems they have. Transforming a table into a normal form to remove duplicated data and other problems is called *normalizing* the table.[2] Thus, when you hear a database designer say, "Those tables are not normalized," she does not mean that the tables have irregular, not-normal data. Instead, she means that the tables have a format that could cause data integrity problems.

Employee

Name	HireDate	Email	DeptNo
Jones	Feb 1, 2002	Jones@ourcompany.com	100
Smith	Dec 3, 2004	Smith@ourcompany.com	200
Chau	March 7, 2004	Chau@ourcompany.com	100
Greene	July 17, 2003	Greene@ourcompany.com	100

Department

DeptNo	DeptName
100	Accounting
200	Marketing
300	Information Systems

Figure 4-22
Two Normalized Tables

[2]See David Kroenke, *Database Processing,* 10th ed. (Upper Saddle River, NJ: Prentice Hall, 2006) for more information.

Figure 4-23
Transforming a Data Model
into a Database Design

- Represent each entity with a table
  - Entity identifier becomes table key
  - Entity attributes become table columns
- Normalize tables as necessary
- Represent relationships
  - Use foreign keys
  - Add additional tables for N:M relationships

Summary of Normalization.   As a future user of databases, you do not need to know the details of normalization. Instead, understand the general principle that every normalized (well-formed) table has one and only one theme. Further, tables that are not normalized are subject to data integrity problems.

Be aware, too, that normalization is just one criterion for evaluating database designs. Because normalized designs can be slower to process, database designers sometimes choose to accept non-normalized tables. The best design depends on the users' requirements.

Representing Relationships

Figure 4-23 shows the steps involved in transforming a data model into a relational database design. First, the database designer creates a table for each entity. The identifier of the entity becomes the key of the table. Each attribute of the entity becomes a column of the table. Next, the resulting tables are normalized so that each table has a single theme. Once that has been done, the next step is to represent relationship among those tables.

For example, consider the E-R diagram in Figure 4-24(a). The *Adviser* entity has a 1:N relationship to the *Student* entity. To create the database design, we construct a table for *Adviser* and a second table for *Student,* as shown in Figure 4-24(b). The key of the *Adviser* table is *AdviserName,* and the key of the *Student* table is *StudentNumber.*

Further, the *EmailAddress* attribute of the *Adviser* entity becomes the *EmailAddress* column of the *Adviser* table, and the *StudentName* and *MidTerm* attributes of the *Student* entity become the *StudentName* and *MidTerm* columns of the *Student* table.

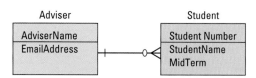

Adviser	Student
AdviserName	Student Number
EmailAddress	StudentName
	MidTerm

a. One-to-Many Relationship between Adviser and Student Entities

Adviser Table—Key is AdviserName.

AdviserName	EmailAddress
Jones	Jones@myuniv.edu
Choi	Choi@myuniv.edu
Jackson	Jackson@myuniv.edu

Student Table—Key is StudentNumber.

StudentNumber	StudentName	MidTerm
100	Lisa	90
200	Jennie	85
300	Jason	82
400	Terry	95

Figure 4-24
Representing a 1:N
Relationship

b. Creating a Table for Each Entity

Adviser Table—Key is AdviserName.

AdviserName	Email
Jones	Jones@myuniv.edu
Choi	Choi@myuniv.edu
Jackson	Jackson@myuniv.edu

Foreign Key Column Represents Relationship

Student—Key is StudentNumber.

StudentNumber	StudentName	MidTerm	AdviserName
100	Lisa	90	Jackson
200	Jennie	85	Jackson
300	Jason	82	Choi
400	Terry	95	Jackson

c. Using the AdviserName Foreign Key to Represent the One-to-Many Relationship

Figure 4-24 (continued)

The next task is to represent the relationship. Because we are using the relational model, we know that we must add a foreign key to one of the two tables. The possibilities are: (1) place the foreign key *StudentNumber* in the *Adviser* table or (2) place the foreign key *AdviserName* in the *Student* table.

The correct choice is to place *AdviserName* in the *Student* table, as shown in Figure 4-24(c). To determine a student's adviser, we just look into the *AdviserName* column of that student's row. To determine the adviser's students, we search the *AdviserName* column in the *Student* table to determine which rows have that adviser's name. If a student changes advisers, we simply change the value in the *AdviserName* column. Changing *Jackson* to *Jones* in the first row, for example, will assign student 100 to Professor Jones.

For this data model, placing *StudentNumber* in *Adviser* would be incorrect. If we were to do that, we could assign only one student to an adviser. There is no place to assign a second adviser.

This strategy for placing foreign keys will not work for all relationships, however. Consider the data model in Figure 4-25(a) (next page); here there is a N:M relationship between advisers and students. An adviser may have many students, and a student may have multiple advisers (for multiple majors). The strategy we used for the 1:N data model will not work here. To see why, examine Figure 4-25(b). If student 100 has more than one adviser, there is no place to record second or subsequent advisers.

It turns out that to represent an N:M relationship, we need to create a third table, as shown in Figure 4-25(c). The third table has two columns, *AdviserName* and *StudentNumber*. Each row of the table means that the given adviser advises the student with the given number.

As you can imagine, there is a great deal more to database design than we have presented here. Still, this section should give you an idea of the tasks that need to be accomplished to create a database. You should also realize that the database design is a direct consequence of decisions made in the data model. If the data model is wrong, the database design will be wrong as well.

▓ Importance of Users' Review

As stated, a database is a model of how the users view their business world. This means that the users are the final judges as to what data the database should contain and how the records in that database should be related to one another.

The easiest time to change the database structure is during the data modeling stage. Changing a relationship from one-to-many to many-to-many in a data model is simply a matter of changing the 1:N notation to N:M. However, once the database has

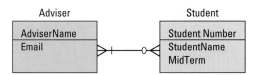

Adviser   Student

| AdviserName |
| Email |

| Student Number |
| StudentName |
| MidTerm |

a. Many-to-Many Relationship between Adviser and Student

Adviser—Key is AdviserName.

AdviserName	Email
Jones	Jones@myuniv.edu
Choi	Choi@myuniv.edu
Jackson	Jackson@myuniv.edu

> No room to place second or third AdviserName

Student—Key is StudentNumber.

StudentNumber	StudentName	MidTerm	AdviserName
100	Lisa	90	Jackson
200	Jennie	85	Jackson
300	Jason	82	Choi
400	Terry	95	Jackson

b. Incorrect Representation of N:M Relationship

Adviser—Key is AdviserName.

AdviserName	Email
Jones	Jones@myuniv.edu
Choi	Choi@myuniv.edu
Jackson	Jackson@myuniv.edu

Student—Key is StudentNumber.

StudentNumber	StudentName	MidTerm
100	Lisa	90
200	Jennie	85
300	Jason	82
400	Terry	95

Adviser_Student_Intersection

AdviserName	StudentNumber
Jackson	100
Jackson	200
Choi	300
Jackson	400
Choi	100
Jones	100

> Student 100 has three advisers.

Figure 4-25
Representing a N:M Relationship

c. Adviser_Student_Intersection Table Represents the Many-to-Many Relationship

been constructed, loaded with data, and application forms, reports, queries, and application programs created, changing a one-to-many relationship to many-to-many means weeks of work.

You can glean some idea of why this might be true by contrasting Figure 4-24(c) with Figure 4-25(c). Suppose that instead of having just a few rows, each table has thousands of rows; in that case, transforming the database from one format to the other involves considerable work. Even worse, however, is that application components will need to be changed as well. For example, if students have at most one adviser, then a single text box can be used to enter *AdviserName*. If students can have multiple advisers, then a multiple-row table will need to be used to enter *AdviserName* and a program will need to be written to store the values of *AdviserName* into the *Adviser_Student_Intersection* table. There are dozens of other consequences as well, consequences that will translate into wasted labor and wasted expense.

The conclusion from this discussion is that user review of a data model is crucial. When a database is developed for your use, you must carefully review the data model. If you do not understand any aspect of it, you should ask for clarification until you do. The data model must accurately reflect your view of the business. If it does not, the database will be designed incorrectly, and the applications will be difficult to use, if not worthless. Do not proceed unless the data model is accurate.

As a corollary, when asked to review a data model, take that review seriously. Devote the time necessary to perform a thorough review. Any mistakes you miss will come back to haunt you, and by then the cost of correction may be very high with regard to both time and expense. This brief introduction to data modeling shows why databases can be more difficult to develop than spreadsheets. This difficulty causes some people to resist the idea of a database, as discussed in the *Opposing Forces Guide* on page 97a.

Database Administration

Databases are valuable and often critical resources. Some multi-user databases have hundreds or thousands of users, all of whom depend on database applications to perform their jobs. Some databases are critical components of operational systems, and the failure of the database can mean stopping the production line. Smaller databases, even personal databases, can contain critical data, and their failure can mean lost opportunities and wasted labor.

In general, the more encompassing the database—the more systems and business functions it touches—the greater the utility of the database. At the same time, the more encompassing the database, the greater the potential for problems. For example, those who work in production and those who work in sales have very different goals and objectives. Long-term planning in production is 3 to 5 years from now; long-term planning in sales is, "What are we doing after lunch?" For a database being designed to serve both groups, a development pace that seems timely to one group can seem glacial to another.

In light of both the importance and the management challenges of databases, most organizations have created a staff function called **database administration**. In smaller organizations, this function usually is served by a single person, sometimes even on a part-time basis. Larger organizations assign several people to an office of database administration. Depending on context, the letters **DBA** either stand for the *database administrator* or for the *office of database administration.*

The purpose of database administration is to manage the development, operation, and maintenance of the database so as to achieve the organization's objectives. This function requires balancing conflicting goals: protecting the database while maximizing its availability for authorized use. It is a staff function; DBAs seldom have direct management authority over either developers or users. Yet to be successful, the DBA must often influence and control the actions of each group.

Figure 4-26 (page 98) summarizes database administration tasks. In the next section, we will describe these tasks as they would be performed by an office of database administration that is supporting a major enterprise database. Database administration for smaller workgroup and personal databases is similar, except that the work is reduced in scale and scope.

DBA Development Responsibilities

Generally, the DBA function is staffed sometime during the first systems development project that requires the database. The earlier in the systems development process the DBA is created, the better. We will say more about project management for systems development in Chapter 6; here we will focus on those aspects that pertain to the DBA.

No, Thanks, I'll Use a Spreadsheet

'm not buying all this stuff about databases. I've tried them and they're a pain—way too complicated to set up, and most of the time, a spreadsheet works just as well. We had one project at the car dealership that seemed pretty simple to me: We wanted to keep track of customers and the models of used cars they were interested in. Then, when we got a car on the lot, we could query the database to see who wanted a car of that type and generate a letter to them.

"It took forever to build that system, and it never did work right. We hired three different consultants, and the last one finally did get it to work. But it was so complicated to produce the letters. You had to query the data in Access to generate some kind of file, then open Word, then go through some mumbo jumbo using mail/merge to cause Word to find the letter and put all the Access data in the right spot. I once printed over two hundred letters and had the name in the address spot and the address in the name spot and no date. And it took me over an hour to do even that. I just wanted to do the query and push a button to get my letters generated. I gave up. Some of the salespeople are still trying to use it, but not me.

"No, unless you are General Motors or Toyota, I wouldn't mess with a database. You have to have professional IS people to create it and keep it running. Besides, I don't really want to share my data with anyone. I work pretty hard to develop my client list. Why would I want to give it away?

"My motto is, 'Keep it simple.' I use an Excel spreadsheet with four columns: Name, Phone Number, Car Interests, and Notes. When I get a new customer, I enter the name and phone number, and then I put the make and model of cars they like in the Car Interests column. Anything else that I think is important I put in the Notes column—extra phone numbers, address data if I have it, email addresses, spouse names, last time I called them, etc. The system isn't fancy, but it works fine.

"When I want to find something, I use Excel's Data Filter. I can usually get what I need. Of course, I still can't send form letters, but it really doesn't matter. I get most of my sales using the phone, anyway."

DISCUSSION QUESTIONS

1. To what extent do you agree with the opinions presented here? To what extent are the concerns expressed here justified? To what extent might they be due to other factors?

2. What problems do you see with the way that the car salesperson stores address data? What will he have to do if he ever does want to send a letter or an email to all of his customers?

3. From his comments, how many different themes are there in his data? What does this imply about his ability to keep his data in a spreadsheet?

4. Does the concern about not sharing data relate to whether or not he uses a database?

5. Apparently, management at the car dealership allows the salespeople to keep their contact data in whatever format they want. If you were management, how would you justify this policy? What disadvantages are there to this policy?

6. Suppose you manage the sales representatives, and you decide to require all of them to use a database to keep track of customers and customer car interest data. How would you sell your decision to this salesperson?

7. Given the limited information in this scenario, do you think a database or a spreadsheet is a better solution?

Category	Database Administration Task	Description
Development	Create and staff DBA function	Size of DBA group depends on size and complexity of database. Groups range from one part-time person to small group.
	Form steering committee	Consists of representatives of all user groups. Forum for community-wide discussions and decisions.
	Specify requirements	Ensure that all appropriate user input is considered.
	Validate data model	Check data model for accuracy and completeness.
	Evaluate application design	Verify that all necessary forms, reports, queries, and applications are developed. Validate design and usability of application components.
Operation	Manage processing rights and responsibilities	Determine processing rights/restrictions on each table and column.
	Manage security	Add and delete users and user groups as necessary; ensure that security system works.
	Track problems and manage resolution	Develop system to record and manage resolution of problems.
	Monitor database performance	Provide expertise/solutions for performance improvements.
	Manage DBMS	Evaluate new features and functions.
Backup and Recovery	Monitor backup procedures	Verify that database backup procedures are followed.
	Conduct training	Ensure that users and operations personnel know and understand recovery procedures.
	Manage recovery	Manage recovery process.
Adaptation	Set up request tracking system	Develop system to record and prioritize requests for change.
	Manage configuration change	Manage impact of database structure changes on applications and users.

Figure 4-26
Summary of Database Administration Tasks

The DBA is not a user of the database or of any of its applications. Instead, the DBA is an auditor, a consultant, sometimes a policeman, and a diplomat who works as a liaison between the users and professional developers. Accordingly, one of the first tasks for the DBA is to create a steering committee that consists of key users. The DBA uses this committee as a forum for community-wide decisions regarding the development, use, and maintenance of the database.

From the start, the DBA needs to ensure that users are appropriately involved in the development process. The requirements specifications must include the needs of all appropriate users. Representatives from all key user groups need to verify and validate the data model during the development process. Also, the DBA needs to ensure that user representatives verify and validate application component designs and implementations.

DBA Operations Responsibilities

Humans struggle to share. We see that played out with toys in the sandbox in preschool, and we see it with databases in organizations at work. People want to process the database to meet their own needs, first. Conflict is inevitable.

For example, suppose an employee leaves the firm. When should that employee's records be deleted from the database? From the point of view of those who write the company's paychecks, they should be deleted at the end of the next pay period. From the

Using the Opposing Forces Guide *(page 97a)*

GOALS

* Explore the differences between a spreadsheet and a database.

* Understand one way that users respond to technology challenges.

BACKGROUND AND PRESENTATION STRATEGIES

The story of the failed database project is, unfortunately, quite common. Often it involves small businesses or workgroups that have attempted to develop a database on their own. On the basis of my experience, the cause of such failures is usually either incompetent database developers or underfunding of the project. (This, by the way, differs from the causes of failure for information systems in general. As we will see in Chapter 6, based on a review of all systems development projects and not just database projects at small businesses, the most likely causes of failure are poor communication between users and systems developers, a lack of clear requirements, and an inability to manage requirements.)

It took this company three consultants to obtain a database that works. *But the one that "works" doesn't meet the requirements*—or at least it doesn't meet the requirements of this salesperson.

Organizations smaller than General Motors or Toyota can develop their own databases, but developing a database and its applications in house does take time, money, and management attention. You, as a future manager, need to know what should be happening.

➤ **We'll talk about systems development techniques in Chapter 6, but to build a database correctly, here's a quick summary of the work that needs to be done:**

- **Determine and document requirements.**

- **Construct a data model and have users validate it.**

- **Design the database.**

- **Implement the database and fill it with data (imported from other sources?).**

- **Design, build, and test database applications.**

- **Write procedures.**

- **Train the users.**

- **Maintain the system.**

➤ **Notice I said** *management attention.* **Suppose you manage the dealership. What role do you see for yourself when a customer database is being developed for your sales staff?**

In light of the amount of work, the dealership might be better off to look for appropriate off-the-shelf software such as Act! or GoldMine. These products, which do use databases, already exist and have interfaces that are purpose-built for sales. Many small business salespeople use and recommend such products.

The issue of whether salespeople should share data is independent of the technology that the salesperson uses. Sharing data is a management policy. If management decides that salespersons' data should be private, there are ways to implement that policy with a database just as well as with a spreadsheet.

It's possible this person is using the failure of the database application to avoid sharing his data. He can hide his spreadsheet from management; they don't know that he's got his own customer data. It could be that he wants to keep his customer data private so that he can take it with him if he decides to work for another dealership. He might be using his disgust with the database project to cover his intentions.

Or, maybe not, but something doesn't fit: He doesn't want to use the database because it's difficult for him to send form letters or email. Yet, he says that he can't send them with his spreadsheet either and that sending letters is not that important to his sales activity.

Another possibility: His data are actually not his. He may have been stealing customers from other salespeople, and he doesn't want them to know that. Putting his data in a centralized database will reveal his actions.

Scrambling all of his data into the *Car Interests* and *Notes* columns will cause enormous problems if he ever wants to import his data to a database. Those problems will also be expensive to fix, because the work of separating the data into proper columns must be done manually. See pages 112–113 of the 10th edition of *Database Processing*[1] for a discussion of these issues.

"Keep it simple" is a great motto, but it shouldn't be simpler than it needs to be. What happens when his customers stop answering their phones because they prefer to use email? He can still send emails one at a time, but without some kind of database application, it will be impossible to send bulk emails announcing the

[1]David Kroenke, *Database Processing,* 10th ed. (Upper Saddle River, NJ: Prentice Hall, 2006).

arrival of new cars, and so on. This person is condemning himself to the old-world style of business.

❓ SUGGESTED RESPONSES FOR DISCUSSION QUESTIONS

1. Ask the students their opinions. I believe users have a right to information systems that allow them to do their jobs. Something doesn't fit here, though. He objects to the database application because it's difficult to send form letters, but then he says they're not that important to the way he sells. What else is going on? (See earlier comments.)

2. He's creating a nightmare for himself. How will he ever disentangle the addresses from the *Notes* column? What a mess!

3. I think some likely themes are *Customer, Auto_Interest, Contact,* and possibly others. *Multiple themes mean: Use a database!*

4. I suspect the concern does relate to using a database, but it ought not. Databases can be private and secure; accounts and roles can be set up so that salespeople do not share each other's data. However, I think he's hiding his desire not to share his data by complaining about the database. He's using frustration with technology to hide from the management policy of sharing data.

   ➤ **If you were a manager, how would you deal with this possibility?**

5. First, management may not be allowing each salesperson to have his or her own format. In fact, they may be trying to discourage it by building the shared database. The question is, who owns the contact data—the salespeople or the dealership? If the salespeople own it, then they can do what they want with it. If the dealership owns the data, then they can specify whatever format they want. The disadvantages to allowing different ways of keeping the data are inconsistent quality, missing data, difficulty of accessing common data, duplicated data, and so on.

6. Well, there's the soft approach and there's the tough one. The soft approach is to explain the need for the database—how it will make everyone more efficient, and how it will help salespeople not lose control of their customers to other salespeople. Also, explain that the database offers better security and control, including better protection, because it will be backed up and stored off-premises. Finally, explain that the database can integrate customer sales data with customer service data, and so forth.

   The tough approach is to mandate it: "We need centralized customer data to beat the competition and, ultimately, to survive. This may require you to make some changes, and it may be difficult for a while, but it's the way we're going to go. Get with it!" Then, provide support to ease the conversion efforts.

   ➤ **Or, as I once heard between a partner in a law firm and a reluctant junior associate: "What possible incentive do I have to use this new system?" asked the junior associate. "Continued employment," responded the partner.**

7. A database is a better solution. Whether it's a database developed in house or one that is embedded in a product like Act! or GoldMine is another question. But this type of problem begs for a database solution.

WRAP UP

➤ **No doubt about it, databases can involve a lot of work and involve management challenges. That's one reason you should read this chapter carefully.**

➤ **Given that databases can be expensive to develop in house (not to mention expensive to maintain, which we'll discuss in Chapter 6), for a common need like customer management for sales, look first to off-the-shelf applications.**

➤ **Sometimes people are frustrated with new systems and technology for justifiable reasons. Other times, they use that frustration for a cover for some other reason. That may have happened here. As a manager, keep that possibility in mind.**

point of view of those who prepare the end-of-quarter financial statements, they should be deleted at the end of the quarter. From the point of view of those who write out W-2 tax forms, they should be deleted at the end of the year. From the point of view of those who respond to an IRS audit of the company, they should be deleted after 3, 7, or more years.

Without someone to help users manage these different views, chaos results. The user with the loudest voice wins. Thus, an important DBA function is to establish community-wide policies for the processing of the database. The DBA uses the steering committee to determine processing rights for each column of each table. These rights include what data users are authorized to read, create, modify, and delete. The DBA also works with development personnel to ensure that a security system is in place to enforce these processing rights.

Finally, the DBA needs to track problems and manage problem solutions. Sometimes the solutions involve new user procedures and training; other times they require changes in application programs or the database. Sometimes solutions involve installing new features of the DBMS. Enterprise DBMS products such as Oracle or DB2 provide many different DBMS features and functions. In some cases, the DBA and development personnel can resolve problems by installing and using additional DBMS functions.

DBA Backup and Recovery Responsibilities

Failures occur. Hardware malfunctions, software has errors, users make mistakes, hurricanes and earthquakes happen. The time to think about these possibilities is long before they occur.

As the protector of the database, the DBA has the responsibility to ensure that appropriate procedures and policies exist for backing up the database and that those procedures are followed. Additionally, the DBA needs to ensure that users and operations personnel are appropriately trained with regard to backup and recovery procedures.

Finally, when failures occur, in many organizations the DBA is responsible for managing the recovery process. Even if the DBA does not have the ultimate responsibility for recovery (it may lie with the operations staff), the DBA has a key role during these times. We will discuss the development of such procedures in Chapter 11.

DBA Responsibilities for Adaptation

Adaptation is the last category of responsibilities in Figure 4-26. Over time, requirements for the database will change. In fact, the database and the systems that process it are often a major cause of the need for change (see the *Reflections Guide* [on page 101a] for an example). Changes that benefit one group in the organization may not benefit other groups. For example, a new feature for one group may mean slower performance for another group. Accordingly, the DBA needs to set up a system for recording and tracking requests for changes. (See *MIS in Use 4-2* on the next page for more on dealing with database growth.)

The steering committee meets periodically to discuss and prioritize the implementation of new features of the database and new functions for database applications. Again, these decisions must be made with a community-wide view. The responsibility of the DBA is to provide the forum and to ensure that requests are considered and acted upon in a responsible manner.

Is the DBA a Technical Person?

The DBA function has broad managerial responsibilities for the database. Part of that function is technical: Monitoring performance, managing the DBMS, and developing backup and recovery procedures all require strong technical DBMS skills. But, for larger organizations, and for databases that touch many different departments and business functions, the DBA's job is more diplomatic than technical. It is a mistake to staff the DBA function only with technical personnel. The DBA is a staff function with little authority. It can only request changes; it cannot order them. Therefore, for the person in this role, much of the time, diplomacy matters more than technical skill.

Dealing with Database Growth

Tektronix Corporation of Beaverton, Oregon, is a world leader in test, measurement, and monitoring electronic equipment. Founded in 1946, Tektronix operates in more than 25 countries, and its revenue in 2004 exceeded $920 million. Tektronix focuses on products that support the convergence of computers and communications. According to its Web site, "Almost any time you view a Web site, you touch the work of Tektronix."

Tektronix uses an Oracle database to store and process all of its financial data. The financial database applications average 800 concurrent users throughout the day, and with so much activity, the database grows rapidly. Unfortunately, such growth has a negative impact on performance. "Despite tuning exercises and hardware upgrades, a growth rate of 1.25GB per month caused performance to decline," said Lois Hughes, a senior systems analyst with Tektronix.

Database administration personnel examined data usage and determined that the system was storing large amounts of seldom-used data. The database contained considerable historical data, but almost all database activity involved recently created data. The unused, older data were causing unacceptable response times for the financial application users.

Database growth is not just a Tektronix problem. According to *Computerworld*, many organizations suffer the same fate. The database at Kennametal, Inc., of Latrobe, Pennsylvania, was growing at 27GB per month when the company decided to do something about it. "Our over-weight database was months away from crashing due to exceeding our production disk-space capacity," says Larry Cuda, global data archiving and migration project leader. "Management determined that we could no longer just keep throwing more disks at the problem."

The obvious answer to these problems is to remove some database data. Unfortunately, that solution can be difficult to implement. Determining which data are still needed is not easy. For example,

data that are still needed to close open transactions cannot be removed. Also, even data that are not needed to close transactions may still be needed for reporting about them.

The problem is compounded by a host of government data retention laws and regulations. Section 302 of The Sarbanes-Oxley Act of 2002 requires the CEO and CFO of a company to certify the accuracy of annual and quarterly reports. Data necessary to support this certification must be kept. Also, organizations engaged in securities trading must comply with SEC Rule 17-A, which sets out very specific data retention rules and requirements. Similarly, the Final Rule adopting HIPAA standards specifies a series of administrative, technical, and physical security procedures for data in hospitals, doctors' offices, and other health-provider organizations.

These three examples are just for the United States. Organizations that operate in foreign countries have even greater problems. Considering just accounts receivable data, for example, China requires data retention for 15 years, Brazil for 10, Italy for 7, and the United States for 3.

Clearly, data archiving is not just a problem for IS technicians. Users and user management must be actively involved with the database administration staff in order to define data archiving requirements, policies, and procedures. Most experts agree with the following guidelines:

1. Convince senior management and end-users of the importance of data archiving and of the need for an approved data archiving policy.
2. Ensure the policy addresses legal requirements for each country in which the organization operates.
3. Create a plan for implementing the archiving policy—ensure the plan prioritizes business requirements ahead of disk space reduction requirements.
4. Structure the plan to never archive data about open transactions
5. Implement the data archiving plan before data volumes cause performance problems.
6. Secure and back up the data archive.

Adapted from: *Computerworld*, March 8, 2004, *www.computerworld.com*, accessed December 2004.

Thanks for Volunteering (continued)

Knowing what you know now, if you were the manager of fundraising at the TV station, you would hire a consultant and expect the consultant to interview all of the key users. From those interviews, the consultant would then construct a data model.

You Be the Guide

Thanks for Volunteering (continued) (page 100)

GOAL

✳ Motivate future users and managers to learn basic database technology in order to be effective consumers of database technology.

RESPONDING TO THE CHALLENGE

This is a happy scenario! What a great ending—they all went off happily into the sunset! It can, by the way, happen just like this. I've seen it many times, both as a user and as a developer. This should offset the negativity in the Opposing Forces Guide.

➤ **Why??? What factors account for the success of this system?**

- **You hired a good consultant. You know what the consultant should be doing, and had she not been doing it, you would have found another consultant.**

- **You encouraged your staff to meet with the consultant (and, though not stated, told your employees that it was important to do so).**

- **You and your employees reviewed and approved the data model.**

- **The consultant knew what she was doing: She knew to switch the data key to a surrogate key (ProspectID) and not to store a value that should be computed.**

- **You stayed involved with the project—and know to gather requirements for future releases.**

Ask the students to examine the data model in Figure 4-27.

➤ **Describe the relationship between *Prospect* and *Work*. What is the maximum cardinality? What is the minimum cardinality? Do these make sense? Why?**

➤ **Describe the relationship between *Prospect* and *Phone*. What is the maximum cardinality? What is the**

minimum cardinality? Do these make sense? Why? If the *Prospect* has just one phone, is this relationship necessary?

➤ **Describe the relationship between *Prospect* and *Contact*. What is the maximum cardinality? What is the minimum cardinality? Do these make sense? Why?**

➤ **Describe the relationship between *Employee* and *Contact*. What is the maximum cardinality? What is the minimum cardinality? Do these make sense? Why?**

➤ **Is there a relationship between *Employee* and *Prospect*? If so, what is it? (It exists, but via the *Contact* entity. Relationships between principal actors often have these "intervening" entities that carry data about how those principal actors relate to each other.)**

Ask the students to correlate the design in Figure 4-28 to the data model in Figure 4-27. As managers and users, they won't need to worry about such designs, but they should understand how closely the data model determines the design, and hence, *by approving the data model, they are in effect approving the design.* Changes afterwards will be *expensive!*

WRAP UP

Sometimes I wrap up by asking the students:

➤ **What did you learn from this vignette?**

➤ **What role do you, as a future manager, need to take?**

➤ **Do you know all you need to know to take that role?**

Also, even if the students are not IS majors, many of them should take our first database class:

➤ **Databases are so important to business today. Every business and almost every information system has a database. We saw in the Ethics Guide how powerful SQL is. If you are an accounting or a marketing manager, you definitely should take our database class.**

➤ **Database knowledge can be an important part of your competitive advantage as an account, a marketer, or other business professional.**

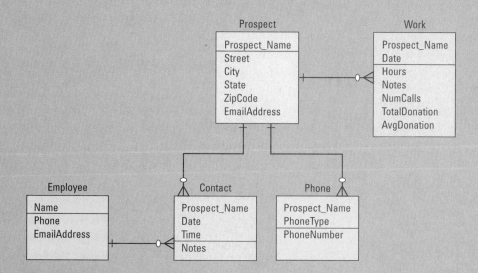

Figure 4-27
Data Model for Volunteer Database

You now know that the structure of the database must reflect the way the users think about their activities. If the consultant did not take the time to interview you and your staff or did not construct a data model and ask you to review it, you would know that you are not receiving good service and would take corrective action.

Suppose you found a consultant who interviewed your staff for several hours and then constructed the data model shown in Figure 4-27. This data model has an entity for *Prospect*, an entity for *Employee*, and three additional entities for *Contact*, *Phone*, and *Work*. The *Contact* entity records contacts that you or other employees have made with the prospective volunteer. This record is necessary so that you know what has been said to whom. The *Phone* entity is used to record multiple phone numbers for each prospective volunteer, and the *Work* entity records work that

the prospect has performed for the station.

After you reviewed and approved this data model, the consultant constructed the database design shown in Figure 4-28. In this design, table keys are underlined, foreign keys are shown in italics, and columns that are both table and foreign keys are underlined and italicized. Observe that the *Name* column is the table key of *Prospect*, and it is both part of the table key and a foreign key in *Phone*, *Contact*, and *Work*.

The consultant did not like having the *Name* column used as a key or as part of a key in so many tables. Based on her interviews, she suspected that prospect names are fluid—and that sometimes the same prospect name is recorded in different ways (e.g., sometimes with a middle initial and sometimes without). If that were to happen, phone, contact, and work data could be misallocated to prospect names. Accordingly, the consultant added

Prospect (<u>Name</u>, Street, City, State, Zip, EmailAddress)
Phone (<u>*Name*</u>, <u>PhoneType</u>, PhoneNumber)
Contact (<u>*Name*</u>, <u>Date</u>, <u>Time</u>, Notes, *EmployeeName*)
Work (<u>*Name*</u>, <u>Date</u>, <u>Time</u>, Notes, NumCalls, TotalDonations)
Employee (<u>EmployeeName</u>, Phone, EmailAddress)

Note:
Underline means table key.
Italics means foreign key.
Underline and italics means both table and foreign key.

Figure 4-28
First Table Design for Volunteer Database

Requirements Creep

Changing requirements is the biggest challenge for creating and managing databases and database applications. Here's a typical scenario: The development team just finishes the order entry database and applications when a user asks, innocently enough, "Where do I enter the second salesperson?"

"What second salesperson?"

"On the order. Sometimes we have joint sales. So where do I put the second salesperson's name?"

"This is the first I've heard of it. Why didn't someone tell me this before?"

"I never thought of it."

Adding a second salesperson means changing the relationship between *Order* and *Salesperson* from 1:N to N:M, which entails considerable rework—and expense. Of course, the best way to solve this problem is not to have it in the first place; it would be better to learn of the need for multiple salespeoples' names long before the system is created. Hence the importance for user involvement in both requirements specification and data model validation.

Unfortunately, however, not all change requests are preventable. Some occur only after a period of system use. Information systems and user organizations do not just influence each other; rather, as in the Escher sketch, they create each other. An information system enables its users to behave in new ways, and as they behave in new ways, they think of new requirements for the system. As the system is adapted to add new features, the users again will be able to behave in new ways, and they will then think of yet additional features and functions.

And so it goes, in a continuous cycle of change throughout the system's development and use. The bottom line is that there will always be new requirements for an information system. As soon as the system is put to use, the need for new features and functions will appear. No one should be surprised at this; it is a fundamental characteristic of the dynamics between users and systems.

This is not to say that the users and the development team can abrogate their responsibilities: They cannot duck and just hope for the best. Instead, they must specify all the requirements that they know about and validate the data model as best they can. Such a review, however, will always be imperfect. There will always be a need for versions 2 and 3 and 4, and so on, as long as the system is used. Plan on it!

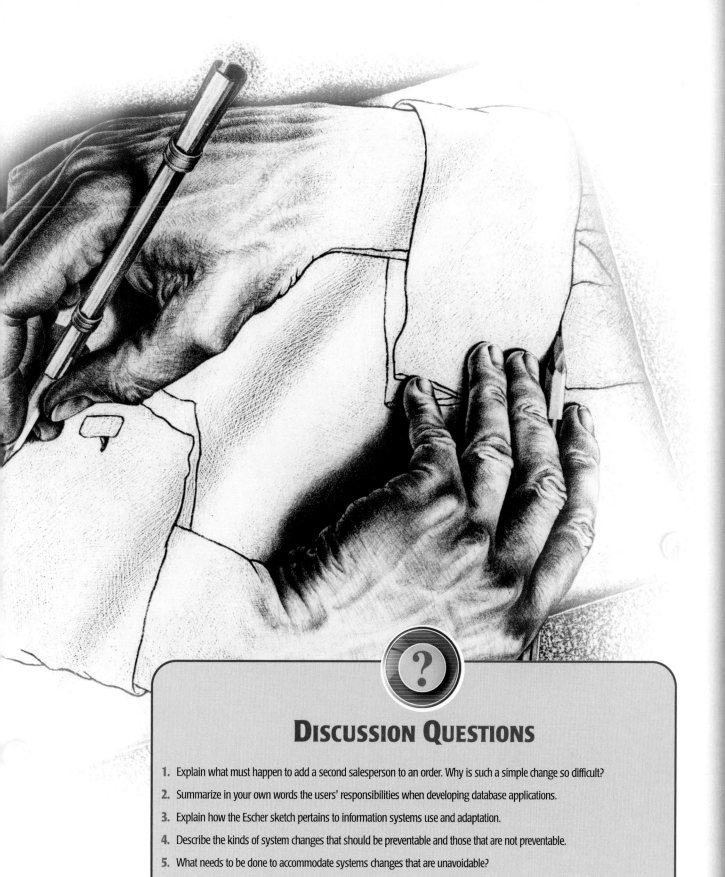

DISCUSSION QUESTIONS

1. Explain what must happen to add a second salesperson to an order. Why is such a simple change so difficult?

2. Summarize in your own words the users' responsibilities when developing database applications.

3. Explain how the Escher sketch pertains to information systems use and adaptation.

4. Describe the kinds of system changes that should be preventable and those that are not preventable.

5. What needs to be done to accommodate systems changes that are unavoidable?

Prospect (*ProspectID*, Name, Street, City, State, Zip, EmailAddress)
Phone (*ProspectID*, PhoneType, PhoneNumber)
Contact (*ProspectID*, Date, Time, Notes, *EmployeeName*)
Work (*ProspectID*, Date, Time, Notes, NumCalls, TotalDonations)
Employee (EmployeeName, Phone, EmailAddress)

Note:
Underline means table key.
Italics means foreign key.
Underline and italics means both
table and foreign key.

Figure 4-29
Second Table Design for
Volunteer Database

a new column, *ProspectID* to the prospect table and created the design shown in Figure 4-29. Values of this ID will have no meaning to the users, but the ID will be used to ensure that each prospect obtains a unique record in the Volunteer database. Because this ID has no meaning to the users, the consultant will hide it on forms and reports that users see.

There is one difference between the data model and the table designs. In the data model, the *Work* entity has an attribute, *AvgDonation*, but there is no corresponding *AvgDonation* column in the *Work* table. The consultant decided that there was no need to store this value in

the database because it could readily be computed on forms and reports using the values in the *NumCalls* and *TotalDonation* columns.

Once the tables had been designed, the consultant created a Microsoft Access database. She defined the tables in Access, created relationships among the tables, and constructed forms and reports. Figure 4-30 shows the primary data entry form used for the Volunteer database. The top portion of the form has contact data, including multiple phone numbers. It is important to know the type of the phone number so that you and your staff know if you're calling someone at work or another setting. The middle

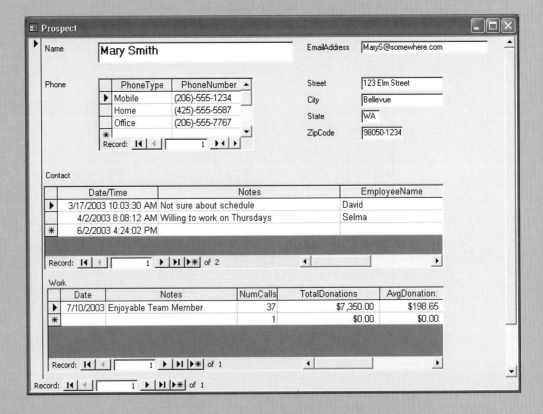

Figure 4-30
Volunteer Prospect Data-
Entry Form

You Be the Guide

Using the Reflections Guide
(page 101a)

GOALS

* Teach students the interdependent relationship between information systems and user organizations.

* Underline the importance of managing requirements creep.

* Illustrate the importance of user review of data models by describing the work necessary to place the second salesperson on the sales order.

* Reinforce the need for user managers to take an active role in systems development.

BACKGROUND AND PRESENTATION STRATEGIES

I love using the Escher sketch when describing requirements creep. In truth, it is not strong enough to say that information systems and users interact with one another. In fact, they *create each other.*

➤ **What does the text mean when it says that information systems and user organizations create each other?**

➤ **What does that statement have to do with databases?**

   As users use a new information system, they will think of new things that they want, and so it goes, around and around.

I think I've heard this same phenomenon referred to as the "freeway effect." The state starts building a freeway, new businesses and homes move into the neighborhood because of the new freeway's presence, and the planned traffic flow doubles. The freeway is crowded the day it opens. (This, by the way, is an easier problem. The freeway designers just have to anticipate traffic flows. Systems designers have to anticipate new features, which, of course, we cannot do.)

Twenty years ago, we were all in search of the right set of clever questions that we could ask the users so that they would tell us "what they really want." Today we know that the users don't know what those requirements will be because the new system, in part, will determine the changes the users want. Use begets changes in behavior and new requirements.

The term *maintenance* is a poor term. It means to fix the system or to adapt it to changing requirements.

Managing requirements creep is a delicate dance. When to decide to modify the requirements during development—thus requiring rework and delay—and when to decide to put off requirements changes for a future release.

   This is a very, very difficult job, and many have failed. The Carnegie Mellon team that analyzed the IRS failure (Chapter 1) cited inability to manage requirements as a significant cause of the (billion dollar) failure.

Managing requirements creep *requires* a strong, open, and honest relationship between systems developer managers and business-user managers. The development managers have to trust that the business managers will prioritize their true requirements and understand the trade-offs and priorities facing developers. User managers have to trust that the development managers are giving fair and honest estimates, and that their reluctance to change requirements isn't pure stubbornness. Both need to balance requirements, costs, and schedules. Knowledge like that in Chapter 4 is essential for future managers.

Imagine the surprise of the user who says, "I need to add a second salesperson," and is told, "That will require two weeks of rework." See question 1.

Think of the data model as a blueprint:

➤ **When is it easiest to move a bathroom? In the blueprint or after the plumbing has been installed and the sheetrock screwed to the walls, taped, and painted?**

 SUGGESTED RESPONSE FOR DISCUSSION QUESTIONS

1. What needs to be done to add the second salesperson?

   • Create the intersection table for the new N:M relationship.

   • Migrate the Order foreign key data to the intersection table.

   • Remove the foreign key from the Order table.

   • Rewrite all queries to use the intersection table.

   • Change all order and salesperson forms to use the new queries.

   • Change all order and salesperson reports to use the new queries.

   • Redesign all order and salesperson forms.

- Redesign all order and salesperson reports.

- Change/redesign application programs that process the relationship between Order and Salesperson.

- Test everything.

This "simple change" isn't simple under the covers. In a finished bathroom, why would it be so difficult to move a bathtub 10 feet? Think of the plumbing that needs to be moved and the work required to get access to that plumbing.

2. One way to address this question is to ask the class what the user is and is not responsible for. Example:

➤ **Is the user responsible for writing the queries?**

➤ **Is the user responsible for creating the data model?**

➤ **Is the user responsible for managing the development schedule?**

➤ **Then what is the user responsible for?**

The user is responsible for providing requirements; giving serious attention when evaluating data models; using prototypes (Chapter 6); trying to think ahead; and helping development manage requirements creep.

3. Users and information systems create each other, just like the two hands in the sketch.

➤ **When is a system finished?**

A system is finished when all users are dead. Until that point, as long as there is one user still using the system, there will be requests for changes. And not because users want to be a pain the neck, but because system use causes changes in behavior, which causes requests for system change.

4. *Preventable changes* occur when users do not take requirements reviews and data model reviews seriously. They stem from requirements that were not thought about because of user carelessness or lack of involvement. They happen, for example, when critical users do not attend review meetings.

Unpreventable changes are requirements that only occur after the users have changed their behaviors by using the new system. Such requirements are just the nature of information systems use within organizations.

5. Things to be done to accommodate unpreventable changes: Document them. Put them into a requirements database. Prioritize them and then make the changes, in accordance with priorities, as time and budget allow.

WRAP UP

➤ **All of this comes down to the following: As a user, if you are asked to review requirements and data models, take that job seriously and do the best job you can. As a manager, make sure your employees take such reviews very seriously. Work collaboratively with development management to ensure that they get the attention they need for requirements.**

➤ **Build the first version as best you can and expect that requirements will change. But don't let the changes occur simply because you or your employees didn't take the time to think seriously about what you need.**

and bottom sections of this form have contact and prior work data. Observe that *AvgDonation* has been computed from the *NumCalls* and *Total Donation* columns.

You were quite pleased with this database application, and you're cer-tain that it helped you to improve the volunteer staffing at the station. Of course, over time, you thought of several new requirements, and you already have changes in mind for next year.

SUMMARY

- The purpose of a database is to keep track of things. A database is a self-describing collection of integrated records. Bytes are grouped into columns, or fields; columns are grouped into rows, or records; and records are grouped into tables, or files. A database consists of a group of tables, relationships among rows in those tables, and metadata.

- With the relational model, data are stored in tables and relationships are represented by column values. A key, or table key, is a column or group of columns that uniquely identifies a row. A foreign key is a column or group of columns in one table that identifies a row in a second table. Foreign keys represent relationships between records. Metadata are data that describe data. Databases include metadata that describe their contents.

- A database application system includes the database, the database management system (DBMS), and database applications. The DBMS is a program used to create, process, and administer a database. Few organizations develop their own DBMSs; such products are licensed from commercial vendors. Popular products include DB2, Access, SQL Server, Oracle, and MySQL. The DBMS is used to create tables, relationships, and other structures. It is also used to read, insert, modify, and delete data.

- Structured Query Language (SQL) is an international standard for defining and processing database data. The DBMS is used to administer the database, which includes establishing and managing a security system, backing up the database, and removing unwanted data.

- A database application consists of forms, reports, queries, and application programs. Forms are used to display, insert, update, and delete data. Reports show data in a meaningful context and may compute values on the fly.

- DBMS products include robust capabilities for querying data. Application programs are used to perform tasks, unique to the application, that a simple form, report, or query cannot accomplish. Special problems occur when more than one user at a time processes the data in a database. Lost-update problems arise when the update of one user overrides the update of a prior user. Locking the data can prevent lost updates, but locking introduces yet other problems.

- DBMS products fall into two groups: Enterprise DBMS products support many users and huge databases and provide 24/7 support. DB2, SQL Server, and Oracle are popular enterprise DBMS products. The only surviving personal DBMS product is Microsoft Access.

- A data model is a logical representation of a database that describes data and relationships. The entity-relationship (E-R) model is the most common data model.

- An entity is something that users want to track. Entities have attributes that describe their characteristics. Most entities have an identifier, which is an attribute (or group of attributes) associated with one and only one entity instance.

- Entities have relationships to one another. The maximum cardinality is the maximum number of entities that a relationship can have. Common examples are 1:N and N:M. The minimum cardinality is the number of entities that a relationship must have. An entity can be optional or required.

- Database design is the process of converting a data model into tables, relationships, and data constraints. Normalization is the process of converting poorly structured tables into tables that are well structured. Tables can be classified into normal forms depending on the types of problems they have. Every well-formed table has one and only one topic or theme.

- The easiest time to change the structure of a database is during the data modeling stage. Only the users can validate the data model, and so they must perform a careful and thorough review of it. Mistakes missed in the data modeling stages can be very difficult and expensive to correct later.

■ The purpose of database administration (DBA) is to manage the development, operation, and adaptation of the database. An office of database administration supports larger enterprise databases. Small databases have a single individual, sometimes working part-time, as a database administrator. Figure 4-26 summarizes database administration tasks.

KEY TERMS AND CONCEPTS

Access **82**
Attribute **89**
Byte **78**
Column **78**
Crow's foot **91**
Crow's-foot diagram version **91**
Data integrity problem **92**
Data model **88**
Database **78**
Database administration **97**
Database application **84**
Database application system **81**
Database management system
   (DBMS) **81**
DBA **97**
DB2 **82**
Enterprise DBMS **87**
Entity **89**
Entity-relationship (E-R) data
   model **88**

Entity-relationship (E-R)
   diagram **90**
Field **78**
File **78**
Firewall **85a**
Foreign key **80**
Form **85**
Identifier **89**
Key **79**
Lost-update problem **87**
Maximum cardinality **91**
Metadata **80**
Minimum cardinality **91**
Multi-user processing **86**
MySQL **82**
Object-relational database **80n**
N:M (many-to-many)
   relationship **91**
Normal forms **93**
Normalization **92**

1:N (one-to-many)
   relationship **91**
Oracle **82**
Query **85**
Personal DBMS **87**
Record **78**
Relation **80**
Relational database **80**
Relationship **90**
Report **85**
Row **78**
SQL Server **82**
Structured Query Language
   (SQL) **82**
Table **78**
Unified Modeling Language
   (UML) **89**
User account **85a**
User role **85a**

ASSIGNMENT MATERIAL

Review Questions

1. What is the purpose of a database?

2. Using your own words, when should you use a spreadsheet to keep track of things? When should you use a database to keep track of things?

3. Identify the components of a database.

4. Explain how keys are used to express relationships.

5. How does metadata make a database more useful?

6. What are the functions of the DBMS?

7. What are the components of a database application?

8. Give an example, other than the one in this chapter, of the lost-update problem.

9. Why should users know how to interpret data models?

10. Define *entity* and give an example other than one in this chapter.

11. Define *attribute* and give examples for the entity in your answer to question 10.

12. Define *identifier* and give an example for the entity in your answer to question 10.

13. Give an example of two entities that have a relationship to the entity in your answer to question 10.

14. Draw an entity-relationship diagram for the entities in your answer to question 13.

15. Show the maximum and minimum cardinalities for your relationships in your answer to question 14.

16. What is the purpose of database administration?

17. Summarize DBA responsibilities for the following activities.

    a. During database development
    b. For operations
    c. For database backup and recovery
    d. For database adaptation

Applying Your Knowledge

18. Draw an entity-relationship diagram that shows the relationships of a database, database applications, and users.

19. Consider the relationship between *Adviser* and *Student* in Figure 4-19. Explain what it means if the maximum cardinality of this relationship is:

    a. N:1
    b. 1:1
    c. 5:1
    d. 1:5

20. In Figure 4-27, the *Contact* entity is dependent on *Prospect*. What would it mean if this entity were dependent on *Employee*?

21. How would you change the E-R diagram in Figure 4-27 if only one phone number is to be recorded for each prospect?

22. The partial E-R diagram in Figure 4-31 is for a sales order. Assume there is only one *Salesperson* per *SalesOrder*.

    a. Specify the maximum cardinalities for each relationship. State your assumptions, if necessary.
    b. Specify the minimum cardinalities for each relationship. State your assumptions, if necessary.

23. a. Construct a data model for the data in Figure 4-2.
    b. The database in Figure 4-2 contains data for a single class. Suppose the professor who uses this database wants to keep data for several classes. Further suppose that some students enroll in more than one of a professor's classes. Revise your data model to show this changed assumption.
    c. Is your first or second data model better?

Application Exercises

24. Suppose that you work in a sales office and your boss asks you to create a "computer file" to keep track of product prices offered to customers. Suppose you decide to use a spreadsheet for this purpose as follows.

    a. Create a spreadsheet with the following columns: *CustomerName, CustomerLocation, MeetingDate, ProductName, UnitPrice, Salesperson,* and *Salesperson_Email.*
    b. Suppose you have three customers: Ajax, Baker, and Champion. Suppose Ajax is located in New York City, Baker is located in Toronto, and Champion is located in New York City. Assume you have two salespeople: Johnson and Jackson. (Make up email addresses for each.)

    Assume you have three products: P1, P2, and P3. Periodically, your salespeople meet with customers, during which meetings they agree on product prices. The salespeople pitch one, two, or three products in each of these meetings. Some customers negotiate better prices than others, so the price varies by customer.

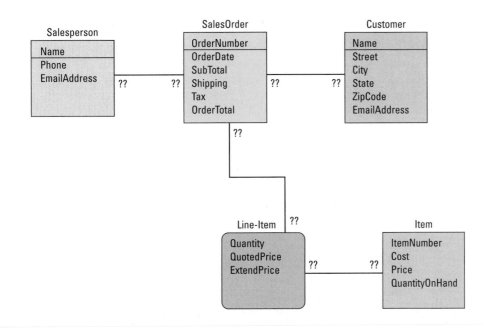

Figure 4-31
Partial E-R Diagram for SalesOrder

Using this information, fill your spreadsheet with at least 20 rows of sample data. Make up the price data. Assume that prices increase and decrease over time. Enter data for some meetings in 2005 and for some meetings in 2006.

c. Copy your spreadsheet to a new worksheet. Suppose that you made a mistake and Champion is based in San Francisco, not New York City. Using this second worksheet, make the necessary changes to correct your mistake.

d. Suppose that you learn that the product P1 was renamed P1-Turbo in 2006. Explain the steps you need to take to correct this mistake.

e. A real sales-tracking application would have hundreds of customers, many salespeople, hundreds of products, and possibly thousands of meetings. For such a spreadsheet, how would you correct the problems in parts c and d? Comment on the appropriateness of using a spreadsheet for such an application.

25. Consider the same problem as in question 24, except use a database to keep track of the price quotations.

a. Create a new database using Microsoft Access and create the following three tables:

CUSTOMER (*CustomerName, Location*)
SALESPERSON (*SalespersonName, Saleperson_Email*)
PRICE_QUOTE (*Date, Product, Price, CustomerName, SalespersonName*)

Assume the following: *CustomerName* is the key of CUSTOMER; *SalespersonName* is the key of SALESPERSON; and the three columns (*Date*, *Product*, and *CustomerName*) are the key of PRICE_QUOTE. Make appropriate assumptions about the data types for each table column.

b. Use Access to create a 1:N relationship between CUSTOMER and PRICE_QUOTE. Create a 1:N relationship between SALESPERSON and PRICE_QUOTE. Check Enforce Referential Integrity for both relationships.

c. Fill your tables using the same data that you used in question 24.

d. Make the changes necessary to record the fact that customer Champion is based in San Francisco rather than in New York City. How many items do you need to change?

e. Make the changes necessary to change the name of product P1 to P1-Turbo for all quotes after 2006.

f. Using the Access Help system, learn about update action queries. Create an update action query to make the change in part e.

g. Compare spreadsheets and databases for this application. Which is better? Why? What are the characteristics of an application that would cause you to choose a database over a spreadsheet? A spreadsheet over a database?

Career Assignments

26. Search the U.S. Department of Labor's Occupational Outlook Handbook (*bls.gov/oco/home.htm*) for the term *database administrator*. Answer the following questions based on the information you find.

a. What are the job prospects for database administrators in the next 5 years?

b. What skills do database administrators need? (*Note:* Sometimes this handbook groups jobs together. Make sure you find the skills necessary for database administrators in particular.)

c. What courses could you take or activities could you engage in to prepare you for such a job?

27. Do a Web search for the term "databases for *x*," filling in your major field of study for *x*. If you are majoring in accounting, for example, search for "databases for accounting." If you are majoring in marketing, fill in "databases for marketing." Read two or three of the links that you find interesting. Look for articles that are less technical and more managerial.

a. Summarize your findings.

b. Describe two or three job opportunities that might exist for someone who has some technical knowledge along with a business degree in a functional area like accounting or marketing. These job opportunities may not be listed as such. Instead, think about what you have read in this chapter and what you learned in part a and imagine what job opportunities there might be.

c. Today, business professionals are required to be more actively involved in the development and use of information systems. Official job descriptions may not have kept up with this requirement. Explain how you could use this fact and your knowledge of IS to create a competitive advantage over other job applicants.

d. Your department maintains relationships with professionals who are active in your major field of study. Describe how you could contact one of those professionals to verify the conclusions you reached in parts a through c. What ancillary benefits might accrue if you do this?

Case Study 4-1

Aviation Safety Network

The mission of the Aviation Safety Network (ASN) is to provide up-to-date, complete, and reliable information on airliner accidents and safety issues to those with a professional interest in aviation. ASN defines an airliner as an aircraft capable of carrying 14 or more passengers. ASN data include information on commercial, military, and corporate airplanes.

ASN gathers data from a variety of sources, including the International Civil Aviation Board, the National Transportation Safety Board, and the Civil Aviation Authority. Data

ASN Aviation Safety Database results

24 occurrences in the ASN safety database:

date	type	registration	operator	fat.	location	pic	cat
26-JUN-1988	Airbus A.320	F-GFKC	Air France	3	France		A1
14-FEB-1990	Airbus A.320	VT-EPN	Indian Airlines	92	India		A1
20-JAN-1992	Airbus A.320	F-GGED	Air Inter	87	France		A1
27-MAR-1993	Airbus A.320	VT-E..	Indian Airlines	0	India		H2
26-AUG-1993	Airbus A.320	G-KMAM	Excalibur Airways	0	U.K.		I2
14-SEP-1993	Airbus A.320	D-AIPN	Lufthansa	2	Poland		A1
22-OCT-1993	Airbus A.320	F-....	Air Inter	0	France		I2
10-DEC-1993	Airbus A.320	F-GF..	Air France	0	France		H2
19-DEC-1996	Airbus A.320	F-OHMK	Mexicana	0	Mexico		A2
10-MAR-1997	Airbus A.320	A4O-EM	Gulf Air	0	U.A.E.		A1
22-MAR-1998	Airbus A.320	RP-C3222	Philippine Air Lines	0	Philippines		A1
12-MAY-1998	Airbus A.320	SU-GB?	EgyptAir	0	Egypt		A2
21-MAY-1998	Airbus A.320	G-UKLL	Air UK Leisure	0	Spain		I2
12-FEB-1999	Airbus A.320	F-GJVG	Air France	0	France		U2
02-MAR-1999	Airbus A.320	F-G...	Air France	0	France		H2
26-OCT-1999	Airbus A.320	VT-ESL	Indian Airlines	0	Myanmar		A2
11-APR-2000	Airbus A.320	F-OHMD	Mexicana	0	Mexico		O1
05-JUL-2000	Airbus A.320		Royal Jordanian	1	Jordan		H2
23-AUG-2000	Airbus A.320	A4O-EK	Gulf Air	143	Bahrain		A1
07-FEB-2001	Airbus A.320	EC-HKJ	Iberia	0	Spain		A1
17-MAR-2001	Airbus A.320	N357NW	Northwest Airlines	0	USA		A2
20-MAR-2001	Airbus A.320	D-AIP.	Lufthansa	0	Germany		I2
24-JUL-2001	Airbus A.320	4R-ABA	SriLankan Airlines	0	Sri Lanka		O1
28-AUG-2002	Airbus A.320	N635AW	America West	0	USA		A1

Source: Aviation Safety Network, *http://aviation-safety.net*.

Figure 1
Incidents and Accidents Involving the Airbus 320 from the ASN Aviation Safety Database

are also taken from magazines, such as *Air Safety Week* and *Aviation Week and Space Technology;* from a variety of books; and from prominent individuals in the aviation safety industry.

ASN compiles the source data into a Microsoft Access database. The core table contains over 10,000 rows of data concerning incident and accident descriptions. This table is linked to several other tables that store data about airports, airlines, aircraft types, countries, and so forth. Periodically, the Access data are reformatted and exported to a MySQL database, which is used by programs that support queries on ASN's Web site (*aviation-safety.net*).

On that site, incident and accident data can be accessed by year, by airline, by aircraft, by nation, and in other ways. For example, Figure 1 (page 107) shows a list of incidents and accidents that involved the Airbus 320. When the user clicks on a particular accident, such as the one on March 20, 2001, a summary of the incident is presented, as shown in Figure 2.

Incident Description   Status: **Final**   [legenda]

Date:	**20 MAR 2001**
Time:	12:00
Type:	Airbus A.320-211
Operator:	Lufthansa
Registration:	D-AIP.
Year built:	1990
Engines:	2 CFMI CFM56-5A1
Crew:	0 fatalities / 6 on board
Passengers:	0 fatalities / 115 on board
Total:	0 fatalities / 121 on board
Airplane damage:	None
Location:	Frankfurt International Airport (FRA) (Germany)
Phase:	Take-off
Nature:	International Scheduled Passenger
Departure airport:	Frankfurt International Airport (FRA)
Destination airport:	Paris

Narrative:
The Airbus 320 hit turbulence just after rotation from runway 18 and the left wing dipped. The captain responded with a slight sidestick input to the right but the aircraft banked further left. Another attempt to correct the attitude of the plane resulted in a left bank reaching ca 22deg. The first officer then said "I have control", and switched his sidestick to priority and recovered the aircraft. The left wingtip was reportedly just 0.5m off the ground. The aircraft climbed to FL120 where the crew tried to troubleshoot the problem. When they found out that the captain's sidestick was reversed in roll, they returned to Frankfurt. Investigation revealed that maintenance had been performed on the Elevator Aileron Computer no. 1 (ELAC). Two pairs of pins inside the connector had accidentally been crossed during the repair.

Source: Aviation Safety Network, *http://aviation-safety.net.*

Figure 2
Incident Description
Summary from the ASN
Aviation Safety Database

Date	Type	Occupants	Survivors	Phase [1]	Safest location
02 MAY 1970	DC-9	63	40	ER	rear
04 APR 1977	DC-9	85	22	ER	rear
12 AUG 1985	Boeing 747	524	4	ER	rear
11 NOV 1965	Boeing 727	91	48	LA	rear
20 NOV 1967	Convair CV-880	82	12	LA	rear
13 JAN 1969	DC-8	45	30	LA	front
08 DEC 1972	Boeing 737	61	18	LA	rear
29 DEC 1972	Lockheed L-1011	176	77	LA	front & rear
30 JAN 1974	Boeing 707	101	4	LA	center
11 SEP 1974	DC-9	82	12	LA	rear
24 JUN 1975	Boeing 727	124	9	LA	rear
27 APR 1976	Boeing 727	88	51	LA	front
11 FEB 1978	Boeing 737	49	7	LA	rear
28 DEC 1978	DC-8	189	179	LA	rear
02 JUN 1983	DC-9	46	23	LA	center
02 AUG 1985	Lockheed L-1011	163	29	LA	rear
15 SEP 1988	Boeing 737	104	69	LA	rear
08 JAN 1989	Boeing 737	126	79	LA	front
19 JUL 1989	DC-10	296	185	LA	center
01 FEB 1991	Boeing 737	89	67	LA	rear
20 JAN 1992	Airbus A.320	96	9	LA	rear
26 APR 1994	Airbus A.300	271	7	LA	center
01 JUN 1999	DC-9	145	134	LA	front & rear
03 DEC 1990	DC-9	44	36	TA	front
27 NOV 1970	DC-8	229	182	TO	front
13 JAN 1982	Boeing 737	79	5	TO	rear
22 AUG 1985	Boeing 737	137	82	TO	front
15 NOV 1987	DC-9	82	54	TO	rear
31 AUG 1988	Boeing 727	108	94	TO	front & center
22 MAR 1992	Fokker F-28	51	24	TO	front & rear
02 JUL 1994	DC-9	57	20	TO	rear
31 OCT 2000	Boeing 747	179	96	TO	front & rear

Source: Aviation Safety Network, *http://aviation-safety.net*.

Figure 3
Safest Location on Aircraft from the ASN Aviation Safety Database

In addition to descriptions of incidents and accidents, ASN also summarizes the data to help its users determine airliner accident trends. For example, Figure 3 shows the safest location on the aircraft for a selection of airliner accidents. (A value of "ER" in the *Phase* column means the accident occurred while the aircraft was en route, "LA" means the accident occurred during landing, and "TO" means that accident occurred during take off.) According to ASN, "there is no significant difference regarding survival for passengers seated in the front or the rear of the plane."

Hugo Ranter of the Netherlands started the ASN Web site in 1995. Fabian I. Lujan of Argentina has maintained the site since 1998. ASN has more than 10,000 email subscribers in 150 countries, and the site receives over 50,000 visits per week.

Questions

1. All of the data included in this database are available in public documents. Since this is the case, what is the value of Aviation Safety Network? Why don't users just consult the online version of the underlying references? In your answer, consider the difference between data and information.

2. What was the cause of the incident shown in Figure 2? That incident, in which no one was injured, occurred in an Airbus 320 airplane that was flown by Lufthansa Airlines out of an airport in Germany. It would be illogical to conclude from this one incident that it is dangerous to fly Airbus 320s, Lufthansa, or out of Germany. Suppose, however, that you wanted to determine whether there is a systematic pattern of maintenance problems with the A320, Lufthansa, or airports in Germany. How would you proceed? How would you use the resources of *aviation-safety.net* to make this determination?

3. The ASN database and Web site were created and are maintained by two individuals. The database may be complete and accurate, or it may not be. To what extent should you rely on these data? What can you do to decide whether you should rely on the data at this site?

4. Consider the data in Figure 3. Do you agree that there appears to be no significant difference between passengers in the front and the rear of the airplane? Why or why not? There does seem to be a difference between the number of accidents and the phase of the flight. What is that difference, and how can you use it to limit your exposure to aircraft accidents?

5. Suppose you work in the marketing department for an airline. Can you use these data in your marketing efforts? If so, how? What are the dangers of basing a marketing campaign on safety?

6. Suppose you are a maintenance manager for a major airline. How can you use these data? Would it be wise to develop your own, similar database? Why or why not?

7. Develop a data model for the database that underlies this site. Your model should include the following entities: *Aircraft_Type*, *Airline*, *Accident*, *Cause*, and *Country*. In your data model, specify the relationships between the entities and include several attributes for each.

Case Study 4-2

Benchmarking, Bench Marketing, or Bench Baloney?

Which DBMS product is the fastest? Which product yields the lowest price/performance ratio? What computer equipment works best for each DBMS product? These reasonable questions should be easy to answer. They are not.

In fact, the deeper you dig, the more problems you find. To begin with, which product is fastest doing *what*? To have a valid comparison, all compared products must do the same work. So, vendors and third parties have defined *benchmarks*, which are descriptions of work to be done along with the data to be processed. To compare performance, analysts run competing DBMS products on the same benchmark and measure the results. Typical measures are number of transactions processed per second, number of Web pages served per second, and average response time per user.

At first, DBMS vendors set up their own benchmark tests and published those results. Of course, when vendor A used its own benchmark to claim that its product was superior to all others, no one believed the results. Clearly, vendor A had an incentive to set up the benchmark to play to its product strengths. So, third parties defined standard benchmarks. Even that led to problems, however. According to *The Benchmark Handbook* (at *benchmarkresources.com/handbook*):

> When comparative numbers were published by third parties or competitors, the losers generally cried foul and tried to discredit the benchmark. Such events often caused benchmark wars. Benchmark wars start if someone loses an important or visible benchmark evaluation. The loser reruns it using regional specialists and gets new and winning numbers. Then the opponent reruns it using his regional specialists, and of course gets even better numbers. The loser then reruns it using some one-star gurus. This progression can continue all the way to five-star gurus.

For example, in July 2002 *PC Magazine* ran a benchmark using a standard benchmark called the *Nile benchmark*. This particular test has a mixture of database tasks that are processed via Web pages. The faster the DBMS, the more pages that can be served. The results of the test were as shown in Figure 1.

The test compared five DBMS products: DB2 (from IBM), MySQL (a free, open-source DBMS product from MySQL.com), Oracle (from Oracle Corporation), SQL Server (from Microsoft), and ASE (from Sybase Corporation). The vertical axis in the graph shows the number of pages processed per second; as the label says, higher is better.

From this graph, you can see that SQL Server's performance was the worst. In the magazine review, the authors stated that they believed SQL Server scored poorly because the test used a new version of a non-Microsoft driver (a program that sends requests and returns results to and from the DBMS).

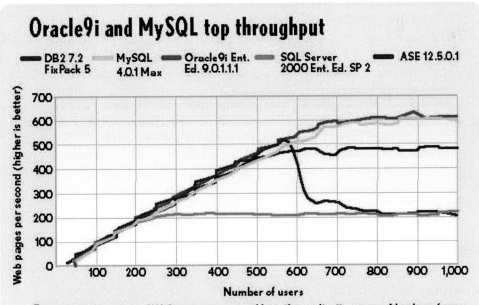

Figure 1
Results of First Nile
Benchmark Test

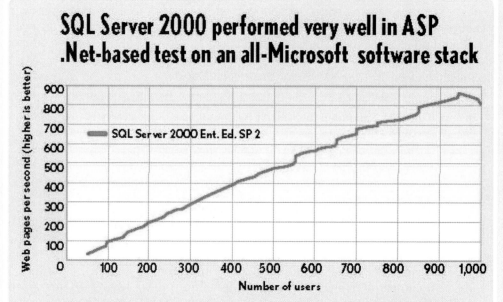

Figure 2
Results of Second Nile
Benchmark Test

As you might imagine, no sooner was this test published than the phones and email server at *PC Magazine* were inundated by objections from Microsoft. *PC Magazine* reran the tests, replacing the suspect driver with a full panoply of Microsoft products. The article doesn't say, but one can imagine that five-star Microsoft gurus chartered the next airplane to PC Labs, where the testing was done. (You can read about both phases of the benchmark at *eweek.com/article2/0,4149,293,00.asp.*)

Rerunning the test with the Microsoft-supporting software, the SQL Server results were as shown in Figure 2.

In the second test, SQL Server performed better than all of the other products in the first test. But now we're comparing apples and oranges. The first test used standard software, and the second test used Microsoft-specific software.

When the five-star gurus from Oracle or MySQL use *their* favorite supporting products and "tune" to this particular benchmark, their re-rerun results will be superior to those for SQL Server. And round and round it will go.

Questions

1. Suppose you manage a business activity that needs a new IS with a database. The development team is divided on which DBMS you should use. One faction wants to use Oracle, a second wants to use MySQL, and a third wants to use SQL Server. They cannot decide among themselves, and so they schedule a meeting with you. The team presents all of the benchmarks shown here. How do you respond?

2. Performance is just one criterion for selecting a DBMS. Other criteria are the cost of the DBMS, hardware costs, staff knowledge, ease of use, ability to tune for extra

performance, and backup and recovery capabilities. How does consideration of these other factors change your answer to question 1?

3. The Transaction Processing Council (TPC) is a not-for-profit corporation that defines transaction processing and database benchmarks and publishes vendor-neutral, verifiable performance data. Visit its Web site at *tpc.org*.
   a. What are TPC-C, TPC-R, and TPC-W?
   b. Suppose you work in the marketing department at Oracle Corporation. How would you use the TPC results in the TPC-C benchmark?
   c. What are the dangers to Oracle in your answer to part b?
   d. Suppose you work in the marketing department for DB2 at IBM. How would you use the TPC results in the TPC-C benchmark?
   e. Do the results for TPC-C change your answer to question 1?
   f. If you are a DBMS vendor, can you ignore benchmarks?

4. Reflect on your answers to questions 1 through 3. On balance, what good are benchmarks? Are they just footballs to be kicked around by vendors? Are advertisers and publishers the only true beneficiaries? Do DBMS customers benefit from the efforts of TPC and like groups? How should customers use benchmarks?

Data Communications and Internet Technology

Learning Objectives

* Know basic telecommunications terminology.
* Know the definition and characteristics of LANs, WANs, and internets.
* Understand the nature of processing in a layered communications protocol.
* Know the purpose of the five layers of the TCP/IP–OSI protocol.
* Understand Ethernet and wireless LANs.
* Understand the characteristics of WANs using personal computers with modems to the Internet, networks of leased lines, PSDNs, and virtual private networks.
* Know basic concepts involved in the operation of the Internet.

Guides

PROBLEM SOLVING GUIDE
Thinking Exponentially Is Not Possible, but. . .

OPPOSING FORCES GUIDE
Where's the OFF Button?

SECURITY GUIDE
Encryption

ETHICS GUIDE
Personal Email at Work?

REFLECTIONS GUIDE
Human Networks Matter More

Chapter Preview

This chapter addresses computer networks and technology. This complex subject involves the interaction of dozens of equipment types, methods, and standards. It is easy to drown in a sea of terms and acronyms. To avoid drowning and to prepare you to work in a rapidly changing field, we begin with some basic networking concepts, followed by a discussion of layered protocols. You can use this framework to help you organize the information in this chapter.

In truth, data communications and networking are difficult and challenging topics, and this chapter is the most technical chapter in this book. Be patient. Your goal should be to learn basic concepts so that you can respond to requests like that of the chief operating officer in the opening scenario.

The last portion of this chapter explains how the Internet works. Because the Internet is the foundation of twenty-first-century commerce, knowing Internet components and their interactions is part of a business professional's literacy. Just as you need to know terms like LIFO and FIFO and understand what it means when marginal revenue equals marginal cost, so, too, you need to know what TCP/IP and related protocols are and how they are used.

The Connectivity Evaluation Project

Suppose you are the accounts payable manager who answered the $80,000 question in Chapter 3. Six months have passed, and you're having success. You answered the hardware question well enough, management is pleased, and you have no hardware budget problems. You've also instigated changes that have increased the productivity of your department. In short, your career is off to a good start.

Still, you are surprised one day when your boss sticks her head in your office and says, "The chief operating officer would like to see you. I think he has a special project for you—could be a good opportunity."

The next day, you meet with the chief operating officer (COO) who says, "We've been really impressed with your work. Your department's doing exceptionally well. But that's not why I wanted to see you. We liked the way you handled your computer budget, and we've got another problem, a little bigger, that we'd like you to address.

"As you probably know, we bought the Lopez manufacturing facility in California. We need to connect the computers there to the computers here in Poughkeepsie. The MIS department has given me a plan for this, but I'm not certain that they've looked at all the alternatives. They're pretty close to the bits and bytes, if you know what I mean, and I don't know that they've taken the broad, management perspective that I need. They may have, but I'm just not sure.

"Here's what I want you to do. Starting Monday, take a week—I've asked your boss to cover your department for you—and investigate the alternatives for connecting the Lopez computers to ours. I know you're not a technical person, and I don't want a technical proposal. I want a business report on the alternatives, costs/benefits, future potential, and so forth. Again, take it from a management perspective.

"If you want to bring in a consultant, that's fine, just as long as they aren't horribly expensive. You can see Aaron to set up that budget. OK? Get back to me if you need anything; otherwise, I'll expect to hear from you within three weeks."

You leave the meeting flattered that you've been given this special task, and you know it's a career-enhancing opportunity. So you spend a good part of your weekend identifying computer communications consultants to contact.

You develop a list of three potential consultants. When you told the first one that you're not a technical person, his tone turned patronizing. In so many words he said, "Write me a check and I'll solve the problem for you." You're pretty sure that's not what the COO had in mind. Another vendor sounds too technical. He made statements like, "Well, you need to wire your business with Cat5e UTP, connect that to RJ-45 plugs on wall plates in each room, and finally connect your PC's NICs to the RJ-45 plugs using connection cables." You suspect he doesn't understand the idea of a broad management perspective. The third consultant sounded more promising; she understands your task and you think she knows what she's doing. Unfortunately, even she used terms like LAN and WAN, leased lines versus PSDN versus VPN, and Internet tunneling. You have no idea what those terms mean. What to do?

The Connectivity Evaluation Project (page 116)

GOALS

* Motivate students to learn data communications and Internet technology.

* Invoke students' curiosity about leased lines, PSDNs, VPNs—data communication alternatives that business managers should know.

WAYS TO STIMULATE STUDENT INVOLVEMENT

This scenario is very typical of activities in smaller companies—those with, say, under $100 million in sales. Larger companies have a CIO and staff to which the COO would delegate responsibility for such decisions.

Important note for future general managers: Effective data communication with the acquired company may be a key to the merger's success. One could fault this company that this issue was not addressed prior to the acquisition.

In companies of this size, the COO has to make a management decision about what technology to use. The consequences of that decision are communications effectiveness, cost, and schedule. The wrong decision will mean later changes, more cost, and delay.

It is very common for senior managers to delegate work like this to trusted subordinates. From the manager's standpoint, it saves work and it gives a chance to provide *on-the-job training to a key junior person.* It also allows the manager to judge the *subordinate's capability for solving loosely defined problems.*

➤ **Notice how different this assignment is from most that you get in school. The question is poorly formulated; the decision method is vague (hire a consultant if you want, but not one that is too expensive, if you do hire one).**

➤ **By implication the manager is saying, "Don't involve me further. I just want your final report." (He can do this because he knows that Aaron will check the consulting expenditure with him before approving it.)**

➤ **The source of the consultant, the amount to pay, what constitutes "too expensive" are all left to the subordinate to figure out. This is often how problems like this are addressed in the real world:** *"Make a plan, find out what you need, do it, and get back to me."*

I think our protagonist started on the wrong foot. Instead of starting with a list of consultants, he should have started with a list of questions that need to be answered.

Normally, the IS department would be a good source of expertise for our protagonist. However, the COO indicates that he has received a proposal from that department, and he's not sure about it. Perhaps he wants a report that is completely separate from the thinking of the IS department. If so, without involvement of that department, our protagonist runs the danger of developing ideas that are infeasible, given (unknown) local conditions. Were I the protagonist, I would be very uncomfortable performing this study without some coordination with the IS department. At least, he should clarify this situation with the COO and make some contact with that department if possible. No matter what, not involving the IS department is awkward. A solid, informal, company network (see Reflections Guide) would help here.

➤ **Recall the Problem Solving Guide from Chapter 3:** *Question your questions.* **Make a list of questions to be answered, and then formulate a strategy for solving them. That solution strategy will indicate whether the consultant is required, and, if so, what type of consultant.**

That list of questions that must be answered will also provide a justification for the consultant. (With the COO's endorsement, he probably doesn't need one. But providing one eases Aaron's job and, through the back channel, shows the COO that he's doing his homework.)

However, it's also possible that a consultant is needed to formulate the list of questions. But, in that case, the protagonist should have started that way with the consultants: "First, I need to learn the questions I should be asking."

➤ **If you had been the protagonist of this story, you would have known to start with the list of questions. You already would have been doing a better job than this person!**

Data communications is an exceedingly important field. *Knowledge of data communications combined with knowledge of data security* would be an exceptionally marketable skill set. You might ask a colleague who teaches your data communications class to speak to the students for 5 minutes or so about that class. A graduate with knowledge of business, data communications, and data security would be a hot prospect.

This chapter contains considerable material on TCP/IP–OSI protocols. Why is this important to the student? Given the importance of the Internet, I think a basic understanding of how it works is essential to any businessperson. Today, people should know what IP is and what an IP address is. They should also know how domain registration works. I think they need to know DHCP and NAT as well; they use them all the time. For example:

➤ **When we get to Chapter 11, we will learn that at least half of home wireless networks are unprotected. Try it: Take a laptop with wireless capability into some busy neighborhood and turn it on. See how many wireless nets are unprotected. Truly amazing!**

➤ **Nothing more than MAC address filtering would lock out all but the very sophisticated criminal. Of course, one first has to know what a MAC address is and how to access the firmware on one's router. This is easy to do, but you need a little knowledge of data communications.**

➤ **Given the level of wireless technology right now, every home user has to be a network administrator, yet almost no one knows how! See Case 5-2 at the end of this chapter.**

If nothing else, students should understand TCP/IP–OSI as part of their professional literacy—to better understand modern commerce, even to be better investors. For example, Cisco makes routers. Altera makes programmable devices that Cisco places in its routers. There is a supply chain relationship between those companies. Without the knowledge students are gaining in this class, they will have no idea of what those companies do and how they relate.

The Larry Jones case (MIS in Use 5-1) is based on a real student. He was very unassuming and did not present himself like a classic "techie" at all. He saw himself as an emerging businessperson who happened to know a lot about data communications. I wonder what his net worth will be in a few years. . . .

WRAP UP

Summary comments:

➤ **The purpose of this chapter is to teach you basic concepts and terminology about data communications and how the Internet works.**

➤ **Given the ubiquity of data communications today, knowing these basics is essential for business literacy.**

➤ **You could be given the task that the Accounts Payable manager was given. Were that to happen, lucky you! What a career-building opportunity this person has!**

Students may complain about the level of technical difficulty in this chapter. I don't let them off the hook; but I do attempt to provide support—at least to those who are making a legitimate effort to learn it. Class "plays" can help. Here are a couple of ideas:

➤ **Bring 10 students to the front of the class and enact the TCP–OSI protocol architecture. Five students are senders and five are receivers. The level-one students hold a rope or something that represents the communications line. Each student plays the role of a protocol at a level—students have to explain what they receive, what they output, and what they do. I explain they are interfacing with the students standing next to them, but communicating with the student at their level in the other group.**

   I find it helps to go slowly and make each student tell me, clearly, what he or she is doing. Often, they are very confused, and this play forces them to ask questions. I may pass three or four messages through this network before they begin to understand what to do.

➤ **Another tack is to send an email to a student in the back of the class. In this case, most of the students are routers. I start with an email, break it into packets, and pass them to the first "router" and tell him/her to pass it to a router that is closer to the back row. Sometimes I go out into the group and take one of the packets and destroy it to show the need for reliability. Eventually the packets arrive (they're numbered) and are placed in order and opened by the recipient.**

➤ **Yet a third "play" can be used to illustrate NAT and DHCP. I have two groups of students, representing two LANs, and the rest of the students are routers. You can use the example in the text in Figures 5-23 and 5-24. In each LAN, one student is the router and is a DHCP server and performs NAT. When students join the LAN they get their local IP address from him/her. (I don't worry about switches unless the students are confused by their omission.)**

I find the students will keep working to learn this material as long as I am making a strong effort to teach it. I don't let them off the hook just because it's difficult.

➤ **This subject can be difficult, so tell me, as your coach, what you need to know. This difficulty can be overcome!**

Fundamental Networking Concepts

A computer **network** is a collection of computers that communicate with one another over transmission lines. As shown in Figure 5-1, the three basic types of networks are local area networks, wide area networks, and internets.

A **local area network (LAN)** connects computers that reside in a single geographic location on the premises of the company that operates the LAN. The number of connected computers can range from two to several hundred. The distinguishing characteristic of a LAN is *a single location.* **Wide area networks (WANs)** connect computers at different geographic locations. The computers in two separated company sites must be connected using a WAN. To illustrate, the computers for a College of Business located on a single campus can be connected via a LAN. The computers for a College of Business located on multiple campuses must be connected via a WAN.

The single versus multiple site distinction is important. With a LAN, an organization can place communications lines wherever it wants, because all lines reside on its premises. The same is not true for a WAN. A company with offices in Chicago and Atlanta cannot run a wire to connect computers in the two cities. Instead, the company must contract with a communications vendor that is licensed by the government and already has lines or has the authority to run new lines between the two cities.

An **internet** is a network of networks. Internets connect LANs, WANs, and other internets. The most famous internet is "**the Internet**" (with an upper-case letter *I*), the collection of networks that you use when you send email or access a Web site. In addition to the Internet, private networks of networks, called internets also exist.

The networks that comprise an internet use a large variety of communication methods and conventions, and data must flow seamlessly across them. To provide seamless flow, an elaborate scheme called a *layered protocol* is used. We consider such schemes next and then turn to LANs, WANs, and internets in more detail.

Layered Protocols

Suppose you are on vacation in Hawaii and you want to send a photo of your amazing surfing skills to a friend in snow-bound Cincinnati, Ohio. You plug your portable computer into your hotel's network, fire up your email program, write the email, attach the photo, and press Send. That's it. In a matter of minutes your friend will be admiring your surfing antics. Even though you may not know it, a techno-miracle occurred.

Video

Figure 5-2 (page 118) shows the networks involved in sending your email message and picture. There is a LAN at your hotel, a LAN at your friend's company, and the Internet connects the two. Assume you sent your message from Computer 3 (C3) at the hotel and that your friend is sitting at Computer 10 (C10) in the company in Ohio.

You know that your email and picture traveled over the Internet, which is a network of networks. But how? A host of problems had to be overcome: Your friend has a Macintosh computer, and you have a Dell. The two of you use different email programs. As shown, both you and your friend are connected to LANs, but your hotel's LAN uses wires, and your friend's company's LAN is wireless. Thus, the LANs are of different types and process messages differently.

Type	Characteristic
Local Area Network (LAN)	Computers connected at a single physical site
Wide Area Network (WAN)	Computers connected between two or more separated sites
The Internet and internets	Networks of networks

Figure 5-1
Major Network Types

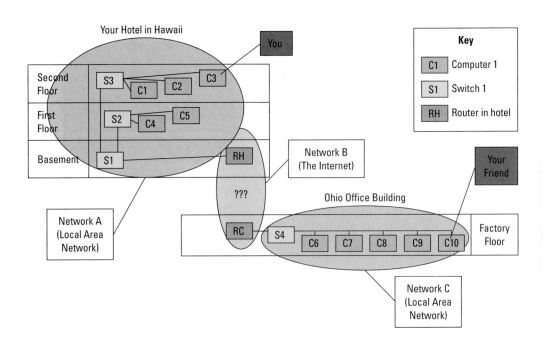

Figure 5-2
Example Networks

Furthermore, your message and picture were sent over an optical fiber cable underneath the sea and received by a computer in San Francisco. But, your picture was too big to send in one big chunk, so it was broken into pieces, and the pieces traveled separately. When the pieces (called *packets*) arrived in San Francisco, a device (called a *router*) determined that the best way to get them to your friend was to send them to a router in Los Angeles, which sent the pieces to a router in Denver, which sent them to a router in Cincinnati, which sent them to a company that contracts with your friend's employer to provide Internet access, which sent them to the email server at your friend's company. Meanwhile, your computer determined that one of the pieces got lost along the way, and it automatically resent that piece.

When all of the pieces have been assembled, your friend gets the "You've got mail" indicator on his computer. He looks at your picture and asks, "How does she do that?" What he should be asking is, "How does the Internet do that?"

The key concept is *divide and conquer*. All of the work is divided into categories, and the categories of work are arranged into layers. To understand this further, we must first explain communications protocols.

Communications Protocols

A **protocol** is a standardized means for coordinating an activity between two or more entities. Humans use social protocols. For example, a protocol exists for introducing two people to one another. Another human protocol, illustrated in Figure 5-3, occurs at the grocery store. This protocol, like all protocols, proceeds through a sequence of ordered steps. If, in response to the clerk's query "Debit or credit," you enter your PIN, you are skipping steps and thus violating the protocol. The clerk will correct you and ask her

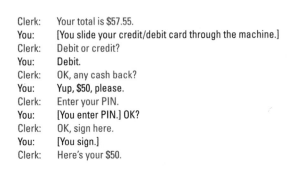

Figure 5-3
Example of a Grocery Store Protocol

question again. Notice, too, that the protocol has a decision branch. If you say "credit," then the clerk will not ask the question about cash back or ask you to enter your PIN.

A **communications protocol** is a means for coordinating activity between two or more communicating computers. Two machines must agree on the protocol to use, and they must follow that protocol as they send messages back and forth. Because there is so much to do, communications protocols are broken up into levels or layers.

The TCP/IP–OSI Architecture

In fact, several different **layered protocol** schemes, or **architectures**, have been proposed. The **International Organization for Standardization (ISO)** developed the **Reference Model for Open Systems Interconnection (OSI)**, an architecture that has seven layers. Another group, the **Internet Engineering Task Force (IETF)**, developed a four-layer scheme called the **TCP/IP (Transmission Control Program/Internet Protocol) architecture**. For reasons that are beyond our discussion, the most commonly used architecture today is a five-layer blend of these two architectures called the **TCP/IP–OSI architecture**.

Figure 5-4 shows the five layers of this hybrid architecture. As shown in the right-most column, the bottom two layers concern the transmission of data within a single network. The next two layers are used for data transmission across an internet (a network of networks, including the Internet). The top layer provides protocols that enable applications to interact.

Layer 5

Examine the networks in Figure 5-2 between your hotel in Hawaii and your friend. Unknown to you or your friend, each of your computers contains programs that operate at all five layers of the TCP/IP–OSI architecture. Your email program operates at Layer 5. It generates and receives email (and attachments like your photo) according to one of the standard email protocols defined for Layer 5. Most likely, it uses a protocol called **Simple Mail Transfer Protocol (SMTP)**.

Layer	Name	Specific Function	Broad Function
5	Application	The application layer governs how two applications work with each other, even if they are from different vendors.	Interoperability of application programs
4	Transport	Transport layer standards govern aspects of end-to-end communication between two end hosts that are not handled by the internet layer. These standards also allow hosts to work together even if the two computers are from different vendors and have different internal designs.	Transmission across an internet
3	Internet	Internet layer standards govern the transmission of packets across an internet—typically by sending them through several routers along the route. Internet layer standards also govern packet organization, timing constraints, and reliability.	
2	Data Link	Data link layer standards govern the transmission of frames across a single network—typically by sending them through several switches along the data link. Data link layer standards also govern frame organization, timing constraints, and reliability.	Transmission across a single network
1	Physical	Physical layer standards govern transmission between adjacent devices connected by a transmission medium.	

Figure 5-4
TCP/IP—OSI Architecture

Source: Used by permission from Ray Panko, *Business Data Networks and Telecommunications*, 5th Ed. (Prentice Hall, 2005), p. 92.

There are many other Layer-5 protocols. **HTTP**, or the **Hypertext Transfer Protocol**, is used for the processing of Web pages. When you type the address *www.ibm.com* into your browser, notice that your browser adds the notation *http://*. (Try this, if you've never noticed that it happens.) By filling in these characters, your browser is indicating that it will use the HTTP protocol to communicate with the IBM site.

By the way, the Web and the Internet are not the same thing. The Web, which is a subset of the Internet, consists of sites and users that process the HTTP protocol. The Internet is the communications structure that supports all application-layer protocols, including HTTP, SMTP, and other protocols.

FTP, or the **File Transfer Protocol**, is another application-layer protocol. You can use FTP to copy files from one computer to another. In Figure 5-2, if Computer 1 wants to copy a file from Computer 9, it would use FTP.

Three important terms lurk in this discussion:

- **Architecture.** An *architecture* is an arrangement of protocol layers in which each layer is given specific tasks to accomplish.
- **Protocol.** At each layer of the architecture, there are one or more *protocols*. Each protocol is a set of rules that accomplish the tasks assigned to its layer.
- **Program.** A *program* is a specific computer product that implements a protocol.

So, for example, the TCP/IP-OSI architecture has five layers. At the top level are numerous protocols, including HTTP, SMTP, and FTP. For each of those protocols, there are program products that implement the protocol. Some of the programs that implement the HTTP protocol of the TCP/IP–OSI architecture are called *browsers*. Two common browsers are Netscape Navigator and Microsoft Internet Explorer.

Layer 4

As Figure 5-5 shows, our email program (which uses SMTP) interacts with another protocol called **TCP**, or **Transmission Control Program (TCP)**. TCP operates at Layer 4 of the TCP/IP–OSI architecture. Note that we are using the acronym TCP in two ways: as the name of a Layer-4 *protocol* and as part of the name of the TCP/IP–OSI protocol architecture. In fact, the architecture gets its name because it usually includes the TCP protocol.

TCP performs many important tasks. Your Dell and your friend's Apple have different operating systems that represent data in different ways. Programs in those operating systems that implement the TCP protocol make conversions from one data representation to the other. Also, a TCP program examines your email and picture and

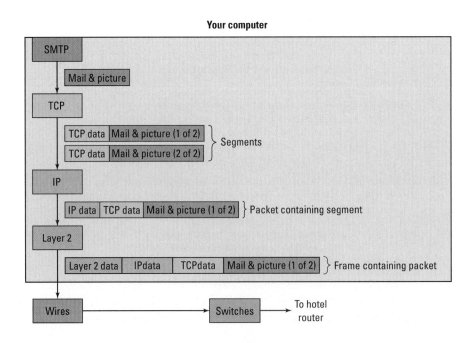

Figure 5-5
TCP/IP—OSI on Your
Computer

breaks lengthy messages (like your picture) into pieces called **segments**. When it does this, it places identifying data at the front of each segment that are akin to the To and From addresses that you would put on a letter for the postal mail.

TCP programs also provide reliability. It was the TCP program on your computer that noticed that one of the pieces did not arrive at your friend's computer and so it resent that piece.

Your friend's Macintosh computer also has a program that runs the TCP protocol. It receives the segments from your computer and sends acknowledgments back to your computer when it receives each segment. The TCP program also translates the segments from Windows (Dell) to Macintosh format, reassembles the segments into a coherent whole, and makes that assembly available to your friend's email program.

Layer 3

TCP interacts with protocols that operate at Level 3, the next layer down. For the TCP/IP architecture, the layer-3 protocol is the **Internet Protocol (IP)**. The chief purpose of IP is to route messages across an internet. In the case of your email, the IP program on your computer does not know how to reach your friend's computer, but it does know how to start. Namely, it knows to send all of the pieces of your email and picture to a device in your hotel's network called a *router*. In Figure 5-2, that router is labeled RH. (This is not a brand of router, it is just the label we will put on the hotel's router in this figure.)

To send a segment to RH, the IP layer program on your computer first packages each segment into a packet. As shown in Figure 5-5, it also places IP data in front of the packet, in front of the TCP data. This action is akin to wrapping a letter inside another envelope and placing additional To/From data in the header of the outer envelope.

Routers are special-purpose computers that implement the IP protocol. The router labeled RH examines the destination of your packets and uses the rules of the IP protocol to decide where to send them. RH does not know how to get them all the way to Ohio, but it does know how to get them started on their way. In this case, it decides to send them to another router located in San Francisco. Dozens of other routers on the Internet will eventually cause the packets containing your message and picture to arrive at a router at your friend's employer. We will explain more about this process later in the chapter.

Layers 1 and 2

As shown in Figure 5-2, your hotel uses a LAN to connect the computers in its hotel rooms. (Lucky you—you're staying at an exclusive hotel with just two floors and five rooms.) Basic computer connectivity is accomplished using Layers 1 and 2 of the TCP/IP–OSI architecture. As you will learn, computing devices called *switches* facilitate that data communication. (See Figure 5-5.)

A program implementing a Layer-2 protocol will package each of your packets into **frames**, which are the containers used at Layers 1 and 2. (Segments go into packets, and packets go into frames.) Then, programs, switches, and other devices cause the pieces of your email and picture to pass from your computer to Switch 3, from Switch 3 to Switch 1, and from Switch 1 to Router RH. (See Figure 5-2.)

Before we can finish the saga of your email, you need to know more about LANs and WANs. We will turn to those topics now and pick up the rest of the email story in the last section of this chapter when we describe how the Internet works.

By the way, any computing device can run the TCP/IP–OSI protocols, even a toaster or a microwave oven. However, read the *Problem Solving Guide* on page 121a before investing in such appliances.

▮ Local Area Networks

A *local area network (LAN)* is a group of computers connected together on a single company site. Usually the computers are located within a half mile or so of each other, although longer distances are possible. The key distinction, however, is that all

Thinking Exponentially Is Not Possible, but...

Nathan Myhrvold, the chief scientist at Microsoft Corporation during the 1990s, once said that humans are incapable of thinking exponentially. Instead, when something changes exponentially, we think of the fastest linear change we can imagine and extrapolate from there, as illustrated in the figure on the next page. Myhrvold was writing about the exponential growth of magnetic storage. His point was that no one could then imagine how much growth there would be in magnetic storage and what we would do with it.

This limitation pertains equally well to the growth of computer network phenomena. We have witnessed exponential growth in a number of areas: the number of Internet connections, the number of Web pages, and the amount of data accessible on the Internet. And, all signs are that this exponential growth isn't over.

What, you might ask, does this have to do with me? Well, suppose you are a product manager for home appliances. When most homes have a wireless network, it will be cheap and easy for appliances to talk to one another. When that day arrives, what happens to your existing product line? Will the competition's talking appliances take away your market share? On the other hand, talking appliances may not satisfy a real need. If a toaster and a coffee pot have nothing to say to each other, you'll be wasting money to create them.

Every business, every organization, needs to be thinking about the ubiquitous and cheap connectivity that is growing exponentially. What are the new opportunities? What are the new threats? How will our competition react? How should we position ourselves? How should we respond? As you consider these questions, keep in mind that because humans cannot think exponentially, we're all just guessing.

So what can we do to better anticipate changes brought by exponential phenomena? For one, understand that technology does not drive people to do things they've never done before, no matter how much the technologists suggest it might. (Just because we can do something does not mean anyone will want to do that something.)

Social progress occurs in small, evolutionary, adaptive steps. Right now, for example, thousands of people are driving to stores to rent a movie. When they get there, they may not find the movie they want, they may wait in a long line, or they may never find a parking spot. Is it likely that someone would want to rent a movie online, over the Internet, if they could? Probably so; online rental is an extension of what people are already doing. It solves a problem that people already have. So, when network capacities support online movie rental, it's likely to be a success.

On the other hand, emerging network technology enables my dry cleaner to notify me the minute my clothes are ready. Do I want to know? How much do I care to know that my clothes are ready Monday at 1:45 rather than sometime after 4:00 on Tuesday? In truth, I don't care. Such technology does not solve a problem that I have.

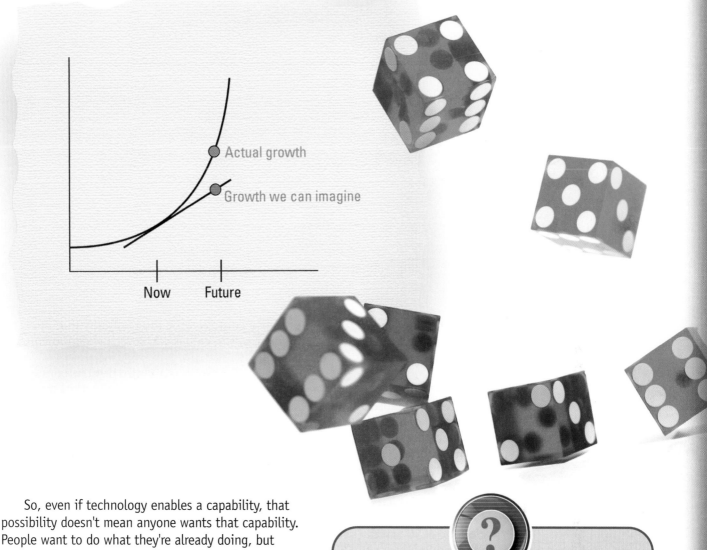

Actual growth

Growth we can imagine

Now   Future

So, even if technology enables a capability, that possibility doesn't mean anyone wants that capability. People want to do what they're already doing, but more easily; they want to solve problems that they already have.

Another response to exponential growth is to hedge your bets. If you can't know the outcome of an exponential phenomenon, don't commit to one direction. Position yourself to move as soon as the direction is clear. Develop a few talking appliances, position your organization to develop more, but wait for a clear sign of market acceptance before going all out.

Finally, notice in the exponential curve that the larger the distance between Now and the Future, the larger the error. In fact, the error increases exponentially with the length of the prediction. So, if you read in this textbook that IPv6 will replace IPv4 in one year, assign that statement a certain level of doubt. On the other hand, if you read in this text that it will replace IPv4 in five years, assign that statement an exponentially greater level of doubt.

DISCUSSION QUESTIONS

1. In your own words, explain the meaning of the claim that no one can think exponentially. Do you agree with this claim?

2. Describe a phenomenon besides connectivity or magnetic memory that you believe is increasing exponentially. Explain why it is difficult to predict the consequences of this phenomenon in three years.

3. To what extent do you think technology is responsible for the growth in the number of news sources? On balance, do you think having many news sources of varying quality is better than having a few with high quality control?

4. List three products or services, like movie rental, that could dramatically change because of increased connectivity. Do not include movie rental.

5. Rate your answers to question 3 in terms of how closely they fit with problems that people have today.

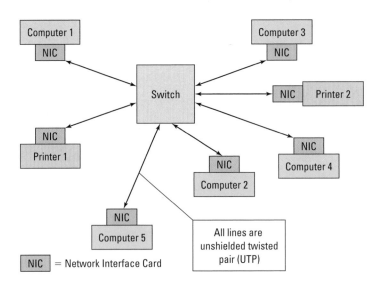

Figure 5-6
Local Area Network

of the computers are located on property controlled by the company that operates the LAN. This means that the company can run cables wherever needed to connect the computers.

Consider the LAN in Figure 5-6. Here, five computers and two printers connect via a **switch**, which is a special-purpose computer that receives and transmits messages on the LAN. In Figure 5-6, when Computer 1 accesses Printer 1, it does so by sending the print job to the switch, which then redirects that data to Printer 1.

Each device on a LAN (computer, printer, etc.) has a hardware component called a **network interface card (NIC)** that connects the device's circuitry to the cable. The NIC works with programs in each device to implement Layer 1 and 2 protocols. On older machines, the NIC is a card that fits into an expansion slot. Newer machines have an **onboard NIC**, which is an NIC built into the motherboard.

Figure 5-7 shows a typical NIC device. Each NIC has a unique identifier, which is called the **MAC (media access control) address**. The computers, printers, switches, and other devices on a LAN are connected using one of two media. Most connections are made using **unshielded twisted pair (UTP) cable**. Figure 5-8 shows a section of UTP cable that contains four pairs of twisted wire. A device called an RJ-45 connector is used to connect the UTP cable into NIC devices on the LAN.

By the way, wires are twisted for reasons beyond aesthetics and style. Twisting the wires substantially reduces the cross-wire signal interference that occurs when wires run parallel for long distances.

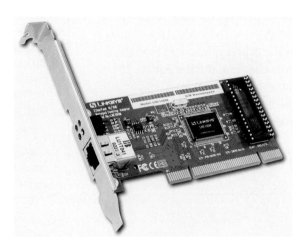

Figure 5-7
NIC Interface Card

You Be the Guide

Using the Problem Solving Guide (page 121a)

GOALS

* Sensitize students to the difficulty (impossibility?) of thinking exponentially.

* Describe strategies that students can use to deal with exponential phenomena in their professional lives.

BACKGROUND AND PRESENTATION STRATEGIES

When Nathan Myhrvold was the chief technology officer at Microsoft, he wrote a paper entitled "Road Kill on the Information Superhighway," a classic that contained the statement, "No one can think exponentially." He was a graduate student of Stephen Hawking, later started his own company, and became a Microsoft employee when his company was acquired by Microsoft. Working at a very senior level at Microsoft during its glory years of the 1990s, he amassed vast wealth (and no longer works for Microsoft).

The graph in this guide shows it all. When told something grows exponentially, we think fast growth, but we do so *linearly*. We just cannot image the changes posed by exponential growth; it is even more difficult to understand the consequences. The exponential growth in the number of Internet users is a case in point. Who would have imagined the changes in politics and the news media that the bloggers have brought forward? So fast that the word *blog* doesn't appear in the current (2005) standard Microsoft Word dictionary.

I underline the words of caution regarding the talking appliances. Although we have the technology for the alarm clock to signal the coffee pot and for the coffee pot to signal the toaster, does anybody really want that capability?

I find it helps to discuss a contemporary example of a possibly exponential phenomenon. RFID could be one example. Another one that has begun to emerge since the text was written is *podcasting*, which is the preparation and distribution of MP3 audio files for playback on iPods and similar devices. Podcasts can be registered with aggregators like podcasting.net for inclusion in podcast directories.

The following sequences of questions use podcasting as the example. They could use RFID or IPv6 instead, if you prefer.

➤ **Podcasting is so recent that the text doesn't address it. What is podcasting?**

➤ **What are potential commercial uses of podcasting? In public relations? In advertising? For employee education and training? Other?**

➤ **How could a company use podcasting to increase the productivity of its sales force while traveling on the road?**

➤ **How can we apply the principles of this guide to podcasting?**

➤ **The guide recommends hedging one's bets when addressing new technology. Put a little money on one or more possibilities; be positioned to move in the direction that the market takes. Watch and wait; move when the direction is clear.**

➤ **How could we hedge our bets with regard to podcasting?**

Notice the impact of time on the size of the disparity between linear and exponential thinking. What will podcasting do in one year? Five years? Ten years?

➤ **Learn to read technology articles critically. Where exponential phenomena are concerned, any statement that begins, "XXX (the phenomenon) will double in 5 years," is so full of uncertainty as to be nearly meaningless.**

Here are two cases in point in our business: RFID and IPv6. For the first, organizations are still trying to figure out how to use it. Everyone seems to say that it will be important, but no one (in 2005, including Wal-Mart) knows how, when, or why. The impetus for IPv6 was that the world was going to run out of IP addresses. With DHCP and NAT, however, the utility of the existing IPv4 address space has expanded dramatically. IPv6 still has advantages over IPv4, but the pressure to convert is much less than most would have thought just three years ago.

❓ SUGGESTED RESPONSES FOR DISCUSSION QUESTIONS

1. I think it's hard to disagree with this statement, but it will be interesting to see what the students think. The goal of the question is to make sure the students understand the point of the remark.

2. See the earlier discussion of podcasting. RFID adoption is another. It hasn't yet caught on, but once RFID becomes a standard in the supply chain, watch

out! Everyone will begin to use it. Overnight it will become a true (as opposed to today's Wal-Mart-dictated) requirement. Another example: What will be the demand for HDTV in three years?

3. It's having a huge impact. Not just the 500 channels of TV, but the blogs and podcasters. Also consider video podcasting (by whatever name it will have). Look at how the blogs influenced the 2004 election; blogs claim they played a key role in the early retirement of Dan Rather at CBS.

   Quality is interesting; a debate is underway right now. Mainstream media (MSM) claims that political blogs are of poor quality. The bloggers respond, "No, way—if I publish junk, other bloggers will be all over it in a matter of hours. It's much easier to publish rubbish in a newspaper than in a blog."

4. Three possibilities are:

   • How-to magazines could supplement or replace how-to articles with video clips. (FineWoodworking.com is doing this now.)

   • Parents could use GPS and embedded-under-the-skin RFID chips to keep track of their children.

   • Insurance companies could use onboard auto video recordings to determine who did what during an accident.

These examples all fit closely with problems that people have today. We know that how-to magazines are meeting a market need because they currently sell well. Parents always need to know where their kids are, and insurance companies could use the video to reduce litigation and other accident expenses. In terms of *closeness to real problems,* I'd rank the three ideas as 2, 1, and 3. Child-embedded RFID is probably socially infeasible, however.

WRAP UP

➤ The *terrific news in this guide is that technology constantly creates new opportunities* for products and services. Your future career can be just as exciting as Steve Jobs's has been. The opportunities will be there.

➤ Don't automatically suppose people will want to do what technology enables them to do. People want to do what they are already doing, but better, faster, or cheaper.

➤ Be careful with exponential phenomena. We don't *know* what all of the ubiquitous, nearly free, ever-faster connectivity means. It will mean something—it will mean substantial change—but we don't know what.

➤ Stay tuned!!! Lots of opportunities will come your way during your career!

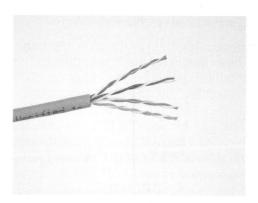

Figure 5-8
Unshielded Twisted Pair
(UTP) Cable

Some LANs, usually those larger than the one in Figure 5-6, use more than one switch. The LAN in your hotel in Figure 5-2 has three switches. Typically, in a building with several floors, a switch is placed on each floor, and the computers on that floor are connected to the switch with UTP cable. The switches on each floor are connected together by a main switch, which is often located in the basement.

The connections between switches can use UTP cable, but if they carry a lot of traffic or are far apart UTP cable may be replaced by **optical fiber cables**. The signals on such cables are light rays, and they are reflected inside the glass core of the optical fiber cable. The core is surrounded by a *cladding* to contain the light signals, and the cladding, in turn, is wrapped with an outer layer to protect it. In Figure 5-2, an optical fiber cable might be used to connect switch S1 with switch S3. Optical fiber cable uses special connectors called ST and SC connectors, which are shown as the blue plugs in Figure 5-9. The meaning of the abbreviations ST and SC are unimportant; they are just the two most common optical connectors.

Figure 5-9
Optical Fiber Cable

The IEEE 802.3, or Ethernet, Protocol

For a LAN to work, all devices on the LAN must use the same protocol. The Institute for Electrical and Electronics Engineers (IEEE, pronounced "I triple E") sponsors committees that create and publish protocols and other standards. The committee that addresses LAN standards is called the *IEEE 802 Committee*. Thus, IEEE LAN protocols always start with the numbers 802.

Today, the world's most popular protocol for LANs is the **IEEE 802.3 protocol**. This protocol standard, also called **Ethernet**, specifies hardware characteristics such as which wire carries which signals. It also describes how messages are to be packaged and processed for transmission over the LAN. Ethernet operates at Layers 1 and 2 of the TCP/IP–OSI architecture.

Most personal computers today are equipped with an onboard NIC that supports what is called **10/100/1000 Ethernet**. These products conform to the 802.3 specification and allow for transmission at a rate of 10, 100, or 1,000 Mbps (megabits per second). Switches detect the speed that a given device can handle and communicate with it at that speed. If you check computer listings at Dell, Hewlett-Packard, Toshiba, and other manufacturers, you will see PCs advertised as having 10/100/1000 Ethernet.

By the way, the abbreviations used for communication speeds differ from those used for computer memory. For communications equipment, k stands for 1,000, not 1,024 as it does for memory. Similarly, M stands for 1,000,000, not $1,024 \times 1,024$; G stands for 1,000,000,000, not $1,024 \times 1,024 \times 1,024$. Thus, 100 Mbps is 100,000,000 bits per second. Also note that communications speeds are expressed in *bits*, whereas memory sizes are expressed in *bytes*.

LANs with Wireless Connections

In recent years, wireless connections have become popular with LANs. Figure 5-10 shows the same LAN as in Figure 5-6 except that two of the computers and one printer have wireless connections. Notice that the NIC for the wireless devices have been replaced by **wireless NIC (WNIC)**. For laptop computers, such devices can be cards that slide into the PCMA slot or they can be built-in, onboard devices.

Several different wireless standards exist, as shown in Figure 5-11. As of 2005, the most popular is IEEE 802.11g. The differences among the variations are beyond the

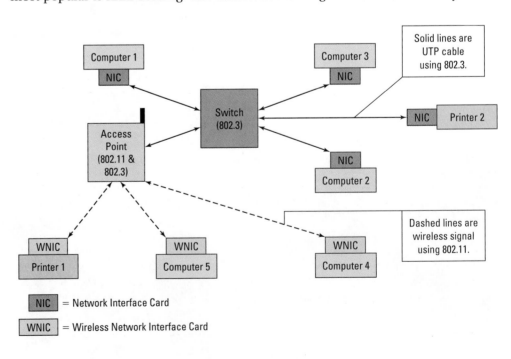

Figure 5-10
Local Area Network with Wireless

802.11 Standard	Rated Speed*	Comment
802.11a	54 Mbps	Not widely used because it operates in a higher frequency band that requires more expensive access points and NICs. Useful where interference is a problem at a lower frequency band.
802.11b	11 Mbps	Widely installed but obsolete because of its low speed. 802.11g equipment will slow down to work with 802.11b equipment, but this loses the usefulness of 802.11g equipment's higher speed.
802.11g	54 Mbps	The dominant WLAN standard today. Operates in a lower frequency band where it is subject to interference from microwave ovens and other devices. Rarely a problem, but can be serious.
802.11n	100 Mbps to 250 Mbps	Standard has not yet been completed.

* Actual speeds are only half as fast or even slower.

Figure 5-11
Wireless Access Standards

Source: Used by permission from Ray Panko, *Business Data Networks and Telecommunications*, 5th ed. (Prentice Hall, 2005), p. 92.

scope of this discussion. Just note that the current standard, 802.11g, allows speeds of up to 54 Mbps. All of the 802.11 standards operate at Layers 1 and 2 of the TCP/IP-OSI model.

Observe that the LAN in Figure 5-10 uses both the 802.3 and 802.11 protocols. The NICs operate according to the 802.3 protocol and connect directly to the switch, which also operates on the 802.3 standard. The WNICs operate according to the 802.11 protocol and connect to an **access point (AP)**. The AP must be able to process messages according to both the 802.3 and 802.11 standards, because it sends and receives wireless traffic using the 802.11 protocol and then communicates with the switch using the 802.3 protocol. Characteristics of LANs are summarized in the top part of Figure 5-12 (page 126).

Knowledge of wireless networks provided an opportunity for one student to start a business, while still in college. Read the *MIS in Use 5-1* (page 127) to see how.

Wide Area Networks

A *wide area network (WAN)* connects computers located at physically separated sites. A company with offices in Detroit and Atlanta must use a WAN to connect the computers together. Because the sites are physically separated, the company cannot string wire from one site to another. Rather, it must obtain connection capabilities from another company (or companies) licensed by the government to provide communications.

Although you may not have realized it, when you connect your personal computer to the Internet, you are using a WAN. You are connecting to computers owned and operated by your **Internet service provider (ISP)** that are not located physically at your site.

An ISP has three important functions. First, it provides you with a legitimate Internet address. Second, it serves as your gateway to the Internet. The ISP receives the communications from your computer and passes them on to the Internet, and it receives communications from the Internet and passes them on to you. Finally, ISPs pay for the Internet. They collect money from their customers and pay access fees and other charges on your behalf.

We begin our discussion of WANs by considering modem connections to ISPs.

Type	Topology	Transmission Line	Transmission Speed	Equipment Used	Protocol Commonly Used	Remarks
Local Area Network	Local area network	UTP or optical fiber	10, 100, or 1, 000 Mbps	Switch NIC UTP or optical	IEEE 802.3 (Ethernet)	Switches connect devices, multiple switches on all but small LANs.
	Local area network with wireless	UTP or optical for non-wireless connections	Up to 54 Mbps	Wireless access point Wireless NIC	IEEE 802.11g	Access point transforms wired LAN (802.3) to wireless LAN (802.11).
Wide Area Network	Dial-up modem to Internet service provider (ISP)	Regular telephone	Up to 55 kbps	Modem Telephone line	Modulation standards (V.32, V90, V92), PPP	Modulation required for first part of telephone line. Computer use blocks telephone use.
	DSL modem to ISP	DSL telephone	Personal: Upstream to 256 kbps, downstream to 768 kbps. Business: to 1.544 Mbps.	DSL modem DSL-capable telephone line	DSL	Can have computer and phone use simultaneously. Always connected.
	Cable modem to ISP	Cable TV lines to optical cable	Upstream to 256 kbps Downstream 300–600 kbps (10 Mbps in theory)	Cable modem Cable TV cable	Cable	Capacity is shared with other sites; performance varies depending on others' use.
	Point to point lines	Network of leased lines	T1–1.5 Mbps T3–44.7 Mbps OC48–2.5 Gbps OC768–40 Gbps	Access devices Optical cable Satellite	PPP	Span geographically distributed sites using lines provided by licensed communications vendors. Expensive to set up and manage.
	PSDN	Lease usage of private network	56 Kbps–40 Mbps+	Leased line to PSDN POP	Frame-relay ATM 10 Gbps and 40 Gbps Ethernet	Lease time on a public switched data network–operated by independent party. Ineffective for inter-company communication.
	Virtual private network (VPN)	Use the Internet to provide private network	Varies with speed of connection to Internet	VPN client software. VPN server hardware and software.	PPTP IPSec	Secure, private connection provides a tunnel through the Internet. Can support inter-company communication

Figure 5-12
Summary of LAN and WAN Networks

Connecting the Personal Computer to an ISP: Modems

Home computers and those of small businesses are commonly connected to an ISP in one of three ways: using a regular telephone line, using a special telephone line called a DSL line, or using a cable TV line.

All three of these alternatives require that the *digital data* in the computer be converted to an **analog**, or wavy, signal. A device called a **modem**, or modulator/demodulator, performs this conversion. Figure 5-13 (page 128) shows one way of converting the digital byte 01000001 to an analog signal.

As shown in Figure 5-14 (page 128), once the modem converts your computer's digital data to analog, that analog signal is then sent over the telephone line or TV cable. If sent by telephone line, the first telephone switch that your signal reaches converts the signal into the form used by the international telephone system.

Larry Jones (Student) Network Services

In 2003, Larry Jones was an entering freshman at Big State University. (This case is real; however, to protect privacy, the student and university names are fictional.) Larry had always been interested in technology and as a high school student had won a scholarship from Cisco Corporation (a maker of routers and other communications hardware). As part of his scholarship, Larry had attended several Cisco training classes on setting up LANs, switches, and routers.

Larry pledged a fraternity at Big State, and when the fraternity leadership learned of his expertise, they asked him to set up a LAN with an Internet connection for the fraternity house. It was a simple job for Larry, and his fraternity brothers were quite satisfied with his solution. He did it for free, as a volunteer, and appreciated the introductions the project gave him to senior leaders of the fraternity. The project enabled him to build his network of personal contacts.

Over the summer of 2003, however, it dawned on Larry that his fraternity was not the only one on the Big State campus that had the need for a LAN with access to the Internet. Accordingly, that summer he developed marketing materials describing the need and the services he could provide. That fall he called on fraternities and sororities and made presentations of his skills and of the network he had built for the fraternity. Within a year, he had a dozen or so fraternities and sororities as customers.

Larry quickly realized that he couldn't just set up a LAN and Internet connection, charge his fee, and walk away. His customers had continuing problems that required him to return to resolve problems, add new computers, add printer servers, and so forth. At first, he provided such support as part of his installation package price. He soon learned that he could charge a support fee for regular support, and even add extra charges for support beyond normal wear and tear. By the end of 2004, the support fees were meeting all of Larry's college expenses, and then some.

When I last saw him, Larry had formed a partnership with several other students to expand his services to local apartment houses and condominiums.

This case is continued as Case Study 5-1 at the end of this chapter (page 148).

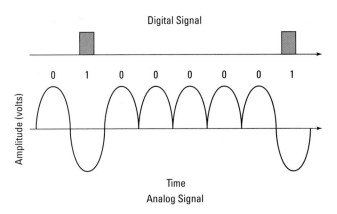

Figure 5-13
Analog vs. Digital Signals

Dial-Up Modems

A **dial-up modem** performs the conversion between analog and digital in such a way that the signal can be carried on a regular telephone line. As the name implies, you dial the phone number for your ISP and connect. The maximum transmission speed for a switch is 56 kbps (in practice, the limit is 53 kbps). By the way, when two devices connected by modems use different speeds, the slower speed is the one at which they operate.

Modulation is governed by one of three standards: V.34, V.90, and V.92. These standards specify how digital signals will be transformed into analog and hence operate at Layer 1, the physical layer, of the TCP/IP–OSI architecture.

The way in which messages are packaged and handled between your modem and the ISP is governed by a protocol known as the **Point-to-Point Protocol (PPP)**. This Layer-2 protocol is used for networks that involve just two computers, hence the term *point-to-point*.

DSL Modems

A **DSL modem** is the second modem type. DSL stands for **digital subscriber line**. DSL modems operate on the same lines as voice telephones and dial-up modems, but they operate so that their signals do not interfere with voice telephone service. DSL modems provide much faster data transmission speeds than dial-up modems. Additionally, DSL modems always maintain a connection, so there is no need to dial up; the Internet connection is available immediately.

Because DSL signals do not interfere with telephone signals, DSL data transmission and telephone conversations can occur simultaneously. A device at the telephone company separates the phone signals from the computer signals and sends the

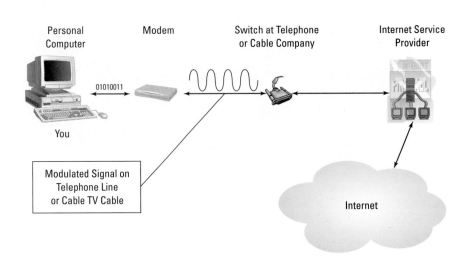

Figure 5-14
Personal Computer (PC)
Internet Access

latter signal to the ISP. DSL modems use their own Layer 1 and 2 protocols for data transmission.

There are gradations of DSL service and speed. Most home DSL lines can download data at speeds ranging from 256 kbps to 768 kbps and can upload data at slower speeds, say 256 kbps. DSL lines that have different upload and download speeds are called **asymmetric digital subscriber lines (ADSL)**. Most homes and small businesses can use ADSL because they receive more data than they transmit (e.g., pictures in news stories), and hence do not need to transmit as fast as they receive.

Some users and larger businesses, however, need DSL lines that have the same receiving and transmitting speeds. They also need performance-level guarantees. **Symmetrical digital subscriber lines (SDSL)** meet this need by offering the same fast speed in both directions. As much as 1.544 Mbps can be guaranteed.

Cable Modems

A **cable modem** is the third modem type. Cable modems provide high-speed data transmission using cable television lines. The cable company installs a fast, high-capacity optical fiber cable to a distribution center in each neighborhood that it serves. At the distribution center, the optical fiber cable connects to regular cable-television cables that run to subscribers' homes or businesses. Cable modems modulate in such a way that their signals do not interfere with TV signals. Like DSL lines, they are always on.

Because up to 500 user sites can share these facilities, performance varies depending on how many other users are sending and receiving data. At the maximum, users can download data up to 10 Mbps and can upload data at 256 kbps. Typically, performance is much lower than this. In most cases, the speed of cable modems and DSL modems is about the same. Cable modems use their own Layer 1 and 2 protocols. Figure 5-12 summarizes these alternatives.

Is *always-on* truly a benefit? For a discussion of the downside of perpetual connectivity, read the *Opposing Forces Guide* on page 129a.

You will sometimes hear the terms *narrowband* and *broadband* with regard to communications speeds. **Narrowband** lines typically have transmissions speeds less than 56 kbps. **Broadband** lines have speeds in excess of 256 kbps. Thus, a dial-up modem provides narrowband access, and DSL and cable modems provide broadband access.

Networks of Leased Lines

As shown in Figure 5-12, a second WAN alternative is to create a **network of leased lines** between company sites. Figure 5-15 shows a WAN that connects computers located at three geographically distributed company sites. The lines that connect

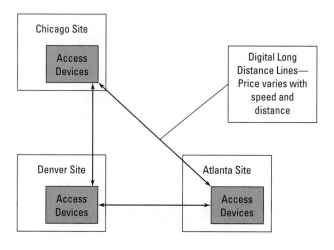

Figure 5-15
Wide Area Network Using Leased Lines

Where's the OFF Button?

DSL modems were the watershed. That was the point at which we lost our independence. Up until then, you had to *dial* up—you had to take action—to get connected. The default mode was Off, and you had to do something to get On. Since DSL, the default mode has been On.

Delbert Scott was a dry-land wheat farmer in western Colorado. He was born in 1920 and for most of his life worked long hours in primitive conditions. He did not have electricity until he was 40, and the ranch never did have indoor plumbing. Delbert was, however, a happy man. He loved the ranch, the range, the solitude. "Some days I go down to the creek and sit and think. And sometimes, I just sit."

Today, perpetual connectivity is terrific: It is useful, and it increases productivity. But what about just sitting? Some may say, "Who cares? Who wants just to sit? It's boring." Have we lost not only the ability to be off line, but also the desire? Is that how *The Matrix* came about? That is, no one enslaved us— we did it ourselves? Today, we are choosing perpetual connectivity because we want to. It's voluntary: We connect because we want the services, the information, the instantaneous gratification. But in the process, what do we lose?

DISCUSSION QUESTIONS

1. What's your response to the idea of "just sitting"? Think about turning off your cell phone, not answering emails, even getting out of town. How many days could you live that way? How many days do you want to live that way?

2. Is independence an illusion? Are we not social animals? Is Delbert's story only a myth? Was he wishing, while he sat, that he could talk to his brother? Doesn't the Internet merely support our basic instincts to connect? And why is that wrong?

3. Today, perpetual connectivity is voluntary—as long as you don't want to enroll in a class, receive email from your professor, arrange meetings with other students, entertain yourself, or find a job. But how "voluntary" is that? Does it matter?

4. Do you use Instant Messaging? If so, do you find it weird to learn when your friends sign on to their computers? Or that your friends find out when you sign on? Why should they know that much about you? What about you, as a future manager? Do you want Instant Messaging to tell your employees when you arrive at work? Is it their business? Is it noticed when you don't sign on?

5. Where does ubiquitous connectivity take us? Is The Matrix inevitable?

these sites are leased from telecommunications companies that are licensed to provide them.

A variety of **access devices** connect each site to the transmission. These devices are typically special-purpose computers; the particular devices required depend on the line used and other factors. Sometimes switches and routers are employed, but other types of equipment are needed as well. The discussion of such access devices is beyond the scope of this text.

A variety of leased-line alternatives exists. As shown in Figure 5-16, lines are classified by their use and speed. A T1 line can support up to 1.544 Mbps; a T3 line can support up to 44.736 Mbps. Using optical fiber cable, even faster lines are possible; an OC-768 line supports 40 Gbps. Except for T1 speeds, faster lines require either optical fiber cable or satellite communication. T1 speeds can be supported by regular telephone wires as well as by optical fiber cable and satellite communication.

Setting up a point-to-point line, once it has been leased, requires considerable work by highly trained, expensive specialists. Connecting the company's LANs and other facilities is a challenging task, and maintaining those connections is expensive. In some cases, organizations contract with third parties to set up and support the lines they have leased.

Notice, too, that with point-to-point lines, as the number of sites increases, the number of lines required increases dramatically. If another site is added to the network in Figure 5-15, up to three new leased lines will be needed. In general, if a network has *n* sites, as many as *n* additional lines need to be leased, set up, and supported to connect a new site to all the other sites.

Furthermore, only predefined sites can use the leased lines. It is not possible for an employee working at a temporary, remote location, such as a hotel, to use this network. Similarly, customers or vendors cannot use such a network, either.

However, if an organization has substantial traffic between fixed sites, leased lines can provide a low cost per bit transmitted. A company like Boeing, for example, with major facilities in Seattle, St. Louis, and Los Angeles, could benefit by using leased lines to connect these sites. The operations of such a company require transmitting huge amounts of data between those fixed sites. Further, such a company knows how to hire and manage the technical personnel required to support such a network.

The most common protocol for leased lines is the Point-to-Point Protocol (PPP), the same protocol used to connect a dial-up modem to an ISP.

Line Type	Use	Maximum Speed
Telephone line (twisted pair copper lines)	Dial-up modem	56 Kbps
	DSL modem	1.544 Mbps
	WAN—T1—using a pair of telephone lines	1.544 Mbps
Coaxial cable	Cable modem	Upstream to 256 Kbps Downstream to 10 Mbps (usually much less, however)
Unshielded twisted pair (UTP)	LAN	100 Mbps
Optical fiber cable	LAN and WAN—T3, OC-768, etc.	40 Gbps or more
Satellite	WAN—OC-768, etc.	40 Gbps or more

Figure 5-16
Transmission Line Types, Uses, and Speeds

Using the Opposing Forces Guide *(page 129a)*

GOAL

* Motivate students to ponder what always-on connectivity means. (Are we losing anything important?)

BACKGROUND AND PRESENTATION STRATEGIES

Every now and then I worry that we are integrating technology into the fabric of our society with no regard for the long-term effects. Where are we going? Are we unthinkingly on the road to the controlled society Orwell described in his book *1984*? By using cell phones, DSL/cable connectivity, wireless from everywhere, integrated phones/computers/entertainment devices, are we setting ourselves up for totalitarian control? Are we like children, blindly following a path of M&M's straight into a swamp from which we cannot extricate ourselves? Or, is this rampant paranoia? I think it's at least worth asking the question.

Many consumers use credit cards to buy food and fill prescriptions at the same grocery store. UPC codes identify every item purchased, and the credit card identifies the customer. If someone is buying medication to control cholesterol, it's possible that the grocery store could prohibit that person from buying ice cream (a food high in cholesterol). Or, put more positively, insurance companies could reduce the healthcare premium for people who buy healthy food. (I mentioned this in class last term, and one of my students said, "That'll make for some interesting parking lot offers: 'Hey, old man, I'll buy you some ice cream, if you buy me some beer.'")

Last month I watched a young mother manage her two-year-old on the slippery slide at the park. The entire time, 30 minutes or so, she was on the cell phone, talking constantly, while she pushed her child around with the other hand. What are the consequences of this?

➤ **Are these worries groundless, or is something being lost? Would either the mother or the child's experiences have been better if the mother had turned off her phone?**

• **Is she an exhausted full-time mother who desperately needs some relief from childrearing, and her cell phone is a great option?**

• **Or maybe she was supposed to be at work and was conducting business while playing with her son. Maybe she'd been on the road for a week and was going back for another week the next day, and this was the *only* time she had—in which case the cell phone was giving her time she would not otherwise have had to spend with her son.**

I do believe DSL marks a watershed. The default was "off," and you had to work to get on. Now, the default is "on," and you have to work to get off.

FYI: Delbert Scott was a cowboy. Born in western Colorado, he was a renowned rodeo rider in the 1940s. He also liked quiet, solitude, and empty spaces. There must still be people like him, but I suppose many cowboys carry cell phones in their saddle bags—trading stock around the campfire. What do they lose by being always on? Anything?

 SUGGESTED RESPONSES FOR DISCUSSION QUESTIONS

1. Depends on student comments. Questions to start the discussion:

   ➤ **Would your life be better if you turned off your cell phone now and then?**

   ➤ **What would happen if you turned off your cell phone for 24 hours? 48 hours? A week?**

   ➤ **What would you lose? What would you gain?**

   ➤ **Are the benefits of always being connected worth the cost?**

2. Is independence an illusion? Probably so. Humans have been gathering in communities for hundreds of thousands of years. Were it not for our instinct to gather, would cell phones sell? Probably not. Delbert may have wanted to talk with his brother, but because he couldn't, he spent his time otherwise.

   ➤ **Was that good or bad?**

   ➤ **You, however, have a choice; you can be connected or not.**

   ➤ **Just remember to ask yourself what life might be like if you turned off your cell phone.**

   ➤ **Even though independence is an illusion, until recently it was possible for people to choose to be alone. With cell phones, email, and instant messaging, has it become impossible for anyone to ever be alone?**

3. Being connected is a *requirement* for any professional person today. Does it matter? Consider the following questions:

   ➤ **In what ways do cell phones free people?**

   ➤ **If your boss can reach you anytime on your cell phone, do you have greater freedom of movement?**

   ➤ **Do cell phones give you greater freedom of movement, but less freedom?**

   ➤ **Do cell phones give your boss more or less control?**

   ➤ **Does connectivity increase or decrease the need for business travel?**

   ➤ **Does connectivity reduce efficiency by increasing the amount of rubbish that business people send one another? Do they ask questions they need not ask? Do they make comments that are obvious and need not be made?**

   ➤ **What do you do with someone who calls you too frequently? Socially? In business? Do you become a slave to communications nuisances?**

   ➤ **How do you know you have not become a communication nuisance yourself?**

4. Big Brother is watching you! Actually, all of your IM chat buddies are watching you, and you are watching them!

   ➤ **IM involves a tremendous loss of privacy and makes you easy prey to friends and business associates who are nuisances. Is it worth it? Why?**

5. *The Matrix* is a science-fiction movie, and the life it portrayed is certainly avoidable. Today and for the near future, I do see a tremendous loss of privacy and loss of control over one's life. Also, connectivity will make it easier for governments to keep track of their citizens. They may do this initially in the name of *security*, but once the infrastructure is in place, who will be able to dismantle it?

WRAP UP

➤ **In Chapter 1, we talked about "waking up to your life." Part of being awake is watching what technology does to your life. Although you need to stay connected, it's worth asking what you lose:**

- **Some privacy**
- **Some independence of action**
- **Some control over your time**
- **Some time to yourself—for reflection or just downtime**

➤ **It may be worth trying an experiment of going 24 hours with your cell phone off and then analyzing the experience.**

Public Switched Data Network

Yet another WAN alternative is a **public switched data network (PSDN),** a network of computers and leased lines that is developed and maintained by a vendor that leases time on the network to other organizations. A PSDN is a utility that supplies a network for other companies to lease. Figure 5-17 shows the PSDN as a cloud of capability. What happens within that cloud is of no concern to the lessees. As long as they get the availability and speed they expect, the PSDN could consist of strings of spaghetti connected by meatballs. (This is not likely to be the case, however.)

When using a PSDN, each site must lease a line to connect to the PSDN network. The location at which this occurs is called a **point of presence (POP)**; it is the access point into the PSDN. Think of the POP as the phone number that one dials to connect to the PSDN. Once a site has connected to the PSDN POP, the site obtains access to all other sites connected to the PSDN.

PSDNs save the setup and maintenance activities required when using leased lines. They also save costs because a company does not have to pay for the entire network; the company can pay just for the traffic that it sends. Further, using a PSDN requires much less management involvement than using leased lines. Another advantage of PSDNs is that only one line is required to connect a new site to all other sites.

Three Layer 1 and 2 protocols are used with PSDNs: Frame Relay, ATM (asynchronous transfer mode), and Ethernet. **Frame Relay** can process traffic in the range of 56 kbps to 40 Mbps. **Asynchronous transfer mode (ATM)** can process speeds from 1 to 156 Mbps. Frame Relay, although slower, is simpler and easier to support than ATM, and PSDNs can offer it at lower cost than ATM. On the other hand, some organizations need ATM's faster speed. Also, ATM can support both voice and data communication.

Often, PSDNs offer both Frame Relay and ATM on their network. Customers can choose whichever technique best fits their needs. Some companies use a PSDN network in lieu of a long-distance telephone carrier.

Ethernet, the protocol developed for LANs, also is used as a PSDN protocol. Newer versions of Ethernet can operate at speeds of 10 and 40 Gpbs.

Virtual Private Network

The **virtual private network (VPN)** is the fourth WAN alternative shown in Figure 5-12. A VPN uses the Internet or a private internet to create the appearance of private point-to-point connections. In the IT world, the term *virtual* means something that

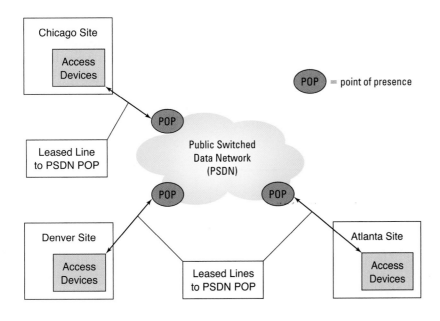

Figure 5-17
Wide Area Network Using PSDN

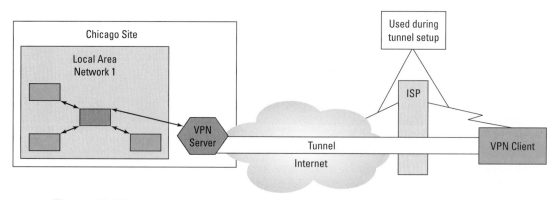

Figure 5-18
Remote Access Using VPN: Actual Connections

appears to exist that does not exist in fact. Here, a VPN uses the public Internet to create the appearance of a private connection.

Figure 5-18 shows one way to create a VPN to connect a remote computer, perhaps an employee working at a hotel in Miami, to a LAN at the Chicago site. The remote user is the VPN client. That client first establishes a connection to the Internet. The connection can be obtained by accessing a local ISP as shown in the figure; or, in some hotels, the hotel itself provides a direct Internet connection.

In either case, once the Internet connection is made, VPN software on the remote user's computer establishes a connection with the VPN server in Chicago. The VPN client and VPN server then have a point-to-point connection. That connection, called a **tunnel**, is a virtual, private pathway over a public or shared network from the VPN client to the VPN server. Figure 5-19 illustrates the connection as it appears to the remote user.

VPN communications are secure, even though they are transmitted over the public Internet. To ensure security, VPN client software *encrypts*, or codes, the original message so that its contents are hidden. (See encryption in the *Security Guide* on page 133a.) Then, the VPN client appends the Internet address of the VPN server to the message and sends that package over the Internet to the VPN server. When the VPN server receives the message, it strips its address off the front of the message, *decrypts* the coded message, and sends the plain text message to the original address on the LAN. In this way, secure private messages are delivered over the public Internet.

Virtual private networks offer the benefit of point-to-point leased lines, and they enable remote access, both by employees and by any others who have been registered with the VPN server. For example, if customers or vendors are registered with the VPN server, they can use the VPN from their own sites. Figure 5-20 shows three tunnels; one supports a point-to-point connection between the Atlanta and Chicago sites and the other two support remote connections.

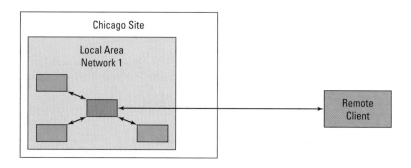

Figure 5-19
Remote Access Using VPN:
Apparent Connection

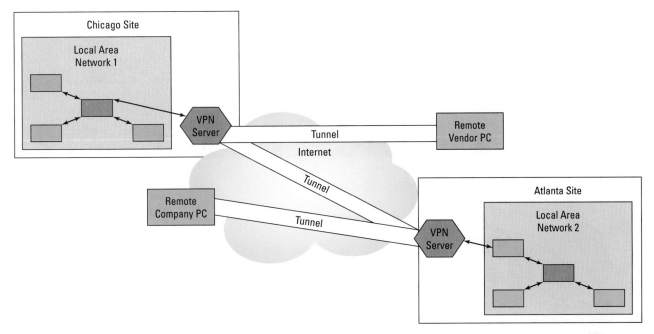

Figure 5-20
Wide Area Network Using VPN

Microsoft has fostered the popularity of VPNs by including VPN support in Windows. All versions of Microsoft Windows have the capability of working as VPN clients. Windows server products can operate as VPN servers.

▌ Criteria for Comparing Network Alternatives

As you have learned, many different computer networking alternatives are available, each with different characteristics. Choosing among them can be a complicated task. Figure 5-21 (page 134) lists three categories of criteria you can use to compare alternatives.

As shown, three types of costs need to be considered. *Setup costs* include the costs of acquiring transmission lines and the necessary equipment, such as switches, routers, and access devices. If lines or equipment are leased, setup fees also may be involved. Additionally, if your company is performing some of the setup work itself, labor costs need to be included. Finally, there are training costs.

Operational costs include lease fees for lines and equipment, charges of the ISP, the cost of ongoing training, as well as other similar costs. The communications equipment will also need to be maintained. *Maintenance costs* include those for periodic maintenance, for problem diagnosis and repair, and for mandatory upgrades.

Figure 5-21 shows six considerations with regard to performance: Line and equipment *speed* are self-explanatory. *Latency* is the transmission delay that occurs due to network congestion during busy periods. *Availability* refers to the frequency and length of service outages. *Loss rate* is the frequency of problems in the communications network that necessitate data retransmission.

Finally, *transparency* is the degree to which the user is unaware of the underlying communications system. For example, a DSL modem that is always connected is more transparent that a dial-up modem, which requires that the modem first obtain a phone line that is not in use and then dial the ISP number. The greater the transparency, the greater the ease of network use.

In many cases, vendors of communications equipment and services are willing to make *performance guarantees* that commit them to levels of service quality. These

Encryption

Encryption is the process of transforming clear text into coded, unintelligible text for secure storage or communication. Considerable research has gone into developing **encryption algorithms** that are difficult to break. Commonly used methods are DES, 3DES, and AES; search the Internet for these terms if you want to know more about them.

A **key** is a number used to encrypt the data. The encryption algorithm applies the key to the original message to produce the coded message. Decoding (decrypting) a message is similar; a key is applied to the coded message to recover the original text. In **symmetric encryption**, the same key is used to encode and to decode. With **asymmetric encryption**, different keys are used; one key encodes the message, and the other key decodes the message. Symmetric encryption is simpler and much faster than asymmetric encryption.

A special version of asymmetric encryption, **public key/private key**, is popular on the Internet. With this method, each site has a public key for encoding messages and a private key for decoding

them. (For now, suppose we have two generic computers, A and B.) To exchange secure messages, A and B send each other their public keys as uncoded text. Thus, A receives B's public key and B receives A's public key, all as uncoded text. Now, when A sends a message to B, it encrypts the message using B's public key and sends the encrypted message to B. Computer B receives the encrypted message from A and decodes it using its private key. Similarly, when B wants to send an encrypted message to A, it encodes its message with the A's public key and sends the encrypted message to A. Computer A then decodes B's message with its own private key. The private keys are never communicated. (There are other uses for public/private keys as you will learn.) Unfortunately, public key/private key encryption is complex and therefore slow. It can only be used for short messages.

Most secure communication over the Internet uses a protocol called **HTTPS**. With HTTPS, data are encrypted using a protocol called the **Secure Socket Layer (SSL)**, also known as **Transport Layer Security (TLS)**. SSL/TLS uses a combination of public key/private key and symmetric encryption. It works as follows: First, your computer obtains the public key of the Web server to which it will connect. Your computer then generates a key for symmetric encryption and encodes that key using the Web site's public key. It sends the encrypted symmetric key to the Web site. The Web site then decodes the symmetric key using its private key.

From that point forward, your computer and the Web site communicate using symmetric encryption. At the end of the session, your computer and the secure site discard the keys. Using this strategy, the bulk of the secure communication occurs using the faster symmetric encryption. Also, because keys are used for short intervals, there is less likelihood they can be discovered.

Use of SSL/TLS makes it safe to send sensitive data like credit card numbers and bank balances. Just be certain that you see https//: in your browser and not just http://.

DISCUSSION QUESTIONS

1. Describe a simple encryption scheme that substitutes one letter for another one. If someone had examples of your coded messages, how would they go about breaking your code? How difficult would that be to do?

2. Explain the difference between symmetric and asymmetric encryption.

3. What is the advantage of symmetric encryption? What is the disadvantage?

4. Explain how public key/private key encryption works. How many keys are involved?

5. Explain how SSL/TLS works. Why is it important that the symmetric key be discarded at the end of the session?

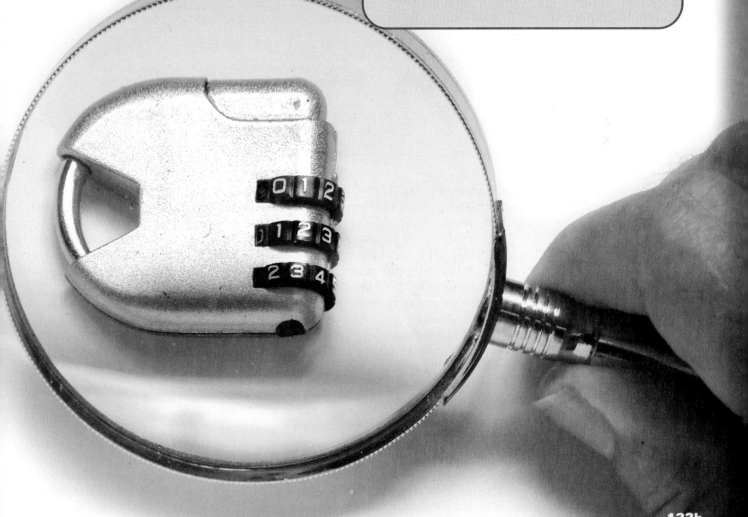

Criteria Category	Criteria	Description
Cost	Initial setup	Transmission line Equipment Setup fees Setup labor Training costs
	Operational	Line lease fees Equipment lease fees ISP and other service fees Ongoing training
	Maintenance	Periodic maintenance costs Problem diagnosis and repair costs Mandatory upgrade costs
Performance	Speed	Line and equipment speed
	Latency	Delays during busy periods
	Availability	Frequency of service outage
	Loss rate	Frequency retransmission required
	Transparency	User involvement in operation
	Performance guarantees?	Vendors agree to cost penalties if levels of service not met
Other	Growth potential	How difficult to upgrade when service needs or capacity increase?
	Commitment periods	Length of leases and other agreements
	Management time	How much management activity is required?
	Financial risk	How much is at stake if system not effective?
	Technical risk	If using new technology, likelihood of failure

Figure 5-21
Criteria for Comparing
Networking Alternatives

levels can include availability, error rate, speeds, and the like. When a performance guarantee is in place, the vendor agrees to cost penalties when agreed-upon levels are not met.

Other criteria to consider when comparing network alternatives include the growth potential (greater capacity) and the length of contract commitment periods. Shorter periods allow for greater flexibility and usually are preferred. Also, how much management time is required? An alternative that requires in-house technical staff will require more management time than one that does not. The final two criteria to consider are the degrees of financial and technical risk.

The criteria in Figure 5-21 could be used to compare and evaluate any of the alternatives in Figure 5-12. Such a comparison is likely what the COO had in mind in the chapter's opening scenario. (See Applying Your Knowledge question 17, page 147.)

How the Internet Works

Given this background, we can now return to your hotel room in Hawaii. You are sending a message and picture of your amazing surfing skills to your friend back in snow-bound Ohio. In the rest of this chapter we will explain, at a high level, how it all works.

This is the most complicated section in this textbook. To understand this material, we will break the discussion into four sections. First, we will consider the addressing of

Using the Security Guide
(page 133a)

GOAL

* Teach students to ensure that they are using SSL when sending confidential data over the Internet.

BACKGROUND AND PRESENTATION STRATEGIES

The discussion in this chapter introduces topics that will be addressed in greater detail in Chapter 11. It seemed unwise, to me, however, to wait until that chapter to explain the importance and need for SSL when sending confidential information.

➤ *Do not send Social Security numbers, driver's license numbers, bank account numbers, or any other confidential data using http. If you choose to send such data over the Internet, make sure you are using https, instead.*

➤ **Whenever you buy something online, ensure the vendor is using https. Look for https:// in your browser's address line.**

SSL is the original name of the protocol invented by Netscape. It was long ago endorsed by Microsoft and other large vendors and has become the *de facto* security standard for http. The later versions of SSL are called *Transport Layer Security,* or *TLS.* Today, SSL and TLS are essentially synonyms.

The SSL protocol operates between the application layer (layer 5) and the transport layer (layer 4) of the TCP/IP–OSI architecture.

Because SSL/TLS operates between the application and transport layers, it can be used by any layer-5 protocol and not just http. For example, some versions of FTP use TLS, and it is possible to use TLS with email protocols. Today, however, *email is not usually protected by TLS.*

Consequently, *email is seldom secure.*

➤ **None of the email that you process via your own ISP is secure, and you should assume that any email you process at work also is insecure.**

➤ **Organizations have the right to inspect emails that are generated or received on the organization's computers and/or transmitted on the organization's**

networks. Therefore, sending or receiving email at work is (a) seldom secure and (b) never private.

➤ **The bottom line:** *Do not send confidential information in email!*

Here's the bottom line on public/private key encryption:

* We want to use symmetric encryption because it's faster.
* But, how do the parties securely obtain the same key?
* Use asymmetric (public/private key) encryption to transmit the symmetric key, then switch to symmetric encryption.
* With an easy way to securely transmit symmetric keys, those keys can be used for shorter periods of time, thus reducing the likelihood they will be compromised.

An interesting and well-written book on encryption is *The Code Book*, by Simon Singh (New York: Doubleday, 1999).

 SUGGESTED RESPONSES FOR DISCUSSION QUESTIONS

1. A simple scheme is just to move one letter up or down the alphabet. Replace the plaintext *a* with a coded *b*, a plaintext *b* with a coded *c*, and so forth. Thus, MIS becomes NJT. Such codes are very easy to break using frequency analysis. See the Singh book for more information.

2. Symmetric uses one key for encrypting. Asymmetric uses two keys.

3. Symmetric encryption is faster. The disadvantage is that both parties must have the same key, and the problem becomes how to get the key to both parties. Furthermore, the longer one uses a key, the greater the chance that someone can decode it. Hence, users should change keys frequently—amplifying the problem of getting the key to both parties.

4. The sender encodes the message with the receiver's public key. The receiver decodes the message with its own private key.

5. Assume a customer is buying something from an e-commerce vendor. The customer obtains the public key from the vendor's site. The customer generates a symmetric key and encrypts that key using the vendor's public key. The vendor receives the encrypted symmetric key and decodes it using

its own private key. From then on, the parties communicate using symmetric encryption. The parties throw away the key after use, because the longer a key is used, the greater the chance that someone could decode it.

➤ **Notice there is a problem here that we will address in Chapter 11: How does the customer know he or she received the vendor's public key and not the public key of a site spoofing the vendor? Chapter 11 will tell the rest of the story.**

WRAP UP

One more time:

➤ **Do not send Social Security numbers, driver's license numbers, bank account numbers, or any other confidential data using http. Make sure you are using https, instead.**

➤ **Email is usually not secure. It is not private at work, either!**

computers and other devices. As you will learn, each computer and device has two addresses, a physical address and a logical one. Next, we will consider how protocols at all five layers of the TCP/IP–OSI model operate to send a request to a Web server within a LAN. Third, we will consider how those same protocols work to send messages across the Internet. Finally, we will wrap up with some details about IP addresses and the domain name system. Be patient, and take your time; you may need to read this section more than once. We begin with addresses.

Network Addresses: MAC and IP

On most networks, and on every internet, two address schemes identify computers and other devices. Programs that implement Layer 2 protocols use *physical addresses*, or *MAC addresses*. Programs that implement Layer 3, 4, and 5 protocols use *logical addresses*, or *IP addresses*. We will consider each type.

Physical Addresses (MAC Addresses)

As stated earlier, every network device, including your computer, has an NIC for accessing the network. Each NIC is given an address at the factory. That address is the device's **physical address**, or **MAC address**. By agreement among computer manufacturers, such addresses are assigned in such a way that no two NIC devices will ever have the same MAC address.

MAC addresses are used within networks at Layer 2 of the TCP/IP–OSI model. Physical addresses are only known, shared, and used within a particular network or network segment. For internets, including the Internet, another scheme of addresses must be used. That scheme turned out to be so useful that it is also used within LANs, in addition to MAC addressing.

Logical Addresses (IP Addresses)

Internets, including the Internet, and many private networks use **logical addresses**, which are also called **IP addresses**. You have probably seen IP addresses; they are written as a series of dotted decimals, for example, 192.168.2.28. We will describe the structure of IP addresses later.

IP addresses are not permanently associated with a given hardware device. They can be reassigned to another computer, router, or other device when necessary. To understand one advantage of logical addresses, consider what happens when an organization like IBM changes the device (a router) that receives requests when users type *www.ibm.com*. That name is associated with a particular IP address (as we will explain later in this chapter). If IP addresses were permanent, like MAC addresses, then when IBM upgrades its entry router, all of the users in the world would have to change the IP address associated with *www.ibm.com* to the new address. Instead, with logical IP addresses, a network administrator need only reassign IBM's IP address to the new router.

Public Versus Private IP Addresses

In practice, two kinds of IP addresses exist. **Public IP addresses** are used on the Internet. Such IP addresses are assigned to major institutions in blocks by the **Internet Corporation for Assigned Names and Numbers (ICANN)**. (More on ICANN later.) Each IP address is unique across all computers on the Internet. In contrast, **private IP addresses** are used within private networks and internets. They are controlled only by the company that operates the private network or internet. (Remember that IP addresses are series of dotted decimals; we are *not* referring here to recognizable words such as *pearson.com*.)

Dynamic Host Configuration Protocol

Today, in most cases, when you plug your computer into a network (or sign on to a wireless network), a program in Windows or other operating system will search that network for a DHCP server, which is a computer or router that hosts a program called **Dynamic Host Configuration Protocol (DHCP)**. When the program finds such a device, your computer will request a temporary IP address from the DHCP server. That IP address is loaned to you while you are connected to the LAN. When you disconnect, that IP address becomes available, and the DHCP server will reuse it when needed.

Of course, within a private network, administrators can assign private IP addresses manually as well. Often, the strategy within a private network is to manually assign IP addresses to computers that operate Web servers or other shared devices for which it is desirable to have a fixed IP address. Today, most users, however, are assigned IP addresses using DHCP.

Private IP Addresses at the Hawaii Hotel

To make sense of the discussion so far, consider Figure 5-22, which shows the LAN operated by your hotel in Hawaii. Let's suppose that you occupy the penthouse suite (more good luck!) and that you plug your computer into the network as Computer C3 in Figure 5-22. When you do so, a program in your operating system will search the network for a DHCP server. It turns out that the router labeled RH is such a server. Your computer asks RH for an IP address, and RH assigns one. It will be a number like 192.168.2.28, but for simplicity let's denote your IP address by the symbol IP3.

Using TCP/IP–OSI Protocols Within the Hotel

Once you have an IP address, protocol programs on your computer at Layers 3, 4, and 5 can communicate with any other computer in your network. Suppose, for example, that the computer labeled HS is running a Web server that provides information to hotel guests. This Web server is private; the hotel wants only guests and others within the hotel to be able to access it. Hence, the server operates only within the LAN.

Suppose the IP address of the server has been assigned by a network administrator; let's denote that address as IP8. The router, RH in Figure 5-22, also has an IP address. Denote that address as IP9. Now, let's see how all of these addresses are used within the hotel's LAN.

Communications Processing on Your Computer

The hotel provides a brochure in your room that tells you how to sign on to the local Web server by entering a name into your browser. When you follow those instructions, your browser constructs a request for the server and uses the HTTP protocol to send it to HS.

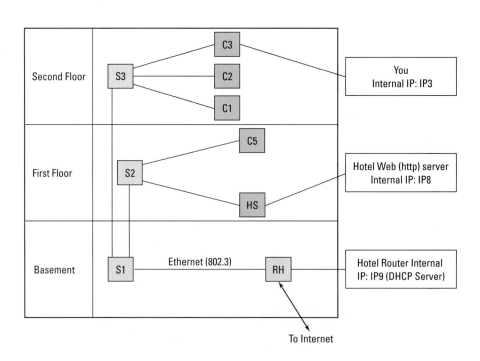

Figure 5-22
Hotel LAN in Hawaii

We can follow the action in Figure 5-23 (page 138). Your browser sends its service request for HS to a program that implements TCP. One function of TCP is to break requests into segments, when necessary. In this case, suppose it breaks the request into two segments. The TCP program adds additional data to the segments. Here we show a header with "IP3 to IP8," but other data, and possibly a trailer, are added as well. We will ignore the real headers and trailers to focus on basic concepts.

The TCP program hands the segment(s) to a program that implements IP. As stated, the major function of that IP program is routing. It determines that the only route to IP8 is through the router at RH, whose IP address is IP9. So, the IP program adds the IP9 header and passes the wrapped packet down to a program that implements Ethernet.

The Ethernet program translates the IP address into a MAC address. Ethernet determines that the device at IP9 has a particular MAC address, which will be a long number. Here, for simplicity, we denote that address as RH. Ethernet will wrap the packet into a frame that is addressed to device RH.

When you signed onto the LAN, your Ethernet program learned that the only way it can connect to other computers is via switch S3 (see Figure 5-22). Accordingly, it sends the frame to S3.

Communications Processing on the Switches

All switches have a table of data called a **switch table**. This table tells the switch where to send traffic to get it to its destination. The table on switch S3 has entries for every other device on the LAN. It knows, for example, that to get a frame to RH, it must send it to switch S1. Accordingly, it sends the frame to S1.

S1 also has a switch table. S1 consults that table and determines that it has a direct connection to RH. Therefore, it sends the frame to RH.

Communications Processing on the Router

When the frame arrives at RH, it has arrived at its destination, and so Ethernet unpacks the frame and sends the contained packet up to IP. IP examines the packet and determines that the packet's destination is IP8. RH, which is a router, has a **routing table** that tells it where to send traffic for IP8. This routing table indicates that IP8 is just one hop away. So, IP changes the destination of the packet to IP8 and passes it back down to Ethernet.

Ethernet determines that the device at IP8 has the MAC address HS. So, it packages the packet into a frame and gives that frame the address HS. It then sends the frame to its switch S1. S1 consults its switch table and sends the frame to S2; S2 sends the frame to HS.

Communications Processing on the Web Server

HS is the destination for the frame, so the Ethernet program unpacks the frame and sends the contained packet to the IP program. IP8 is the destination for the packet, so the IP program strips off the IP header and sends the contained segment up to a program that implements TCP. That program examines the segment and determines that it is the first of two. TCP sends an acknowledgment back to your computer to indicate that it received the first segment. (Of course, the acknowledgment must be routed and switched as well.) TCP waits for the second segment to arrive.

Once both segments have arrived, the TCP program sends the complete request up to the Web server program that processes the HTTP protocol. (Whew!)

To summarize:

- *Switches* work with *frames* at *Layer 2*. They send frames from switch to switch until they arrive at their destination. They use *MAC addresses*.
- *Routers* work with *packets* at *Layer 3*. They send packets from router to router until they arrive at their destination. They use *IP addresses*.

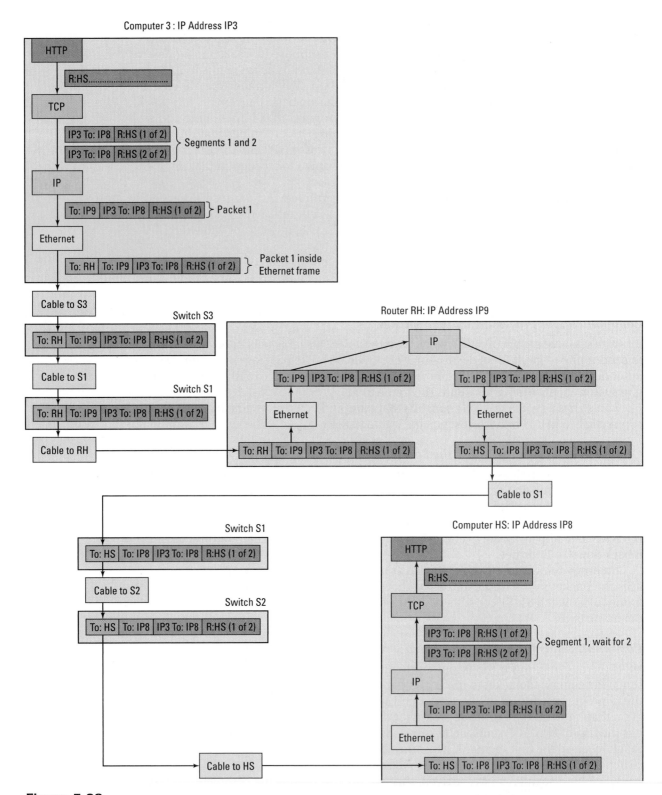

Figure 5-23
Accessing the (Private) Hotel Web Server

Using TCP/IP-OSI Protocols over the Internet

Finally, we are in position to describe how your email gets from you at the hotel in Hawaii to your friend in the company in Ohio. In fact, you need to know just one more topic to understand the techno-miracle that occurs: how private and public IP addresses are converted.

Network Address Translation

All of the IP addresses described in the prior section were private IP addresses. They are used within the LAN at your hotel. For Internet traffic, however, only public IP addresses can be used. These addresses are assigned in blocks to large companies and organizations like ISPs.

Your hotel has an ISP that it uses to connect to the Internet. That ISP assigned one of its public IP addresses to the router in your hotel. We will denote that IP address as IPx. (Again, it will be a dotted-decimal number, but ignore that right now.)

Therefore, as shown in Figure 5-24 (page 140), router RH has two IP addresses: a private one, IP9, and a public one, IPx. All Internet traffic aimed at any computer within the hotel LAN will be sent over the Internet using IP address IPx. The router will receive all packets for all computers at the hotel. When it receives a packet, it determines the internal IP address within the LAN for that computer. It then changes the address in the packet from IPx (the router's IP address) to the internal IP address of a computer in the hotel—the packet's true destination. Thus, if the router receives some traffic intended for you, it will change the packets's address from IPx to IP3 and send it to you.[1]

The process of changing public IP addresses into private IP addresses, and the reverse, is called **Network Address Translation (NAT)**. NAT uses a concept called ports. . . . But, let's stop there. We've had enough. If you major in IS, you can learn about NAT. Let's just move on and trust that NAT works.

All of the techniques described in this chapter are in use, every day, throughout the world. Consider, for example, *MIS in Use 5-2* (page 141), which describes the equipment used in a small home office.

Your Email (!)

Finally, we can describe how your email gets to your friend in Ohio. Before we describe that process, though, let's address a related side issue—whether personal email at work crosses ethical boundaries. See the *Ethics Guide* on page 141a.

If you decide it is ethical to send the email to your friend, you start your email program, and you enter your friend's email address. Suppose that your friend's name is Carter, and his email address is CarterK@OhioCompany.com. Your email program works at the application layer, and it implements SMTP. According to this protocol, your email will be sent to a mail server at the Internet address *OhioCompany.com*.

Your email program will use the domain name system (described later) to obtain the public IP address for the mail server at *OhioCompany.com*. Let's denote that address as IPz.

The message to IPz is then sent to the router RH as follows: Your email program implements SMTP, which sends the message to TCP. There it is broken into segments, and each segment is sent to IP, where they are placed into packets and routed to RH. Then, each packet is sent to your Ethernet program, where it is placed in a frame and sent to switch S3, and then S1, and then the router.

When one of the packets from your email and picture arrives at the router, it implements NAT and replaces your private IP address, IP3, with its public IP address, IPx. Router RH consults its routing table and determines how best to get the packet to IPz. Suppose that it determines that it should send the packet to Internet router R2.

---

[1]Believe it or not, we are simplifying here. This description is typical for a SOHO network. A real hotel and company would use devices in addition to the router for DHCP and NAT.

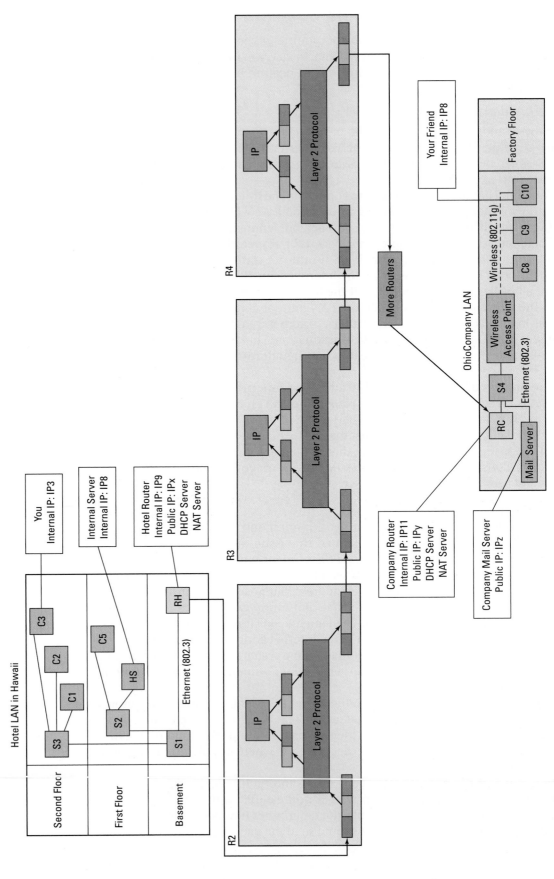

Figure 5-24
Hawaii Hotel to OhioCompany via Internet

Networks in Action: What's in the Box?

The following picture shows LAN and Internet hardware used in a **SOHO (small office, home office)** company. This messy set of wires, devices, and office paraphernalia illustrates the use of many of the concepts in this chapter.

A SOHO Network

The small, flat, black box is a DSL modem that is connected to a telephone line. The DSL modem also connects to the silver, upright box with the small dark gray antenna. That silver box is a Microsoft Wireless Base Station. *Wireless Base Station* is a marketing term that Microsoft uses to soften the complexity of what's actually in that gray box. Amazingly, that little box contains an Ethernet LAN switch, an 802.11g wireless access point, and a router. Notice the several UTP cables that connect the Wireless Base Station to computers and other devices on the LAN. A generic term for Microsoft's Wireless Base Station is **device access router**, the term you should use when you go shopping for one.

In addition to the switch, access point, and router, the Wireless Base Station also contains a small special-purpose computer that has firmware programs installed. These programs provide DHCP service as well as NAT. The Wireless Base Station also has programs for administration and for setting up wireless security.

Notice the printer (behind the tape dispenser). The printer has a small black box with a gray UTP cable and a small black power line going into it. The black box is an NIC that connects the printer to the LAN. This NIC is called a *printer server*, and it, too, has a special-purpose computer with firmware that allows for setting up and administering the printer server and printer. Using the printer server, the printer is not directly connected to any computer. Any of the users on the LAN can use the printer without turning on a computer to serve the printer.

This case is continued as Case Study 5-2 at the end of this chapter (page 150).

The processing of the packet over the Internet is just the same as described for the hotel in Figure 5-22. Packets are sent from router to router until they reach the router RC, the gateway router at your friend's company, which sends them to the mail server.

At that server, segments will be unpacked from packets and sent to a TCP program on the mail server that will send an acknowledgment back to your computer. Then TCP will wait for all of the segments in your mail (and picture) to arrive. TCP will then send the entire message and photo attachment to the program that implements SMTP. That program, which operates at Layer 5, will place the message and photo in the mailbox for CarterK.

When your friend checks his mail, the mail program on his computer will use all five layers of the TCP/IP–OSI architecture to send his mail check request to the mail server. His computer, which is also operating behind a router that provides NAT, has the internal IP address IP8. Notice that he has the same IP address as the server HS at

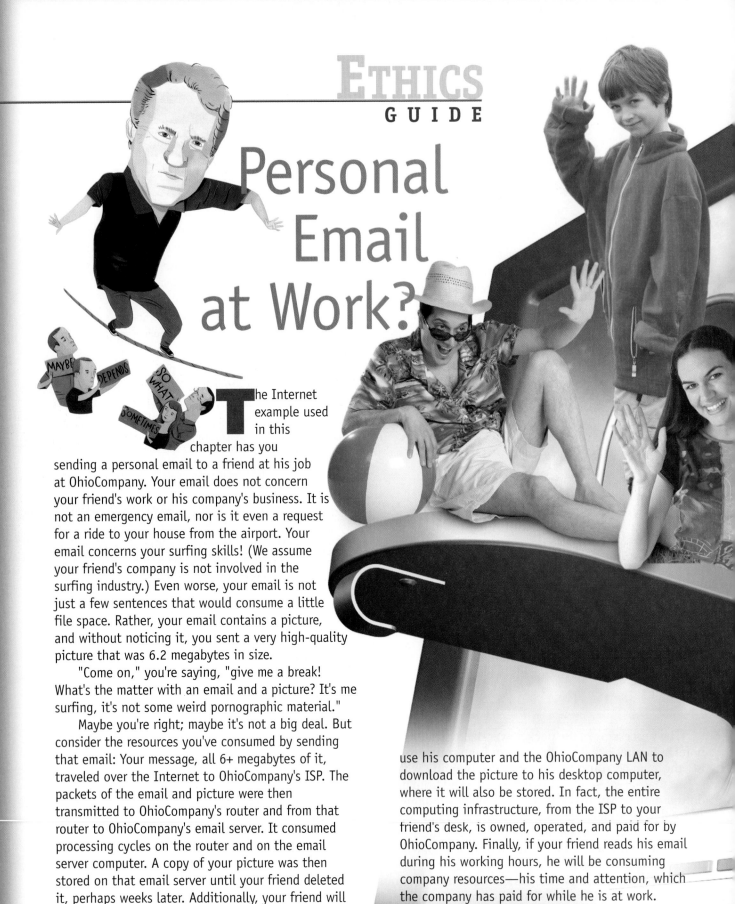

ETHICS GUIDE

Personal Email at Work?

The Internet example used in this chapter has you sending a personal email to a friend at his job at OhioCompany. Your email does not concern your friend's work or his company's business. It is not an emergency email, nor is it even a request for a ride to your house from the airport. Your email concerns your surfing skills! (We assume your friend's company is not involved in the surfing industry.) Even worse, your email is not just a few sentences that would consume a little file space. Rather, your email contains a picture, and without noticing it, you sent a very high-quality picture that was 6.2 megabytes in size.

"Come on," you're saying, "give me a break! What's the matter with an email and a picture? It's me surfing, it's not some weird pornographic material."

Maybe you're right; maybe it's not a big deal. But consider the resources you've consumed by sending that email: Your message, all 6+ megabytes of it, traveled over the Internet to OhioCompany's ISP. The packets of the email and picture were then transmitted to OhioCompany's router and from that router to OhioCompany's email server. It consumed processing cycles on the router and on the email server computer. A copy of your picture was then stored on that email server until your friend deleted it, perhaps weeks later. Additionally, your friend will use his computer and the OhioCompany LAN to download the picture to his desktop computer, where it will also be stored. In fact, the entire computing infrastructure, from the ISP to your friend's desk, is owned, operated, and paid for by OhioCompany. Finally, if your friend reads his email during his working hours, he will be consuming company resources—his time and attention, which the company has paid for while he is at work.

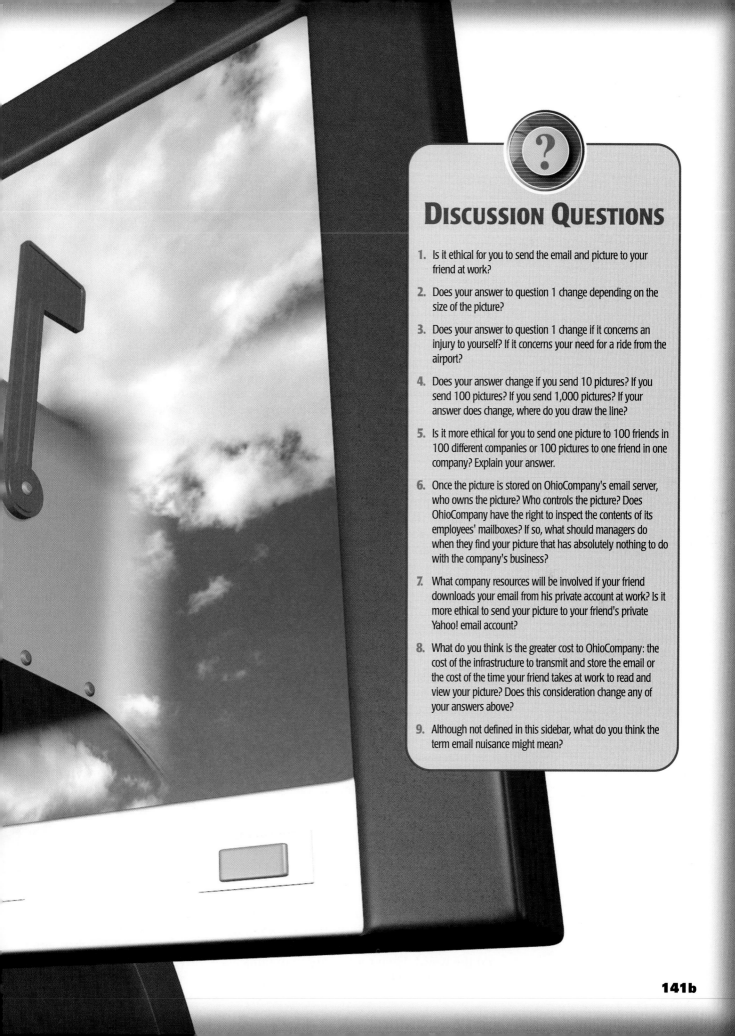

DISCUSSION QUESTIONS

1. Is it ethical for you to send the email and picture to your friend at work?

2. Does your answer to question 1 change depending on the size of the picture?

3. Does your answer to question 1 change if it concerns an injury to yourself? If it concerns your need for a ride from the airport?

4. Does your answer change if you send 10 pictures? If you send 100 pictures? If you send 1,000 pictures? If your answer does change, where do you draw the line?

5. Is it more ethical for you to send one picture to 100 friends in 100 different companies or 100 pictures to one friend in one company? Explain your answer.

6. Once the picture is stored on OhioCompany's email server, who owns the picture? Who controls the picture? Does OhioCompany have the right to inspect the contents of its employees' mailboxes? If so, what should managers do when they find your picture that has absolutely nothing to do with the company's business?

7. What company resources will be involved if your friend downloads your email from his private account at work? Is it more ethical to send your picture to your friend's private Yahoo! email account?

8. What do you think is the greater cost to OhioCompany: the cost of the infrastructure to transmit and store the email or the cost of the time your friend takes at work to read and view your picture? Does this consideration change any of your answers above?

9. Although not defined in this sidebar, what do you think the term email nuisance might mean?

your hotel. This duplication will not cause a problem, because these IP addresses are used only in local, private networks. Neither address is used on the public Internet.

Carter's computer connects to the mail server using a wireless protocol, 802.11g, but the essence of his communications to the mail server is the same as that on your hotel LAN. The mail server will send your email and picture to a TCP program on the mail server, from there to an IP program for routing to IP8, and from there to a program that processes Ethernet. Switch S4 will then convert the Ethernet frames into 802.11g frames and send them to your friend's computer.

That's how it works!

Domain Name System

IP addresses are useful for computer-to-computer communication, but they are not well suited for human use. I want to be able to enter a name like *www.icann.org* into my browser and not have to remember and enter its public IP address, which is 192.0.34.65. The purpose of the **domain name system (DNS)** is to convert user-friendly names into their IP addresses. Any registered, valid name is called a **domain name**. The process of changing a name into its IP address is called *resolving the domain name*.

This process requires the solution of two problems. First, to be useful, every domain name must be unique, worldwide. To ensure that duplicates do not occur, an agency registers names and records the corresponding IP addresses in a global directory. Second, when the user enters a domain name into her browser or other Layer-5 application, there needs to be some way for the application to resolve the domain name. We will consider each problem in turn.

Domain Name Registration

ICANN is a nonprofit organization that is responsible for administering the registration of domain names. ICANN does not register domain names itself; instead, it licenses other organizations to register names. ICANN is also responsible for managing the *domain name resolution system*.

The last letters in any domain name are referred to as the **top-level domain (TLD)**. For example, in the domain name *www.icann.org* the top-level domain is *.org*. Similarly, in the domain name *www.ibm.com*, *.com* is the top-level domain. For non-U.S. domain names, the top-level domain is often a two-letter abbreviation for the country in which the service resides. For example, a name like *www.somewhere.cn* would be a domain name in China, and *www.somewhere.uk* would be a domain name in the United Kingdom.

Figure 5-25 shows the U.S. top-level domains as of 2005. Some of these TLDs are restricted to particular industries, purposes, or organizations. The TLD *.aero*, for example, is restricted for use by organizations in the air transport industry. Similarly, *.name* is intended for use by individuals, and *.mil* is reserved for use by the U.S. military.

If you want to register a domain name, the first step is to determine the appropriate TLD. You should then visit *icann.org* and determine which agencies ICANN has licensed to register domains for that TLD. Finally, follow the registration process as required by one of those agencies. Again, if the domain name you want is already in use, your registration will be disallowed, and you will need to select another domain name.

Domain Name Resolution

A **uniform resource locator** (**URL**, pronounced either by saying the three letters or as "Earl") is a document's address on the Web. URLs begin with a domain name and then are followed by optional data that locates a document within that domain. Thus, in the URL *www.prenhall.com/kroenke*, the domain name is *www.prenhall.com*, and */kroenke* is a directory within that domain.

Domain name resolution is the process of converting a domain name into a public IP address. The process starts from the TLD and works to the left across the URL. As of 2005, ICANN manages 13 special computers called **root servers** that are distributed around the world. Each root server maintains a list of IP addresses of servers that resolve each type of TLD.

You Be the Guide

Using the Ethics Guide
(page 141a)

GOALS

* Alert students to the need to learn organizational policies regarding personal computer and network use at work.

* Stimulate thinking about professional and ethical responsibilities for sending email to people who are at work.

BACKGROUND AND PRESENTATION STRATEGIES

I wrote this chapter using the example of someone sending a picture of herself surfing in Hawaii so as to capture the students' attention. But, as I wrote it, I realized that somewhere along the line, we need to question the ethics of this action. I didn't want to leave the student thinking that such behavior shouldn't at least be *examined for appropriateness.*

This situation is complicated because the woman sending the email has no relationship to OhioCompany. Her friend, who is an employee of OhioCompany, is the passive recipient. This makes the ethics a bit difficult to untangle, but leads to a better discussion, I think.

First, there is no law that prohibits a person from sending or receiving personal emails at work, so the *action is certainly legal.*

If we fall back on the definition of ethical as "consistent with agreed principles of correct moral conduct," then we need to ask, "What are the agreed principles that pertain?" Most likely OhioCompany *has a corporate policy about personal use of computers and networks at work.* If so, that policy stipulates what the "agreed principles" are—at least from the company's standpoint—and the company's standpoint should be paramount, it seems to me, because it pays for the computers and networks.

So, at their first jobs, students *should learn the corporate policy for personal use of computers at work.* If they are not informed about that policy when they are hired, they should ask the human resources department about it. Asking their boss about such a policy at work may not set the right impression—maybe they can wait a week or so before asking that question.

This still leaves two possible ethical dilemmas:

> What if OhioCompany has no such policy? Does that mean they don't care, and employees should feel free to use the computers and networks without restriction?

I think not; I think a sense of business professionalism should limit personal computer use at work, even in the absence of a policy.

> The second dilemma occurs if OhioCompany has such a policy, but employees disregard or ignore it. In that case the agreed principles, at least among the employees, are that such use is OK. Do you agree?

I think it depends. If the employer knows about such use and doesn't take any action or issue any advisories about the policy, it would be hard to claim that such use is unethical. If, however, the company regularly asks employees not to use computers and networks for personal business at work and employees ignore that policy, then I think the action is unethical.

This leads to an important consideration for students as they join their employer:

> When you take your first job, you might want to restrict the people to whom you give your work email address to a few close friends and relatives. Use a private email account for most friends.

> Of course, if you generate an email at work and send it to someone, they will automatically obtain your work email address.

Nearer to home, you might also address computer-use policies on your campus.

> What are the policies for computer use at our campus?

> Where do we go to find out?

> Are the policies different for students than for professors?

> *Should* they be different? Professors are employees, and students are clients

 ### SUGGESTED RESPONSES FOR DISCUSSION QUESTIONS

Warning: These questions ask about the ethical responsibility of the woman sending the email, who is not an employee of OhioCompany. If the person at work was sending the emails, the answers would more clear.

I find it useful to consider the ethical situation from the standpoint of both parties, as described in the comments for each question.

1. First, consider the wording of the question:

   ➤ **This question is asking whether it is ethical for you to send email to your friend at work,** *not* **whether it is ethical for you, at work, to receive your friend's email.**

   Unless your friend has asked you not to send email to him at work, I think you have no ethical problem, but see further considerations in subsequent questions.

   ➤ **What if the question were, "Is it ethical for you to send personal email from work"?**

   In that case, I think the answer depends on organizational policy.

2. Your answer *might* change depending on the size of the picture. Even though it is your friend who is at work and not you, and even though you have no relationship to OhioCompany, a sense of business professionalism might cause you to pause before sending a large picture file to your friend's work email address. A very large file may attract unwanted attention to your friend's email account. A better course of action might be to send the picture to your friend's personal email account and a short email to your friend at work telling him that you did so.

   What about the person at OhioCompany? Do the ethics change for him depending on the size of the picture? Probably, depending on OhioCompany policy.

3. I think a short email about an injury would be appropriate to send to your friend—especially if it concerned something that your friend needed to do to help you. Most organizational policies allow personal email for emergency situations. I think the same could be said for the ride from the airport.

4. Again, the answer is complicated because it is asking if the non-OhioCompany employee is behaving ethically by sending all of these pictures. The friend, the OhioCompany employee, is a passive recipient. So the question is asking, "Do you have an ethical responsibility to recognize that your friend is at work and to limit what you send to him there?"

   I think so—if not an ethical responsibility, at least a responsibility as a friend not to embarrass your friend at work.

   Now, depending on OhioCompany's policy, the friend at work probably has an ethical responsibility to ask you not to send so much email to him at work. He also has a responsibility to delete all of these files from his computer. Again, though, it depends on the company's policy.

5. I think it is unprofessional and unethical to send 100 pictures to a friend; it's also a silly waste. Instead, post the album on a picture Web site. Then the question becomes, "Is your friend violating organizational policy by looking at your pictures on that site?" It depends on company policy. See question 8.

   Sending one picture to 100 friends at work is unprofessional. I think you're becoming an email nuisance. See question 9.

6. OhioCompany owns the bits (not the rights to the image—an important difference). They can delete those bits at their option. Yes, OhioCompany has the right to inspect; it owns the computers. Again, managers' actions depend on organizational policy.

7. If you send the email to your friend's private account, then you have moved any possible professional or ethical burden from yourself to your friend. So, it is preferable for you to do so. By sending the email to the private account, the picture will be stored on the private ISP's servers and not OhioCompany's. Otherwise, the cost of your friend reading the email and viewing the picture is the same to OhioCompany.

8. Probably the opportunity cost of the friend's not working is greater than the cost of the computing infrastructure. By sending a lot of pictures, you are wasting your friend's time. Again, one picture seems OK, as long as your friend hasn't asked you not to send such email to him at work. More than that is at least inconsiderate and unfriendly, and probably unethical.

9. Ask the students their opinions. Sending 100 emails to a friend at work in a short period of time seems like a nuisance to me. But where between 1 and 100 does nuisance begin?

WRAP UP

➤ **At work, you have a responsibility to learn your organization's policy for personal computer and network use. It is always unwise and probably unethical not to follow that policy.**

➤ **You have a professional, and maybe an ethical, responsibility not to embarrass your friends by sending too much email to them at work. At least ask your friends if they would prefer you use their private accounts.**

TLD	Introduced	Purpose	Sponsor/Operator
.aero	2001	Air-transport industry	Societe Internationale de Telecommunications Aeronautiques SC (SITA)
.biz	2001	Businesses	
.com	1995	Unrestricted (but intended for commercial registrants)	VeriSign, Inc.
.coop	2001	Cooperatives	DotCooperation, LLC
.edu	1995	United States educational institutions	EDUCAUSE
.gov	1995	United States government	U.S. General Services Administration
.info	2001	Unrestricted use	Afilias, LLC
.int	1998	Organizations established by international treaties between governments	Internet Assigned Numbers Authority
.mil	1995	United States military	U.S. DoD Network Information Center
.museum	2001	Museums	Museum Domain Management Association (MuseDoma)
.name	2001	For registration by individuals	Global Name Registry, LTD
.net	1995	Unrestricted (but intended for network providers, etc.)	VeriSign, Inc.
.org	1995	Unrestricted (but intended for organizations that do not fit elsewhere)	Public Interest Registry; Global Registry Services
.pro	2002	Accountants, lawyers, physicians, and other professionals	RegistryPro, LTD

Figure 5-25
Top-Level Domains, 2005

For example, to resolve the address *www.somewhere.biz*, you would first go to a root server and obtain the IP address of a server that resolves *.biz* domain names. To resolve the address *www.somewhere.com*, you would go to a root server and obtain the IP address of a server that resolves *.com* domain names. In the first case, given the address of the server that resolves *.biz*, you would query that server to determine the IP address of the server that resolves the particular name *somewhere.biz*. Then you would go to that server to determine the IP address of the server that manages *www.somewhere.biz*.

In practice, domain name resolution proceeds more quickly because there are thousands of computers called **domain name resolvers** that store the correspondence of domain names and IP addresses. These resolvers reside at ISPs, at academic institutions, at large companies, at governmental organizations, and so forth. A domain name resolver may even be located on your campus. If so, whenever anyone on your campus resolves a domain name, that resolver will store, or **cache**, the domain name and IP address on a local file. Then, when someone else on campus needs to resolve that same domain name, there is no need to go through the entire resolution process. Instead, the resolver can supply the IP address from the local file.

Of course, domain names and their IP addresses can change. Therefore, from time to time the domain name resolvers delete old addresses from their lists or refresh old addresses by checking their correctness.

In this chapter, you've learned about *computer* networks. Read the *Reflections Guide* on page 143a to learn how better to manage your *human* networks as well.

Human Networks Matter More

In case you missed it, *Six Degrees of Separation* is a play by John Guare that was made into a movie starring Stockard Channing and Donald Sutherland. The title is related to the idea, originated by the Hungarian writer Frigyes Karinthy, that everyone on earth is connected to everyone else by five (Karinthy) or six (Guare) people.[2] For example, according to the theory, you are connected to Eminem by no more than five or six people, because you know someone who knows someone, who knows someone, etc. By the same theory, you are also connected to a Siberian seal hunter. Today, in fact, with the Internet, the number may be closer to three people than to five or six, but in any case, the theory points out the importance of human networks.

Suppose you want to meet your university's president. The president has a secretary who acts as a gatekeeper. If you walk up to that secretary and say, "I'd like a half an hour with President Jones," you're likely to be palmed off to some other university administrator. What else can you do?

If you are connected to everyone on the planet by no more than six degrees, then surely you are connected to your president in fewer steps. Perhaps you play on the tennis team, and you know that the president plays tennis. In that case, it is likely that the tennis coach knows the president. So, arrange a tennis match with your coach and the president. Voilà! You have your meeting. It may even be better to have the meeting on the tennis court than in the president's office.

The problem with the six-degree theory, as Stockard Channing said so eloquently, is that even though those six people do exist, we don't know who they are. Even worse, we often don't know who the person is with whom we want to connect. For example, there is someone, right now who knows someone who has a job for which you are perfectly suited. Unfortunately, you don't know the name of that person.

It doesn't stop when you get your job, either. When you have a problem at work, like the $80,000 question in Chapter 3, there is someone who knows exactly how to help you. You, however, don't know who that is.

Accordingly, most successful professionals consistently build personal human networks. They keep building them because they know that somewhere there is someone whom they need to know or will need to know. They meet people at professional and social situations, collect and pass out cards, and engage in pleasant conversation (all part of a social protocol) to expand their networks.

You can apply some of the ideas about computer networks to make this process more efficient. Consider the network diagram to the left.

Assume that each line represents a relationship between two people. Notice that the people in your department tend to know each other, and the people in the accounting department also tend to know each other. That's typical.

Now suppose you are at the weekly employee after-hours party and you have an opportunity to introduce yourself either to Linda or Eileen. Setting aside personal considerations, thinking just about network building, which person should you meet?

---

[2] See "The Third Link" in Albert Laszlo Barabasi's book *Linked* (New York: Perseus Publishing, 2002) for background on this theory.

If you introduce yourself to Linda, you shorten your pathway to her from two steps to one and your pathway to Shawna from three to two. You do not open up any new channels because you already have them to the people in your floor.

However, if you introduce yourself to Eileen, you open up an entirely new network of acquaintances. So, considering just network building, you use your time better by meeting Eileen and other people who are not part of your current circle. It opens up many more possibilities.

The connection from you to Eileen is called a weak tie in social network theory,[3] and such links are crucial in connecting you to everyone in six degrees. *In general, the people you know the least contribute the most to your network.*

This concept is simple, but you'd be surprised by how few people pay attention to it. At most company events, everyone talks with the people they know, and if the purpose of the function is to have fun, then that behavior makes sense. In truth, however, no business social function exists for having fun, regardless of what people say. Business functions exist for business reasons, and you can use them to create and expand networks. Given that time is always limited, you may as well use such functions efficiently.

---

[3] See Terry Granovetter, "The Strength of Weak Ties," *American Journal of Sociology*, May 1973.

? DISCUSSION QUESTIONS

1. Determine the shortest path from you to your university's president. How many links does it have?

2. Give an example of a network to which you belong that is like your floor in the figure on the preceding page. Sketch a diagram of who knows whom for six or so members of that group.

3. Recall a recent social situation and identify two people, one of whom could have played the role of Linda (someone in your group whom you do not know) and one of whom could have played the role of Eileen (someone in a different group whom you do not know). How could you have introduced yourself to either person?

4. Does it seem too contrived and calculating to think about your social relationships in this way? Even if you do not approach relationships like this, are you surprised to think that others do? Under what circumstances does this kind of analysis seem appropriate, and when does it seem inappropriate?

5. Consider the phrase, "It's not what you know, it's whom you know that matters." Relate this phrase to the diagram. Under what circumstances is this likely to be true? When is it false?

6. Describe how you can apply the principle, "The people you know the least contribute the most to your network" to the process of a job search.

IP Addressing Schemes

Two IP addressing schemes exist. The first and more common scheme is called **IPv4**, and it constructs addresses having 32 bits. The bits are divided into four groups of 8 bits, and a decimal number represents each group.

IPv4 addresses are displayed by placing periods between each group of 4 bits. A typical IPv4 address appears as 63.224.57.59. Because the largest decimal number that can be represented with 8 bits is 255, the numbers between the periods are always between 0 and 255. The following could *never be* an IPv4 address: 444.200.209.001.

When IPv4 was developed, the Internet had few users; 32-bit addresses, which allow for 4,294,967,295 distinct addresses, seemed more than enough. In recent years, however, the growth of the Internet has challenged that assumption. Therefore, a new IP addressing scheme, called **IPv6,** has been developed. Currently, both IPv4 and IPv6 addresses are used on the Internet. Over the coming years, however, IPv6 will replace IPv4.

IPv6 addresses have 128 bits, which allows for 2^{128} distinct addresses, or an address for just about every dust particle in the universe. Why do we need so many addresses?

The answer is that for both IPv4 and IPv6, not all of the addresses are used. This occurs because large blocks of IP addresses are allocated to major organizations such as government agencies and commercial enterprises. Organizations may not use all of the addresses in the block assigned to it. Thus, many IP addresses go unused.

The ways in which IP address blocks are allocated are complicated, and the allocation scheme differs between IPv4 and IPv6. This topic is not important for our purposes. For now, just realize that every computer on the Internet is assigned a unique IP address that consists of either 32 or 128 bits.

By the way, IPv6 has many advantages over IPv4 besides more IP addresses. See *ipv6.org* for more information.

The Connectivity Evaluation Project (continued)

At the start of this chapter, we left you with the project of giving your COO a high-level management report on the communication alternatives available for integrating the home office with the new facility acquired in California. From this chapter, you know that a LAN won't do the job. You will most likely have a LAN at both the Poughkeepsie and California facilities, but you cannot use a LAN to connect the two sites.

Instead, you will need to use some sort of WAN or internet or the Internet. One option is to acquire leased lines between the two facilities, and that might be the way to go. But leased lines have some disadvantages. Similarly, you could buy time on a PSDN, and that, too, would solve the problem, but it, too, has disadvantages. You could also set up some type of VPN, but you're not sure that it would handle the traffic load.

Still, you think you've identified three potentially workable solutions. To evaluate those alternatives further, you'll need to dig deeper and possibly hire the consultant. You will have an opportunity to do that in question 17 of Applying Your Knowledge (page 147).

You Be the Guide

Using the Reflections Guide
(page 143a)

GOALS

✳ Teach students the importance of networking.

✳ Emphasize that business social functions are always business functions.

BACKGROUND AND PRESENTATION STRATEGIES

Successful business people are constantly networking. They constantly add to their set of acquaintances. This is true even at the highest levels: Every summer Microsoft has a meeting of the CEOs of the world's 100 largest corporations. Almost all attend, not so much because of the presentations, but because they have so few opportunities to meet each other informally. When the CEO of 3M bumps into the CEO of Citibank at the coffee pot, who knows what transpires? The start of a new board seat for someone?

Business is nothing but relationships. People do business *with people.* Meeting the right people in an informal context makes it possible to better accomplish work in formal contexts. At the weekly softball game, when Brenda makes (or doesn't make) a double play with Don and Bill, a bond is formed that makes it more likely that Brenda and Bill will come to Don's network requirements meeting. It may not make sense, but that's just the way people are. In business, relationships are everything.

So, even though it may seem contrived and awkward, students should learn to attend business social events and to use those events for network building. Sometimes people go to events because they want to meet someone in particular, and sometimes they go just to expand their networks.

➤ **Go to business social events and don't spend all your time talking to people you already know. Make a point of meeting new people who work in other departments.**

Warning: Business social events are business events. There is a difference between a softball game with your friends and one at work. There is a difference between a holiday party with your friends and one at work. The goal of all business social events is to expand networks and to enable people to relate to one another informally. A holiday party is not an opportunity for the company to reward its employees with unlimited free alcohol.

➤ **Party with your friends, but network at business social functions.**

I once managed an exceedingly capable C++ developer who got drunk at the holiday party and made a fool of himself. The next Monday, our business unit manager wanted me to fire him. He was critical to our project, and I was able to help him keep his job. Our relationship, however, was never the same, and his stature at the company fell dramatically.

➤ *Business social functions are business events.*

It is important, too, for students to use social organizations outside of their company for network building. The local chapter of professional accountants or marketers or software entrepreneurs or financial executives is an important source of professional relationships. The best way to build a network is not just to go to a meeting; rather, get involved with the group. Help run a meeting, become an officer, work on the membership committee.

➤ **As the guide points out, there is someone out there who knows someone or something that you need to know. Because you don't and can't know who that person is, your only alternative is to meet as many interesting people as you can.**

⍰ SUGGESTED RESPONSES FOR DISCUSSION QUESTIONS

1. The answer depends on the student and your local situation.

2. Use a fraternity or sorority, a student club, a church community, a dorm, a professional group, a job.

3. It's easier to meet Linda because she's in your group. You and she have many acquaintances in common. You also have your department's business in common, so you'll likely have much to say. It's more awkward to meet Eileen. You have no acquaintances in common; you may not know what group she works in or what she does. You may have little to say to one another.

➤ **It may be awkward to meet strangers, but it is important. Try it. Practice while you're in school. Get used to meeting people and talking with them. Learn to be better at it. If you're shy, force yourself to do it.**

4. Business social events are business events. Period.

➤ **You wouldn't go into an important meeting without having an agenda of what you want to** accomplish. So, too, don't go to a business social function without having an objective; for example, "Today I'm going to meet two people from manufacturing and ask about the new MRP system." Having an idea about what you want to know will make it easier to meet people. Just don't turn an informal event into a formal meeting.

➤ You probably don't want to treat parties with your friends this way, but a business social function is not a party. It's a business function.

5. First, regarding the phrase, professionals need to know their profession. Accountants need to know accounting, financial analysts need to know finance, and network administrators need to know TCP/IP–OSI. That said, however, what differentiates two people with about the same level of knowledge? Their relationships!

When you're designing a computer network, knowledge of data communications technology is critical; but when you're an Accounts Payable manager who's been asked to prepare a high-level management statement of networking alternatives, then knowing who to call for help is more important than your particular knowledge of data communications.

➤ Knowledge of data communications at the basic level of this chapter will help you better talk with experts in the field. It will help you build your network.

6. Get out and meet people. Go to every possible business speaker event. Talk with the speaker afterward. Ask interesting questions about his or her talk. Get that person's business card. Follow up with an email thanking them and asking another pertinent question or two. Join relevant business clubs on campus. Get involved. When business people come to campus, volunteer to greet them and buy them a cup of coffee before or afterward. Do everything you can to expand your network. All of these actions increase the likelihood that you'll meet that person who knows about the job that would be ideal for you. And, by the way, your life on campus will be more enjoyable and interesting, too.

WRAP UP

One way to wrap up is to challenge the students to keep thinking about it:

➤ Networking is important—very important. In some ways, for the purposes of getting a job, developing a good network is more important than your GPA. Look how much time you put into your GPA. Just put some of that time into building your network.

➤ Network building is, by the way, a lifelong activity. It may be that some relationships you build here on campus will pay dividends many years down the road.

➤ Think seriously about these ideas. Discuss them with your friends. Determine what you believe about the relative importance of knowledge and networks. When is one more important than the other?

➤ Again, it's your life, your career. I'm just trying to coach you into behaviors that will help you become a successful business professional. Give it some thought!

The Connectivity Evaluation Project (continued) (page 144)

The text explains that a LAN won't do because the sites are geographically separated. That exclusion leaves a WAN, an intranet, and the Internet—specifically, either leased lines, a PSDN, or a VPN. The next task is to dig deeper and possibly hire a consultant.

RESPONDING TO THE CHALLENGE

A number of questions to ask the students:

➤ **Why does the text say a LAN is infeasible?**

➤ **How, in general terms, would leased lines solve this problem?**

➤ **How, in general terms, would buying time on a PSDN solve this problem?**

➤ **How, in general terms, would a VPN solve the problem?**

A good way to discuss this situation is to make a list of questions that need to be answered. Then, given the list, the students can devise a strategy for obtaining answers. (This activity overlaps question 17 in the text. If you have assigned that question, you can use this material to discuss answers to that question.)

➤ **We can organize the question list according to categories:**

DATA REQUIREMENTS

➤ **What types of data do the two sites need to communicate?**

➤ **How much data do they need to exchange?**

➤ **What level of reliability do they need?**

➤ **Is there a need for remote access from outside either facility? From hotels? Customer sites? Employee's homes?**

➤ **Others?**

APPLICATIONS REQUIREMENTS

➤ **Do the two sites need an integrated email system?**

➤ **If so, what are its communications requirements?**

➤ **Do the sites share a common database? Where does that database reside?**

➤ **What are the communications requirements of database applications?**

➤ **Do the sites share internal Web sites?**

➤ **Others?**

SECURITY REQUIREMENTS

➤ **What level of security does each site require?**

➤ **What level of security does the traffic between the sites require?**

➤ **Will nonemployees need to access the network? If so, how and why?**

➤ **Others?**

FUTURE REQUIREMENTS

➤ **Will there be substantial growth at either site?**

➤ **Will site growth impact the communications requirements between the sites?**

➤ **Are additional database or other applications anticipated? For example, does the company plan an ERP system between the two sites?**

(ERP is discussed in Chapter 7, but you might give a thumbnail sketch of it now. Or, just use a generic statement like: *integrated applications, such as integrated manufacturing*.)

ALTERNATIVES

➤ **How well would leased lines (or PSDN or VPN) meet these requirements?**

➤ **Using Figure 5-21 as a guide, how would we go about evaluating these alternatives?**

➤ **What about risk? Do the alternatives vary in the likelihood of failure? How would we find out?**

Given the list of questions, how would the students go about solving them? Which could they answer on their own? Which could they answer from sources within the company? Which would they need to ask the paid consultant? Where else could they go to get answers? Other companies? Industry trade groups? Microsoft, Cicso, Oracle, SAP, PSDN companies, leased line vendors, or other vendors?

WRAP UP

Questions to use for wrap-up:

➤ **What did you learn from this vignette?**

➤ **Can you see yourself in this person's position? Do you think you'd know how to proceed?**

➤ **Do you believe that you need to understand the technology in this chapter to be a well-rounded manager in the future?**

➤ **How does this knowledge give you a competitive advantage?**

SUMMARY

■ A computer network is a collection of computers that communicate with one another over transmission lines. Three types of computer networks are LANs, WANs, and internets, including the Internet. LANs connect computers at one site, on the premises of the company that operates the LAN. WANs connect computers at separated sites. Finally, internets (note the lowercase *i*) are networks of networks.

■ A protocol architecture divides communications activities among several layers. Each layer has specific functions to perform. A protocol is a set of rules for accomplishing the functions of a particular layer. Software programs implement protocols.

■ The TCP/IP–OSI architecture has the five layers shown in Figure 5-4 (page 119). LAN and WAN protocols relate to Layers 1 and 2 of this model and are used within a single network. Protocols for internets use all five layers of this model. SMTP, HTTP, and FTP are three of the most important protocols at Layer 5. The TCP protocol operates at Layer 4; the IP protocol operates at Layer 3; and the IEEE 802 protocols operate at Layers 1 and 2.

■ LANs consist of computers at a single organizational site that are connected via UTP or optical fiber cables. Each computer has a network interface card (NIC), which is a special-purpose computer that connects to the LAN's cabling. A switch is a special-purpose computer that receives traffic from one computer and sends it to another computer. Many LANs have multiple switches.

■ IEEE 802.3, or Ethernet, is the most popular LAN standard. 10/100/1000 Ethernet allows communications at 10, 100, or 1,000 Mbps. Some LANs are supported by wireless connections; wireless computers need a wireless NIC. The most popular wireless standard today is IEEE 802.11g. Both 802.3 and 802.11 operate at Layers 1 and 2 of the TCP/IP-OSI protocol model. Figure 5-12 (page 126) summarizes LAN and WAN network alternatives.

■ WAN alternatives consist of PC to ISP via a modem, networks of leased lines, public switched data networks (PSDNs), and virtual private networks (VPNs). A modem is a device that converts digital signals to analog ones. An ISP, or Internet service provider, is a company that provides Internet addresses, serves as a gateway to the Internet, and charges its customers to pay for the Internet. Three types of modems are dial-up, DSL, and cable. Narrowband communications lines provide transmission speeds less than 56 kbps. Broadband lines have speeds in excess of 256 kbps.

■ Networks of leased lines consist of high-speed lines that connect two points. The Point-to-Point Protocol (PPP) is used to manage such lines. Leased lines are most useful when an organization has large amounts of traffic between two sites.

■ A public switched data network (PSDN) is a network of computers and leased lines that is developed and maintained by a vendor that leases time on the network to other organizations. PSDNs are clouds of capability that other organizations can lease. Three common PSDN protocols are Frame Relay, ATM, and 10 and 40 Gbps Ethernet.

■ A virtual private network (VPN) uses the Internet or other internet to create the appearance of private, point-to-point connections. A VPN client and a VPN server create a tunnel, which is a virtual, private pathway over a public or shared network. VPNs offer the benefit of point-to-point lines to fixed sites as well as to individuals working in remote locations and also to anyone else who has been registered with the VPN server.

■ The TCP/IP–OSI protocols can be used by applications within a LAN or across the Internet or other internet.

■ Communicating devices have two addresses, a physical address (MAC) and an IP address (logical address). Private IP addresses are valid within a LAN or other private network or internet. Public IP addresses are valid on the Internet. DHCP is a service that provides temporary private IP addresses to computer users. *Switches* work with *frames* at *Layer 2*. They send frames from switch to switch until they arrive at their destination, and they use *MAC addresses*. *Routers* work with *segments* at *Layer 3*. They send segments from router to router until they arrive at their destination, and they use *IP addresses*.

■ The process of converting IP addresses from private to public and public to private is called Network Address Translation (NAT). NAT is provided by routers and other devices.

■ The domain name system (DNS) resolves domain names into IP addresses. ICANN licenses other agencies to register unique domain names and their associated IP addresses. The last letters in a domain name are called the top-level domain. Examples are *.com*, *.org*, and *.cn*. Different agencies are licensed to register domain names on different top-level domains. To resolve a domain name, it is necessary to obtain the IP address of a computer that resolves the top-level domain from one of the DNS root servers. That IP address is then used to obtain the IP address of the next part of the domain name, and so forth, until the IP address of the entire domain name is resolved. Domain name resolver computers save work by caching resolved domain names. IPv4 addresses consist of 32 bits, and IPv6 addresses consist of 128 bits. Both IPv4 and IPv6 are used on the Internet today.

KEY TERMS AND CONCEPTS

ASSIGNMENT MATERIAL

Review Questions

1. Give an example of a human protocol other than one discussed in this chapter.

2. Name the five layers of the TCP/IP-OSI layered protocol. Briefly describe the function of each layer.

3. Explain the following statement: "In a layered protocol, each layer interfaces with the layers above and below it, but except for the bottom layer, does not share an interface with layers at the same level."

4. When a manufacturer offers a computer with built-in Ethernet 10/100/1000 capability, what does that mean?

5. What TCP/IP-OSI layers does Ethernet support?

6. List four different WAN alternatives and explain the advantages and disadvantages of each.

7. What purposes does an ISP serve?

8. Explain the differences between:
    a. Dial-up, DSL, and cable modems
    b. Switches and routers
    c. Frames and segments
    d. MAC addresses and IP addresses
    e. Private IP addresses and public IP addresses

9. Explain, at a high level, how DHCP works.

10. Explain what is happening in Figure 5-24.

11. Explain, at a high level, why router RH in Figure 5-24 needs two IP addresses.

12. What does *ICANN* stand for? What does it do?

13. What is the function of the domain name system?

14. Explain the steps necessary to register a domain name.

Applying Your Knowledge

15. Suppose you manage a group of seven employees in a small business. Each of your employees wants to be connected to the Internet. Consider two alternatives:

    - Alternative A: Each employee has his own modem and connects individually to the Internet
    - Alternative B: The employees' computers are connected using a LAN and the network uses a single modem to connect.

    a. Sketch the equipment and lines required for each alternative.
    b. Explain the actions you need to take to create each alternative.
    c. Compare the alternatives using the criteria in Figure 5-21.
    d. Which of these two alternatives do you recommend?

16. Consider the situation of a company that has two offices at physically separated sites. Suppose each office has a group of 15 computers.

    a. If the two offices are retail art galleries, what is likely to be the most common interoffice communication? Given your answer, what type of WAN do you think is most appropriate?
    b. Suppose the two offices are manufacturing sites that communicate via email and that regularly exchange large drawings and plans. What are the advantages and disadvantages of each of the four WAN types for these offices? Under what circumstances would you recommend a leased-line WAN?
    c. Suppose the two offices are the same as described in part b, but that in addition, each has salespeople on the road who need to connect to the office computers. How would your answer to part b change?
    d. Would you change your answer to part c if both offices are located in the same building? Why or why not?
    e. What additional factors would you need to consider if one of the offices in part c was in Los Angeles and the other was located in Singapore?

17. Consider the *Connectivity Evaluation Project* that begins on page 116.

    a. Using the alternatives stated in the *Connectivity Evaluation Project* on page 116 and Figure 5-21, formulate a list of questions that you need to answer for each alternative. If you can state the answer to any of these questions, given what you know now, do so.
    b. Given your question list, do you need to hire a consultant? If so, indicate which questions you need the consultant to answer and which, with further study, you can answer yourself.
    c. Given the data you have, are there any communications alternatives that you can eliminate without further study?
    d. Suppose that while you're conducting your study you learn that IS is recommending setting up a VPN. List the advantages and disadvantages of this recommendation. If the COO asks you what you think of a VPN for this situation, how would you respond?

18. Suppose that you are a marketing consultant named Taylor Blitherspoon and that you want to set up a Web site for your business. You want to use the domain name *TaylorBlitherspoon*.

    a. Explain the general process for registering a domain.
    b. Which top-level domain do you think is appropriate?
    c. Access *icann.org* and obtain the name of an agency that can register a domain for the TLD you selected. What is the name of that agency?
    d. Access the Web site for that agency to learn the process that you must use. How much will it cost initially to register your domain name? How much will it cost to maintain it in the future?

Application Exercise

19. Suppose you work for a company that installs computer networks. Assume that you have been given the task of creating spreadsheets to generate cost estimates.

    a. Create a spreadsheet to estimate hardware costs. Assume that the user of the spreadsheet will enter the number of pieces of equipment and the standard cost for each type of equipment. Assume that the networks can include the following components: NIC cards, WNIC cards, wireless access points, switches of two types, one faster, one slower, at two different prices, and routers. Also assume that the company will use both UTP and optical fiber cable and that prices for cable are stated as per foot.

    b. Show how you can use the spreadsheet from part a to estimate the costs of networks having different performances. Use the network layout in Figure 5-2 and assume different kinds of devices at different prices. Make assumptions about distances between computers and devices.

    c. Modify your spreadsheet to include labor costs. Assume there is a fixed cost for the installation of each type of equipment and a per foot cost for the installation of cable.

Career Assignments

20. Suppose you are interested in working in sales of products and services for computer networking and related industries. Query your favorite Web search engine for job opportunities such as PSDN sales job opportunities, WAN sales job opportunities, and network sales job opportunities. Also, search the Web sites of communication vendors such as Cisco, Juniper, Redback, Nortel, and others for possible job leads.

    a. Describe the characteristics of jobs that that are currently available.

    b. Search the Department of Labor's Occupational Outlook Handbook (*bls.gov/oco/*) and related resources to determine the outlook for such jobs.

    c. What classes or other activities, such as internships, could you take to prepare for such jobs?

21. Answer question 20, but suppose you are interested in network customer support job opportunities.

22. Answer question 20, but suppose you are interested in network management job opportunities.

Case Study 5-1

Larry Jones Network Services

SOHO networks are increasing in popularity. Today, many homes have multiple computers, and although they have a need to share resources like printers, the major drive for networking home computers is to share an Internet connection. Each home user must have Internet access, but no one wants (or needs) to pay for a separate connection for each.

The situation is likely to become more complex in the future as computer networks are used for entertainment as well as for information. We can see the start of that movement in Internet games, but those games require little networking compared to what will be needed when TV, radio, movies, and music are downloaded over the Internet. At that point, every computing device in the home will need to be networked.

Reread the case concerning Larry Jones on page 127 and then answer the following questions.

Questions

1. Consider the first fraternity house that Larry equipped. Explain how a LAN could be used to connect all of the computers in the house. Would you recommend an Ethernet LAN, an 802.11 LAN, or a combination? Justify your answer.

2. This chapter did not provide enough information for you to determine how many switches the fraternity house might need. However, in general terms, describe how the fraternity could use a multiple-switch system. Compare your solution to that for the hotel in Figure 5-2.

3. Considering the connection to the Internet, would you recommend that the fraternity house use a dial-up, a DSL, or a cable modem? Although you can rule out at least one of these alternatives with the knowledge you already have, what additional information do you need in order to make a specific recommendation?

4. Explain how the fraternity house could use DHCP. Would you recommend it?

5. Explain how the fraternity house could use NAT. Would you recommend it?

6. Should Larry develop a standard package solution for each of his customers? What advantages accrue from a standard solution? What are the disadvantages?

7. Do you perceive an opportunity at your campus for a service like Larry's? If you do not have fraternities and sororities, are there apartments and condos for which you could provide such services?

8. Using Larry Jones's experience as a guide, what opportunities will exist for small, local consulting companies for setting up SOHO networks?

9. Few home entertainment consumers will want to learn about DHCP, NAT, IP address settings, and the like. In response, vendors will attempt to ease the setup of home entertainment networks by hiding the technology. Ultimately, they will be successful, but in the near-term, customer support will be a burden to them. Although some of that support can be outsourced and sent overseas, the installation and setup of equipment must be done locally. Describe business opportunities that exist for you to provide customer support for vendors.

10. Are there local retailers selling home entertainment equipment that might be interested in a home network setup service? If so, describe their needs and the services you could provide.

Case Study 5-2

SOHO Network Administration

This project is a continuation of the SOHO network case begun on page 141.
Figure 1 illustrates the structure of the SOHO network:

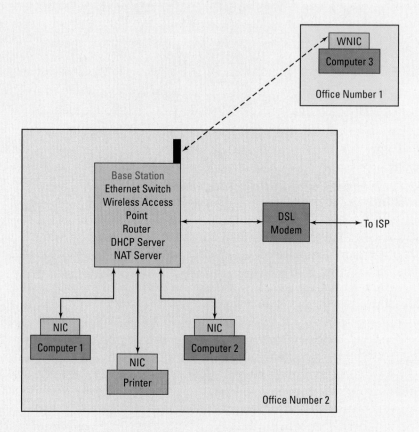

Figure 1

Both of these offices are in the same building. As shown, the base station includes an Ethernet switch, a wireless access point, a router, a DHCP server, and a NAT server. The base station, which is more generally called a *device access router,* has room for up to four physical connections from computers and servers.

Questions

1. Using the concepts from this chapter, answer the following questions:
   a. What hardware is needed to add an additional computer to the LAN using Ethernet?
   b. Describe the advantages of using DHCP for the new computer.
   c. The line between the base station and the modem is not a telephone line. Which line(s) will be telephone line(s)?
   d. Which lines will be UTP cables?
   e. What hardware is needed to add another wireless computer?
   f. The computer user in Office 2 must enter Office 1 to access the printer. This is a problem to the occupants of both offices. What must be done to move the printer to a neutral location between the two offices?

g. With regard to part f, suppose the users of this LAN decide to use a wireless printer server. Go to *cnet.com* or another site that lists computer hardware and determine the approximate cost of a wireless printer server. Under what conditions is it better to buy a wireless printer server? Under what conditions is it better to buy a second printer for Office 2 instead of a printer server?

h. The base station has room to connect only four Ethernet devices. If three computers and the printer are already connected using Ethernet, what options are available for adding yet another computer to the LAN?

i. All of the computers in this LAN run Microsoft Windows. A user at Computer 1 clicked the LAN icon at the bottom of his screen and the screen shown in Figure 2 appeared.
   i. Are the IP addresses in this screen internal or public IP addresses?
   ii. What computer is located at IP address 192.168.2.19?
   iii. What device is located at IP address 192.168.2.1?

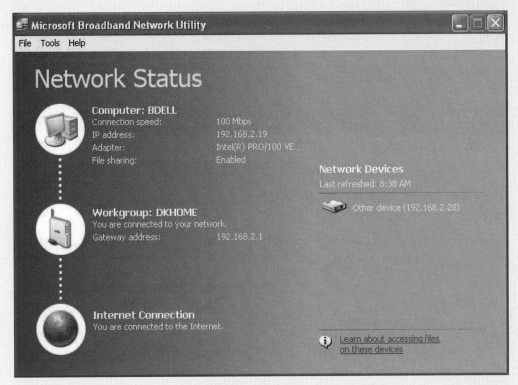

Source: Microsoft product screen shot reprinted with permission from Microsoft Corporation.

Figure 2

2. The user did not know what device was located at IP address 192.168.2.28, so he opened his browser and typed: *http://192.168.2.28*. The screen shown in Figure 3 (page 152) appeared.
   a. Which device on the SOHO LAN has been assigned this IP address?
   b. Which device created this display?
   c. What is the purpose of this display?

3. Out of curiosity, the user then entered *http:// 192.168.2.1* into his browser. The display shown in Figure 4 (page 152) resulted. In this chapter, you have not learned what a *subnet mask* is. However, you should be able to figure out the meanings of the data in this display.

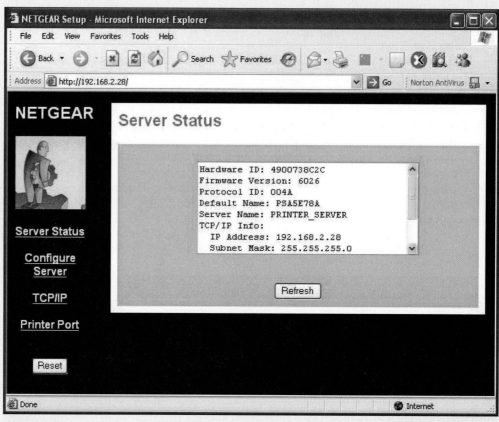

Figure 3   *Source*: Used with permission of NETGEAR, Inc.

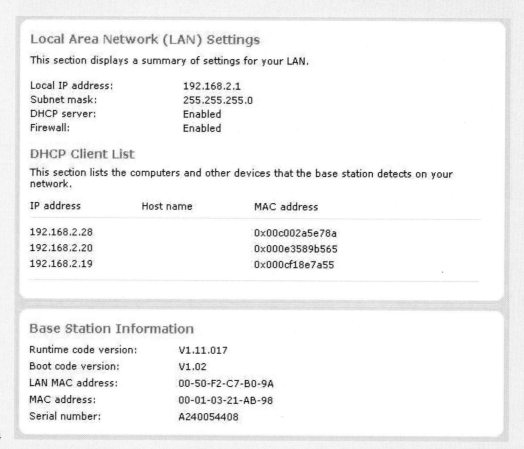

Figure 4

a. Which device produced this display?
b. What does "DHCP server: enabled" mean?
c. Explain the entries in the DHCP section.
d. The base station has two MAC addresses. What two devices inside the base station do you think they refer to?
e. What is the MAC address of the printer server? (Use data from the last two displays.)
f. The network administrator for this SOHO LAN can access a management utility within the base station. She did so and navigated to the display shown in Figure 5.

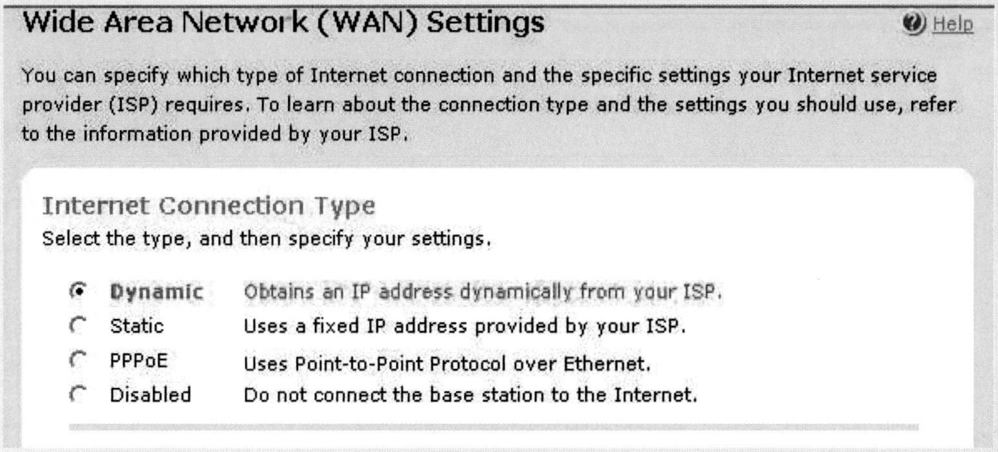

Wide Area Network (WAN) Settings ⓗ Help

You can specify which type of Internet connection and the specific settings your Internet service provider (ISP) requires. To learn about the connection type and the settings you should use, refer to the information provided by your ISP.

Internet Connection Type
Select the type, and then specify your settings.

- ⦿ **Dynamic** — Obtains an IP address dynamically from your ISP.
- ○ Static — Uses a fixed IP address provided by your ISP.
- ○ PPPoE — Uses Point-to-Point Protocol over Ethernet.
- ○ Disabled — Do not connect the base station to the Internet.

Figure 5

---

a. Do the data in this display pertain to the Ethernet switch or the router?
b. This chapter showed the use of DHCP within a LAN. This screen allows the base station to use DHCP to obtain its own public IP address from the ISP. What benefits does the ISP accrue by using DHCP?
c. When would the network administrator *not* use DHCP to connect to the ISP?
d. Under what circumstances would someone use a base station and not connect it to the Internet?

Systems Development

Learning Objectives

* Know the characteristics of systems development.

* Understand what professional systems analysts do.

* Understand how program development and systems development differ.

* Learn the major challenges of systems development.

* Know the nature and phases of the classical systems development cycle (SDLC).

* Know the nature and development tools used for rapid application development (RAD).

* Know the nature and phases of object-oriented development (OOD) using the unified process (UP).

* Understand the nature and advantages of extreme programming (XP).

Guides

ETHICS GUIDE
Estimation Ethics

PROBLEM SOLVING GUIDE
Aim for What You Want

OPPOSING FORCES GUIDE
The Real Estimation Process

SECURITY GUIDE
Security and Systems Development

REFLECTIONS GUIDE
Dealing with Uncertainty

This chapter introduces processes for developing information systems. We begin by discussing the nature of development work and the challenges inherent in systems development. We then survey four different development methodologies: the classical systems development life cycle (SDLC), rapid application development (RAD), object-oriented development (OOD), and extreme programming (XP).

Throughout these discussions, we will indicate the roles that you, as a future business professional and manager, should play. Pay particular attention to these discussions. Your goal should be to learn not only how to become an effective consumer of computer expertise and services, but also how to serve as an active user representative on a development project.

Baker, Barker, and Bickel

Baker, Barker, and Bickel met in June 2005 at a convention of resort own- ers and tourism operators. They sat next to each other by chance while waiting for a presentation, and after introducing themselves and laughing at the odd sound of their three names, they were surprised to learn that they managed similar businesses. Wilma Baker lives in Santa Fe, New Mexico, and specializes in renting homes and apartments to visitors to Santa Fe. Jerry Barker lives in Whistler Village, British Columbia, and specializes in renting condos to skiers and other visitors to the

Whistler/Blackcomb Resort. Chris Bickel lives in Chatham, Massachusetts, and specializes in renting homes and condos to vacationers to Cape Cod.

The three agreed to have lunch after the presentation. During lunch, they shared frustrations about the difficulty of obtaining new customers. As the conversation developed, they began to wonder if there was some way to combine forces (i.e., they were seeking a competitive advantage from an alliance). So, they decided to skip the next day's presentations and meet to discuss ways to form an alliance. Ideas they wanted to discuss further were sharing customer data, developing a joint reservation service, and exchanging property listings.

As they talked, it became clear they had no interest in merging their businesses; each wanted to stay independent. They also discovered that each was very concerned, paranoid even, about protecting their existing customer base from poaching. Still, the conflict wasn't as bad as it first seemed. Barker's business was primarily the ski trade, and winter was his busiest season; Bickel's business was mostly Cape Cod vacations, and she was busiest during the summer. Baker's high season was the summer and fall. But, it did appear that there was enough difference in their high seasons that they would not necessarily cannibalize their businesses by selling the others' offerings to their own customers.

The question then became how to proceed. Given their desire to protect their own customers, they did not want to develop a common customer database. The best idea seemed to be to share data about properties. That way they could keep control of their customers but still have an opportunity to sell time at the others' properties.

They discussed several alternatives. Each could develop her or his own property database, and the three could then share those databases over the Internet. Or, they could develop a centralized property database that they would all use. Or, they could find some other way to share property listings.

Baker, Barker, and Bickel needed to develop an information system to support their new alliance. As we proceed through this chapter, we will see how they can go about doing so.

◼ Systems Development Fundamentals

Systems development, or **systems analysis and design** as it is sometimes called, is the process of creating and maintaining information systems. Notice that this process concerns *information systems*, not just computer programs. Developing an *information system* involves all five components: hardware, software, data, procedures, and people. Developing a *computer program* involves software programs, possibly with some focus on data and databases. Figure 6-1 shows that systems development has a broader scope than computer program development.

MIS in Use 6-1 discusses the nature of large-scale corporate information systems and why such systems need formal methods of development.

Because systems development addresses all five components, it requires more than just programming or technical expertise. Establishing the system's goals, setting up the project, and determining requirements require business knowledge and management skill. Tasks like building computer networks and writing computer programs require technical skills, but developing the other components requires nontechnical,

Baker, Barker, and Bickel

(page 155)

GOALS

* Motivate students to learn basic systems development processes.

* Establish a case to illustrate the phases of different systems development processes.

WAYS TO STIMULATE STUDENT INVOLVEMENT

Notice that BBB met because they were *networking at a convention*. Had they not attended the conference, and had they not introduced themselves to each other, this possible alliance would not have started. As discussed in the Reflections Guide in Chapter 5, students must learn to develop their networks just at these professionals did.

Given the small size of their businesses, the BBB owners will need to be close to the systems development project. They have no staff of systems developers to call upon. They will have to plan the project themselves, get it started, and call in additional expertise as necessary. They will need to communicate frequently with one another about the project, and *the more they know about systems development, the better off they will be.*

An alliance like this one has a good chance of falling apart. An idea that seems promising while away from the pressures of everyday work may turn out to be unrealistic when back to work. Even if the project gets off the ground, the owners may find it difficult to keep it going while running their businesses. When the first bump in the road comes along, BBB will be tempted to abandon the project. For these reasons, BBB will be wise to start with a simple project. They need a project that will be easy to implement so they can determine the value of the alliance.

Consider two alternatives:

➤ **Once a week, the partners send each other an email with an attachment that lists 15 top properties/specials that are available for rent.**

➤ **The partners develop a shared property database and hire consultants to write a series of application programs that enable each office to rent properties using a VPN over the Internet. The system automates the calculation of revenue sharing.**

The first project can be implemented in about 10 minutes with little risk. The second project will require—well, ask the students what tasks BBB need to perform to create the database and to prepare the VPN:

➤ **You already know many tasks that will need to be done to implement the second alternative. Start with the database. Tell me what BBB will need to do just to design and implement the database.**

➤ **What tasks will they need to perform to obtain VPN access over the Internet? Why do they need a VPN?**

It seems to me that a good course of action for BBB is to lean toward a simple solution like the first one. If they find value in the alliance—that BBB are each able to rent others' properties and that the problems in doing so are surmountable—then they can proceed to a more elaborate system, and do that in easy stages.

If they do begin with a simple system, they will learn many of the requirements for the more elaborate one. Running the simple system will, for example, help them build an appropriate data model more quickly.

Regardless of which system they choose, even if they choose one as simple as emailing a list of properties, they should go through the definition phase of the SDLC. That will cause them to create a mutual view of the need and problem and to assess feasibility. See the discussion in the "Baker, Barker, and Bickel (Continued)" annotation.

WRAP UP

One way to introduce this chapter is to ask the students what they think they need to know if they are Baker, Barker, or Bickel. Have the students break into groups of three and ask the groups to respond to the following questions:

➤ **What do you need to know about systems development?**

➤ **What do you need to know to decide if you want to proceed?**

➤ **What criteria should you use to decide if this system is a good idea?**

➤ **How are you going to evaluate alternatives?**

➤ **Do you hire a consultant or systems developer? How do you decide?**

➤ **What other questions do you need to address?**

➤ Here you are, in class, and you have an opportunity to learn systems development fundamentals and you have me as your consultant. What questions do you have?

➤ Make a list of the top five questions you want to answer from our sessions on systems development.

Save your list. We'll use it again when we finish this chapter.

(You can ask the students to assess whether they've answered their questions when you pick up the continuation of BBB at the chapter's end.)

Computer programming concerned
with programs, some data

| Hardware | Software | Data | Procedures | People |

Scope of Systems Development

Figure 6-1
Systems Development vs.
Program Development

human relations skills. Creating data models requires the ability to interview users and understand their view of the business activities. Designing procedures, especially those involving group action, requires business knowledge and an understanding of group dynamics. Developing job descriptions, staffing, and training all require human resource and related expertise.

Thus, do not suppose that systems development is exclusively a technical task undertaken by programmers and hardware specialists. Rather, it requires coordinated teamwork of both specialists and nonspecialists with business knowledge.

Information Systems Are Never Off-the-Shelf

In Chapter 3, you learned there are three sources for software: off-the-shelf, off-the-shelf with adaptation, and tailor-made. Although all three sources pertain to software, only two of them pertain to information systems. Unlike software, *information systems are*

MIS in Use 6-1

Thinking Big About Systems Development

Many students do not appreciate the need for systems development processes. You may have worked only with an accounting spreadsheet or a single-user contact manager database. These are small systems with easily understood requirements. If you have not worked with large-scale corporate information systems, you have not seen their scope, and so you may not know why systems development processes are so important.

Consider the IRS case discussed in Chapter 1. The IRS has over 100,000 employees at more than a thousand sites. The development team for the IRS system includes more than 500 professionals. How do you manage them? How do you ensure that they are working to the same set of goals and requirements and using the same design? (See the case starting on page 185 for more on this situation.)

Or, consider the problems of international organizations. Suppose The Coca-Cola Corporation wants to standardize on a single information system for beverage production. Coca-Cola plants exist in almost every country in the world; a new system will involve tens of thousands of people and more than 50 different languages. How do you develop such a system? Clearly, you must follow a comprehen-

sive process, and you must do so consistently, despite the different languages and cultures.

Or, think about a company like The 3M Company. 3M has over 50 business units that sell thousands of products in more than 90 nations. 3M is concerned about the proper and safe use of its products worldwide. Suppose the 3M legal department asks you to develop an information system that stores product information, product safety requirements, and the relationship of product requirements to international, national, and local labor laws. Suppose you are given 3 years and a $10 million budget for the new system. How do you proceed?

As you will learn in Chapter 7, enterprise-wide information systems seldom just automate existing procedures. Instead, most information systems are *process-design oriented*. The idea is first to modernize and streamline the underlying business processes and then to develop an information system to support and enforce those new business processes. However, the new system will change the way people work; it will change habits, authorities, reporting structures, and the like. These are very difficult changes for people to make. Designing such a system for a global organization is a monumental task.

Large-scale systems have wide-reaching effects. Therefore, development of such projects must be carefully planned and executed, using an effective and comprehensive development process. Without such a process, chaos and disaster are the likely result.

never off-the-shelf. Because information systems involve your company's people and procedures, you must construct or adapt procedures to fit your business and people, regardless of how you obtain the computer programs.

As a future business manager, you will have a key role in information systems development. In order to accomplish the goals of your department, you need to ensure that effective procedures exist for using the information system. You need to ensure that personnel are properly trained and are able to use the IS effectively. If your department does not have appropriate procedures and trained personnel, you must take corrective action. Although you might pass off hardware, program, or data problems to the IT department, you cannot pass off procedural or personnel problems to that department. Such problems are your problems. The single most important criterion for information systems success is for users to take ownership of their systems.

Information Systems Maintenance

Systems development is defined as a process for creating and *maintaining* information systems. Before we continue, you need to understand that, in truth, *maintenance* is a poor term. Maintenance connotes someone changing the oil or putting air in the tires. It implies activities to keep the system running, which is an incorrect image. For information systems, *maintenance* means one of two things: either fixing a system to make it do what it should have done in the first place or adapting it to changing requirements. Although neither of those actions is well described by the term *maintenance*, that term is fixed in the industry, and so we will use it in this text. Understand, however, that in the context of IS, **maintenance** means to fix or adapt.

Systems Development Challenges

Systems development is difficult and risky. Many projects are never finished. Of those that are finished, some are 200 or 300 percent over budget. Still other projects finish within budget and schedule, but never satisfactorily accomplish their goals. (See *Case Study 6-2*, page 187, for more statistics on development failures.)

You may be amazed to learn that systems development failures can be so dramatic. You might suppose that with all the computers and all the systems developed over the years, by now there must be some methodology for successful systems development. In fact, there *are* systems development methodologies that can result in success, and we will discuss four of them in this chapter. But, even when competent people follow one of these methodologies, the risk of failure is still high.

In the following sections, we will discuss the following major challenges to systems development:

- The difficulty of determining requirements
- Changes in requirements
- Scheduling and budgeting difficulties
- Changing technology
- Diseconomies of scale

The Difficulty of Requirements Determination

First, requirements are difficult to determine. Think about the system that Baker, Barker, and Bickel want to develop. What does it mean to share property listings? Specifically, what property data need to be shared? What should the data entry forms look like? What reports do the owners need? How do they want to query the data? Are the data the same for each company, or do they vary from one to another?

Further, how will one of the agencies go about reserving another agency's property? How will such reservations be communicated to the other agency? How will payments be processed? The questions go on and on. Each of the development processes that we will describe in this chapter is designed to ensure that such questions are both asked and answered.

Changes in Requirements

Even more difficult, systems development aims at a moving target. Requirements change as the system is developed, and the bigger the system and the longer the project, the more the requirements change.

When requirements do change, what should the development team do? Stop work and rebuild the system in accordance with the new requirements? If they do that, the system will develop in fits and starts and may never be completed. Or, should the team finish the system, knowing that it will be unsatisfactory the day it is implemented and will therefore need immediate maintenance?

Scheduling and Budgeting Difficulties

Other challenges involve scheduling and budgeting. How long will it take to build a system? That question is not easy to answer. Suppose you are building the property-tracking system for Baker, Barker, and Bickel. How long will it take to create the data model? Even if you know how long it takes to build one complete data model, Baker, Barker, and Bickel may disagree with each other. How many times will you need to rebuild the data model until they agree?

Data modeling is just one element of the project. Suppose Baker, Barker, and Bickel decide to use a public switched data network to connect their three companies. How long will it take to lease the lines to connect to the PSDN vendor? How long will it take to negotiate a contract? How long will it take to determine what hardware and software are required? How long will it take to get the system up and running?

Consider the applications. How long will it take to build the forms, reports, queries, and application programs? How long will it take to test all of them? What about procedures and people? What procedures need to be developed, and how much time should be allowed to create and document them, develop training programs, and train the personnel?

Further, how much will all of this cost? Labor costs are a direct function of labor hours; if you cannot estimate labor hours, you cannot estimate labor costs. Moreover, if you cannot estimate how much a system costs, then how do you perform a financial analysis to determine if the system generates an appropriate rate of return?

Changing Technology

Yet another challenge is that while the project is underway, technology continues to change. For example, while you are developing Baker, Barker, and Bickel's property-sharing system, Microsoft, Sun, and IBM are working on a new technology called XML Web Services. You learn that this new technology could drastically shorten your development time, halve the costs, and result in a better system. That is, it will do those things if it actually works the way vendors say it will.

Even if you believe the new technology is a viable answer, do you want to stop your development to switch to the new technology? Would it be better to finish developing according to the existing plan?

Diseconomies of Scale

Unfortunately, as development teams become larger, the average contribution per worker decreases. This is true because as staff size increases, more meetings and other coordinating activities are required to keep everyone in sync. There are economies of scale up to a point, but beyond a workgroup of, say, 20 employees, diseconomies of scale begin to take over.

A famous adage known as **Brooks's Law** points out a related problem: *Adding more people to a late project makes the project later.*[1] Brooks's Law is true not only because a larger staff requires increased coordination, but also because new people

---

[1] Fred Brooks was a successful senior manager at IBM in the 1960s. After retiring from IBM, he wrote a classic book on IT project management called *The Mythical Man-Month.* Published by Addison-Wesley in 1975, the book is pertinent today and should be read by every IT or IS project manager. It's an enjoyable book, too.

need training. The only people who can train the new employees are the existing team members, who are thus taken off productive tasks. The costs of training new people can overwhelm the benefit of their contribution.

In short, managers of software development projects face a dilemma: They can increase work per employee by keeping the team small, but in doing so, they extend the project's timeline. Or, they can reduce the project's timeline by adding staff, but because of diseconomies of scale, they will have to add 150 or 200 hours of labor to gain 100 hours of work. And, due to Brooks's Law, once the project is late, both choices are bad.

Furthermore, schedules can be compressed only so far. According to one other popular adage, "Nine women cannot make a baby in one month."

Is It Really So Bleak?

Is systems development really as bleak as the list of challenges makes it sound? Yes and no. All of the challenges just described do exist, and they are all significant hurdles that every development project must overcome. As noted previously, once the project is late and over budget, no good choice exists. "I have to pick my regrets," said one beleaguered manager of a late project.

The IT industry has over 50 years of experience developing information systems, and over those years, methodologies have emerged that successfully deal with these problems. In the next four sections, we will consider four different systems development processes:

- Systems development life cycle (SDLC)
- Rapid application development (RAD)
- Object-oriented systems development (OOD)
- Extreme programming (XP)

You may be wondering why there are *four* different methodologies. Why not just one? Because information systems differ, no single process works for all situations. As you learned in Chapter 2, some systems automate business processes and decision making, whereas others augment them. An automated system must be a complete solution; an augmentation system can have gaps that users fill.

Also, the scale of information systems varies widely. Personal systems support one person with a limited set of requirements. Workgroup systems support a group of people, normally with a single application. Enterprise systems support many work-groups with many different applications. Interenterprise systems support many different organizations with different organizational cultures; some support users in different countries with different cultural heritages.

So, given the variety of possible systems, it is not surprising that there are different development processes. Different processes are appropriate for different types of systems. We begin with the classical systems development process.

▨ The Systems Development Life Cycle Development Process

The **systems development life cycle (SDLC)** is the classical process used to develop information systems. The IT industry developed the SDLC in the "school of hard knocks." Many early projects met with disaster, and companies and systems developers sifted through the ashes of those disasters to determine what went wrong. By the 1970s, most seasoned project managers agreed on the basic tasks that need to be performed to successfully build and maintain information systems. These basic tasks are combined into phases of systems development.

Different authors and organizations package the tasks into different numbers of phases. Some organizations use an eight-phase process, others use a seven-phase process, and still others use a five-phase process. In this text, we will use the following five-phase process:

1. System definition
2. Requirements analysis
3. Component design
4. Implementation
5. System maintenance (fix or enhance)

Figure 6-2 shows how these phases are related. Development begins when a business-planning process identifies a need for a new system. We address IS planning processes in Chapter 10. For now, suppose that management has determined, in some way, that the organization can best accomplish its goals and objectives by constructing a new information system.

Developers in the first SDLC phase, system definition, use management's statement of the system need to begin to define the new system. The resulting project plan is the input to the second phase, requirements analysis. Here, developers identify the particular features and functions of the new system. The output of that phase is a set of approved user requirements, which become the primary input used to design system components. In phase 4, developers implement, test, and install the new system.

Over time, users will find errors, mistakes, and problems. They will also think of new features that they need. The need for these changes is input to a system maintenance phase. The maintenance phase starts the process all over again, which is why the process is considered a cycle.

In the following sections, we will consider each phase of the SDLC in more detail.

The System Definition Phase

In response to the need for the new system, the organization will assign a few employees, possibly on a part-time basis, to define the new system, to assess its feasibility, and to plan the project. Typically, someone from the IS department leads the initial team, but the members of that initial team are both users and IS professionals.

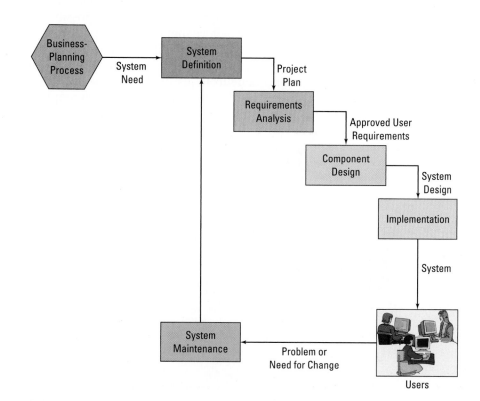

Figure 6-2
Phases in the SDLC

Define System Goals and Scope

As shown in Figure 6-3, the first step is to define the goals and scope of the new information system. Recall from Chapter 2 that information systems are developed for one of three reasons: to obtain a competitive advantage, to solve a problem, or to assist in decision making. At this step, the team defines the goal or purpose of the new system in terms of one or more of these reasons.

Consider the property listing sharing system for Baker, Barker, and Bickel. What is the purpose of that system? Each owner wants to protect his customer base but use the alliance to expand his product offerings. This goal is both achieving a competitive advantage and solving the problem of not having enough customers.

During project definition, the project's scope is delineated. Baker, Barker, and Bickel partially defined the scope when they said they do not want to merge their businesses nor their business operations. Also, they do not want to share customer data with each other. They only want to share property listings in such a way that each agency preserves its own customer base.

There is one aspect of Baker, Barker, and Bickel's project definition that we have not addressed. How will the members of the alliance compensate each other? What incentive does Baker have to lease one of Barker's properties? And what incentive does Barker have to allow Baker to do so? An important issue like this needs to be part of the project's goals and scope. For our purposes in illustrating systems development, the particular arrangement is unimportant. It needs to be defined, however. For now, we will assume that when Baker leases one of Barker's properties, they split the commission on the lease 50-50.

Assess Feasibility

Once we have defined the project's goals and scope, the next step is to assess feasibility. This step answers the question, "Does this project make sense?" The aim here is to eliminate obviously nonsensible projects before forming a project development team and investing significant labor.

Feasibility has four dimensions: **cost**, **schedule**, **technical**, and **organizational feasibility**. Because IS development projects are difficult to budget and schedule, cost and schedule feasibility can be only an approximate, back-of-the-envelope analysis. The purpose is to eliminate any obviously infeasible ideas as soon as possible.

For example, if Baker, Barker, and Bickel believe that they must have some type of integrated, Web-based database, they can ask a consultant how much such databases generally cost to develop. If the answer is a minimum of $30,000, then they can decide if they can reasonably expect to receive benefits to justify this expense. If they do not expect sufficient benefits, they can cancel the project or agree to accomplish their goals using some other system, say by using email messages. For a discussion of ethical issues relating to cost estimates, see the *Ethics Guide* on page 163a.

Like cost feasibility, *schedule feasibility,* is difficult to determine because it is difficult to estimate the time it will take to build the system. However, if, for example, Baker, Barker, and Bickel determine that it will take at least 6 months to develop the

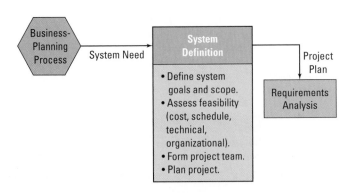

Figure 6-3
SDLC: System Definition
Phase

system and put it into operation, they can then decide if they can accept that minimum schedule. At this stage of the project, the company should not rely on either cost or schedule estimates; the purpose of these estimates is simply to rule out any obviously unacceptable projects.

Technical feasibility refers to whether existing information technology is likely to be able to meet the needs of the new system. For a small system, like that for Baker, Barker, and Bickel, technical feasibility is certain. For larger, more complicated projects with demanding performance requirements, feasibility may not be certain. Technical feasibility is used mostly to eliminate projects based on naïve notions about what IT can do. Examples today are systems that require humanlike computer robots and so forth.

The team that proposed the CADE system for the IRS (see Chapter 1, page 7) should have investigated technical feasibility in greater depth. From the public documents it appears that senior IRS managers were not aware they were pushing the limits of technology when they agreed to the CADE system. See *Case Study 6-1* for more.

Finally, *organizational feasibility* concerns whether the new system fits within the organization's customs, culture, charter, or legal requirements. For example, if Baker, Barker, or Bickel has an investor who has a conflict with one of the other person's businesses, the proposed system might be organizationally infeasible. Or, if the combined sales listings would violate antitrust law, the new system would be organizationally infeasible.

Form a Project Team

If the defined project is determined to be feasible, the next step is to form the project team. Normally the team consists of both IT personnel and user representatives. The project manager and IT personnel can be in-house personnel or outside contractors. We will describe various means of obtaining IT personnel using outside sources and the benefits and risks of outsourcing when we discuss IS management in Chapter 10.

Typical personnel on a development team are a manager (or mangers for larger projects), system analysts, programmers, software testers, and users. **Systems analysts** are IT professionals who understand both business and technology. They are active throughout the systems development process and play a key role in moving the project through the systems development process. Systems analysts integrate the work of the programmers, testers, and users. Depending on the nature of the project, the team may also include hardware and communications specialists, database designers and administrators, and other IT specialists.

The team composition changes over time. During requirements definition, the team will be heavy with systems analysts. During design and implementation, it will be heavy with programmers, testers, and database designers. During integrated testing and conversion, the team will be augmented with testers and business users.

User involvement is critical throughout the system development process. Depending on the size and nature of the project, users are assigned to the project either full or part time. Sometimes users are assigned to review and oversight committees that meet periodically, especially at the completion of project phases and other milestones. Users are involved in many different ways. The important point is for users to have active involvement and to take ownership of the project throughout the entire development process.

The first major task for the assembled project team is to plan the project. Members of the project team specify tasks to be accomplished, assign personnel, determine task dependencies, and set schedules. You will learn more about project planning in your operations management classes, if you have not done so already.

Requirements Analysis Phase

The primary purpose of the requirements analysis phase is to determine and document the specific features and functions of the new system. For most development projects, this phase requires interviewing dozens of users and documenting potentially

Estimation Ethics

A *buy-in* occurs when a company agrees to produce a system or product for less than it knows the project will require. An example for Baker, Barker, and Bickel would be if a consultant agreed to build the system for $50,000 when good estimating techniques indicate it will take $75,000. If the contract for the system or product is written for "time and materials," the customer will ultimately pay the $75,000 for the finished system. Or, the customer will cancel the project once the true cost is known. If the contract for the system or product is written for a fixed cost, then the developer will eat the extra costs. The latter strategy is used if the contract opens up other business opportunities that are worth the $25,000 loss.

Buy-ins always involve deceit. Most would agree that buying in on a time-and-materials project, planning to stick the customer with the full cost later, is unethical and wrong. Opinions on buying in on a fixed-priced contract vary. Some would say buying in is always deceitful and should be avoided. Others say that it is just one of many different business strategies.

What about in-house projects? Do the ethics change if an in-house development team is building a system for use in house? If team members know there is only $50,000 in the budget, should they start the

project if they believe its true cost is $75,000? If they do start, at some point senior management will either have to admit a mistake and cancel the project or find the additional $25,000. Project sponsors can make all sorts of excuses for such a buy-in. For example, "I know the company needs this system. If management doesn't realize it and fund it appropriately, then we'll just force their hand."

These issues become even stickier if team members disagree about how much the project will cost. Suppose one faction of the team believes the project will cost $35,000, another faction estimates $50,000, and a third thinks $65,000. Can the project sponsors justify taking the average? Or, should they describe the range of estimates?

Other buy-ins are more subtle. Suppose you are a project manager of an exciting new project that is possibly a career-maker for you. You are incredibly busy, working 6 days a week and long hours each day. Your team has developed an estimate for $50,000 for the project. A little voice in the back of your mind says that maybe not all costs for every aspect of the project are included in that estimate. You mean to follow up on that thought, but more pressing matters in your schedule take precedence. Soon you find yourself in front of management, presenting the $50,000 estimate. You probably should have found the time to investigate the estimate, but you didn't. Is your behavior unethical?

Or, suppose you approach a more senior manager with your dilemma. "I think there may be other costs, but I know that $50,000 is all we've got. What should I do?" Suppose the senior manager says something like, "We'll let's go forward. You don't know of anything else, and we can always find more budget elsewhere if we have to." How do you respond?

You can buy in on schedule as well as cost. If the marketing department says, "We have to have the new product for the trade show," do you agree, even if you know it's highly unlikely? What if marketing says, "If we don't have it by then, we should just cancel the project." Suppose it's not impossible to make that schedule, it's just highly unlikely. How do you respond?

DISCUSSION QUESTIONS

1. Do you agree that buying in on a cost-and-materials project is always unethical? Explain your reasoning. Are there circumstances in which it could be illegal?

2. Suppose you learn through the grapevine that your opponents in a competitive bid are buying in on a time-and-materials contract. Does this change your answer to question 1?

3. Suppose you are a project manager who is preparing a request for proposal on a cost-and-materials systems development project. What can you do to prevent buy-ins?

4. Under what circumstances do you think buying in on a fixed-price contract is ethical? What are the dangers of this strategy?

5. Explain why in-house development projects are always time-and-materials projects.

6. Given your answer to question 5, is buying in on an in-house project always unethical? Under what circumstances do you think it is ethical? Under what circumstances do you think it is justifiable, even if it is unethical?

7. Suppose you ask a senior manager for advice as described in the guide. Does the manager's response absolve you of guilt? Suppose you ask the manager and then do not follow her guidance. What problems result?

8. Explain how you can buy in on schedule as well as costs.

9. For an in-house project, how do you respond to the marketing manager who says that the project should be cancelled if it will not be ready for the trade show? In your answer, suppose that you disagree with this opinion—suppose you know the system has value regardless of whether it is done by the trade show.

STANDARD VEHICLE PRICE
Options Installed by Manufacturer

MANUFACTURER'S SUGGESTED RETAIL PRICE

CONVENIENCE PACKAGE
• REMOTE KEYLESS ENTRY W/ALARM $14,410.00
• POWER WINDOWS
• POWER REMOTE EXTERIOR MIRRORS
• CRUISE CONTROL
TRAVEL PACKAGE
• MAP LIGHTS
• AUTO-DIMMING INSIDE MIRROR   825.00
EXTERIOR TEMPERATURE GAUGE
DIGITAL COMPASS
FLOOR MATS - FRONT AND REAR
POWER SUNROOF   200.00
ANTI-LOCK BRAKES W/TRAC CTRL
50-STATE EMISSIONS
TOTAL OPTIONS

                                   80.00
                                   725.00
                                   400.00
                                   N/C
                                   2,230.00

hundreds of requirements. Requirements definition is thus expensive. It is also difficult, as you will see.

Determine Requirements

Determining the system's requirements is the most important phase in the systems development process. If the requirements are wrong, the system will be wrong. If the requirements are determined completely and correctly, then design and implementation will be easier and more likely to result in success.

Examples of requirements are the contents of a report or the fields in a data entry form. Requirements include not only what is to be produced, but also how frequently and how fast it is to be produced. Some requirements specify the volume of data to be stored and processed.

If you take a course in systems analysis and design, you will spend weeks on techniques for determining requirements. Here, we will just summarize that process. Typically, systems analysts interview users and record the results in some consistent manner. Good interviewing skills are crucial; users are notorious for being unable to describe what they want and need. Users also tend to focus on the tasks they are performing at the time of the interview. Tasks performed at the end of the quarter or end of the year are forgotten if the interview takes place mid-quarter. Seasoned and experienced systems analysts know how to conduct interviews to bring such requirements to light.

As listed in Figure 6-4, sources of requirements include existing systems as well as the forms, reports, queries, and application features and functions desired in the new system. Security is another important category of requirements.

If the new system involves a new database or substantial changes to an existing database, then the development team will create a data model. As you learned in Chapter 4, that model must reflect the users' perspective on their business and business activities. Thus, the data model is constructed on the basis of user interviews and must be validated by those users.

Sometimes the requirements determination is so focused on the software and data components that other components are forgotten. Experienced project managers ensure consideration of requirements for all five IS components, not just for software and data. Regarding hardware, the team might ask: Are there special needs or restrictions on hardware? Is there an organizational standard governing what kinds of hardware may or may not be used? Must the new system use existing hardware? What requirements are there for communications and network hardware?

Similarly, the team should consider requirements for procedures and personnel: Do accounting controls require procedures that separate duties and authorities? Are there restrictions that some actions can be taken only by certain departments or specific personnel? Are there policy requirements or union rules that restrict activities to certain categories of employees? Will the system need to interface with information

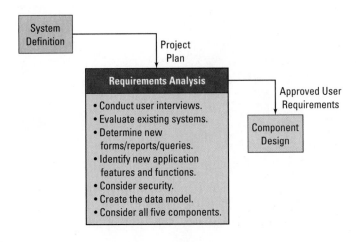

Figure 6-4
SDLC: Requirements Analysis
Phase

You Be the Guide

Using the Ethics Guide
(page 163a)

GOALS

* Introduce the concept of *buy-in* as it pertains to information systems.

* Assess the ethics of buy-ins in different settings.

BACKGROUND AND PRESENTATION STRATEGIES

I was first introduced to *buy-in* when I worked in procurement in the defense industry in the late 1960s. At that time, it was common for large government contractors to buy in on initial system production and to make up the difference by selling expensive spare parts over the 20-year or more life of that system. Senator Proxmire attained national prominence when he discovered the U.S. Navy was paying $250 for submarine toilet seats. Another cost-recovery technique was to claim that all but the most obvious corrections to plans were "out of scope" changes that required supplemental payment.

I was a very junior person, and I do not know what the thinking was at senior levels. But, I suspect it involved a degree of "wink-wink" collusion between high-level defense and aerospace executives. Congress had only so much money in the budget for a given system. The contractor would bid within that limit and make up the differences via supplemental appropriations in later years. I suspect that none of this was a surprise to Congress. It was a way of obtaining a system in the face of competing demands for the government budget. Some called it a "game that we must play." It was not illegal, and it involved some risk on the contractor's part; there was always the chance that a project would be cancelled before the buy-in costs could be recovered.

Buy-ins are prevalent in everyday life, too. We all know the ads for cars that loudly announce a price of $15,000, but the small print indicates that there will be supplemental charges for "additional items."

All types of custom building also can involve buy-ins. Building a custom home, a custom boat, a custom landscaping job—all are susceptible to buy-ins.

The best defense against buy-ins is experience in the industry. Or, as Donald Trump put it during his Senate testimony on the United Nations remodeling project, if you don't have experience working with New York construction contractors, "You'll go to school while they eat your lunch."

So, one of the major goals of this guide is to see how buy-ins apply to information systems projects. Future managers need to know this so that they can guard against, or at least consider the possibility of a buy-in.

Future managers also need to consider their own values and principles. At what point is a buy-in within accepted boundaries of conduct, and when does it exceed those boundaries? When will you be willing to put your job on the line when resisting a buy-in on ethical principles?

Finally, note that the guide points out that buy-ins can occur for both cost and schedule. They also can occur for technical feasibility when a team asserts that some new technology is further developed than it is. (I suspect that happened with the IRS CADE project discussed at the end of Chapter 1.) Ultimately, however, technical buy-ins become both cost and schedule buy-ins.

 ### SUGGESTED RESPONSES FOR DISCUSSION QUESTIONS

1. Again, using the definition of *ethical* as "consistent with agreed principles of correct moral conduct," I don't think it's possible to say that every buy-in is unethical. All buy-ins involve deceit, but that deceit may be an accepted practice in the industry (see previous comments). It's a very slippery slope, however. What level of deceit is allowable? Senator Proxmire's discovery of a $250 submarine toilet seat seems to indicate that someone went over the line.

   Yes, a buy-in could be illegal, especially for public projects. The contractor might have agreed to comply with a law that pertains to honesty in bidding. Also, some states may have enacted laws that require a certain level of truth in advertising. Such laws lie behind the auto ads in which someone quickly reads the serial number of autos that are being advertised.

2. First, your company may have a policy about buy-ins that requires you to submit a complete and honest bid. If so, you should follow that policy. If not, you need to wonder how reliable the grapevine is and assess how widespread and accepted buy-ins are in your industry. You also need to check with your

management. Consider the impact of a buy-in on your reputation for future jobs (see question 3). As a general rule, I'd say avoid the buy-in, bid honestly, and keep looking for other jobs on which to bid.

3. Create as comprehensive a list of features and functions as you can. Ensure that the proposal requires an estimate for every feature and function. Check bids to ensure that every item was included. Employ experts to determine the reasonableness of the bid items. For this activity, there is no substitute for experience. Check the reputation of the vendor. Are they known for buy-ins or for honest bids? What percent overrun is typical for the vendor's projects?

4. The obvious danger is that you never have a chance to get your money back. The customer never approves any "out of scope" changes and cancels the project before you have a chance to recoup losses on spare or replacement parts.

   Some vendors buy-in in order to gain experience and/or reputation on a particular technology. Someone might buy-in, for example, on building a database for a Web site so as to learn how to build such databases. If the vendor considers the difference between the buy-in bid and the actual cost as an investment and has no intent of recovering that loss, then the behavior is ethical, at least to my mind. Otherwise, is the buy-in consistent with agreed-on principles in that industry?

5. There is no fixed bid.

6. What hard questions! Is it ever appropriate to deceive your own management? If so, when? I think, over the long haul, nothing is more serviceable than the truth. I don't think I'd ever recommend deceiving one's own management. There may be exceptions to that, but I'd say they'd be very rare. I'd say it's unethical, unwise, and seldom justifiable. In some organizations, that attitude might be called naïve. (If so, I'd rather work somewhere else.)

7. If I were the junior person, I'd go with the manager's recommendation. The statement, "We can always find the money someplace else," suggests to me that the manager has flexibility in the budget that I don't know about. I think the statement "absolve you of guilt" puts it a little strongly, but, yes, I think I could go forward on solid ethical ground. Not following the advice is a form of betrayal. If you aren't going to follow that advice, at least tell your manager ahead of time and explain why you cannot. Or, determine the other costs and show them to your manager.

8. You can buy-in on schedule by agreeing to produce something on a schedule that you believe you cannot meet. When schedule delays occur, the customer is so committed to the project that they cannot cancel it.

9. Again, nothing is more serviceable than the truth. I'd call the marketing manager's bluff: "OK, let's cancel the project." If the project is important enough, that person will back down. Then, I'd say, "We'll do the best we can, but we operate under the risk that it won't be done by then. Plan accordingly." I'd then try to negotiate having some limited version of the project ready by the trade show.

   This happened to me once when a senior sales manager said a version of a software product had to be ready by that year's fall Comdex show. I did exactly as described previously. It turned out he was speaking rashly and backed down. We delivered a solid working version for use in the computers in the trade-show booth. The full version was shipped to customers two months later.

WRAP UP

➤ **Be aware that buy-ins occur and that some vendors make a practice of them. Scrutinize unbelievably low bids. They probably are unbelievable.**

➤ **There is no substitute for experience. Hire expertise to evaluate bids.**

➤ **Consider your own position on buy-ins. When can you justify one? Ever? If so, when?**

systems from other companies and organizations? In short, requirements need to be considered for all of the components of the new information system.

These questions are examples of the kinds of questions that must be asked and answered during requirements analysis.

Obtain User Approval

Once the requirements have been specified, the users must review and approve them before the project continues. The easiest and cheapest time to alter the information system is in the requirements phase. Changing a requirement at this stage is simply a matter of changing a description. Changing a requirement in the implementation phase may require weeks of reworking applications components and the database.

The *Problem Solving Guide* on page 165a discusses the need to have accurate requirements as a starting point, whether you are developing information systems or aiming toward a goal of any sort.

Component Design Phase

Each of the five components is designed in this stage. Typically, the team designs each component by developing alternatives, evaluating each of those alternatives against the requirements, and then selecting among those alternatives. Accurate requirements are critical here; if they are incomplete or wrong, then they will be poor guides for evaluation.

Figure 6-5 shows that design tasks pertain to each of the five IS components.

Hardware Design

For hardware, the team determines specifications for the hardware that they want to acquire. (The team is not designing hardware in the sense of building a CPU or a disk drive.)

For the Baker, Barker, and Bickel system, for example, various hardware communications alternatives are possible:

1. They can use PC and LANs connected over the public Internet.
2. They can lease three separate point-to-point leased lines.
3. They can lease time on some type of PSDN.
4. They can create a VPN over the Internet.

The development team evaluates each of these alternatives against the requirements using criteria like those in Figure 5-22 (page 136).

Program Design

Program design depends on the source of the programs. For off-the-shelf software, the team must determine candidate products and evaluate them against the requirements. For off-the-shelf with alteration programs, the team identifies products to be acquired off-the-shelf and then determines the alterations required. For custom-developed programs, the team produces design documentation for writing program code.

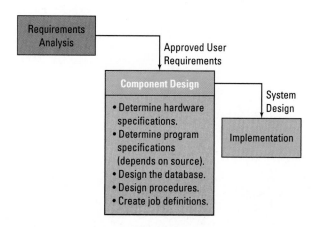

Figure 6-5
SDLC: Component Design Phase

ProblemSolving
GUIDE

Aim for What You Want

Have you ever watched someone ride a bicycle between two closely spaced posts? Hoping not to crash, the rider first looks at one post, lurches toward it, looks at the other post, and lurches over that way. With luck, despite flopping back and forth, the rider passes through the gap, narrowly averting a crash.

Race-car drivers know how to avoid all that lurching. They advise, "Always put your eyes where you want to go. Don't look at the other cars. Look where you want to go, look at the spot between the other cars." Try it the next time you ride a bicycle through a narrow gap. Stare at a spot in the middle of the gap, between the posts, and 5 or 10 feet beyond them. Fixing your attention where you want to go, you'll ride straight to that spot, moving smoothly between the posts. It works.

Why does this strategy work? Possibly, the anatomy of our brains is such that we unconsciously bring about what we focus on. Although consciously we may be thinking, "This is what I don't want to happen," somehow the don't part of that statement doesn't reach our subconscious. Focusing on the post, we crash into it.

Rather than focusing on what you want to avoid, focus on what you want and where you want to go. These simple ideas work well in business, too. Put your attention on the desired outcome, and manage your efforts to that outcome.

Of course, to use this strategy, you have to know what you want. And therein lies the rub. You want a great job. OK, but what sort of great job? What specific tasks and responsibilities do you want? Do you want to manage people? Money? Projects? Maybe you want to be a financial analyst. If so, what kinds of analysis do you want to do? In what industry? Focus on the details of the job you want, and it will be easier to obtain. Any job recruiter will agree.

Suppose you say, "I just don't know. I know I should know, but I don't." As soon as you make those statements, you're focusing on the post and not on the job you want. Instead, focus on what you can do to determine the job you want. Or, just pick a job that's close to what you want and start focusing on it. That strategy will take you out of the mire of self-criticism.

What does this discussion have to do with IS? Requirements. What do you want the new system to do? Without accurate requirements, the system cannot be built. You need to know what you want before you or anyone else can build it. Furthermore, you need consistent requirements. If one part of the team focuses on one set of requirements and another part of the team focuses on a different, inconsistent set, the result will be chaos, or worse.

As a future user, your most important systems development task is to manage your requirements. Are they complete? Consistent? Does the development team understand them? Is the team focused on them?

Do you have a system for tracking requirements? Are your requirements prioritized? Do you have a way of tracking deferred requirements? Do you meet regularly with developers to ensure that everyone understands the same set of requirements and is working toward the same goal?

Perhaps the project is too big for all the requirements to be known. In that case, build the system incrementally. You may want to move the risk forward (as is done with RAD and UP, which are discussed later in the chapter). If so, focus on defining the requirements for the most uncertain part of the project. Define that aspect and accomplish that part of the system.

Put your attention where you want to go.

DISCUSSION QUESTIONS

1. On a stretch of remote highway, a car slides off the road in a snowstorm. A power line runs along the highway. A driver in a car behind stares incredulously as the car steers off the road and straight into the only pole within 1,000 feet. (A true story.) What happened? Why did the driver not slide into the 500 feet of open space on either side of the pole?

2. "Baloney, this is just psycho-babble. It may work for race-car drivers, but race-car driving takes different skills than job hunting." Do you agree or disagree with this statement? Why or why not?

3. Consider the following statement made by a retired senior manager: "As a general rule, I think you find in your employees whatever you look for. If you think they're lazy and incompetent, that's what you'll find. If you think they're bright, motivated, and want to do good work, you'll find that as well." How does this statement relate to the race-car driver's strategy? Do you agree or disagree with it?

4. In your own words, describe how the race-car driver's strategy applies to systems development. What are some of the posts to be avoided? Where should users place their attention? Where should developers place their attention? Where should management place its attention?

	Users	**Operations Personnel**
Normal processing	• Procedures for using the system to accomplish business tasks	• Procedures for starting, stopping, and operating the system
Backup	• User procedures for backing up data and other resources	• Operations procedures for backing up data and other resources
Failure recovery	• Procedures to continue operations when the system fails • Procedures to convert back to the system after recovery	• Procedures to identify the source of failure and get it fixed • Procedures to recover and restart the system

Figure 6-6
Procedures to Be Designed

Database Design

If developers are constructing a database, then during this phase they convert the data model to a database design using techniques like those described in Chapter 4. If developers are using off-the-shelf programs, then little database design needs be done; the programs will handle their own database processing.

Procedure Design

For a business information system, the system developers and the organization must also design procedures for both users and operations personnel. Procedures need to be developed for normal, backup, and failure recovery operations, as summarized in Figure 6-6. Usually teams of systems analysts and key users design the procedures.

Design of Job Descriptions

With regard to people, design involves developing job descriptions for both users and operations personnel. Sometimes new information systems require new jobs. If so, the duties and responsibilities for the new jobs need to be defined in accordance with the organization's human resources policies. More often, organizations add new duties and responsibilities to existing jobs. In this case, developers define these new tasks and responsibilities in this phase. Sometimes, the personnel design task is as simple as statements like, "Jason will be in charge of making backups." As with procedures, teams of systems analysts and users determine job descriptions and functions.

Design for Baker, Barker, and Bickel

Because we have not detailed Baker, Barker, and Bickel's requirements, we cannot describe specific design decisions. In general, however, they first need to decide how elaborate an information system they want to construct. On the one hand, they could build a simple system centered on email. With it, each company sends property descriptions to the others via email. Each independent company then forwards these descriptions to its own customers, also using email. When a customer makes a reservation for a property, that request is then forwarded back to the property manager via email.

Using the Problem Solving Guide (page 165a)

GOALS

* Teach students to focus on what they want and not on what they fear.

* Apply the "focus on what you want" strategy to systems development.

BACKGROUND AND PRESENTATION STRATEGIES

In Chapter 1, we discussed the idea that, although people cannot change their IQ, they can improve the way they use the IQ they have. This guide is a perfect example of one such technique.

Focus on what you want, not on what you fear. The nature of our minds seems to be that we get whatever we focus on. If we focus on limitations, we'll find our limitations. As Richard Bach wrote in *Jonathan Livingston Seagull* (Avon, 1976), "Focus on your limitations and, sure enough, they're yours."

Sometimes *students become curmudgeons* with me about this guide.

• "Oh, come on, this is just the 'power of positive thinking.' You sound like my mother!"

Here are some possible responses:

➤ **Maybe so, but it works. Try it on your bicycle—go ride between two posts and see which strategy works better. Staring at the posts or staring at the space between the posts. And don't forget your helmet!**

➤ **Next time you have a meeting with a group of students, focus on the positive aspects of the other students. Focus on the ideas they're producing, the things you're learning from them, the enjoyable time you're spending. Tell your fellow students that their comments are insightful and interesting (when they are, that is). Contrast this with the results you get from a meeting in which everyone one doubts and criticizes everyone else.**

➤ **Or, try this strategy on me. Consider the different results you'll get from me by using one of these two statements:**

• **Professor XXX, I think the Baker, Barker, Bickel case is really interesting. Tell me how you think they should address feasibility. I have a problem like that right now!**

• **This systems development stuff is really boring. Do I have to learn it? Will it be on the exam?**

Students should be applying this strategy to their job search right now. They need to know what job they want and how they are going to get it. There are hundreds of jobs out there. Some will be perfect, setting the student up for a great career, or at least for an interesting and fruitful first job. Others will be a bad fit and provide little more than a paycheck. The students need to be thinking, NOW, about which jobs they want.

➤ **Here's an assignment for you tonight: Write a paragraph that describes the job you want after graduation. Don't think about your limitations, don't wonder how you're going to get that job. Just think as hard as you can about what you want, and describe that job. Be realistic (you're not going to be CEO of 3M), but be aggressive in what you want.**

How does all of this relate to systems development? Requirements!!! No one can build a system if they don't know what that system is supposed to do. Classical SDLC and RAD have a formal requirements phase, with documented requirements and user reviews. UP has use cases, and XP integrates users into the process. In all cases, it is a matter of focusing the team on building what is wanted.

Case Study 6-2 works well with this guide. That case study addresses failures caused by a lack of user involvement in requirements. You might combine this guide with a discussion of that case.

In short, for over 30 years, studies have consistently shown that a lack of user involvement and poor requirements are the leading causes of information systems failures. Our students, once they become business professionals, need to know how to help the development team focus on what is wanted!

 SUGGESTED RESPONSES FOR DISCUSSION QUESTIONS

1. The driver was focused on the power pole. Had the driver focused on the space between the poles, the accident would have been most unlikely. "Gosh, I hope I don't hit that pole" somehow becomes, "Hit the pole." It's as if our bodies only hear *hit the pole* during a time of stress.

2. Use this question to bring forth objections from the students. Some ideas for dealing with resistance to this idea appear under the curmudgeon point in the Background discussion.

3. There is no single secret to effectively managing every employee in every situation. If there were, there wouldn't be courses on management and miles of books on "effective people management." People are so different; their talents, hopes, and goals vary so much; and every project presents different challenges.

However, as a general rule, I know of no better guide to good management than realizing that *you're likely to find what you look for.* If you expect your employees to be lazy and undependable, you will eventually find evidence to support your expectation, even in the best employees. However, if you expect your employees to be interested in their work, to be motivated, to want to excel, to want to accomplish their job goals, then you will find evidence to support those characteristics as well. My experience managing software development projects is that when a project has a culture of wanting to excel, any employees who do not have that attitude will leave the project.

(This applies to students as well. I find the supply of maturity rises to meet the expectation. When I expect my students to be responsible, to take assignments seriously, to do their homework, to act like the business professionals they say they want to become, then they tend to act that way. Not always, but almost. And, if nothing else, my high expectation raises the level of professionalism at least a bit. Focus your thinking on a classroom full of interested, motivated students who are asking interesting questions and with whom you're having fun. You'll get it!)

4. Use the BBB case. BBB should focus on the result they want, which is greater revenue by being able to rent one another's properties. Given that focus, they should deal with problems that crop up as nuisances to be eliminated. Deal with the problem and get back to the primary focus: increased revenue.

Such a focus will mean that the team does not get bogged down in alternatives that won't lead to increased revenue. If an email with an attachment enables them to achieve their goals, they need do nothing more. If, however, a more sophisticated system will help them achieve greater revenue, then they should build that system.

Possible systems development "posts" to avoid:

- Lack of clear communication of requirements/ needs (among BBB and in general)

- Lack of knowledge of systems development processes

- Focus on problems rather than solutions to those problems

- Starting with too elaborate a system

- Becoming distracted from the system's goals

Everyone should place their attention on the BBB system's goals: increase revenue by renting one another's properties.

WRAP UP

➤ Ironically, this simple idea, *focus on what you want, focus on the space between the posts,* is among the most important ideas you'll learn in this class.

➤ It pertains to systems development, and it pertains to your wider life as well.

➤ The trick is to remember it: *Focus on what you want.*

On the other hand, they could construct a more complex system using a Web-based, shared database that contains data on all their properties and reservations. Because reservations tracking is a common business task, it is likely that they can license an existing application with this capability. If so, during design, they need to choose the product to license and design a system for transferring their property data into that new product. They also need to design procedures and job descriptions for operating and using the new system. Finally, they need to decide among communications capabilities like those listed earlier.

If they do not license an existing product, but build their own data-base and applications instead, then they must do much more design work. This alternative is likely to be very expensive and probably not cost justifiable for their needs.

Because Baker, Barker, and Bickel is a loose association, and because they have no experience working together, there is considerable risk that this alliance will fail to generate the anticipated benefits. Accordingly, Baker, Barker, and Bickel will likely invest as little as possible, until they know what the true benefits are. In this circumstance, a good plan would be to design the simplest possible system, assess the benefits, and later build a more elaborate system if needed.

Implementation Phase

Once the design is complete, the next phase in the SDLC is implementation. Tasks in this phase are to build, test, and convert the users to the new system (see Figure 6-7). Developers construct each of the components independently. They obtain, install, and test hardware. They license and install off-the-shelf programs; they write adaptations and custom programs as necessary. They construct a database and fill it with data. They document, review, and test procedures, and they create training programs. Finally, the organization hires and trains needed personnel.

System Testing

Once developers have constructed and tested all of the components, they integrate the individual components and test the system. So far, we have glossed over testing as if there is nothing to it. In fact, software and system testing are difficult, time-consuming, and complex tasks. Developers need to design and develop test plans and record the

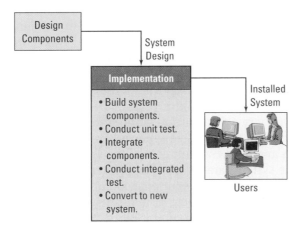

Figure 6-7
SDLC: Implementation Phase

results of tests. They need to devise a system to assign fixes to people and to verify that fixes are correct and complete.

A **test plan** consists of sequences of actions that users will take when using the new system. Test plans include not only the normal actions that users will take, but also incorrect actions. A comprehensive test plan should cause every line of program code to be executed. The test plan should thus cause every error message to be displayed. Testing, retesting, and re-retesting consume huge amounts of labor. Often, developers can reduce the labor cost of testing by writing programs that invoke system features automatically.

Today, many IT professionals work as testing specialists. Testing, or **product quality assurance (PQA)** as it is often called, is an important career. PQA personnel usually construct the test plan with the advice and assistance of users. PQA test engineers themselves perform testing, and they also supervise user test activity. Many PQA professionals are themselves programmers who write automated test programs.

In addition to IT professionals, users should be involved in system testing. Users participate in the development of test plans and test cases. They also can be part of the test team, usually working under the direction of PQA personnel. Users have the final say on whether the system is ready for use. If you are invited to participate as a user tester, take that responsibly seriously. It will become much more difficult to fix problems after you have begun to use the system in production.

Beta testing is the process of allowing future system users to try out the new system on their own. Software vendors like Microsoft often release beta versions of their products for users to try and to test. Such users report problems back to the vendor. Beta testing is the last stage of testing. Normally products in the beta test phase are complete and fully functioning; they typically have few serious errors. Organizations that are developing large new information systems sometimes use a beta-testing process just as software vendors do.

System Conversion

Once the system has passed integrated testing, the organization installs the new system. The term **system conversion** is often used for this activity because it implies the process of *converting* business activity from the old system to the new.

Organizations can implement a system conversion in one of four ways:

- Pilot
- Phased
- Parallel
- Plunge

IS professionals recommend any of the first three, depending on the circumstances. In most cases, companies should avoid "taking the plunge"!

With **pilot installation**, the organization implements the entire system on a limited portion of the business. An example would be for Baker to try the system when renting Bickel's properties. The advantage of pilot implementation is that if the system fails, the failure is contained within a limited boundary. This reduces exposure of the business and also protects the new system from developing a negative reputation throughout the organization(s).

As the name implies, with **phased installation** the new system is installed in phases across the organization(s). With the Baker, Barker, and Bickel example, phased installation would be to try only a portion of the system, say that for sending property descriptions to each other, for all three agencies. Once a given piece works, then the organization installs and tests another piece of the system, until the entire system has been installed. Some systems are so tightly integrated that they cannot be installed in phased pieces. Such systems must be installed using one of the other techniques.

With **parallel installation**, the new system runs in parallel with the old one until the new system is tested and fully operational. Parallel installation is expensive because the organization incurs the costs of running both systems. Users must work double time, if you will, to run both systems. Then, considerable work is needed to determine if the results of the new system are consistent with those of the old system.

However, some organizations consider the costs of parallel installation to be a form of insurance. It is the slowest and most expensive style of installation, but it does provide an easy fallback position if the new system fails.

The final style of conversion is **plunge installation** (sometimes called **direct installation**). With it, the organization shuts off the old system and starts the new system. If the new system fails, the organization is in trouble: Nothing can be done until either the new system is fixed or the old system is reinstalled. Because of the risk, organizations should avoid this conversion style if possible. The one exception is if the new system is providing a new capability that is not vital to the operation of the organization.

The Baker, Barker, and Bickel system is an example of such an exception. There is no old system; the agencies are not currently renting each other's properties. If the new system fails, it just means that they will continue not to rent each others' properties. In cases like this, the plunge method can be justified. Otherwise, avoid it.

Figure 6-8 summarizes the tasks for each of the five components during the design and implementation phases. Use this figure to test your knowledge of the tasks in each phase.

Maintenance Phase

The last phase of the SDLC is maintenance. As noted earlier, maintenance is a misnomer; the work done during this phase is either to *fix* the system so that it works correctly or to *adapt* it to changes in requirements.

Figure 6-9 (page 170) shows tasks during the maintenance phase. First, there needs to be a means for tracking both failures[2] and requests for enhancements to meet new

	Hardware	Software	Data	Procedures	People	
Design	Determine hardware specifications.	Select off-the-shelf programs. Design alterations and custom programs as necessary.	Design database and related structures.	Design user and operations procedures.	Develop user and operations job descriptions.	
Implementation	Obtain, install, and test hardware.	License and install off-the-shelf programs. Write alterations and custom programs. Test programs.	Create database. Fill with data. Test data.	Document procedures. Create training programs. Review and test procedures.	Hire and train personnel.	Unit test each component
	Integrated Test and Conversion					

Note: Cells shaded tan represent software development.

Figure 6-8
Design and Implementation for the Five Components

---

[2] A *failure* is a difference between what the system does and what it is supposed to do. Sometimes you will hear the term *bug* used instead of failure. As a future user, call failures *failures,* for that's what they are. Don't have a *bugs list,* have a *failures list.* Don't have an *unresolved bug,* have an *unresolved failure.* A few months of managing an organization that is coping with a serious failure will show you the importance of this difference in terms.

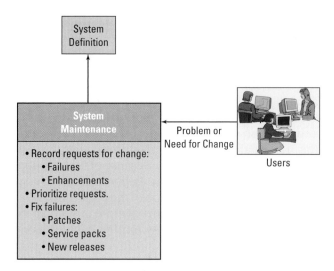

Figure 6-9
SDLC System Maintenance
Phase

requirements. For small systems, organizations can track failures and enhancements using word-processing documents. As systems become larger, however, and as the number of failure and enhancement requests increases, many organizations find it necessary to develop a tracking database. Such a database contains a description of the failure or enhancement. It also records who reported the problem, who will make the fix or enhancement, what the status of that work is, and whether the fix or enhancement has been tested and verified by the originator.

Typically, IS personnel prioritize system problems according to their severity. They fix high-priority items as soon as possible, and they fix low-priority items as time and resources become available.

With regard to the software component, software developers group fixes for high-priority failures into a **patch** that can be applied to all copies of a given product. As described in Chapter 3, software vendors supply patches to fix security and other critical problems. They usually bundle fixes of low-priority problems into larger groups called **service packs**. Users apply service packs in much the same way that they apply patches, except that service packs typically involve fixes to hundreds or thousands of problems.

By the way, you may be surprised to learn this, but all commercial software products are shipped with known failures. Usually vendors test their products and remove the most serious problems, but they seldom, if ever, remove all of the defects they know about. Shipping with defects is an industry practice; Microsoft, Adobe, Oracle, RedHat, and many others all ship products with known problems.

Because an enhancement is an adaptation to new requirements, developers usually prioritize enhancement requests separate from failures. The decision to make an enhancement includes a business decision that the enhancement will generate an acceptable rate of return. Although minor enhancements are made using service packs, major enhancement requests usually result in a complete new release of a product.

As you read this, keep in mind that although we usually think of failures and enhancements as applying to software, they can apply to the other components as well. There can be hardware or database failures or enhancements. There can also be failures and enhancements in procedures and people, though the latter is usually expressed in more humane terms than failure or enhancement. The underlying idea is the same, however.

As stated earlier, note that the maintenance phase starts another cycle of the SDLC process. The decision to enhance a system is a decision to restart the systems development process. Even a simple failure fix goes through all of the phases of the

SDLC; if it is a small fix, a single person may work through those phases in an abbreviated form. But each of those phases is repeated, nonetheless.

Problems with the SDLC

Although the industry has experienced notable successes with the SDLC process, there have also been many problems with it, as discussed next.

The SDLC Waterfall

One of the reasons for SDLC problems is due to the **waterfall** nature of the SDLC. Like a series of waterfalls, the process is supposed to operate in a sequence of not-repeated phases. For example, the team completes the requirements phase and goes over the waterfall into the design phase, and on through the process (look back to Figure 6-2, page 161).

Unfortunately, systems development seldom works so smoothly. Often, there is a need to crawl back up the waterfall, if you will, and repeat work in a prior phase. Most commonly, when design work begins and the team evaluates alternatives, they learn that some requirements statements are incomplete or missing. At that point, the team needs to do more requirements work, yet that phase is supposedly finished. On some projects, the team goes back and forth between requirements and design so many times that the project seems to be out of control.

Requirements Documentation Difficulty

Another problem, especially on complicated systems, is the difficulty of documenting requirements in a usable way. I once managed the database portion of a software project at Boeing in which we invested more than 70 labor-years into a requirements statement. The requirements document was 20-some volumes that stood 7 feet tall when stacked on top of one another.

When we entered the design phase, no one really knew all the requirements that concerned a particular feature. We would begin to design a feature only to find that we had not considered a requirement buried somewhere in the documentation. In short, the requirements were so unwieldy as to be nearly useless. Additionally, during the requirements analysis interval, the airplane business moved on. By the time we entered the design phase, many requirements were incomplete and some were obsolete. Projects that spend so much time documenting requirements are sometimes said to be in **analysis paralysis**.

Scheduling and Budgeting Difficulties

For a new, large-scale system, schedule and budgeting estimates are so approximate as to become nearly laughable. Management attempts to put a serious face on the need for a schedule and a budget, but when you are developing a large multiyear, multimillion-dollar project, estimates of labor hours and completion dates are approximate and fuzzy. The employees on the project, who are the source for the estimates, know how little they know about how long something will take and how much they guessed. They know that the total budget and timeline is a summation of everyone's similar guesses. Many large projects live in a fantasy world of budgets and timelines. The *Opposing Forces Guide* on page 171a states the difficulties with project estimation.

In truth, the software community has done much work to improve software development forecasting. But for large projects with large SDLC phases, just too much is unknown for any technique to work well. So, development methodologies other than the SDLC have emerged for developing systems through a series of small, manageable chunks. Rapid application development, object-oriented development, and extreme programming are three such methodologies.

The Real Estimation Process

I'm a software developer. I write programs in an object-oriented language called C++. I'm a skilled object-oriented designer, too. I should be—I've been at it 12 years and worked on major projects for several software companies. For the last 4 years, I've been a team leader. I lived through the heyday of the dot-com era and now work in the IT department of a giant pharmaceutical company.

"All of this estimating theory is just that—theory. It's not really the way things work. Sure, I've been on projects in which we tried different estimation techniques. But here's what really happens: You develop an estimate using whatever technique you want. Your estimate goes in with the estimates of all the other team leaders. The project manager sums all those estimates together and produces an overall estimate for the project.

"By the way, in my projects, time has been a much bigger factor than money. At one software company I worked for, you could be 300 percent over your dollar budget and get no more than a slap on the wrist. Be 2 weeks late, however, and you were finished.

"Anyway, the project managers take the project schedule to senior management for approval, and what happens? Senior management thinks they are negotiating. 'Oh, no,' they say, 'that's way too long. You can surely take a month off that schedule. We'll approve the project, but we want it done by February 1 instead of March 1.

"Now, what's their justification? They think that tight schedules make for efficient work. You know that everyone will work extra hard to meet the tighter timeframe. They know Parkinson's Law—'the time required to perform a task expands to the time available to do it.' So, fearing the possibility of wasting time because of too-lenient schedules, they lop a month off our estimate.

"Estimates are what they are; you can't knock off a month or two without some problem, somewhere. What does happen is that projects get behind, and then management expects us to work longer and longer hours. Like they said in the early years at Microsoft, 'We have flexible working hours. You can work any 65 hours per week you want.

"Not that our estimation techniques are all that great, either. Most software developers are optimists. They schedule things as if everything will go as planned, and things seldom do. Also, schedulers usually don't allow for vacations, sick days, trips to the dentist, training on new technology, peer reviews, and all the other things we do in addition to writing software.

"So we start with optimistic schedules on our end, then management negotiates a month or two off, and voilà, we have a late project. After a while, management has been burned by late projects so much that they mentally add the month or even more back onto the official schedule. Then both sides work in a fantasy world, where no one believes the schedule, but everyone pretends they do.

"I like my job. I like software development. Management here is no better or worse than in other places. As long as I have interesting work to do, I'll stay here. But I'm not working myself silly to meet these fantasy deadlines."

DISCUSSION QUESTIONS

1. What do you think of this developer's attitude? Do you think he's unduly pessimistic or do you think there's merit to what he says?

2. What do you think of his idea that management thinks they're negotiating? Should management negotiate schedules? Why or why not?

3. Suppose a project actually requires 12 months to complete. Which do you think is likely to cost more: (a) having an official schedule of 11 months with at least a 1-month overrun or (b) having an official schedule of 13 months and following Parkinson's Law, having the project take 13 months?

4. Suppose you are a business manager and an information system is being developed for your use. You review the scheduling documents and see that little time has been allowed for vacations, sick leave, miscellaneous other work, and so forth. What do you do?

5. Describe the intangible costs of having an organizational belief that schedules are always unreasonable.

6. If this developer worked for you, how would you deal with his attitude about scheduling?

7. Do you think there is something different when scheduling information systems development projects than when scheduling other types of projects? What characteristics might make such projects unique? In what ways are they the same as other projects?

8. What do you think managers should do in light of your answer to question 7?

▧ Rapid Application Development

James Martin, one of the pioneers in information systems, popularized the term *rapid application development* in the title of his 1991 book. The basic idea of **rapid application development (RAD)** is to break up the design and implementation phases of the SDLC into smaller chunks and to design and implement those chunks using as much computer assistance as possible. Figure 6-10 shows the process Martin envisioned.

Like SDLC, RAD has a requirements phase, but it interweaves the design and implementation phases. That is, developers design, implement, and fix a piece of the new system until the users are satisfied with that piece. Then, developers move on to design, implement, and fix another section of the system, and so forth, until the entire system has been developed in pieces. This process, sometimes called **incremental development**, reduces development challenges by using a divide-and-conquer strategy.

The RAD requirements analysis can be less detailed and less complete than with SDLC, because the users are actively involved during design and implementation. In effect, during the design/implement/fix process, the users provide detailed requirements in context.

RAD Characteristics

The main RAD characteristics are as follows:

1. The design/implement/fix development process (as just discussed)
2. Continuous user involvement throughout
3. Extensive use of prototypes
4. Joint application design
5. Use of CASE tools

With RAD, users are actively involved throughout the development process and become key members of the development team. Having users as part of the team not only increases the accuracy and completeness of the requirements, it also promotes a better environment for conversion. The new system will be installed not by strangers, but rather with the active participation of involved users.

The final three characteristics are discussed in detail in the following sections.

Prototypes

Another RAD characteristic is the use of prototypes. A **prototype** is a mock-up of an aspect of the new system. A prototype could be a mock-up of a form, report, query,

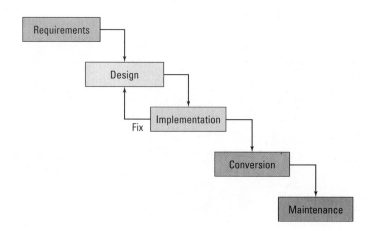

Figure 6-10
Martin's RAD Process

Using the Opposing Forces Guide (page 171a)

GOALS

* Sensitize students to the challenges of software scheduling.

* Alert students to possible consequences when negotiating a schedule.

BACKGROUND AND PRESENTATION STRATEGIES

There are many formal methods for scheduling, and I've worked at companies that have attempted to implement some of those methods. But invariably, requirements change, personnel depart, management loses patience with the discipline required to manage to schedules, or some other factor invalidates the good intentions of the project's managers. Companies that have an effective process for scheduling software projects are extremely rare.

If anyone had figured software scheduling out, you'd think it would be Microsoft. But look how late both Vista and SQL Server 2005 are. Clearly, they don't know how to do it, either.

The Software Institute at Carnegie Mellon developed the software maturity model that rates organizations on their use of effective development processes. Perhaps some of that model's level-4 or level-5 companies know how to schedule software development and how to manage to that schedule.

For complex software, with real users and with real requirements-management problems, I'm skeptical that anyone has figured it out. I think schedule risk is one of the major reasons that organizations choose to license software. The schedule (and attendant cost) risks of in-house software development are just too great.

Perhaps there's something about the nature of software that means you can't know how long it will take until you've done it. If so, the only organizations that can afford that kind of risk are vendors who can amortize the cost (whatever it turns out to be) over hundreds or thousands of users.

The protagonist of this guide has been burned many times. He's been asked to work weekends, holidays, and nights and to put in 80- and 90-hour work weeks during "crunch time," and he's not doing it anymore. He'll give what he thinks is a fair contribution—and he'll

probably do quite a bit more than that—but he no longer believes in heroics. "The more rabbits you pull out of the hat, the more rabbits they expect you to pull out of a hat, until all you're doing is pulling rabbits out of the hat. Nope, not anymore!"

Two important takeaways for the students:

➤ **Software developers are optimists. Ensure that they have not planned schedules assuming that people work full time. People can't work all the time—they get sick, go to the dentist, serve jury duty, write employee evaluations, sit on design reviews, apply for patents, and so on. Plans should apply a factor like 0.6 to compute the number of effective labor hours for each employee.**

➤ **Be aware of the consequences of negotiating a schedule. If the developers have used a sensible process for creating the schedule, it is seldom worth reducing it. They're optimists, anyway, and chances are the project will take longer than they think. If you trust that developer management is making effective use of the developers' time, leave the schedules alone.**

One important point not brought out by this guide: *Large projects are much harder to schedule than small ones.* Also, if the project lasts longer than a year, watch out! Longer projects mean more chance for technology change, requirements change, and employee turnover. All of these factors increase the likelihood of schedule delays.

 ### SUGGESTED RESPONSES FOR DISCUSSION QUESTIONS

1. I think the developer has been burned many times. We can learn a lot by understanding his points.

2. There's a risk when management attempts to negotiate schedules. As stated in the takeaway, noted previously, if management trusts that development management has used a sensible process to obtain the schedules, and if they trust development management to effectively utilize developers' time, leave the schedule alone.

   Alternatively, if the product must be produced more quickly, remove requirements. But do so realistically, and not as part of a negotiating ploy.

   As a manager, consider, too, the implications of negotiating a schedule. You're essentially telling the developers that you do not trust them, that you think they're attempting to deceive you with a relaxed schedule.

Rather than a harsh negotiation with the implications just stated, you might ask the developers to show you their schedule, to discuss their scheduling methodology with you, and then, as a team, work together to determine if there are any tasks for which the schedule could be compressed, or ways of rearranging tasks for greater schedule efficiency.

3. Without any further information about the costs of the one-month difference, I'd prefer the 13-month shipment. Software that is produced when in "late mode" is typically lower in quality than software that is produced on a planned schedule. I'd bet (absent more information) that such quality matters will translate into costs high enough to swamp the costs of the two extra months of development.

4. Return the plan to development management and tell them to plan more realistically. This planning mistake would raise serious flags in my mind about the competency of the development team. I'd do something to get that team more training, bring in consulting expertise, or start looking for new development managers.

5. If schedules are always unreasonable, then nobody believes anything. Schedules lose relevance, importance, and meaning. "Everybody knows this is a phony schedule. Don't knock yourself out."

6. I'd listen. I'd ask them to help me develop a plan and a process that would not have the result they fear. I'd work with them to develop that plan and to implement it.

7. This is a good question for the students to discuss. Some factors that may make software scheduling harder are:

   • Changing technology.
   • Changing requirements.

   • Software is mental—it's logical poetry. It's as varied as the human mind.
   • Large differences exist in the amount of quality code that different developers generate. These differences complicate planning.
   • Different tasks require different amounts of time. Writing an application where the tools and techniques are known is far simpler than inventing or applying a new technology. This complicates the planning process. Consider the IRS's CADE example.

   In other ways, software is similar to managing any other complex project. It requires clearly defined tasks and schedules, unambiguous assignments of personnel to tasks, careful follow-up on assignments, management of critical paths and schedules, effective communication, and other skills students will learn in their project management classes.

8. Learn project management skills. Be aware of the difficulty of scheduling software projects. Understand the need to manage requirements creep. Be willing to remove features and functions if the schedule must be kept. Always plan on delays in software projects. Don't assume that because a project is late that software management is incompetent. It may be, but it may also be that unavoidable factors intervened.

WRAP UP

➤ **What did you learn from this guide?**

➤ **As a future manager, how will you plan your activities around software schedules?**

➤ **How useful are the insights of this contrarian?**

➤ **What characteristics make some contrarians' comments more useful than others?**

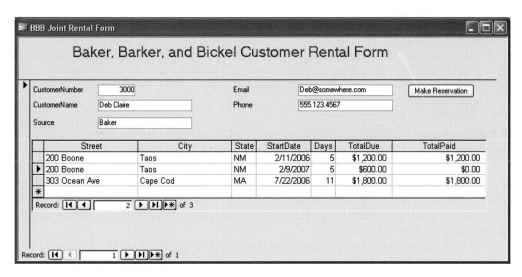

Figure 6-11
Example of Prototype Form

or other element of the user interface. Figure 6-11 shows a prototype of a data entry form for the Baker, Barker, and Bickel property rental system. This particular form was generated using Microsoft Access, which developers frequently use as a prototyping tool.

Prototypes vary in functionality and utility. Some prototypes are just visual mockups of eventual system components. Others are working prototypes from which users can activate some of the system's features. Furthermore, some prototypes are just demonstrations—they are designed to be thrown away. Other prototypes are kept and evolve into the final form, report, or other system component.

Prototypes help users evaluate requirements because they show actual data in context. A user reviewing the form in Figure 6-11, for example, might realize that the system should sort the data in the grid by *StartDate*. This requirement would be difficult to know or specify without the prototype.

Prototypes also can provide an opportunity for users to test the user interface. The user can employ the form in Figure 6-11 to enter, modify, or delete data.

Prototypes are more understandable than data models. For example, the prototype in Figure 6-12 illustrates that each customer has many rentals, and it implies that each rental has at most one customer. It also shows that the same customer can rent the same property on different dates. We can show the same facts using a data model, as shown in Figure 6-12, but the form is usually easier for users to understand.

Unfortunately, prototypes can imply that the application is more complete than it actually is. For example, the form in Figure 6-11 is only a mock-up. If you click the *Make Reservation* button, nothing happens. The program code that will actually create the reservation does not yet exist. Because writing this code may take three or four or

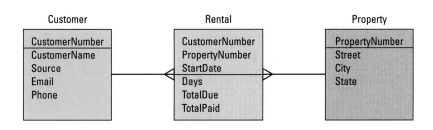

Figure 6-12
Data of Prototype Form in Figure 6-11

more times more effort than generating the mock-up, the users on the team will believe the system is closer to being done than it is.

Prototypes are very useful as communication devices between users and developers. As long as the developers limit the users' expectations, prototypes are helpful tools.

Joint Application Design

Joint application design (JAD) is another key element of RAD. The term *joint* is used because a *team* of users, developers, and PQA personnel conducts design activities. Prior to 1990, only professional developers participated in design, and the idea of including users and PQA personnel was radical. JAD came about because developers wanted to incorporate feedback and testing earlier in the development process. Ultimately, developers decided that the best place to get feedback was during design creation.

A *JAD session* is a design meeting of short duration, perhaps an afternoon or a day or two at most. During the session, attendees develop the design of a particular component of the system. The goal is to keep the scope of the component small enough that the design can be completed in a short period.

Organizations vary in the degree of structure given to JAD sessions. Some organizations have strict guidelines for both the JAD process and for the documents created both before and after the JAD sessions. Other organizations are less formal in process and documentation. If you are invited as a user to a JAD session, learn the rules and expectations ahead of time. Also, devote time and attention to the meeting; such meetings are important.

CASE and Visual Development Tools

CASE stands for **computer-assisted software engineering** or **computer-assisted systems engineering**, depending on who is using the term. The first meaning focuses on program development; the second focuses on development of systems having the five components. You will encounter both meanings.

For either meaning, the basic idea is to use a computer system, called a **CASE tool**, to help develop computer programs or systems. CASE tools vary in their features and functions. Some such tools address the entire systems development process from requirements to maintenance; others address just the design and implementation phases. Either way, most CASE tools have a **repository**, which is a database that contains documents, data, prototypes, and program code for the software or system under development.

Most CASE products have tools for creating prototypes, and many have **code generators**, which are programs that generate application code for commonly performed tasks. The idea is to improve developer productivity by having the tool generate as much code as possible. The developer can then add code for application-specific features.

To give you an idea of how a code generator works, examine Figure 6-13, which illustrates the use of Microsoft FrontPage, a product used to generate Web pages. FrontPage is not a CASE tool, but because it has code generation capabilities we will use it for illustration.

In Figure 6-13a, the developer has created a Web page with text, labels, and data entry boxes. The developer can resize elements on the page, move them around, change colors, and so forth, all using the graphical tools and symbols. Behind the scenes, FrontPage is generating code in HTML, a language used by browsers to define Web pages. Figure 6-13b shows the code that corresponds to Figure 6-13a.

As you can imagine, using the graphical facilities in Figure 6-13a is much easier than writing the code in Figure 6-13b. Code generators in CASE tools provide similar functionality. They can do more than just write code for forms and reports, however. Some CASE tools, for example, generate code for common actions like reading, inserting, updating, and deleting rows of tables in a relational database.

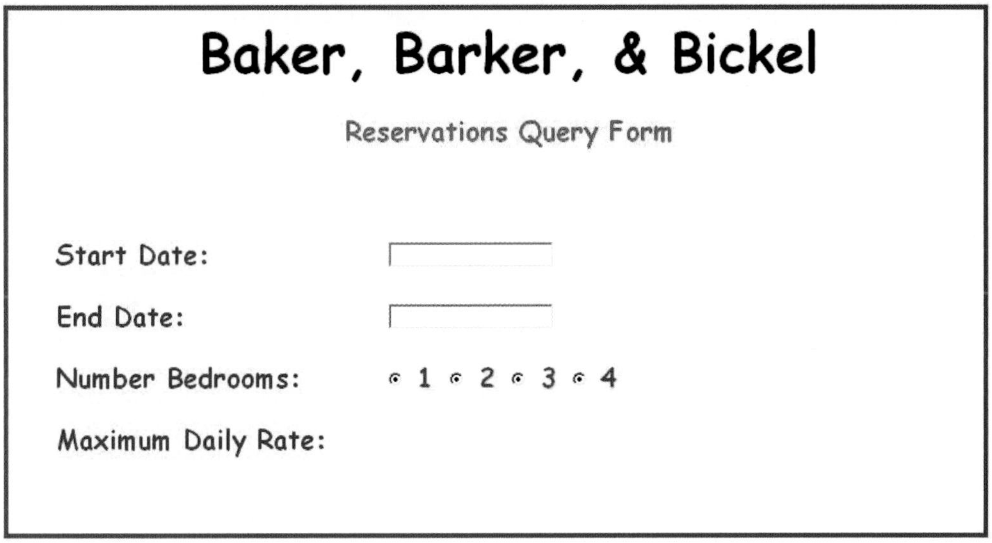

Baker, Barker, & Bickel

Reservations Query Form

Start Date:

End Date:

Number Bedrooms: ⊙ 1 ⊙ 2 ⊙ 3 ⊙ 4

Maximum Daily Rate:

Figure 6-13a
Visual Web Page Development

```
<meta name="ProgID" contents="FrontPage.Editor.Document">
<title>IS300 – Classes</title>
<meta name="MicroSoft Border" content="1">
<link rel="File-List" href="Figure%206-13_files/filelist.xml">
</head>
<body>
<h1 align="center"><font face="Comic Sans MS" size="7">Baker, Barker, &amp; Bickle</font></h1>
<p align="center"><b><font face="Comic Sans MS" size="5" color="#FF0000">
Reservations Query Form<font/></b></p>
<blockquote>
<p align="left"><b><font face="Comic Sans MS" color="#ff0000" size="5">     </font> </b></p>
<p align="left"><b><font face="Comic Sans MS" size="5" color="#0000FF">
Start Date:              </font></b>
<input type="text" name="T1" size="20"></p>
   <p align="left"><b><font face="Comic Sans MS" size="5" color="#0000FF">End
   Date:             
   </font></b><input type="text" name="T1" size="20"><b><font face="Comic Sans MS" size="5"color="#0000FF">   
   </font></b></p>
   <p align="left"><b><font face="Comic Sans MS" size="5" color="#0000FF">
   Number Bedrooms:       </font>
   <font face="Comic Sans MS"><font size="5" color="#008000">
   <input type="radio" Value="V1" checked name="R1"> 1 </font>
   <font size="5" color="#008000">
   <input type="radio" Value="V1" checked name="R1"> 2
   <input type="radio" Value="V1" checked name="R1"> 3
   <input type="radio" Value="V1" checked name="R1"> 4 </font></font></b></p>
   <p align="left"><!--[if gte vml 1]><v:rect id="_x0000_s1027"
 alt="" style='position:absolute;left:3.75pt;top:8.25pt;width:663.75pt;
 height:347.25pt;z-index:-1' strokecolor="#930" strokeweight="3pt"/><![endif]--><![if !vml]><span
style='mso-ignore:vglayout;position:absolute;z-index:-1;left:3px;top:9px;
width:899px;height:467px'><img width=889 height=467
src="Figure%206-13_files/image001.gif" v:shapes="_x0000_s1027"></span><![endif]>
<b><font face="Comic Sans MS" size="5" color="#0000FF">Maximum
  Daily Rate:</font></b></p>
</blockquote>

</body>

</html>
```

Figure 6-13b
Code Behind Visual Web Page

Visual development tools also are used in RAD projects to improve developer productivity. Figure 6-14 (page 176) shows the use of Microsoft's Visual Studio.Net. The window in the bottom center has code for processing the form shown in the top center. Visual Studio.Net wrote the program code shown here. The developer starts with that code as a skeleton and adds features and functions to it.

By the way, even though we are introducing visual development tools here, in the discussion of RAD, do not be misled into thinking that such tools are used only in RAD projects. They are used for software development projects of all types.

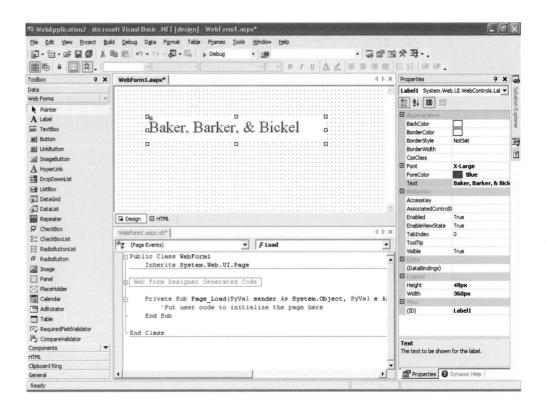

Figure 6-14
Visual Programming Tool
Example

Object-Oriented Systems Development

A third development methodology arose from the discipline of object-oriented programming and is called **object-oriented development (OOD)**. As you will see, OOD has a number of characteristics in common with RAD, but it extends those concepts as well. OOD use began after RAD, in the early to mid-1990s.

Object-oriented development arose in response to the judgment that there is too much freedom in computer programming. Fred Brooks, author of *The Mythical Man-Month,* wrote that computer programs are logical poetry. Just as there are a myriad of ways to write poetry, so, too, there are a myriad of ways to write computer programs. Unlike poetry, however, programs must work together. A large system like Windows has thousands of programs that work together in a unified way. To create such a product, programmers must follow consistent practices; if they do not, chaos results.

OOD develops programs using the techniques of **object-oriented programming (OOP)**, which is a discipline for designing and writing computer programs. Programs developed using OOP are easier and cheaper to fix and adapt than those developed using traditional techniques. For this reason and various others, almost every software vendor today writes programs using OOP. Microsoft Windows and Office, for example, were written using OOP techniques.

Developers of business applications have been slower to adopt OOP, in part because they must integrate new programs with existing, non-OOP programs. Still, OOP sees increased use for business applications each year and will soon be the standard for such applications, too.

A series of diagramming techniques called the **Unified Modeling Language (UML)** facilitates OOP development. UML has dozens of different diagrams for all phases of system development. In fact, one complaint about UML is that there are so many diagrams that projects bog down in diagramming to the detriment of finishing the system. UML proponents argue that use of the diagrams is optional and that good project managers will select which ones to use.

UML itself does not require or promote any particular development process. There is, however, one methodology, called the **unified process (UP)**, which was designed for use with UML. We will summarize that process here. Be aware, however, that UML and UP are just examples of OOD diagrams and processes. Your organization may use different techniques. Also note that although UP is primarily a process for developing computer programs and not information systems, the ideas of UP can be broadened to include development of systems having the five components.

The Unified Process

Figure 6-15 shows the basic UP phases. Three of the five phases are similar to phases in the SDLC:

- The *inception* phase is similar to the first part of the SDLC definition phase.
- The *transition* phase is similar to the conversion phase in SDLC implementation.
- The *maintenance* phase is similar to maintenance in the SDLC.

The remaining two phases—*elaboration* and *construction*—are very different from SDLC, as you will see.

Elaboration Phase

During the elaboration phase, developers construct and test the framework and architecture of the new system. The result is a working system with basic capabilities. Elaboration includes requirements determination, design, programming, and testing.

With UML and UP, developers express requirements in the form of *use cases*. A **use case** is simply a description of an application of the new system. Figure 6-16 (page 178)shows a sample use case for the Baker, Barker, and Bickel property reservation system. As shown, a use case consists of one or more scenarios that describe how the system will be used. The main success scenario describes how the system is used to create the desired outcome. This is the so-called *happy scenario*. Alternative scenarios describe other situations. They can be other versions of success or scenarios for different cases of failure.

Use cases drive the elaboration iterations. For example, in one iteration developers would implement scenario 1 in the use case in Figure 6-16. With subsequent iterations, they would implement other scenarios. Each iteration terminates with a functioning, tested system. Developers will not implement all of the use cases or use-case scenarios in an iteration, but those that they do implement will work.

According to the UP, the elaboration phase addresses the aspects of the system that have the most risk and uncertainty. Developers save the creation of features and functions for which there is little risk for the construction phase.

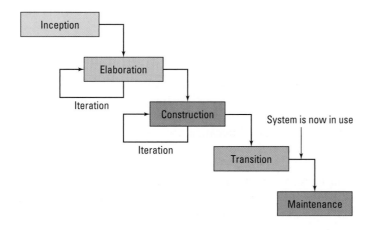

Figure 6-15
Stages in the Unified Process

Baker Reserves Barker or Bickel Property

Main success scenario:
1. Customer calls Baker and wants to make a reservation in Barker or Bickel's territory. Customer states needs. Baker agent queries system for properties meeting those needs. Customer states dates desired. Agent checks availability for those dates. Property is available. Agent states prices and customer agrees to term. Agent takes credit card information. Agent sends notification to the relevant Barker or Bickel and confirmation to customer.

Alternative scenarios:
2. Property is found and dates are available. Customer wants to think about it. Agent sends more information to customer and holds property reservation for 48 hours.

3. Property is found, and dates are available. Customer says price is too high.
   a. Agent seeks another property.
   b. Agent asks customer for budget and seeks price change from external agent at Barker or Bickel.
   (1) Price change is OK and customer accepts terms.
   (2) Price change is not OK. Agent seeks another property.

4. Property is found and dates are not available.
   a. Agent seeks another property.
   b. Customer changes dates required.

Figure 6-16
Use Case Example

In today's world, security is an important source of system requirements. Developers need to address security needs, regardless of the style of development used. For the SDLC and RAD, developers obtain security requirements during requirements analysis. For UP, developers normally would address security during the elaboration phase. See the *Security Guide* on page 179a to understand important security issues for systems development.

Construction Phase

During the UP construction phase, developers design, implement, and test the easier, lower-risk features and functions that were not addressed during elaboration. Just as with the elaboration phase, construction consists of multiple iterations, each of which ends with a tested, working version of the system. Once developers have constructed all features and functions, the system is ready for deployment.

As noted earlier, the last two UP phases, transition and maintenance, are similar to phases in the SDLC, and we will not consider them further.

At this point in the chapter, we have studied three different development processes—the SDLC process, RAD, and UP. Do companies choose one process for use with all of their IT projects? Some do, but others do not. *MIS in Use 6-2* discusses how Sears, Roebuck and Company found itself using a variety of development processes and the steps the company took to standardize the development process.

UP Principles

Figure 6-17 summarizes the principles that underlie the UP. We have already discussed the first five. Considering the sixth principle, UP continuously involves users throughout the development process. Because the elaboration and construction phases proceed in iterations, and because users provide requirements for each iteration, there is a continuous need for user involvement. In addition, users provide test criteria and may even perform incremental testing.

One of the dangers of incremental development is that the project is never finished. Users add more and more requirements, and so there is always a need for another iteration. Continual iterations are less likely if the users are paying for the sys-

Sears Standardizes Development

Sears, Roebuck and Company sells home merchandise, apparel, and auto products throughout the United States and Canada. Sears operates 2,300 retail outlets and sells over the Web at *sears.com* and *landsend.com*. It also offers products through a variety of specialty catalogs. Additionally, Sears operates the largest home-product repair service in the United States, making more than 14 million service calls per year.

Sears employs over 1,000 IT professionals who were using a variety of different system development methodologies, including SDLC, RAD, and versions of UP. This variety of different development methodologies resulted in systems having inconsistent quality and timeliness. According to John Morrison, IT Methodology Consultant at Sears,

> One of our central challenges was the use of multiple methodologies throughout IT. Associates were interpreting these methodologies in different ways. . . . [A]t the start of every project, the team had to establish roles for the project, decide which artifacts were going to be used. . . . [W]ithout a

consistent, repeatable methodology, you have no way to pass on the process knowledge you've acquired.

To solve this problem, Sears created a single, consistent, enterprise-wide development process. This process is backed by software development tools licensed from IBM and based on a version of the unified process called the Rational Unified Process (RUP)® Methodology. These tools provide Sears' developers the ability to manage requirements, development documentation, defects and testing results, and changes to requirements. RUP was chosen as the standard because teams within Sears had obtained success using it on isolated projects.

The results so far have been encouraging. IT personnel are more effective because they need learn only one development process. Furthermore, the improved management of development projects has reduced the costs related to system defects and failures by 20 percent. The IT department expects further cost savings as developers gain more experience with the methods and tools.

Source: "Sears Builds Enterprise-wide Solution Delivery Framework," *306.ibm.com/software/success/cssdb.nsf/CS/MGER-5S3N9N?OpenDocument&Site=software* (accessed June 2005).

tem (as they would be at Baker, Barker, and Bickel) or if they need the system to solve a troublesome problem. But, there is always the chance that different user groups will insist on different sets of requirements. To keep the project from spinning out of control and to ensure that the system does eventually finish, the project team managers must prioritize requirements and have a process for deferring some requirements when necessary.

Similar comments apply to managing changes. As developers complete iterations, the users may want to change aspects of the system that have already been developed. Some changes are unavoidable and should be expected. If developers and the organization allow too many changes, however, the system can go into paralysis and never move forward.

1. Develop incrementally.
2. State requirements with use cases.
3. Address high-risk functions early.
4. Build cohesive architecture early.
5. Test and verify quality early and often.
6. Involve users continuously.
7. Manage requirements.
8. Manage change requests.

Figure 6-17
UP Principles

Source: Adapted from Craig Larman, *Applying UML and Patterns: An Introduction to Object – Oriented Analysis and Design and the Unified Process* 2nd Edition. Adapted by permission of Pearson Education, Inc, Upper Saddle River, NJ.

Security and Systems Development

What makes for a secure system? Particular requirements depend on the features and functions of the information system, but a useful, general definition is the following: *A secure information system is one in which only authorized users can take authorized actions.*

The process of creating a secure system can be summarized in the following five steps:

» Decide how users will be authenticated.

» Determine user groups.

» List primary features and functions of the system.

» Determine how restrictions will be enforced.

» Allocate permissions to user groups for specific features and functions.

The first step is to decide how the system will authenticate users. How does the IS know that the person signed on as John Adams is, in fact, John Adams? There are two possibilities. The IS can rely on the authentication performed by the operating system or a computer network or it can perform its own authentication.

Systems that are used exclusively within an organization can rely on authentication by the operating system or network. For example, when you sign on to your university's network, a security application authenticates your system name and password. Once you have been authenticated to the network, other information systems—say, those for class scheduling—can use that authentication.

Applications that operate outside of an organizational network must perform their own authentication. At Amazon.com, for example, the Your Account application authenticates users by name and password. User name and password is the lowest level of user authentication. Other authentication methods are described in Chapter 11 (page 344).

Once authenticated, users can perform authorized actions. Although it is possible to define allowed actions for each authenticated user, such a policy becomes an administrative headache. If there are, say, 200 users, then 200 sets of permissions will be defined. When permissions change, each of the 200 accounts must be examined. Of course, the situation gets worse if there are 2,000 or 20,000 users.

Instead, users are assigned to one or more user groups; and permissions are defined for each user group. Therefore, the second step in developing a secure system is to determine user groups. With the Baker, Barker, and Bickel system, for example, there could be an Owner users group, a Reservations Agent group, and a Systems Administrator group. In a sense, user groups are roles that users can take. A single individual can belong to several groups, just as a user can take several roles. For example, Baker, Barker, and Bickel would be assigned to both the Owner and Reservations Agent groups. Office employees would be assigned only to the

Reservations Agent group. Other personnel who maintain the system for Baker, Barker, and Bickel would be assigned to the Systems Administrator group.

The next step is to list features and functions of the system. This list is a direct result of systems design activity. With the Baker, Barker, and Bickel system, system features and functions include: Query for Property; Obtain Property Availability Dates; Make, Change, or Delete Reservation; and so forth. Later, user groups will either be given permission or not given permission to use or not to use system features and functions as appropriate.

Also during design, the developers must determine how to enforce restrictions. The most primitive way to limit an action is to allow the user to attempt it and then slap the user's hand by issuing an error message like, "You are not allowed to perform this action." Such a message is insulting, and this technique is not recommended.

An improvement on the "slap your hand" strategy is to disable features and functions that the user cannot perform. In Microsoft Office, disabled functions are shown in a light shade of gray, and most users have learned that nothing will happen when they click on a grayed-out option. Some applications follow this same convention by "graying out" functions disabled by the security system.

A variation on this technique is to disable and gray out the portions of a data entry form that the user cannot change. With the Baker, Barker, and Bickel system, for example, the Price field of the Reservations form could be shown in gray type. The color of that field would indicate to the agents that it is disabled, and hence they cannot change the value of Price.

The third and best alternative is not to display actions that the user is unauthorized to perform. This alternative not only prohibits unauthorized use, but it also hides features and functions from unauthorized personnel. Because they cannot see

it, they do not even know that the feature or function exists.

Applications involving financial transactions like accounts payable, accounts receivable, and payroll require special security consideration. In particular, the system needs to be designed to provide appropriate separation of duties and authorities. For example, the same person should not be allowed to authorize a payment and to generate a check. For such applications, good security requires that job descriptions, user procedures, and program security features and functions be designed to work together. You will learn more about appropriate controls in your accounting classes. For now, just be aware that computer programs, by themselves, cannot provide effective accounting controls for financial systems. Programs must be augmented by appropriate manual procedures and job descriptions.

DISCUSSION QUESTIONS

Consider the inventory application system at your local grocery store. Assume that this system is used to record item sales and returns at cash registers, the arrival of goods from the warehouse, ordering of items, and related inventory management activities. Answer the following questions. As you do so, make assumptions as necessary and state your assumptions.

1. Explain why this system needs to address security. Describe three ways this system is vulnerable to misuse or crime.

2. State the definition of a secure system. How does this definition apply to the grocery store inventory application?

3. Which type of authentication would be used for this application?

4. Define potential user groups.

5. List five application features and functions. Describe how those features and functions would be allocated to the user groups you defined in question 5.

6. Although not discussed in this feature, it is possible to have too much security. Describe what you think happens when a system has too much security. How do you think systems developers should decide how much security is appropriate?

Most successful UP projects prioritize change requests and implement them in accordance with that priority. To ensure that requests are not lost or duplicated, developers use some sort of change-tracking system.

Extreme Programming

We conclude this chapter with a short discussion of **extreme programming (XP)**, which is an emerging technique for developing computer programs. It is not useful for developing large systems that require new business processes and procedures. Organizations have used it successfully, however, in developing application programs.

Extreme programming represents the ultimate in iterative development. Programmers create only features and functions of the new program that they can complete in 2 weeks or less. If many programmers are working on the project, each person's work must be done in such a way that all of their work can be combined and assembled at the end of that period. Users and PQA professionals test the developed code continuously through the process.

In addition to this extremely iterative style, XP is distinguished by three key characteristics: It (1) is customer centric, (2) it uses just-in-time design, and (3) it involves paired programming.

Customer-Centric Nature

With XP, the customer or user of the new program is a critical part of the development team. The customer works full time on the project and consults closely with programmers and test engineers. The customer actively and personally defines requirements to the development team, fleshing out requirement details as they are needed by the programmers. The customer also helps testing personnel develop test plans and automated tests and performs application testing on a regular and recurring basis.

JIT Design

As you will learn in Chapter 7, the acronym JIT means *just-in-time*. The JIT design of XP means that programmers defer program design until the last possible moment. Programmers create the minimal design they need to accomplish the requirements of the current iteration, and nothing more. Unlike other development techniques, developers prepare no overarching program design until the code to be written requires it.

As the project proceeds and as an existing design becomes unworkable, the development team discards that design and creates a new design. (The new design might be more or less complex than the discarded one, depending on the nature of the developing system.) Developers then alter existing programs as necessary to conform to the new design. Such a design technique means that developers will change and adapt programs dozens of times during the development process. Although this reprogramming may be expensive, the JIT design process means that the final programs will be as simple as possible.

Paired Programming

Paired programming is the most unconventional characteristic of XP. With it, two programmers work together, side by side, on the very same computer. They look over each other's shoulders, and they continuously communicate as they program on that single machine. According to XP proponents, studies show that two programmers working in this way can do at least as much work as two programmers working separately, and the resulting program code has fewer errors and is more easily main-

Using the Security Guide

(page 179a)

GOAL

* Teach fundamentals of system security.

BACKGROUND AND PRESENTATION STRATEGIES

This guide is a straightforward explanation of basic security concepts. Accordingly, I believe it works better as homework than as an in-class exercise.

The primary purpose of having this discussion in this chapter is to drive home the point that security is an important systems feature that a company needs to consider throughout the development process. For example, using SDLC, security has requirements, it needs design, security features need to be implemented and tested, and they need to be maintained. Thus security features are developed just as other system features; they may be among the most important system features.

Security varies from system to system. A system for scheduling tee times at a golf course needs less security than one for trading gold futures on the world market.

The five steps shown in the guide summarize a means for designing system security. They are useful, once security requirements are known. Once the design is created using these steps, the security system must be implemented.

We will discuss authentication in more detail in Chapter 11. Meanwhile, you might mention that users can be authenticated on the basis of what they *know* (passwords and PINs), what they *have* (smart cards), and what they *are* (biometrics, retina scans, etc.).

Also, as mentioned with regard to passwords in the Security Guide in Chapter 1, once a user is authenticated to one system or network, that system may authenticate the user to other systems or networks. This saves the user from repeatedly authenticating him or herself, but at the expense of greater damage if the user's identity is compromised. One more time: *Protect your passwords.*

This material repeats some of the discussion of users and user groups from the Security Guide in the database chapter (Chapter 4). There, we illustrated how the DBMS can be used to enforce permissions on the database. This chapter extends those ideas to apply

them to application programs as opposed to just database access. The two security systems interact. The application can authenticate the user and pass the user's credentials to the DBMS. The DBMS will then check its security metadata to determine the groups to which the user has been assigned. The user's identity and those groups determine the data access that the user has been assigned.

It is possible to design the security system so that the permissions available to a user are those granted to the user by the application programs, or that the permissions available to a user are those granted to the user by the DBMS, or by the lesser of the two. It just depends on the security system design.

The particulars of security system design are beyond the scope of this class. However, users should understand the importance of identities and groups. If they are asked to assist network, database, or system administrators in the definition of groups and permissions, they should know to take such work seriously.

 SUGGESTED RESPONSES FOR DISCUSSION QUESTIONS

1. This system involves both money and goods; it is an easy target for theft. *Possible vulnerabilities:* (a) Sales and returns: Clerk logs on as someone else, enters fictitious customer return, pockets money. (b) Inventory ordering: An unauthorized user orders goods, then removes them from inventory without payment. (c) Inventory management: An unauthorized user declares undamaged received goods as damaged, and removes goods without payment.

    ➤ **Has anyone worked in a grocery store?**

    ➤ **Could you describe the security system?**

    ➤ **Were there any security problems while you worked there?**

2. A secure system is one that only allows authorized users to take authorized actions. One example: Clerks who order dairy foods ought not be able to order beer and wine (assuming the store has such a separation of duties and authorities).

3. Could use user name and password authentication.

4. Inventory management could be allocated by major food groups: dairy-ordering group, beer-and-wine-ordering group, produce-ordering group, and so on. Assign different employees authorities to order different items. The inventory supervisor group

could be given authorities for special actions for all inventory groups. The checker group could be divided into checker and manager groups. The store-manager group could have authority for special actions on all store activities.

5. Approve small-dollar return cash payments—all checkers.

   Approve large-dollar return cash payments—checker manager, only.

   Enter small-dollar damaged goods—all ordering employees.

   Enter large-dollar damaged goods—inventory supervisor.

   Allow dairy-group manager to order beer and wine—store manager, only.

6. Too much security occurs when the system provides protections that the users don't need or want. Too much security occurs if the systems developers design a security system that is overly burdensome for the users to employ.

   Note, however, that it *is not within the job descriptions of systems developers to decide how much security is appropriate*. The users decide how much security is appropriate. The systems developers' job is to implement the security system that the users say they need.

   Within the context of that remark, if the systems developers believe that a security system is likely to become so burdensome that users will come to hate the system, then the systems developers have a responsibility to inform the users of that fact, and both groups should work together to identify security system features that will provided needed protection but not be burdensome.

WRAP UP

➤ **Security is an important source of requirements. When systems are being developed on your behalf, be sure that developers address security requirements. If not, raise the issue, and keep raising it until it is addressed.**

➤ **When asked to help assign users to user groups, take that work seriously.**

➤ **As a future manager, protect your passwords (and other forms of authentication). You should also insist that your employees protect their passwords as well. Do not allow password use to become lackadaisical.**

tained.[3] According to the same source, 90 percent of programmers who have tried paired programming for 3 weeks or more prefer it.

At each iteration of the project, one of the programmers moves to a different team. In this way, many different programmers see the same code. Over time, the jointly developed code attains a consistent look and feel. Also, the project never becomes dependent on one programmer for her specialized expertise. Many programmers know many different sections of code.

Extreme programming is not suited for every project or for every organization, but it does offer at least the promise of advantages over traditional programming methods.

Comparison of the Four Development Methodologies

Figure 6-18 compares the four different development techniques described in this chapter. Both the SDLC and RAD address information *systems* consisting of the five components. OOD with UP and XP are primarily concerned with the development of computer *programs*. Software development vendors such as Microsoft or Oracle are more likely to use the latter two techniques. Companies that are developing organizational information systems, say, an inventory or order entry system, are more likely to use the SDLC and RAD.

You should be familiar with each of these techniques because you may be asked to participate as a user or customer of one of these systems. If so, take that responsibility seriously. User involvement is crucial to systems success as described in the *Reflections Guide* on page 181a.

Systems Development Methodology	Scope	Advantages	Disadvantages
SDLC	All five components	• Comprehensive. • Addresses both business and technical issues. • Tried and tested.	• Requirements analysis may lead to analysis paralysis. • Waterfall nature unrealistic.
RAD	All five components	• Iterative nature reduces risk. • JAD improves design. • Use of prototypes and CASE tools increases productivity.	• Requirements analysis may lead to analysis paralysis. • Less suited to very large projects.
OOD with UP	Primarily object-oriented programs	• Use cases are effective requirements documents. • Risk moved forward to elaboration phase. • Each iteration terminates with a working system.	• Less useful for business systems development than for program development. • Danger of sinking into elaboration black hole.
Extreme Programming	Programs	• Customer (user) is always involved. • Paired programming improves quality and reduces risk. • Most useful when requirements evolve with systems development.	• Focus is on programming. • JIT design can require wasteful redesign. • Less useful when system involves many users having different, possibly conflicting, requirements.

Figure 6-18
Comparison of Development Techniques

---

[3]Ron Jeffries, "What Is Extreme Programming?" *XP Magazine,* November 11, 2001, *xprogramming.com/xpmag/whatisxp.htm#pair* (accessed May 2005).

Dealing with Uncertainty

In the mid-1970s, I worked as a database disaster repairman. As an independent consultant, I was called by organizations that licensed the then-new database management systems but had little idea of what to do with them.

One of my memorable clients had converted the company's billing system from an older-technology system to the new world of database processing. Unfortunately, after they cut off the old system, serious flaws were found in the new one, and from mid-November to mid-January the company was unable to send a bill. Of course, customers who do not receive bills do not pay, and my client had a substantial cash flow problem. Even worse, some of its customers used a calendar-year tax basis and wanted to pay their bills prior to the end of the year. When those customers called to find the amount they owed, accounts receivable clerks had to say, "Well, we don't know. The data's in our computer, but we can't get it out." That was when the company called me for database disaster repair.

The immediate cause of the problem was that the client used the plunge conversion technique. But looking deeper, how did that organization find itself with a new billing system so full of failures?

In this organization, management had little idea about how to communicate with IT, and the IT personnel had no experience in dealing with senior management. They talked past one another.

Fortunately, this client was, in most other respects, a well-managed company. Senior management only needed to learn to manage their IS projects with the same discipline as they managed other departments. So, once we had patched the billing system together to solve the cash flow problem, the management team began work to implement policies and procedures to instill the following principles:

» Business users, not IS, would take responsibility for the success of new systems.

» Users would actively work with IS personnel throughout systems development, especially during the requirements phase.

» Users would take an active role in project planning, project management, and project reviews.

» No development phase would be considered complete until the work was reviewed and approved by user representatives and management.

» Users would actively test the new system.

» All future systems would be developed in small increments.

I cannot claim that all future development projects at this company proceeded smoothly after the users began to practice these principles. In fact, many users were slow to take on their new responsibilities; in some cases, the users resented the time they were

asked to invest in the new practices. Also, some were uncomfortable in these new roles. They wanted to work in their business specialty and not be asked to participate in IS projects about which they knew little. Still others did not take their responsibilities seriously; they would come to meetings ill prepared, not fully engage in the process, or approve work they did not understand.

However, after that billing disaster, senior management understood what needed to be done. They made these practices a priority, and over time user resistance was mostly overcome. When it was not overcome, it was clear to senior management where the true problem lay.

DISCUSSION QUESTIONS

1. In general terms, describe how the billing system might have been implemented using pilot conversion. Describe how it might have been implemented using parallel conversion.

2. If you were the billing system project manager, what factors would you consider when deciding the style of conversion to use?

3. If the billing system had been converted using either pilot or parallel, what would have happened?

4. Explain in your own words the benefits that would accrue using the new principles.

5. Summarize the reasons that users resisted these new principles. What could be done to overcome that resistance?

6. Suppose you work in a company where users have little to no active involvement in systems development. Describe likely consequences of this situation. Describe five actions you could take to correct this situation.

Baker, Barker, and Bickel (Continued)

Throughout this chapter, we have discussed the application of many of the principles of systems development to the new system for Baker, Barker, and Bickel. Accordingly, we will not consider their situation further here. However, Applying Your Knowledge question 31 (page 184) asks you to apply these principles by planning a development project using the SDLC. Answering that question will help to prepare you to be a better user representative on development projects at your future employer.

SUMMARY

- Systems development is the process of creating and maintaining information systems. It requires the coordinated teamwork of both IS professionals and users. Systems analysts are IS professionals who have both business and technical knowledge.

- Because information systems involve all five components, they are never off-the-shelf.

- Systems development concerns the creation and maintenance of IS. In this context, maintenance means either to *fix* the system to make it work as it should have in the first place or to *adapt* it to changing requirements.

- Major challenges of systems development include difficulty in determining requirements, changes in requirements, difficulties in scheduling and budgeting, changing technology, and diseconomies of scale.

- The major phases of the systems development life cycle (SDLC) process are system definition, requirements analysis, component design, implementation, and system maintenance. Four dimensions of feasibility are cost, schedule, technical, and organizational feasibility. Defining specific system requirements is the most important task in the systems development process. Each of the five components is designed during the component design phase.

- During implementation, developers construct, test, and install the components of the IS. Product quality assurance (PQA) personnel specialize in the vital task of system testing. Four styles of system conversion are pilot, phased, parallel, and plunge.

Normally, organizations should avoid the plunge method.

- During maintenance, developers either fix or adapt the system. Organizations must maintain a system for tracking failures and requests for enhancements. SDLC is a *cycle* because the decision to enhance a system is a decision to start another trip through the SDLC phases. The SDLC is called a *waterfall model* because it assumes that the process operates as a sequence of not-repeated phases.

- Rapid application development (RAD) breaks up the design and implementation phases using incremental development and uses as much computer assistance as possible in those phases. RAD interweaves the design and implementation phases, and it uses prototypes, which are mock-ups of aspects of the new system. A danger in using prototypes is that they make the system appear more finished than is actually the case.

- Joint application development (JAD) is another RAD practice. With it, teams of users, development personnel, and test personnel work together to design portions of the system in meetings lasting no longer than a few days. RAD also uses computer-assisted software/system engineering (CASE) tools.

- A third development methodology is object-oriented development (OOD). OOP results in programs that are much easier to fix and adapt than programs developed using other techniques. The Unified Modeling Language (UML) is a set of diagramming techniques that support OOD. The unified process (UP) is an example of an OOD development methodology.

You Be the Guide

Using the Reflections Guide
(page 181a)

GOALS

✳ Reinforce the dangers of the plunge style of implementation.

✳ Introduce principles of effective IS management.

BACKGROUND AND PRESENTATION STRATEGIES

System conversion of critical business functions like billing is important and usually difficult. Regardless of the style of implementation, problems usually occur. Pilot and piecemeal conversion reduce the risk, but they still demand careful attention—from both users and developers. Parallel implementation is expensive and requires users to perform double duty. If parallel implementation is used, the plan should include hiring additional, temporary personnel to ease the users' workload.

The story recounted in this guide occurred around 1980. I hope that the plunge conversion of a critical system like billing would be rare today. I suppose, though, that in smaller companies, it still must occur.

At the time of the billing system disaster, this company had about $70 million in sales. Its credit was excellent, and borrowing money for the cash flow crisis was thankfully not a problem. Interest rates were high then, however, and borrowing was expensive.

The person in charge of the company's IS department had been promoted from within. He was in over his head. I worked with him for a year or so after this billing system disaster; the company wanted him to succeed. Ultimately, however, the job required him to grow faster than he could. He left the company and took a job managing computer operations at another company. That job was a better fit for his skills. The company then hired a more senior and experienced person as its IS director.

The billing disaster caught the attention of the CEO. Up until then, he'd not paid too much attention to his information systems. Until the billing system, the company's information systems were primarily calculating systems (see Figure 7-1) and had been managed with a light touch by the CFO. The billing system changed the CEO's posture.

At the time of the disaster, the attitude of the entire company mirrored that of the CEO. No one knew exactly what the IS department did, and as long as they got their paychecks on time, they didn't much care. Once the CEO decided that users need to be more closely involved, once he understood and believed the criticality of user involvement in information systems, he embarked on a program to get the users involved.

As stated in the guide, employee attitudes did not change overnight, however. To facilitate a change in attitude, he asked me to conduct a series of meetings with key users in headquarters and other major offices, explaining the importance of user involvement in information systems development and use.

You might forewarn your students about how difficult it can be to choose to actively participate in systems requirements:

• It's easy to de-prioritize requirement meetings because the new system is usually months away, and you'll have jobs that need to be done today.

• The new system may involve discussions about technology that you find tedious and boring.

• The systems development personnel may not be terribly skilled at communicating with you.

• Meetings may require lots of preparation.

• Possibly none of your managers will see the importance of your involvement and will not reinforce your activities.

• You may know that you'll be long gone into a new position or new job by the time the system comes along.

• Users may differ with each other and with you. Meetings can become tedious.

All of these factors can make it difficult for you to participate. It's still *very important* for you to do so, however.

Over time, user resistance was overcome, at least for most user managers. The next system the company developed was an order entry and production scheduling system. It had active user involvement, and though that process, too, had problems, that system's development was a vast improvement over the billing system.

See Case Study 6-2. Even today, active user management of requirements is a serious problem. We have 30 years' experience with this phenomenon, and yet it still continues. Why? I hope someone will someday do research that will lead us out of this continuing, unsolved problem. It's a puzzle.

ⓘ SUGGESTED RESPONSES FOR DISCUSSION QUESTIONS

1. Pilot conversion: Implement for one product line, for a set of a few customers, or for one production plant. Parallel conversion: Run both the old billing system and the new one at the same time. Reconcile the two systems.

2. Risk, cost, and disruption of business activities would be good factors to consider. It's a balancing of trade-offs.

3. It would have become obvious that the system was not finished and was not ready for use. For piecemeal conversion, the damage would have been limited to a section of the business, and the company would have needed to borrow less money, or possibly none at all. Damage to the company's reputation by not being able to send bills would have been limited to a few customers. In the case of parallel conversion, no customers would have been impacted at all, and there would have been no need to borrow money.

4. The ultimate result is better information systems: information systems that meet user requirements; information systems that are easy to use; information systems with appropriate security. I think, too, that ultimately, it results in lower cost. Although the cost of development may be higher because of the cost of users' labor in creating such systems, over the long haul, an information system that meets user needs and is easy to use will result in less operations labor, and if the system is in use long enough, will recoup the greater initial investment.

5. Users resisted because the system required more work from them. They had to devote time and attention to the new system. Also, they could no longer sit on the sidelines and criticize whatever result occurred. They also became partly responsible for the new system. If the system did not meet user needs, they would be held accountable for the failure by their peers. In this particular company, however, the major form of resistance was from the extra work.

Some of the factors in this company were senior management's posture that user involvement and user training were going to be required. Consistency was also important; when users balked at attending meetings, senior management made it clear that attendance at such meetings was required. When users came to meetings ill-prepared, senior management objected. (We will address change management in more detail in Chapter 7.)

6. Systems for which users have little active involvement will not meet users' needs; they will be difficult to use; they will constantly be "in development." Users will be frustrated and unproductive. They will hold the IS department responsible for the systems failures.

What the student could do depends on his or her job description and management level in the organization. Apply the five principles stated in the middle of the guide in a way that is appropriate for that job and level.

➤ **Tell me a job you'd like to have, and how you could use the principles in this guide to change the situation.**

WRAP UP

➤ **Unless the system has an inconsequential impact on operations, do not take the plunge. (And why develop a system that has an inconsequential impact?)**

➤ **Active user involvement is key! As a future manager and business professional, take the principles in the middle of this guide seriously.**

➤ **The bottom, bottom line: *Users are ultimately responsible for the quality of the information systems they have!***

■ Phases in the UP are inception, elaboration, construction, and transition. The elaboration and construction phases differ from the phases in the SDLC; they consist of iterations of requirements/design/construction work. Each iteration concludes with a functioning, tested system. Use cases express requirements for both elaboration and construction. In the elaboration phase, developers build the system architecture and implement high-risk features. In the construction phase, developers construct lower-risk system features and functions.

■ Extreme programming (XP) is an emerging technique for developing computer programs. With it, projects are divided into very short iterations, usually 2 weeks or less. XP is customer centric, uses JIT design, and involves programmers working in pairs.

KEY TERMS AND CONCEPTS

Analysis paralysis   **171**
Beta testing   **168**
Brooks's Law   **159**
CASE tool   **174**
Code generator   **174**
Computer-assisted software/
   systems engineering
   (CASE)   **174**
Cost feasibility   **162**
Extreme programming
   (XP)   **180**
Incremental development   **172**
Joint application design
   (JAD)   **174**
Maintenance   **158**
Object-oriented development
   (OOD)   **176**

Object-oriented programming
   (OOP)   **176**
Organizational feasibility   **162, 163**
Paired programming   **180**
Parallel installation   **169**
Patch   **170**
Phased installation   **168**
Pilot installation   **168**
Plunge (direct) installation   **169**
Product quality assurance
   (PQA)   **168**
Prototype   **172**
Rapid application development
   (RAD)   **172**
Repository   **174**
Schedule feasibility   **162**

Service pack   **170**
System analyst   **163**
System conversion   **168**
Systems analysis and
   design   **157**
Systems development   **157**
Systems development life cycle
   (SDLC)   **160**
Technical feasibility   **162, 163**
Test plan   **168**
Unified Modeling Language
   (UML)   **176**
Unified process (UP)   **177**
Use case   **177**
Visual development tools   **177**
Waterfall   **171**

ASSIGNMENT MATERIAL

Review Questions

1. Explain the difference between systems development and computer program development. Which is more relevant for business professionals?

2. Who has responsibility for fixing procedure and people problems in an information system?

3. Explain why computer requirements are difficult to determine. Use an example other than one in this chapter.

4. Explain why systems development aims at a moving target. Use an example other than one in this chapter.

5. Explain why scheduling and budgeting is difficult for systems development. Use an example other than one in this chapter.

6. Explain the dilemma posed by changing technology.

7. What are diseconomies of scale? How do they pertain to systems development?

Questions 8 through 18 refer to the SDLC.

8. List the five phases of the SDLC.

9. Summarize the major tasks of the requirements phase.

10. What is the purpose of feasibility assessment?

11. What role do users serve on an IS development project team?

12. List sources of requirements.

13. Describe a situation in which the procedure component is a source of requirements. Describe a situation in which the people component is a source of requirements.

14. What happens if the requirements definition is incorrect or incomplete?

15. Summarize design tasks for each of the five components.

16. Describe implementation activities for each of the five components.

17. List and describe the four styles of conversion.

18. What is the problem with waterfall model of information systems development?

Questions 19 through 22 refer to RAD.

19. How does the RAD process differ from the SDLC process?

20. Describe the nature of incremental development.

21. What is the danger of using prototypes?

22. Describe a JAD session.

Questions 23 through 27 refer to OOD and UP.

23. Explain the statement, "The problem with computer programming is that there is too much freedom."

24. What tasks are accomplished during the inception phase?

25. Describe the nature of the elaboration phase. What tasks should be addressed during this phase?

26. Describe the nature of the construction phase.

27. In your own words, how does UP differ from SDLC? How does it differ from RAD?

28. Summarize the key characteristics of XP.

Applying Your Knowledge

29. Reread the description of the project for developing a database to track volunteers at the TV station in Chapter 4 (pages 76 and 100–103). Consider this project from a systems development perspective.

    a. Develop a brief plan for this project using the SDLC. List major tasks that need to be performed at each phase.

    b. Develop a brief plan for this project using RAD. List major tasks that need to be performed at each phase.

    c. Develop a brief plan for this project using the UP. List major tasks that need to be performed at each phase.

    d. Which of these three techniques do you think is most appropriate for developing this database?

30. Reread the description of the project to connect the computers of the newly acquired company in Chapter 5 (pages 116 and 144). Consider this project from a systems development perspective. Using the SDLC, develop a project plan. In your plan, describe tasks that need to be performed for each of the phases of the SDLC. Also, include a description of work to be done for each of the five components, as appropriate.

31. Suppose that you are one of the members of the Baker, Barker, and Bickel alliance and that the other members have asked you to take the lead on planning the project to develop an IS that will allow the three agencies to rent each other's properties. Because the actual value of the alliance is unknown, you and the other members want to limit your front-end exposure. Use the SDLC to create a plan.

    a. List specific tasks that you need to perform during the requirements phase.

    b. Assume that you will not be developing your own programs but will be licensing programs from a vendor and adapting them. List specific tasks that you need to perform during design. Consider all five components in your answer.

    c. List tasks that you will need to perform during implementation. Consider all five components. Describe how you would implement each of the four conversion techniques.

    d. Describe maintenance activities. Include activities you need to perform to better determine the true value of this alliance.

Application Exercises

32. Suppose you are given the task of keeping track of the number of labor hours invested in meetings for systems development projects. Assume your company uses the traditional SDLC and that each phase requires two types of meetings: *Working meetings* involve users, systems analysts, programmers, and PQA test engineers. *Review meetings* involve all of those people, plus level-1 and level-2 managers of both user departments and the IS department.

    a. Construct a spreadsheet that computes the total labor hours invested in each phase of a

You Be the Guide

Baker, Barker, and Bickel (Continued) (page 183)

The case can be used for the students to review and apply what they've learned from this chapter. Also, if the students made a list of what they wanted to learn about systems development when this case was introduced, they can check that list to see if they've accomplished those goals. (Be sure to read the annotations at the start of the BBB case.)

RESPONDING TO THE CHALLENGE

One way to provide a broad-brush review is to ask:

➤ **What style of systems development seems most appropriate for BBB?**

➤ **What would be the advantages of using SDLC?**

Review the phases of SDLC and then ask the class if BBB could use SDLC. I think the definition phase would be very appropriate for BBB.

➤ **Would RAD be appropriate?**

Review RAD and then ask the class to comment on how BBB could use it. (Probably not appropriate until it is known that there is a need for developing programs as part of the systems solution.)

➤ **What about UP?**

Review UP and then ask the class to comment on how BBB could use it. (Probably not appropriate—at least not until customer programs need to be developed.)

➤ **What about XP?**

Review XP and then ask the class to comment on how BBB could use it. (Probably not appropriate, for same reasons as UP.)

I like to spend some time applying the definition phase of SDLC to the following problem:

➤ **What tasks are to be done during the definition phase?**

• Define system goals and scope.

• Assess feasibility: cost, organizational, schedule, technical.

• Form the project team.

• Plan the project.

➤ **How would you define the system goals and scope?**

The primary goal is to increase revenue by renting each others' properties. Scope is to be limited to keep the businesses separate, as well as because there's a good chance the system won't be useful in the long term (see intro to BBB, at start of chapter).

➤ **What are elements of cost, organizational, schedule, and technical feasibility?**

Take technical first: Nothing here that can't be done, so it can be dismissed as a concern.

➤ **What about organizational feasibility?**

Lots to say here: What will the owners actually do with the system? Do they really want it? Will their employees actually use it? Will it deliver sufficient value that the project stays alive? Will the boundaries of the businesses be threatened so that at some point BBB won't want to use it? What happens if one of the B's loses interest?

➤ **What can we say about cost feasibility?**

There are so many ways of proceeding; some will be cheap and easy, like emailing a Word attachment. Others, like the VPN access of the database, will be quite costly. We'd have to reassess cost feasibility after we knew more about requirements and had sketched out a few alternatives. *(This is an excellent example, by the way, of why the waterfall nature doesn't work. After requirements and a bit of design, we have to redo feasibility assessment.)*

➤ **What can we say about schedule feasibility?**

When do BBB need the system? Schedule feasibility then depends on which system they choose to implement. A simple one like a Word attachment to email could be done fast.

I don't think we can go much farther with this case here. We need to know more about how seriously BBB take this new system, how important it will be to them, and how much incremental revenue they will make.

Even though we don't know those factors, however, we do know what stages of the SDLC would be next: requirements, design, implementation, and maintenance.

➤ **What are the major tasks for BBB for determining requirements?**

➤ **What are the major design tasks for BBB? (Keep all five components in mind.)**

➤ **What are the major tasks for BBB during implementation?**

➤ **What are the major tasks for BBB during maintenance?**

WRAP UP

If you asked the students to make a list of what they wanted to learn, now is a good time to discuss that list.

➤ **What have you learned about systems development?**

➤ **Did the items in your list change as you learned more about it?**

➤ **Do you have any objectives that weren't accomplished?**

➤ **The bottom line: Users and user management have key roles in systems development. Read the list of principles in the middle of the Reflections Guide (page 181a). Attend to that list when information systems are developed on your behalf!**

project. When a meeting occurs, assume you enter the project phase, the meeting type, the start time, the end time, and the number of each type of personnel attending. Your spreadsheet should calculate the number of labor hours and should add the meeting's hours to the totals for that phase and for the project overall.

b. Change your spreadsheet to include a budget of the number of labor hours for each type of employee for each phase. In your spreadsheet, show the difference between the number of hours budgeted and the number actually consumed.

c. Change your spreadsheet to include the budgeted cost and actual cost of labor. Assume that you enter, once, the average labor cost for each type of employee.

33. Use Access to develop a failure-tracking database application. For each failure, your application should record the following:

FailureNumber (Use an Access autonumber data type.)

DateReported

FailureDescription

ReportedBy (the name of the PQA engineer reporting the failure)

FixedBy (the name of the programmer who is assigned to fix the failure)

DateFailureFixed

FixDescription

DateFixVerified

VerifiedBy (the name of the PQA engineer verifying the fix)

a. Create a Failure table, a PQA Engineer table, and a Programmer table. The last two tables should have a *Name* (assume names are unique in each table) and *Email*. Add other appropriate columns to each table.

b. Create one or more forms that can be used to report a failure, to report a failure fix, and to report a failure verification. Create the form(s) so that the user can just pull down the name of a PQA engineer or programmer from the appropriate table to fill in the *ReportedBy*, *FixedBy*, and *VerifiedBy* fields.

c. Construct a report that shows all failures sorted by reporting PQA engineer and then by *DateReported*.

d. Construct a report that shows only fixed and verified failures

e. Construct a report that shows only fixed but unverified failures.

Career Assignments

34. Use your favorite Web search engine to search for the term *systems analyst job opportunities*. Click on four or five of the links you find interesting and answer the following questions.

a. Describe educational requirements for this job.

b. Describe the qualifications necessary to obtain such a job.

c. Describe internships and part-time jobs you could take to prepare for this job.

d. Summarize the employment prospects for this job.

e. Are you interested in this job? Explain why or why not.

35. Answer question 34, but search for the term *PQA test engineer job opportunities*.

36. Answer question 34, but search for the term *application programmer*.

Case Study 6-1

The Need for Technical Feasibility

The United States Internal Revenue Service (IRS) Business Systems Modernization (BSM) project has been a multiyear attempt to replace the existing tax-processing information systems with systems based on modern technology. Review pages 7 and 21 for a discussion of the underlying need, problems, and suggested problem solutions.

The subsystem that has generated the most controversy and been the cause of the most serious delays is the Customer Account Data Engine (CADE). The heart of CADE is a database of business rules. Unlike most databases that contain facts and figures like CustomerName, Email, Balance, and so forth, the CADE database contains business rules, which are statements about how an organization conducts its business. In the context of the IRS, this database contains rules about tax laws and the processing of tax forms. An example of such a rule is:

> Rule 10:
>   IF the amount on line 7 of Form 1040EZ is greater than zero,
>   THEN invoke Rule 15.

With a rule-based approach, the IRS need only develop programs that access the database and follow the rules. No other programs need to be developed.

Rule-based systems differ substantially from traditional application programs. Using traditional technology, the developers interview the users, determine what the business rules are, and then write computer code that operates in accordance with the rules. The disadvantage of such traditional programming is the only technically trained programmers can decipher the rules in the program code. Also, only trained programmers can add, change, or delete rules.

The advantage of rule-based systems like CADE is that the business rules are stored in the database and can be read, added, changed, or deleted by personnel with business knowledge but little computer training. Hence, in theory, CADE is more adaptable to changing requirements than a system written with traditional programming languages.

Unfortunately, the technical feasibility of using a rule-based system for a problem as large and complex as IRS tax processing is unknown. It appears, at least from public records, that no one ever tried to estimate that feasibility. The result has been a string of schedule delays and cost overruns. The first CADE release, which processes only the simplest individual tax returns (those using IRS Form 1040EZ), was to be completed by January 2002. It was delayed once until August 2003, and then delayed again to September 2004. At that point, a limited version of this first release was demonstrated.

The database for these simple returns has some 1,200 business rules, but no reliable estimate has yet been developed for the number of rules required for the full system. The lack of an estimate is particularly serious because some experts believe the difficulty and complexity of creating rules increases geometrically with the number of rules. Meanwhile, $33 million was invested in 2003, and another $84 million was spent in 2004.

Given the history of problems, the IRS hired the Software Engineering Institute of (SEI) Carnegie Mellon University to conduct an independent audit of the project. SEI verified that no one knows with any certainty how many business rules will eventually be required. Additionally, according to the SEI report,

> We believe that harvesting the business rules, not coding them, will drive the cost and schedule of future CADE releases. By harvesting, we mean capturing, adjudicating, and cataloging the rules. CADE has invested many resources exploring rules engines, but few resources exploring the rules themselves. The IRS needs to understand and document their business rules as well as the rules' complicated interactions. Some of the delays that have already plagued CADE are a direct result of an imperfect understanding of the business rules. This situation will only grow as the number and complexity of the implemented rules increases.

According to the SEI testimony, without reliable estimates of the number of business rules,

> No one knows how long rule harvesting will take, how many people will be required, the background, training and experience of the people required, or how much it will cost. Based on anecdotal information presented to us, we believe the time will be measured in years and cost will be measured in the tens of millions of dollars.

Until sound, supported cost and schedule estimates for rule harvesting are available, future CADE plans and schedules are only tentative and likely subject to delays and missed milestones.

Sources: U.S. House, Committee on Ways and Means, Subcommittee on Oversight, Statement of M. Steven Palmquist, Chief Engineer for Civil and Intelligence Agencies, Acquisition Support Program, Software Engineering Institute, Carnegie Mellon University, Pittsburgh, Pennsylvania, February 12, 2004; and *treas.gov/irsob/documents/special_report1203.pdf* (accessed June 2005).

Questions

1. Ignoring developments that have occurred since this case was written, what statement can be made about the technical feasibility, cost feasibility, and schedule feasibility of this project?

2. Use your imagination to try to understand how this situation came about. The IRS selected a team of contractors to develop the information systems that would support the modernization effort. Those contractors proposed a rule-based system, but apparently no one asked whether such a system would work on a problem this large. How could that come about? Suppose you were a non-IT manager at the IRS. Would you know to ask? Suppose you were a senior manager at one of the contractors. Would you know to ask? If you did ask and your technical people said, "No problem," what would you do?

3. Suppose you are a senior IRS manager. In defense of your management, you say, "We hired reputable contractors who had extensive experience developing large and complicated systems. When they told us that a rule-based approach was the way to go, we agreed. Should we be required to second-guess the experts?" Comment on that statement. Do you believe it? Do you think it's a justification?

4. Does it seem remarkable that, according to the SEI review, no one has yet considered the time, cost, and difficulty of harvesting the rules? Clearly, the need to allocate time and labor to that problem was visible from the start of the project. How do you think such an oversight occurred? What are the consequences of that oversight?

5. Suppose it turns out that a rule-based system is infeasible for processing more complicated tax returns. What alternatives are available to the IRS? As a taxpayer, which do you recommend?

6. Google "IRS CADE problems" and read three or four articles and reports on recent developments. Comment on any recent information that sheds light on your answers to questions 1 through 5. What strategy for solving this problem does the IRS seem to be following? How likely is that strategy to succeed?

Case Study 6-2

Slow Learners, or What?

In 1974, when I was teaching at Colorado State University, we conducted a study of the causes of information systems failures. We interviewed personnel on several dozen projects and collected survey data on another 50 projects. Our analysis of the data revealed that the single most important factor in IS failure was a lack of user involvement. The second major factor was unclear, incomplete, and inconsistent requirements.

At the time, I was a devoted computer programmer and IT techie, and frankly, I was surprised. I thought that the significant problems would have been technical issues.

I recall one interview in particular. A large sugar producer had attempted to implement a new system for paying sugar beet farmers. The new system was to be implemented at some 20 different sugar beet collection sites, which were located in small farming communities, adjacent to rail yards. One of the benefits of the new system was significant cost savings, and a major share of those savings occurred because the new system eliminated the need for local comptrollers. The new system was expected to eliminate the jobs of 20 or so senior people.

The comptrollers, however, had been paying local farmers for decades; they were popular leaders not just within the company, but in their communities as well. They were well liked, highly respected, important people. A system that caused the elimination of their jobs was, using a term from this chapter, *organizationally infeasible*, to say the least.

Nonetheless, the system was constructed, but an IS professional who was involved told me, "Somehow, that new system just never seemed to work. The data were not entered on a timely basis, or they were in error, or incomplete; sometimes the data were not entered at all. Our operations were falling apart during the key harvesting season, and we finally backed off and returned to the old system." Active involvement of system users would have identified this organizational infeasibility long before the system was implemented.

That's ancient history, you say. Maybe, but in 1994 the Standish Group published a now famous study on information systems failures. Entitled "The CHAOS Report," the study indicated the leading causes of IS failure are, in descending order, (1) lack of user input, (2) incomplete requirements and specifications, and (3) changing requirements and specifications (*standishgroup.com*). That study was completed some 20 years after our study.

More recently, in 2004, Professor Joseph Kasser and his students at the University of Maryland analyzed 19 system failures to determine their cause. They then correlated their analysis of the cause with the opinions of the professionals involved in the failures. The correlated results indicate the first-priority cause of system failure was "Poor requirements"; the second-priority cause was "Failure to communicate with the customer" (*softwaretechnews.com/technews2-2/trouble.html*).

In 2003, the IRS Oversight Board concluded the first cause of the IRS BSM failure (see *Case Study 6-1*) was "inadequate business unit ownership and sponsorship of projects. This resulted in unrealistic business cases and continuous project scope 'creep.'"

For over 30 years, studies have consistently shown that leading causes of system failures are a lack of user involvement and incomplete and changing requirements. Yet, failures from these very failures continue to mount.

Sources: standishgroup.com; softwaretechnews.com/technews2-2/trouble.html.

Questions

1. Using the knowledge you have gained from this chapter, summarize the roles that you think users should take during an information systems development project. What responsibilities do users have? How closely should they work with the IS team? Who is responsible for stating requirements and constraints? Who is responsible for managing requirements?

2. If you ask users why they did not participate in requirements specification, some of the common responses are the following:
   a. "I wasn't asked."
   b. "I didn't have time."

   c. "They were talking about a system that would be here in 18 months, and I'm just worried about getting the order out the door today."
   d. "I didn't know what they wanted."
   e. "I didn't know what they were talking about."
   f. "I didn't work here when they started the project."
   g. "The whole situation has changed since they were here; that was 18 months ago!"

   Comment on each of these statements. What strategies do they suggest to you as a future user and as a future manager of users?

3. If you ask IS professionals why they did not obtain a complete and accurate list of requirements, common responses are:
   a. "It was nearly impossible to get on the users' calendars. They were always too busy."
   b. "The users wouldn't regularly attend our meetings. As a result, one meeting would be dominated by the needs of one group, and another meeting would be dominated by the needs of another group."
   c. "Users didn't take the requirement process seriously. They wouldn't thoroughly review the requirements statements before review meetings."
   d. "Users kept changing. We'd meet with one person one time and another person a second time, and they'd want different things."
   e. "We didn't have enough time."
   f. "The requirements kept changing."

   Comment on each of these statements. What strategies do they suggest to you as a future user and a future manager of users?

4. If it is widely understood that one of the principal causes of IS failures is a lack of user involvement, and if that factor continues to be a problem after 30 years of experience, does this mean that the problem cannot be solved? For example, everyone knows that you can maximize your gains by buying stocks at their annual low price and selling them at their annual high price, but doing so is very difficult. Is it equally true that although everyone knows that users should be involved in requirements specification, and that requirements should be complete, it just can't be done? Why or why not?

PART III

Information Systems

The three chapters in this part describe the principal information systems used in organizations today. Each of these systems applies the information technology that you learned about in Chapters 3 through 6 to help businesses and organizations gain competitive advantage, solve problems, and make decisions.

Chapter 7 considers information systems within organizations. It describes both functional applications that benefit a single business function as well as integrated applications that support cross-departmental processes. Chapter 8 addresses information systems among firms. It discusses e-commerce and supply chains and describes how information systems are used to solve problems and integrate the activities of multiple organizations. Chapter 9 describes business intelligence and knowledge management systems. It describes reporting systems, data warehouses, data mining applications, and knowledge management systems.

Information Systems Within Organizations

Learning Objectives

- Understand the differences between functional systems and integrated, cross-departmental, process-based systems.

- Know the features and purposes of functional information systems for human resources, accounting, sales and marketing, operations, and manufacturing.

- Understand the problems caused by the isolation of functional systems.

- Understand the basic concepts of Porter's models for competitive strategy and value chains.

- Understand how value chains and business process redesign led to the development of integrated applications.

- Know the features and functions of three types of integrated systems: customer relationship management (CRM), enterprise resource planning (ERP), and enterprise application integration (EAI).

Guides

ETHICS GUIDE
Dialing for Dollars

PROBLEM SOLVING GUIDE
Thinking About Change

OPPOSING FORCES GUIDE
The Flavor-of-the-Month Club

SECURITY GUIDE
Centralized Vulnerability

REFLECTIONS GUIDE
ERP and the Standard, Standard Blueprint

Chapter Preview

This chapter discusses how organizations apply the technologies you learned in Chapters 3 through 6. Companies' goals in applying these technologies are to create information systems that provide competitive advantages, help solve problems, and facilitate decision making. As the title indicates, this chapter addresses only information systems for business processes within organizations. Information systems for processes that span organizations are also important, and we will discuss them in Chapter 8.

The discussion is organized into three parts. First, we survey functional systems that support human resources, accounting, sales and marketing, operations, and manufacturing. Such functional systems help businesses achieve their goals and objectives, but they have important limitations, which we describe at the end of the section.

The next section of the chapter describes and applies two models of organizations that Michael Porter developed. As you will see, Porter's models point the way for the development of integrated information systems. Such systems provide features and functions that cross departmental boundaries. Finally, the chapter concludes by describing three important integrated systems: customer relationship management (CRM), enterprise resource planning (ERP), and enterprise application integration (EAI).

Universal Electronics

Suppose you are the customer service manager for Universal Electronics, an electronics-equipment producer. Your company makes small electronic instruments like voltmeters, multimeters, and circuit-testing equipment. The equipment you manufacture provides essential capability at the lowest possible price.

At present, Universal collects and stores limited customer data. For some equipment, your department saves customer names and addresses in case of an equipment safety recall, but seldom uses that data. In truth, your department provides little customer service beyond handling returns and dealing with order problems.

You are a capable and ambitious professional, and you have been reading about the latest trends in customer service and support. You know that if your company were to maintain a database of customer characteristics and their purchases, you could provide much better support. You could also analyze those data to determine sales and purchase patterns. For example, you could determine that customers who purchase automotive-tuning equipment are also likely to purchase multimeters. The sales department could use such data for sales promotions and sales leads.

You describe these ideas to your boss, and she is interested enough to allow you to spend half time for 2 weeks developing this idea. Using the systems development techniques you learned about in your MIS class, you decide to assess the feasibility of such a system. You know that you will need the support of the IS department to develop this system, so you approach the IS director. He's intrigued and assigns a systems analyst to work with you. Together, you analyze the feasibility and develop a project plan.

You present the completed plan to your boss and the IS director, and with a few modest changes, they approve it. Your company has a committee of senior managers that reviews potential new projects, and your boss arranges for you to present this plan to the committee.

At the committee's next monthly meeting, you present your idea and plan. Universal's COO (chief operating officer) chairs the committee, and this is your first opportunity to present to him. Understandably, you're nervous as you start, but your enthusiasm and thorough understanding of the problem and your proposal enable you to make a superb presentation. At the conclusion, the COO thanks you for your excellent work and says the committee will give you a response at the end of the day after they've had a chance to review other proposals.

You know you have a great idea, you know you did your homework, and you know that you clearly presented the idea and the benefits of this system to your organization. You have little doubt that your proposal will be accepted and that you'll soon be involved in its development. You are therefore shocked and surprised, even stunned, when your boss calls you into her office to say that the committee rejected your idea. The members do not want you or anyone else at the company to spend any more time on this project. Period.

"Frankly," she says, "I'm surprised. I really thought they'd go for it. The COO did say, however, that if you want to learn the committee's reasoning, you can schedule a one-on-one appointment with him."

You're depressed and angry. The benefits of this new system are so obvious and the payback is so great that you just don't understand the

Universal Electronics (page 194)

GOALS

* Introduce competitive strategy by discussing a project concept that *fails* to meet an organization's competitive strategy.

* Motivate student discussion in this and the next chapter by asking the students to recommend an IS that does meet an organization's competitive strategy.

WAYS TO STIMULATE STUDENT INVOLVEMENT

I find the material in Chapters 7 and 8 difficult to teach to undergraduates. One of the key problems is that the business experience of most of my students is that *they've been lifeguards,* or held other low-level jobs. It can be difficult to discuss competitive advantage in any meaningful way with students having such experience.

The purpose of this vignette is to enliven the teaching of competitive advantage by describing *one employee's failed project proposal.* I use it to drive home the idea that organizations have a competitive strategy and that the actions of all employees should enforce that strategy. Also, the character, features, and functions of every IS should reinforce that strategy.

However, if I create a PowerPoint slide that says, "(1) Organizations have a competitive strategy, (2) all activities must support that strategy, (3) all information systems must support that strategy," my students don't learn anything, and they often go to sleep!

So, I try to use this story to cause the students to arrive at these points.

Playing devil's advocate, I sometimes ask the following sequence of questions:

► **What's wrong with the management of this company?**

► **Why is the COO so closed minded?**

► **How many of you agree** with me **that this person should change companies, and soon?**

If the students have read this story, they will respond.

If I'm not getting a response, it's because they didn't read the story. So, I have them open their books and read it now! (And I also explain that not reading is not acceptable behavior. I know this can seem like a losing battle, but I keep after it nonetheless. If I don't, their not-reading just gets worse.)

To my mind, the answer to the prior questions is that there is absolutely *nothing wrong* with the company's enforcing its strategy. The COO is not closed minded, but *is doing his job,* and our protagonist would be *foolish to change companies.* The protagonist has a good shot at becoming the protégé of the COO and having the COO as a mentor, and that's a great spot to be in!

But, I want the students to tell me that. Sometimes I have to carry the devil's advocate to extreme lengths before they catch on (e.g., "The COO should be fired for enforcing the corporate strategy," etc.). And sometimes, in frustration, I have to say, "Hello, is anyone out there thinking? What's wrong with what I'm saying?"

The company has been remiss, however, in not explaining its strategy to its employees. The COO admits as much midway through his one-on-one with our protagonist. The company has also figured that out and is going to correct it.

Bottom line: Every employee action and every information system should enforce the organization's competitive strategy! But, I want the students to tell me that.

WRAP UP

I find a good way to wrap up this introduction to the scenario is to ask the following questions:

► **Did our protagonist's project fail?**

(Yes, certainly.)

► **Did our protagonist fail?**

(Definitely not!)

► **Failure in a single project doesn't necessarily mean job or career failure. It's what you do next that matters most. It would have been a failure for this employee not to meet with the COO, given the generous offer to meet. It would have been a failure to quit and join another company without learning why the project plan was rejected.**

► **In fact, this "failure" resulted in huge gains for our protagonist. The protagonist has received high-level attention and a special project. Also, for the COO to make time to explain all of this and to offer an alternative option is great news for this employee's future in that company. Now the employee is being taught basic business principles by the COO. This employee's initiative is receiving very positive results.**

► **The failure in this story is with the managers who met with our protagonist and let him or her go all the way to the planning committee with an idea that was so obviously in conflict with their competitive strategy. My suspicion is that the COO had some hard conversations with those people, along the lines of: "Don't you understand our strategy? Why are you letting people waste their, your, and my time on projects that are so obviously in conflict with our strategy?" I doubt it was a pleasant week for those managers.**

This vignette sets up the Porter competitive strategy model that starts on page 206. You might bring that model in here as a wrap-up to this discussion.

This book uses three different Porter models, two in this chapter and one in the next chapter. In this chapter, *competitive strategies* and the *value chain* set up process-based systems. Porter's *Five Forces model* sets up the discussion of interorganizational systems and the supply chain in Chapter 8.

This vignette continues in Chapter 8. This is the only opening vignette in the text that is not wrapped up in a single chapter.

committee's decision. You begin to question your company's management. Maybe they just don't know what they're doing? Maybe you should be thinking about working for another company?

Over the weekend, you decide you will look for another job. You also decide, however, to take up the COO's offer to meet. What do you have to lose if you're going to change companies, anyway? So you schedule the appointment with the COO.

Late the next Thursday, as you sit down in the COO's large corner office, he begins, "Great job last Friday. We were impressed with the quality of your work. Interesting idea and well presented."

"I don't get it, then," you stammer, "why did you reject it? Was it too expensive?"

"Oh, we can afford it, there's not that much to it. No, that wasn't it at all."

"Then why?"

"It's not who we are. It's not our strategy."

"What do you mean?"

"Look, our goal is to provide the lowest-cost electronic equipment in the market. We are and will continue to be the cost leader. Everything we do must further that goal. You might be interested to know that your presentation really stirred things up in the committee. If someone as bright and ambitious as you doesn't understand our strategy, then we senior managers are not doing our job of communicating. You'll see the fall-out from that realization in the coming weeks as we engage in new communication programs to our employees."

"But," you continue, "I was able to show a tremendous return on investment by developing the system to keep the customer data."

"Well, you did. But it's not about ROI. It's about strategy. As a company, we don't want to build that customer database—someone might actually use it. If they do, then we're spending labor hours that keep us from being the cost leader. That is the one thing that we must be— that is who we are. It is how we're known in the industry, by our customers, and if we fail at that, we fail as a business."

"But this new system could save costs . . . ."

"Ah, different story," interrupts the COO. "But your proposal didn't say that, did it? Your proposal focused on better customer service, support, and sales. Those are important goals for our competitors, because they aren't the cost leader. They're trying to be the product leader."

"So if I had shown how to save costs . . . ?"

"Yes, but don't go down that path, at least not yet . . . . I'll tell you what. Take some time and think about how we can use information systems to save costs. The system you proposed might be a way to save costs, but it might not be the best one. Think about it. I'll be in Asia for the next 3 weeks. Then, I've got meetings here that will keep me busy for a couple of weeks. Call Brenda and get on my calendar 6 weeks from now. Show me then how we can save costs using information systems. Oh, by the way. Take this out of your own time. I want you running your department. We can't afford to have someone else run your department while you do this. So do both."

As you walk back to your office, your mind is a muddle.

To respond to the COO's query, we need the concepts of both this and the next chapter. We will revisit this story at the end of this chapter and will finish it at the end of the next chapter.

▌ Three Categories of Information Systems

Information systems within organizations will be easier to understand if we begin with a short history. Figure 7-1 shows three eras in IS evolution.

Calculation Systems

The very first information systems, **calculation systems**, seem antiquated today, but they were in use not very long ago. In fact, they could have been used in the business world by your grandfather.

The purpose of those early systems was to relieve workers of tedious, repetitive calculations. The first systems computed payroll and wrote paychecks; they applied debits and credits to the general ledger and balanced the company's accounting records. They also kept track of inventory quantities; quantities that were verified by physical item counts about once a quarter. As calculating machines, they were more accurate than humans—as long as the systems actually worked. (Computer failure rates were high.) Those systems were labor-saving devices; but in truth, they produced little information. None of them survive today, and we will not consider them further.

Functional Systems

The **functional systems** of the second era facilitated the work of a single department or function. They grew as a natural expansion of the capabilities of the systems of the first era. For example, payroll expanded to become human resources, general ledger became financial reporting, and inventory was merged into operations or manufacturing. The changes were more than just in name. In each functional area, companies added features and functions to encompass more activities and to provide more value and assistance.

The problem with functional applications is their isolation. In fact, functional applications are sometimes called **islands of automation** because they work independently of one another. Unfortunately, independent, isolated systems cannot produce many of the efficiencies desired in business. Purchasing influences inventory, which influences production, which influences customer satisfaction, which influences future sales. Decisions that are appropriate when considering only a single function like purchasing may create gross inefficiencies when the entire process is considered.

Name	Era	Scope	Perspective	Example	Technology Symbols
Calculation systems	1950–1980 (Your grandfather)	Single purpose	Eliminate tedious human calculations. "Just make it work!"	Payroll General ledger Inventory	Mainframe Punch card
Functional systems	1975–20?? (Your mother)	Business function	Use computer to improve operation and management of individual departments.	Human resources Financial reporting Order entry Manufacturing (MRP and MRP II)	Mainframe Stand-alone PCs Networks and LANs
Integrated systems (also cross-functional or process-based systems)	2000 ... (You)	Business process	Develop IS to integrate separate departments into organization-wide business processes.	Customer relationship management (CRM) Enterprise resource planning (ERP)	Networked PCs Client-servers The Internet Intranets

Figure 7-1
History of IS Within Organizations

Integrated, Cross-Functional Systems

The isolation problems of functional systems led to the third era of information systems. In this era, systems are designed not to facilitate the work of a single department or function, but rather to integrate the activities in an entire business process. Because those activities cross departmental boundaries, such systems are sometimes called **cross-departmental** or **cross-functional systems**. Because they support complete business processes, they are sometimes also called **process-based systems**.

Transitioning from single-purpose to functional applications was relatively easy. The newer systems provided increased functionality within a single department or function. The line of authority was clear, and little interdepartmental coordination was necessary. Unfortunately, the transition from functional systems to integrated systems is difficult. Integrated processing requires many departments to coordinate their activities. There is no clear line of authority, peer competition can be fierce, and interdepartmental rivalries can subvert the development of the new system.

Most organizations today are a mixture of functional and integrated systems. To successfully compete internationally, however, organizations must eventually achieve the efficiencies of integrated, cross-departmental, process-based systems. Thus, during your career, you can expect to see more and more integrated systems and fewer functional systems. In fact, you will likely be one of the business leaders asked to implement new integrated systems.

By the way, do not assume that the systems and processes discussed in the remainder of the chapter apply only to commercial, profit-making organizations. Not-for-profit and government organizations have most of these same processes, but with a different orientation. Your state Department of Labor has both employees and customers, for example. The Girl Scouts of America has a general ledger and financial statements, as well as operational systems. Information systems for not-for-profit and of government organizations are oriented toward quality of service and efficiency rather than toward profit, but those systems still exist.

■ Survey of Functional Systems

Figure 7-2 (page 198) lists primary functional systems. As stated, each of these serves the needs of a particular business function. We will consider each category in turn.

Human Resources Systems

Human resources systems support recruitment, compensation, evaluation, and development of the organization's employees and affiliated personnel. The first-era human resources (HR) applications did little more than compute payroll. Modern HR applications concern all dimensions of HR activity, as listed in Figure 7-3 (page 198).

Depending on the size and sophistication of the company, recruiting methods may be simple or very complex. In a small company, posting a job may be a simple task requiring one or two approvals. In a larger, more formal organization, posting a new job may involve multiple levels of approval requiring use of tightly controlled and standardized procedures.

Compensation includes payroll for both salaried employees and nonsalaried employees (those who are paid by the hour). It may also include pay to consultants and permanent, but nonemployee, workers such as contractors and consultants. Compensation means not only pay, but also the processing and tracking of vacation, sick leave, and health care and other benefits. Compensation activities also support retirement plans, company stock purchases, and stock options and grants. They can also include transferring employee contribution payments to organizations like the United Way and others.

Employee assessment includes the publication of standard job and skill descriptions as well as support for employee performance evaluations. Such support may

Function	Example Information Systems
Human resources	Recruiting Compensation Assessment Development and training Human resources planning
Accounting and finance	General ledger Financial reporting Cost accounting Budgeting Accounts receivable Accounts payable Cash management Treasury management
Sales & marketing	Lead tracking Sales forecasting Customer management Product management
Operations	Order entry Order management Finished-goods inventory management Customer service
Manufacturing	Inventory Planning Scheduling Manufacturing operations

Figure 7-2
Typical Functional Systems

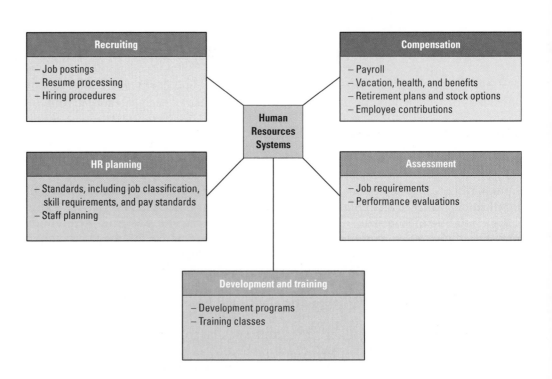

Figure 7-3
Functions Supported by
Human Resources Systems

include systems that allow employees to create self-evaluations as well as evaluation of peers and subordinates. Employee assessment is used for the basis of compensation increases as well as promotion.

Development and training activities vary widely from firm to firm. Some organizations define career paths formally, with specific jobs, skills, experience, and training requirements. HR systems have features and functions to support the publication of these paths. Some HR applications track training classes, instructors, and students.

Finally, HR applications must support planning functions. These include the creation and publication of organizational standards job classifications and compensation ranges for those classifications. Planning also includes determining future requirements for employees by level, experience, skill, and other factors.

Accounting and Finance Systems

Typical **accounting and finance systems** are listed in Figure 7-4. You know what a general ledger is from your accounting classes. Financial reporting applications use the general ledger data to produce financial statement and other reports for management, investors, and federal reporting agencies like the Securities and Exchange Commission (SEC).

Cost-accounting applications determine the marginal cost and relative profitability of products and product families. Budgeting applications allocate and schedule revenues and expenses and compare actual financial results to the plan.

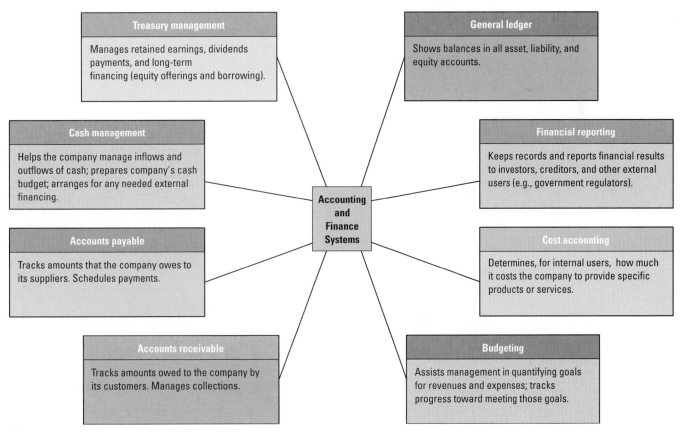

Figure 7-4
Accounting and Finance Systems

Accounts receivable includes not just recording receivables and the payments against receivables, but also account aging and collections management. Accounts payable systems include features to reconcile payments against purchases and to schedule payments according to the organization's payment policy.

Cash management is the process of scheduling payments and receivables and planning the use of cash so as to balance the organization's cash needs against cash availability. Other financial management applications concern checking and other account reconciliation as well as managing electronic funds transfer throughout the organization. Finally, treasury applications concern the management and investment of the organization's cash, as well as the payment of cash dividends.

Sales and Marketing Systems

Typical **sales and marketing systems** are shown in Figure 7-5. They store data about potential customers, their product interests, and contacts with them by sales personnel for lead-tracking purposes. Sales management uses sales forecasting systems to predict future sales. Typically, such systems add projections from individual salespeople together to obtain a territory projection and then add the territory projections together to obtain a regional projection, and so forth. Management uses the result of these calculations to plan company operations as well as to produce revenue projections for the investment community.

Customer management systems maintain customer contact data, credit status, past orders, and other data. The difference between a customer and a lead is that customers have actually ordered. In some organizations, lead tracking and customer management data are processed by a single system.

Marketing personnel use product management systems, which include a variety of different functions. Some systems report product sales by product, product category, location, channel, and so forth. The marketing staff uses this information to evaluate the success of products and to assess the effectiveness of marketing activities, including promotions, advertising, sales channels, and so forth.

Operations Systems

Operations activities concern the management of finished-goods inventory and the movement of goods from that inventory to the customer. **Operations systems** are especially prominent for nonmanufacturers, such as distributors, wholesalers, and retailers. For manufacturing companies, many, if not all, of the operations functions are merged into manufacturing systems.

Figure 7-6 lists the principal operations systems. Order entry systems record customer purchases. Typically, an order entry system obtains customer contact and ship-

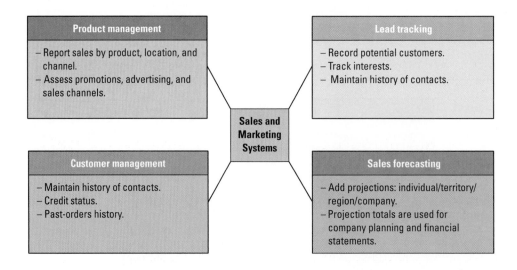

Figure 7-5
Sales and Marketing Systems

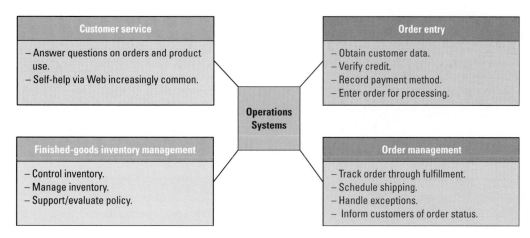

Figure 7-6
Operations Systems

ping data, verifies customer credit, validates payment method, and enters the order into a queue for processing. Order management systems track the order through the fulfillment process, arrange for and schedule shipping, and process exceptions such as out-of-stock products. Order management systems inform customers of order status and scheduled delivery dates.

In nonmanufacturing organizations, operations systems include systems to manage finished-goods inventory. We will not address those systems here; see the discussion of inventory in the discussion of manufacturing systems in the next section. As you read that discussion, just realize that nonmanufacturers do not have raw materials or goods-in-process inventories. They only have finished-goods inventories.

Customer service is the last operations system in Figure 7-6. Customers call customer service to ask questions about products, order status, and problems and to make complaints. Today, many organizations are placing as much of the customer service function on Web pages as they can. Many organizations allow customers direct access to order status and delivery information. Also, organizations are increasingly providing product-use support via Web systems.

Manufacturing Systems

Manufacturing systems facilitate the production of goods. As shown in Figure 7-7 (page 202), manufacturing systems include inventory, planning, scheduling, and manufacturing operations. We begin with inventory.

Inventory Systems

Information systems facilitate inventory control, management, and policy. In terms of inventory control, inventory applications track goods and materials into, out of, and between inventories. Inventory tracking requires that items be identified by a number. In the least sophisticated systems, employees must enter inventory numbers manually. Today, however, most systems use UPC bar codes (the familiar bar code you find on items at the grocery store) to scan product numbers as items move in and out of inventories.

In the future, **radio frequency identification tags (RFIDs)** will be in widespread use. In fact, in 2003 Wal-Mart dictated that all of its suppliers will be required to place RFIDs on all products they supply. An RFID is a computer chip that transmits data about the container or product to which it is attached. RFID data include not just product numbers, but also data about where the product was made, what the components are, special handling requirements, and, for perishable products, when the contents will expire. RFIDs facilitate inventory tracking by signaling their presence to scanners as they are moved throughout the manufacturing facility.

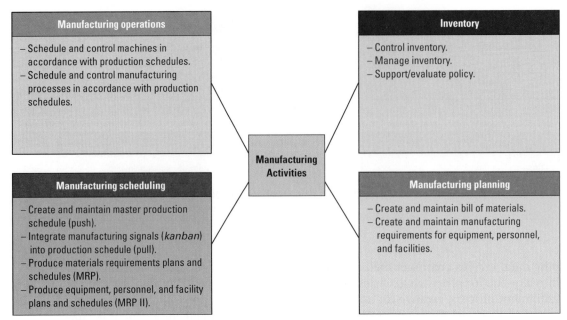

Figure 7-7
Manufacturing Activities Supported by Information Systems

Inventory management applications use past data to compute stocking levels, reorder levels, and reorder quantities in accordance with inventory policy. They also have features for assisting inventory counts and for computing inventory losses from those counts and from inventory-processing data.

With regard to inventory policy, there are two schools of thought in modern operations management. Some companies view inventories primarily as assets. In this view, large inventories are beneficial. Their cost is justified because large inventories minimize disruptions in operations or sales due to outages. Large finished-goods inventories increase sales by offering greater product selection and availability to the customer.

Other companies, such as Dell, view inventories primarily as liabilities. In this view, companies seek to keep inventories as small as possible and to eliminate them completely if possible. The ultimate expression of this view is demonstrated in the **just-in-time (JIT) inventory policy**. This policy seeks to have production inputs (both raw materials and work-in-process) delivered to the manufacturing site just as they are needed. By scheduling delivery of inputs in this way, companies are able to reduce inventories to a minimum.

Still others use both philosophies: Wal-Mart, for example, has large inventories in its stores, but minimizes all other inventories in its warehouses and distribution centers.

Inventory applications help an organization implement its particular philosophy and determine the appropriate balance between inventory cost and item availability, given that philosophy. Features include computing the inventory's return on investment (ROI), reports on the effectiveness of current inventory policy, and some means of evaluating alternative inventory policies by performing what-if analyses.

Manufacturing-Planning Systems

In order to plan materials for manufacturing, it is first necessary to record the components of the manufactured items. A **bill of materials (BOM)** is a list of the materials that comprise a product. This list is more complicated than it might sound, because the materials that comprise a product can be subassemblies that need to be manufactured. Thus, the BOM is a list of materials, and materials within materials, and materials within materials within materials, and so forth.

In addition to the BOM, if the manufacturing application schedules equipment, people, and facilities, then a record of those resources for each manufactured product is required as well. The company may augment the BOM to show labor and equipment requirements or it may create a separate nonmaterial requirements file.

Figure 7-8 shows a sample BOM for a child's red wagon having four components: handle bar, wagon body, front-wheel assembly, and rear-wheel assembly. Three of these have the subcomponent parts shown. Of course, each of these subcomponents could have sub-subcomponents, and so forth, but these are not shown. Altogether, the BOM shows all of the parts needed to make the wagon and the relationships of those parts to each other.

Manufacturing-Scheduling Systems

Companies use three philosophies to create a manufacturing schedule. One is to generate a **master production schedule (MPS)**, which is a plan for producing products. To create the MPS, the company analyzes past sales levels and makes estimates of future sales. This process is sometimes called a **push manufacturing process**, because the company wants to push the products into sales (and customers) according to the MPS.

Figure 7-9 (page 204) shows a manufacturing schedule for wagon production at a toy company. This plan includes three colors of wagons and shows subtle production increases prior to the summer months and prior to the holiday season. Again, the company obtains these production levels by analyzing past sales. The MPS for an actual manufacturer would, of course, be more complicated.

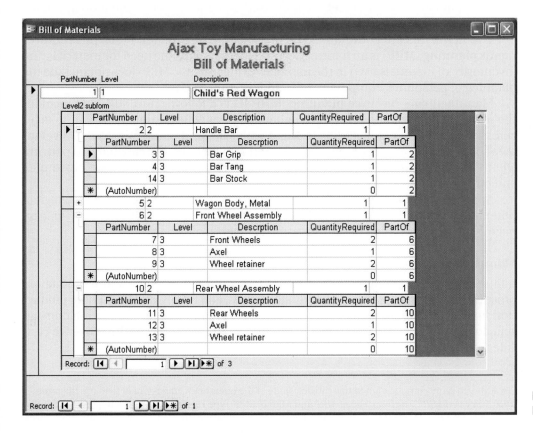

Figure 7-8
Bill of Materials Example

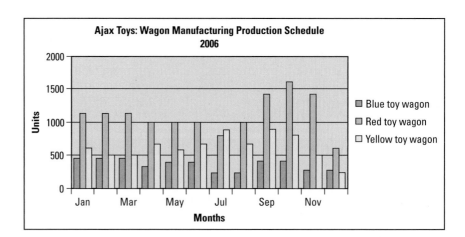

Figure 7-9
Sample Manufacturing Plan

A second philosophy is not to use a preplanned, forecasted schedule, but rather to plan manufacturing in response to signals from customers or downstream production processes that products or components are currently needed. The Japanese word *kanban*, which means "card," is sometimes used to refer to the signal to build something. Manufacturing processes that respond to kanbans must be more flexible than those that are MPS based. A process based on such signals is sometimes called a **pull manufacturing process**, because the products are pulled through manufacturing by demand.

Finally, a third philosophy is a combination of the two. The company creates an MPS and plans manufacturing according to the MPS, but it uses kanban-like signals to modify the schedule. For example, if the company receives signals that indicate increased customer demand, it might add an extra production shift for a while in order to build inventory to meet the increased demand. This combination approach requires sophisticated information systems for implementation.

Two acronyms are common in the manufacturing domain: **Materials requirements planning (MRP)** is an information system that plans the need for materials and inventories of materials used in the manufacturing process. MRP does not include the planning of personnel, equipment, or facilities requirements.

Manufacturing resource planning (MRP II) is a follow-on to MRP that includes the planning of materials, personnel, and machinery. MRP II supports many linkages across the organization, including linkages with sales and marketing via the development of a master production schedule. MRP II also includes the capability to perform what-if analyses on variances in schedules, raw materials availabilities, personnel, and other resources.[1]

Applications that integrate the activities of two or more departments have great potential to streamline manufacturing operations. However, read the *Ethics Guide* on page 205a for a discussion of some possible dangers.

Manufacturing Operations

A fourth category of IS in manufacturing is the control of machinery and production processes. Computer programs operate lathes, mills, and robots, and even entire production lines. In a modern facility, these programs have linkages to the manufacturing-scheduling systems. Because they are not information systems in the sense we consider in this text, we will not consider them further.

---

[1]To add even more complication to this subject, some in the operations management field use the terms *MRP Type I* and *MRP Type II* instead of *MRP* and *MRP II*. MRP Type I refers to materials requirements planning; MRP Type II refers to manufacturing resource planning. When used this way, the different interpretations of the letters MRP are ignored, as if MRP were not an acronym. Unfortunately, such sets of confusing terminology cannot be avoided in a growing field.

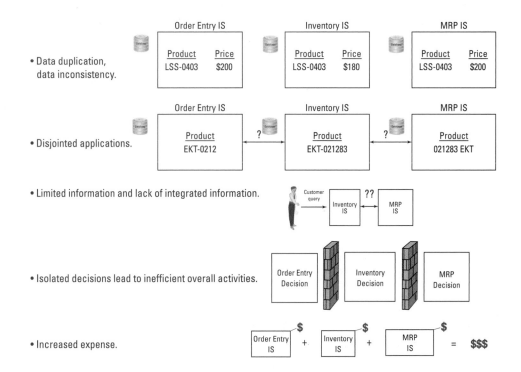

- Data duplication, data inconsistency.

- Disjointed applications.

- Limited information and lack of integrated information.

- Isolated decisions lead to inefficient overall activities.

- Increased expense.

Figure 7-10
Major Problems of Isolated Functional Systems

The Problems of Functional Systems

Functional systems provide tremendous benefits to the departments that use them, but as stated earlier, they are limited because they operate in isolation. In particular, functional systems have the problems listed in Figure 7-10. First, with isolated systems, data are duplicated because each application has its own database. For example, customer data may be duplicated and possibly inconsistent when accounting and sales/marketing applications are separated. As you learned in Chapter 4, the principal problem of duplicated data is a potential lack of data integrity. Changes to product data made in one system may take days or weeks to reach the other systems. During that period, inconsistent data will cause inconsistent application results.

Additionally, when systems are isolated, business processes are disjointed. There is no easy way for the sales/marketing system, for example, to integrate activity with the accounting system. Just sending the data from one system to the other can be problematic.

Consider the simple example in Figure 7-11. Suppose the order entry system defines a product number as four characters, a dash, and nine numeric digits. Yet, suppose the MRP system in the same company defines a product as eight digits followed by four characters. (That is, the MRP system does not use the first digit of the order entry's nine-digit product number.) Every time parts data are exported from order entry and imported into MRP (or the reverse), the data must be converted from one scheme to the other. Multiply this conversion process by several hundred data items, and possibly dozens of other systems, and you can see why processing is disjointed across functional applications.

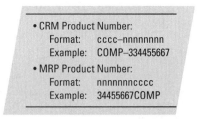

- CRM Product Number:
    Format: cccc–nnnnnnnn
    Example: COMP–334455667
- MRP Product Number:
    Format: nnnnnnnncccc
    Example: 34455667COMP

Figure 7-11
Example of System Integration Problem

Dialing for Dollars

Suppose you are a salesperson and your company's sales forecasting system predicts that your quarterly sales will be substantially under quota. You call your best customers to increase sales, but no one is willing to buy more.

Your boss says that it has been a bad quarter for all of the salespeople. It's so bad, in fact, that the VP of Sales has authorized a 20 percent discount on new orders. The only stipulation is that customers must take delivery prior to the end of the quarter so that accounting can book the order. "Start dialing for dollars," she says, "and get what you can. Be creative."

Using your customer management system, you identify your top customers and present the discount offer to them. The first customer balks at increasing her inventory, "I just don't think we can sell that much."

"Well," you respond, "how about if we agree to take back any inventory you don't sell next quarter?" (By doing this, you increase your current sales and commission, and you also help your company make its quarterly sales projections. The additional product is likely to come back next quarter, but you think, "Hey, that's then and this is now.")

"OK," she says, "but I want you to stipulate the return option on the purchase order."

You know that you cannot write that on the purchase order because accounting won't book all of the order if you do. So you tell her that you'll send her an email with that stipulation. She increases her order, and accounting books the full amount.

With another customer, you try a second strategy. Instead of offering the discount, you offer the product at full price, but agree to pay a 20 percent credit in the next quarter. That way you can book the full price now. You pitch this offer as follows: "Our marketing department analyzed past sales using our fancy new CRM computer system, and we know that increasing advertising will cause additional sales. So, if you order more product now, next quarter we'll give you 20 percent of the order back to pay for advertising."

In truth, you doubt the customer will spend the money on advertising. Instead, they'll just take the credit and sit on a bigger inventory. That will kill your sales to them next quarter, but you'll solve that problem then.

Even with these additional orders, you're still under quota. In desperation, you decide to sell product to a fictitious company that is "owned" by your brother-in-law. You set up a new account, and when accounting calls your brother-in-law for a credit check, he cooperates with your scheme. You then sell $40,000 of product to the fictitious company and ship the product to your brother-in-law's garage. Accounting books the revenue in the quarter, and you have finally made quota. A week into the next quarter, your brother-in-law returns the merchandise.

Meanwhile, unknown to you, your company's MRP II system is scheduling production. The program that creates the MPS reads the sales from your activities (and those of the other salespeople) and finds a sharp increase in product demand. Accordingly, it generates an MPS that calls for substantial production increases and schedules workers for the production runs. The MRP system, in turn, schedules the material requirements with the inventory application, which increases raw materials purchases to meet the increased production schedule.

DISCUSSION QUESTIONS

1. Is it ethical for you to write the email agreeing to take the product back? If that email comes to light later, what do you think your boss will say?

2. Is it ethical for you to offer the "advertising" discount? What effect does that discount have on your company's balance sheet?

3. Is it ethical for you to ship to the fictitious company? Is it legal?

4. Describe the impact of your activities on next quarter's inventories.

A consequence of such disjointed systems is the lack of integrated enterprise data. When a customer inquires about an order, several systems may need to be queried. For example, some order information is in the order entry system, some is in the finished-goods inventory system, and some is in the MRP system. Obtaining a consolidated statement about the customer's order will require processing each of these systems, with possibly inconsistent data.

A fourth consequence of isolated systems is inefficiency. When using isolated functional systems, a department can make decisions based only on the isolated data that it has. So, for example, raw materials inventory systems will make inventory replenishment decisions based only on costs and benefits in that single inventory. However, it might be that the overall efficiency of the sales, order entry, and manufacturing systems, considered together across the enterprise, will be improved by carrying a less than optimal number of products in raw materials inventory.

Finally, isolated functional systems can result in increased cost for the organization. Duplicated data, disjointed systems, limited information, and inefficiencies all mean higher costs.

Organizations recognized the problems of isolated systems back in the 1980s, and business consultants began searching for ways to build more integrated systems. In the mid-1980s, Michael Porter published important models that laid the foundation for the development of integrated systems. We consider those models next.

Competitive Strategy and Value Chains

When Michael Porter wrote the now-classic book *Competitive Advantage* in the mid-1980s, his ideas laid the groundwork for solving the problems of isolated information systems.[2] In his book, Porter defined and described *value chains*, which are networks of business activity that exist within an organization. Value chains pointed the way for moving away from the isolation of functional systems.

In addition to value chains, Porter's book also developed a model of competitive strategies that helps organizations choose which information systems to develop. We will begin with competitive advantage and then define value chains. After that, we will explain how organizations use value chains for process-oriented systems. (Chapter 8 addresses another aspect of Porter's work—his model of five competitive forces.)

Competitive Strategies

According to Porter, a firm can engage in one of the four fundamental competitive strategies shown in Figure 7-12. An organization can focus on being the cost leader or it can focus on differentiating its products from the competition. Further, the organization can employ the cost or differentiation strategy across an industry or it can focus its strategy on a particular industry segment.

Consider the car rental industry, for example. According to the first column of Figure 7-12, a car rental company can strive to provide the lowest-cost car rentals across the industry or it can seek to provide the lowest-cost car rentals to an industry segment, say, U.S. domestic business travelers.

As shown in the second column, a car rental company can seek to differentiate its products from the competition. It can do so in various ways: for example, by providing a wide range of high-quality cars, by providing the best reservations system, by having the cleanest cars or the fastest check-in, or by some other means. The company can strive to provide product differentiation across the industry or within particular segments of the industry, such as U.S. domestic business travelers.

---

[2]Michael Porter, *Competitive Advantage* (New York: Free Press, 1985).

You Be the Guide

Using the Ethics Guide

(page 205a)

GOALS

* Understand how business pressures motivate people to act unethically and sometimes illegally.

* Illustrate how deception in the use of an interdepartmental information system may cause unintended consequences.

BACKGROUND AND PRESENTATION STRATEGIES

The stock market is *brutal to companies that miss their quarterly sales projections.* The pressure on a company to make its numbers can be over the top—especially on small-cap companies that are new, have a limited track record, and have limited cash reserves. Stock prices on such companies can fall by two-thirds of their value in a day.

The software industry has used all three of the techniques in this guide, especially during the 1990s and early 2000s. These techniques, when applied to distributor-customers, are often referred to as *stuffing the channel.* It's a risky strategy; the company is just putting this quarter's problem into the next quarter, where, unless there is a substantial increase in sales demand, the problem will be worse. Managers do it or look the other way when it's being done, because putting off the stock price slaughter for one quarter is at least putting it off for one quarter.

The three techniques used here are:

• The side letter

• The delayed discount

• The fictitious account

I believe that *all three of the stuffing techniques are unethical.* Furthermore, the first and third violate SEC rules and regulations and the *last one is criminally fraudulent.*

In class, I've used the following sequence of questions to introduce this guide:

➤ **Why is the company doing this?**

➤ **What are the techniques used here?**

➤ **Which of these techniques is criminally fraudulent?**

➤ **Which are violations of SEC rules and regulations?**

➤ **Which are unethical?**

The *surprise in this guide* is the impact these actions have on manufacturing scheduling. Given cross-departmental systems, the fictitious increased sales activity *generates increased production activity,* thus compounding the company's problems in the next quarter. The company will have a huge finished goods inventory—from returns and also from the increased production activity. The stock market will note the increased inventory, and even more pressure will come to the beleaguered company (though they brought it on themselves).

Such ethical issues are, by the way, not new: *"Oh, the tangled web we weave, when first we practice to deceive!"* (Sir Walter Scott, *Marmion*). Here, we've automated the tangled web—*increased the productivity of entanglement.*

This company is in serious trouble. At this point, *all choices are bad.* It's a "pick your least regret" situation. I believe that this company, unlike Universal, is a company to leave, and soon. These practices are unethical, and the company will ultimately fail. The bloodbath, when it happens, will be huge.

 SUGGESTED RESPONSES FOR DISCUSSION QUESTIONS

1. To me, *the email involves deception.* The reason for writing it is to avoid a control placed by the accounting department. In almost every case, actions taken for the purpose of deception are unethical. The second part of this question is a good one to ask the class:

   ➤ **If the email comes to light later, what will your boss say?**

   Your boss will likely deny direct involvement. You boss won't deny that such letters are written, but he or she will never admit (nor will there be evidence to prove) that it was encouraged. You'll be left holding the bag, so to speak.

   Additional questions to add reality to this vignette:

   ➤ **What would you do if you found yourself employed by a company that encouraged such practices?**

   Suppose you like where you live, your kids are happy in school, and your spouse has a great job.

   ➤ **Would you change jobs just because of this problem?**

2. I think the delayed discount via the advertising letter is deceptive, and hence unethical. But sometimes I play devil's advocate as follows:

➤ **Is this clearly less unethical than the email? The customer might use the discount for advertising. If they don't, it's not my fault.**

Yes, that might be, but the entire action is based on deception. And there's an additional lie:

➤ **How likely is it that the salesperson's "fancy CRM" produced information about the utility of advertising?**

➤ **Can any course of action that involves a lie ever be ethical? Why or why not?**

To answer the rest of the question in the text, the impact on the balance sheet is to overstate revenue in this quarter.

3. Shipping to the fictitious company is both *illegal and unethical*. This is *"Go to jail"* activity. DO NOT engage in such activity. Enough said!

4. The email and the fictitious company actions will cause excessive inventory next quarter. All of this is "behind the scenes," so no information system will have been programmed to expect the large returns that are going to occur. And, as pointed out in the next question, the sales this quarter may cause the MPS to increase production.

Another question to ask:

➤ **What would you do if you worked as an inventory manager in this company? How would you plan your inventory?**

This organization *is in a very interesting bind*. Inventories are going to go up unless someone tells production to ignore the depletion of inventory. But this means that someone has to explain to why. If they explain why, however, then what was a "dirty little secret" *in sales* becomes a "dirty little secret" *across the company*. Is this the culture that any company wants to create? And yet, if they miss their numbers badly, the organization will be in trouble.

➤ **Which is better: Work in a company with a culture of keeping "dirty little secrets" or work in a troubled company?**

5. The sales manager will probably begin to reduce sales activity by some factor in his planning. He'll have to guess, because no one is likely to tell him which sales are phony. Long-term production planning becomes impossible.

To me, this is a fascinating consequence of these unethical practices. If top management is not aware of the channel stuffing that sales is doing (unlikely, but possible), the production manager might be called on the carpet—at least for increasing production because of the perceived phony sales.

In my experience, *production people and sales people have very different personalities with very different values.* Production people crave organization, accuracy, and quality. Sales people crave human interaction, flexibility, optimism, and "we can do it" attitudes. The two types are like oil and water. I see a possibly explosive meeting between these two groups.

If the class is willing, it might be worthwhile to *conduct a mock hallway interchange*—have one student (majoring in, say, marketing) represent the sales person and another (majoring in, say, production management) represent the production manager. You can be the CEO!

Cue the students: *The production manager is irate and righteous;* the salesperson is *guilty,* but thrilled to have *made the numbers.* The salesperson feels like he or she has *pulled the company* out of a disaster.

6. It will take a miracle to stop this cycle. The company will have to have an incredibly strong next quarter. Without that, they'll be dialing for dollars again. And next quarter, the problem will be amplified; they'll be dialing for even more dollars. This cannot go on. Ultimately, they will have a bad quarter—with consequences much worse than they would have had if they'd have taken the hit in the first bad quarter.

WRAP UP

➤ **The easiest response to this scenario is to say "I'll never work for a company like that." But, what if you like the company and situations like this only come around every 18 months or so—and then it's only the occasional side letter?**

➤ **Would you stay here?**

➤ **Last point: With process-based, interdepartmental systems, the actions of one department influence those of another. In this case, deception breeds deception.**

	Cost	Discrimination
Industry-wide	Lowest cost across the industry	Better product/service across the industry
Focus	Lowest cost within an industry segment	Better product/service within an industry segment

Figure 7-12
Porter's Four Competitive Strategies

According to Porter, to be effective, the organization's goals, objectives, culture, and activities must be consistent with the organization's strategy. To those in the MIS field, this means that all information systems in the organization must facilitate the organization's strategy.

The Value Chain

Although competitive strategy is important, it is Porter's concept of the value chain that is most helpful in defining integrated, process-based information systems. **Value**, in Porter's model, is the total revenue that a customer is willing to spend for a product or service. Porter stressed value rather than cost, because an organization that has a differentiation strategy may intentionally raise costs in order to create value. Such an organization must ensure, however, that cost increases provide sufficient additional value to obtain a positive **margin**, which is the term Porter uses as the difference between value and cost.

A **value chain** is a network of value-creating activities. Figure 7-13 shows the generic value chain model as developed by Porter. That generic chain consists of five **primary activities** and four **support activities**.

Primary Activities in the Value Chain

To understand the essence of the value chain, consider a small manufacturer—say, a bicycle maker. First, the manufacturer acquires raw materials using the inbound logistics activity. This activity concerns the receiving and handling of raw materials and other inputs. The accumulation of those materials adds value in the sense that even a pile of unassembled parts is worth something to some customer. A collection of the parts needed to build a bicycle is worth more than an empty space on a shelf. The value is not only the parts themselves, but also the time required to contact vendors

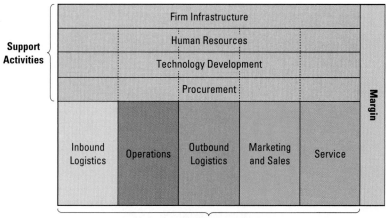

Figure 7-13
Porter's Value Chain Model

Source: Reprinted with the permission of The Free Press, a Division of Simon & Schuster Adult Publishing Group, from Competitive Advantage: Creating and Sustaining Superior Performance, Copyright © 1985, 1998 by Michael E. Porter. All rights reserved.

for those parts, to maintain business relationships with those vendors, to order the parts, to receive the shipment, and so forth.

In the operations activity, the bicycle maker transforms raw materials into a finished bicycle; a process that adds more value. Next, the company uses the outbound logistics activity to deliver the finished bicycle to a customer. Of course, there is no customer to send the bicycle to without the marketing and sales value activity. Finally, the service activity provides customer support to the bicycle users.

Each stage of this generic chain accumulates costs and adds value to the product. The net result is the total margin of the chain, which is the difference between the total value added and the total costs incurred. Figure 7-14 summarizes the primary activities of the value chain.

The value chain in Figure 7-13 is generic. It must be adapted to specific businesses. Consider, for example, adapting that generic chain to your university, say, to the business of undergraduate education. Think about the activities on your campus for each of these five primary activities.

Support Activities in the Value Chain

The support activities in the generic value chain contribute indirectly to the production, sale, and service of the product. They include procurement, which consists of the processes of finding vendors, setting up contractual arrangements, and negotiating prices. (This differs from inbound logistics, which is concerned with ordering and receiving in accordance with agreements set up by procurement.)

Porter defined technology broadly. It includes research and development, but it also includes other activities within the firm for developing new techniques, methods, and procedures. He defined human resources in the same way that we defined it for functional systems. Finally, firm infrastructure includes general management, finance, accounting, legal, and government affairs.

Supporting functions add value, albeit indirectly, and they also have costs. Hence, as shown in Figure 7-13, supporting functions produce a margin. In the case of supporting functions, it would be difficult to calculate the margin because the specific value added of, say, the manufacturer's lobbyists in Washington, D.C., is difficult to know. But, there is a value added, there are costs, and there is a margin, even if it is only in concept.

Linkages in the Value Chain

Porter's model of business activities includes **linkages**, which are interactions across value activities. Linkages are important sources of efficiencies and are readily supported by information systems. For example, MRP and MRP II are functional systems that use linkages to reduce inventory costs. Manufacturing uses sales forecasts to plan production; it then uses the production plan to determine raw materials needs, and

Figure 7-14
Task Descriptions for Primary Activities of the Value Chain

Source: Reprinted with the permission of The Free Press, a Division of Simon & Schuster Adult Publishing Group, from Competitive Advantage: Creating and Sustaining Superior Performance, Copyright © 1985, 1998 by Michael E. Porter. All rights reserved.

Primary Activity	Description
Inbound logistics	Receiving, storing, and disseminating inputs to the product
Operations	Transforming inputs into the final product
Outbound logistics	Collecting, storing, and physically distributing the product to buyers
Marketing and sales	Inducing buyers to purchase the product and providing a means for them to do so
Service	Assisting customer's use of the product and thus maintaining and enhancing the product's value

then uses the material needs to schedule purchases. The end result is just-in-time inventory, which reduces inventory sizes and costs.

By describing value chains and their linkages, Porter started a movement to create integrated, cross-departmental business systems. Over time, Porter's work led to the creation of a new discipline called *business process design.*

Business Process Design

Video

Porter's work resonated with the thinking of many business consultants, analysts, and other professionals. The idea of the value chain as a network of value-creating activities became the foundation of a movement called **business process design**, or sometimes *business process redesign*. The central idea is that organizations should not automate or improve existing functional systems. Rather they should create new, more efficient business processes that integrate the activities of all departments involved in a value chain.

Thus, in the early 1990s some organizations began to design cross-departmental business processes. The goal was to take advantage of as many activity linkages as possible. For example, a cross-departmental customer management process integrates all interactions with the customer, from prospect, through initial order, through repeat orders, including customer support, credit, and accounts receivable.

Challenges of Business Process Design

Unfortunately, process design projects are expensive and difficult. Highly trained systems analysts interview key personnel from many departments and document the existing system as well as one or more system alternatives. Managers review the results of the analysts' activity, usually many times, and attempt to develop new, improved processes. Then new information systems are developed to implement those new business processes. All of this takes time, and meanwhile, the underlying processes are changing, which means the process design may need to be redesigned before the project is completed.

Once these difficulties have been overcome and the new integrated systems designed, an even greater challenge arises: Employees resist change. People do not want to work in new ways, they do not want to see their department reorganized or abolished, and they do not want to work for someone new. Even if the system can be implemented over this resistance, some people will continue to resist. All of these difficulties translate into labor hours, which translate into costs. Thus, business process design is very expensive.

Even worse, the ultimate outcome is uncertain. An organization that embarks on a business process design project does not know ahead of time how effective the ultimate outcome will be.

Some businesses were successful in their process design activities, but many others failed. In some cases, millions of dollars were spent on projects that ultimately were abandoned. The idea of designing business processes for greater integration was floundering when it received a boost from an unexpected source: integrated application vendors.

Benefits of Inherent Processes

Many early business process design projects failed because they were tailor-made. They were custom-fit to a particular organization, and so just one company bore the cost of the design effort. In the mid-1990s, a number of successful software vendors began to market premade integrated applications, with built-in processes. See, for example, the companies discussed in the *MIS in Use 7-1* (page 210) case.

When an organization acquires, say, a business application from Oracle or SAP, the processes for using the software are built-in or **inherent processes**. In most cases,

Business Process Application Vendors

The following figure lists the largest and most successful vendors of business process applications. With one exception, all of these vendors began by specializing in an application for a single business process. As each vendor achieved success with its first application, it developed applications for other processes or obtained them via acquisition. Ultimately, the successful vendors had applications for all major business processes. They then merged those applications into a suite of products and called that suite their enterprise resource planning (ERP) solution. (This solution will be discussed later in this chapter.)

PeopleSoft is a typical business process application vendor. PeopleSoft began with a payroll application that it broadened to a complete human resources application. Then, the company added more and more applications to its suite. In 2003, it acquired JD Edwards, a company that specialized in inventory and manufacturing applications. By combining its in-house developed applications with those obtained from JD Edwards, PeopleSoft has applications for a

majority of organizational value chain activities and can now claim it offers an integrated IS solution. (In fall 2004, Oracle acquired PeopleSoft.)

SAP is the exception to this strategy. SAP invented the integrated-IS category. Instead of developing an application for one or two value chain activities, SAP began with a design for a full suite of applications that supported all organizational activities.

SAP took the early lead in ERP, but is being challenged today by the other vendors that developed integrated information systems by adding more and more applications to their suites. Over time, the offerings of all of these companies begin to look more and more alike. Sometime soon, organizational information systems will become an "ERP commodity," with one suite barely distinguishable from another in terms of functionality.

Major software vendors like Oracle and Microsoft didn't wait on the sidelines while these new software businesses emerged. IBM, Oracle, and Microsoft began in-house development and acquisition programs to obtain organizational applications software. Today, these three firms claim to offer full, integrated IS solutions; ultimately, given their financial strength, they will probably spend until they are successful. Time will tell.

Major Applications Vendors		
PeopleSoft	Human resources	Acquired by Oracle in 2004
JD Edwards	Manufacturing	Acquired by PeopleSoft in 2003
Siebel Systems	Salesforce automation Customer relationship management	$1.339 billion in 2004; acquired by Oracle in 2005
SAP	Enterprise resource management	$10.179 billion in 2004
Great Plains	Accounting	Acquired by Microsoft in 2003
Oracle	Application suite developed on DBMS sales	$10.156 billion in 2004
Microsoft	Application suite from acquisitions and in-house development	$36.835 billion in 2004

the organization must conform its activities to those processes. If the software is designed well, the inherent processes will effectively integrate activities across departments. These prebuilt processes will save the organization the substantial, sometimes staggering, costs of designing new processes itself.

Figure 7-15 (page 212) shows an example of an inherent process in a software product called SAP R/3, a product licensed by SAP. When an organization licenses this product, SAP provides hundreds of diagrams just like this one. These diagrams show the business processes that must be created in order to effectively use the software.

This diagram shows the flow and logic of one set of inherent processes. In the top lines, if the purchase requisition does not exist and if the RFQ (request for quotation) is to be created, then the purchasing department creates an RFQ and sends it to potential vendors. You can read through the rest of this sample diagram to obtain the gist of this process snippet.

To some, when an organization licenses cross-departmental software, the primary benefit is not the software, but the inherent processes in the software. Licensing an integrated application not only saves the organization the time, expense, and agony of process design, it also enables the organization to benefit immediately from tried and tested cross-departmental processes.

Of course, there is a disadvantage. The inherent processes may be very different from existing processes and thus require the organization to change substantially. Such change will be disruptive to ongoing operations and very disturbing to employees. The *Problem Solving Guide* on page 211a discusses the effects of organizational change in more detail.

Three Examples of Integrated, Cross-Functional Information Systems

We conclude this chapter with three examples that demonstrate the nature of integrated, cross-functional information systems:

- Customer relationship management (CRM)
- Enterprise resource planning (ERP)
- Enterprise application integration (EAI)

The first, customer relationship management, integrates all of the processes that touch the customer. The second, enterprise resource planning, integrates all the direct activities in the organization: logistics, operations, manufacturing, sales and marketing, and support. Finally, the third, enterprise application integration, is a hybrid that provides many (but not all) of the benefits of integration, but without the agony of replacing existing systems.

One warning: When you read descriptions of business processes and applications at vendor sites on the Web, in trade magazines and journals, and in vendor product descriptions, you will find inconsistent terminology. Each vendor defines terms to present its products most advantageously. For example, Oracle's Siebel Systems, which began with applications to help salespeople prioritize prospects, defines CRM with an emphasis on new-customer, presale activities. On the other hand, SAP defines CRM very broadly, relating customer information to every value chain activity and making the entire business "customer centric." Thus, vendors and authors use the same terms, but with different meanings and emphasis.

You may find the inconsistent terminology frustrating, but imagine the problem that inconsistent terminology creates for an organization that wishes to license one of these applications. Because vendors define CRM differently, when the company evaluates the applications, it will be comparing apples to oranges. What is a

PROBLEMSOLVING
G U I D E

Thinking About Change

New information systems, especially those that cross departmental boundaries, require employees to change. Employees may do their jobs differently, they may be assigned to a new job or a new boss or a new department, and they will probably work with new people. At the very least, they will certainly use new information systems forms, reports, and other features. Many organizations have found that implementing such change is the most difficult part of IS implementation.

Because organizational change is a common problem, a change management industry has emerged to help organizations deal with it. Change management is a blend of business, engineering, sociology, and psychology that strives to understand the dynamics of organizational change and to develop and communicate theories, methods, and techniques that enable successful organizational change.

According to Adel Aladwani (2001), the top obstacle to successful change is employee resistance. Employees resist change for several reasons. For one, change requires adapting to a new situation or system, and, for a while, all changes make work harder, not easier. Unless employees understand the need for change, they will be unwilling to devote the extra energy and work required.

To be willing to change, employees need to understand the importance of and need for the new system or project. The CEO or other senior manager needs to sponsor the new system. The sponsor should explain the rationale for the system at the onset and throughout the project. Many managers, when reviewing their projects after implementation, say that they did not communicate the need for the new system frequently enough. Experience shows that employees want to hear about the necessity for change from two people: the CEO and their immediate boss.

Another reason that employees resist change is fear of the unknown. Recent motivational research focuses on the concept of self-efficacy. Self-efficacy means that people believe they have the knowledge and skills necessary to be successful at their jobs. When employees feel that way, they not only are happier, but they also work better. Self-efficacy breeds success: When employees feel confident, they bring more and more of their natural abilities to the problems they face.

Change, however, threatens self-efficacy. When change is underway, people ask questions like, "Will I understand how to use the new system?" "Will I be as successful with it as I was in the past?" "Will I be asked to do things I don't know how to do?" Just having such questions impairs one's ability to work.

Because change is threatening, organizations need to take steps to increase employees' sense of self-efficacy. These steps must go beyond explaining the need for the system. Employees need to be shown how the new system will improve their work situation. They need to be trained on new procedures. If possible, employees should be given opportunities to gain confidence in the new system and in their ability to use it. They also need to see others, either employees in their own organization or other organizations, achieve positive outcomes from the new system. Some organizations find that creating networks or alliances of employees helps to reduce the stress of the change.

In a recent study, Siebel Systems identified a number of key factors in successful change management. Of those factors, two emerged as most important: bosses' behavior and communication. Employees respond to how the boss responds. If their boss supports the change, not just with words, but also with his attitude and actions, then employees are more likely to accept the change. Also, frequent two-way communication is important. Management frequently needs to explain the rationale and importance of the change, and employees need frequent opportunities to express their thoughts and feelings about the change.

Employees tend to support what they create. When employees are given an opportunity to participate in the change and to express their thoughts about the change (how it could be improved and so forth), they have a stake in the change and are more likely to support it.

Sources: Adel Aladwani, "Change Management Strategies for Successful ERP Implementation," *Business Process Management Journal*, vol. 7, no. 3, 2001, page 266; Siebel Systems, "Applied Change Management: A Key Ingredient for CRM Success," Siebel eBusiness, June 2003, *www.siebel.com/resource-library/reg-resource.shtm* (accessed June 2005); Tom Werner, "Change Management and E-Learning," *www.brandon-hall.com* (accessed September 2004).

DISCUSSION QUESTIONS

Imagine that your university announces that next semester students will be required to use a new information system to enroll in classes.

1. What is your first feeling (not thought) on hearing that news?

2. What would you like the university administration to communicate to you about the change?

3. Explain the term self-efficacy in relation to this change. What could the university do to increase your sense of self-efficacy?

4. Suppose a good friend tries the new system and says, "Hey, it's much better than the old one. Very easy to use." How does that affect your feelings about the change? What if your friend says, "It's terrible, such a hassle." How does that affect your feelings?

5. Given your answer to question 4, what programs could the university develop to reduce resistance to the change?

6. What might your professors say about the change that would cause you to feel better about it? What might your professors say that would cause you to feel worse about it?

7. In this situation, which is more powerful, the opinions of your good friend or the opinion of your professor? Explain your response. In business, which would be more important, your coworkers' opinions or those of your boss's?

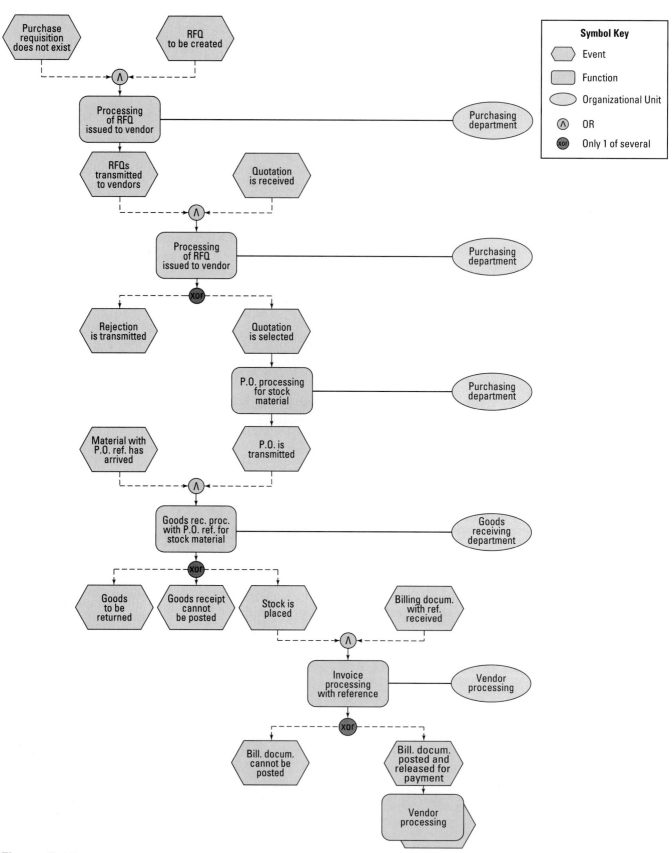

Figure 7-15
Example of SAP R/3 Ordering Process

Source: Curran, Thomas A.; Ladd, Andrew; Ladd, Dennis, *SAP R/3 Reporting and E-Business Intelligence*, 1st Edition,
© 2000. Reprinted by permission of Pearson Education, Inc., Upper Saddle River, NJ.

Using the Problem Solving Guide (page 211a)

Note: This guide works well with this chapter's Opposing Forces Guide.

GOALS

* Explain, demonstrate, or illustrate that humans resist change.

* Suggest ways that managers can reduce employee resistance to change.

BACKGROUND AND PRESENTATION STRATEGIES

Humans resist change. Whether from fear, anxiety, extra work, or loss of self-efficacy, humans do not like to change. One way to bring home the resistance to change is to play a hoax on the students.

HOAX PRESENTATION **(Alternatively, use the nonhoax presentation that follows.)**

The hoax: Start your presentation by reading the following *fake memo from the Dean:*

> *Starting this term, all students will be required to perform 100 hours of community service as part of their graduation requirement. The College of Business will provide a list of organizations that the students can serve. Students, especially seniors, are encouraged to visit their adviser as soon as possible to plan their community service. Advisers have been given special training to help students adapt to this change. See your adviser as soon as possible.*

(Possibly have a colleague read the memo as a special announcement.)

Now, to continue the hoax, ask questions like:

➤ **Can I answer any questions about this important new program?**

➤ **Are there any seniors in the class? You will need to get started right away!**

➤ **I can see that this program will place a burden on you. But it seems like an excellent idea. How many of you have done public service before?**

➤ **Has anyone heard whether past public service will count?**

Attempt to develop an emotional outrage, a belief that this just cannot be, and so forth. At some point, *reveal the hoax.*

➤ **How did you feel about this change?**

➤ **What did you think about this change?**

➤ **What if this were your job, and the issue was that your department had been broken up and you now worked for someone new?**

NONHOAX PRESENTATION (Skip if you used the hoax.) Suppose a business issues the following statement:

> *Because of efficiencies brought about by our new ERP system, your department has been abolished. You have been assigned to a new department. Your new boss is Ms. Jones, and you should see her immediately to learn your new job responsibilities.*

Some questions to ask the students:

➤ **As an employee, what is your first response?**

➤ **How likely are you, as an employee, to support the new program?**

➤ **How does the concept of self-efficacy apply to this situation?**

➤ **Consider two alternative statements from your boss:**

- **"I don't know why they did this. I think it's stupid. They're just trying to reduce costs and the whole program will cause a mess for years."**

- **"These new changes are important in order to compete internationally. If we don't make changes like this, unemployment will be rampant. I know this is awkward, but in the long run, this change will benefit the health of our organization and increase opportunities for the future."**

➤ **Explain the impact of your boss's statement on your attitude.**

 SUGGESTED RESPONSES FOR DISCUSSION QUESTIONS

Note: If you used the hoax, base these questions on the hoax situation. If not, use the new information system example in the questions.

1. Likely first feelings are fear, anger, resentment, frustration. All negative responses. Good questions to ask:

➤ **What do they fear?**

➤ **What are they angry about?**

➤ **Suppose the new system will actually make their lives easier. Will they still feel negatively? Why?**

2. According to the text, the communication should include not just why the change is necessary, but also how the students will be able to succeed with it—how it will make life easier *for the student* and how the student will have self-efficacy (see question 3).

Suppose the university says (adapt if you used the hoax):

➤ **This system will reduce administrative costs.**

➤ **This system will reduce administrative costs and enable a reduction in tuition.**

➤ **This system will make registration easier for you.**

➤ **What if the university says nothing at all?**

Which of these statements is most reassuring and helpful? Why?

3. Examples of self-efficacy are:

• "Will I be able to get the classes I want?"

• "How long will it take me?"

• "How long will it take me to learn the system?"

Another form of self-efficacy is the loss of the utility of knowledge.

• "I know how to manipulate the existing system to get what I want. Now, all that knowledge will be wasted."

The university could increase self-efficacy with training and examples of how easy the system will be to use. It could also provide testimonials from students who have used the new system.

4. In general, friends' opinions matter very much. However, people also adjust those opinions based on what they think of the friend: "Oh, she's an engineer; of course it will be easy for her" or "If he can do it, then so can I." Peer opinions are very important, but they are also hard to manage, and their consequences are difficult to predict. As stated in question 3, testimonials can be effective means for instituting change.

5. A resistance-reducing program could be a pilot program of students using the system. Then, have those students become coaches to others. Or, the university's Web site could post testimonials of the ease of use of the new system, and so on. All such efforts should be aimed at increasing student self-efficacy.

6. If the professor is viewed as a part of the administration, that is, as a paid voice for the administration, nothing positive the professor says will be trusted. Certainly, though, no matter how the professor is viewed, any negative statements the professor makes will have a seriously deleterious impact on student attitudes.

The parallel between students/professors and employees/managers may not be strong. Employees and managers are "all in it together" in a way that students and professors are not. The department manager works with the employees 40+ hours per week. The employees' frustrations will quickly become the manager's frustrations. Students and professors are more isolated from one another.

7. The students are likely to have some interesting comments here. If they feel unthreatened, they may reveal how they view professors, which could lead to some interesting discussion quite apart from the topic of this guide.

In my opinion, it depends on what they think of their professor/boss and what they think of their fellow students/co-workers. If the professor/boss seems trustworthy, that person's opinion probably means more than the student's/co-worker's.

Opinions vary, though. It will be interesting to see what your students say.

WRAP UP

List the five components of an information system: hardware, software, data, procedures, and people. Remind the students that these components are *listed in increasing order of difficulty of change.* Changing procedures and altering the organization, altering job descriptions, and creating new reporting structures can be incredibly difficult, as we have seen.

Self-efficacy is the key. Ask the students to summarize actions that management can take to offset the consequences of procedural and people (organizational and reporting to) changes.

feature of one product is an add-on to another and is not available in a third. Let the buyer beware.

Customer Relationship Management Systems

Customer relationship management (CRM) is the set of business processes for attracting, selling, managing, and supporting customers. The difference between CRM systems and traditional functional applications is that CRM addresses all activities and events that touch the customer and provides a single repository for data about all customer interactions. With functional systems, data about customers are sprinkled in databases all over the organization. Some customer data exist in customer management databases, some in order entry databases, some in customer service databases, and so forth. CRM systems store all customer data in one place and thus make it possible to access all data about the customer.

By the way, some CRM systems include activities that occur at the customer's site. Such systems thus support linkages between two organizations and hence are broader than the scope of this chapter. Accordingly, we will consider the within-organization aspects of CRM in this chapter and the among-organizations aspects of CRM in the next chapter when we discuss supply chain management.

Figure 7-16 shows four phases of the customer life cycle: marketing, customer acquisition, relationship management, and loss/churn. Marketing sends messages to the target market to attract customer prospects. When prospects order, they become customers who need to be supported. Additionally, resell processes increase the value of existing customers. Inevitably, over time the organization loses customers. When this occurs, win-back processes categorize customers according to value and attempt to win back high-value customers.

Figure 7-17 (page 214) shows the major components of a CRM system. Notice there are components for each stage of the customer life cycle. Information systems that support

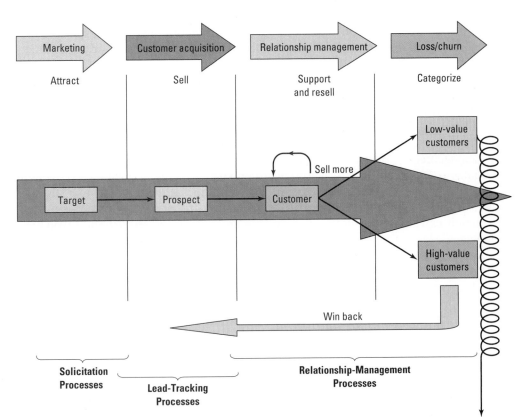

Figure 7-16
The Customer Life Cycle

Source: Douglas MacLachlan, University of Washington.

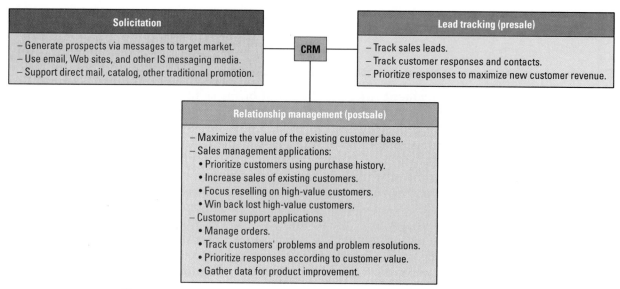

Figure 7-17
CRM Components

solicitation include email applications and organizational Web sites. Additionally, some information systems support traditional direct mail, catalog, and other solicitations.

The organizational Web site is an increasingly important solicitation tool. Web addresses are easy to promote (and remember), and a once a target prospect is on the site, product descriptions, use cases, success stories, and other solicitation materials can be provided easily. Further, the cost of distributing these materials via the Web is substantially less than the cost of creating and distributing printed materials. Many Web sites require customer name and contact information before releasing high-value promotional materials. That contact information then feeds lead-tracking applications.

The purpose of lead-tracking, or presale, applications is to turn prospects into customers. Such applications track sales leads and record customer responses and contacts. Most of these applications enable the sales department to prioritize contacts so as to focus on high-potential prospects.

Lead tracking is particularly important when multiple salespeople call on the same customer. Often salespeople may join forces to work out a strategy for sales calls and follow-ups. If nothing else, consolidated lead tracking can keep sales personnel from duplicating efforts and from interfering with one another.

With the first order, a prospect becomes a customer and is a candidate for relationship management applications. The purpose of relationship management applications is to maximize the value of the existing customer base. As Figure 7-17 shows, two types of applications are used. Sales management applications support sales to existing customers. They have features to prioritize customers according to their purchase history. Salespeople can increase sales to existing customers by focusing on customers who have already made large purchases, by focusing on large organizations that have the potential to make large purchases, or both. The goal of such applications is to ensure that sales management has sufficient information to prioritize and allocate sales time and effort.

Sales management applications also have features to prioritize lost customers, to determine which of those are high-value lost customers, and to help the sales team to develop a strategy to win those customers back. Surprisingly, it can be difficult for a company to know when it has lost a customer. A telephone company will know it has lost a customer when the customer cancels the service, but an online retailer many not know when it has lost a customer. In such a case, only an analysis of past purchase history can indicate that the customer is gone.

Of course, it is cheaper to keep an existing customer than to acquire a new customer or win back a lost one. Accordingly, another important component to relation-

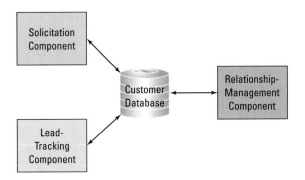

Figure 7-18
CRM Centered on Integrated
Customer Database

ship management is customer support. Order management applications help the customer to determine the status of an order, how and when it was shipped, the status of returns, and so forth. Additionally, other customer support applications track customer problems and resolutions and ensure that customers need not repeat their problem history to each new support representative.

Integrated CRM applications store data in a single database, as shown in Figure 7-18. Because all customer data reside in one location, CRM processes can be linked to one another. For example, customer service activities can be linked to customer purchase records. In this way, both sales and marketing know the status of customer satisfaction, both on an individual customer basis for future sales calls and also collectively for analyzing customers' overall satisfaction. Also, many customer support applications prioritize customers to avoid giving $10,000 worth of support to a customer with a lifetime value of $500. Finally, customer support has an important linkage to product marketing and development; it knows more than any other group what customers are doing with the product and what problems they are having with it.

Enterprise Resource Planning

Enterprise resource planning (ERP) integrates all of the organization's principal processes. ERP is an outgrowth of MRP II, and the primary ERP users are manufacturing companies. The first and most successful vendor of ERP software is SAP (SAP AG Corp., headquartered in Germany). More than 12 million people use SAP in over 88,000 SAP installations worldwide (*sap.com/company*, accessed March 2005).

Thus far, ERP represents the ultimate in cross-departmental process systems. ERP integrates sales, order, inventory, manufacturing, and customer service activities. ERP systems provide software, predesigned databases, procedures, and job descriptions for organization-wide process integration. For such changes, there can be resistance and opposition, as shown in the *Opposing Forces Guide* on page 215a.

Before continuing, be aware that some companies misapply the term ERP to their systems. It is a hot topic, and there is no truth-in-ERP-advertising group to ensure that all of the vendors that claim ERP capability have anything remotely similar to what we describe here. Again, let the buyer beware.

ERP Characteristics

Figure 7-19 (page 216) lists the major ERP characteristics. First, as stated, ERP takes a cross-functional, process view of the entire organization. With ERP, the entire organization is considered a collection of interrelated activities.

Second, true ERP is a formal approach that is based on documented, tested business models. ERP applications include a comprehensive set of inherent processes for all organizational activities. SAP defines this set as the **process blueprint** and documents each process with diagrams that use a set of standardized symbols. The process diagram in Figure 7-15 is a SAP process diagram.

Because ERP is based on formally defined procedures, organizations must adapt their processing to the ERP blueprint. If they do not, the system cannot operate effectively, or

TQM

The Flavor-of-the-Month Club

KNOWLEDGE MANAGEMENT

O h, come on. I've been here 30 years and I've heard it all. All these management programs. . . . Years ago, we had Zero Defects. Then was Total Quality Management, and after that, Six Sigma. We've had all the pet theories from every consultant in the Western Hemisphere. No, wait, we had consultants from Asia, too.

"Do you know what flavor we're having now? We're redesigning ourselves to be 'customer centric.' We are going to integrate our CRM system into an ERP system to transform the entire company to be 'customer focused.'

"You know how these programs go? First, we have a pronouncement at a 'kick-off meeting' where the CEO tells us what the new flavor is going to be and why it's so important. Then a swarm of consultants and 'change management' experts tell us how they're going to 'empower' us. Then HR adds some new item to our annual review, such as, 'Measures taken to achieve customer-centric company.'

"So, we all figure out some lame thing to do so that we have something to put in that category of our annual review. Then we forget about it because we know the next new flavor of the month will be along soon. Or worse, if they actually force us to

ZERO DEFECTS

use the new system, we comply, but viciously. You know, go out of our way to show that the new system can't work, that it really screws things up.

"You think I sound bitter, but I've seen this so many times before. The consultants and rising stars in our company get together and dream up one of these programs. Then they present it to the senior managers. That's when they make their first mistake: They think that if they can sell it to management, then it must be a good idea. They treat senior management like the customer. They should have to sell the idea to those of us who actually sell, support, or make things. Senior management is just the banker; the managers should let us decide if it's a good idea.

"If someone really wanted to empower me, she would listen rather than talk. Those of us who do the work have hundreds of ideas of how to do it better. Now it's customer centric? As if we haven't been trying to do that for years!

"Anyway, after the CEO issues the pronouncements about the new system, he gets busy with other things and forgets about it for a while. Six months might go by, and then we're either told we're not doing enough to become customer centric (or whatever the flavor is) or the company announces another new flavor.

JIT

CHANGE MANAGEMENT

SIX SIGMA

"In manufacturing they talk about push versus pull. You know, with push style, you make things and push them onto the sales force and the customers. With pull style, you let the customers' demand pull the product out of manufacturing. You build when you have holes in inventory. Well, they should adapt those ideas to what they call 'change management.' I mean, does anybody need to manage real change? Did somebody have a 'Use the cell phone' program? Did some CEO announce, 'This year, we're all going to use the cell phone'? Did the HR department put a line into our annual evaluation form that asked how many times we'd used a cell phone? No, no, no, and no. Customers pulled the cell phone through. We wanted it, so we bought and used cell phones. Same with color printers and Palm Pilots and wireless networks.

"That's pull. You get a group of workers to form a network, and you get things going among the people who do the work. Then you build on that to obtain true organizational change. Why don't they figure it out?

"Anyway, I've got to run. We've got the kick-off meeting of our new initiative—something about supply chain management. Now they're going to empower me to buy things from our suppliers. Like I haven't been doing that all these years. Oh, well, I plan to retire soon.

"Oh, wait. Here, take my t-shirt from the knowledge management program 2 years ago. I never wore it. It says, 'Empowering You through Knowledge Management.' That one didn't last long."

? DISCUSSION QUESTIONS

1. Clearly, this person is bitter about new programs and new ideas. What do you think might have been the cause of his antagonism? What seems to be his principal concern?

2. What does he mean by "vicious" compliance? Give an example of an experience you've had that exemplifies such compliance.

3. Consider his point that the proponents of new programs treat senior managers as the customer. What does he mean? To a consultant, is senior management the customer? What do you think he's trying to say?

4. What does he mean when he says, "If someone wants to empower me, she would listen rather than talk"? How does listening to someone empower that person?

5. His examples of "pull change" all involve the use of new products. To what extent do you think pull works for new management programs?

6. How do you think management could introduce new programs in a way that would cause them to be pulled through the organization? Consider the suggestion he makes, as well as your own ideas.

7. If you managed an employee who had an attitude like this, what could you do to make him more positive about organizational change and new programs and initiatives?

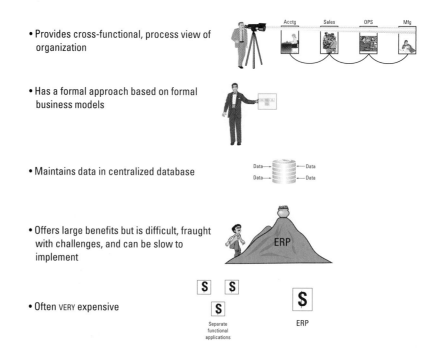

- Provides cross-functional, process view of organization

- Has a formal approach based on formal business models

- Maintains data in centralized database

- Offers large benefits but is difficult, fraught with challenges, and can be slow to implement

- Often VERY expensive

Figure 7-19
Characteristics of ERP

even correctly. In some cases, it is possible to adapt ERP software to procedures that are different from the blueprint, but such adaptation is expensive and often problematic.

As stated, with isolated systems, each application has it own database. This separation makes it difficult for authorized users to readily obtain all of the pertinent information about customers, products, and so forth. With ERP systems, organizational data are processed in a centralized database. Such centralization makes it easy for authorized users to obtain needed information from a single source. However, such integration has a downside, as discussed in the *Security Guide* on page 217a.

Once an organization has implemented an ERP system, it can achieve large benefits. However, as shown in Figure 7-19, the process of moving from separated, functional applications to an ERP system is difficult, fraught with challenge, and can be slow. In particular, changing organizational procedures has proved to be a great challenge for many organizations, and in some cases was even a pitfall that prevented successful ERP implementation. Finally, the switch to an ERP system is very costly—not only because of the need for new hardware and software, but also due to the costs of developing new procedures, training employees, converting data, and other developmental expenses.

Benefits of ERP

Figure 7-20 summarizes the major benefits of ERP. First, the processes in the business blueprint have been tried and tested over hundreds of organizations. The processes are always effective and often very efficient. Organizations that convert to ERP do not need to reinvent business processes. Rather, they gain the benefit of those processes that have already made many organizations successful.

By taking an organization-wide view, many organizations find they can reduce their inventory, sometimes dramatically. With better planning, it is not necessary to

- Efficient business processes
- Inventory reduction
- Lead-time reduction
- Improved customer service
- Greater, real-time insight into organization
- Higher profitability

Figure 7-20
Potential Benefits of ERP

You Be the Guide

Using the Opposing Forces Guide *(page 215a)*

GOALS

* Engage students' resistance to change-management theories.

* Encourage students to think about the reality of change management and how to deal with forces that oppose it.

BACKGROUND AND PRESENTATION STRATEGIES

The person on whom this vignette is based believed that *management never listened* to him. He thought he was *smarter than management* (and he probably was), and he thought most attempts at change management were silly—almost as if management went to a training program, learned certain words to recite, and then recited those words, without any real care for the employees.

People who deal closely with the customer often identify more with the customers' needs and problems than they do with their own management. Because they spend more time with the customer than they do with their managers, they begin to identify more with the customer than with the company. They blame management for the customers' problems. This is especially true if they have no ready fix for the customers' problems.

Outside consultants can be highly demotivating to employees. Employees quite naturally feel resentful when some highly paid person from outside comes along and "tells management what I've been telling them all along." They feel, "Management won't listen to me, but they will listen to them."

A single "kick-off" meeting is insufficient to launch a new program. The program must have *regular, recurring follow-up* at all levels of management (especially first-line management).

Companies sometimes encounter *vicious compliance:* "You control my paycheck, but you don't control my heart and mind. I'll do what you say, but angrily, and I won't do a very good job at it." This is an incredibly immature response, but sometimes employees feel that is their only possible response. Communication is nil.

Scenario for class discussion: To illustrate how difficult change management can be, consider the following scenario: Suppose an organization changes its competitive strategy from a *differentiating strategy* to a *cost-leader strategy.*

➤ **How will this change alter the way the organization treats its existing customers?**

➤ **How will the customers respond to those changes?**

➤ **How will the employees respond to the customers' responses?**

➤ **What kind of change management program needs to be created when shifting to a cost-leader strategy?**

➤ **What changes, besides customer service, will be affected? For example, how might that strategy change employee travel accommodations or computer equipment?**

➤ **How will the employees respond to those changes?**

Ask the students to specify five or six features of a change-management program to implement a change to a cost-leader strategy.

➤ **Even with such a program, how popular will such a change be?**

➤ **Is it conceivable that there could be a pull style of change management? If so, how?**

➤ **Is it even possible for an organization to make the shift from a differentiation strategy to a cost-leadership strategy?**

➤ **How popular will management be during such a change? Does unpopularity justify not making the change?**

 SUGGESTED RESPONSES FOR DISCUSSION QUESTIONS

1. Begin by asking the students:

➤ **What causes someone to have such an attitude?**

➤ **What has management done in the past to cause him to feel this way?**

➤ **What would you do if you had an employee like this?**

Some of the causes I perceive: Management doesn't listen to his good ideas, but they will listen to an outside consultant. Management is insincere in its efforts to help employees deal with changes.

2. Vicious compliance means employees do something because they have to. They don't believe in it, but they'll do it because they want their paychecks. It is horrible to feel like this and horrible to manage people who act like this.

> ➤ **Have you every worked in an organization in which vicious compliance was practiced?**

> ➤ **What causes vicious compliance?**

> ➤ **What would you do if you managed a department with employees who were complying viciously?**

> ➤ **Can information systems play a role in causing vicious compliance?**

3. He wants to focus on the needs of the company's customers, not the needs of the company's managers. Sometimes, senior management is treated as the person to convince, yet revenue depends on the customers' response.

For example, you can convince management that a new IS will be terrific, but if its features cause employees to hate it, then it was not terrific. By the way, employees have a different relationship to senior managers than consultants do. If management buys the consultants' story, the consultants have convinced their customer, but the employees will be left with the duty of convincing the company's customers.

> ➤ **What does he mean by the statement, "Senior management is just the banker"?**

> ➤ **What happens when employees are more focused on pleasing their management than on pleasing the customer?**

> ➤ **What is the proper balance between pleasing management and pleasing the customer?**

4. The employee is saying that he has great ideas that he believes no one listens to. He doesn't need someone to give him more power, he needs someone to let him use the power he already has.

> ➤ **How does listening to someone empower them?**

> ➤ **What is the difference between *telling* someone what they should do and *listening* to them say what they want to do?**

> ➤ **How does that difference empower someone?**

5. The contrarian has a point: When people truly see the benefit of something, there really is no need to manage change. But, is all change like that?

> ➤ **Is there a way, for example, to pull the changes to implement a new ERP system through the organization? How?**

> ➤ **If not, how could management push the changes for the new ERP system?**

Pull can work if employees have been the source of a change or have had a vital role in implementing that change. Maybe quality circles succeed because employees will pull the change to them.

6. Management could listen to the employees, incorporate employees' ideas for implementation, communicate early and often, and take active steps to show value for employees. Management also must deal with self-efficacy issues (see the Problem Solving Guide on page 211a).

7. He needs to be listened to, and more than once. He will be quick to sense any insincerity, and if he's promised anything, he'll be furious (as well as smug because he *knew* it was only a ruse) that management has let him down once again. Involve him in a leadership role for new programs and initiatives. This employee will be high-maintenance for a long time. The extra effort might be worth the manager's time, if he has lots to add to the group.

WRAP UP

> ➤ **What did you learn about change management from this exercise?**

> ➤ **How does change management pertain to IS in particular?**

> ➤ **Side note: Interesting career opportunities are available in helping organizations adapt to changes brought by information systems, but such jobs can be hard to find. Not all go by the title of change-management consultant. Sometimes the titles are user support, user training, systems analyst, and related titles. If you're interested in this topic, you should take our systems development class.**

maintain large buffer stocks. Additionally, items remain in inventory for shorter periods of time, sometimes no longer than a few hours or a day.

Another advantage is that ERP helps organizations reduce lead times. Because of the more efficient processes and better information, organizations can respond more quickly to process new orders or changes in existing orders. This means they can deliver goods to customers faster. In some cases, ERP-based companies can receive payments on orders shipped before they pay for the raw materials used in the parts on the order.

As discussed earlier, data inconsistency problems are not an issue because all ERP data are stored in an integrated database. Further, because all data about a customer, order, part, or other entity reside in one place, the data are readily accessible. This means that organizations can provide better information about orders, products, and customer status to their customers. All of this results not only in better, but also less costly, customer service.

Finally, ERP-based organizations often find that they can produce and sell the same products at lower costs due to smaller inventories, reduced lead times, and cheaper customer support. The bottom-line result is higher profitability. The trick, however, is getting there.

Implementing an ERP System

Figure 7-21 summarizes the major tasks in the implementation of an ERP system. The first task is to model the current business processes. Managers and analysts then compare these processes to the ERP blueprint processes and note the differences. The company then must find ways to eliminate the differences, either by changing the existing business process to match the ERP process or by altering the ERP system.

Modeling the current business processes is a difficult and time-consuming task. Trained and skilled analysts are needed to observe, investigate, and document current practices. Often, existing procedures are not documented and are known only by those who perform them. Many meetings, interviews, and observations can be necessary to tease out and document these procedures. This activity is crucial because the organization must understand what procedural changes will be necessary before converting to the new system.

To appreciate the magnitude of these tasks, consider that the SAP blueprint contains over a thousand process models. Organizations that are adopting ERP must review those models and determine which ones are appropriate to them. Then, they compare the ERP models to the models developed based on their current practices. Inevitably, some current-practice models are incomplete, vague, or inaccurate, so the team must repeat the existing process models. In some cases, it is impossible to reconcile any existing system against the blueprint model. If so, the team must adapt, cope, and define new procedures, often to the confusion of current employees.

Once the differences between as-is processes and the blueprint have been reconciled, the next step is to implement the system. Before implementation starts, however,

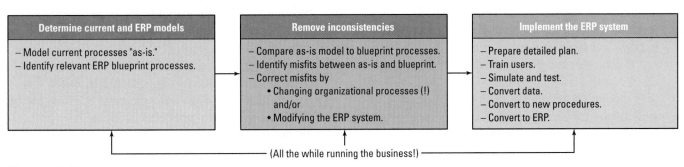

Figure 7-21
ERP Implementation

Centralized Vulnerability

Organizational information systems have evolved from those that support business activities in isolation to those that support integrated processing among several or many business functions. This evolution allows organizations to obtain efficiencies via linkages among business functions. A side consequence, however, is increased vulnerability.

With ERP and other multifunction systems, a centralized database enables authorized users to obtain integrated information. However, a centralized database also makes it easier for unauthorized users and criminals to obtain that same integrated information. Further, in the event of a catastrophic data loss, all of the applications in the ERP suite will be unavailable. The entire organization can become paralyzed.

In short, databases that support ERP, and even functional applications that span several business activities, increase organizational vulnerability. Because of this increased vulnerability, security, backup, and recovery become critical.

If you take an accounting information systems class, you will learn about controls and procedures that should be used to reduce the risk of unauthorized activity and catastrophic loss. There are several types of such controls. One is to ensure that appropriate security measures exist to protect the organizational

network and organizational databases, as described in Chapters 4 and 5.

Another type of control is to ensure that appropriate roles are defined for application users and that permissions and passwords are set to enforce those roles. The goal of such controls is to promote appropriate separation of duties and authorities. For example, no one person should be able to enter and approve a purchase requisition.

In addition to these restrictions on user activities, the organization must protect data assets from loss due to natural disaster or other catastrophic loss. We will discuss this further in Chapter 11.

All of these comments make good sense, given the organization's vulnerability due to ERP and other centralized databases. However, these measures may result in undesirable side effects. First, security is expensive. Organizations must continually answer the question, "How much is enough?" As with insurance, senior managers must balance the benefits of increased security against the costs of implementing a stronger security system.

Second, increased security always means reduced flexibility. For example, in a tightly controlled CRM, a customer support representative will be unable to make changes to certain customer data. This restriction may seem unreasonable to both the customer and the support representative, but it may be necessary to provide an appropriate level of control.

Tight security is particularly a problem in smaller organizations or departments. In a small medical office, for example, there may be only one person who is allowed to make changes to patient billing records. When that person is sick or on vacation, who performs this task? The office may not be able to defer the changes until the person returns, which means that someone else, possibly someone not trained to make the changes, must perform them. That second person will then be assigned new roles and possibly given passwords to additional accounts. When the authorized person returns, all of this activity then needs to be undone. This can be a hassle for everyone and often leads to disrespect for the security system and circumvention of its controls.

The bottom line is that with information security, one size does not fit all. Each system and each organization must design security systems that provide appropriate protection given its objectives, its security budget, and its tolerance for information system inflexibility.

DISCUSSION QUESTIONS

1. Do you think that increased centralization of data and systems always leads to increased vulnerability? Are there situations where this does not occur?

2. List three types of information systems control.

3. Describe the trade-off that must occur between increased security and cost.

4. Describe the trade-off that must occur between increased security and flexibility.

5. How does an organization decide the best trade-offs in questions 3 and 4?

6. Explain why tight security is more difficult to implement in smaller organizations and departments.

users must be trained on the new processes, procedures, and use of the ERP system features and function. Additionally, the company needs to conduct a simulation test of the new system to identify problems. Then, the organization must convert its data, procedures, and personnel to the new ERP system. All of this happens while the business continues to run on the old system.

As you learned in Chapter 6, plunging the organization into the new system is an invitation to disaster. Instead, a thorough and well-planned test of the new system is necessary, followed by a careful cutover to the new system. Realize, too, that while the new ERP system is being installed, normal business activity continues. Somehow the employees of the organization must continue to run the company while the cutover is underway. It is a difficult and challenging time for any organization that undergoes this process. *MIS in Use 7-2* describes how one company, the Brose Group, implemented ERP.

Implementing an ERP system is not for the faint of heart. Because so much organizational change is required, all ERP projects must have the full support of the CEO and executive staff. Because ERP processes cross departmental boundaries, no single departmental manager has the authority to force an ERP implementation. Instead, full support for the task must come from the top of the organization. Even with such support, there is bound to be second-guessing and griping, as was shown in the *Opposing Forces Guide* on page 215a.

MIS in Use 7-2

The Brose Group Implements SAP— One Site at a Time

The Brose Group supplies windows, doors, seat adjusters, and related products for more than 40 auto brands. Major customers include General Motors, Ford, DaimlerChrysler, BMW, Porsche, Volkswagen, Toyota, and Honda. Founded as an auto and aircraft parts manufacturer in Berlin in 1908, the company today has facilities at more than 30 locations in 20 different countries. Revenue for 2004 exceeded 2 billion euros.

In the 1990s, Brose enjoyed rapid growth but found that existing information systems were unable to support the company's emerging needs. Too many different information systems meant a lack of standardization and hampered communication among suppliers, plants, and customers. Brose decided to standardize operations on R/3, an ERP application licensed by SAP that supports more than a thousand different business processes. Rather than attempt to implement those processes on its own, Brose hired SAP Consulting to lead the project.

The SAP team provided process consulting and implementation support, and it trained end users. According to Christof Lutz, SAP project manager, "Our consultants and the Brose experts worked openly, flexibly, and constructively together. In this atmosphere of trust, we created an implementation module that the customer can use as a basis for the long term."

The Brose/SAP consulting team decided on a pilot approach. The first installation was conducted at a new plant in Curitiba, Brazil. The team constructed the implementation to be used as a prototype for installations at additional plants. Developing the first implementation was no small feat, because it involved information systems for sales and distribution, materials management, production planning, quality management, and financial accounting and control.

Once the initial system was operational at the Curitiba plant, the prototype was rolled out to additional facilities. The second implementation, in Puebla, Mexico, required just 6 months for first operational capability, and the next implementation in Meerane, Germany, was operational in just 19 weeks.

The conversion to the ERP system has contributed to dramatically increased productivity. In 1994, Brose achieved sales of 541 million euros with 2,900 employees, or 186,000 euros per employee. Ten years later, in 2004, Brose attained sales of 2 billion euros with 8,200 employees, or 240,000 euros per employee.

This case continues at the end of this chapter on page 225.

Sources: brose.de/en/pub/company (accessed November 2004); *sap.com/industries/automotive/pdf/CS_Brose_Group.pdf* (accessed November 2004).

Using the Security Guide
(page 217a)

GOALS

✴ Introduce important security side effects of centralized, interdepartmental systems:

- Increased centralization of data (as in ERP databases) increases organizational vulnerability.

- Increased security means (1) greater expense and (2) less flexibility.

✴ Demonstrate that security programs are difficult for smaller organizations.
(Chapter 11 addresses organizational security in greater depth.)

BACKGROUND AND PRESENTATION STRATEGIES

The Security Guide in Chapter 4 (pages 85a and b) discussed database security, user roles, and user permissions; you may want to review this material.

Trade-offs are a key element of this guide. With enterprise systems, we integrate separate business functions, but we increase vulnerability. To reduce vulnerability, we add security, but now we've reduced flexibility and raised costs. To reduce costs, we eliminate some security, and then we face more vulnerability. These sorts of trade-offs are common with all information systems and, in fact, are common with all business activity. *That's why they pay decision makers the big bucks!*

The problem of security for small organizations is especially important. Unlike large organizations that have offices staffed by trained security experts, a small organization has limited access to such expertise. The small office may have licensed software from a vertical market software vendor, and, if so, that vendor may provide some security expertise. That expertise, however, will pertain to the licensed product and not to overall organizational security.

Early in their careers, the students may be managers of departments or workgroups. Even if those departments reside in a larger organization, they may be subject to some of the security problems of a small office. For example, they may have one or two key users who are given special accounts with extra privileges. What will they do when those key people are absent from work?

 SUGGESTED RESPONSES FOR DISCUSSION QUESTIONS

1. I know of no situation in which centralization doesn't create more vulnerability. In general, if we reduce many things to one thing, then the likelihood that that one thing could be destroyed is higher than it is for the many things. I sometimes ask these questions to see if they're following:

➤ **Is the Internet centralized or decentralized?**

(Decentralized)

➤ **Does the design of the Internet increase or decrease vulnerability?**

(I'd say decrease, and by far.)

2. The controls mentioned in the text are: (a) protect networks and databases from unauthorized activities, (b) define accounts with appropriate permissions, (c) protect assets from natural disasters and catastrophic loss. Many more controls are possible; accounting students should be able to list additional controls.

Sometimes, if some students have had a course in accounting information systems, I ask them to describe controls in more detail. I treat them like consultants and give them a chance to display their knowledge. If no one has such knowledge, sometimes I give two or three students an assignment to ask their accounting professors about controls and report back to the class. Such assignments provide cross-discipline connections, *which are so important.* I think most students enjoy the chance to report back to class on the subject of a different class.

3. For this and question 4, ask the students about the concept of trade-offs:

➤ **What is a trade-off?**

➤ **What are examples of personal trade-offs in your life? Work versus school? Relationships versus individual activity? Other?**

➤ **Is there a fixed rule for deciding about trade-offs?**

➤ **Are there general principles for trade-off decisions?**

Trade-offs that involve cost, such as the one here, are easier than the trade-off in question 4. Here, the question becomes, *"How much do you want to pay?"*

At some point (in theory at least) one could do a cost-benefit analysis to determine the point at which the marginal benefit of increased security is not worth the marginal cost.

4. Consider an information system in which users have to change their password every day, and the system requires that the new password be both strong and different from every password used in the past. This provides high authorization security, but it results in aggravation and loss of flexibility. Or, consider an information system in which every user is allowed to take any action on any database record. This would have very high flexibility with little security.

➤ **What are examples of the security versus flexibility trade-off for the IS on campus?**

All organizations must balance these two factors. Many organizations want to empower their employees to take direct action to solve problems, but they wish to maintain security and control as well. Consider this vignette:

> *On a bus in Mexico, a bus driver shut the door too quickly when a passenger exited the bus, and the door smashed and ruined the passenger's cake. The passenger complained to the driver. The driver looked at the passenger, looked at the cake, reached into the till, and handed the passenger 300 pesos, about the cost of the cake. The passenger departed more or less satisfied.*

➤ **Where did the driver's authority lie on the trade-off between security and flexibility?**

➤ **What are the risks of allowing so much flexibility?**

➤ **What are the benefits?**

➤ **How does this story pertain to the design of information systems?**

5. The cost trade-off is easier. Students should be learning in accounting and finance how (at least in theory) to make such cost trade-offs. (Again, you might ask the students to ask their accounting and finance professors about this and report back to class next time.)

The security versus flexibility trade-off is harder. Someone might say you can make it using a cost analysis as well, but costing the value of flexibility is likely to be very hard.

Example: On my campus, whenever I wish to request the loan of a book from an off-campus library, I must

enter a 12-digit identifying code and then a PIN that is particular to my library account. It's aggravating to do, and the system has no "Remember me on this computer" function, so no matter how many times I've done it from my office computer, I must still enter that number.

The design of this system makes it less likely that someone could spoof my library account. The cost, however, is that I'm less likely to request an off-campus book, because it's such a pain to do.

Now, if we are designing that system, how do we make the trade-off? How would one go about computing the cost of someone spoofing my library account? How would one go about computing the cost of my being reluctant to request a book?

These are tough trade-offs to analyze. Sometimes it's the loudest voice that wins. There are no easy answers.

6. Because there are a limited number of employees and critical functions lay with just one or two, vulnerability is increased.

➤ **How many of you have worked in small offices?**

➤ **Was everyone in the office able to have unrestricted access to the data, or were permissions set up on different users' accounts and groups?**

➤ **What happened when a critical person was absent from work?**

➤ **How important was security to that organization? Did management seem to understand the organization's vulnerability?**

➤ **Should HIPAA requirements be reduced for small offices?**

➤ **If not, how does a small office cope?**

(HIPAA is discussed in Chapter 11, page 343a.)

WRAP UP

➤ **Centralization almost always involves increased vulnerability.**

➤ **In your future career, whenever anyone proposes a system, project, or organizational structure that increases centralization, learn to raise the vulnerability question.**

Enterprise Application Integration

ERP systems are not for every organization. For example, some nonmanufacturing companies find the manufacturing orientation of ERP inappropriate. Even for manufacturing companies, some find the process of converting from their current system to an ERP system too daunting. Others are quite satisfied with their MRP systems and do not wish to change them.

Companies for which ERP is inappropriate still have the problems of isolated systems, however, and some choose to use **enterprise application integration (EAI)** to solve those problems. EAI integrates existing systems by providing layers of software that connect applications together. EAI does the following:

- It connects system "islands" via a new layer of software/system.
- It enables existing applications to communicate and share data.
- It provides integrated information.
- It leverages existing systems—leaving legacy/functional applications as is, but providing an integration layer over the top.
- It enables a gradual move to ERP.

The purpose of the layers of EAI software (a sort of IS connective tissue) is to enable existing applications to communicate with each other and to share data. For example, EAI software can be configured to automatically make the data conversion required in Figure 7-11. When the CRM applications send data to the MRP system, for example, the CRM system sends its data to an EAI software program. That EAI program makes the conversion and then sends the converted data to the ERP system. The reverse action is taken to send data back from the ERP to the CRM.

Although there is no centralized EAI database, the EAI software keeps files of metadata that describe where data are located. Users can access the EAI system to find the data they need. In some cases, the EAI system provides services that provide a "virtual integrated database" for the user to process.

The major benefit of EAI is that it enables organizations to use existing applications while eliminating many of the serious problems of isolated systems. Converting to an EAI system is not nearly as disruptive as converting to ERP, and it provides many of the benefits of ERP. Some organizations develop EAI applications as a stepping-stone to complete ERP systems.

The benefits of inherent processes and procedures are clear, but there may be an unintended consequence. See the *Reflections Guide* on page 219a to consider the risk.

Universal Electronics (continued)

The COO assigned you the task of recommending one or more information systems to save costs. From the chapter's discussion of competitive advantage, you now understand that Universal's goal is to be the cost leader across its market.

In this chapter, you also learned that integrated systems are preferable to functional systems because they avoid the problems of isolated processing. But you suspect your COO will not be open to the costs of either a CRM or an ERP system. You could consider EAI as option, but it is not clear that the primary benefit of EAI is cost savings, and you know that you will be grilled on that issue more than any other.

As you ponder, you conclude that the major source of costs to Universal is inventory. Is there some way to reduce inventory expense? Is there some way Universal could dramatically reduce its inventory—not by 5 percent, but by 40 or 50 percent?

ERP and the Standard, Standard Blueprint

Designing business processes is difficult, time consuming, and very expensive. Highly trained experts conduct seemingly countless interviews with users and domain experts to determine business requirements. Then, even more experts join those people, and together this team invests thousands of labor hours to design, develop, and implement effective business processes that meet those requirements. All of this is a very high-risk activity that is prone to failure. And it all must be done before IS development can even begin.

ERP vendors such as SAP have invested millions of labor hours into the business blueprints that underlie their ERP solutions. These blueprints consist of hundreds or thousands of different business processes. Examples are processes for hiring employees, processes for acquiring fixed assets, processes for acquiring consumable goods, and processes for custom "one-off" (a unique product with a unique design) manufacturing, to name just a few.

Additionally, ERP vendors have implemented their business processes in hundreds of organizations. In so doing, they have been forced to customize their standard blueprint for use in particular industries. For example, SAP has a distribution-business blueprint that is customized for the auto parts industry, for the electronics industry, and for the aircraft industry. Hundreds of other customized solutions exist as well.

Even better, the ERP vendors have developed software solutions that fit their business-process blueprints. In theory, no software development is required at all if the organization can adapt to the standard blueprint of the ERP vendor.

As described in this chapter, when an organization implements an ERP solution, it first determines any differences that exist between its business processes and the standard blueprint. Then, the organization must remove that difference, which can be done in one of two ways: It changes business processes to fit the standard blueprint. Or, the ERP vendor or a consultant modifies the standard blueprint (and software solution that matches that blueprint) to fit the unique requirements.

In practice, such variations from the standard blueprint are rare. They are difficult and expensive to implement, and they require the using organization to maintain the variations from the standard as new versions of the ERP software are developed. Consequently, most organizations choose to modify their processes to meet the blueprint, rather than the other way around. Although such process changes also are difficult to implement, once the organization has converted to the standard blueprint, they no longer need to support a "variation."

So, from a standpoint of cost, effort, risk, and avoidance of future problems, there is a huge incentive for organizations to adapt to the standard ERP blueprint.

Initially, SAP was the only true ERP vendor, but other companies have developed and acquired ERP

solutions as well. Because of competitive pressure across the software industry, all of these products are beginning to have the same sets of features and functions. ERP solutions are becoming a commodity.

All of this is fine as far as it goes, but it introduces a nagging question: If, over time, every organization tends to implement the standard ERP blueprint, and if, over time, every software company develops essentially the same ERP features and functions, then won't every business come to look just like every other business? How will organizations gain a competitive advantage if they all use the same business processes?

If every auto parts distributor uses the same business processes, based on the same software, are they not all clones of one another? How will a company distinguish itself? How will innovation occur? Even if one parts distributor does successfully innovate a business process that gives it a competitive advantage, will the ERP vendors be conduits to transfer that innovation to competitors? Does the use of "commoditized" standard blueprints mean that no company can sustain a competitive advantage?

DISCUSSION QUESTIONS

1. Explain in your own words why an organization might choose to change its processes to fit the standard blueprint. What advantages does it accrue by doing so?

2. Explain how competitive pressure among software vendors will cause the ERP solutions to become commodities. What does this mean to the ERP software industry?

3. If two businesses use exactly the same processes and exactly the same software, can they be different in any way at all? Explain why or why not.

4. Explain the statement that an ERP software vendor can be a conduit to transfer innovation. What are the consequences to the innovating company? To the software company? To the industry? To the economy?

5. In theory, such standardization might be possible, but worldwide there are so many different business models, cultures, people, values, and competitive pressures, can any two businesses ever be exactly alike?

You're thinking maybe such dramatic reductions would be possible if Universal worked more closely with its suppliers.

In fact, there may well be cost savings by working more closely with suppliers. Such systems are the subject of the next chapter. So we will defer your recommendation until after you have read that chapter.

SUMMARY

- Three categories of information systems are calculation systems, functional systems, and integrated systems.

- Functional systems support a single business function. Functional systems support human resources, accounting and finance, sales and marketing, and manufacturing activities. (Refer to Figures 7-2 through 7-7.)

- A master production schedule (MPS) is a plan for producing products. It is used for push-style manufacturing scheduling. Pull scheduling responds to signals, or kanbans, from customers that indicate that a product is needed. Some organizations combine these two styles to create an initial MPS that is then modified in accordance with demand signals.

- Materials requirements planning (MRP) links manufacturing to inbound logistics by planning the need for materials and inventories. Manufacturing resource planning (MRP II) expands on MRP by including the planning of personnel and machinery as well as materials.

- According to Michael Porter, a firm can engage in one of four competitive strategies: low cost across an industry or within an industry segment, or product differentiation across an industry or within an industry segment. An organization's information systems must be designed to support the firm's competitive strategy.

- In the Porter model, value is the total revenue that a customer is willing to spend for a product or service.

- A value chain is a network of value-creating activities.

- The five primary activities in Porter's value chain model are inbound logistics, operations, outbound logistics, marketing and sales, and customer service. Support activities are procurement, technology development, human resources, and firm infrastructure. Linkages are interactions across value chain activities.

- With business process design, new information systems do not automate existing business practices; rather, such systems use technology to enable new, more efficient business processes.

- Customer relationship management (CRM) supports solicitation, lead tracking, and relationship management activities. CRM makes customer data more accessible by storing all customer data in a single database.

- Enterprise resource planning (ERP) systems support all major business activities within the organization. ERP is based on a blueprint of standard business processes, which have been tried and tested over hundreds of organizations. Organizations that adopt an ERP system must either convert their processes to the blueprint or modify the blueprint and ERP software to match their processes.

- Enterprise application integration (EAI) is an alternative to ERP that can provide many of the benefits of integrated IS. EAI integrates existing applications by providing layers of software that connect applications.

KEY TERMS AND CONCEPTS

Accounting and finance
    systems   199
Bill of materials (BOM)   202

Business process design   209
Calculation systems   196
Cross-departmental systems   197

Cross-functional systems   197
Customer relationship
    management (CRM)   213

You Be the Guide

Universal Electronics (continued) (page 219)

The protagonist of this story is a fortunate person. A senior manager has given our protagonist an interesting and important task, and if that person can deliver anything useful on this task, his or her future with this company will be very bright. Even though the original project was rejected, he/she has accumulated considerable personal capital. Failure in a project doesn't mean failure in person or career, depending on what happens next.

RESPONDING TO THE CHALLENGE

Make the following points in discussing how to respond to this challenge:

Considering cross-functional, integrated applications and given the response to his first proposal, not considering a CRM system is probably wise. The benefits of CRM are not primarily cost reduction, and some aspects of CRM are too close to his original proposal. An ERP system is likely to be very expensive, and although cost reduction may ultimately occur from an ERP investment, I think cost reduction is unlikely to be an early benefit.

The protagonist might have been too quick to dismiss EAI as a cost-saving alternative. Further investigation into EAI was probably warranted. Using EAI might save on inventory costs, and integrating sales data with purchasing and inventory data will not necessarily require the cooperation of suppliers, which the supply chain solution may do.

WRAP UP

This ending, how shared information among companies in the supply chain can help Universal save inventory costs, sets up the next chapter. This solution is discussed at the end of that next chapter.

➤ **This is interesting: Thinking about ways of implementing competitive strategy using information systems. There is a lot more to it than just building a Web site.**

You Be the Guide

Using the Reflections Guide
(page 219a)

GOALS

＊ Reinforce the importance of inherent processes in ERP and other licensed software and the expense and challenges of variances from those processes.

＊ Introduce possible longer-range consequences of adapting to vendors' inherent processes.

＊ Demonstrate an example of long-range thinking.

BACKGROUND AND PRESENTATION STRATEGIES

Warning: Before using this guide, ensure the students understand what an ERP system is and how much it integrates the organization's activities. It may be a good idea to start with a review of ERP systems.

Are organizations that enforce the standard ERP blueprint for their industry condemning themselves to industry-wide uniformity?

I don't know if this problem is real or not. But, in theory, as ERP packages become commodities (and we do know that competitive software products always becomes a commodity), then every business will be run just like every other business. If that is the case, then how will one business gain a competitive advantage? Possibly, the company that executes the ERP processes most efficiently becomes the leader, but that is a difference in scale more than a difference in kind.

Even more worrisome, once ERP systems are solidly integrated into the organization, *will they stifle creativity?* Employees already complain that they are forced to do silly things because the "software requires them to." Will the software mean that it is a waste of time to develop improved ways of doing business, because the improved way is incompatible with the "always-enforced" ERP way?

I posed this question to a PeopleSoft salesperson who said the answer lay with business intelligence applications of the data generated by the ERP system. "Organizations can gain a competitive advantage," he said, "*by reporting and mining the data* that we generate in their databases."

Is that answer credible? If the information created by the business intelligence system can be applied in the context of the existing ERP or other system, then his answer may have merit. But what if the information created indicates the need for a change to a system that cannot be changed because of the structure of an existing ERP system?

Side effect: When an organization requests a feature change in the ERP system, that action may mean that every other customer of that vendor, and ultimately the entire industry, will have that change. *Thus, the competitive advantage will be unsustainable.*

What to do? No organization today that can benefit from ERP would choose not to implement it. But, having done so, has the organization entered a *conformity trap?*

 SUGGESTED RESPONSES FOR DISCUSSION QUESTIONS

1. The vendors would say that customers should adapt because the standard blueprint, the inherent processes, are the "best-of-class solutions." They also know that variances are expensive and difficult to maintain. Life for the vendor and for the IS department is a lot easier if the company converts to the standard process.

   ➤ **What does the organization lose by converting to the standard blueprint?**

   ➤ **What are the costs of that conversion? (Also consider nonmonetary costs.)**

2. Ask the marketing students what causes products to become commodities. Software is no different. (*This point, by the way, opens the door to talk about careers in software sales, marketing, and support. These are great, high-paying jobs, and this class is the first step toward one.*)

   The process: No vendor can allow another vendor to have a competitive advantage, so they all copy the features and functions from one another. Ultimately, like cans of tomatoes on the grocery shelf, they all look the same.

3. This is the key question, and I don't know a definite answer. The answer may come down to the issue of whether they can be better in the execution of the inherent processes in the software.

   ➤ **If a company executes the standard blueprint better than its competitors, will that give it a competitive advantage?**

➤ **Is it possible for a company to engage in a differentiation strategy if all companies use the same inherent processes?**

➤ **Consider Lowe's and Home Depot. They have the same business processes. What will make one better than the other? If they're both using the same ERP package, the differentiation won't be in IS innovation.**

There is no obvious nor easy answer.

4. Such transfer of innovation happens when a company has an exception to the ERP system for which it asks the ERP vendor to program supporting software. If the exception represents an improved process, the ERP vendor can put it into its new software versions. Voila! The ERP vendor has been a conduit of innovation from one company to an industry.

Ultimately, this phenomenon is beneficial to the industry and the economy. That may be small consolation to the company that cannot maintain its competitive advantage. Then again, innovation should be a continuous process. As Rudyard Kipling wrote,

> "They copied all they could follow, but they couldn't copy my mind,
>
> And I left 'em sweating and stealing a year and a half behind."

(*The Mary Gloster*, 1894)

5. It is probably not possible for two companies ever to be completely alike, but they may be close enough to make sustainable competitive advantages difficult, if not impossible. Example: Lowe's versus Home Depot.

One way to teach this is to play devil's advocate (or, depending on your views, an honest critic). Say something like:

➤ **This essay is much ado about nothing. It has no real issue; the points it makes are hair-splitting, unrealistic, theoretical, and vapid. We're wasting our time.**

See how the students respond. If they take an opposing position, continue in this vein. If they don't, ask them if they think they've wasted their time by considering this essay. To me, thinking about something that might be important and concluding that it is not important is hardly a waste of time.

WRAP UP

➤ **From time to time, it's worth thinking about the long-range consequences of technology trends. In this case, we find that adapting to industry-wide inherent processes may create competitive advantages but—at least for interdepartmental processes—those advantages may not be sustainable.**

➤ **By the way, most medium to large-scale companies have a person called the CTO, or chief technology officer. You'll learn more about that person in Chapter 10. One of the key roles of that person is to think about the longer-range consequences of technology use. The job of CTO is fascinating, and it is one that some of you might want to consider.**

ASSIGNMENT MATERIAL

Review Questions

1. Summarize the three eras of information systems development. Why was the movement from calculation systems to functional systems easier than the movement from functional systems to integrated systems?
2. Choose one area of interest from human resources, accounting and finance, sales and marketing, operations, or manufacturing. Summarize information systems used in that area of interest.
3. Summarize the problems of functional systems. Which single problem do you believe is the most serious? Does your answer depend on a particular company or industry? Why or why not?
4. Explain how the organization's competitive strategy relates to information systems design.
5. List the five primary activities in Porter's value chain model and explain the function of each.
6. List the four support activities in Porter's value chain model and explain the function of each.
7. Why are activity linkages important?
8. Summarize the activities in business process redesign.
9. Explain why business process redesign is both difficult and expensive.
10. Explain how integrated application vendors gave a boost to business process redesign.
11. Describe three different business processes used at your university.
12. Describe the customer life cycle.
13. Explain how CRM systems support the product life cycle. Why are customer data more easily accessed with CRM systems?
14. List the major advantages of an ERP system.
15. Summarize the process of implementing an ERP system.
16. Explain the basic concept of EAI.

Applying Your Knowledge

17. Apply the value chain model to a retailer such as Target (*target.com*). What is its competitive strategy? Describe the tasks Target must accomplish for each of the primary value chain activities. How does Target's competitive strategy and the nature of its business influence the general characteristics of Target's information systems?
18. Apply the value chain model to a mail-order company such as L.L Bean (*llbean.com*). What is its competitive strategy? Describe the tasks L.L. Bean must accomplish for each of the primary value chain activities. How does L.L. Bean's competitive strategy and the nature of its business influence the general characteristics of its information systems?
19. Choose one of the following basic business processes: inventory management, operations and manufacturing, HR management, or accounting/financial management. Use the Internet to identify three vendors that license a product to support that process. Compare offerings from the three vendors as follows.
    a. Determine differences in terminology, especially differences in the ways that the vendors use the same terms.
    b. Compare features and functions of each of the product offerings.
    c. For each vendor, specify the characteristics of a company for which that vendor's offering would be ideal.

20. Access the Web sites for SAP, Siebel, and PeopleSoft.

    a. Determine how each vendor uses the term *ERP*. In what ways are their uses of the term similar? In what ways are they different?

    b. Does each vendor have a single ERP product or does each vendor offer different products that, taken together, form an ERP solution?

    c. If you were looking for an ERP solution for your company, how would you deal with the differences in the use of the term *ERP*? How would you compare product offerings to determine which product is most appropriate for your organization?

    d. How does your answer to part c change if you assume that (1) your company is a manufacturer, (2) your company is a distributor, and (3) your company is a hotel chain?

Application Exercises

21. Suppose your manager asks you to create a spreadsheet to compute a production schedule. Your schedule should stipulate a production quantity for seven products that is based on sales projections made by three regional managers at your company's three sales regions.

    a. Create a separate worksheet for each sales region. Assume that each sheet contains monthly sales projections for each of the past four quarters. Assume that it also contains actual monthly sales for each of those past four quarters. Finally, assume that each sheet contains a projection for each month in the coming quarter.

    b. Fill in sample data for each of the worksheets in part a.

    c. On each of the worksheets, use the data from the prior four quarters to compute the discrepancy between the actual sales and the sale projections. This discrepancy can be computed in several ways: You could calculate an overall average, you could calculate an average per quarter or per month. You could also weight recent discrepancies more heavily than earlier ones. Choose a method that you think is most appropriate. Explain why you chose the method you did.

    d. Modify your worksheets to use the discrepancy factors to compute an adjusted forecast for the coming quarter. Thus, each of your spreadsheets will show the raw forecast and the adjusted forecast for each month in the coming quarter.

    e. Create a fourth worksheet that totals sales projections for all of the regions. Show both the unadjusted forecast and the adjusted forecast for each region and for the company overall. Show month and quarter totals.

    f. Create a bar graph showing total monthly production. Display the unadjusted and adjusted forecasts using different colored bars.

22. Figure 7-8, the sample bill of materials, is a form produced using Microsoft Access. Producing such a form is a bit tricky, so this exercise will guide you through the steps required. You can then apply what you learn to produce a similar report. You can also use Access to experiment on extensions of this form.

    a. Create a table named PART with columns PartNumber, Level, Description, QuantityRequired, and PartOf. Description and Level should be text, PartNumber should be AutoNumber, and QuantityRequired and PartOf should be numeric, long integer. Add the PART data shown in Figure 7-8 to your table.

    b. Create a query that has all columns of PART. Restrict the view to rows having a value of 1 for Level. Name your query **Level1**.

    c. Create two more queries that are restricted to rows having values of 2 or 3 for Level. Name your queries **Level2** and **Level3**, respectively.

    d. Create a form that contains PartNumber, Level, and Description from **Level1**. You can use a wizard for this if you want. Name the form **Bill of Materials**.

    e. Using the subform tool in the Toolbox, create a subform in your form in part d. Set the data on this form to be all of the columns of **Level2**. After you have created the subform, ensure that the Link Child Fields property is set to PartOf and that the Link Master Fields property is set to PartNumber. Close the Bill of Materials form.

    f. Open the subform created in part e and create a subform on it. Set the data on this subform to be all of the columns of **Level3**. After you have created the subform, ensure that the Link Child Fields property is set to PartOf and that the Link Master Fields property is set to PartNumber. Close the Bill of Materials form.

    g. Open the Bill of Materials Form. It should appear as in Figure 7-8. Open and close the form and add new data. Using this form, add sample BOM data for a product of your own choosing.

h. Following the process similar to that just described, create a Bill of Materials Report that lists the data for all of your products.

i. **(Optional, challenging extension)** Each part in the BOM in Figure 7-8 can be used in at most one assembly (there is space to show just one PartOf value). You can change your design to allow a part to be used in more than one assembly as follows. First, remove PartOf from PART. Next, create a second table that has two columns: AssemblyPartNumber and ComponentPartNumber. The first contains a part number of an assembly and the second a part number of a component. Every component of a part will have a row in this table. Extend the views described above to use this second table and to produce a display similar to Figure 7-8.

Career Assignments

23. Use your favorite search engine to search the Web for the term *MRP job opportunities*.

Investigate several of the sites that you find to answer the following questions.

a. Describe the two jobs in the search results that you find to be the most interesting.
b. Describe the educational requirements for each of these jobs.
c. Describe internships and other experience that you could gain to better prepare you for each of these jobs.
d. Using both Web resources and your own experience, describe the employment outlook for these jobs.

24. Same as question 23, but search for the term *ERP job opportunities*.

25. Same as question 23, but search for the term *EAI job opportunities*.

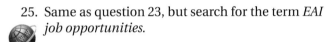

Case Study 7-1

Enterprise IS and the Physical Workplace

Knoll, Inc. (*knoll.com*) is a leading manufacturer of office equipment. Founded in 1938, Knoll has always been known for its groundbreaking, innovative, and fashionable designs. Today, such innovation includes not only modern, contemporary designs, but also designs that recognize changes in the nature of the work environment. Knoll understood early on that the move from hierarchical thinking to a focus on cross-departmental business processes dramatically impacts the physical design of workers' environments.

According to Christine Barber, Director of Workplace Research at Knoll, "The explosion of information technology has caused a fundamental shift in company offices away from clerical and toward professional, managerial, and creative work. . . . Whereas white-collar labor in the nineteenth and most of the twentieth century involved an army of clerical workers performing rote tasks under the supervision of an elite corps of managers, most of the grunt work has now been turned over to computers. . . . Two-thirds [of office workers] describe themselves as 'problem solvers,' 'information analyzers,' and 'idea generators'. . . . Half of those working in midsize to large companies characterize their work as 'collaborative' in nature" (Barber and Yee, 2004).

Because of the importance of workplace changes to its market, Knoll commissioned a study involving 1,500 interviews of 350 office workers. Researchers asked those workers to rate the importance of office factors in terms of their contribution to productivity. The following are the top five factors, rated in decreasing order of productivity impact:

- State-of-the-art computer technology
- Ample storage space for work items
- Control over temperature
- Quiet workspace
- Space that can be personalized

In this study, Knoll also found a curious paradox in workers' attitudes toward privacy. Most workers want it both ways: They want their own office or private space in which to concentrate, perform uninterrupted work, and hold private meetings, but they also want open space for collaboration, a feeling of teamwork, and a sense of family. Modern workers, according to Knoll's study, "crave both privacy and intimacy." They want an open space design rather than a cubicle configuration. In fact, according to the research study, "the cubicle is the symbol of everything 'old economy' in workplace design, evoking images of 'prison,' conformity, being a number or stamped with a barcode" (Barber and DYG, Inc., 2004).

According to Barber, "As the workforce of the new economy performs increasingly cerebral, self-directed, and multidisciplinary tasks, the gap between managers and managed narrows dramatically in terms of skills, experience, and responsibility. But the flattening of the organizational pyramid has not inspired any real change in office space" (Barber and DYG, Inc., 2004).

These are intriguing statements. We know that information systems improve communication and that they foster cross-departmental, process thinking. Do they also change the shape of the workplace? They should, at least according to Barber: "Businesses feel compelled to invest in cutting-edge information technology to stay competitive; but they persist in seeing offices as assembly lines, rather than as think tanks, for producing knowledge-based products and services" (Barber and Yee, 2004).

Sources: Christine Barber and DYG, Inc., "The 21st Century Workplace"; Christine Barber and Roger Yee, "Brave New Workplace," 2004, *knoll.com/research/index.htm* (accessed March 2005).

Questions

1. Given the fact that Knoll sponsored the research described here, is Knoll more likely to be engaging in a cost leader or differentiator competitive strategy? Explain your answer.

2. How will the change from hierarchical to cross-departmental, process thinking affect the design of office furniture and equipment? Do you think there will be sufficient impact to justify Knoll's concern and research? What are the dangers to a company like Knoll of not considering these trends?

3. Describe two nontechnology-related industries, other than the office furniture industry, that are likely to be changed by cross-departmental, enterprise-wide information systems and related organizational changes. Explain the nature of the impact on those industries.

4. Suppose you are a product manager in Knoll's marketing group. Describe three ways you could use the five productivity factors listed in this case to design new products, product features, or product enhancements.

5. Suppose you manage a sales department with two types of salespeople: those who call on prospects to obtain new customers and those who sell to existing customers. Assume that each salesperson works in a personal cubicle and that salespeople are assigned to cubicles regardless of the type of sales they perform.

Suppose your department is converting to a new CRM system, and you take that opportunity to propose an improvement to your sales team's workplace.

a. Given the information in this case, what changes would you make?

b. Suppose you ask the manager of the new CRM project for funds to purchase new office furniture and equipment. Suppose she rejects your request saying, "New furniture has absolutely nothing to do with the success of our new system." How do you respond?

c. Rank the importance of the workspace arrangement for the users of a new information system. Is the environment equally important as the system's features? More important? Less important? Explain your answer.

Case Study 7-2

Manufacturing Planning at the Brose Group

Reread *MIS in Use 7-2*, about the Brose Group (page 218) before you proceed with this case.

Modern manufacturing seeks to improve productivity by reducing waste, which means eliminating:

- Overproduction that leads to excess inventories
- Unavailable needed parts, which idle workers and facilities
- Wasted motion and processing due to poorly planned materials handling and operations activities

Manufacturing that eliminates these wastes is called *lean manufacturing*.

To accomplish lean manufacturing, SAP has invented a business process it calls just-in-sequence (JIS) manufacturing. JIS is an extension to just-in-time (JIT), the pull manufacturing philosophy described in this chapter. JIS extends JIT so that parts not only arrive just in time, but also arrive in just the correct sequence.

For example, the Brose Group factory in Brazil manufactures doors for General Motors. When General Motors starts the construction of a new auto, it sends a signal of the need for doors to the Brose Group. That signal, a kanban, starts the construction of the four doors on four separate production lines in Brazil. Brose schedules the work on each of these lines so as to produce the four doors and their related equipment and deliver them at the correct time and in the correct sequence at General Motors. Thus, if General Motors needs the rear-door frames, then the front-door frames, then the front doors, and finally the rear doors, Brose will schedule manufacturing and delivery accordingly.

To achieve JIS, Brose used SAP R/3 combined with a supplementary SAP module called SAP for Automotive with JIS. Like all ERP software, these applications include inherent processes. In this case, those business processes include manufacturing planning methods and procedures for JIS performance.

Sources: brose.de/en/pub/company (accessed November 2004); *sap.com/industries/automotive/pdf/ CS_Brose_Group.pdf*, 2003 (accessed March 2005).

Questions

1. Reflect on the nature of JIS planning. In general terms, what kinds of data must Brose have in order to provide JIS to its customers? What does Brose need to know? It certainly needs a bill of materials for the items it produces. What other categories of information will Brose need?

2. According to the description on page 218, the SAP system included applications for sales and distribution, materials management, production planning, quality management, and financial accounting and control. Describe, in general terms, features and functions of these applications that are necessary to provide JIS.

3. The Brose factory in Brazil produces more than doors for General Motors. The factory must coordinate the door orders with orders for other products and orders from other manufacturers. What kinds of information systems are necessary to provide such coordinated manufacturing planning?

4. Brazilians speak Portuguese, workers in the United States speak English and Spanish, and personnel at the Brose headquarters speak German. Summarize challenges to Brose and SAP Consulting when implementing a system for users who speak four different languages and live in four (at least) different cultures.

5. Visit *sap.com/industries/automotive* and investigate SAP for Automotive with JIS. What features and functions does this product have that standard SAP R/3 does not have? What advantages does SAP obtain by creating and licensing this product? What advantages do SAP's customers obtain from this product? In your response, consider both R/3 customers who are and who are not automotive manufacturers.

6. Brose seeks to provide JIS service to its customers. Does this goal necessitate that Brose suppliers also provide JIS service to Brose? What can Brose do if its suppliers do not provide such service? Is there any reason why Brose would not want them to provide such service? Do you think that before one company in a supply chain can offer JIS, all companies in the supply chain must offer the service?

CHAPTER 8

E-commerce and Supply Chain Systems

Learning Objectives

* Understand Porter's five competitive forces model.
* Define e-commerce and important e-commerce terms.
* Understand the effect of e-commerce on market efficiency.
* Learn technology for supporting commerce servers.
* Understand the structure, profitability, and dynamics of supply chains.
* Know the purpose, concepts, advantages, and disadvantages of EDI.
* Know the purpose, concepts, advantages, and disadvantages of XML.

Guides

PROBLEM SOLVING GUIDE
Interorganizational Information Exchange

OPPOSING FORCES GUIDE
The Lawyer's Full-Employment Act

ETHICS GUIDE
The Ethics of Supply Chain Information Sharing

SECURITY GUIDE
A Trojan Horse?

REFLECTIONS GUIDE
XML and the Future of Computing

Chapter Preview

Chapter 7 surveyed information systems within an organization. This chapter builds on that discussion and describes information systems among or across organizations. Such interorganizational information systems have increased in importance in recent years because of the increased availability of computer networks—the Internet as well as private and proprietary networks. As recently as 10 or 15 years ago, organizations communicated primarily by telephone and fax. Today, those primitive communications methods have been replaced by computer communications.

We begin the chapter with a discussion of Porter's five competitive forces model and how it relates to interorganizational processing. We then define e-commerce and related terms and assess the impact of e-commerce activity on market efficiency. We then present the technology that supports e-commerce activities. Next, we describe the structure and characteristics of supply chains. We describe two important supply chain problems and then introduce EDI and XML, two technologies used for exchanging messages and data on supply chains. We conclude with a brief discussion of XML Web services, a new and important technology for interorganizational information systems.

Universal Electronics (continued)

At the end of Chapter 7, we left you in the middle of the task that your COO had given you. He had rejected your idea for a new, extended customer support system for Universal Electronics because it did not fit the organization's strategy of being the industry cost leader. He did not want to hear how your proposed system could save costs in customer service; at least "not yet," he said. He wanted you to look for other cost-saving applications throughout the company. By the end of Chapter 7, you had decided to consider an application for reducing Universal's inventory, but that required knowledge of interorganizational systems. We consider such systems in this chapter and conclude this saga at the end of the chapter.

■ Porter's Five Competitive Forces Model

Video

In the previous chapter, you learned about Porter's model of competitive strategies and his model of value chains. We used the concept of value chains to show the importance of moving from functional information systems to process-based, cross-departmental information systems.

Porter developed a third model that helps to introduce the notion of interorganizational systems. That model, illustrated in Figure 8-1, is called the **Porter's five competitive forces model**. According to this model, five competitive forces determine industry profitability: bargaining power of suppliers, bargaining power of customers,

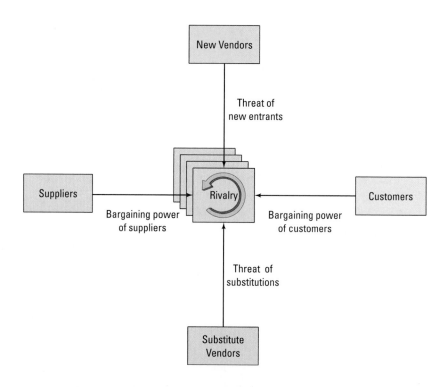

Figure 8-1
Porter's Model of Industry Structure

Universal Electronics (page 230)

GOALS

* Use the case introduced in Chapter 7 to discuss the inventory savings possible with interorganizational information systems.

* Motivate students to learn about interorganizational IS by considering cost savings in addition to those from inventory.

WAYS TO STIMULATE STUDENT INVOLVEMENT

Universal's competitive strategy is to be the cost leader. The COO and steering committee rejected the proposal to build a customer support database because "someone might actually use it," meaning employees would spend labor hours on service rather than on cost reduction.

Our protagonist has been challenged to find information systems that will reduce costs. The system he/she proposed might do that, but he/she has been asked to look more broadly.

By the end of Chapter 7, our protagonist had decided to focus on inventory, wondering if there was a way to reduce inventory not by 5 percent, but by 40 to 50 percent. There might be a way, but it would require Universal to integrate its inventory needs with its suppliers' inventory systems. Some type of interorganizational system would be required.

➤ **Do you think an inventory reduction of 40 to 50 percent is possible?**

➤ **What does 40 to 50 percent mean? Percent of what? Percent of items in inventory? Percent of inventory costs?**

➤ **Is there a difference?**

➤ **Which should Universal focus on?**

You can use the following series of questions to set up the topics in this chapter:

➤ **Our protagonist may have settled on reducing costs via inventory too soon. Maybe there were better alternatives.**

➤ **What is e-commerce?**

➤ **Could Universal use e-commerce to sell its goods to its customers?**

➤ **Would e-commerce substantially reduce costs?**

➤ **What additional information do you need to decide if e-commerce is a cost-reduction solution that Universal should investigate?**

As you will see, the text introduces four drivers of supply chain performance:

• Facilities (number, size, location, design)

• Inventory (balance between availability and cost)

• Transportation (how and when to move goods)

• Information (about customers, orders, inventories, suppliers, transportation alternatives, etc.)

➤ **How could information impact the cost of the other three drivers?**

➤ **Does a consideration of these drivers suggest ways that an information system could reduce cost besides reducing inventory?**

➤ **We'll return to these questions at the end of this chapter.**

WRAP UP

The following are some possible questions to set up the topic of interorganizational systems:

➤ **What is the difference between intra-organizational IS and interorganizational IS?**

➤ **Did the COO ask our protagonist specifically to investigate interorganizational systems?**

(No, but he would have been disappointed, I'd think, if they weren't considered.)

➤ **What did the COO ask?**

(Find a way to reduce costs.)

➤ **What do you need to know about interorganizational IS to be able to assess whether intra- or interorganizational IS are more likely to result in cost savings?**

new entrants to the market, rivalry among firms in the market, and the threat of substitutions for an organization's products or services.

These factors determine not only how organizations gain competitive advantages, but also how **sustainable** those advantages are. For example, when an organization adds value to its product and obtains an increase in price, it may not be able to sustain that price. Suppliers upstream may demand a portion of the value added by raising their prices. Similarly, depending on how competitive an industry is, other firms may copy the value added by the firm: Competitors who copy the value added may soon bargain away the price premium from that addition. Then both organizations may find themselves with reduced profitability. They both continue to provide the new service, but at a reduced price.

Information systems play a key role in obtaining sustainable advantages among organizations. In Chapter 2, we discussed how information systems can provide barriers to entry to reduce the risk of new entrants, competitor rivalry, and substitutions. In this chapter, we will consider how information systems can create sustainable advantages among customers and suppliers. We begin with e-commerce and then turn to supply chain management.

■ E-Commerce

E-commerce is the buying and selling of goods and services over public and private computer networks. Notice that this definition restricts e-commerce to buying and selling transactions. Checking the weather at *yahoo.com* is not e-commerce, but buying a weather service subscription that is paid for and delivered over the Internet is.

Figure 8-2 lists categories of e-commerce companies. The U.S. Census Bureau, which publishes statistics on e-commerce activity, defines **merchant companies** as those that take title to the goods they sell. They buy goods and resell them. It defines **nonmerchant companies** as those that arrange for the purchase and sale of goods without ever owning or taking title to those goods. Regarding services, merchant companies sell services that they provide; nonmerchant companies sell services provided by others. We will consider merchants and nonmerchants separately in the following sections.

E-Commerce Merchant Companies

There are three main types of merchant companies: those that sell directly to consumers, those that sell to companies, and those that sell to government. Each uses slightly different information systems in the course of doing business. **B2C**, or **business-to-consumer**, e-commerce concerns sales between a supplier and a retail customer (the consumer). A typical information system for B2C provides a Web-based application or **Web storefront** by which customers enter and manage their orders. Amazon.com, REI.com, and LLBean.com are examples of companies that use B2C information systems.[1]

The term **B2B**, or **business-to-business**, e-commerce refers to sales between companies. As Figure 8-3 (page 232) shows, raw materials suppliers use B2B systems to sell to manufacturers, manufacturers use B2B systems to sell to distributors, and distributors uses B2B systems to sell to retailers.

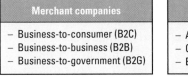

Merchant companies	Nonmerchant companies
– Business-to-consumer (B2C) – Business-to-business (B2B) – Business-to-government (B2G)	– Auctions – Clearinghouses – Exchanges

Figure 8-2
E-Commerce Categories

---

[1]Strictly speaking, B2C is not commerce between two organizations. However, because it is commerce between two independently owned entities (the retailer and the consumer), we include it in this chapter.

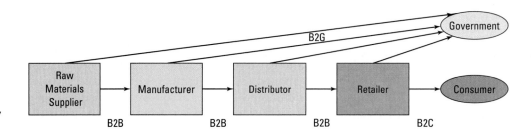

Figure 8-3
Example of Use of B2B, B2G, and B2C

B2G, or **business-to-government**, refers to sales between companies and governmental organizations. As Figure 8-3 shows, a manufacturer that uses an e-commerce site to sell computer hardware to the U.S. Department of State is engaging in B2G commerce. Suppliers, distributors, and retailers can sell to the government as well.

B2C applications first captured the attention of mail-order and related businesses. However, companies in all sectors of the economy soon realized the enormous potential of B2B and B2G. The number of companies engaged in B2B and B2G commerce now far exceeds those engaging in B2C commerce.

Furthermore, today's B2B and B2G applications implement just a small portion of their potential capability. Their full utilization is some years away. Although most experts agree that these applications involve some sort of integration of CRM and SRM (supplier relationship management) systems, the nature of that integration is not well understood and is still being developed. Consequently, you can expect further progress and development in B2B and B2G applications during your career. Later in this chapter we will discuss some of the problems of B2B and the technology that is used to solve those problems.

Nonmerchant E-Commerce

The most common nonmerchant e-commerce companies are auctions and clearinghouses. E-commerce **auctions** match buyers and sellers by using an e-commerce version of a standard auction. This e-commerce application enables the auction company to offer goods for sale and to support a competitive bidding process. The best-known auction company is eBay, but many other auction companies exist; many serve particular industries. *MIS in Use 8-1* describes a B2B e-commerce site for the steel industry.

Clearinghouses provide goods and services at a stated price and they arrange for the delivery of the goods, but they never take title. One division of Amazon.com, for example, operates as a nonmerchant clearinghouse and sells books owned by others. As a clearinghouse, Amazon matches the seller and the buyer and then takes payment from the buyer and transfers the payment to the seller, minus a commission. Figure 8-4 shows a typical Amazon.com listing for selling books that it does not own.

Other examples of clearinghouse businesses are **electronic exchanges** that match buyers and sellers; the business process is similar to that of a stock exchange. Sellers offer goods at a given price through the electronic exchange, and buyers make offers to purchase over the same exchange. Price matches result in transactions from which the exchange takes a commission. Priceline.com is an example of an exchange used by consumers.

E-Commerce Improves Market Efficiency

The debate continues among business observers as to whether e-commerce is something new or if it is just a technology extension to existing business practice. During the dot-com heyday in 1999–2000, some claimed that e-commerce was ushering in a new era and a "new economy." Although experts differ as to whether a "new economy" was created, all agree that e-commerce does lead to greater market efficiency.

For one, e-commerce leads to **disintermediation**, which is the elimination of middle layers in the supply chain. You can buy a flat-screen LCD HDTV from a typical electronics store or you can use e-commerce to buy it from the manufacturer. If you

Steel Spider

Steel Spider (*steelspider.com*) is a nonmerchant Web site that helps steel suppliers promote their companies, generate sales leads, and sell steel. It helps buyers locate and purchase steel. Sellers pay a fee to advertise their steel products and sponsor invitational steel auctions on Steel Spider. Buyers participate without charge.

Suppliers make dozens of different types and formats of steel. Buyers search Steel Spider for the type and format of steel they require. If the steel they need is not currently available, buyers can register their ongoing needs with the site. A software agent, named Boris, on the Steel Spider site watches new supplier listings and notifies registered buyers when steel of the desired type and format becomes available. Another feature allows a buyer to describe an

immediate need and Steel Spider transmits a notification of that need to its existing suppliers who can contact the buyer directly if they desire.

Steel Spider also provides a platform for invitational auctions. Suppliers schedule an auction with the site and specify date, time, and length of the sale. They also provide a description of the steel to be sold, the minimum acceptable bid, and the minimum bid increment. Additionally, the supplier provides a list of the email addresses of buyers who are allowed to bid. Steel Spider then conducts the auction for these terms. The auction process is similar to that on a public auction site like eBay. The major differences are the seller pays a fixed fee per auction and that bidders must be preapproved by the seller.

Source: steelspider.com (accessed May 2005). Used with permission of Mountain Hawk Corporation.

take the latter route, you eliminate the distributor, the retailer, and possibly more. The product is shipped directly from the manufacturer's finished goods inventory to you. You eliminate the distributor's and retailer's inventory carrying costs, and you eliminate shipping overhead and handling activity. Because the distributor and associated inventories have become unnecessary waste, disintermediation increases market efficiency.

E-commerce also improves the flow of price information. As a consumer, you can go to any number of Web sites that offer product price comparisons. You can search for the HDTV you want and sort the results by price and vendor reputation. You can find vendors that avoid your state sales tax or that omit or reduce shipping charges.

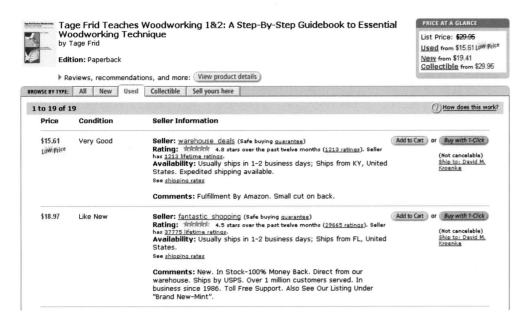

Figure 8-4
Amazon Clearinghouse Sales

The improved distribution of information about price and terms enables you to pay the lowest possible cost and serves ultimately to remove inefficient vendors. The market as a whole becomes more efficient.

From the seller's side, e-commerce produces information about **price elasticity** that has not been available before. Price elasticity measures the amount that demand rises or falls with changes in price. Using an auction, a company can learn not just what the top price for an item is, but also learn the second, third, and other prices from the losing bids. In this way, the company can determine the shape of the price elasticity curve.

Similarly, e-commerce companies can learn price elasticity directly from experiments on customers. For example, in one experiment, Amazon.com created three groups of similar books. It raised the price of one group 10 percent, lowered the price of the second group 10 percent, and left the price of the third group unchanged. Customers provided feedback to these changes by deciding whether to buy books at the offered prices. Amazon.com measured the total revenue (quantity times price) of each group and took the action (raise, lower, or maintain prices) on all books that maximized revenue. Amazon.com repeated the process until it reached the point at which the indicated action was to maintain current prices.

Managing prices by direct interaction with the customer yields better information than managing prices by watching competitors' pricing. By experimenting with customers, companies learn how customers have internalized competitors' pricing, advertising, and messaging. It might be that customers do not know about a competitor's lower prices, in which case there is no need for a price reduction. Or, it may be that the competitor is using a price that, if lowered, would increase demand sufficiently to increase total revenue. Figure 8-5 summarizes e-commerce market consequences.

Many B2B and other interorganizational information systems require meetings among the companies involved to design the joint processes that will be used and eventually to negotiate contracts. You may be asked to participate in such meetings, and, if so, you need to know how to behave in them, as described in the *Problem Solving Guide* on page 235a.

E-Commerce Economics

Although there are tremendous advantages and opportunities for many organizations to engage in e-commerce, the economics of some industries may disfavor e-commerce activity. Companies need to consider the following economic factors:

- Channel conflict
- Price conflict
- Logistics expense
- Customer service expense

Figure 8-3 (page 232) shows a manufacturer selling directly to a government agency. Before engaging in such e-commerce, the manufacturer must consider each of the economic factors just listed. First, what *channel conflict* will develop? Suppose the manufacturer is a computer maker that is selling directly, B2G, to the State Department. When the manufacturer begins to sell goods B2G that State Department employees used to purchase from a retailer down the street, that retailer will resent the competition and may drop the manufacturer. If the value of the lost sales is greater than the value of the B2G sales, e-commerce is not a good solution, at least not on that basis.

Figure 8-5
E-Commerce Market
Consequences

Greater market efficiency	Knowledge of price elasticity
– Disintermediation – Increased information on price and terms	– Losing-bidder auction prices – Price experimentation – More accurate information obtained directly from customer

Furthermore, when a business engages in e-commerce it may also cause *price conflict* with its traditional channels. Because of disintermediation, the manufacturer may be able to offer a lower price and still make a profit. However, as soon as the manufacturer offers the lower price, existing channels will object. Even if the manufacturer and the retailer are not competing for the same customers, the retailer still will not want a lower price to be readily known via the Web.

Also, the existing distribution and retailing partners do provide value; they are not just a cost. Without them, the manufacturer will have the increased *logistic expense* of entering and processing orders in small quantities. If the expense of processing a 1-unit order is the same as that for processing a 12-unit order (which it might be), the average logistic expense per item will be much higher for goods sold via e-commerce.

Similarly, *customer service* expenses are likely to increase for manufacturers that use e-commerce to sell directly to consumers. The manufacturer will be required to provide service to less sophisticated users and on a one-by-one basis. For example, instead of explaining to a single sales professional that the recent shipment of 100 Gizmo 3.0s requires a new bracket, the manufacturer will need to explain that 100 times to less knowledgeable, frustrated customers. Such service requires more training and more expense.

All four economic factors are important for organizations to consider when they contemplate e-commerce sales.

E-Commerce and the World Wide Web

As stated, e-commerce is the buying and selling of products and services over public and private networks. Most B2C commerce conducted over the World Wide Web (WWW) uses Web storefronts supported by commerce servers. A **commerce server** is a computer that operates Web-based programs that display products, support online ordering, record and process payments, and interface with inventory-management applications. If you are involved in managing your company's e-commerce activity, you will need to understand how commerce servers work. However, first we need to discuss the structure and components of the World Wide Web.

Web Technology

Chapter 4 explained how the Internet works and introduced you to several prominent Internet protocols, shown in Figure 8-6. To review, SMTP (Simple Mail Transport Protocol) is used for email; FTP (File Transfer Protocol) is used to exchange files. Those protocols are important for email and file transfer, but for e-commerce and Web applications, most sites generate HTML and transmit it using HTTP (Hypertext Transfer Protocol).

Web Pages and Hypertext Markup Language

HTTP is used to exchange **Web pages** over the Internet. Such pages are documents encoded in a language called **HTML**, or **Hypertext Markup Language**. This language defines the structure and layout of Web pages. An HTML **tag** is a notation used to define a data element for display or other purposes. The HTML code at the top of page 236 illustrates a typical heading tag.

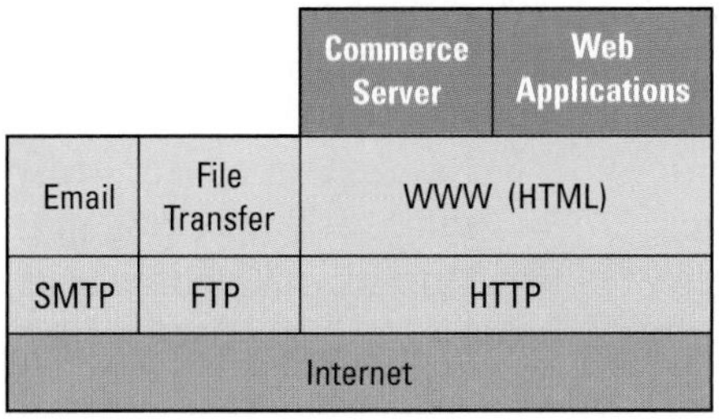

Figure 8-6
Internet Protocols and Uses

PROBLEMSOLVING
GUIDE

Interorganizational Information Exchange

Interorganizational information systems—information systems that connect two or more organizations—require collaborative agreements among independent companies and organizations. Such agreements can be successful only if all parties have a clear idea of the goals, benefits, costs, and risks of working together. The creation of collaborative agreements requires many joint meetings in which the parties make their goals and objectives clear and decide how best to share information and other resources.

During your career, you may be asked to participate is such meetings. You should understand a few basic guidelines before participating.

First, when you meet with employees of another company, realize that you must apply stronger limits on your conversation than when you meet with employees in your own firm. For all you know, the company you are meeting with may become your strongest competitor. In general, you should assume that whatever you say to an employee of another company could be general knowledge in your industry the next day.

Of course, the goal of such meetings is to develop a collaborative relationship, and you cannot accomplish that goal without saying something. The best strategy, however, is to reveal exactly what you must reveal and no more.

Before you meet with another company, you and your team should have a clear and common understanding of the purpose of the meeting. Your team needs to agree beforehand on the topics that are to be addressed and those that are to be avoided. Relationships often develop in stages: Two companies meet, establish one level of understanding, meet again with another level of understanding, and so forth, feeling one another out on the way to some type of relationship.

You may be asked to sign a nondisclosure agreement. Such agreements are contracts that stipulate the responsibilities of each party in protecting the other's proprietary information. Such agreements vary in length; some are a page long and some are 30 pages long. You need to understand the policy of your organization with regard to such agreements before the meeting starts. Sometimes, companies exchange their standard nondisclosure agreements before the meeting so that the respective legal departments can review and approve the agreements ahead of time.

In your remarks, stick to the purpose of the meeting. Avoid conversations about your company or about third parties that do not relate to the meeting topic. You never know the agenda of the other party; you never know what other companies they are meeting; and you never know what other information about your company they may want.

Realize that a meeting isn't over until it's over. The meeting is still underway in the hallway waiting for the elevator. It's still underway at lunch. And it's still underway as you share a cab to the airport. By the way,

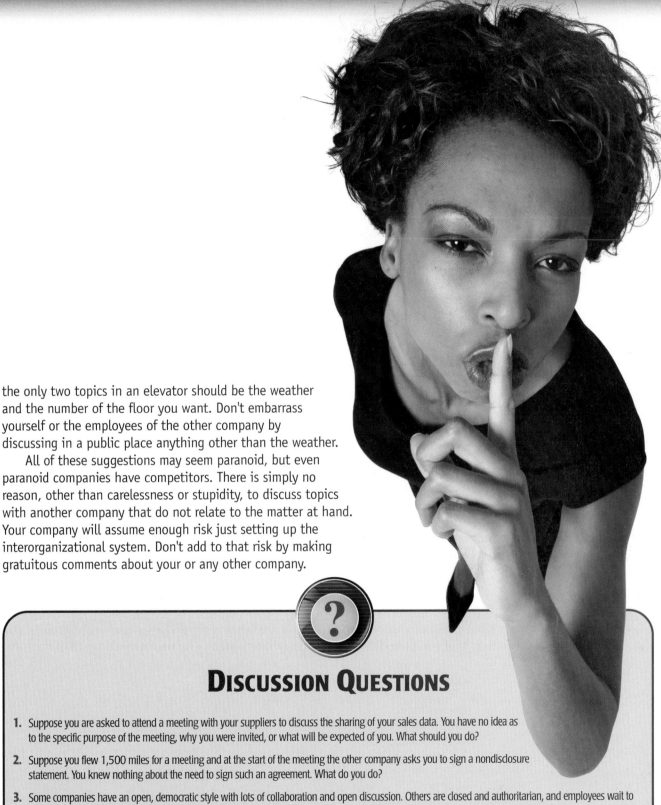

the only two topics in an elevator should be the weather and the number of the floor you want. Don't embarrass yourself or the employees of the other company by discussing in a public place anything other than the weather.

All of these suggestions may seem paranoid, but even paranoid companies have competitors. There is simply no reason, other than carelessness or stupidity, to discuss topics with another company that do not relate to the matter at hand. Your company will assume enough risk just setting up the interorganizational system. Don't add to that risk by making gratuitous comments about your or any other company.

DISCUSSION QUESTIONS

1. Suppose you are asked to attend a meeting with your suppliers to discuss the sharing of your sales data. You have no idea as to the specific purpose of the meeting, why you were invited, or what will be expected of you. What should you do?

2. Suppose you flew 1,500 miles for a meeting and at the start of the meeting the other company asks you to sign a nondisclosure statement. You knew nothing about the need to sign such an agreement. What do you do?

3. Some companies have an open, democratic style with lots of collaboration and open discussion. Others are closed and authoritarian, and employees wait to be told what to do. Describe what will happen when employees from two such companies meet. What can be done to improve the situation?

4. Suppose during lunch an employee of another company asks you, "What are you all doing about XML Web services?" (We discuss this topic later in the chapter on page 252.) Assume that this topic has little to do with the purpose of your meeting. You think about it and decide that it doesn't seem too risky to respond, so you say, "Not much." What information have you conveyed by this statement? What is a better way to respond to the question?

5. Suppose you are in a joint meeting and you are asked, "So who else are you working with on this problem?" Describe guidelines you could use in deciding how to answer this question.

6. Explain the statement, "A meeting isn't over until it's over." How might this statement pertain to other meetings—say, a job interview?

```
<h2>Price of Item</h2>
```

Notice that tags are enclosed in < > (called *angle brackets*) and that they occur in pairs. The start of this tag is indicated by <h2>, and the end of the tag is indicated by </h2>. The words between the tags are the value of the tag. This HTML tag means to place the words "Price of Item" on a Web page in the style of a level-two heading. The creator of the Web page will define the style (font size, color, and so forth) for headings and other tags.

Web pages include **hyperlinks**, which are pointers to other Web pages. A hyperlink contains the URL (Uniform Resource Locator; see Chapter 5, page 142) of the Web page to obtain when the user clicks the hyperlink. The URL can reference a page on the server that generated the page containing the hyperlink or it can reference a page on another server.

Figure 8-7(a) shows a simple HTML document. The document has a heading that provides metadata about the page and a body that contains the content. The tag <h1> means to format the indicated text as a level-one heading; <h2> means a level-two heading. The tag <a> defines a hyperlink. This tag has an **attribute**, which is a variable used to provide properties about a tag. Not all tags have attributes, but many do. Each attribute has a standard name. The attribute for a hyperlink is *href,* and its value indicates which Web page is to be displayed when the user clicks the link. Here, the page *prenhall.com/kroenke* is to be returned when the user clicks the hyperlink. Figure 8-7(b) shows this page as rendered by Internet Explorer.

HTML documents are transmitted by **Web servers** and are consumed by (used by) **browsers**. A Web server is a program that processes the HTTP protocol and transmits Web pages on demand. When you type *http://ibm.com,* you are issuing a request via HTTP for the server at the domain name *ibm.com* to send you its default Web page. The two most popular Web server programs are Apache, commonly used on Linux, and IIS (Internet Information Server), a component of Windows XP Professional and other Windows products.

A browser is a program that processes the HTTP protocol; receives, displays, and processes HTML documents; and transmits responses. Common browsers are Internet Explorer, Netscape Navigator, and Mozilla's FireFox. By the way, some HTML documents contain snippets of program code. That code is sent from the Web server to the user's browser and is processed by the browser on the user's computer.

Three-Tier Architecture

Most commerce server applications use what is called **three-tier architecture**. The tiers refer to three different classes of computers. The **user tier** consists of comput-

```
<html>

<head>
<meta http-equiv="Content-Language" content="en-us">
<title>Using MIS</title>
</head>

<body>

<h1 align="center"><font color="#800080">Using MIS</font></h1>
<p> </p>
<h2><font color="#000080">Example HTML Document</font></h2>

<p> </p>
<p>Click here for textbook web site at Prentice-Hall: 
<a href="http://www.prenhall.com/kroenke">Web Site Link</a></p>

</body>

</html>
```

Figure 8-7a
Sample HTML Document

You Be the Guide

Using the Problem Solving Guide *(page 235a)*

GOALS

* Help students become better business professionals by teaching them proper etiquette at intercompany meetings.

* Forewarn the students of common blunders that can occur when meeting with personnel from other companies.

BACKGROUND AND PRESENTATION STRATEGIES

Supply chain and other interorganizational information systems require meetings between people from different companies. In such meetings, communication behaviors should be more limited than when meeting with personnel from your own company.

Intercompany meetings usually begin with everyone going around the table and introducing him or herself. The students should anticipate that first activity and *prepare an introduction ahead of time.* Once they have a title like Senior VP of International Sales, they won't have to say much. However, while they are still in junior positions they need to find a way to positively introduce themselves without appearing conceited. They need to steer between:

➤ **"Hello, my name is XXX. I'm a very junior employee, and I can't imagine why anyone would want me in this meeting."**

and

➤ **"Hello, my name is XXX, and I invented the Internet. You are so fortunate that I'm here."**

Because a personal introduction is such a common communication requirement, I have my students practice it on me and the class. Each class session, I ask two or three students to introduce themselves. (Actually, I start this practice in the second or third lecture, but it's especially relevant to intercompany meetings where a strong first impression is important.)

Nondisclosure statements are common, at least in the high-tech industry. Employees should *know their company's policy about signing such agreements* long before they schedule their travel. See question 2 for a suggestion about how to handle surprise requests for signing such agreements.

It is so important, especially for people in junior positions, to *know the purpose of the meeting* and to understand *what can and cannot be communicated.* Once something inappropriate has been said, there is no way to take it back. Again, the best way to solve a problem is not to have it at all.

A good guideline is to exchange only that information that needs to be exchanged and no more. Even innocuous statements can be revealing. For social chat, focus on the weather, sporting events, local attractions, antics of your children, or the leading article in today's *Wall Street Journal* (unless it relates to the matter at hand).

A meeting isn't over until it's over. I learned that lesson the hard way. In the heyday of the PC industry between 1985 and 1995, Stuart Alsop was an important columnist and industry pundit for *PCWeek, PC Magazine,* and other such magazines. For several years, he published his own industry newsletter. Alsop's behavior was so unassuming, almost bumbling, that you'd let your guard down. At least I did. And, of course, he was "dumb like a fox." I probably had four or five meetings with him during those years, and in every one I found myself revealing information that I had no intention of revealing. Even worse, after the first meeting, I even knew what he was doing. In that first meeting, he suggested that we get out of the office for some fresh air and walk around the building. Sure enough, in that relaxed and informal atmosphere, I was blathering on and on, as if I was talking to a fellow manager in our company, about what I hoped we'd accomplish in the next year or so. When news of our plans appeared in his next newsletter, our CEO had a serious discussion with me, beginning with a question relating to my IQ. *The meeting isn't over until it's over!*

Corollary to the above: Be especially vigilant at meals.

➤ **When you all go out to lunch, watch what you say in the car, at the restaurant, and on the drive back. You're not having lunch with your family. You're having it with a potential partner, but one who is also meeting with your competitors, the press, and who knows whom else. This person may become your competitor someday.**

➤ **There is no need to make an issue of it in front of the person. Just be aware of the need for care.**

➤ **Stick to the agenda of the meeting. Know what is supposed to be accomplished. Think through ahead of time what you need to communicate and communicate only that.**

➤ Be *exceedingly careful if alcohol is served* at the meal. If you like to drink, do it some other time with your friends. These people are professional associates, not your friends. Don't mix your personal and professional lives.

❓ SUGGESTED RESPONSES FOR DISCUSSION QUESTIONS

1. Find out what you need to know to function effectively. Get answers to all of those questions. What is the purpose of this meeting? Why are you being invited? Ask your manager or someone to help you.

   ➤ **If you're not sure of your role, keep quiet until you are sure. As you rise to higher levels of management, you will have experience to extemporize. Don't start that way, however. You need experience.**

2. When I am caught by surprise by a request to sign a nondisclosure and I have any doubt about whether I want to sign one, I say something like:

   ➤ **I didn't realize we were going to be exchanging confidential information. For now, why don't we just keep our conversation to the nonconfidential aspects of our business together? I'll take your nondisclosure form home with me and let our lawyers OK it. If we need to discuss confidential information in future meetings, we can sign then. OK?**

   If that doesn't work, then, depending on the policy of my company, I may need to fax the form to our attorneys for immediate review, reschedule the meeting, or sign the form.

3. These are very odd and awkward meetings, full of long silences and awkward pauses. (By the way, there is nothing wrong with silence—and it's not for you, as a junior staff member, to fill awkward pauses, anyway.) The key is to know the purpose of the meeting and to stick with that agenda. If you're with the more open company, beware. Just do your business and go home.

   When personnel from another company act odd, there may be something going on. Maybe they've already decided to go with another partner, maybe they have lost interest in the project, maybe they're about to be acquired by your number one competitor. Any of this may have occurred, but they may not have been able to cancel the meeting without revealing what is going on.

4. Don't talk about company business that is not related to the purpose of the meeting. By replying, "Not much," you've said something—maybe that your company is behind the times. A better response would be:

   ➤ **"I don't work in that area, and I wouldn't be able to give you a good answer. How about those Red Sox?"**

5. Answer only if the question is pertinent to the purpose of the meeting and within the scope of what your team has agreed to reveal. Otherwise, duck the question with a response like:

   ➤ **"We're here to work with you, and we're excited to be doing so."**

   A more aggressive—and not recommended response—is:

   ➤ **"Who, besides yourselves, would you recommend?"**

6. The job interview starts with the initial phone call or email, and it isn't over until you've either been hired or not. Every interaction you have with an employee of your future employer is part of your job interview. If someone picks you up at the airport or hotel, the interview begins when you first meet. It's going on while having breakfast, standing in line for a taxi, waiting for the elevator, combing your hair in the bathroom, or walking down the hall to the coffee room. Everything you say is part of the job interview.

WRAP UP

➤ **Business is a social activity. It is in our nature to communicate with one another, and most of us want to appear friendly, or at least not rude. All of that is fine.**

➤ **But always keep in mind, especially when meeting with employees from another company, that you are talking with business associates, not friends. If you say something revealing, you cannot take it back.**

➤ **Stick to the agenda!**

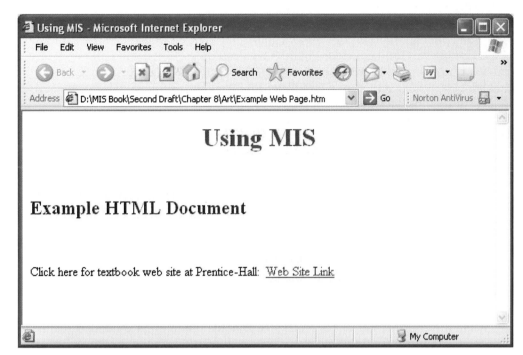

Figure 8-7b
HTML Document on page 236
in Figure 8-7a, rendered
using Internet Explorer

Source: Microsoft product screen
shot reprinted with permission from
Microsoft Corporaton.

ers that have browsers that request and process Web pages. The **server tier** consists of computers that run Web servers and in the process generate Web pages in response to requests from browsers. Web servers also process application programs. In Figure 8-8, the server computers are running both a commerce server and other applications.

To ensure acceptable performance, commercial Web sites usually are supported by several or even many Web server computers. A facility that runs multiple Web servers is sometimes called a **Web farm**. Work is distributed among the computers in a Web farm so as to minimize customer delays. The coordination among multiple Web server computers is a fantastic dance, but, alas, we do not have space to tell that story here. Just imagine the coordination that must occur as you add items to an online order when, to improve performance, different Web servers receive and process each addition to your order.

The third tier is the **database tier**. The computer at this tier receives and processes SQL requests to retrieve and store data (see Chapter 4, page 82–84). Figure 8-8 shows only one computer at the database tier. Although multicomputer database tiers exist, such tiers are less common than multicomputer server tiers.

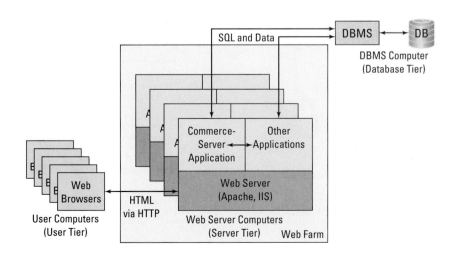

Figure 8-8
Three-Tier Architecture

An Active Example

To see an application of this discussion, go to your favorite Web site, place something in a shopping cart, and consider Figure 8-8 as you do so. When you enter an address into your browser, the browser sends a request for the default site page to the server at that address. A Web server on a computer in a Web farm somewhere processes your request and sends back the default page.

As you click that Web page and others to find products you want, a commerce server on a computer in the Web farm accesses one or more databases to fill the pages with data for the products you want. The commerce server creates pages according to your selections and sends the results back to your browser. Again, different computers on the server tier may process your series of requests and must constantly communicate about your activities.

In Figure 8-9a, the user has navigated through climbing equipment at REI.com to find a particular item. To produce this page, the commerce server accessed a database to obtain the product picture, price, special terms (a 5 percent discount for buying six or more), product information, and related products.

The user placed six items in her basket, and you can see the response in Figure 8-9(b). Again, trace the action in Figure 8-8 and imagine what occurred to produce the second page. Notice that the discount was applied correctly.

When the customer checks out, other commerce server programs will be called to process payments, schedule inventory processing, and arrange for shipping. Most likely the commerce server interfaces with CRM applications for processing the order. Truly this is an amazing capability!

For another example of how companies are conducting Web-based e-commerce, see *MIS in Use 8-2* (page 240).

Figure 8-9a

Sample of Commerce Server Pages: Product-Offer Page

Source: Used with permission of REI.

Figure 8-9b
Shopping-Cart Page

Source: Used with permission of REI.

So far, we have considered only the technology used to support B2C commerce. Before we can consider B2B commerce and other types of information systems that connect two or more organizations, we need to describe the nature of the supply chain that exists among businesses and explore two important supply chain problems. We turn to those topics next.

Supply Chain Management

A **supply chain** is a network of organizations and facilities that transforms raw materials into products delivered to customers. Figure 8-10 (page 241) shows a generic supply chain. Customers order from retailers, who in turn order from distributors, who in turn order from manufacturers, who in turn order from suppliers. In addition to the organizations shown here, the supply chain also includes transportation companies, warehouses, and inventories and some means for transmitting messages and information among the organizations involved.

Because of disintermediation, not every supply chain has all of these organizations. Dell, for example, sells directly to the customer. Both the distributor and retailer organizations are omitted from its supply chain. In other supply chains, manufacturers sell directly to retailers and omit the distribution level.

The term *chain* is misleading. *Chain* implies that each organization is connected to just one company up (toward the supplier) and down (toward the customer) the chain. That is not the case. Instead, at each level, an organization can work with many organizations both up and down the supply chain. Thus, a supply chain is a network.

To understand the operation of a supply chain, consider Figure 8-11 (page 241). Suppose you decide to take up cross-country skiing. You go to REI (either by visiting

Dun and Bradstreet Sells Reports Using E-Commerce

Dun and Bradstreet (D&B) collects and publishes corporate and financial data and data analysis about public and private companies. Customers use D&B's products to assess the creditworthiness of potential customers, to find and evaluate customer leads, to select potential suppliers, and to facilitate supplier negotiations. In business for over 160 years, D&B stores data about 80 million businesses in over 200 countries worldwide. To provide the latest, most up-to-date information, D&B updates its databases more than one million times a day.

Throughout the years, D&B has used the latest technology to deliver its reports. In the beginning, reports were on paper and delivered via mail. Later, reports were faxed to customers, and still later they were delivered via private communications networks. With the advent of the Internet, however, D&B has an even more effective delivery medium: Web-based e-commerce.

Figure 1 shows a search page from the D&B Web site (*dnb.com*). The user has selected a credit report and is using the form shown to

find a credit report available for Georgia-Pacific, a building-products company located in the state of Georgia in the United States. Available reports are shown in the response in Figure 2. These reports can be purchased online via the D&B commerce server.

Consider the advantages to D&B of delivering these reports via the Web. First, the site is up and running 24/7, including holidays. Second, to purchase a report the user enters all customer data, saving D&B data entry and related administrative costs. Furthermore, by using Web-based e-commerce, D&B can change or extend its product offerings simply by making a few changes to its commerce server database. There is no need to create, print, inventory, or mail a new catalog. Finally, the commerce server records customer purchase data that can be mined for information to guide future product offerings (as you will learn in the next chapter). Thus, by using e-commerce technology, D&B sells 24/7, saves costs, distributes more current data, and gains marketing information.

This case is continued as Case Study 8-2 on page 261.

Figure 1
D&B Web Storefront

Source: Used with permission of D&B Corportation

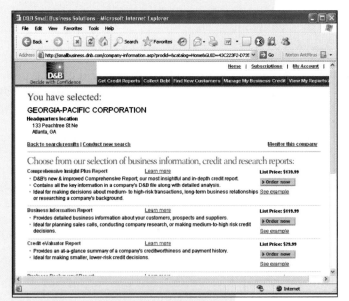

Figure 2
Example of D&B Product Offerings

Source: Used with permission of D&B Corportation

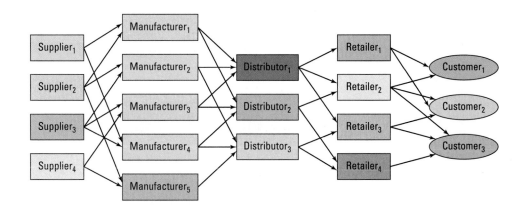

Figure 8-10
Supply Chain Relationships

one of its stores or its Web site) and purchase skis, bindings, boots, and poles. To fill your order, REI removes those items from its inventory of goods. Those goods have been purchased, in turn, from distributors. According to Figure 8-11, REI purchases the skis, bindings, and poles from one distributor and boots from a second. The distributors in turn purchase the required items from the manufacturers, which in turn buy raw materials from their suppliers.

The only source of revenue in a supply chain is the customer. In the REI example, you spend your money on the ski equipment. From that point all the way back up the supply chain to the raw material suppliers, there is no further injection of cash. The money you spend on the ski equipment is passed back up the supply chain as payments for goods or raw materials. Again, the customer is the only source of revenue.

Drivers of Supply Chain Performance

Four major factors, or *drivers*, affect supply chain performance: facilities, inventory, transportation, and information.[2] Figure 8-12 (page 242) lists these drivers of supply chain performance. We will summarize the first three factors in this text and focus our attention on the fourth factor, information. (You can learn in detail about the first three factors in operations management classes.)

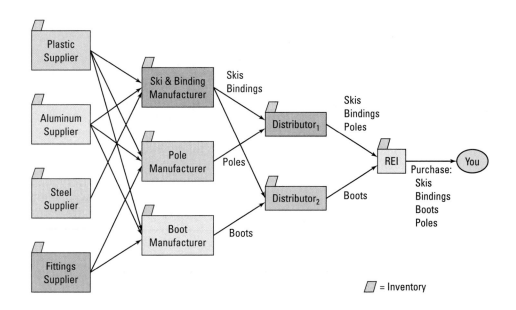

= Inventory

Figure 8-11
Supply Chain Example

---

[2]Sunil Chopra and Peter Meindl, *Supply Chain Management* (Upper Saddle River NJ: Prentice Hall, 2004), pp. 51–53.

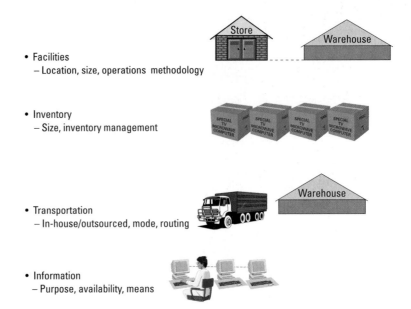

Figure 8-12
Drivers of Supply Chain
Performance

As Figure 8-12 indicates, *facilities* concern the location, size, and operations methodology of the places where products are fabricated, assembled, or stored. The optimal design of facilities is a complicated subject. For example, given all of REI's stores and its e-commerce site, where should it locate its warehouses? How large should they be? How should items be stored and retrieved from the inventories? If one considers facilities for the entire supply chain, these decisions become even more complicated.

Inventory includes all of the materials in the supply chain, including raw materials, in-process work, and finished goods. Each company in Figure 8-11 maintains an inventory. When you and others purchase items from REI, its inventory is reduced, and at some point REI reorders from its distributors. The distributors, in turn, maintain their inventories, and at some point they reorder from the manufacturers, and so forth.

Managing an inventory requires balancing between availability and cost. Inventory managers can increase product availability by increasing inventory size. Doing so, however, increases the cost of the inventory and thus reduces the company's profitability. However, decreasing the size of the inventory increases the odds that an item will be unavailable for purchase. If that happens, the customer may order from a different source, which will reduce the company's revenue and profit. Inventory management is always a balance between availability and cost.

Inventory management decisions include not only the size of the inventory, but also the frequency with which items are reordered and the size of reorders. For example, assume that REI determines that it needs an inventory of 1,000 boots per month. It can order the full 1,000 at the start of the month or it can order 250 four times per month. Decisions like this and other inventory management decisions have a major impact on supply chain performance.

Transportation, the third driver in Figure 8-12, concerns the movement of materials in the supply chain. Some organizations have their own transportation facilities; others use outsourced vendors such as Roadway, UPS, and FedEx, still others use a combination. The transportation mode (such as surface versus air) influences both speed and cost. Routing decisions affect how goods are moved from stage to stage throughout the supply chain.

The fourth driver, *information*, is the factor that most concerns us. Information influences supply chain performance by affecting the ways that organizations in the supply chain request, respond, and inform one another. Figure 8-12 lists three factors of information: purpose, availability, and means. The *purpose* of the information can be transactional, such as orders and order returns, or it can be informational, such as the sharing of inventory and customer order data. *Availability* refers to the ways in which organizations share their information; that is, which organizations have access to which information and when. Finally, *means* refers to the methods by which the information is transmitted. EDI and XML are two types of means discussed later in this chapter.

We will expand on the role of information in the supply chain throughout this chapter. For now, however, we consider two of the ways that information can affect supply chain performance: supply chain profitability and the bullwhip effect.

Supply Chain Profitability Versus Organizational Profitability

Each of the organizations in Figures 8-10 and 8-11 is an independent company, with its own goals and objectives. Each has a competitive strategy that may differ from the competitive strategies of the other organizations in the supply chain. Left alone, each organization will maximize its own profit, regardless of the consequences of its actions on the profitability of the others.

Supply chain profitability is the difference between the sum of the revenue generated by the supply chain and the sum of the costs that all organizations in the supply chain incur to obtain that revenue. In general, the maximum profit to the supply chain *will not* occur if each organization in the supply chain maximizes its own profits in isolation. Usually, the profitability of the supply chain increases if one or more of the organizations operates at less than its own maximum profitability.

To see why this is so, consider your purchase of the ski equipment from REI. Assume that you purchase either the complete package of skis, bindings, boots, and poles or you purchase nothing. If you cannot obtain boots, for example, the utility of skis, bindings, and poles is nil. In this situation, an outage of boots causes a loss of revenue not just for the boots, but also for the entire ski package.

According to Figure 8-11, REI buys boots from distributor 2 and the rest of the package from distributor 1. If boots are unavailable, distributor 2 loses the revenue of selling boots, but does not suffer any of the revenue loss from the nonsale of skis, bindings, and poles. Thus, distributor 2 will carry an inventory of boots that is optimized considering only the loss of boot revenue—not considering the loss of revenue for the entire package. In this case, the profitability to the supply chain will increase if distributor 2 carries an inventory of boots that is larger than optimal for it.

In theory, the way to solve this problem is to use some form of transfer payment to induce distributor 2 to carry a larger boot inventory. For example, REI could pay distributor 2 a premium for the sale of boots in packages and recover a portion of this premium from distributor 1, who would recover a portion of it from the manufacturers, and so forth, up the supply chain. In truth, such a solution is difficult to implement, as illustrated in the *Opposing Forces Guide* on page 243a. For higher-priced items or for items with very high volume, there can be an economic benefit for creating an information system to identify such a situation. If the dynamic is long-lasting, it will be worthwhile to negotiate the transfer-payment agreements. All of this requires a comprehensive supply-chain-wide information system, as you will see.

The Bullwhip Effect

The **bullwhip effect** is a phenomenon in which the variability in the size and timing of orders increases at each stage up the supply chain, from customer to supplier (in Figure 8-11, from *You* all the way back to the suppliers). Figure 8-13 (page 244) summarizes the situation. In a famous study,[3] the bullwhip effect was observed in Procter & Gamble's supply chain for diapers.

---

[3]Hau L. Lee, V. Padmanabhan, and S. Whang, "The Bullwhip Effect in Supply Chains," *Sloan Management Review*, Spring 1997, pp. 93–102.

The Lawyer's Full-Employment Act

I don't think this supply chain profitability thing is likely to work the way it's described here. It sounds like some head-in-the-clouds idea dreamed up by economists.

"First of all, how many products does REI sell? Thousands. And how many distributors does it have? Dozens. How would the company ever know that outages on boots were limiting sales of ski packages? It's got 40-some stores, all over the United States; a Web storefront; and telephone sales. How would REI ever know about patterns like that?

"But, for the sake of argument, let's say it did know. Then what? Suppose REI figured out that every time it runs out of ski boots, on average it loses some number of ski-package sales. Pick any number—say, one out of five. And say that REI makes $200 profit on a ski package. So every time it runs out of ski boots, let's say it loses $40 in profit.

"Knowing that, REI decides to pay a premium to the boot distributor to carry a larger-than-normal inventory of boots. First of all, you wonder why REI doesn't just carry that inventory itself. But anyway, somehow it is going to make a payment to the distributor to carry more boot inventory. All of that, of course, supposes that the distributor is managing inventory that closely, which it probably isn't. Anyway, now REI is going to recoup that payment from the ski, binding, and pole distributor. How—with a check?

"Let's just abandon all sense of reason and say, 'OK, that's what they're going to do.' Now REI has to negotiate an agreement among at least three companies, and probably more if you include the manufacturers. Know what it's like to negotiate an agreement among multiple companies? It takes forever. Just setting up the meetings is tough because everyone's busy, and then the discussions start! And every time you add another company, the required time doubles, at least.

"But, let's suppose that somehow REI does get an agreement. Then what happens? The parties take it to the lawyers. And what may have started as a simple, 1-page agreement becomes a booklet, maybe 20 or 30 pages. Of course none of the people who are trying to get the agreement know 'legalese,' so they have to take it to *their lawyers*, and voilà, you've an ego contest among lawyers and law firms. All of this not only delays the project, but now you're running up the price tag. Those lawyers are expensive.

"By the time you get all of this done, it's no longer ski season, and you're not selling any ski equipment. By the time next year rolls around, you're working with different distributors. It just won't work."

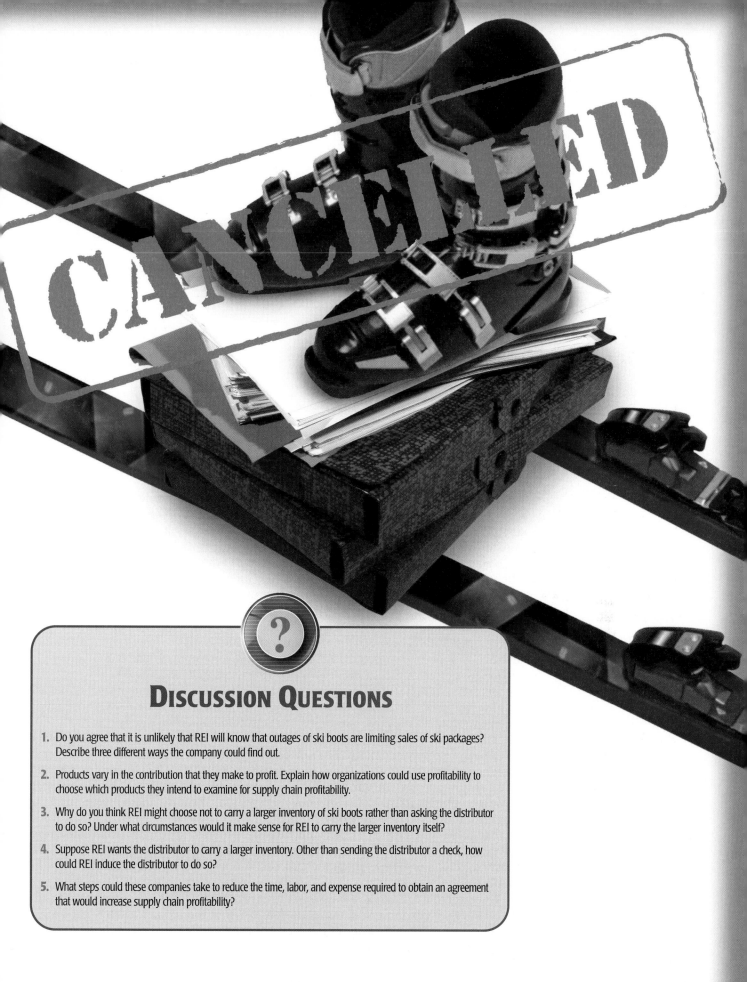

DISCUSSION QUESTIONS

1. Do you agree that it is unlikely that REI will know that outages of ski boots are limiting sales of ski packages? Describe three different ways the company could find out.

2. Products vary in the contribution that they make to profit. Explain how organizations could use profitability to choose which products they intend to examine for supply chain profitability.

3. Why do you think REI might choose not to carry a larger inventory of ski boots rather than asking the distributor to do so? Under what circumstances would it make sense for REI to carry the larger inventory itself?

4. Suppose REI wants the distributor to carry a larger inventory. Other than sending the distributor a check, how could REI induce the distributor to do so?

5. What steps could these companies take to reduce the time, labor, and expense required to obtain an agreement that would increase supply chain profitability?

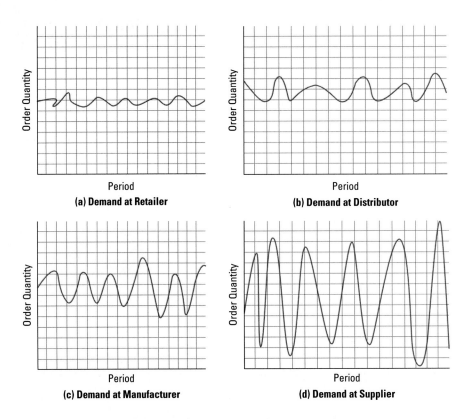

Figure 8-13
The Bullwhip Effect

As you can imagine, except for random variation, diaper demand is constant. Diaper use is not seasonal; the requirement for diapers doesn't change with fashion or anything else. The number of babies determines diaper demand, and that number is constant or possibly slowly changing.

Retailers do not order from the distributor with the sale of every diaper package. The retailer waits until the diaper inventory falls below a certain level, called the *reorder quantity*. Then the retailer orders a supply of diapers, perhaps ordering a few more than it expects to sell to ensure that it does not have an outage.

The distributor receives the retailer's orders and follows the same process. It waits until its supply falls below the reorder quantity, and then it reorders from the manufacturer, with perhaps an increased amount to prevent outages. The manufacturer, in turn, uses a similar process with the raw-materials suppliers.

Because of the nature of this process, small changes in demand at the retailer are amplified at each stage of the supply chain. As shown in Figure 8-13, those small changes become quite large variations on the supplier end.

The bullwhip effect is a natural dynamic that occurs because of the multistage nature of the supply chain. It is not related to erratic consumer demand, as the study of diapers indicated. You may have seen a similar effect while driving on the freeway. One car slows down, the car just behind it slows down a bit more abruptly, which causes the third card in line to slow down even more abruptly, and so forth, until the thirtieth car or so is slamming on its brakes.

The large fluctuations of the bullwhip effect force distributors, manufacturers, and suppliers to carry larger inventories than should be necessary to meet the real consumer demand. Thus, the bullwhip effect reduces the overall profitability of the supply chain.

One way to eliminate the bullwhip effect is to give all participants in the supply chain access to consumer-demand information from the retailer. Each organization can thus plan its inventory or manufacturing based on the true demand (the demand from the only party that introduces money into the system) and not on the observed demand from the next organization up the supply chain. Of course, an *interorganizational information system* is necessary to share such data.

Using the Opposing Forces Guide *(page 243a)*

GOALS

✳ Understand the difference between supply chain profit and individual company profit.

✳ Investigate the feasibility of maximizing supply chain profit.

✳ Teach some of the inhibitors to obtaining interorganizational agreements.

BACKGROUND AND PRESENTATION STRATEGIES

The primary purpose of this guide is to *underline the difference between supply chain profit and individual company profit:*

• Supply chain profit is the difference between revenue paid by the consumers (the only source of cash) and the costs incurred by all of the companies in the supply chain.

• Individual company profit is the difference between revenue received by the company and that company's costs.

Supply chain profit is *not maximized when each company maximizes its own profit.* Instead, as in the example of the ski boots and ski packages, supply chain profit will be greater if some of the companies operate at other-than-maximal profit for them. Of course, for any company to do that, that company needs to be compensated by other members of the supply chain— at least as much as the forgone profit, but likely even more as an inducement.

In practice, as our contrarian points out, pragmatic issues may make this issue moot. His important points:

• Difficulty (impossibility?) in determining which items need to be managed from a supply chain, rather than individual company, basis.

• Difficulty negotiating contract terms.

• Difficulty getting lawyers to approve.

• Time delays make agreement schedule infeasible.

If it is (or ever becomes) possible to determine how to maximize supply chain profits, that computation *will rely heavily on interorganizational information systems.* Information is the key to determining how to maximize

supply chain profit—no other driver (facility, inventory, or transportation) can accomplish that task.

Even if supply chain profit maximization is not feasible today, it is an important goal for the future. Perhaps future supply-chain-wide use of Web services (later in chapter) will enable supply chains to be managed from the standpoint of supply-chain-wide profitability.

Nothing so facilitates interorganizational activity as a well-written contract that clearly specifies the responsibilities and obligations of each party. A clearly worded contract simplifies life for everyone, and the benefits continue for years. Furthermore, every organization that needs its day in court is thankful for competent legal representation. It's hard to remember that, though, when you've negotiated the deal, the opportunity awaits (or is passing), and the only thing holding up progress is groups of lawyers wrangling over seemingly innocent terminology!

SUGGESTED RESPONSES FOR DISCUSSION QUESTIONS

1. It might be difficult to compute the effect that the boot outage is having, or to know other than anecdotally, but experienced salespeople probably know some of the major patterns. Three possible ways to learn this effect is to ask salespeople, to survey customers, or to compute it by comparing sales of individual items versus sales of packages. (Note: *This question sets up the discussion of market-basket analysis in the next chapter.*)

2. To choose which products to examine for supply chain profitability, organizations could constrain the analysis of purchasing patterns to high-margin items. Look carefully at which items tend to be purchased with high-margin items. Ask customers and salespeople if the absence of those companion items constrains the purchase of the high-margin item.

   This answer has a problem, however. First, ask the students:

➤ **Do you see a problem of constraining the analysis to high-margin items?**

The companies in the supply chain are concerned with total margin, not individual-item margin. If it turns out that, because of higher volume, REI earns more total margin on packages of dehydrated corn, peas, and a spoon than it earns on sales of ski packages, then the analysis should examine corn-package sales before ski-package sales. Even though the margin on a ski package might be $40 and the margin on a package of corn, peas, and a spoon might be $1, volume differences can make the sale of corn packages contribute more to the total margin.

3. Ostensibly, the distributor is selling to more vendors than just REI. If the distributor carries the larger inventory, it can balance REI's needs against its other customers' needs. The total profit for the supply chain that includes both REI and its competitors will be higher.

   In practice, REI probably doesn't consider total supply chain management, including its competitors. It may want the distributor to carry the larger inventory just to save its (REI's) inventory costs. REI would carry the larger inventory if the cost of doing so was compensated by greater sales of ski packages and if the distributor would not agree to do so (or if it was too difficult to induce the distributor to do so).

4. Several alternative inducements are to threaten to take one's business elsewhere; to threaten to buy directly from the manufacturer; and to negotiate penalties for out-of-stock situations.

5. They could negotiate a blanket agreement that would pertain to all members of the supply chain and would pertain to a large group of goods. The terminology of the blanket agreement would be negotiated once, approved by attorneys of all the involved firms, and be used over and over. Such an agreement would need to be drawn carefully, however, to avoid restraint of trade concerns and the appearance of collusion or a trust. The lawyers really do need to be involved on this one!

WRAP UP

➤ **Supply chain profitability is an interesting concept, but it may only be a concept, at least right now. It may be difficult to take practical action to take advantage of the additional profits that companies could make by optimizing supply chain profit over individual company profit.**

➤ **If it ever becomes possible to have a pragmatic solution to the supply chain profitability problem, that solution will involve information systems. Stay tuned!**

Interorganizational Information Systems

Figure 8-14 shows the three fundamental information systems involved in supply chain management: supplier relationship management (SRM), inventory, and customer relationship management (CRM). Note that a manufacturer may also have manufacturing applications such as MRP, MRP II, or ERP systems. We discussed all of these applications except SRM in Chapter 7. We discuss it next.

Supplier Relationship Management

Supplier relationship management (SRM) is a business process for managing all contacts between an organizational and its suppliers. The term *supplier* in *supplier relationship management* is broader than the use of the term *supplier* in Figures 8-10 and 8-11. In those figures, the term refers to the supplier of raw materials and assemblies to a manufacturer. *Supplier* in SRM is used generically: It refers to *any organization* that sells something to the organization that has the SRM application. Thus, in this generic sense, a manufacturer is a supplier to a distributor.

SRM is an integrated system in the same sense of CRM, MRP, and EAI described in Chapter 7. With regard to Porter's model, an SRM supports both the inbound logistics primary activity and the procurement support activity. Considering business processes, SRM applications support three basic processes: source, purchase, and settle, as summarized in Figure 8-15 (page 246).

Considering sourcing, the organization needs to find possible vendors of needed supplies, materials, or services; to assess the vendors that it does find; to negotiate terms and conditions; and to formalize those terms and conditions in a procurement contract. SRM software is especially relevant to finding and assessing vendors. Some SRM applications have features to search for product sources and to find evaluations of vendors and products. You see something akin to this functionality when you search for electronics products on a site such as *cnet.com*. There you can readily determine which vendors provide which products, and you can also obtain evaluations of products and vendors. Similar capabilities are built into SRM packages.

Once the company has identified vendors and has procurement contracts in place, the next stage is to procure the goods. The SRM application requests information, quotations, and proposals from would-be suppliers. The company then can use the SRM to manage the approval workflow in order to approve the purchase and issue the order.

The third major SRM activity is to settle. Here, the accounting department reconciles the receipt of the goods or services against the purchase documents and schedules the vendor payment. The payment portion of the SRM typically connects to the cash management subsystem in the financial management application.

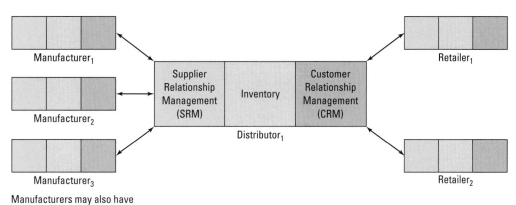

Manufacturers may also have
MRP, MRP II, or ERP applications.

Figure 8-14
B2B in One Section of the
Supply Chain

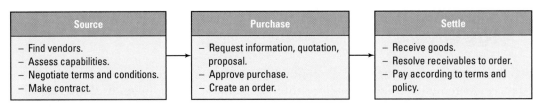

Figure 8-15
Summary of SRM Processes

Some SRM packages include features to support procurement auctions. Generally, companies use auctions to obtain large amounts of materials, energy, or other consumables. In these procurement auctions, an organization indicates its desire to purchase a product or service and invites would-be sellers to submit bids. Typically, the low bid wins the auction. Organizational auctions can attract a large number of vendors and often result in substantial cost savings.

Integrating SRM with CRM

According to Figure 8-16, the supplier's CRM application interfaces with the purchaser's SRM application. In fact, from a process standpoint, these two systems are two sides of the same coin and share the same process goals. Both the supplier and the customer want to perform the ordering process as cheaply and efficiently as possible. To do this, the CRM and SRM applications need to be integrated.

Recall from Chapter 7 that one function of a CRM is to increase the value of existing customers. One way to do that is to connect the CRM to the customer's SRM so that recurring purchases are automated. The SRM examines inventory, determines that items are required, and automatically creates the order via its connection to the supplier's CRM.

According to the Hackett Group, by focusing purchases to a few vendors and by automating the procurement process, companies can operate with a procurement cost about 70 percent lower than the average.[4]

Some companies initially are uncomfortable with the idea of linking their supply chain information systems to those of other organizations. They may fear a loss of corporate data or a loss of autonomy or control, which could occur if the information sharing is not done well. The *Ethics Guide* on page 247a discusses some of the ethical issues involved in supply chain information sharing.

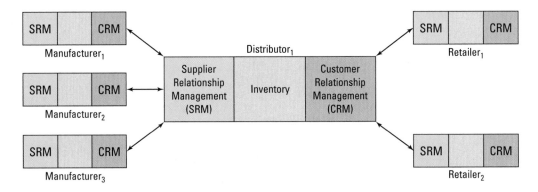

Figure 8-16
ERP II in One Section of the Supply Chain

---

[4]The Hackett Group, *Achieving World-Class Source to Settlement Through Best Practices*, Miami, Florida, March 2003, *thehackettgroup.com* (accessed October 2004).

Information Technology for Data Exchange

Web commerce-server applications are useful for B2C, but they are not sufficient for B2B needs. In general, organizations need to exchange data and messages in more general and flexible ways than they can do with commerce servers. As you can see from the previous discussion, they may need to exchange orders, order confirmations, requests for quotations, item inventory status data, accounts payable and accounts receivable data, and a myriad of other types of data and documents.

Figure 8-17 summarizes alternatives for exchanging data and messages. The most basic are telephone calls and documents exchanged via fax or postal mail. Another alternative is to exchange messages and documents via email. None of these requires information technology beyond what you already know.

The next three alternatives do involve additional technology. *Electronic Data Interchange (EDI)* is a standard for exchanging documents from machine to machine, electronically. In the past, EDI was used over point-to-point or value-added networks. Recently, EDI systems have been developed that use the Internet as well. Another alternative is *eXtensible Markup Language (XML)*, a standard that offers advantages over EDI and that most believe will eventually replace EDI. We will discuss both EDI and XML in the next section.

In addition to sharing documents, some SCM applications allow programs to communicate directly with each other. In the past, two organizations needed to design a proprietary system developed specifically to meet this need. More recently, a set of standards called *XML Web services* has been developed that many organizations use for interprogram communication. We will discuss this topic later in the chapter.

Electronic Data Interchange

Electronic Data Interchange (EDI) is a standard of formats for common business documents. To understand the need for EDI, consider the supply chain in Figure 8-10, and suppose that there are 5 distributors and 10 manufacturers. Further, suppose that each distributor wants to send orders electronically to all of the manufacturers. Because the transmissions are electronic, the distributors and manufacturers must agree on a format for the orders. This format will include how many data fields will be sent, in what order they will be sent in, how many characters will be sent in each data field, and so forth. This is not difficult work; it merely requires a common design for the order transmissions.

However, if each distributor designs a *different* electronic order format for each manufacturer, then a total of 5 times 10, or 50, different formats must be designed. When you consider that the companies may wish to exchange not only orders, but also requests for quotations, order confirmations, order shipping notices, and so forth, you can see that the distributors and manufacturers would have to develop thousands of different document formats.

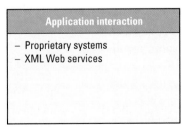

Message exchange
– Telephone
– Paper (fax, postal mail)
– Email
– Electronic Data Interchange (EDI)
– EDI over Internet
– eXtensible Markup Language (XML)

Application interaction
– Proprietary systems
– XML Web services

Figure 8-17
Alternatives for Inter-organizational Message and Data Exchange

The Ethics of Supply Chain Information Sharing

Suppose that you work for a distributor that has developed information systems to read inventory data both up and down the supply chain. You can query the finished goods inventories of your manufacturers and the store inventories of your retailers. These systems were developed to increase supply chain efficiency and profitability. Consider the following situations:

Situation A: You notice that the store inventories of all retailers are running low on items in a particular product family. You know the retailers will soon send rush orders for some of those items, and in anticipation, you accumulate an oversupply of those items. You query the manufacturers' inventory data, and you find that the manufacturers' finished goods inventories are low. Because you believe you have the only supply of those items, you increase their price by 15 percent. When the retailers ask why, you claim extra transportation costs. In fact, all of the increase is going straight to your bottom line.

Situation B: Unknown to you, one of your competitors has also accumulated a large inventory of those same items. Your competitor does not increase prices on those items, and consequently you sell none at your increased price. You decide you need to keep better track of your competitors' inventories in the future.

You have no way direct way to read your competitors' inventories, but you can infer their inventories by watching the decrease of inventory levels on the manufacturer side and comparing that decrease to the sales on the retail side. You know what's been produced, and you know what's been sold. You also know how much resides in your inventory. The difference must be held in your competitor's inventories. Using that process, you now can estimate your competitors' inventories.

Situation C: Assume that the agreement that you have with the retailers is that you are able to query all of their current inventory levels, but only for the orders they have with you. You are not supposed to be able to query orders they have with your competitors. However, the information system contains a flaw, and by mistake you are able to query everyone's orders, your own as well as those of your competitors.

Situation D: Assume the same agreement with your retailers as in situation C. One of your developers, however, notices a hole in the retailer's security system and writes a program to exploit that hole. You now have access to all of the retailers' sales, inventory, and order data.

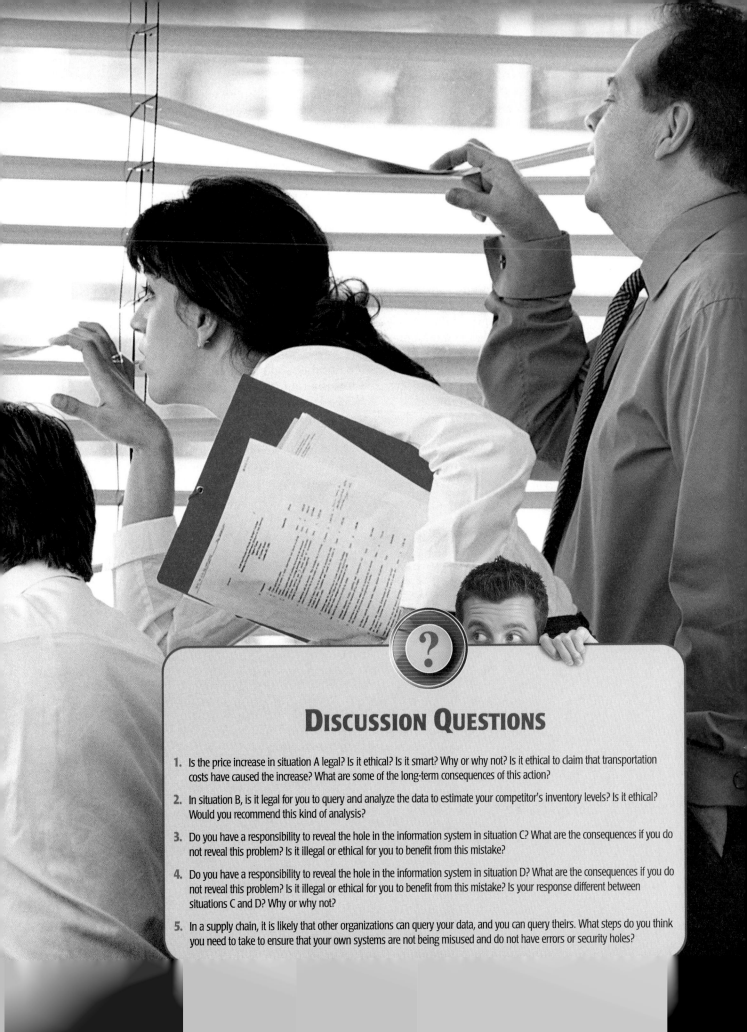

DISCUSSION QUESTIONS

1. Is the price increase in situation A legal? Is it ethical? Is it smart? Why or why not? Is it ethical to claim that transportation costs have caused the increase? What are some of the long-term consequences of this action?

2. In situation B, is it legal for you to query and analyze the data to estimate your competitor's inventory levels? Is it ethical? Would you recommend this kind of analysis?

3. Do you have a responsibility to reveal the hole in the information system in situation C? What are the consequences if you do not reveal this problem? Is it illegal or ethical for you to benefit from this mistake?

4. Do you have a responsibility to reveal the hole in the information system in situation D? What are the consequences if you do not reveal this problem? Is it illegal or ethical for you to benefit from this mistake? Is your response different between situations C and D? Why or why not?

5. In a supply chain, it is likely that other organizations can query your data, and you can query theirs. What steps do you think you need to take to ensure that your own systems are not being misused and do not have errors or security holes?

This work is needlessly repetitive. None of these companies considers the design of such forms to be a proprietary secret; these designs are just necessary clerical work. To reduce this clerical workload, more than 30 years ago companies began to define standard formats for the electronic transmission of documents.

The EDI X12 Standard

In the United States, the X12 Committee of the American National Standards Institute (ANSI) manages EDI standards. Today, the **EDI X12 standard** includes hundreds of documents. They have standard names like EDI 850 (purchase order), EDI 856 (advance ship notices), and EDI 810 (electronic invoice).

An EDI document definition consists of a set of segments, each of which has a defined set of fields. Figure 8-18 shows a segment of the EDI 850 (purchase order) standard that specifies the items that are being ordered. There is one segment of this type for each item on the order. For this example, the segment is named P01, and each of the data fields within that segment are named P01*xx*, as in P0101, P0102, and so forth. Each data element has a number, a description, and attributes, including whether the data element is required, the type of data that should be used for that data element, and the required number and maximum number of characters written in the form *nn/mm*, where *nn* is the required number of characters and *mm* is the maximum number.

You do not need to memorize the information in Figure 8-18; instead, just use that figure to appreciate the nature of EDI standards. Understand the amount of detailed work that must go into the development of such formats and why companies decided they needed standards for them. Without standards, specifications like those in Figure 8-18 need to be negotiated for each trading partner.

Segment: **P01**–Baseline item data
Usage: Mandatory
Max Use: 99
Purpose: To specify basic and most frequently used line item data

Segment Number	Data Element	Name	Attributes
P0101	350	Assigned Identification *Purchase Order Line Number*	M AN 1/11
P0102	330	Quantity Ordered	X R 1/7
P0103	355	Unit or Basis for Measurement *Code*	M ID 2/2
P0104	212	Unit Price *Three Decimal Places*	X R 1/9
P0106	235	Product ID Qualifier *UI – UPC Consumer Package Code* *UP – UPC Consumer Package Code*	M ID 2/2
P0107	234	Product ID *UPC Code*	M AN 12
Etc.			

Figure 8-18
Portion of EDI 850
(Purchase Order)
Standard

Using the Ethics Guide
(page 247a)

GOAL

* Investigate the differences between aggressive, unwise, unethical, and illegal activity using information systems in the supply chain.

BACKGROUND AND PRESENTATION STRATEGIES

The situations are sorted in increasing order of questionability. The first one is certainly legal and ethical; it may or may not be wise. The last one is certainly unethical, and it may be illegal, or at least a violation of a contract.

These scenarios are similar to those in the Ethics Guide in Chapter 1. They involve the use or misuse of information. The difference is that the information systems here are far more sophisticated than the email systems described in Chapter 1.

One of the challenges in attempting to view systems from a supply-chain-wide perspective is that there is no Supply Chain Company. The supply chain has no owners, no stockholders, and no employees, and no organization is concerned about the economic welfare of the supply chain to the exclusion of its own economic welfare.

Because of this characteristic, every organization views the supply chain through the prism of its own goals and objectives. Any information system developed to support supply-chain-wide integration is subject to use or misuse to further the goals of the individual companies. An information system might provide information to enable supply-chain-wide optimization, but an organization could use that same system to further its own interests, as in the examples described here.

A supply chain is a complex network. Adding information systems to this network further increases the complexity of the interactions. It would be exceedingly difficult, probably impossible, to predict the consequences of the addition of a new information system. Therefore, companies in the supply chain are wise to proceed slowly when sharing information about their inventories, orders, demand patterns, and related matters. The consequences could be surprising, and possibly undesirable.

As a result, supply-chain-wide information systems are likely to be implemented much more slowly than the technology could possibly support.

➤ In terms of Chapter 6, all of these concerns fall into the category of organizational feasibility. Supply chain information systems can be cost, schedule, and technically feasible, but fail organizationally because of the lack of control over the side consequences of sharing information.

 SUGGESTED RESPONSES FOR DISCUSSION QUESTIONS

1. I think situation A is both legal and ethical. At least the action of using the information to know to accumulate inventory is legal and ethical. Increasing prices also is legal and ethical.

➤ **Is lying to provide a justification of the price increase ethical?**

It does not seem ethical to me. In fact, I think the need to lie is an indication that something has been done that is not right—or that needs to be sheltered from the hard light of truth.

Probably the best question here, though, is:

➤ **Setting aside the lie and assuming that all this behavior is otherwise ethical, is increasing the prices in this situation wise?**

So much depends on the perceptions of the retailers. They might view it as smart—as your ability to read trends and to increase prices on scarce goods. They might respect your operations more because of it. However, they might perceive it as greedy and ruthless. It could reduce trust and encourage the retailers to find a different distributor, one that wouldn't "put the screws to them" when it could.

2. I see no legal or ethical problem in any of this analysis. It's an analysis that's available to everyone in the supply chain. You're just using the information that you have at your disposal to better run your business.

3. Much depends on whatever contracts exist among the organizations in the supply chain. If you have signed a contract that stipulates that you will query only your own orders, then using this flaw violates that contract. Even if you have just agreed verbally to this limitation, that verbal agreement could be binding. Even if it is not binding, if you did agree verbally to read data only about your orders, then using the flaw is unethical.

➤ **Setting aside contractual or ethical obligations, do you see a problem in not revealing the flaw?**

As long as the flaw exists, there is the possibility that other distributors are using it to query the retailers' orders with you. It's a double-edged sword that can cut both ways. All in all, it would seem a wise course of action to reveal the flaw, possibly for contractual reasons, certainly for ethical reasons. As long as the flaw exists, you cannot control its consequences.

➤ **By the way, if one such flaw exists, there's always the possibility of two such flaws. You don't know about the ethics of your competitors. What are the consequences?**

➤ **How do you spell paranoia? This flaw could be the downfall of the information-sharing initiative in this supply chain.**

See also question 5.

4. You may or may not have a contractual obligation to reveal the hole in situation D, but, in my opinion, you certainly have an ethical responsibility to reveal the hole. Also:

➤ **Where there is one hole, there may be two. How do you know that other organizations are not exploiting it to obtain data about your operations?**

You have culpability here that you did not have in situation C. In this situation, your developer actively sought a way to obtain unauthorized access.

➤ **Do you think other organizations in the supply chain would see a difference in your behavior between situations C and D?**

You bet they would. The one in C just happened. The other you caused!

5. This is a very tough question. Whenever you open any of your information systems to the outside, you run a risk of inadvertently releasing confidential information. There is no way around it. Some thoughts about possible safeguards are:

- Use a careful and methodical development process (see Chapter 6).

- Thoroughly test the systems you implement.

- Observe usage patterns in your data. Attempt to identify spurious queries.

- Protect your network from unauthorized access.

- Hire a white-hat hacker (see Chapter 11).

- Buy insurance.

- Other???

WRAP UP

➤ **We've considered two types of integration in this and in the prior chapter. In Chapter 7, we examined interdepartmental, cross-functional systems that integrated departmental activity and eliminated the silos of isolation caused by functional systems.**

➤ **In this chapter, we considered systems that provide a similar integrative function, but across businesses in a supply chain, and not just departments in an organization.**

➤ **From the standpoint of databases to build, applications to write, and procedures to develop, the integration of departments into process-based systems and the integration of separate organizational information systems into supply chain systems are very similar.**

➤ **Yet, there are substantial differences—differences that we can state in different ways. In terms of systems development, we can say that supply chain systems have organizational feasibility issues that interdepartmental, intracompany systems don't have.**

➤ **What are some examples of organizational feasibility issues that supply chain systems have but that interdepartmental, intracompany systems do not have? (Many important differences among companies may become problematical: company objectives, goals, competitive strategy, priorities, and culture are just a few.)**

➤ **How do those differences impact supply chain information systems development?**

(Different companies will value the supply chain IS differently; some may see it as essential, and some may see it as barely worthwhile. They will have different priorities, varying degrees of willingness to invest, different requirements, various levels of patience with delays, and others.)

Other EDI Standards

Unfortunately, the X12 standard is not the only EDI standard. A second standard, called the **EDIFACT standard**, is used internationally. A third standard, called the **HIPAA standard**, is used for medical records. Because of the existence of multiple standards, when two organizations today wish to exchange documents electronically, they must first agree on which standard they will use.

One further complication is that the standards do not stand still. With usage, organizations find a need to make adjustments to the standards. Thus, there are various versions of each of the X12, EDIFACT, and HIPAA standards. So, to exchange documents, two companies need to agree on the standard and the version of the standard that they will use. From that point on, however, the companies can exchange documents without further configuration work.

eXtensible Markup Language

At this point, you may be asking a burning question—namely, why not use HTML for document interchange? Why mess around with EDI or anything else when the greatest success story in modern history involves the sharing of Web pages over the Internet? Why not use HTML to create purchase order, price quotations, or other business documents? They could then be transmitted using HTTP, just as Web pages are.

In fact, organizations have used HTML to share documents. However, doing so presents several problems. We will first summarize those problems and then describe a successor markup language called XML that overcomes them.

Problems with HTML

Three problems with HTML are:

- HTML tags have no consistent meaning.
- HTML has a fixed number of tags.
- HTML mixes format, content, and structure.

The first problem is that tags are used inconsistently. For example, in standard use, heading tags should be arranged in outline format. The highest-level heading tag should be an h1; within h1, there should be one or more h2 tags; and within the h2 tags, there should be h3 tags; and so forth, for as many heading levels as the author of a document wants.

Unfortunately, there is no feature of HTML that forces consistent use. An h2 tag can appear anywhere—above an h1 heading, below an h4 heading, or anyplace else. An h2 tag can represent a level-two heading, but it can also be used just to obtain a particular type of formatting. If I want the words "Prices guaranteed until Jan. 1, 2005" to appear in the formatting of a level-two heading, I can code:

```
<h2>Prices guaranteed until Jan. 1, 2005</h2>
```

This statement is not intended to be a level-two heading, but it will be given the font size, weight, and color that such headings have.

The possibility of tag misuse means that we cannot depend on tags to infer the document's structure. An h2 tag may not be a heading at all. This limitation means that organizations cannot use HTML tags to reliably exchange documents.

A second problem with HTML is that it defines a fixed set of tags. If two businesses want to define a new tag, say <PriceQuotation>, there is no way in HTML for them to define it. HTML documents are limited to the predefined tags.

The third problem with HTML is that HTML mixes the structure, formatting, and content of a document. Consider the following line of HTML code:

```
<h2 align="center"><font color="#FF00FF">Price of Item</font></h2>
```

This heading mixes the structure (h2) with the formatting (alignment and color) with the content (Price of Item). Such mixing makes HTML difficult to work with. Ideally, the structure, format, and content should be separate.

Importance of XML

To overcome the problems in HTML, the computer industry designed a new markup language called the **eXtensible Markup Language (XML)**. XML is the product of a committee that worked under the auspices of the **World Wide Web Consortium (W3C)**, a body that sponsors the development and dissemination of Web standards. By the way, W3C publishes excellent tutorials, and you can find an XML tutorial on its Web site, *w3c.org*.

XML provides a superior means for organizations to exchange documents. It solves the problems mentioned for HTML, and it has become a significant standard for computer processing. For example, all Microsoft Office 2003 products can save their documents in XML format. XML is also a key part of standards for Web services, and it is particularly important for supply chain management, as you will see.

Application of XML to the Supply Chain

XML has the potential to improve, sometimes drastically, the efficiency of supply chain processes and activities. To understand how, consider REI and its relationship to its distributors. Suppose REI wants to transmit counts of inventory items to all of its suppliers. To do so, REI designs an XML document for sending the item counts. (For now, think of an XML document as a sequence of tags and data, like HTML documents.) Once it has designed the document, REI records the structure of that document in what is called an **XML schema**. Such a schema is just another XML document, but one that records the structure (or schema) of the first (item count) document. Call that schema the item count schema.

Next, REI prepares inventory count documents according to its design. Before sending those documents to its distributors, REI double-checks that the documents are valid by comparing them to the schema. Fortunately, there are hundreds of readily available programs that can validate an XML document against its schema. For example, both Internet Explorer and Netscape Navigator can validate any XML document. This validation feature means significant cost savings because no human labor is required to check documents.

Before sending item count documents to the distributors, REI shares the item count schema with them, possibly by publishing it on a Web site that the distributors have permission to access. When a distributor receives an inventory count document from REI, it uses the published schema to validate the received document. In this way, the distributors ensure that they receive correct and complete documents and that no part of the document has been lost in transmission. Again, this automated process saves labor because it frees the distributors from manually validating the correctness of the documents they receive. This automated validation can mean enormous labor savings.

Using XML in an Industry

Now broaden this idea from two businesses to an entire industry. Suppose, for example, that the real estate industry agrees on an XML schema document for property listings. Every real estate company that can produce data in the format of the schema can then exchange listings with every other such real estate company. Given the schema, each company can ensure that it is transmitting and receiving valid documents.

Figure 8-19 lists some XML-standards work that is underway in various industries.

Application Interaction in the Supply Chain

You have learned how companies can use EDI and XML to exchange documents. What if two organizations want their computer programs to interact? What if a company wants its SRM application program to connect directly to a supplier's CRM application? Neither the EDI nor the XML standard, by itself, supports such activity.

The process of a program on one computer accessing programs on a second computer is called **remote computing** or **distributed computing**. Several different techniques are used. Two important ones are the use of proprietary designs and Web services.

Industry	Example XML Standards
Accounting	American Institute of Certified Public Accountants (AICPA): Extensible Financial Reporting Markup Language
Automotive	Society of Automotive Engineers (SAE): XML for the Automotive Industry—SAE J2008
Banking	Financial Services Technology Consortium (FSTC): Bank Internet Payment System (BIPS)
Human Resources	HR-XML Consortium
Insurance	ACORD: Property and Casualty
Real Estate	OpenMLS: Real Estate Listing Management System
Workflow	Internet Engineering Task Force (IETF): Simple Workflow Access Protocol (SWAP)

Figure 8-19
XML Industry Standards

Distributed Computing Using Proprietary Designs

One way to develop distributed computer programs is to develop proprietary distributed applications. *Proprietary* means that the solution is unique to and is owned by the organizations that develop and pay for the distributed systems. It is a one-of-a-kind solution.

To develop a proprietary design, teams of developers from the companies involved work together using a development process like that described in Chapter 6. The teams determine application requirements, develop a design, and write and test programs according to that design. Such projects are distinguished from other development projects only in the requirement for remote processing.

Consider an example. Suppose the companies in a supply chain decide they want to eliminate the bullwhip effect. To do this, the retailers in the supply chain must share sales data with all companies up the chain. Accordingly, the companies in the supply chain organize a development team consisting of IT personnel from all of the major companies.

The joint development team designs this application to use a particular communications capability, particular operating systems, and particular distributed computing techniques. A major portion of the development effort is in selecting which communications technologies, operating systems, and distributed techniques are to be used and how program code will use those techniques.

An alternative proprietary method is for one company to develop all of the necessary programs itself and then to install some of its programs on another company's computers. In the past, some manufacturers developed order entry programs that they installed on their customers' computers. These programs call directly into the manufacturer's CRM application. The customers need only install the programs that the manufacturer provides.

Of course, this process is much simpler to describe than it is to do. Inevitably, there are differences on the customers' computers that the manufacturer did not expect, and so the manufacturer has to make special-purpose program versions for different distributors. Sometimes this happens dozens of times, resulting in a software configuration management nightmare for the manufacturer. The *Security Guide* on page 251a discusses another set of risks associated with using another company's software programs.

Proprietary solutions are difficult and expensive to develop and operate. If they provide sufficient business value, however, the return on investment can make them worthwhile. Even so, however, considerable management time and attention is necessary. Because of the difficulty, expense, and time involved in developing such solutions,

A Trojan Horse?

Suppose you work for a distributor that manages its inventory very closely. One of your major manufacturers says that it can dramatically shorten the lead time on most of its products if your purchasing personnel order directly from the manufacturer's CRM. To make that possible, the manufacturer needs to install some of its programs on the computers in your purchasing department. Your staff will use those programs to order from the manufacturer's system.

Reduced lead time has high value to you because it translates directly into a smaller inventory, something your company is fanatical about. You contact other companies that have allowed the manufacturer to install such programs, and no one reports any difficulty. There were a few installation glitches, and once in a while the manufacturer's CRM is unavailable, but no one has reported serious problems. Given all that, you agree to try it for a 3-month period.

You negotiate the details of your agreement with the manufacturer, and the legal departments of both companies sign an agreement. All is proceeding smoothly until the chief information officer (CIO) of your company gets wind of this project. He refuses to allow the programs to be installed on the computers in purchasing. He also directs building security personnel not to allow anyone from the manufacturer into your company's building.

When you learn of the CIO's actions, you immediately schedule an appointment with him. At the meeting, you can tell he's barely controlling his fury. "First," he says, "have you thought about the consequences of putting someone else's programs on our network? Behind our firewall? We go to huge trouble and enormous expense to build these firewalls, and then you put somebody else's software inside them? Do you know what a Trojan horse is?"

"But," you stammer, "other companies have done this without a problem."

"Maybe so, and maybe they've had security problems that they don't know about. I can't believe you got this far on this project and no one thought to even contact me. It's unbelievable!"

"Well," you counter, "I see your point and I'm sorry we didn't contact you sooner. But what can we do now? Using their system could mean huge cost savings to us."

DISCUSSION QUESTIONS

1. Why is the CIO so concerned? The company regularly installs software from Microsoft, Oracle, IBM, Sun, and other vendors. Why is he so worried about this one?

2. Explain in your own words the problems of installing another company's software inside your own network. How does the term Trojan horse apply here?

3. Was it irresponsible not to involve the CIO in this project? Even if you didn't know to contact the CIO, should the legal department have done so? What does this situation tell you about the position of the IS department at this company?

4. What can be done? Is this issue serious enough to cause the cancellation of this project? What steps can the CIO take to reduce the risk? What steps can you take? How about the legal department? Or accounting? If your firm has a risk management department, how should it be involved?

5. At some point, so much extra work is involved to protect the security of your computer system that you begin to wonder if the direct order-entry system is worth it. Is the CIO wrong? If you can't manage your inventory effectively, you won't be in business anyway. Is the CIO being too restrictive? Why or why not?

many organizations today are beginning to use another technology that uses a different strategy—XML Web services. We consider it next.

XML Web Service Applications

XML Web services, sometimes called simply *Web services*, are a set of standards that facilitate distributed computing using Internet technology. Web services are the latest and greatest tool for application interaction, and they will be important in the early years of your career. Every major software vendor has products that support Web services. For example, Microsoft provides .Net development tools, and IBM provides J2EE development tools. (Because of the standards, by the way, applications developed by these different tools will work together without problem.)

Fundamental Web Services Concepts The goal of Web services is to provide a standardized way for programs to access one another remotely, without the need to develop proprietary solutions. Because they are standardized, worldwide, they are immediately accessible. Right now, for example, without a meeting or even a conversation, you can access Amazon.com and use Web services standards to write your own personal front-end to Amazon's catalog. (To learn more, see *amazon.com/webservices.*) There is no need for developer meetings to create designs for interprogram communication. Everything necessary is already part of the Web services standards.

A number of important standards have been defined to make Web services possible, but a discussion of those standards is beyond the scope of this book. In general, these standards enable programs on one computer to obtain a **service description** that details what programs exist on another computer and how to communicate with those programs.

Once the service user has the service description, it uses the information it contains to invoke the service. In the case of Amazon.com, a service user can invoke the Amazon.com service to find a particular book, to find a set of books, or to provide additional Amazon.com catalog information. Remarkably, it appears to the service user that all of the Amazon.com programs are actually on the service user's computer. If you were the service user, it would be as if you had Amazon.com's catalog programs (and database) on your own machine.

All Web service data are transmitted in XML documents. These documents have XML schemas defined, and all program components of the XML Web services architecture can automatically validate them. See the *Reflections Guide* on page 253a for more thoughts on the emerging importance of XML.

Web Services and the Supply Chain Web services have the potential to simplify the automation of supply chain interactions. Any organization in the supply chain can develop Web services and publish those services to other organizations in the supply chain. Developers in those other organizations can access the service description and write programs that call the Web services.

Consider an example: Suppose that, to reduce the bullwhip effect, a retailer develops a Web service to share its CRM sales data with companies in the supply chain. Other companies in the supply chain, such as distributors and manufacturers, consume this service to plan their inventory and production activities. As Figure 8-20 shows, the retailer publishes a service description and makes that description available to distributors and manufacturers. Developers in those companies write programs according to the Web service description.

To obtain sales data, the Web service programs of the distributor or manufacturer create a service request. Those Web service programs transmit that request to the service provider at the retailer's computer. The message goes to the retailer and is processed by the Web service programs. Those programs call the CRM application to read data in the CRM database. They then format a response in an XML document and send the response to the service consumer (the distributor or manufacturer).

Because of the standards, no joint development meetings or other coordination activities are required among the organizations to enable the use of these Web services.

You Be the Guide

Using the Security Guide
(page 251a)

GOALS

* Sensitize students to the problems of installing other companies' software.

* Illustrate problems that can occur when not involving the CIO or other IS professionals in business initiatives that involve computing infrastructure.

BACKGROUND AND PRESENTATION STRATEGIES

Warning: This guide uses the term *firewall,* but we won't discuss firewalls until Chapter 11. For now, I explain that a *firewall* is a computing device that filters Internet and other network traffic for security.

Unfortunately, the problem presented in this scenario is common. Recently I visited my doctor's office for routine blood tests. While sitting in the office laboratory, I noticed that the lab technician's computer was running an application program from an independent medical lab. (The screen showed a logo that I recognized from the lab's billing statements.)

I asked the technician if that program belonged to the doctors' group or if it was from the lab. She said, "Oh, it's not ours, it's one the lab wrote." I asked if they sent her an installation disk with the program or if she installed it over the Internet. "Oh, no, they come over here from time to time and install their programs on our computers."

This doctors' group, consisting of 30+ physicians and staff, is located in a major medical center in Seattle, and the doctors have privileges at a major university teaching hospital. I would think they are in at least the top quartile of their business (I hope so, anyway), and they send me all sorts of notices about how they protect my data according to HIPAA standards, and so on. While I sat there, a number of questions popped into my mind. But, first, ask the students:

➤ **What questions pop into your mind when you hear this scenario?**

Here are some of the questions I was asking:

➤ **How do they know that program is free of viruses, malicious Trojan horses, and other malware?**

➤ **How do they know that the people from the lab who install those programs aren't installing some other, malicious program as well?**

➤ **Their computers are connected to a network and via that network to the Internet. How do they know that a program installed by the lab software person is not sending patient data out the door?**

➤ **What stipulations exist in their contract with the lab to protect the doctors in case of a malicious Trojan horse or other malware?**

➤ **Does their insurance policy protect them for this type of liability?**

➤ **What do they know about the personnel who are installing these programs on their computers? Are they employees of the lab? Are they employees of another company? Are they recent graduates of the state's white-collar crime incarceration program?**

➤ **Here's a pertinent announcement:**

➤ **Do NOT let ANYONE outside your IS organization install programs on your computers!**

 ### SUGGESTED RESPONSES FOR DISCUSSION QUESTIONS

1. The CIO is right to be very concerned.

   ➤ **What's the difference between software from Microsoft or Oracle and software from ABC Manufacturing?**

   (No, the answer is not what one student quipped in my class, "Software from ABC Manufacturing actually works.") The difference is that Microsoft and Oracle are very experienced vendors with substantial talent and expertise for ensuring that their software does not contain malware. ABC Manufacturing may or may not have such talent and expertise.

2. Once inside the organization's network, the Trojan horse program can wreak havoc on the organization's computing infrastructure. It can steal data; it can disrupt operations; it can maliciously destroy data. As the CIO says, they go to incredible effort and expense to protect the perimeter of the organization's network, and this installation will bypass all of those protections.

3. Yes, it was incredibly irresponsible not to involve the CIO!

   ➤ **Do not install any programs on your computer that have not been approved by your IS department. Do not let anyone you manage install them, either.**

I hope this was just an oversight on the part of a junior person in the legal department. Every organization should have a policy of notifying the CIO of any initiative that involves installing computer software on the organization's computers.

If this was not an oversight, then the CIO has little stature in the organization. Some corrective action needs to be taken.

4. It will be interesting to see how the students respond. I think it is potentially serious enough to cause cancellation of the project. The CIO needs a chance to have his or her staff check into the program and find out who wrote it, what it does, how it's been tested, the experience of the manufacturer, and the experiences of other businesses that use the program. Perhaps, too, computers that use this program can be set up in a special security zone within the organization's network. Lots can be done, but the CIO needs time and a chance to participate.

To avoid such problems, you could be certain to involve the CIO from the start. Legal could ensure that the contract protects the organization from problems in the manufacturer's software. Accounting could be instructed not to approve budget for projects that involve computer software without concurrence from the IS department. If there is a separate risk management department, it too should be notified of this issue; there may be a need to obtain a special liability insurance policy or take other risk-reduction action.

5. Questions to ask the class:

➤ **Is the CIO being too restrictive?**

➤ **Should the company just install the software and hope for the best?**

➤ **If you were a proponent of the direct order-entry system, what would you do?**

I don't think the CIO is too restrictive at all. The company should not install the software and just hope for the best. That's no way to run a business!!! There are many alternatives between closing one's eyes to the risk and canceling the project.

WRAP UP

➤ **In this world of viruses, worms, Trojan horses, spyware, adware, data thefts, identity thefts, and other problems, the CIO and the IS department have every right—even duty—to restrict the installation of programs on computers within the organization's network.**

➤ **Work with the IS department when you have an initiative that will require new software. Give them fair notice.**

➤ **We will be discussing these issues further when we discuss IS management in Chapter 10 and security in Chapter 11.**

Web service provider
Web service consumer

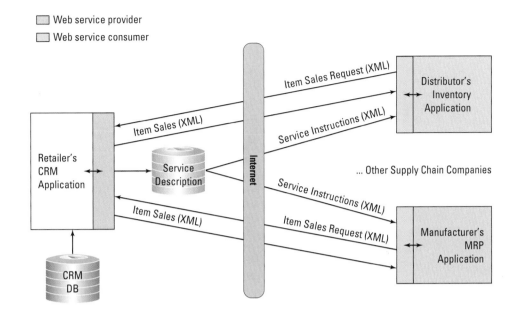

Figure 8-20
Example of Web Services for Sharing Sales Data

The developers are all working on the same page, so to speak. They all use the same Web services standards.

Web services not only provide cost savings for the development of interorganizational IS, they also drastically reduce the time required to achieve operational capability. Furthermore, the use of Web services provides tremendous flexibility. A manufacturer, for example, can combine Web services from several different companies into a single application. The manufacturer can also readily change and adapt those combinations to meet new business requirements.

Universal Electronics (continued)

Given what you have learned about interorganizational systems in this chapter, we can now pick up the Universal story as you develop a cost-savings proposal.

Over the weekend and in the evenings you begin to think more broadly about Universal. What are its most significant costs? With the sponsorship of the COO, you approach accounting, and the comptroller assigns an employee to work with you.

Together, you analyze Universal's financial statements, and you find that its largest costs are in inventory. Recalling that the best way to solve a problem is not to have it, you ask yourself what it would take to eliminate Universal's inventory. A few nights of study (remember, you have to run your department during the day) convince you that although it is impossible to eliminate inventory altogether, you could reduce inventory costs, maybe substantially, by shipping many products directly from your suppliers to your customers.

You set up a meeting with the manager of the purchasing department to explore this idea. When asked about this possibility, she says, "We tried that once, or at least we experimented with it, and it didn't work. We didn't have reliable, up-to-date information about the manufacturers' inventories. We would promise deliveries to our customers and then find out the manufacturer didn't have the items in stock. So we decided we had to keep buffer stock in our inventory."

"What if we had reliable data on the manufacturer's inventories?" you ask. "Would shipping directly from them to our customers make any sense?"

"Possibly. I don't know how we'd get that data, however."

XML and the Future of Computing

Once upon a time, computers were used solely for computing. They were valued for their ability to perform arithmetic and complex calculations. Today, few computers are valued primarily as computational tools. Today they are valued because they *communicate*.

Consider the systems in this chapter. What's the primary purpose of an IS in the supply chain? It is to communicate orders, invoices, or other documents or to send and receive data among programs. More broadly, watch a football game or TV show with a 20- to 40-year-old audience demographic, and the commercials will show you what computers are used for: communications and entertainment (which is a type of communication).

Communication cannot occur without common standards. Two people cannot communicate if they do not speak the same language, and a language is just a standard way for people to exchange sounds and written symbols. So, too, computers must share standards to communicate. You learned about some of these standards in Chapter 5: TCP/IP, IPv6, and URLs are all examples of computer standards. Those standards address the packaging of messages; however, they do not address message content.

That's where XML enters the picture. Bill Gates called XML the *"lingua franca of the Internet."* A lingua franca is a common language widely used by speakers of other languages. With his ability to anticipate the future of computing, Gates may be a bit ahead of the curve. If XML is not yet the language of the Internet, it is likely to be that within the next 5 years.

Right now, today, there are hundreds of manufacturers with rooms full of people checking orders. Those orders may arrive via postal mail, fax, as attachments to emails, or through information systems. Regardless, without XML, every one of those orders must be manually validated. Is the order complete? Are all of the customer's data present? Are the shipping address and the billing address complete and valid? Do we have all of the data we need to process the order? Are any part numbers, styles, colors, or quantities missing? Are the shipping instructions complete and clear? The result is hundreds of clerks validating orders, hour after hour.

As you learned in this chapter, XML provides a clear separation of structure, content, and format. Once an XML order schema is written, all of the order checking is automated. No humans are required. And writing an XML schema isn't that hard: It doesn't take that long, and it's easy to fix. No staff of highly trained programmers is required; regular people can write XML schemas with a week or so of training. Given the schema, any of hundreds of different programs can validate an XML document against that schema. No new programs need to be written. You already have everything you need on your home computer.

A startling possible consequence of the growth of XML on the future of computing relates to databases.

As you learned in Chapter 4, databases store tables, not XML documents. So the process is as follows: Take the data out of the database, put it into an XML document, send that document somewhere, receive the XML document, strip the data, and return it to a relational database. That process can be a bottleneck.

But, why put the data in relational databases? Why not store the XML documents as XML documents? To many, this is heresy: "Not put the data into a relational database?"

Before this can happen, significant problems must be overcome: how to efficiently query stores of XML documents, how to process duplicated data, and how to make XML data available to table-oriented programs like Excel. Yes, there are problems to overcome. But I'm willing to bet that by the end of your career, relational databases will be a thing of the past. No one will remember (or care) why we had them. It will be XML storage all the way![5]

---

[5]See David Kroenke, "Beyond the Relational Database Model," *IEEE Computer*, May 2005.

DISCUSSION QUESTIONS

1. What is a lingua franca and how does having one save time?

2. In your own words, explain the benefits of XML. Use both the comments in this editorial and material from the discussion of XML earlier in this chapter.

3. Describe the savings that would accrue if XML documents were stored in XML format.

4. What resistance is likely to the idea of storing XML documents in XML format? How will existing IS departments react to such a proposal? How will DBMS vendors react? How will database consultants react?

5. Do you think the resistance in question 4 is likely to be overcome? Why or why not? What factors will influence whether relational databases are eliminated?

6. What role could a DBMS product that is a hybrid of XML and relational data play? Is there evidence of such a hybrid at either *www.microsoft.com* or *www.oracle.com*?

At this point, you know you are on to something. If you can find a way to deliver current, accurate manufacturers' inventory data to your salespeople, then you could ship at least some of your orders directly to your customers and save the costs of inventory handling and inventory storage. *That* would be a cost savings that would meet the challenge given you by the COO.

With this idea, you and the purchasing manager identify seven different manufacturers who supply products for which the inventory cost is high and for which it is feasible to ship direct. You contact those companies and discover that two of them have developed XML Web services that publish their inventory data.

Armed with this knowledge, you approach the IS department and explain your thinking. Together with personnel in that department you develop a plan for a test program in which the IS department would develop a program to access one of the manufacturer's Web services and obtain the inventory data. IS agrees to support your idea, but wants to participate with you in the presentation to the COO. "Even if we develop just a test application with minimal features, it will require extra budget."

You develop a presentation of these ideas and schedule a meeting with the COO, the purchasing manager, and the IS manager. Just to make sure there are no surprises for anyone, you give that presentation to the latter two people prior to the presentation to the COO. Your plan includes a request for extra budget for you, purchasing, and IS. With a few changes, everyone is on board with the idea.

Your meeting with the COO is very different from the first one. For one, the COO knows you are sincere and capable (and is appreciative that you did all of this while running your department in parallel), and he generally seems more receptive. He listens to your presentation, asks a few questions, and at the end says,

"Done. Get on with it. You can have the budget you request."

Surprised, you stammer, "But what about my department?"

"OK," he says, "we'll get someone to take over your department while you run this special project. You can have 6 weeks to bring me the first results. At that point, we'll decide what we're going to do with you. Make it happen!"

And that's why you, the reader of this text, need to know about XML and XML Web services!

SUMMARY

- Porter defined five competitive forces: bargaining power of suppliers, bargaining power of customers, new entrants to the market, rivalry among firms in the market, and the threat of substitutions for an organization's products or services.

- E-commerce is the buying and selling of goods and services over public and private networks. Merchant companies take title to the goods they sell. Nonmerchant companies arrange for purchase and sale without owning the goods.

- B2C refers to e-commerce between businesses and consumers; B2B refers to e-commerce among businesses; B2G is e-commerce conducted between businesses and governments. Additional forms of e-commerce are auctions, clearinghouses, and electronic exchanges.

- E-commerce improves market efficiency by disintermediation, improved flow of price information, and knowledge of price elasticity obtained directly from the customer.

Universal Electronics (continued)
(page 253)

It's a happy story with a happy ending. It's possible to leave the case as it is written and move on to the next chapter. Maybe wrap up with a discussion of all of the things that our protagonist did right. And, there were many:

➤ **He/she showed initiative, self-reliance, creativity, ability to work with others, consideration of others (prebriefing the IS manager and the purchasing manager), a willingness to take direction from the COO, and an ability to learn and adapt to what he/she had been taught.**

So, all things considered, it's a great success.

However, one could make the argument that our protagonist jumped at the first opportunity and didn't consider as many possibilities as he/she might have considered. There may have been other more dramatic ways to save costs; at least he/she should have considered a few more before settling on the XML solution (which, given the few vendors that have an XML interface, is just a partial solution).

RESPONDING TO THE CHALLENGE

One way to wring even more learning from this case is to consider three potential cost-savings categories of information systems:

• *E-commerce systems* for customer sales

• *Inventory management systems* (systems that don't strive to eliminate inventory, but rather attempt to manage it better)

• Information systems that reduce supply chain costs regarding *facilities and transportation*

We don't have sufficient data about Universal's sales activities, inventory management, facilities, or transportation to decide if information systems for them would result in greater cost savings than the systems our protagonist proposed. However, the following activity can be used to help the students to review all of the systems we've discussed in this and the last chapter.

You could consider the following sets of questions for the entire class or, to save time, you might break up the class into groups and assign each group to address one of the three question sets.

QUESTION SET 1

➤ Could the company use e-commerce information systems to save costs?

➤ Is an e-commerce storefront cheaper than one full-time telesales person? Cheaper than two? Cheaper than five? Cheaper than a telesales department? How would you find out?

➤ How would you predict the relative effectiveness of a Web storefront compared to telesales?

➤ Are they even comparable? Why or why not?

➤ If you can't reduce costs by replacing telesales, is there some other way that a Web storefront reduces costs?

➤ Examine Figure 7-16. In what aspects of the customer life cycle do you think e-commerce systems could be used for cost savings?

➤ Do you think you could successfully argue that e-commerce systems could result in greater cost savings than the inventory-elimination alternative our protagonist recommended? Explain your answer.

QUESTION SET 2

➤ Rather than attempting to eliminate inventory for a few vendors, why not create information systems that better manage inventory for all products from all vendors?

➤ Could better inventory management result in greater cost savings than eliminating inventory for a few vendors? How would you find out?

➤ What information systems can result in better inventory management? How will these systems save costs?

➤ Could auctions be used to reduce inventory costs? How?

➤ The case ends with an approval to implement a prototype system using XML Web services. That prototype may indicate substantial costs savings for those manufactures that do provide such an interface. What about those that do not? How could information systems be used to improve inventory management for products that those manufacturers supply?

➤ Do you think you could successfully argue that new inventory management systems could result in greater cost savings than the inventory-elimination alternative our protagonist recommended? Explain your answer.

QUESTION SET 3

➤ Besides inventory, two other drivers of supply chain performance are facilities and transportation. What kinds of information systems could be used to better manage facilities?

➤ Could better facility management save more costs than the proposal our protagonist made? How would you decide?

➤ How could information systems use RFIDs to better manage the inventory facility?

➤ Could information systems be used to decide the size, location, and contents of inventory facilities? Is this a one-time assessment, or could inventory contents be managed more dynamically? Would such dynamic management be likely to save costs?

➤ How could the company use information systems to save transportation costs?

➤ Would information systems be better able to save transportation costs from the manufacturer to inventory or from inventory to the customer?

➤ Do you think you could successfully argue that information systems to support facility management and transportation will result in greater cost savings than the inventory elimination alternative our protagonist recommended? Explain your answer.

WRAP UP

➤ We've traveled a lot of ground since we first met our protagonist and his/her failed project proposal at the start of Chapter 7.

➤ One important generalization is that information systems must support the organization's competitive strategy.

➤ What else have you learned from this?

➤ Did our protagonist ultimately succeed?

➤ Why was the COO so quick to approve the project?

➤ Might the COO have talked with the purchasing manager and the IS manager prior to the meeting? If so, what had our protagonist done that facilitated those conversations?

➤ What are two things you've learned about business professionalism from this case?

(Possible answers: Practice initiative, self-reliance, creativity, ability to work with others, consideration of others, a willingness to take direction, willingness to learn.)

➤ What are two things you've learned about interorganizational systems from this case?

(Possible answers: (1) Some organizations can best achieve their competitive strategy by cooperative programs with other organizations in the supply chain. (2) XML offers the promise of a customizable standard that could reduce the time, cost, and risk of development of interorganizational IS.)

Using the Reflections Guide
(page 253a)

GOALS

* Reinforce the differences between relational tables and XML documents.

* Introduce XML data stores.

* Illustrate the kinds of technology assessments that CTOs and others need to make as they help prepare their organizations for the future (a theme introduced in the Reflections Guide in Chapter 7).

BACKGROUND AND PRESENTATION STRATEGIES

I have a strong opinion on the value of XML data stores and their future as a replacement of relational databases. However, this belief is not shared by everyone, or even most people, in the IS industry. Given my strong bias, I think you might do the best by your students by taking a devil's-advocate position with regard to this guide.

(I did put my more aggressive thoughts into the editorial referenced in the guide. Responses to the editorial were bimodal: Some IEEE members were "irritated at such claptrap," whereas others were intrigued and thought there might be merit in the idea.)

First, students need to understand the difference between a relational database and an XML data store. Relational databases store data in tables; in most cases, users need information that is taken from several or even many tables. For example, to obtain information about salespeople, orders, customers, and products, users must combine data from many different tables.

Within an organization, the combination of data from these tables is manageable (perhaps expensive, but manageable). Developers agree on how to extract and combine data, and they produce the information that users want.

For interorganizational systems, however, this situation becomes far more difficult to manage. If there are 10 companies in a supply chain, then the developers in those 10 companies will have at least 10 different ways of extracting the data from the relational database.

XML documents get around this problem; the members of the supply chain agree on the XML schema to use, and they can each fill that schema by any means they want. Thus, coordination activity is greatly simplified.

Today, with data in relational databases, we have to take the data out of the relational tables and use a combination of SQL statements and program logic to format it into XML documents. We then transport the XML document to some destination, where we then take that document apart and place the data back into a set of tables.

But, this means that each company must pay for programmers to write applications that extract data from the database and put it into the XML document, or take data that is in the XML document and store it in the database. Why do this? Even though tools like ADO.NET provide great utility for making the transformation, why bother? Why not store the XML document as an XML document? We wouldn't need to break the data up into tables. But, how realistic is that?

This idea *could be* nothing more than an interesting possibility. But, I think it's worth at least discussing with the students. If nothing else, it will illustrate the kind of thinking that CTOs and others need to do as they assess technology trends for their organizations. Here's a series of questions that you might use to examine this question with your class:

➤ **The author claims that XML data stores will replace the relational model. Could this be correct?**

➤ **First, let's review. What characterizes a relational database?**

(Data stored in tables with relationships represented by foreign keys.)

➤ **What characterizes an XML document?**

(Outline-like arrangement of data. Structure formally defined by an XML schema. Automatic validation. Clean separation of structure, content, and format.)

➤ **Is XML a good way to communicate structured data from one site, user, or system to another?**

(Yes.)

➤ **Is there work involved in transforming relational tables of data into XML documents and from XML documents back to relational data?**

(Yes, and it can be expensive.)

➤ **So, why bother making the transformation back to relational tables?**

(My question!)

➤ **But, what about the billions of bytes of data that are already in relational databases? Who wants to reformat all of that?**

(No one.)

➤ **We cannot just stop the world, reformat all of the world's data into XML documents, and then restart the world.**

(Right!)

➤ **So, for a while, relational data and XML data must peacefully coexist. Will this be expensive and confusing?**

(Yes.)

➤ **How many organizations will want to go through that mess?**

(Well, some, but possibly not many . . .)

➤ **So, although there might be some advantages to XML data stores, the relational model will be with us for some time. right . . . at least 10 or 20 years.**

(Right!)

➤ **And, we know that predictions for 10 or 20 years are silly in this business.**

(Right!)

➤ **So, what do you conclude is responsible thinking with regard to this issue?**

➤ **Who in an organization is responsible for thinking about such matters? What happens if no one thinks about such issues? What happens if the company invests in XML data stores and they never become a reality?**

 ## SUGGESTED RESPONSES FOR DISCUSSION QUESTIONS

1. A *lingua franca* is a common language, often used for commerce. It makes it possible for many people, entities, or systems to communicate.
2. The benefits of XML are clean separation of structure, content, and format; automatic validation; and structured data, well-marked by extendible tags. (See other advantages in background. Those advantages are beyond the scope of the text.)
3. Companies would not have to hire programmers to write programs to convert relational data to XML format, and the reverse.

4. The established relational industry will resist this idea. People's relational expertise will be threatened. IS departments will see a lot of work, a lot of risk, and questionable benefits. Many would prefer to hire programmers to make the conversion only when absolutely necessary. DBMS vendors are already placing XML features into their products. It may be that they see the writing on the wall, or perhaps they are just hedging their bets: They want to have XML features in case XML standards take off. Some database consultants will hang on to their relational expertise and resist all they can. Others will see an opportunity to sell more database consulting services, especially during the era when both relational and XML data stores need to be supported. The latter group will be willing to consider the strengths of XML and may get on board.
5. Nothing succeeds like success. When (if) organizations, supply chains, industries, or others obtain a competitive advantage by processing XML documents and storing them as XML documents, then resistance will gradually be overcome. If there is no clear success, if the relational model continues to meet the needs of organizations, then XML will be used for data transport and no more.
6. Technology always advances via hybrids. Something new is incorporated into something old. Sails were added to rowboats until sails replaced oars. Paddlewheels were added to sailboats until paddlewheels replaced sails. Direct-drive propellers were added to paddle-wheeled boats until propellers replaced paddlewheels. This is progress by incremental adoption. DBMS products that have both relational and XML features will play a crucial role. Yes, both Oracle and SQL Server have XML features, and both are adding more.

WRAP UP

I think the best possible way to wrap up is for you to state your own conclusions. What do you think is likely to happen? Ask the class what they think.

Probably more important than this particular issue is to demonstrate to the students that these kinds of assessments go on all the time. As stated in the Reflections Guide in Chapter 7, it is the job of the CTO to assess such trends. What a fun job!

- Organizations should address four economic factors when considering e-commerce activity: channel conflict, price conflict, logistics expense, and customer service expense.

- Most B2C commerce is conducted using commerce servers. Such servers use Web pages encoded in HTML. Web pages are created by Web servers and consumed by browsers. The three-tier architecture consists of user, server, and database tiers.

- A supply chain is a network of organizations and facilities that transforms raw materials into finished goods for customers. Most supply chains have suppliers, manufacturers, distributors, and retailers. Supply chains also include transportation companies, warehouses, inventories, and some means of transmitting messages and information. The four drivers of supply chain performance are facilities, inventories, transportation, and information.

- In general, the maximum profits to the supply chain will not occur if each independent organization within it maximizes its own profit in isolation.

- The bullwhip effect is a phenomenon in which the variability in the size and timing of orders increases at each stage up the supply chain.

- Three fundamental supply chain information systems are supplier relationship management (SRM), inventory, and CRM. An SRM application is a cross-functional application with features and functions for sourcing, procuring, and settling accounts. Integrating SRM with CRM applications allows organizations to reduce procurement costs substantially.

- Organizations can exchange documents and data between programs using various alternatives. Two important document-exchange standards are EDI and XML.

- EDI is a standard of formats for common business documents. EDI standards define documents as a series of segments and the data fields in each segment. Common EDI standards are X12, EDIFACT, and HIPAA.

- XML is a markup language like HTML, but it improves upon HTML by requiring standard use of XML elements, by allowing users to extend the elements, and by clearly separating document structure, content, and format.

- An XML schema is an XML document that defines the structure of other XML documents.

- XML has wide applicability in the supply chain. Two organizations can agree on a common XML schema and use it to format and validate documents they exchange. XML can also be used to define document standards for an industry.

- Two standard ways for applications to share data are to use a proprietary means and to use XML Web services. Proprietary solutions have been used in the past, but are time consuming, laborious, and expensive.

- XML Web services allow programs to exchange data in a standardized way. A Web service provider publishes a service description, which is used to develop programs that call the Web service. All XML Web service data are exchanged using automatically validated XML documents.

KEY TERMS AND CONCEPTS

ASSIGNMENT MATERIAL

Review Questions

1. Explain how Porter's five competitive forces relate to interorganizational information systems.

2. Give examples of merchant and nonmerchant companies other than those mentioned in this chapter.

3. If disintermediation leads to market efficiencies, why do distributors and retailers still exist?

4. Describe characteristics of industries in which distributors and retailers are vulnerable to disintermediation. What characteristics make an industry not vulnerable to disintermediation?

5. Explain the importance of price elasticity to a retailer. How can a retailer best use knowledge about price elasticity?

6. Describe economic factors that organizations should address before engaging in e-commerce.

7. Go to your favorite Web storefront and place two items into a shopping cart. Using Figure 8-8 as a guide, explain the activities that occur behind the scenes between each of your clicks on a Web page.

8. Explain why the word *chain* in supply chain is misleading.

9. What is the only source of revenue for the supply chain?

10. List characteristics of four drivers that effect supply chain performance.

11. Give an example, other than one in this text, of a situation in which supply chain profitability is not maximized when each organization maximizes its own profitability.

12. Explain the term *bullwhip effect*. How can an information system be used to eliminate the bullwhip effect?

13. Explain the statement, "From a process standpoint, CRM and SRM are two sides of the same coin."

14. Describe the general character of an EDI document description.

15. What are X12, EDIFACT, and HIPAA standards?

16. Why are the EDI Internet standards not likely to be important?

17. Describe three characteristics of HTML that limit its usefulness for document interchange.

18. Explain how two organizations can benefit by sharing XML schema documents.

19. Explain how an industry can benefit by sharing XML schema documents.

20. What are the disadvantages of developing proprietary solutions for application interaction?

21. Explain how Web services could be used to eliminate the bullwhip effect.

Applying Your Knowledge

22. Suppose you are a manufacturer of high-end consumer kitchen appliances, and you are about to bring out a new line of mixers that will make an existing model obsolete. Assume you have 500 mixers of that existing model in finished-goods inventory. Describe three different strategies for using an electronic auction for unloading that inventory. Which strategy do you recommend?

23. Search the Microsoft, Oracle, and SAP Web sites for SRM applications. Compare the features and functions you find to those described in this chapter. Are these products commodities or do they have different features and functions? Is their use of terminology consistent? If not, describe important inconsistencies.

24. This chapter contends that over time XML Web services will replace EDI. Search the Web for evidence that either supports or contradicts this contention. Do you find applications that are being converted from EDI to Web services? Are EDI vendors adding Web services applications to their product suites? On a site for a vendor like SAP, do you see more evidence of EDI or of Web services features and functions?

25. Search the Web for case histories on the use of Web services and supply chain management. You can start by searching for the terms *supply chain* and *Web services*. See where that takes you. Find

an article about a major company's use of Web services in the supply chain. Summarize the experience of that company.

26. Amazon.com makes it exceedingly easy for developers to use its Web services. Why do you think Amazon.com does that? What competitive advantage does it receive? Describe another B2C business, in another industry, that might achieve similar benefits by developing an easily used Web service.

Application Exercises

27. Assume you have been asked to create a spreadsheet to help make a buy-versus-lease decision for the servers on your organization's Web farm. Assume you are considering the servers for a 5-year period, but that you do not know exactly how many servers you will need. Initially, you know you will need 5 servers, but you might need as many as 50, depending on the success of your organization's e-commerce activity.

    a. For the buy-alternative calculations, set up your spreadsheet so that you can enter the base price of the server hardware, the price of all software, and a maintenance expense that is some percentage of the hardware price. Assume that the percent you enter covers both hardware and software maintenance. Also assume that each server has a 3-year life, after which it has no value. Assume straight-line depreciation for computers used less than 3 years, and that at the end of the 5 years, you can sell the computers you have used for less than 3 years for their depreciated value. Also assume that your organization pays 2 percent interest on capital expenses. Assume the servers cost $5,000 each, and the needed software costs $750. Assume maintenance expense varies from 2 to 7 percent.

    b. For the lease-alternative calculations, assume that the leasing vendor will lease the same computer hardware as you can purchase. The lease includes all the software you need as well as all maintenance. Set up your spreadsheet so that you can enter various lease costs, which vary according to the number of years of the lease (1, 2, or 3). Assume the cost of a 3-year lease is $285 per machine per month, of a 2-year lease is $335 per machine per month, and of a 1-year lease is $415 per machine per month. Also, the lessor offers a 5 percent discount if you lease from 20 to 30 computers and a 10 percent discount if you lease from 31 to 50 computers.

    c. Using your spreadsheet, compare the costs of buy versus lease under the following situations. (Assume you either buy or lease. You cannot lease some and buy some.) Make assumptions as necessary and state those assumptions.

        i. Your organization requires 20 servers for 5 years.

        ii. Your organization requires 20 servers for the first 2 years and 40 servers for the next 3 years.

        iii. Your organization requires 20 servers for the first 2 years, 40 servers for the next 2 years, and 50 servers for the last year.

        iv. Your organization requires 10 servers the first year, 20 servers the second year, 30 servers the third year, 40 servers the fourth year, and 50 servers the last year.

        v. For the previous case, does the cheaper alternative change if the cost of the servers is $4,000? If it is $8,000?

28. Assume you have been given the task of compiling evaluations that your company's purchasing agents make of their vendors. Each month, every purchasing agent evaluates all of the vendors that it has worked with in the past month on three factors: price, quality, and responsiveness. Assume the ratings are from 1 to 5, with 5 being the best. Because your company has hundreds of vendors and dozens of purchasing agents, you decide to use Access to compile the results.

    a. Create a database with three tables: VENDOR (*VendorNumber, Name, Contact*), PURCHASER (*EmpNumber, Name, Email*), and RATING (*EmpNumber, VendorNumber, Month, Year, PriceRating, QualityRating, ResponsivenessRating*). Assume *VendorNumber* and *EmpNumber* are the keys of VENDOR and PURCHASER, respectively. Decide what you think is the appropriate key for RATING.

    b. Create appropriate relationships using Tools/Relationships.

    c. Using the table view of each table, enter sample data for vendors, employees, and ratings.

    d. Create a query that shows the names of all vendors and their average scores.

    e. Create a query that shows the names of all employees and their averages scores. *Hint:* In this and in question f, you will need to use the Group By function in your query.

    f. Create a parameterized query that you can use to obtain the minimum, maximum, and average ratings on each criterion for a particular vendor. Assume you will enter *VendorName* as the parameter.

Career Assignments

29. Use your favorite search engine and search the Web for the term *e-commerce marketing job opportunities*. Investigate several of the sites that you find to answer the following questions:

    a. Describe the two jobs in the search results that you find most interesting.
    b. Describe the educational requirements for each of these jobs.
    c. Describe internships and other experience that you could gain to better prepare you for each of these jobs.
    d. Using both Web resources and your own experience, describe the employment outlook for these jobs.

30. Same as question 29, but search for the term *supply chain management job opportunities*. In your answer, focus on jobs that have some relationship to information systems.

31. Same as question 29, but search for the term *XML programmer job opportunities*.

Case Study 8-1

Getty Images Serves Up Profit

Getty Images was founded in 1995 with the goal of consolidating the fragmented photography market by acquiring many small companies, applying business discipline to the merged entity, and developing modern information systems. The advent of the Web drove the company to e-commerce and in the process enabled Getty to change the workflow and business practices of the professional visual content industry. Getty Images has grown from a startup to become, by 2004, a global, $600 million plus, publicly traded (NYSE: GYI), very profitable company.

Getty Images obtains its imagery (both still and movie) from photographers under contract, and it owns the world's largest private archive of imagery. Getty also employs staff photographers to shoot the world's news, sport, and entertainment events. In the case of photography and film that it does not own, it provides a share of the revenue generated to the content owner. Getty Images is both a producer and a distributor of imagery, and all its products are sold via e-commerce on the Web.

Getty Images employs three licensing models: The first is *subscription*, by which customers contract to use as many images as they want as often as they want (this applies to the news, sport, and entertainment imagery). The second model is *royalty free*. In this model, customers pay a fee based on the file size of the image and can use the image any way they want and as many times as they want. However, under this model, customers have no exclusivity or ability to prevent a competitor from using the same image at the same time.

The third model, *rights managed,* also licenses creative imagery. In this model, which is the largest in revenue terms, users pay fees according to the rights that they wish to use—size, industry, geography, prominence, frequency, exclusivity, and so forth. According to its Web site:

> Getty Images has been credited with the introduction of royalty-free photography and was the first company to license imagery via the Web, subsequently moving the entire industry online. The company was also the first to employ creative researchers to anticipate the visual content needs of the world's communicators, and Getty Images remains the first and only publicly traded imagery company in the world. (*corporate.gettyimages.com/source/company*, accessed December 2004)

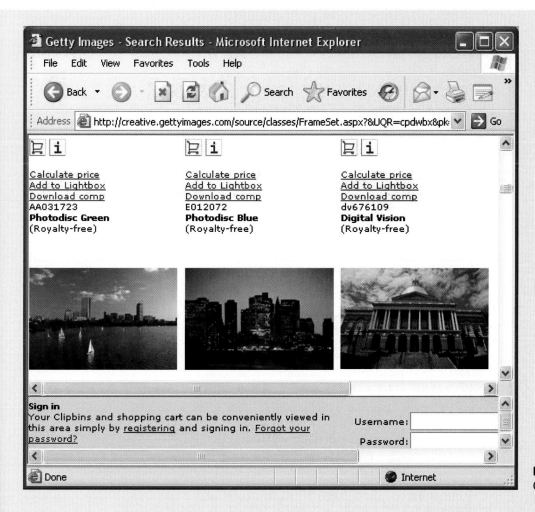

Figure 1
Getty Images Search Results

In 2003, Getty Images' Web site, *gettyimages.com*, received more than 51 million visits and served over 1.3 billion pages. Visitors to the site viewed more than 6.7 billion photo thumbnails in the third quarter of 2004 alone.

Because Getty Images licenses photos in digital format, its variable cost of production is essentially zero. Once the company has obtained a photo and placed it in the commerce server database, the cost of sending it to a customer is zero. Getty Images does have the overhead costs of setting up and operating the e-commerce site, and it does pay some costs for its images—either the costs of employing the photographer or the cost of setting up and maintaining the relationship with out-of-house photographers. For some images, it also pays a royalty to the owner. Once these costs are paid, however, the cost of producing a photo is nil. This means that Getty Images' profitability increases substantially with increased volume.

Figure 1 shows a page that the Getty Images commerce server produced when the user selected creative, royalty-free photography and searched on the term *Boston*.

When the user clicked "Calculate price" for the image named Photodisc Green, the commerce server produced the page shown in Figure 2 (page 260). This Web page shows a default price. Users in different countries may have a different price depending on agreements, taxes, and local policies.

Source: gettyimages.com (accessed December 2004).

Questions

1. Visit *gettyimages.com* and select "Creative, Royalty Free Photography." Search for an image of a city close to your campus. Select a photo and determine its default

Figure 2
Price Calculation for an
Image of Boston

prices. Using Figure 8-8 as a guide, list the actions that must occur on the Getty Images Web site as you click through the site.

2. Considering the relationship of fixed and variable costs at Getty Images, why do you think that it "employs creative researchers to anticipate the visual content needs of the world's communicators?" Why is that research important? What justifies the cost of such research?

3. With regard to question 2, describe how Getty Images could use records of customer activity on its own Web site to anticipate future needs. What data could it process and what information could it develop?

4. Investigate the Getty Images Web site and determine how it uses its site to attract new photographers.

5. Some of the key elements in the valuation of Getty Images are the following: customers, photo inventory, photographer relationships, and IT infrastructure.
   a. Rank these elements in decreasing order of importance and justify your ranking.
   b. Explain which, if any, of these key elements can serve as a barrier to entry to other online photo companies.

6. Because of e-commerce, Getty Images has the enviable position of near-zero variable cost of production. Describe two other industries that could use e-commerce to attain the same advantage.

Case Study 8-2

Dun and Bradstreet Data via Web Services

As stated in the Dun and Bradstreet (D&B) case on page 240, D&B collects data on more than 80 million businesses and sells it to customers who use the data for analyzing customer credit, selecting customer prospects, and identifying potential suppliers.

Some customers are willing to buy company reports using the commerce server illustrated in the previous D&B case. For others, this process is too slow and cumbersome. For example, consider the customers that use D&B data to assess creditworthiness. Because of competitive pressure, some companies must make credit assessments immediately, in real time, while interacting with their customers. For such applications, buying a prewritten report over the D&B commerce server will not suffice.

Instead, these customers want to use automated processes to access the D&B databases. They want to write credit-analysis programs that obtain needed data from D&B in real time. Consider, for example, the needs of a computer distributor or retailer (such as CDW in Chapter 3, page 50). The distributor's customers can place large orders using the distributor's Web storefront. The equipment price for a medium-sized network could total $40,000 or $50,000, and before accepting the order, the distributor needs to assess the creditworthiness of the customer. In situations like this, the distributor wants its commerce server programs to access D&B data and to use it to evaluate credit programmatically.

To meet this need, D&B developed a version of Web services that its customers' programs can access. Although the D&B version uses XML documents for data exchange, it does not use all of the XML Web service standards. In particular, it does not provide a standard service description nor use standard services protocols. Instead, the D&B service provides a proprietary interface for customers. The D&B Web service could not use the current, modern standards because those standards were not finalized when D&B developed its Web services system.

Still, D&B's Web services do use XML. Consequently, its users can realize the advantages of schema validation, and both D&B and its customers can use XML standards to reformat documents automatically.

In order to use the D&B Web services, customers must enter into an agreement with D&B that specifies which data will be accessed and what and how they will pay for that data access. Then, the customers must learn the D&B interface and develop programs accordingly. D&B provides some technical assistance to customer program developers.

By using Web services to obtain data, customers obtain the latest, up-to-the-minute data. This advantage is important because D&B makes over a million updates to its database every day. Furthermore, D&B Web services provide a single, consistent interface for customers to use. Customers save costs because they need to develop D&B access programs only once; all applications can use those programs to obtain D&B data. Finally, D&B customers can use the Web services interface to request alerts when particular data are updated. Alerts enable customers to update their own databases with the most current data.

Sources: Sean Rhody, "Dun and Bradstreet," *Web Services Journal,* Vol. 1, Issue 1, *sys-con.com/webservices* (accessed December 2004); Dun and Bradstreet, "Data Integration Toolkit," PowerPoint Presentation, *globalaccess.dnb.com* (accessed December 2004).

Questions

1. Summarize the difference between obtaining D&B data by purchasing reports from the D&B Web server and by obtaining D&B data via Web services.

2. Explain how schema validation improves the quality of the data exchange. How can D&B and its Web services customers use schema validation to advantage?

3. As stated, D&B did not describe their Web services in the standard way. What are the consequences to D&B? What are the consequences to D&B's customers? D&B could upgrade its Web services to use these standards. If you worked at D&B, how would you decide whether to make that upgrade? Consider the consequences of the upgrade on both new and existing D&B Web services customers.

4. Besides credit reporting, D&B customers use D&B data to find and assess customer prospects and to determine potential sources of suppliers. Explain how Web services could be used for these applications as well as for credit analysis.

5. D&B is an international organization that provides data to customers worldwide. What advantages does the use of Web services provide for non–U.S. customers?

6. How does the D&B Web services interface give D&B a competitive advantage over other data providers?

Business Intelligence and Knowledge Management

Learning Objectives

- Understand the need for business intelligence systems.
- Know the characteristics of reporting systems.
- Know the purpose and role of data warehouses and data marts.
- Understand fundamental data-mining techniques.
- Know the purpose, features, and functions of knowledge management systems.

Guides

SECURITY GUIDE
Semantic Security

PROBLEM SOLVING GUIDE
Counting and Counting and Counting

ETHICS GUIDE
The Ethics of Classification

OPPOSING FORCES GUIDE
Data Mining in the Real World

REFLECTIONS GUIDE
Justifying the Justification?

Chapter Preview

The information systems described in Chapters 7 and 8 generate enormous amounts of data. Most of these data are used for operational purposes such as tracking customer orders, inventories, shipments, receivables, payables, employee assignments, and so forth. These operational data have a potential windfall: They contain patterns, relationships, clusters, and other information that can facilitate management, especially planning and forecasting. Business intelligence systems are information systems that produce such information from operational data.

In addition to information in data, even more important sources of information are employees themselves. Employees come to the organization with expertise, and as they gain experience in the organization, they add to that expertise. Vast amounts of collective knowledge exist in the minds of every organization's employees. The question is, how can that knowledge be shared? How does an employee with a particular problem learn that another employee knows exactly how to solve that problem? Knowledge management applications address this need, and we will conclude this chapter with a description of the purpose, features, and functions of these applications.

Carbon Creek Gardens

Mary Keeling owns and operates Carbon Creek Gardens, a retailer of trees, garden plants, perennial and annual flowers, and bulbs. "The Gardens," as her customers call it, also sells bags of soil, fertilizer, small garden tools, and garden sculptures. Mary started the business 10 years ago when she bought a section of land that, because of water drainage, was unsuited for residential development. With hard work and perseverance, Mary has created a warm and inviting environment with a unique and carefully selected inventory of plants. The Gardens has become a favorite nursery for serious gardeners in her community.

"The problem," she says, "is that I've grown so large, I've lost track of my customers. The other day, I ran into Tootsie Swan at the grocery store, and I realized I hadn't seen her in ages. I said something like, 'Hi, Tootsie, I haven't seen you for a while,' and that statement unleashed an angry torrent from her. It turns out that she'd been in over a year ago and wanted to return a plant. One of my part-time employees waited on her and had apparently insulted her or at least didn't give her the service she wanted. So, she decided not to come back to the Gardens.

"Tootsie was one of my best customers. I'd lost her, and I didn't even know it! That really frustrates me. Is it inevitable that as I get bigger, I lose track of my customers? I don't think so. Somehow, I have to find out when regular customers aren't coming around. Had I known Tootsie had stopped shopping with us, I'd have called her to see what was going on. I need customers like her.

"I've got all sorts of data in my sales database. It seems like the information I need is in there, but how do it get it out?"

■ The Need for Business Intelligence Systems

According to a study done at the University of California at Berkeley,[1] a total of 403 petabytes of new data were created in 2002. Undoubtedly, even greater amounts are being generated today, but just consider that number. As shown in Figure 9-1, 403 **petabytes** is roughly the amount of all printed material ever written. The print collection of the Library of Congress is .01 petabytes, so 400 petabytes equals 40,000 copies of the print collection of the Library of Congress. That is indeed a lot of data, and it's the amount generated in just one year. By 2007, nearly 2,500 petabytes, or 2.5 **exabytes**, of data will have been generated.

The generation of all these data has much to do with Moore's Law. The capacity of storage devices increases as their costs decrease. Today, storage capacity is nearly unlimited. Figure 9-2 shows that at the end of 2003, total hard disk storage capacity exceeded 41 exabytes, which is eight times the number of words ever spoken by all human beings throughout history. Not all of that storage is used for business. Much of it is used to store music, digital pictures, video, and phone conversations. However, much of that capacity is also used to store the data from business information

---

[1]"How Much Information, 2003," *sims.berkeley.edu/research/projects/how-much-info-2003* (accessed May 2005).

Carbon Creek Gardens

(page 266)

GOALS

* Introduce the students to a common business intelligence (BI) problem in a realistic, but comprehensible, setting.

* Set up a business scenario that can be used to augment the lecture throughout the chapter.

* Encourage the students to think about using IS for innovative solutions to business problems.

WAYS TO STIMULATE STUDENT INVOLVEMENT

I begin with the question:

➤ **How does a business know when it has lost a customer?**

What an important question! If you know that you've lost a customer, you can do something to win back that person or company. But, if you don't know, you'll suffer the consequences without being able to do anything about them.

➤ **Have you ever decided not to go back to a shop, retailer, restaurant, or some other business? Why?**

➤ **Was there anything the company could have done to win you back?**

➤ **Do you think the company would have been willing to do that, had it known?**

Another important question:

➤ **What is the cost of a lost customer? Is it just the value of the lost sale?**

No, clearly the loss is the value of the annuity of all of that customer's future sales.

When viewed from this perspective, it's easy to see why some companies, like Nordstrom, do everything possible not to lose a customer. (Again, the easiest way to solve a problem is not to have it.)

So, it's an important question. But,

➤ **How can you determine if a customer has been lost? What sort of analysis needs to be done?**

➤ **What records exist that could be processed to find lost customers? Is the analysis watertight? Could someone be misclassified as a lost customer?**

➤ **Does the cost of misclassifying a customer as lost make the analysis not worthwhile?**

OK, so it's an important question, and one that probably has a cost-feasible IS solution.

➤ **Assume that you work as a sales or marketing analyst. What kind of system would be useful for you to find lost customers?**

The answer to that question is the subject of this chapter.

WRAP UP

I wrap up this initial discussion with the following statement:

➤ **Think about this problem as we discuss business intelligence systems. Some of the systems we describe will be appropriate for this problem, others will not be. Those others have utility for other problems, however.**

Note: I recommend an RFM solution at the end of the chapter. However, partway through the chapter, on page 272, the text suggests a way that Mary could compare two reports from different periods to determine whether she'd lost one of her top-50 customers.

Kilobyte (KB)	*1,000 bytes OR 10³ bytes* 2 Kilobytes: A typewritten page 100 Kilobytes: A low-resolution photograph
Megabyte (MB)	*1,000,000 bytes OR 10⁶ bytes* 1 Megabyte: A small novel OR a 3.5-inch floppy disk 2 Megabytes: A high-resolution photograph 5 Megabytes: The complete works of Shakespeare 10 Megabytes: A minute of high-fidelity sound 100 Megabytes: One meter of shelved books 500 Megabytes: A CD-ROM
Gigabyte (GB)	*1,000,000,000 bytes OR 10⁹ bytes* 1 Gigabyte: A pickup truck filled with books 20 Gigabytes: A good collection of the works of Beethoven 100 Gigabytes: A library floor of academic journals
Terabyte (TB)	*1,000,000,000,000 bytes OR 10¹² bytes* 1 Terabyte: 50,000 trees made into paper and printed 2 Terabytes: An academic research library 10 Terabytes: The print collections of the U.S. Library of Congress 400 Terabytes: National Climactic Data Center (NOAA) database
Petabyte (PB)	*1,000,000,000,000,000 bytes OR 10¹⁵ bytes* 1 Petabyte: Three years of EOS data (2001) 2 Petabytes: All U.S. academic research libraries 20 Petabytes: Production of hard-disk drives in 1995 200 Petabytes: All printed material
Exabyte (EB)	*1,000,000,000,000,000,000 bytes OR 10¹⁸ bytes* 2 Exabytes: Total volume of information generated in 1999 5 Exabytes: All words ever spoken by human beings

Source: sims.berkeley.edu/research/projects/how-much-info/datapowers.html (accessed May 2005).

Figure 9-1
How Big Is an Exabyte?

Source: Used with permission of Peter Lyman and Hal R. Varian, University of California at Berkeley.

Year	Disks Sold (Thousands)	Storage Capacity (Petabytes)
1992	42,000	
1995	89,054	104.8
1996	105,686	183.9
1997	129,281	343.63
1998	143,649	724.36
1999	165,857	1394.60
2000	200,000 (IDEMA)	4,630.5
2001	196,000 (Gartner)	7,279.14
2002	**213,000 (Gartner projection)**	**10,849.56**
2003	235,000	15,892.24
TOTAL	**1,519,527 (1.5 billion drives)**	**41,402.73 (41 exabytes)**

Source: sims.berkeley.edu/research/projects/how-much-info/datapowers.html (accessed May 2005).

Figure 9-2
Hard-Disk Storage Capacity

Source: Used with permission of Peter Lyman and Hal R. Varian, University of California at Berkeley.

systems. For example, in 2004 Verizon's SQL Server database contained more than 15 tera-bytes of data. If that data were published in books, a bookshelf 450 miles long would be required to hold them.

With all of that data, we are drowning in data and starving for information. How can we go about finding information in that sea of data?

Business Intelligence Tools

Astronomers use telescopes to search the heavens for meaningful patterns. We need the equivalent of a telescope for data, with which to search the immense sea of data for patterns. Tools for searching business data in an attempt to obtain such information are called **business intelligence (BI) tools**. In this chapter, we will consider two types of BI tools: reporting tools and data-mining tools.

Reporting tools are programs that read data from a variety of sources, process that data, produce formatted reports, and deliver those reports to the users who need them. The processing of the data is simple: Data are sorted and grouped, and simple totals and averages are calculated, as you will see. Reporting tools are used primarily for *assessment*. They are used to address questions like: What has happened in the past? What is the current situation? How does the current situation compare to the past?

Data-mining tools process data using statistical techniques, many of which are sophisticated and mathematically complex. We will explore data mining in some detail later in the chapter. For now, it's enough to say that *data mining* involves searching for patterns and relationships among data. In most cases, data-mining tools are used to make *predictions*. For example, we can use one form of analysis to com-pute the probability that a customer will default on a loan or the probability that a customer is likely to respond positively to a promotion. Another data-mining tech-nique predicts products that tend to be purchased together. In one famous example, a data-mining analysis determined that customers who buy diapers are likely to buy beer.[2] That information enabled store managers to locate beer and diapers near each other in store displays.

Although reporting tools *tend to be* used to assess and data-mining tools *tend to be* used to predict, that distinction is not always true. A better way to distinguish between these two BI tools is that reporting tools use simple operations like sorting, grouping, and summing and data-mining tools use sophisticated statistical techniques. You will learn more as this chapter progresses.

Business Intelligence Systems

As you know by now, there is a difference between a tool and an information system. A *tool* is a computer program. An *information system* is a collection of hardware, soft-ware, data, procedures, and people.

The purpose of a **business intelligence (BI) system** is to provide the right informa-tion, to the right user, at the right time. A tool produces the information, but the sys-tem ensures that the right information is delivered to the right user at the right time.

BI systems help users accomplish their goals and objectives by producing insights that lead to actions. For example, a reporting *tool* can generate a report that shows a customer has canceled an important order. A reporting *system*, however, alerts that customer's salesperson with this unwanted news, and does so in time for the salesper-son to try to alter the customer's decision.

Similarly, a data-mining *tool* can create an equation that computes the probability that a customer will default on a loan. A data-mining *system*, however, uses that equa-tion to enable banking personnel to assess new loan applications. Again, BI systems help users turn insights into actions.

---

[2]Michael J. A. Berry and Gordon Linoff, *Data Mining Techniques for Marketing, Sales, and Customer Support* (New York: John Wiley, 1997).

Reporting Systems

The purpose of a **reporting system** is to create meaningful information from disparate data sources and to deliver that information to the proper user on a timely basis. Before we describe the components of a reporting system, first consider how reporting operations can be used to construct meaningful information.

Creating Information Using Reporting Operations

Chapter 1 defined the difference between data and information. Data are recorded facts or figures; information is knowledge derived from data. Alternatively, information is data presented in a meaningful context. Reporting systems generate information from data as a result of four operations:

- Filtering data
- Sorting data
- Grouping data
- Making simple calculations on the data

To illustrate the use of these operations, consider Figure 9-3, which shows a portion of a file of raw data on the price of the NDX.X, an index fund of 100 stocks traded on the NASDAQ stock exchange. As shown, the data consist of the trading date, the opening price, the closing price, and the volume of shares traded. Figure 9-3 is a simple list of data. As it stands, this list shows little information.

Information can be constructed from these data, however, by applying the four reporting operations listed earlier. Specifically, suppose you believe the up/down

TDate	Open	Close	Volume
2003-08-27	1305.98	1318.93...	13497300.0
2003-08-26	1298.23	1309.05	13828600.0
2003-08-25	1302.5	1306.64...	11178400.0
2003-08-22	1338.19...	1304.54	17052000.0
2003-08-21	1309.56...	1314.65...	17224700.0
2003-08-20	1289.43...	1299.73	15067600.0
2003-08-19	1291.37...	1299.69...	17243900.0
2003-08-18	1258.18...	1284.80...	14763100.0
2003-08-15	1250.45	1253.63...	7039500.0
2003-08-14	1241.17...	1251.90...	13115700.0
2003-08-13	1247.55...	1240.37...	14492000.0
2003-08-12	1227.5	1240.7	13298400.0
2003-08-11	1209.35...	1223.14...	12037800.0
2003-08-08	1223.66...	1207.28	13363300.0
2003-08-07	1214.89...	1217.17...	16380400.0
2003-08-06	1221.99	1215.13...	18622700.0
2003-08-05	1263.79	1229.72	17433800.0
2003-08-04	1263.62...	1267.38...	15734100.0
2003-08-01	1274.61...	1264.33...	14840400.0
2003-07-31	1278.29	1276.94...	18584700.0
2003-07-30	1276.57...	1263.78	15137600.0
2003-07-29	1284.24	1275.17...	17038000.0
2003-07-28	1281.5	1280.53	15358200.0
2003-07-25	1252.62...	1278.30...	15879800.0

Figure 9-3
Trade Data for NDX.X
(NASDAQ 100)

Day of Week	2003 AverageChangeInClosePrice
Monday	3.77
Tuesday	4.41
Wednesday	−1.70
Thursday	5.71
Friday	−2.48

Figure 9-4
Report Based on Trade Data in Figure 9-3

direction of the price on this index fund depends on the day of the week. To assess your belief, you create a report on the trading data for 2003. In your report, you *filter* the trading data to obtain data for trades in 2003. Then, you *compute* the change in closing price from day to day. You then *group* the data by day of week, and finally, you *sort* the results according to the order of the days in the week.

Figure 9-4 shows the result of these operations. Indeed, in 2003, on average, NDX.X traded up on Monday, Tuesday, and Thursday and down on Wednesday and Friday.[3] To restate, Figure 9-3 shows data; Figure 9-4 shows information.

The construction of such reports is not particularly difficult. (Figure 9-4 was generated using SQL, the database processing language you learned about in Chapter 4. Programmers can create reasonably complex data transformations using simple statements from this language.)

In the remainder of this section, we look at various aspects of reporting systems, including components and functions of these systems, and some examples.

Components of Reporting Systems

Figure 9-5 shows the major components of a reporting system. Data from disparate data sources are read and combined, using filtering, sorting, grouping, and simple calculating, to produce information. Figure 9-5 combines data from an Oracle database, a SQL Server database, and other nondatabase data. Some data are generated within the organization, other data are obtained from public sources, and still other data may be purchased from data utilities.

A reporting system maintains a database of reporting metadata. The metadata describes reports, users, groups, roles, events, and other entities involved in the reporting activity. The reporting system uses the metadata to prepare and deliver reports to the proper users on a timely basis.

As shown in Figure 9-5, organizations can prepare reports in a variety of formats. Figure 9-6 lists report characteristics by type, media, and mode, which we discuss in the following sections.

Report Type

In terms of **report type**, reports can be *static* or *dynamic*. **Static reports** are prepared once from the underlying data, and they do not change. A report of past year's sales, for example, is a static report. Other reports are **dynamic**; at the time of creation, the reporting system reads the most current data and generates the report using that fresh data. A report on sales today and a report on current stock prices are both dynamic reports.

Query reports are prepared in response to data entered by users. Google provides a handy example of a query report: You enter the keywords you want to search on, and the reporting system within Google searches its database and generates a response that

---

[3]Wait! Before you rush off to trade on this pattern, realize this is just one year's data. In fact, this pattern did not hold in 2002, nor in 2004. Most analysts believe that day of week is a poor indicator of market direction. Although the report produces the information, the insight (and action) is up to the human interpreter of the information.

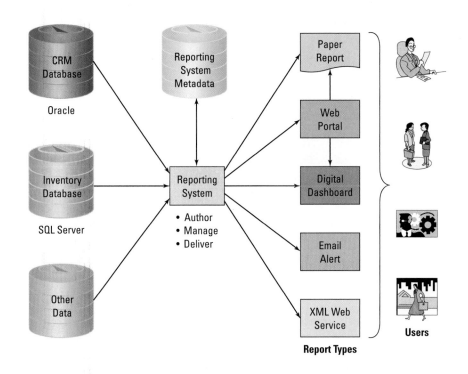

Figure 9-5
Components of a Reporting System

Type	Media	Mode
Static	Paper	Push
Dynamic	Computer screen via application	Pull
Query	Web site	
Online Analytical Processing (OLAP)	Digital dashboard	
	Alerts, via email or cell phone	
	Export to Excel, Quicken, TurboTax, QuickBooks, or other application	
	XML Web service	

Figure 9-6
Summary of Report Characteristics

is particular to your query. Within an organization, a query report could be generated to show current inventory levels. The user enters item numbers, and the reporting system responds with inventory levels of those items at various stores and warehouses.

Online analytical processing (OLAP) is a fourth type of report. OLAP reports allow the user to dynamically change the report grouping structures. An OLAP reporting application is illustrated later in this chapter.

Report Media

Today, reports are delivered via many different **report media** or channels. Some reports are printed on paper, and others are created in a format like PDF whereby they can be printed or viewed electronically. Other reports are delivered to computer screens. Applications for CRM and ERP systems, for example, include dozens of different reports that users view online. Additionally, companies sometimes place reports on internal corporate Web sites for employees to access. For example, an organization might place a report of its latest sales on the sales department's Web site or a report on customers serviced on the customer service department's Web site.

Another report medium is a **digital dashboard,** which is an electronic display that is customized for a particular user. Vendors like Yahoo! and MSN provide common

Figure 9-7
Digital Dashboard Example

examples. Users of these services can define content they want—say, a local weather forecast, a list of stock prices, or a list of news sources—and the vendor constructs the display customized for each user. Figure 9-7 shows an example.

Other dashboards are particular to an organization. Executives at a manufacturing organization, for example, might have a dashboard that shows up-to-the-minute production and sales activities.

Alerts are another form of report. Users can declare that they wish to receive notification of events, say, via email or on their cell phones. Of course, some cell phones are capable of displaying Web pages, and digital dashboards can be delivered to them as well.

Some reports are exported from the report generator to another program such as Excel, Quicken, QuickBooks, and so forth. For example, application programs at many banks can export customer checking account transactions into Excel, Quicken, or Money.

Finally, reports can be published via a Web service. The Web service produces the report in response to requests from the service-consuming application, as discussed in Chapter 8. This style of reporting is particularly useful for interorganizational information systems like supply chain management.

Report Mode

The final report characteristic in Figure 9-6 is the **report mode**. Organizations send a **push report** to users according to a preset schedule. Users receive the report without any activity on their part. In contrast, users must request a **pull report**. To obtain a pull report, a user goes to a Web portal or digital dashboard and clicks a link or button to cause the reporting system to produce and deliver the report.

Carbon Creek Gardens (continued)

Before we continue, examine Figure 9-6 again and consider the situation at Carbon Creek Gardens. Mary wants to know when she's lost a customer. One way to help her would be to produce a static report, say in PDF format, showing the top 50 customers from the prior year. Mary could print that report

or we could place it on a private section of her Web site so that she could download it from wherever she happens to be.

Periodically, say once a week, Mary could request a dynamic report that shows the top buyers for that week. That report could also be in PDF format or it could just be produced onscreen. Mary could compare the two reports to determine who's missing. If she wonders whether a customer such as Tootsie has been ordering, she could request a query report on Tootsie's activities.

This solution places the burden of locating a missing customer on Mary, however, and she might not notice that someone is missing. We will consider other alternatives later in this chapter.

Functions of Reporting Systems

In the middle of Figure 9-5, under the drawing of the reporting system, three functions of a reporting system are listed: author, manager, and deliver.

Report Authoring

Authoring a report involves connecting to data sources, creating the report structure, and formatting the report. Figures 9-8 and 9-9 show the use of a Microsoft developer tool called Visual Studio.Net for authoring a report. In Figure 9-8, the developer has already specified a database that contains the NASDAQ trading data and has just entered a SQL statement, shown in the lower-center portion of this display, to generate this report.

In Figure 9-9, (page 274) the report author is creating the format of the report by specifying the headings and format of the data items. In a more complicated report, the author would specify sorting and grouping of data items, as well as page headers and footers. The developer sets values for item properties using the property list in the right-hand side of the display in Figure 9-9.

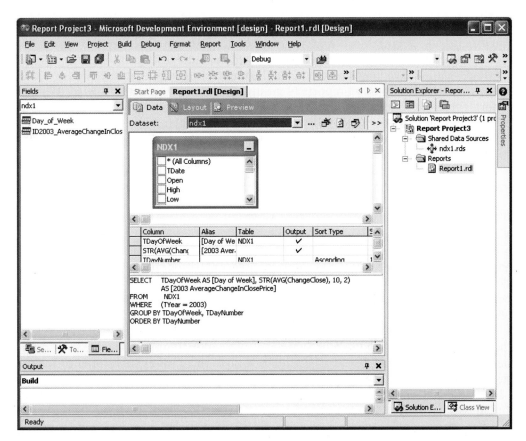

Figure 9-8
Connecting to a Report Data Source Using VisualStudio.Net

Source: Microsoft product screen shot reprinted with permission from Microsoft Corporaton.

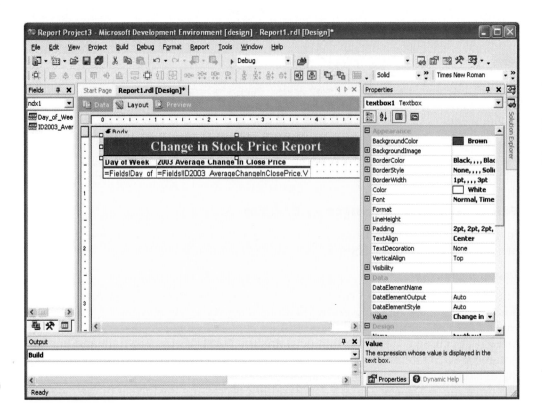

Figure 9-9

Formatting a Report Using VisualStudio.Net

Source: Microsoft product screen shot reprinted with permission from Microsoft Corporaton.

Report Management

The purpose of *report management* is to define who receives what reports, when, and by what means. Most report-management systems allow the report administrator to define user accounts and user groups and to assign particular users to particular groups. For example, all of the salespeople would be assigned to the sales group, all of the executives assigned to the executive group, and so forth. All of these data are stored in the reporting system's metadata shown in Figure 9-5.

Reports that have been created using the report-authoring system are assigned to groups and users. Assigning reports to groups saves the administrator work: When a report is created, changed, or removed, the administrator need only change the report assignments to the group. All of the users in the group will inherit the changes.

As stated, the report-management metadata indicate which format of this report is to be sent to which user. The metadata also indicates what channel is to be used and whether the report is to be pushed or pulled. If the report is to be pushed, the administrator declares whether the report is to be generated on a regular schedule or as an alert.

Report Delivery

The report-delivery function of a reporting system pushes reports or allows them to be pulled according to report-management metadata. Reports can be delivered via an email server, via a Web site, via XML Web services, or by other program-specific means. The report-delivery system uses the operating system and other program security components to ensure that only authorized users receive authorized reports. It also ensures that push reports are produced at appropriate times.

For query reports, the report-delivery system serves as an intermediary between the user and the report generator. It receives user query data, such as the item numbers in an inventory query, passes the query data to the report generator, receives the resulting report, and delivers the report to the user.

For discussion of security issues relating to reporting systems, see the *Security Guide* on page 275a.

Examples of Reporting Systems

So far, our discussion of reporting systems has focused on their features and functions. Such a discussion gives you an idea of the capabilities of reporting system, but not much information on how you might use them. In this section, we consider two applications of reporting systems. The first concerns a simple report often used in marketing. The second illustrates the power of OLAP analysis.

RFM Analysis

RFM analysis is a way of analyzing and ranking customers according to their purchasing patterns.[4] It is a simple technique that considers how *recently* (R) a customer has ordered, how *frequently* (F) a customer orders, and how much *money* (M) the customer spends per order. We consider this technique here because it is a useful analysis that can be readily implemented using a reporting system.

To produce an RFM score, the program first sorts customer purchase records by the date of their most recent (R) purchase. In a common form of this analysis, the program then divides the customers into five groups and gives customers in each group a score of 1 to 5. Thus, the 20 percent of the customers having the most recent orders are given an R score of 1, the 20 percent of the customers having the next most recent orders are given an R score of 2, and so forth, down to the last 20 percent, who are given an R score of 5.

The program then re-sorts the customers on the basis of how frequently they order. The 20 percent of the customers who order most frequently are given an F score of 1, the next 20 percent of most frequently ordering customers are given a score of 2, and so forth, down to the least frequently ordering customers, who are given an F score of 5.

Finally, the program sorts the customers again according to the amount spent on their orders. The 20 percent who have ordered the most expensive items are given an M score of 1, the next 20 percent are given an M score of 2, and so forth, down to the 20 percent who spend the least, who are given an M score of 5.

Figure 9-10 shows sample RFM data. The first customer, Ajax, has ordered recently and orders frequently. The company's M score of 3 indicates, however, that it does not order the most expensive goods. From these scores, the sales team can surmise that Ajax is a good and regular customer, but that they should attempt to up-sell more expensive goods to Ajax.

The second customer in Figure 9-10 could be a problem. Bloominghams has not ordered in some time, but when it did order in the past, it ordered frequently, and its orders were of the highest monetary value. This data suggests that Bloominghams may have taken its business to another vendor. Someone from the sales team should contact this customer immediately.

No one on the sales team should be talking to the third customer, Caruthers. This company has not ordered for some time; it did not order frequently; and when it did order, it bought the least-expensive items, and not many of them. The sales team should not waste any time on this customer; if Caruthers goes to the competition, the loss would be minimal.

The last customer, Davidson, is right in the middle. Davidson is an OK customer, but probably no one in sales should spend much time with them. Perhaps sales can set up an automated contact system or use the Davidson account as a training exercise for an eager departmental assistant or intern.

A reporting system can generate the RFM data and deliver it in many ways. For example, a report of RFM scores for all customers can be pushed to the vice president of sales; reports with scores for particular regions can be pushed to regional sales managers; and reports of scores for particular accounts can be pushed to the account salespeople. All of this reporting can be automated.

Customer	RFM Score		
Ajax	1	1	3
Bloominghams	5	1	1
Caruthers	5	4	5
Davidson	3	3	3

Figure 9-10
Example of RFM Score Data

---

[4]Arthur Middleton Hughes, "Boosting Response with RFM," *Marketing Tools,* May 1996. See also *dbmarketing.com.*

Semantic Security

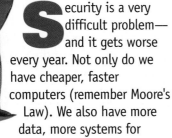

Security is a very difficult problem—and it gets worse every year. Not only do we have cheaper, faster computers (remember Moore's Law). We also have more data, more systems for reporting and querying that data, and easier, faster, and broader communication. All of these combine to increase the chances that we inadvertently divulge private or proprietary information.

Physical security is hard enough: How do we know that the person (or program) that signs on as Megan Cho really is Megan Cho? We use passwords, but files of passwords can be stolen. Setting that issue aside, we need to know that Megan Cho's permissions are set appropriately. Suppose Megan works in the HR department, so she has access to personal and private data of other employees. We need to design the reporting system so that Megan can access all of the data she needs to do her job, and no more.

Also, the report-delivery system must be secure. A reporting server is an obvious and juicy target for any would-be intruder. Someone can break in and change access permissions. Or, a hacker could pose as someone else to obtain reports. Reporting servers help the authorized user, resulting in faster access to more information. But, without proper security reporting servers also ease the intrusion task for unauthorized users.

All of these issues relate to physical security. Another dimension to security is equally serious and far more problematic: semantic security. **Semantic security** concerns the unintended release of protected information through the release of a combination of reports or documents that are independently not protected.

Take an example from class. Suppose I assign a group project, and I post a list of groups and the names of students assigned to each group. Later, after the assignments have been completed and graded, I post a list of grades on the Web site. Because of university privacy policy, I cannot post the grades by student name or identifier; so instead, I post the grades for each group. If you want to get the grades for each student, all you have to do is combine the list from Lecture 5 with the list from Lecture 10. You might say that the release of grades in this example does no real harm—after all, it is a list of grades from one assignment.

But go back to Megan Cho in HR. Suppose Megan evaluates the employee compensation program. The COO believes salary offers have been inconsistent over time and that they vary too widely by department. Accordingly, the COO authorizes Megan to receive a report that lists *SalaryOfferAmount* and *OfferDate*, and a second report that lists *Department* and *AverageSalary*.

Those reports are relevant to her task and seem innocuous enough. But Megan realizes that she could use the information they contain to determine individual salaries—information she does not have and is not authorized to receive. She proceeds as follows.

Like all employees, Megan has access to the employee directory on the Web portal. Using the directory, she can obtain a list of employees in each department, and using the facilities of her ever-so-helpful report-authoring system, she combines that list with the department and average-salary report. Now she has a list of the names of employees in a group and the average salary for that group.

Megan's employer likes to welcome new employees to the company. Accordingly, each week the company publishes an article about new employees who have been hired. The article makes pleasant comments about each person and encourages employees to meet and greet them.

Megan, however, has other ideas. Because the report is published on the Web portal, she can obtain an electronic copy of it. It's an Acrobat report, and using Acrobat's handy Search feature, she soon has a list of employees and the week they were hired.

She now examines the report she received for her study, the one that has *SalaryOfferAmount* and the offer date, and she does some interpretation. During the week of July 21, three offers were extended: one for $35,000, one for $53,000, and one for $110,000. She also notices from the "New Employees" report that a director of marketing programs, a product test engineer, and a receptionist were hired that same week. It's unlikely that they paid the receptionist $110,000; that sounds more like the director of marketing programs. So, she now "knows" (infers) that person's salary.

Next, going back to the department report and using the employee directory, she sees that the marketing director is in the marketing programs department. There are just three people in that department, and their average salary is $105,000. Doing the arithmetic, she now knows that the average salary for the other two people is $102,500. If she can

find the hire week for one of those other two people, she can find out both the second and third person's salaries. You get the idea. Megan was given just two reports to do her job. Yet she combined the information in those reports with publicly available information and is able to deduce salaries, for at least some employees. These salaries are much more than she is supposed to know. This is a semantic security problem.

DISCUSSION QUESTIONS

1. In your own words, explain the difference between physical security and semantic security.

2. Why do reporting systems increase the risk of semantic security problems?

3. What can an organization do to protect itself against accidental losses due to semantic security problems?

4. What legal responsibility does an organization have to protect against semantic security problems?

5. Suppose semantic security problems are inevitable. Do you see an opportunity for new products from insurance companies? If so, describe such an insurance product. If not, explain why not.

Online Analytical Processing

Online analytical processing (OLAP), a second type of reporting system, is a more a generic category of applications than is RFM. OLAP provides the ability to sum, count, average, and perform other simple arithmetic operations on groups of data. The remarkable characteristic of OLAP reports is that they are dynamic. The viewer of the report can change the report's format, hence the term *online*.

An OLAP report has measures and dimensions. A **measure** is the data item of interest. It is the item that is to be summed or averaged or otherwise processed in the OLAP report. Total sales, average sales, and average cost are examples of measures. A **dimension** is a characteristic of a measure. Purchase date, customer type, customer location, and sales region are all examples of dimensions.

Figure 9-11 shows a typical OLAP report. Here, the measure is *Net Store Sales*, and the dimensions are *Product Family* and *Store Type*. This report shows how net store sales vary by product family and store type. Stores of type *Supermarket* sold a net of $36,189 worth of nonconsumable goods, for example.

A presentation of a measure with associated dimensions like that in Figure 9-11 is often called an **OLAP cube**, or sometimes simply a *cube*. The reason for this term is that some products show these displays using three axes, like a cube in geometry. The origin of the term is unimportant here, however. Just know that an *OLAP cube* and an *OLAP report* are the same thing.

The OLAP report in Figure 9-11 was generated by SQL Server Analysis Services and is displayed in an Excel pivot table. The data were taken from a sample instructional database, called Food Mart, that is provided with SQL Server. It is possible to display OLAP cubes in many ways besides with Excel. Some third-party vendors provide more extensive graphical displays. For more information about such products, check for OLAP vendors and products at the Data Housing Review at *dwreview.com/OLAP/index.html*. Note, too, that OLAP reports can be delivered just like any of the other reports described for report management systems.

As stated earlier, the distinguishing characteristic of an OLAP report is that the user can alter the format of the report. Figure 9-12 (page 277) shows such an alteration. Here, the user added another dimension, store country and state, to the horizontal display. Product-family sales are now broken out by the location of the stores. Observe that the sample data include only stores in the United States and only in the western states of California, Oregon, and Washington.

With an OLAP report, it is possible to **drill down** into the data. This term means to further divide the data into more detail. In Figure 9-13 (page 278), for example, the user has drilled down into the stores located in California; the OLAP report now shows sales data for the four cities in California that have stores.

Notice another difference between Figures 9-12 and 9-13. The user has not only drilled down, she has also changed the order of the dimensions. Figure 9-12 shows *Product Family* and then store location within *Product Family*. Figure 9-13 shows store location and then *Product Family* within store location.

	A	B	C	D	E	F	G
1							
2							
3	Store Sales Net	Store Type ▼					
4	Product Family ▼	Deluxe Supermarket	Gourmet Supermarket	Mid-Size Grocery	Small Grocery	Supermarket	Grand Total
5	Drink	$8,119.05	$2,392.83	$1,409.50	$685.89	$16,751.71	$29,358.98
6	Food	$70,276.11	$20,026.18	$10,392.19	$6,109.72	$138,960.67	$245,764.87
7	Non-Consumable	$18,884.24	$5,064.79	$2,813.73	$1,534.90	$36,189.40	$64,487.05
8	Grand Total	$97,279.40	$27,483.80	$14,615.42	$8,330.51	$191,901.77	$339,610.90

Figure 9-11
OLAP Product Family by Store Type

You Be the Guide

Using the Security Guide
(page 275a)

GOALS

* Discuss the trade-off between information availability and security.

* Introduce, explain, and discuss ways to respond to *semantic security*.

BACKGROUND AND PRESENTATION STRATEGIES

This guide briefly discusses physical security and mentions some of its problems, especially authorization. We will address authorization in detail in Chapter 11, thus here I recommended focusing on the second theme: *semantic security*.

Semantic security is the "unintended release of protected information through the release of a combination of reports or documents that individually do not contain protected information."

In this guide, Megan was able to combine data in reports that she receives for her job with data in a combination of public documents to infer at least one employee's salary, and possibly several others. She is not supposed to have this information. The fact that both the new-employee report and the employee newsletter were *delivered electronically* greatly simplified her task. This fact enabled her to readily search those documents.

In truth, this problem has existed for as long as records have been kept. It is becoming a larger factor today because more and more reports are being produced, and those reports are being produced *in readily searchable form*. Thus, more data can be searched faster.

The critical question is: *What can be done about it?* Who has the time to consider every possible inference from combinations of every available document? Who has the ability to make every possible inference? No one.

We consider those issues in the following questions.

? SUGGESTED RESPONSES FOR DISCUSSION QUESTIONS

1. *Physical security* ensures that only authorized users can take authorized actions at appropriate times. *Semantic security* concerns information that is inadvertently released via a combination of information that is obtained via authorized methods. Questions to ask:

   ➤ **Did Megan break into any security system?**

   (No.)

   ➤ **Did Megan violate any corporate policy?**

   (No.)

   ➤ **Was she able to obtain, through her efforts, information she was not authorized to have?**

   (Yes.)

2. Reporting systems increase the risk because they deliver information in formats that are readily searched electronically.

   ➤ **Should (or even can) anything be done to make electronic documents not searchable?**

   (No.)

   ➤ **So, do we stop producing electronic reports?**

   (Obviously not, but this leads to question 3.)

3. This is a tough question to answer. Organizations need to understand that combinations of documents can give away sensitive data. With that awareness, managers need to manage with the expectation that some confidential data will ultimately be released. We just don't know what or when.

   ➤ **Is there a way for organizations to eliminate this possibility?**

   It is difficult to imagine that there is a way. Even investigating the possibilities would be incredibly expensive.

   ➤ **How would you know if you found all of the possibilities?**

   ➤ **If you know your organization is subject to a threat, what can you do?**

   One answer: While hoping that confidential data stays that way, manage as if it won't. See the Wrap Up discussion. Also, the next two questions provide some guidance.

4. Organizations have a responsibility to comply with privacy law. Federal organizations must comply with the Privacy Act of 1974. Medical offices must comply with HIPAA. The Gramm-Leach-Bliley (GLB) Act requires financial institutions to protect their clients' data. (See the Ethics Guide in Chapter 11, page 343a, for more information.)

Most of these laws require basic accounting controls for security. They do not address semantic security. However, I believe lawyers will require corporations to take reasonable and prudent steps to avoid obvious semantic security problems.

5. Most business insurance policies contain clauses that cover some liability for semantic security lapses. There might be an opportunity for a new type of policy that addresses such risks. It seems doubtful, but for enough money you can get someone to insure anything. These are good questions for students to ask their insurance-course professor.

WRAP UP

It is not possible to protect against all semantic security problems. Too much information is published, and the world is full of clever, curious people.

➤ **Given this fact, what can we do?**

Where possible, *design business programs for transparency.* Insofar as possible, design business programs *assuming sensitive data will become known.*

In the encryption discipline, it has long been recognized that any security technique that relies on a secret algorithm will *eventually be breached.* The technique must assume that the algorithm is in the public domain; secrecy is provided by the keys that are used with the technique.

Another point relates to salaries, a sensitive topic for most people:

➤ **Suppose you manage a department in which salaries are to be kept confidential. Are they?**

➤ **Knowing that salaries may not always be confidential, what do you do if there's a serious salary imbalance in your department?**

You can hope it never becomes public; you can try to correct it by raising someone's salary; you can prepare yourself for the lower-paid employee to come angrily in your door some day. There's no way around it, you're exposed to a risk.

For a second example, if it is important that the number of employees and the revenue of a given division remain confidential, then do all you can to keep that data confidential. But, expect that reporters, business analysts, stock pickers, and many others will be able to infer that data. *Do not construct a business plan that relies on such secrecy.* Someone will find a way to discover the information.

	A	B	C	D	E	F	G	H	I
1									
2									
3	Store Sales Net			Store Type					
4	Product Family	Store	Store State	Deluxe Superma	Gourmet Supermar	Mid-Size Groce	Small Grocery	Supermarket	Grand Total
5	Drink	USA	CA		$2,392.83		$227.38	$5,920.76	$8,540.97
6			OR	$4,438.49				$2,862.45	$7,300.94
7			WA	$3,680.56		$1,409.50	$458.51	$7,968.50	$13,517.07
8		USA Total		$8,119.05	$2,392.83	$1,409.50	$685.89	$16,751.71	$29,358.98
9	Drink Total			$8,119.05	$2,392.83	$1,409.50	$685.89	$16,751.71	$29,358.98
10	Food	USA	CA		$20,026.18		$1,960.53	$47,226.11	$69,212.82
11			OR	$37,778.35				$23,818.87	$61,597.22
12			WA	$32,497.76		$10,392.19	$4,149.19	$67,915.69	$114,954.83
13		USA Total		$70,276.11	$20,026.18	$10,392.19	$6,109.72	$138,960.67	$245,764.87
14	Food Total			$70,276.11	$20,026.18	$10,392.19	$6,109.72	$138,960.67	$245,764.87
15	Non-Consumable	USA	CA		$5,064.79		$474.35	$12,344.49	$17,883.63
16			OR	$10,177.89				$6,428.53	$16,606.41
17			WA	$8,706.36		$2,813.73	$1,060.54	$17,416.38	$29,997.01
18		USA Total		$18,884.24	$5,064.79	$2,813.73	$1,534.90	$36,189.40	$64,487.05
19	Non-Consumable Total			$18,884.24	$5,064.79	$2,813.73	$1,534.90	$36,189.40	$64,487.05
20	Grand Total			$97,279.40	$27,483.80	$14,615.42	$8,330.51	$191,901.77	$339,610.90

Figure 9-12
OLAP Product Family and Store Location by Store Type

Store Sales Net				Store Type ▾					
Store Country	Store Sta	Store City	Product Family ▾	Deluxe Super	Gourmet Supermar	Mid-Size Groce	Small Grocery	Supermarket	Grand Total
USA	CA	Beverly Hills	Drink		$2,392.83				$2,392.83
			Food		$20,026.18				$20,026.18
			Non-Consumable		$5,064.79				$5,064.79
		Beverly Hills Total			$27,483.80				$27,483.80
		Los Angeles	Drink					$2,870.33	$2,870.33
			Food					$23,598.28	$23,598.28
			Non-Consumable					$6,305.14	$6,305.14
		Los Angeles Total						$32,773.74	$32,773.74
		San Diego	Drink					$3,050.43	$3,050.43
			Food					$23,627.83	$23,627.83
			Non-Consumable					$6,039.34	$6,039.34
		San Diego Total						$32,717.61	$32,717.61
		San Francisco	Drink				$227.38		$227.38
			Food				$1,960.53		$1,960.53
			Non-Consumable				$474.35		$474.35
		San Francisco Total					$2,662.26		$2,662.26
	CA Total				$27,483.80		$2,662.26	$65,491.35	$95,637.41
	OR		Drink	$4,438.49				$2,862.45	$7,300.94
			Food	$37,778.35				$23,818.87	$61,597.22
			Non-Consumable	$10,177.89				$6,428.53	$16,606.41
	OR Total			$52,394.72				$33,109.85	$85,504.57
	WA		Drink	$3,680.56		$1,409.50	$458.51	$7,968.50	$13,517.07
			Food	$32,497.76		$10,392.19	$4,149.19	$67,915.69	$114,954.83
			Non-Consumable	$8,706.36		$2,813.73	$1,060.54	$17,416.38	$29,997.01
	WA Total			$44,884.68		$14,615.42	$5,668.24	$93,300.57	$158,468.91
USA Total				$97,279.40	$27,483.80	$14,615.42	$8,330.51	$191,901.77	$339,610.90
Grand Total				$97,279.40	$27,483.80	$14,615.42	$8,330.51	$191,901.77	$339,610.90

Figure 9-13
OLAP Product Family and Store Location by Store Type

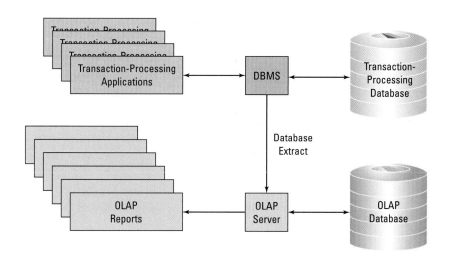

Figure 9-14
Role of OLAP Server and OLAP Database

Both displays are valid and useful, depending on the user's perspective. A product manager might like to see product families first and then store location data. A sales manager might like to see store locations first and then product data. OLAP reports provide both perspectives, and the user can switch between them while viewing the report.

Unfortunately, all of this flexibility comes at a cost. If the database is large, doing the necessary calculating, grouping, and sorting for such dynamic displays will require substantial computing power. Although standard, commercial DBMS products do have the features and functions required to create OLAP reports, they are not designed for such work. They are designed, instead, to provide rapid response to transaction processing applications such as order entry or manufacturing planning.

Accordingly, special-purpose products called **OLAP servers** have been developed to perform OLAP analysis. As shown in Figure 9-14, an OLAP server reads data from an operational database, performs preliminary calculations, and stores the results of those calculations in an OLAP database. Several different schemes are used for this storage, but the particulars of those schemes are beyond this discussion. (Search the Web for the terms *MOLAP, ROLAP,* and *HOLAP* if you want to learn more.) Normally, for performance and security reasons, the OLAP server and the DBMS run on separate computers.

MIS in Use 9-1 (page 280) discusses the successful implementation of OLAP to improve the productivity of business intelligence analysts.

Data Warehouses and Data Marts

Basic reports and simple OLAP analyses can be made directly from operational data. For the most part, such reports display the current state of the business, and if there are a few missing values or small inconsistencies with the data, no one is too concerned. However, operational data are unsuited to more sophisticated analyses, particularly data-mining analyses that require high-quality input for accurate and useful results. Therefore, many organizations choose to extract operational data into facilities called **data warehouses** and **data marts**, both of which are facilities that prepare, store, and manage data specifically for data mining and other analyses. (We'll explain the differences between data warehouses and data marts in a few pages.)

Figure 9-15 (page 280) summarizes data warehouses. Programs read operational data and extract, clean, and prepare that data for BI processing. The prepared data are stored in a data-warehouse database using a data-warehouse DBMS, which can be different from the organization's operational DBMS. For example, an organization might use Oracle for its operational processing, but use SQL Server for its data

Business Intelligence at Avnet, Inc.

In 2004, Avnet, Inc., generated over $10 billion in revenue by selling a wide array of electronics products and services to more than 100,000 companies in 68 countries. Avnet, based in Phoenix, Arizona, operates several divisions and sells many product lines. It operates as a wholesale distributor of electronic components, and it adapts some of those components to the needs of large enterprises. It also creates, markets, and sells special-purpose embedded computing systems. Given its size and breadth, Avnet is a key player in the electronics supply chain.

Avnet accelerated its growth by acquiring more than 30 different companies over the past 10 years. As a result, according to Steve Slatzer, Avnet's director of strategic finance, "We had growing pains." Integrating the disparate information systems of these acquired companies while supporting strong growth in sales trans-actions caused accounting and financial reporting nightmares.

Between 1997 and 2001, Avnet had developed OLAP applica-tions that enabled financial managers to drill down into the financial data, depending on their unique requirements. Unfortunately, as the company grew, the OLAP applications slowed considerably. Updates to the structure of the OLAP cubes required so much time that the OLAP-based financial reporting application was unreliable.

To respond to these challenges, the company decided to redesign its business intelligence systems. Because some divisions of Avnet were using SAP for operational processing, the company decided to acquire the add-on SAP product called Business Information Warehouse (SAP BW). SAP BW not only provided better OLAP performance and reliability, but also eased the data integra-tion task.

Today, Avnet has used SAP BW to integrate not only the SAP data sources but also data from the non-SAP legacy systems used by companies Avnet acquired. According to Slatzer,

Now that we can pull information from all our data sources into one place, we can create a very rich reporting environment. It lets users drill down to all kinds of underlying detail—detail that wouldn't have been visible with the old system . . . For example, they can drill from the general ledger into the fixed-asset system, in order to see what fixed assets are currently assigned to a particular location.

With the new system, users do not need to switch back and forth between different information systems with different user inter-faces, become familiar with different data presentations, or worry about getting data from one system to another. Instead, they can focus their efforts on analyzing results, which is both what they are paid to do and also what they want to do.

Sources: avnet.com (accessed January 2005); *sap.com* (accessed January 2005).

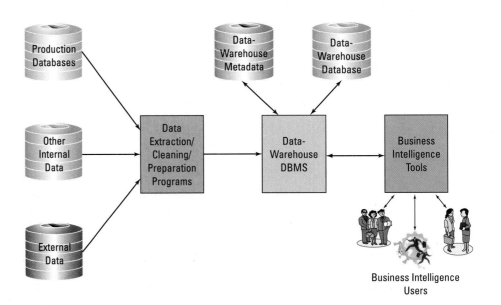

Figure 9-15
Components of a Data Warehouse

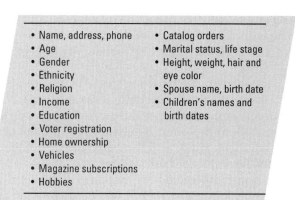

- Name, address, phone
- Age
- Gender
- Ethnicity
- Religion
- Income
- Education
- Voter registration
- Home ownership
- Vehicles
- Magazine subscriptions
- Hobbies

- Catalog orders
- Marital status, life stage
- Height, weight, hair and eye color
- Spouse name, birth date
- Children's names and birth dates

Figure 9-16
Consumer Data Available for Purchase from Data Vendors

warehouse. Other organizations use SQL Server for operational processing, but use DBMSs from statistical package vendors such as SAS or SPSS in the data warehouse.

Data warehouses include data that are purchased from outside sources. A typical example is customer credit data. Figure 9-16 lists some of the consumer data than can be purchased from commercial vendors today. An amazing (and from a privacy standpoint, frightening) amount of data is available.

Metadata concerning the data—its source, its format, its assumptions and constraints, and other facts about the data—is kept in a data-warehouse metadata database. The data-warehouse DBMS extracts and provides data to business intelligence tools such as data-mining programs.

Problems with Operational Data

Unfortunately, most operational and purchased data have problems that inhibit their usefulness for business intelligence. Figure 9-17 lists the major problem categories. First, although data that are critical for successful operations must be complete and accurate, data that are only marginally necessary need not be. For example, some systems gather demographic data in the ordering process. But, because such data are not needed to fill, ship, and bill orders, their quality suffers.

Problematic data are termed **dirty data**. Examples are a values of *B* for customer gender and of *213* for customer age. Other examples are a value of *999-999-9999* for a U.S. phone number, a part color of *gren*, and an email address of WhyMe@ GuessWhoIAM.org. All of these values can be problematic for data-mining purposes.

Purchased data often contain missing elements. Most data vendors state the percentage of missing values for each attribute in the data they sell. An organization buys such data because for some uses, some data are better than no data at all. This is especially true for data items whose values are difficult to obtain, such as *Number of Adults in Household, Household Income, Dwelling Type,* and *Education of Primary Income Earner.* For data-mining applications, though, a few missing or erroneous data points can be worse than no data at all because they bias the analysis.

Inconsistent data, the third problem in Figure 9-17, are particularly common for data that have been gathered over time. When an area code changes, for example, the

- Dirty data
- Missing values
- Inconsistent data
- Data not integrated

- Wrong granularity
  - Too fine
  - Not fine enough
- Too much data
  - Too many attributes
  - Too many data points

Figure 9-17
Problems of Using Transaction Data for Analysis and Data Mining

phone number for a given customer before the change will not match the customer's number after the change. Likewise, part codes can change, as can sales territories. Before such data can be used, they must be recoded for consistency over the period of the study.

Some data inconsistencies occur from the nature of the business activity. Consider a Web-based order entry system used by customers worldwide. When the Web server records the time of order, which time zone does it use? The server's system clock time is irrelevant to an analysis of customer behavior. Coordinated Universal Time (formerly called Greenwich Mean Time) is also meaningless. Somehow, Web server time must be adjusted to the time zone of the customer.

Another problem is nonintegrated data. Suppose, for example, that an organization wants to perform an RFM analysis but wants to consider customer payment behavior as well. The organization wants to add a fourth factor (which we will call P) and scale it from 1 to 5 on the basis of how quickly a customer pays. Unfortunately, however, the organization records such payment data in a PeopleSoft financial management database that is separate from the Siebel CRM database that has the order data. Before the organization can perform the analysis, the data must somehow be integrated.

Data can also be too fine or too coarse. For the former, suppose we want to analyze the placement of graphics and controls on an order entry Web page. It is possible to capture the customers' clicking behavior in what is termed **clickstream data**. Those data, however, include everything the customer does at the Web site. In the middle of the order stream are data for clicks on the news, email, instant chat, and a weather check. Although all of that data may be useful for a study of consumer computer behavior, it will be overwhelming if all we want to know is how customers respond to an ad located differently on the screen. To proceed, the data analysts must throw away millions and millions of clicks.

Data can also be too coarse. For example, a file of order totals cannot be used for a market-basket analysis. For market-basket analysis, we need to know which items were purchased with which others. This doesn't mean the order-total data are useless. They can be adequate for an RFM analysis, for example; they just won't do for a market-basket analysis.

If data are in the wrong format, that condition is sometimes expressed by saying the data have the wrong **granularity**. Generally it is better to have too fine a granularity than too coarse. If the granularity is too fine, the data can be made coarser by summing and combining. Only analysts' labor and computer processing are required. If the granularity is too coarse, however, there is no way to separate the data into constituent parts.

The final problem listed in Figure 9-17 concerns too much data. As shown in the figure, we can have either too many attributes or too many data points. Think of the tables in Chapter 4. We can have too many columns or too many rows.

Consider the first problem: too many attributes. Suppose we want to know the factors that influence how customers respond to a promotion. If we combine internal customer data with purchased customer data, we will have more than a hundred different attributes to consider. How do we select among them? Because of a phenomenon called the **curse of dimensionality**, the more attributes there are, the easier it is to build a model that fits the sample data but that is worthless as a predictor. There are other good reasons for reducing the number of attributes, and one of the major activities in data mining concerns efficient and effective ways of selecting attributes.

The second way to have too much data is to have too many data points—too many rows of data. Suppose we want to analyze clickstream data on CNN.com. How many clicks does that site receive per month? Millions upon millions! In order to meaningfully analyze such data we need to reduce the amount of data. There is a good solution to this problem: statistical sampling. Organizations should not be reluctant to sample data in such situations, as explained in the *Problem Solving Guide* on page 283a.

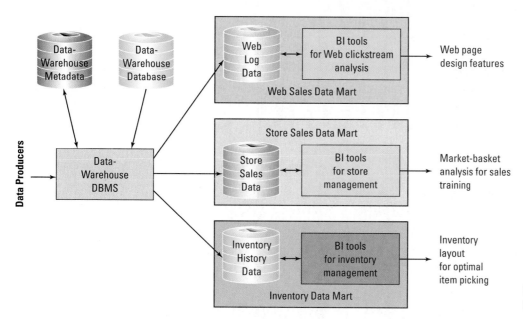

Figure 9-18
Data Mart Examples

Data Warehouses Versus Data Marts

So, how is a data warehouse different from a data mart? In a way, you can think of a *data warehouse* as distributor in a supply chain. The data warehouse takes data from the data manufacturers (operational systems and purchased data), cleans and processes the data, and locates the data on the shelves, so to speak, of the data warehouse. The people who work with a data warehouse are experts at data management, data cleaning, data transformation, and the like. However, they are not usually experts in a given business function.

A *data mart* is a data collection, smaller than the data warehouse, that addresses a particular component or functional area of the business. If the data warehouse is the distributor in a supply chain, then a data mart is like a retail store in a supply chain. Users in the data mart obtain data that pertain to a particular business function from the data warehouse. Such users do not have the data management expertise that data warehouse employees have, but they are knowledgeable analysts for a given business function.

Figure 9-18 illustrates these relationships. The data warehouse takes data from the data producers and distributes the data to three data marts. One data mart is used to analyze clickstream data for the purpose of designing Web pages. A second analyzes store sales data and determines which products tend to be purchased together. This information is used to train salespeople on the best way to up-sell to customers.

The third data mart is used to analyze customer order data for the purpose of reducing labor for item picking from the warehouse. A company like Amazon.com, for example, goes to great lengths to organize its warehouses to reduce picking expenses.

As you can imagine, it is expensive to create, staff, and operate data warehouses and data marts. Only large organizations with deep pockets can afford to operate a system like that shown in Figure 9-18. Smaller organizations operate subsets of this system; they may have just a simple data mart for analyzing promotion data, for example.

▉ Data Mining

Data mining is the application of statistical techniques to find patterns and relationships among data and to classify and predict. As shown in Figure 9-19 (page 284) data mining represents a convergence of disciplines. Data-mining techniques emerged from statistics and mathematics and from artificial intelligence and machine-learning

Counting and Counting and Counting

Not long ago, in a very large software company, a meeting occurred between a group of highly competent product managers and a group of equally competent data miners. The product managers wanted the data miners to analyze customer clicks on a Web page to determine customer preferences for particular product lines. The products were competing with one another for resources, and the results of the analysis were important in allocating those resources.

The meeting progressed well until one of the data miners started to explain the sampling scheme that they would use.

"Sampling?" asked the product managers in a chorus. "Sampling? No way. We want all the data. This is important, and we don't want a guess."

"But there are millions, literally, millions of ad clicks to analyze. If we don't sample, it will take hours, maybe even days, to perform the calculations. You won't see the results from each day's analysis until several days later if we don't sample." The data miners were squirming.

"We don't care," said the product managers. "We must have an accurate study. Don't sample!"

This leads us to a statistical concept you need to know: *There's nothing wrong with sampling.*

Properly done, the results from a sample are just as accurate as results from the complete data set. Studies done from samples are also cheaper and faster. Sampling is a great way to save time and money.

Suppose you have a bag of blue and red balls randomly mixed. Let's say the bag is big enough to contain 100,000 balls. How many of those balls do you need to examine to calculate, accurately, the proportion of each color?

You go to the park on a sunny day, sit down with your bag, and start pulling balls out of the bag. After 100 balls, you conclude the ratio of blue to red is 3 to 4. After 500 balls, you conclude the ratio of blue to red balls is 3 to 4. After 5,000 balls, you conclude the ratio of blue to red balls is 3 to 4. After 10,000 balls, you conclude the ratio of blue to red balls is 3 to 4. Do you really need to sit there until next week, counting balls day and night, to examine every ball in the bag? And, if you're the manager who needs to know that ratio, do you really want to pay someone to count all those balls? You knew the answer after you had counted 100 balls.

That's why the data miners were so depressed after their meeting with the product managers. They knew they had to count Web clicks long, long after there was any more information to be gained from continuing to count. To add to the pain of their situation, they had to do it only because of the product managers' ignorance.

In truth, skill is required to develop a good sample. The product managers should have listened

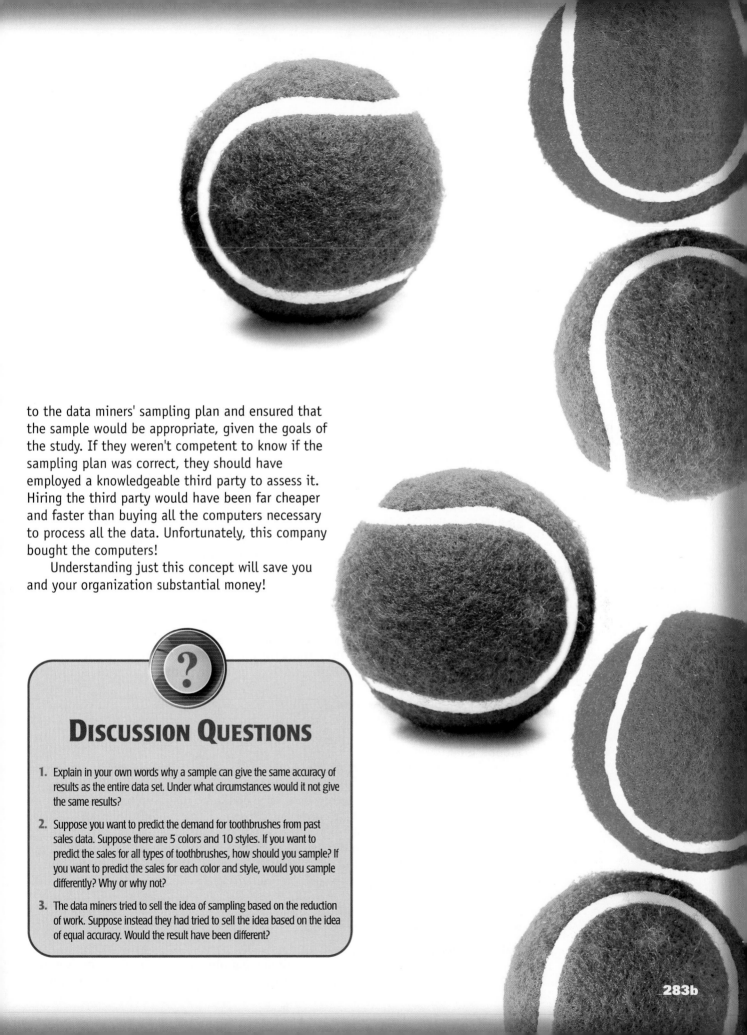

to the data miners' sampling plan and ensured that the sample would be appropriate, given the goals of the study. If they weren't competent to know if the sampling plan was correct, they should have employed a knowledgeable third party to assess it. Hiring the third party would have been far cheaper and faster than buying all the computers necessary to process all the data. Unfortunately, this company bought the computers!

Understanding just this concept will save you and your organization substantial money!

DISCUSSION QUESTIONS

1. Explain in your own words why a sample can give the same accuracy of results as the entire data set. Under what circumstances would it not give the same results?

2. Suppose you want to predict the demand for toothbrushes from past sales data. Suppose there are 5 colors and 10 styles. If you want to predict the sales for all types of toothbrushes, how should you sample? If you want to predict the sales for each color and style, would you sample differently? Why or why not?

3. The data miners tried to sell the idea of sampling based on the reduction of work. Suppose instead they had tried to sell the idea based on the idea of equal accuracy. Would the result have been different?

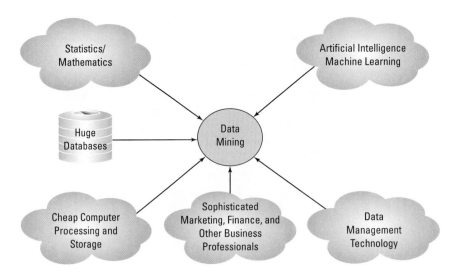

Figure 9-19
Convergence Disciplines
for Data Mining

fields in computer science. As a result, data-mining terminology is an odd blend of terms from these different disciplines. Sometimes people use the term *knowledge discovery in databases* (KDD) as a synonym for data mining.

Data-mining techniques take advantage of developments in data management for processing the enormous databases that have emerged in the last 10 years. Of course, these data would not have been generated were it not for fast and cheap computers, and without such computers, the new techniques would be impossible to compute.

Most data-mining techniques are sophisticated, and many are difficult to use well. Such techniques are valuable to organizations, however, and some business professionals, especially those in finance and marketing, have become expert in their use. In fact, today there are many interesting and rewarding careers for business professionals who are knowledgeable about data-mining techniques.

Data-mining techniques fall into two broad categories: unsupervised and supervised. We explain both types below.

Unsupervised Data Mining

With **unsupervised data mining**, analysts do not create a model or hypothesis before running the analysis. Instead, they apply the data-mining technique to the data and observe the results. With this method, analysts create hypotheses after the analysis to explain the patterns found.

One common unsupervised technique is **cluster analysis**. With it, statistical techniques identify groups of entities that have similar characteristics. A common use for cluster analysis is to find groups of similar customers from customer order and demographic data.

For example, suppose a cluster analysis finds two very different customer groups: One group has an average age of 33, owns at least one laptop and at least one PDA, drives an expensive SUV, and tends to buy expensive children's play equipment. The second group has an average age of 64, owns vacation property, plays golf, and buys expensive wines. Suppose the analysis also finds that both groups buy designer children's clothing.

These findings are obtained solely by data analysis. There is no prior model about the patterns and relationship that exist. It is up to the analyst to form hypotheses, after the fact, to explain why two such different groups are both buying designer children's clothes.

Supervised Data Mining

With **supervised data mining**, data miners develop a model prior to the analysis and apply statistical techniques to data to estimate parameters of the model. For example, suppose marketing experts in a communications company believe that cell phone

Using the Problem Solving Guide (page 283a)

GOALS

* Teach the students that:
  * Proper sampling leads to valid results and can save time and money.
  * Not all sampling plans are valid. The sampling plan should be evaluated.
* Illustrate a practical application of empathetic thinking.

BACKGROUND AND PRESENTATION STRATEGIES

As the start of the chapter indicates, information systems are generating enormous amounts of data. Attempts to process all of the data are wasteful, time consuming, and foolish. There is nothing wrong with a proper sample!

The marketing analysts in this guide were MBA-level analysts working for a famous and very successful software company. They were highly paid and very successful in their careers. In this case, they also caused their employer to waste a large amount of money.

One caveat: Sampling is every bit as accurate as nonsampling, *as long as the sampling plan is valid*. So, rather than refusing to allow sampling, the product managers should have evaluated the sampling plan— or hired someone to do it if they were not qualified. What a waste!

Question 2 can't be answered based on the information in this guide. Its purpose is to show *the need for a sampling plan* and possibly the need to bring in outside expertise to evaluate that plan.

I wasn't in the meeting between the data miners and the product managers, but from the reports I heard, I think the data miners erred in stating their objection as avoiding useless work. The product managers didn't care about the data miners' workload; they cared about their products. If the data miners thought empathetically, they would have explained how sampling would enable them to do more studies, faster, with quicker turnaround, and thus provide better guidance to the product managers. In fairness to the data miners, however, they were blindsided by this issue. They didn't expect to have any resistance to

sampling, and responded extemporaneously with their concerns. See question 3.

 ### SUGGESTED RESPONSES FOR DISCUSSION QUESTIONS

1. Once you have sampled enough items, additional sampling does not add more value. You're just wasting your time and money.

   ➤ **How do you know if you've sampled enough?**

   Intuitively, you know you've sampled enough when continued sampling provides little new information. Principles and formulas exist that specify how many items you need to sample. They are the subject of a statistics class, not this class. For now, just understand that sampling can provide accurate results.

   By the way, the number required for a good sample is surprisingly small. Many good samples for political attitudes for the U.S. population use fewer than 4,000 people.

2. The question indicates the need for a sampling plan, and, as should have happened in this guide, for someone with statistical expertise to evaluate the appropriateness of the sampling plan. The answer to this question cannot be determined from the information in this guide. The point:

   ➤ **Sampling can be tricky: If you don't know what you're doing, hire someone who does.**

   The following sequence of questions will indicate the general nature of a solution to the problem. Suppose one out of every 1,000 toothbrush sales is for the style Macho and the color Pink.

   ➤ **If we sample 1,000 items, how likely are we to find a sale for Macho, Pink toothbrushes?**

   (Very unlikely.)

   Suppose that we sample 100,000 items. Suppose the most popular color and style is {Pink, Grandmother}, and it accounts for 70 percent of our sales. On average then, 70,000 of those in the sample will be sales for {Pink, Grandmother} toothbrushes. With a straight sample of 100,000, we oversampled {Pink, Grandmother} and likely undersampled {Pink, Macho}.

   The conclusion: Sampling is fine, but if there is any complexity at all, and if you don't know what you're doing, call in an expert.

3. I think the result would have been different. This answer takes us back to empathetic thinking, which was first discussed in Chapter 2 (page 33a). The data miners responded with what was important to *them*, which was all the unnecessary work that they had to do. But the product managers didn't care about how much work the data miners had; they cared about the future of their products.

If the data miners had thought about the problem from the perspective of the product managers, they would have focused on the benefit of *equal accuracy with results available faster*. They needed to focus on benefits *to the product managers* instead of cost to *them*.

➤ **After the meeting was over, was there anything the data miners might have done to reverse the non-sampling decision?**

Product managers are incredibly busy people with packed schedules. It might be impossible to reschedule a meeting with the product managers to revisit this issue. But the issue might be too loaded to revisit via email. This could well be a decision that needs to be reversed but never will be because the necessary people cannot be regrouped to revisit it. Because of the way the matter was left, the product managers think the data miners are just trying to avoid work; they won't agree to remeet for that reason.

➤ **How would you write an email to justify a subsequent meeting?**

➤ **How likely is this email to succeed?**

(I think unlikely. In this situation, the data miners had one shot, and they missed. I doubt they'll get another.)

➤ **When you're not getting the decision you want, remember to reframe the question using empathetic thinking. Doing so, you might avoid situations like this!**

WRAP UP

The conclusions of this guide are simple:

➤ **Use sampling and, if you need to, hire an expert to evaluate the sampling plan.**

➤ **Possibly the most important learning in this guide, though, is the ineffective communication strategy used by the data miners (see question 3). They should have sold sampling by focusing on the benefit of equally accurate results, delivered faster.**

usage on weekends is determined by the age of the customer and the number of months the customer has had the cell phone account. A data-mining analyst would then run an analysis that estimates the impact of customer and account age. One such analysis, which measures the impact of a set of variables on another variable, is called a **regression analysis**. A sample result for the cell phone example is:

```
CellPhoneWeekendMinutes =
12 + (17.5 * CustomerAge) + (23.7 * NumberMonthsOfAccount)
```

Using this equation, analysts can predict the number of minutes of weekend cell phone use by summing 12, plus 17.5 times the customer's age, plus 23.7 times the number of months of the account.

As you will learn in your statistics classes, considerable skill is required to interpret the quality of such a model. The regression tool will create an equation, such as the one shown. Whether that equation is a good predictor of future cell phone usage depends on statistical factors like *t* values, confidence intervals, and related statistical techniques.

Neural networks are another popular supervised data-mining technique used to predict values and make classifications such as "good prospect" or "poor prospect" customers. The term *neural networks* is deceiving because it connotes a biological process similar to that in animal brains. In fact, although the original *idea* of neural nets may have come from the anatomy and physiology of neurons, a neural net is nothing more than a complicated set of possibly nonlinear equations. Explaining the techniques used for neural networks is beyond the scope of this text. If you want to learn more, search *kdnuggets.com* for the term *neural network*.

In the next sections, we will describe and illustrate two typical data-mining techniques—market-basket analysis and decision trees—and show applications of those techniques. From this discussion, you can gain a sense of the nature of data mining. These examples should give you, a future manager, a sense of the possibilities of data-mining techniques. You will need additional coursework in statistics, data management, marketing, and finance, however, before you will be able to perform such analyses yourself.

Market-Basket Analysis

Suppose you run a dive shop and one day you realize that one of your salespeople is much better at up-selling to your customers. Any of your sales associates can fill a customer's order, but this one salesperson is especially able to sell customers items *in addition to* those for which they ask. One day you ask him how he does it.

"It's simple," he says. "I just ask myself what is the next product they would want to buy. If someone buys a dive computer, I don't try to sell her fins. If she's buying a dive computer, she's already a diver and she already has fins. But, these dive computer displays are hard to read. A better mask makes it easier to read the display and get the full benefit from the dive computer."

A **market-basket analysis** is a data-mining technique for determining sales patterns. A market-basket analysis shows the products that customers tend to buy together. Several different statistical techniques can be used. Here we will discuss a technique that involves *probabilities*.

Figure 9-20 (page 286) shows hypothetical data from 1,000 transactions at a dive shop. The first row of numbers under each column is the total number of transactions that include the product in that column. For example, the 270 in the first row of *Mask* means that 270 of the 1,000 transactions include the purchase of a mask. The 120 under *Dive Computer* means that 120 of the 1,000 purchased transactions included a dive computer.

We can use the numbers in the first row to estimate the probability that a customer will purchase an item. Because 270 out of 1,000 transactions included a mask, we can estimate the probability that a customer will buy a mask to be 270/1,000, or .27.

1,000 Transactions	Mask	Tank	Fins	Weights	Dive Computer
	270	200	280	130	120
Mask	20	20	150	20	50
Tank	20	80	40	30	30
Fins	150	40	10	60	20
Weights	20	30	60	10	10
Dive computer	50	30	20	10	5
No additional product	10	—	—	—	5

Support $= P(A \& B)$ Example: P (Fins & Mask) $= 150/1{,}000 = .15$

Confidence $= P(A \mid B)$ Example: P (Fins $\mid$ Mask) $= 150/270 = .55556$

Lift $= P(A \mid B)/P(A)$ Example: P (Fins $\mid$ Mask)/P (Fins) $= .55556/.28 = 1.98$

Note: P(Mask $\mid$ Fins)/P (Mask) $= (150/280)/.27 = 1.98$

Figure 9-20
Market-Basket Example

In market-basket terminology, **support** is the probability that two items will be purchased together. For the data in Figure 9-20, 150 of the transactions include both fins and a mask, and thus the support for fins and a mask is 150/1,000, or .15. Similarly, the support for fins and weights is 60/1,000, or .06, and the support for fins along with a second pair of fins is 10/1,000, or .01.

These data are interesting by themselves, but we can refine the analysis by taking another step and considering additional probabilities. For example, what proportion of the customers who bought a mask also bought fins? There are 270 transactions that involve a mask, and of those, 150 bought fins. Thus, given that a customer bought a mask, we can estimate the probability that he will buy fins to be 150/270, or .5556. In market-basket terminology such a conditional probability estimate is called the **confidence**.

Reflect on the meaning of this confidence value. The likelihood of someone walking in the door and buying fins is 280/1,000, or .28. But, the likelihood of someone buying fins, given that he bought a mask, is .5556. Thus, if someone buys a mask, the likelihood that he will also buy fins almost doubles, from .28 to .5556. Thus, all sales personnel should be trained to try to sell fins to anyone buying a mask.

Now consider dive computers and fins. Of the 1,000 transactions, fins were sold 280 times, so the probability that someone walks into the store and buys fins is .28. But, of the 120 purchases of dive computers, only 20 transactions also included fins. So the likelihood of someone buying fins, given she bought a dive computer, is 20/120 or .1666. Thus, when someone buys a dive computer, the likelihood that she will also buy fins falls from .28 to .1666.

The ratio of confidence to the base probability of buying an item is called **lift**. Lift shows how much the base probability increases or decreases when other products are purchased. The lift of fins and a mask is the confidence of fins given a mask, divided by the base probability of fins. In Figure 9-20, the lift of fins and a mask is .5556/.28, or 1.98. Thus, the likelihood that someone buys fins when they buy a mask almost doubles. Surprisingly, it turns out that the lift of fins and a mask is the same as the lift of a mask and fins. Both are 1.98.

We need to be careful here, though, because this analysis only shows shopping carts with two items. We cannot say from this data what the likelihood is that customers, given that they bought a mask, will buy both weights and fins. To assess that probability, we need to analyze shopping carts with three items. This statement illustrates, once again, that we need to know what problem we're solving before we start to build the information system to mine the data. The problem definition will help us decide if we need to analyze three-item, four-item, or some other sized shopping cart.

Many organizations are benefiting from market-basket analysis today. You can expect that this technique will become a standard CRM analysis during your career.

By the way, the study that showed the correlation of beer and diapers (cited earlier) used market-basket analysis. That correlation was strongest on Thursdays. Interviews indicated that customers were buying goods for the weekend, goods which included both beer and diapers.

Decision Trees

A **decision tree** is a hierarchical arrangement of criteria that predict a classification or a value. Here we will consider decision trees that predict classifications. Decision tree analyses are an unsupervised data-mining technique: The analyst sets up the computer program and provides the data to analyze, and the decision tree program produces the tree.

A Decision Tree for Student Performance

The basic idea of a decision tree is to select attributes that are most useful for classifying entities on some criterion. Suppose, for example, that we want to classify students according to the grades they earn in the MIS class. To create a decision tree, we first gather data about grades and attributes of students in past classes.

We then input that data into the decision tree program. The program analyzes all of the attributes and selects an attribute that creates the most disparate groups. The logic is that the more different the groups, the better the classification will be. For example, if every student who lived off campus earned a grade higher than 3.0, and every student who lived on campus earned a grade lower than 3.0, then the program would use the variable *live-off-campus* or *live-on-campus* to classify students. In this unrealistic example, the program would be a perfect classifier, because each group is pure, with no misclassifications.

More realistically, consider Figure 9-21, which shows a hypothetical decision tree analysis of MIS class grades. Again, assume we are classifying students depending on whether their grade was greater than 3.0 or less than or equal to 3.0.

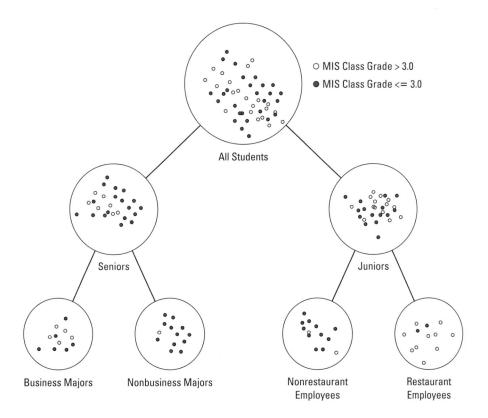

Figure 9-21
Grades of Students from Past MIS Class (Hypothetical Data)

The decision tree tool that created this tree examined student characteristics such as their class (junior or senior), their major, their employment, their age, their club affiliations, and other student characteristics. It then used values of those characteristics to create groups that were as different as possible on the classification grade above or below 3.0.

For the results shown here, the decision tree program determined that the best first criterion is whether the students are juniors or seniors. In this case, the classification was imperfect, as shown by the fact that neither of the senior nor the junior groups consisted only of students with GPAs above or below 3.0. Still, it did create groups that were less mixed than in the *All Students* group.

Next, the program examined other criteria to further subdivide *Seniors* and *Juniors* so as to create even more pure groups. The program divided the senior group into subgroups: those who are business majors and those who are not. The program's analysis of the junior data, however, determined that the difference between majors is not significant. Instead, the best classifier (the one that generated the most different groups) is whether the junior worked in a restaurant.

Examining this data, we see that junior restaurant employees do well in the class, but junior nonrestaurant employees and senior nonbusiness majors do poorly. Performance in the other senior group is mixed. (Remember, these data are hypothetical.)

A decision tree like the one in Figure 9-21 can be transformed into a set of decision rules having the format, **If... then....** Decision rules for this example are:

- If student is a junior and works in a restaurant, then predict grade > 3.0.
- If student is a senior and is a nonbusiness major, then predict grade < = 3.0.
- If student is a junior and does not work in a restaurant, then predict grade < = 3.0.
- If student is a senior and is a business major, then make no prediction.

As stated, decision tree algorithms create groups that are as pure as possible, or stated otherwise, as different from each other as possible. The algorithms use several metrics for measuring difference among groups. Further explanation of those techniques is beyond the scope of this text. For now, just be sure to understand that maximum difference among groups is used as the criterion for constructing the decision tree.

There are many problems with classification schemes, especially schemes that classify people. The *Ethics Guide* on page 289a examines some of them.

Let's now apply the decision tree technique to a business situation.

A Decision Tree for Loan Evaluation

A common business application of decision trees is to classify loans by likelihood of default. Organizations analyze data from past loans to produce a decision tree that can be converted to loan-decision rules. A financial institution could use such a tree to assess the default risk on a new loan. Sometimes, too, financial institutions sell a group of loans (called a loan portfolio) to one another. The results of a decision tree program can be used to evaluate the risk in a given portfolio.

Figure 9-22 shows an example provided by Insightful Corporation, a vendor of business intelligence tools. This example was generated using its Insightful Miner product. This tool examined data from 3,485 loans. Of those loans, 72 percent had no default and 28 percent did default. To perform the analysis, the decision tree tool examined values of six different loan characteristics.

In this example, the decision tree program determined that the percentage of the loan that is past due (*PercPastDue*) is the best first criterion. Reading Figure 9-22, you can see that of the 2,574 loans with a *PercPastDue* value of .5 or less (more than half paid off), 94 percent were not in default. Hence, any loan that is more than half paid off has little risk of default.

Reading down several lines in this tree, 911 loans had a value of *PercPastDue* greater than .5; of those loans, 89 percent were in default.

These two major categories are then further subdivided into three classifications: *CreditScore* is a creditworthiness score obtained from a credit agency; *MonthsPastDue*

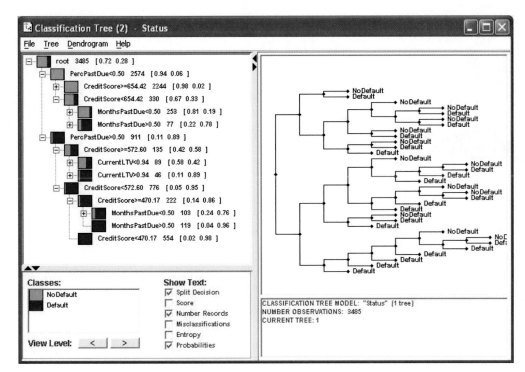

Figure 9-22
Credit Score Decision Tree

Source: Used with permission of Insightful Corporation. Copyright © 1999–2005 Insightful Corporation. All Rights Reserved.

is the number of months since a payment; and *CurrentLTV* is the current ratio of outstanding balance of the loan to the value of the loan's collateral.

With a decision tree like this, the financial institution can develop decision rules for accepting or rejecting the offer to purchase loans from another financial institution. For example:

- If the loan is more than half paid, then accept the loan.
- If the loan is less than half paid and
  - If *CreditScore* is greater than 572.6 and
    - If *CurrentLTV* is less than .94, then accept the loan.
- Otherwise, reject the loan.

Of course, the financial institution will need to combine these risk data with an economic analysis of the value of each loan to determine which loans to take.

Decision trees are easy to understand and, even better, easy to implement using decision rules. They also can work with many types of variables, and they deal well with missing values. Organizations can use decision trees by themselves or combine them with other techniques. In some cases, organizations use decision trees to select variables that are then used by other types of data-mining tools. For example, decision trees can be used to identify good predictor variables for neural networks.

Knowledge Management

We conclude this chapter with an introduction to knowledge management and knowledge management systems. Whereas data mining relies heavily on statistical techniques for acquiring unknown information from hidden patterns in the data, knowledge management systems concern the sharing of knowledge that is already known to exist, either in libraries of documents, in the heads of employees, or in other known sources.

Knowledge management (KM) is the process of creating value from intellectual capital and sharing that knowledge with employees, managers, suppliers, customers, and others who need that capital. Although KM is supported by IS technology, KM is not technology. It is a *process* supported by the five components of an information

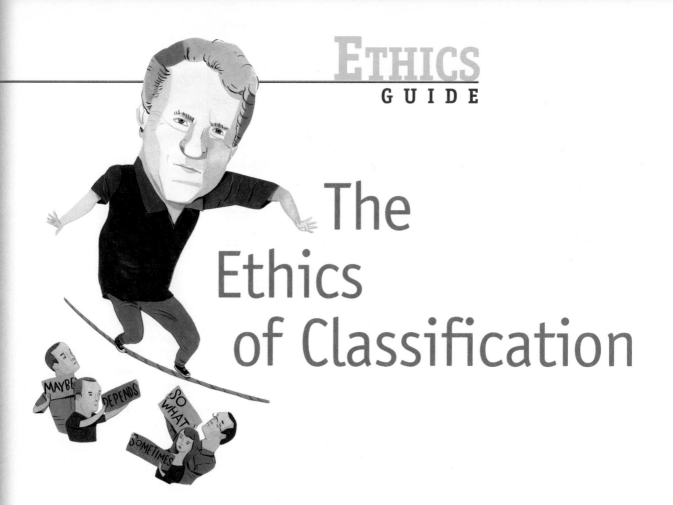

The Ethics of Classification

Classification is a useful human skill. Imagine walking into your favorite clothing store and seeing all of the clothes piled together on a center table. T-shirts and pants and socks intermingle, with the sizes mixed up. Retail stores organized like this would not survive, nor would distributors or manufacturers who managed their inventories this way. Sorting and classifying are necessary, important, and essential activities. But those activities can also be dangerous.

Serious ethical issues arise when we classify people. What makes someone a good or bad "prospect"? If we're talking about classifying customers in order to prioritize our sales calls, then the ethical issue may not be too serious. What about classifying applicants for college? As long as there are more applicants than positions, some sort of classification and selection process must be done. But what kind?

Suppose a university collects data on the demographics and the performance of all of its students. The admissions committee then processes these data using a decision tree data-mining program. Assume the analysis is conducted properly and the tool uses statistically valid measures to obtain statistically valid results. Thus, the following resulting tree accurately represents and explains variances found in the data; no human judgment (or prejudice) was involved.

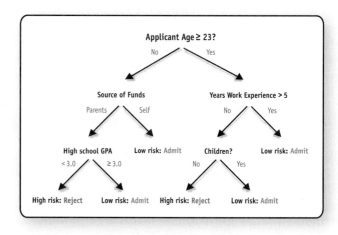

Applicant Age ≥ 23?

No — Yes

Source of Funds | Years Work Experience > 5

Parents — Self | No — Yes

High school GPA | Low risk: Admit | Children? | Low risk: Admit

< 3.0 — ≥ 3.0 | No — Yes

High risk: Reject | Low risk: Admit | High risk: Reject | Low risk: Admit

Source: Reprinted through the courtesy of CIO. Copyright © 2005 CXO Media Inc.

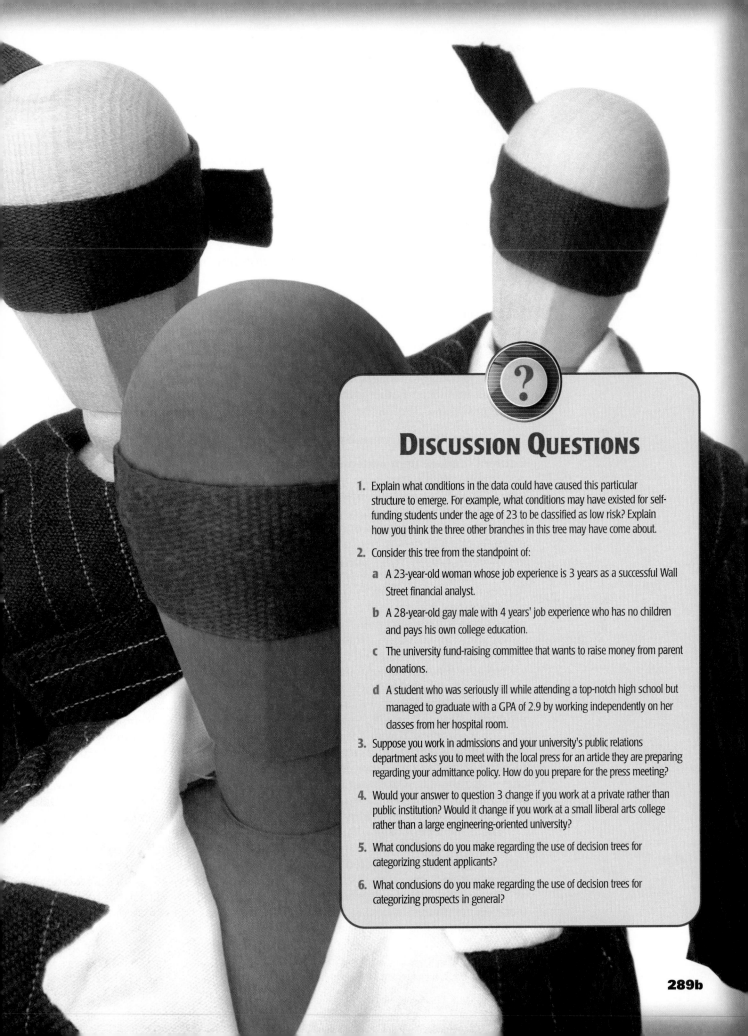

DISCUSSION QUESTIONS

1. Explain what conditions in the data could have caused this particular structure to emerge. For example, what conditions may have existed for self-funding students under the age of 23 to be classified as low risk? Explain how you think the three other branches in this tree may have come about.

2. Consider this tree from the standpoint of:

   a A 23-year-old woman whose job experience is 3 years as a successful Wall Street financial analyst.

   b A 28-year-old gay male with 4 years' job experience who has no children and pays his own college education.

   c The university fund-raising committee that wants to raise money from parent donations.

   d A student who was seriously ill while attending a top-notch high school but managed to graduate with a GPA of 2.9 by working independently on her classes from her hospital room.

3. Suppose you work in admissions and your university's public relations department asks you to meet with the local press for an article they are preparing regarding your admittance policy. How do you prepare for the press meeting?

4. Would your answer to question 3 change if you work at a private rather than public institution? Would it change if you work at a small liberal arts college rather than a large engineering-oriented university?

5. What conclusions do you make regarding the use of decision trees for categorizing student applicants?

6. What conclusions do you make regarding the use of decision trees for categorizing prospects in general?

system. Its emphasis is on people, their knowledge, and effective means for sharing that knowledge with others.

The benefits of KM concern the application of knowledge to enable employees and others to leverage organizational knowledge to work smarter. Santosus and Surmacz cite the following as the primary benefits of KM:

1. KM fosters innovation by encouraging the free flow of ideas.
2. KM improves customer service by streamlining response time.
3. KM boosts revenues by getting products and services to market faster.
4. KM enhances employee retention rates by recognizing the value of employees' knowledge and rewarding them for it.
5. KM streamlines operations and reduces costs by eliminating redundant or unnecessary processes.[5]

In addition, KM preserves organizational memory by capturing and storing the lessons learned and best practices of key employees.

There are three major categories of knowledge assets: data, documents, and employees. We have addressed information derived from data already in the reporting and data-mining sections of this chapter. In this last section, we will consider KM as it pertains to content management and the sharing of employee knowledge.

Data mining and other business intelligence systems are useful, but not without problems, as discussed in the *Opposing Forces Guide* on page 291a.

Content Management Systems

Content management systems are information systems that track organizational documents, Web pages, graphics, and related materials. Such systems differ from operational document systems in that they do not directly support business operations. An insurance company, for example, scans every document it receives and stores those documents as part of its client-processing application. This is not an example of a KM system because it is part of an operational, transaction-processing application. KM content management systems are not concerned with operational documents. Instead, they are concerned with the creation, management, and delivery of documents that exist for the purpose of imparting knowledge.

The largest collection of documents ever assembled exists on the Internet, and the world's best-known document search engine is Google. When you search for a term, or "Google it," you are tapping into the world's largest content management system. This system, however, was not designed for a particular KM purpose; it just emerged. Here we are concerned with content management systems that are created and used by organizations for a specific KM purpose.

Typical users of content management systems are companies that sell complicated products and want to share their knowledge of those products with employees and customers. Someone at Toyota, for example, knows how to change the timing belt on the four-cylinder 2000 Toyota Camry. Toyota wants to share that knowledge with car owners, mechanics, and Toyota employees. Cisco wants to share with network administrators its knowledge about how to determine if a Cisco router is malfunctioning. Microsoft wants to share with the data miners of the world its knowledge about how to use its Data Transformation Services product to move data from an Oracle database into Excel.

The basic functions of content management systems are the same as for report management systems: author, manage, and deliver. However, the authoring of documents is generally considered to be outside the domain of the content manager. Documents and other resources have been prepared using Word, FrontPage, Acrobat, or some other document product. The only requirement that content managers place on document authoring is that the document has been created in a standardized format.

---

[5]Megan Santosus and John Surmacz, "The ABCs of Knowledge Management," *CIO Magazine*, May 23, 2001. *cio.com/research/knowledge/edit/kmabcs.html* (accessed July 2005).

You Be the Guide

Using the Ethics Guide

(page 289a)

GOAL

* Explore difficult ethical issues about using decision trees for classifying people.

BACKGROUND AND PRESENTATION STRATEGIES

Classification, especially the classification of people, poses many ethical problems. But, organizations must classify; they must decide which students to admit, which people to promote, or which people to deny loans. *It has to be done.*

Decision trees are a classification scheme that analyzes data to create the most dissimilar groups. As such, it is *free of human bias.* The analysis is performed, and the data speak for themselves.

Thus, even though the results of such an analysis may be *unpopular,* such as the example in the guide, these results come directly from the data. The data are speaking for themselves. No subjective human judgment entered into this analysis, and the results *should be less biased* than when using human categorizers.

However, *not all decision trees are equally valid.* Like all statistics techniques, decision tree analyses vary in the degree of fit. Some data analyses have clear separation of groups—the criteria really do split the data. For others, the split is less clear, even murky. However, the analysis software will show the criteria, even if they are weak. Unless the analysts know to investigate standard errors, confidence intervals (see the Problem Solving Guide), and related measures, they will not be able to discriminate a strong classification scheme from a weak one. From the data presented, we have no idea of how strong this decision tree analysis was.

However, the results of a decision tree analysis may tend to reinforce negative social stereotypes and may be organizationally, legally, and socially infeasible.

? SUGGESTED RESPONSES FOR DISCUSSION QUESTIONS

1. Of course, this question has no correct answer. Often, the students' answers are fascinating.

Sometimes, the students become angry, even though they know this is an example, and I need to remind them that this is only an example.

2. None of these people will like this scheme. The people in a, b, and d would be furious. You might let students role-play and speak for each of them. By the way, what relevance is the sexual preference of the person in b? It will have been more difficult for him to have children by 28 than it would have been for a straight man. He might prevail in a discrimination suit against the university.

   The university fund-raising committee in c won't like this scheme because it is biased toward students who are paying their own way. There may be many students under age 23 with high school GPA under 3.0 who have parents who would be pleased to donate, but not if their children aren't admitted.

3. Would anyone want that job? What will happen if the press finds out about the person in 2(d)? It will be a public relations nightmare.

   One teaching possibility: *Conduct a mock press interview in class.* Divide the students into two groups—one group of university admissions personnel who must defend this scheme and a second group of press reporters. Conduct the interview. If the class is large, bring three to five members of each group to the front of the class and conduct the interview in front of the class.

CUES FOR THE UNIVERSITY PERSONNEL:

➤ **Our analysis is based on a reliable data about the success of past students.**

➤ **We provided no human input to obtain these results. We are only responding to what the data tell us.**

➤ **We used the best, most up-to-date statistical techniques.**

➤ **We will review this policy each year and rerun our analysis when appropriate.**

QUESTIONS FROM THE PRESS:

➤ **We hear you are operating a harsh and inhumane computer-based system for school admissions. Is this true?**

➤ **Are you actually turning away people because they were sick in high school?**

➤ **Please describe the scheme you use.**

➤ **We've heard of a discrimination suit from one of the rejected students. Does the system, in fact, discriminate against gay people?**

Good luck!

4. Private institutions may have some leeway that public institutions don't. I doubt there would be much difference depending on the type of school. The students may have other opinions.

5. You might also ask:

➤ **Does the answer depend on the statistical strength of the results?**

I think that any university using decision trees would at least have to (a) ensure their tree was defensible to the public, (b) provide human review to overrule the classification for exceptional situations, and (c) ensure the results are *statistically* valid.

6. Ensure that the results are statistically strong. Be sure that the results are publicly defensible. Consult corporate legal about the risk of antidiscriminatory practices and other legal risks.

WRAP UP

To wrap up, I say that many different opinions are possible with regard to the use of decision trees, but that each business professional should take the time to consider what his or her own opinions are. Here are some questions that help the students form their own opinions. The answers depend on each students' perspective and values.

➤ **Do individuals who are classified by an automated process have a right to know this is being done? For example, when applying for a loan, does the applicant have a right to know that the approval or rejection notification is made by an automated process and not by a human?**

➤ **Are decision tree classification schemes more appropriate for single events, such as a loan approval, than they are for life-changing events, such as college admissions?**

➤ **Can decision trees be used to advantage to eliminate situations that have substantial human bias?**

➤ **Should decision trees be used when they reinforce negative social stereotypes? Does it matter if the data strongly support the negative social stereotype?**

➤ **Can techniques like decision trees offer an organization an easy way to hide its social bias? What if the organization chooses to use analyses that have results that reinforce their biases, but ignore analyses the do not reinforce them? Isn't this just a smokescreen to hide behind?**

(On this point, see the Reflections Guide, pages 295a and b.)

- 110GB of content
- 3.2 million files
- Content created/changed 24/7 at rate of 5GB per day
- 1,100 databases
- Multiple languages
- 125 million unique users per month
- 999 million page views per month

Figure 9-23
Document Management at Microsoft.com (as of December 2003)

Source: microsoft.com/backstage/inside.htm (accessed February 2004). © 2003 Microsoft Corporation. All rights reserved.

Content Management Problems

Content management functions are, however, exceedingly complicated. First, most content databases are huge; some have thousands of individual documents, pages, and graphics. Figure 9-23 shows the scale of the content management problem at Microsoft.com. Although the size of the content store is impressive (recall from Figure 9-1 that 110GB is equivalent to 110 pickup trucks of books), the more critical number is the amount of new or changed content per day: 5GB. This means that roughly 5 percent of the content of Microsoft.com changes *every day*.

Another complication for content management systems is that documents do not exist in isolation from each other. Documents may refer to one another or multiple documents may refer to the same product or procedure. When one of them changes, others must change as well. Some content management systems keep semantic linkages among documents so that content dependencies can be known and used to maintain document consistency.

A third complication is that document contents are perishable. Documents become obsolete and need to be altered, removed, or replaced. Consider, for example, what happens when a new product is announced. The document in Figure 9-24 was first written before Microsoft Reporting Services was available to the public. It was written to build the business case for the product. Once the product became available, however, the description in this document needed to be changed. As shown here, the second paragraph states that the product is now available. As originally written, however, that paragraph stated that the product would be available soon. The day that Reporting Services shipped, every document that referenced that product on Microsoft.com had to be checked and possibly revised or removed.

Finally, consider the content management problem for multinational companies. Microsoft publishes Microsoft.com in over 40 languages. In fact, at Microsoft.com,

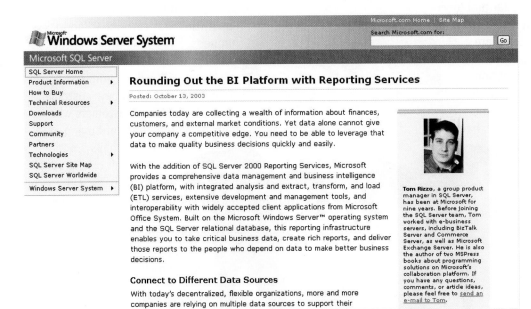

Figure 9-24
Reporting Services: United States

Source: Used with permission of Tom Rizzo of Microsoft Corporation.

Data Mining in the Real World

I'm not really a contrarian about data mining. I believe in it. After all, it's my career. But data mining in the real world is a lot different from the way it's described in textbooks.

"There are many reasons it's different. One is that the data are always dirty, with missing values, values way out of the range of possibility, and time values that make no sense. Here's an example: Somebody sets the server system clock incorrectly and runs the server for a while with the wrong time. When they notice the mistake, they set the clock to the correct time. But all of the transactions that were running during that interval have an ending time before the starting time. When we run the data analysis, and compute elapsed time, the results are negative for those transactions.

"Missing values are a similar problem. Consider the records of just 10 purchases. Suppose that two of the records are missing the customer number and one is missing the year part of transaction date. So you throw out three records, which is 30 percent of the data. You then notice that two more records have dirty data, and so you throw them out, too. Now you've lost half your data.

"Another problem is that you know the least when you start the study. So you work for a few months and learn that if you had

another variable, say the customer's Zip code, or age, or something else, you could do a much better analysis. But those other data just aren't available. Or, maybe they are available, but to get the data you have to reprocess millions of transactions, and you don't have the time or budget to do that.

"Overfitting is another problem, a huge one. I can build a model to fit any set of data you have. Give me 100 data points and in a few minutes, I can give you 100 different equations that will predict those 100 data points. With neural networks, you can create a model of any level of complexity you want, except that none of those equations will predict new cases with any accuracy at all. When using neural nets, you have to be very careful not to overfit the data.

"Then, too, data mining is about probabilities, not certainty. Bad luck happens. Say I build a model that predicts the probability that a customer will make a purchase. Using the model on new-customer data, I find three customers who have a .7 probability of buying something. That's a good number, well over a 50-50 chance, but it's still possible that none of them will buy. In fact, the probability that none of them will buy is .3 3 .3 3 .3, or .027, which is 2.7 percent.

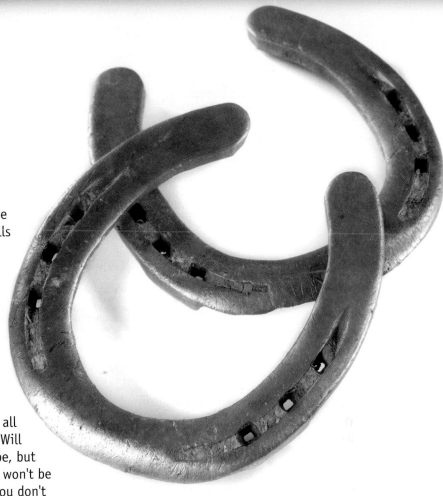

"Now suppose I give the names of the three customers to a salesperson who calls on them, and sure enough, we have a stream of bad luck and none of them buys. This bad result doesn't mean the model is wrong. But what does the salesperson think? He thinks the model is worthless and can do better on his own. He tells his manager who tells her associate, who tells the Northeast Region, and sure enough, the model has a bad reputation all across the company.

"Another problem is seasonality. Say all your training data are from the summer. Will your model be valid for the winter? Maybe, but maybe not. You might even know that it won't be valid for predicting winter sales, but if you don't have winter data, what do you do?

"When you start a data-mining project, you never know how it will turn out. I worked on one project for 6 months, and when we finished, I didn't think our model was any good. We had too many problems with data: wrong, dirty, and missing. There was no way we could know ahead of time that it would happen, but it did.

"When the time came to present the results to senior management, what could we do? How could we say we took 6 months of our time and substantial computer resources to create a bad model? We had a model, but I just didn't think it would make accurate predictions. I was a junior member of the team, and it wasn't for me to decide. I kept my mouth shut, but I never felt good about it. Fortunately, the project was cancelled later for other reasons.

"However, I'm only talking about my bad experiences. Some of my projects have been excellent. On many, we found interesting and important patterns and information, and a few times, I've created very accurate predictive models. It's not easy, though, and you have to be very careful. Also, lucky!"

? DISCUSSION QUESTIONS

1. Summarize the concerns expressed by this contrarian.

2. Do you think the concerns raised here are sufficient to avoid data-mining projects altogether?

3. If you were a junior member of a data-mining team and you thought that the model that had been developed was ineffective, maybe even wrong, what would you do? If your boss disagrees with your beliefs, would you go higher in the organization? What are the risks of doing so? What else might you do?

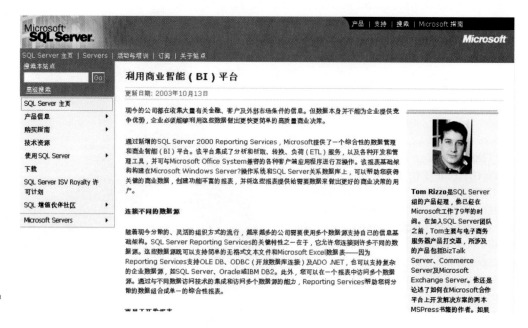

Figure 9-25
Reporting Services: China

Source: Used with permission of Tom
Rizzo of Microsoft Corporation.

English is just another language. Every document, in whatever language it was authored, must be translated into all languages before it can be published on Microsoft.com. Figure 9-25 shows the Chinese version of the article in Figure 9-24.

Content Delivery

Delivery for content management systems is, at least in one major way, much simpler than for report management systems. Almost all users of content management systems *pull* the contents. Unlike reporting systems, there is no need to set up elaborate structures of users, user groups, reports, and schedules in order to push content accordingly. Instead, the content is available simply to be pulled as needed.

Of course, users cannot pull content if they do not know it exists. So, the content must be arranged and indexed, and a facility for searching the content devised. Here, however, organizations get a break, at least for their publicly accessible content.

As stated, the world's largest and most popular search engine is Google. Google searches through all public sites of all organizations. This means that Google is usually the fastest and easiest way to find a document. This often is true even within an organization. It may be easier, for example, for a General Motors employee to find a General Motors document using Google than using an in-house search engine. Google will have crawled through the General Motors site and will have indexed all documents using its superior technology.

Documents that reside behind a corporate firewall, however, are not publicly accessible and will not be reachable by Google or other search engines. Organizations must index their own proprietary documents and provide their own search capability for them.

One last consideration concerns the formatting of documents when they are delivered. Web browsers and other programs can readily format content expressed in HTML, PDF, or another standard format. Also, XML documents often contain their own formatting rules that browsers can interpret. The content management system will have to determine an appropriate format for content expressed in other ways.

KM Systems to Facilitate the Sharing of Human Knowledge

Nothing is more frustrating for a manager to contemplate than the situation in which one employee struggles with a problem that another employee knows how to solve easily. Similarly, it would be frustrating to learn of a customer who returns a large order because the customer couldn't perform a basic operation with the product that many employees (and other customers) can readily perform.

You Be the Guide

Using the Opposing Forces Guide (page 291a)

GOAL

* Teach real-world issues and limitations for data mining.

BACKGROUND AND PRESENTATION STRATEGIES

The contrarian whom I interviewed for this guide had 15 years' experience as a data miner, most of that in the automotive industry. He'd come back to the university because he was having a career crisis. He wasn't sure that data mining was worth it. He'd begun to question the validity of many data-mining techniques. His concerns and misgivings are summarized in this guide.

Judging by his experience, especially his last comment about luck, we can conclude that data mining shares risk characteristics with other forms of mining. Sometimes you find the gold or the oil, and sometimes you do not.

A *difficult ethical dilemma* is buried in this guide—one that I softened in writing the text. At the end of 6 months, this person had determined that the model that he had developed was, in fact, useless. They had overfit the data, and *he believed the predictive power of the model was nil.* He did not believe that the model should be implemented. But he was a junior member of the team, and his boss did not want to admit the model they had developed would be a bad predictor. His response was to leave that company within a few months. He still feels guilty about it—guilty that he didn't get a better result and guilty that he wasn't more honest and forthcoming. See question 3.

? SUGGESTED RESPONSES FOR DISCUSSION QUESTIONS

1. The problems he identifies are:

   • Dirty data

   • Missing values

   • Lack of knowledge at start of project

   • Overfitting

   • Probabilistic—good model may have unlucky first uses

   • Seasonality

   • High risk—cannot know outcome

The students may not understand overfitting. It's not discussed in the main part of the text. Overfitting occurs when you create a model that is too complicated. Basically, your model captures not only the essence of the underlying phenomena, but also the random error that happened to be present in the data you used. When you try to use that model to predict, it predicts both the phenomena and the error; but the error, because it's random, will be different than it was for the sample study data. Thus, the model is terrific for explaining the sample data, but horrible as a predictor.

Overfitting is a huge problem in data mining, especially when using neural nets. They can produce such a complicated set of equations that they can predict any sample, including all of the sample's error.

2. Like gold mining, data mining is fraught with risk. I would say:

   ➤ **Have a clear business objective in mind. Don't just "see what the data show."**

   ➤ **Understand how the results of data mining can lead to action—not just insight.**

   ➤ **If possible, run a pilot study with a limited amount of data and determine the utility of the analysis.**

   (A pilot study may not be possible. If the only difference between the pilot and the full analysis is the amount of data processed, then the complete study infrastructure may need to be finished just to do the pilot.)

   ➤ **Be aware of the problem of overfitting—one can create a model that will fit the sample data perfectly, but that will have no utility for prediction.**

   ➤ **Keep in mind the risky nature data mining.**

3. In considering this question, a great question for the class is:

   ➤ **If you, as a junior employee, were in his circumstances and had developed a model that you didn't believe was useful, what would you do?**

   Some possible responses:
   First would be to discuss your misgivings with your boss. Maybe you are wrong about the quality of the model. Maybe there are other factors in the background that make your fears ungrounded. Maybe your boss agrees and wants to strategize with you about what to do.

➤ If your boss disagrees, would you go higher in the organization?

Maybe. But only after very careful questioning of my situation and motives. I'd ask myself whether the problems and risks of going higher are worth the gain.

Risks:

- This will end my relationship with my boss.

- My boss will become my enemy within the company.

- I may expose both of us to the risk of being fired.

- My boss's boss may think I'm a whiner and a problem maker.

- My boss's boss may not want to know.

Gain:

- Saving the organization time and money.

- If the data-mining project involves people, saving the harm that will be done by miscategorizing people.

- Preserving the reputation of data mining within the organization.

Other courses of action are to quit the company, to transfer to another group, or to not do anything at all.

All in all, this is a very difficult situation with no clear and obvious solution.

WRAP UP

➤ This case has two major themes: realistic problems in data mining and an ethical dilemma—when you know something that it will be possibly self-defeating to reveal. Both are important.

➤ You may not be a data miner in your career, but you will most likely encounter, sometime during your career, a situation when you may have to take self-defeating actions in order to act ethically. You need to keep thinking about such situations and what YOU will do.

1. Portals, discussion groups, email
    – Idea publishing
    – Bulletin boards
    – Frequently asked questions (FAQs)
2. Collaboration systems
    – Net presentations
    – Video conferencing
    – Net meetings
3. Expert systems
    – Human-derived decision trees
    – Some major success in the 1980s and 1990s
    – Unexpected side consequences cause large maintenance costs
    – Can work well in narrow domain

Figure 9-26
Technology Support of
Sharing Human Knowledge

KM systems are concerned with the sharing not only of content, as just described, but also with the sharing of knowledge among humans. How can one person share her knowledge with another? How can one person learn of another person's great idea?

As shown in Figure 9-26, three forms of technology are used for knowledge-sharing among humans:

- Portals, discussion groups, and email
- Collaborations systems
- Expert systems

The following pages describe each type of system. As you read these descriptions, keep in mind that KM is not really about technology. It is about humans sharing ideas with other humans. The technology is simply an enabler for this process.

Portals, Discussion Groups, and Email

Consider the following story:

> Around the holidays in 2000, a Giant Eagle deli manager thought of a way to display the seafood delicacy that proved irresistible to harried shoppers, accounting for an extra $200 in 1-week sales. But uncertain of his strategy, he first posted the idea on the KnowAsis portal. Other deli managers ribbed him a bit, but one tried the idea in his store and saw a similar boost in sales. The total payoff to the company, for this one tiny chunk of information, was about $20,000 in increased sales in the two stores. The company estimates that if it had implemented the display idea across all its stores during this period, the payoff might have been $350,000. Previously, "there was no tradition of sharing ideas in the store environment," says Jack Flanagan, executive vice president of Giant Eagle business systems.[6]

An employee may have a good idea, a novel approach, or a better way to solve a problem, and KM systems allow that employee to share that knowledge with others. Notice in this example that the employee shared the idea gratuitously; no one asked him about how to arrange the seafood delicacy, the employee just posted the good idea on the Web portal. It was up to other managers and employees to pull that knowledge down from the portal.

Discussion groups are another form of organizational KM. They allow employees or customers to post questions and queries seeking solutions to problems they have. Oracle, IBM, PeopleSoft, and other vendors support product discussion groups where users can post questions and where employees, vendors, and other users can answer them. Later, the organization can edit and summarize the questions from such discussion groups into **frequently asked questions (FAQs)**, another form of knowledge-sharing.

---

[6]Lauren Gibbons Paul, "Why Three Heads Are Better than One," *CIO Magazine*, December 1, 2003, *cio.com/archive/120103/km.html* (accessed July 2005).

Basic email can also be used for knowledge-sharing, especially if email lists have been constructed with KM in mind. For example, an email list of all product-quality engineers, across all plants, across the organization, can facilitate communication among those employees.

Two human factors inhibit knowledge-sharing, however. The first is that employees can be reluctant to exhibit their ignorance. Out of fear of appearing incompetent, employees may not post their queries on bulletin boards or use email groups. Such reluctance can sometimes be reduced by the attitude and posture of the managers of such groups. One strategy for employees in this situation is to use email lists to identify a smaller group of people who have an interest in a specific problem. Members of that smaller group can then discuss the issue in a less-inhibiting forum.

The other inhibiting human factor is employee competition. "Look," says the top salesperson. "I earn a substantial bonus from being the top salesperson. Why would I want to share my sales techniques with others? I'd just be strengthening the competition." This understandable perspective may not be changeable. A KM application may be ill-suited to a competitive group. Or, the company may be able to restructure rewards and incentives to foster sharing of ideas among employees (e.g., giving a bonus to the *group* that develops the best idea).

Even in situations where there is no direct competition, employees may be reluctant to share ideas out of shyness, fear of ridicule, or inertia. In these cases, a strong management endorsement for knowledge-sharing can be effective, especially if that endorsement is followed by strong positive feedback. As one senior manager said, "There is nothing wrong with praise or cash, and especially cash."

Collaboration Systems

Collaboration systems are information systems that enable people to work together more effectively. For centuries, meetings have been the primary means for humans to exchange knowledge and information. Today's information technology can foster meetings in several ways. For one, the Internet can be used as a broadcast medium for speeches, panel discussions, and other types of meetings. *Web broadcasts*, because they are digital, can be readily saved and replayed at the viewer's convenience. Web broadcasts can also be made interactive by combining them with discussion group bulletin boards that are live during the broadcast. Normally, the sponsoring organization controls publication of the discussion group so as to filter inappropriate comments.

Video conferencing is another popular form of IT-supported meetings. Video conferencing equipment is expensive, however, so normally it is located in selected sites in the organization. Employees go to those sites to participate in the meeting.

Net meetings are a means by which individuals can participate in remote meetings without leaving their desks. With a speaker and a Web camera, virtual meetings can be conducted among employees who sit in their own offices. See Figure 9-27.

Expert Systems

Expert systems, the last form of KM applications we will consider, are rule-based systems that use If . . . then rules similar to those created by decision tree analysis. However, whereas decision trees If . . . then rules are created by mining data, those in **expert systems** are created by interviewing experts in a given business domain and codifying the rules stated by those experts. Also, decision trees typically have a fewer than a dozen rules, whereas expert systems can have hundreds or thousands of rules.

Many expert systems were created in the late 1980s and early 1990s, and some of them have been successful. They suffer from three major disadvantages, however. First, they are difficult and expensive to develop. They require many labor hours from both experts in the domain under study and designers of expert systems. This expense is compounded by the high opportunity cost of tying up domain experts. Such experts are normally some of the most sought-after employees in the organization.

Second, expert systems are difficult to maintain. Because of the nature of rule-based systems, the introduction of a new rule in the middle of hundreds of others can

Figure 9-27
Net Meeting Graphic

have unexpected consequences. A small change can cause very different outcomes. Unfortunately, such side-effects cannot be predicted or eliminated. They are the nature of complex rule-based systems.

Finally, expert systems were unable to live up to the high expectations set by their name. Initially, proponents of expert systems hoped to be able to duplicate the performance of highly trained experts like doctors. It turned out, however, that no expert system has the same diagnostic ability as knowledgeable, skilled, and experienced doctors. Even when expert systems were developed that came close in ability, changes in medical technology required constant changing of the expert system, and the problems caused by unexpected consequences made such changes very expensive.

Today, however, there are successful, less ambitious expert systems. Typically these systems address more restricted problems than duplicating a doctor's diagnostic ability. One example, discussed in *MIS in Use 9-2* (page 296), is a system at Washington University Medical School.

The BI systems described in this chapter can provide substantial benefits to the organizations that use them. Unfortunately, however, the results can be unintentionally biased by the process in which they are used, as described in the *Reflections Guide* on page 295a.

Carbon Creek Gardens (continued)

Recall that Mary Keeling was both embarrassed and frustrated when she learned she had lost a customer and didn't know about it. We described one solution for Mary in the section on reporting, but that solution is unsatisfactory. It requires Mary to search for missing customers by comparing data in two reports, looking for a customer that appears in one and does not appear in another. After a long day at work, Mary is unlikely to want to do this, and she is likely to make mistakes when she does.

Another technique covered in this chapter should jump out at you as an excellent solution to Mary's problem. Rather than describe that

Justifying the Justification?

From 1971 to 1973, I worked at the Pentagon, helping to build a computer simulation of World War III. It was a huge project, probably one of the largest software projects up to that time. Today, compared to an operating system like Windows, it would be trivial. Back then, it was a BIG project.

I helped to build the database management system that supported the simulation, so I wasn't very close to the analysis process. But one run of the simulation would take 24 hours of computer time, which meant that all of us in the group took turns babysitting a large mainframe computer through each run. I spent many a night perched between two keypunch machines, hoping that nothing would go awry. (For example, one morning I forgot, in my sleepy haze, to print the results—which meant 24 hours of computer time went down the drain!)

Anyway, here is how the analysis process appeared from my keypunch perch: We would run the simulation and obtain a set of results. The military analysts and weapons experts would examine the results, and if the results weren't quite what was expected or wanted, the analysts would ask us to change some of the inputs or a portion of the model and run the simulation again. If the results of that next run were closer to what was wanted, we would keep them. Otherwise, the analysts would discard those results too. We would change something else and run the simulation again.

Over time, we accumulated a set of results that the analysts approved. Those accumulated results were presented to the four-star generals and other senior Pentagon managers. Sometimes these senior people

would see problems in the analyses, and we would discard some of the results, or run the simulation again. When the senior managers approved the analyses, we would take a summary of the accumulated results to Congress to justify a portion of the military budget.

I do not believe that anyone thought they were deceiving anyone else. The top managers didn't realize that the results they saw left out a substantial portion of the unfavorable simulations. They never knew about those other results. Even the analysts who were filtering the outcomes by throwing out the numbers they didn't like weren't being dishonest. They simply thought that those results were wrong or unrealistic. I do not think they realized they were using the computer to promulgate their prior ideas about military needs.

Many, many years later, I did a market-basket analysis for a major retailer. The analysis found that orders having a product in the tools category almost never included a product from another category. However, orders having items from the clothing/tops category included items from 33 other subclasses of products. I suspect that phenomenon is why few men enjoy shopping with women, but that's projecting my own shopping attitudes on the results.

Which is just the point. What did the retailer do with the information about that shopping pattern? Some people wanted to redesign the stores to put items from more categories in the tools department. Others wanted to expand the size of the clothing departments. Still others wanted to redesign Web

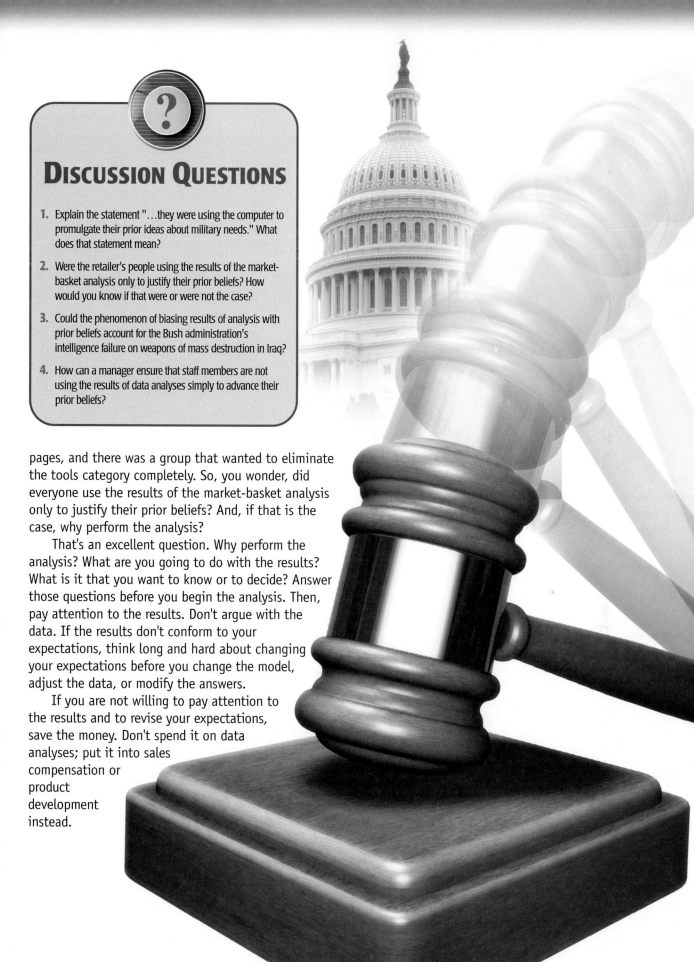

DISCUSSION QUESTIONS

1. Explain the statement "…they were using the computer to promulgate their prior ideas about military needs." What does that statement mean?

2. Were the retailer's people using the results of the market-basket analysis only to justify their prior beliefs? How would you know if that were or were not the case?

3. Could the phenomenon of biasing results of analysis with prior beliefs account for the Bush administration's intelligence failure on weapons of mass destruction in Iraq?

4. How can a manager ensure that staff members are not using the results of data analyses simply to advance their prior beliefs?

pages, and there was a group that wanted to eliminate the tools category completely. So, you wonder, did everyone use the results of the market-basket analysis only to justify their prior beliefs? And, if that is the case, why perform the analysis?

That's an excellent question. Why perform the analysis? What are you going to do with the results? What is it that you want to know or to decide? Answer those questions before you begin the analysis. Then, pay attention to the results. Don't argue with the data. If the results don't conform to your expectations, think long and hard about changing your expectations before you change the model, adjust the data, or modify the answers.

If you are not willing to pay attention to the results and to revise your expectations, save the money. Don't spend it on data analyses; put it into sales compensation or product development instead.

solution here, however, you should answer it for yourself in question 22 on page 298. By this point in the book, you should be able to conceptualize a system to solve Mary's problem.

Expert Systems for Pharmacies

The Medical Informatics group at Washington University School of Medicine in St. Louis, Missouri, develops innovative and effective information systems to support decision making in medicine. The group has developed several expert systems that are used as a safety net to screen the decisions of doctors and other medical professionals. These systems help to achieve the hospital's goal of state-of-the-art, error-free care.

Medical researchers developed early expert systems to support and in some cases to replace medical decision making. MYCIN was an expert system developed in the early 1970s for the purpose of diagnosing certain infectious diseases. Physicians never routinely used MYCIN, but researchers used its expert system framework as the basis for many other medical systems. For one reason or another, however, none of those systems has seen extensive use.

In contrast, the systems developed at Washington University are routinely used, in real time, every day. One of the systems, DoseChecker, verifies appropriate dosages on prescriptions issued in the hospital. Another application, PharmADE, ensures that patients are not prescribed drugs that have harmful interactions. The pharmacy order entry system invokes these applications as a prescription is entered. If either system detects a problem with the prescription, it generates an alert like the sample shown in Figure 1.

A pharmacist screens an alert before sending it to the doctor. If the pharmacist disagrees with the alert, it is discarded. If the pharmacist agrees there is a problem with either the dosage or a harmful drug interaction, she sends the alert to the doctor. The doctor can then alter the prescription or override the alert. If the doctor does not respond, the system will escalate the alert to higher levels until the potential problem is resolved.

Neither DoseChecker nor PharmADE attempts to replace the decision making of medical professionals. Rather, they operate behind the scenes, as a reliable assistant helping to provide error-free care.

MIS in Use 9-2

Figure 1
Alert from Pharmacy Clinical Decision Support System

Apparently, the systems work. According to the Informatics Web site, "Over a 6 month period at a 1,400 bed teaching hospital, the system {DoseChecker} screened 57,404 orders and detected 3,638 potential dosing errors." Furthermore, since the hospital implemented the system, the number of alerts has fallen by 50 percent, indicating that the prescribing process has been improved because of the feedback provided by the alerts.

Source: The Division of Medical Informatics at Washington University School of Medicine for the Department of Pharmacy at Barnes Jewish Hospital. *informatics.wustl.edu* (accessed January 2005). Used with permission of Medical Informatics at Washington University School of Medicine and BJC Healthcare.

Carbon Creek Nursery (continued) (page 295)

The solution using the two reports (in midchapter) has the disadvantage that Mary must compare the report data and look for names that are on one and not on the other. This is too much work for her, and thus not an effective solution.

RESPONDING TO THE CHALLENGE

The obvious solution to Mary's problem is to develop an RFM analysis. But, rather than providing this solution, you might lead the students through the various types and discuss the applicability of each type to this problem:

➤ **Reporting system?**

(We've already rejected this solution.)

➤ **OLAP?**

(It could be used to solve this problem, but not directly, and it would require substantial work on her part.)

➤ **Data warehouse?**

(No, she's way too small a company for that.)

➤ **Market-basket analysis?**

(No, she's not considering product groupings.)

➤ **Decision trees?**

(No, she's not classifying.)

➤ **Neural network?**

(No, she's not predicting or classifying.)

➤ **Knowledge management system?**

(No, not relevant.)

➤ **RFM?**

(Yes!)

RFM analyses are easy (and cheap) to perform and give results that are readily understood and actionable. *I do not know why every retailer does not perform such analyses.* I think it should be a module in every retail sales software package.

Had Mary performed an RFM analysis at the start of the spring season, the RFM result for Tootsie Swan would have been 511, a clear danger signal that Tootsie was a lost customer.

To perform such an analysis, Mary needs only the simplest of data: the customer identity, the order date, and the order amount for each customer purchase.

One problem for many small retailers is that they do not record customer identity with each purchase. However, most small businesses have some type of frequent-buyer program that does track customer identity. The data in those systems could be used to perform the RFM analysis. Granted, those records have a bias in that they contain sales data only from customers who have chosen to enroll in the frequent-buyer program. But those customers are normally the most important ones. The interpretation of the results should change, however, because the RFM scores will be biased upward. A 5 for the frequent buyer program is probably a 3 or so for customers overall.

The SQL statements for performing an RFM analysis are simple. I show a complete set of them in my database book.[1]

WRAP UP

Possible wrap-up statements:

➤ **You've learned a lot about business intelligence and data mining in this chapter. You should be able to take an active role in providing requirements for reporting systems, OLAP analysis, and knowledge management.**

➤ **Unless you become a specialist, you are unlikely to perform data mining yourself. Still, knowing about the possibility of data mining enables you to suggest it when it might be appropriate.**

➤ **These techniques could be an important part of your competitive advantage. Many businesses are not using business intelligence as well as they should. You may be able to introduce such techniques.**

➤ **If you are interested in learning more about these techniques and maybe specializing in one of them, you should take our database processing class. Drop me an email if you want to know more.**

[1]David Kroenke, *Database Processing*, 10th ed. (Upper Saddle River, NJ: Prentice Hall, 2006), 539–541.

You Be the Guide

Using the Reflections Guide
(page 295a)

GOALS

* Demonstrate how bias in communication along the management chain can dramatically change a message.

* Explore ways in which personal bias influences the interpretation of results.

BACKGROUND AND PRESENTATION STRATEGIES

This guide addresses two types of bias and how that bias influences interpretation of study results: bias within an individual and bias that results from chains of interpersonal communication.

Biases within humans influence the way we interpret our world. We cannot help it. In fact the word *interpret* implies some mental processing in reference to currently held ideas and beliefs. Because such bias is inevitable, it is important for businesspeople to understand what their biases are. With such understanding, we at least know what we are doing and how we differ from others.

Understanding one's biases isn't easy. "I don't know who discovered water, but it probably wasn't a fish." We are afloat in our biases.

How do we discover our biases? We can discover our biases through honest and forthright conversation with our colleagues. That, of course, helps us only if we listen to what others are saying and, in particular, listen to what they are saying about our interpretations. Here's a hint I give my students: *Be guided by your strong emotional responses.* Those emotions often reveal one's biases.

Discovering your biases is one of the most important achievements in college.

Considering intercommunication bias, a fun way to introduce the topic of upward bias is to play a version of the children's game of telephone. Make several copies of the following message:

> *For long-term investors, IBM could be a good investment in the next quarter, if the stock can be purchased for $3 under its current price.*

Now tell the students that they work for the person to the left of them and that they manage the person to the right of them. (That assignment alone will get the students' attention!)

Give the written message to students who are lowest in the hierarchy, who manage no one. Make a copy of the message for each row of students. Ask the students with the messages to whisper the statement to their boss (the person on their left). Do not pass the written message along. Restrict the students to saying the message once or twice. Then ask the second person to whisper the message to their boss (a third student), and so forth, through at least five or six students. (More is better.)

Given the many layers of management, the last person to receive the message must be the equivalent of the worldwide CEO. Ask the worldwide CEOs to write the message they received. When all messages have crossed the room, ask the worldwide CEOs to read what they've written.

The resulting messages should show the results of upward bias.

Now imagine the results if each person in this chain had filtered the data by choosing only the results from certain studies. (They wouldn't consider this as filtering, they would see it as "Improving the results".) We can see how the message that is received at the top level will be stated in far more certain (either optimistic or pessimistic) terms than when it was created at the bottom.

There are two phenomena lurking here: (1) the distortion that naturally occurs when a message is passed up the management hierarchy and (2) the bias that occurs when people use analyses to justify their beliefs. Those two operating together can drastically bias the message received at the top. (This game leads naturally to question 4, What can we do about it?)

 SUGGESTED RESPONSES FOR DISCUSSION QUESTIONS

1. Any results that didn't conform with prior beliefs were either adjusted or rejected. These people thought that was their job. And, indeed, when performing any sort of data-mining activity, analysts must examine results for reasonability. If the results are unreasonable, then there may be something wrong with the model.

   But this is a slippery slope. Models must be adjusted, but:

   ➤ **How do you know if you are correcting a model appropriately or whether you are just forcing the model to generate the desired results?**

This is a sophisticated question, and the students may have trouble with it. You may need to back up and talk more about model building and model correction for them to understand the question. All of this is aimed at the goal of encouraging the students to understand how their biases impact what they do.

2. Yes, I think the retailers were using the results to justify prior beliefs. Everyone wanted to use the results to promulgate their pet project. A big factor in this situation was that the business did not start the market-basket analysis with a clear business objective. They just wanted to do market basket to see what they would learn about data mining.

3. This is obviously a loaded question whose answer depends on one's personal bias. So, one place to start the discussion is with that bias:

➤ **To what extent does your personal political bias impact your answer or even your ability to this question? Can you address this question impartially?**

Consider the following statement:

➤ **It's hard to believe the Colin Powell would have perjured himself when he testified about those weapons before the United Nations on February 5, 2003.**

➤ **Was he the victim of upward bias, as described in this guide? Or, was he lied to by others in the administration?**

This question may lead to a raucous discussion. At some point, conclude it with:

➤ **So, now we have firsthand experience about the ways in which biases influence our interpretation of our world.**

4. This is obviously a difficult-to-answer question. Some factors to consider:

Is the interpretation well supported by the model results? Or, is the interpretation a bit of a stretch?

To what extent did the staff have influence over the model construction and maintenance? Could they have biased the model unintentionally?

How do the staff members present themselves? Are their statements expressed in emotionally laded terminology?

Do the staff members have a big stake in the outcome? Is this analysis obviously self-serving? (These biases don't make the analysis wrong, but they may call for careful scrutiny.)

WRAP UP

➤ **All of this comes back to a statement in Chapter 1: Your thinking is the most important part of any information system that you use! The business intelligence applications will provide the information, but the way that you bias and communicate that information is up to you!**

SUMMARY

- Enormous amounts of data are generated each year. Business intelligence (BI) tools search these increasing amounts of data for useful information. Two types of BI tools exist: reporting and data mining. Reporting tools, which tend to be used for assessment, process data using simple calculations such as sums and averages. Data-mining tools, which tend to be used for prediction, process data using sophisticated statistical and mathematical techniques. The purpose of a BI system is to provide the right information to the right user at the right time.

- Reporting systems create meaningful information from disparate data sources and deliver that information to the proper user on a timely basis. Reporting systems generate information by filtering, sorting, grouping, and making calculations. The components of a reporting system are shown in Figure 9-7. Reports vary by type, media, and mode. The three major functions of a reporting system are authoring, managing, and delivering.

- RFM and OLAP are two examples of report applications. RFM is used to classify customers on the basis of how recently, how frequently, and how much they order. OLAP, or online analytical processing, is used to categorize data and to drill up and down dimensions of that data.

- Data warehouses and data marts are facilities that prepare, store, and manage data for data mining and other analyses. Data warehouses must clean and process data because of problems that occur when using operational data for data mining. A data warehouse is like a distributor in a supply chain, and a data mart is like a retailer in the supply chain. Data marts contain data that are used for particular business activities or departments.

- Data mining can be unsupervised or supervised. Unsupervised techniques have no prior model. Supervised techniques require the development of a prior model. Cluster analysis, market-basket analysis, and decision trees are unsupervised techniques. Neural networks are a supervised technique.

- Market-basket analysis determines groups of products that customers tend to purchase together. Decision trees are used to construct "If… Then…" rules for predicting classifications. Neural networks, which are only loosely based on the anatomy of neurons, are devices for constructing complicated arrays of nonlinear equations.

- Knowledge management is the process of creating value from intellectual capital and sharing that knowledge with employees, managers, suppliers, customers, and others who need that capital. Knowledge management systems organize the sharing of knowledge that is known to exist, either in libraries of documents or in the minds of employees. Content management systems manage documents, Web pages, and graphics, so that they can be readily accessed and searched.

- Human knowledge-sharing systems use portals, bulletin boards, and email to facilitate knowledge interchange. Collaboration systems include net conferencing, video conferencing, and expert systems.

KEY TERMS AND CONCEPTS

ASSIGNMENT MATERIAL

Review Questions

1. How does Moore's Law influence data storage?

2. Explain the difference in typical usage between reporting and data-mining tools.

3. Explain the difference in processing techniques between reporting and data-mining tools.

4. Name the major components of a reporting system and show their relationship.

5. Explain what actions a sales team should take with customers that have RFM scores of [4, 1, 1], [1, 1, 3], and [5, 5, 5].

6. What is the remarkable characteristic of an OLAP report?

7. Explain the differences between the reports in Figures 9-12 and 9-13.

8. Summarize five potential problems that can occur when using operational data for data mining.

9. What is the difference between a data warehouse and a data mart? How do they relate to a supply chain?

10. According to this chapter, what is the most important point to consider when thinking about the data-mining process?

11. Explain why the term *neural network* is misleading.

12. Give an example of four "If. . .Then. . ." rules for the decision tree on page 289 (the student classification).

13. Explain the difference between knowledge management and data mining.

14. Give an example of the need for a content management system other than one mentioned in this chapter.

15. Summarize four complications in content management.

16. Explain how and when organizations can rely on Google to index the content of their Web sites. What is the danger of that policy?

17. What factors inhibit knowledge-sharing among employees? How can managers reduce the impact of those factors?

18. According to this chapter, what is the best use for an expert system?

Applying Your Knowledge

19. Reflect on the differences between reporting systems and data-mining systems. What are their similarities and differences? What are likely to be differences in their costs? What are differences in their benefits? How would an organization choose between the two BI tools?

20. Suppose you are a member of the Audubon Society, and the board of the local chapter asks you to help them analyze its member data. The group wants to analyze the demographics of its membership against members' activity, including events attended, classes attended, volunteer activities, and donations. Describe two different reporting applications and one data-mining application that they might develop. Be sure to include a specific description of the goals of each system.

21. Suppose you are the director of student activities at your university. Recently, some students have charged that your department misallocates its resources. They claim the allocation is based on outdated student preferences. Funds are given to activities that few students find attractive, and insufficient funds are allocated to new activities in which students do want to participate. Describe how you could use reporting and/or data-mining systems to assess this claim.

22. Consider Mary Keeling's problem at Carbon Creek Nursery. One of the following techniques is an excellent solution to her problem: OLAP report, decision tree, RFM report, neural network, or market-basket analysis.

a. Which of these techniques will solve her problem and why?

b. Explain why the technique you selected is better than each of the other alternatives.

c. Why is the technique you selected better than the reporting solution on page 272–273?

d. Describe the data Mary will need to use the technique you recommend.

e. Suppose the reporting system on page 272–273 is half as expensive to implement than the technique you recommend. How would Mary decide between the two?

Application Exercises

23. OLAP cubes are very similar to Microsoft Excel *pivot tables*. If you are unfamiliar with pivot tables, open Excel and search the help system for pivot tables. Select one of the demos to see how pivot tables work. Or, you can just follow the instructions below. For this exercise, assume that in your organization the purchasing agents rate vendors (similar to the situation in question 28, in Chapter 8, page 257). You can use a pivot table to display the data in flexible and informative ways.

a. Open Excel and add the following column headings to your spreadsheet: *VendorName, EmployeeName, Date, Year*, and *Rating*. Enter sample data under these headings. Add ratings for at least three vendors and at least three rows for each vendor. Add sufficient data so that each vendor will have at least five ratings, and each employee will have entered at least five ratings. Also, add data for at least two different months and two different years.

b. Under the Data tab in Excel, select Pivot Table and Pivot Chart. (From here on, the exact menu names may vary depending on the version of Excel you have. Look for names that are close to those used here.) A wizard will open. Select Excel and Pivot table in the first screen. Click Next.

c. When asked to provide a data range, drag your mouse over the data you entered so as to select all of the data. Be sure to include the column headings. Excel will fill in the range values in the open dialog box. Click Next, Select New worksheet, and then Finish.

d. Excel will create a field list on the right-hand side of your spreadsheet. Drag and drop the field named *VendorName*, on the words 'Drop Row Fields Here.' Drag and drop *EmployeeName*, on the words 'Drop Column Fields Here.' Now drag and drop the field named *Rating* on the words 'Drop Data Items Here.' Voilà! You have a pivot table.

e. To see how the table works, drag and drop more fields on the various sections of your pivot table. For example, drop *Year* on top of *Employee*. Then move year below *Employee*. Now move *Year* below *Vendor*. All of this action is just like an OLAP cube, and in fact, OLAP cubes are readily displayed in Excel pivot tables. The major difference is that OLAP cubes are usually based on thousands or more rows of data.

f. (**Extra credit**) If you answered question 28 in Chapter 8 on page 257, you can import the data you created there into a pivot table. To do that, select External data in the first panel of the wizard. Then, use the Excel Help system to figure out how to import your data. Your job will be easier if you first create a query in Access that contains the data from all three tables.

24. It is surprisingly easy to create a market-basket report using table data in Access. To do so, however, you will need to enter SQL expressions into the Access query builder. Here, you can just copy SQL statements to type them in. If you take a database class, you will learn how to code SQL statements like those you will use here.

a. Create an Access database with a table named ORDERS having columns *OrderNumber, ItemName*, and *Quantity*, with data types Number (*LongInteger*), Text (50), and Number (*LongInteger*), respectively. The key of this table is (*OrderNumber, ItemName*), but you will not need to define it for this exercise. (If you want to know how to define it, after you have entered the data type definitions of those two columns, drag your mouse to highlight both of them in the design window and then click the key icon.)

b. Now enter sample data. Make sure that there are several items on each order and that some orders have items in common. For example, you might enter [100, 'Cup', 4], [100, 'Saucer', 4], [200, 'Fork', 2], [200, 'Spoon', 2], [200, 'Knife', 2], and [200, 'Cup', 3]. Enter data for at least five orders.

c. Now, to perform the market basket analysis, you will need to enter several SQL statements into Access. To do so, click the queries tab and select Create query in Design view. Click Close when the Show Table dialog box appears. Now right-click in the gray section above the grid in the Select Query window. Select SQL View. Now enter the following expression exactly as it appears here:

```
SELECT T1.ItemName as FirstItem,
   T2.ItemName as SecondItem
FROM ORDERS T1, ORDERS T2
WHERE T1.OrderNumber = T2.OrderNumber
AND T1.ItemName <> T2.ItemName
```

Click the red exclamation point in the toolbar to run the query. Correct any typing mistakes and, once it works, save the query using the name *TwoItemBasket*.

d. Now enter a second SQL statement. Again, click the queries tab and select Create query in Design view. Click Close when the Show Table dialog box appears. Now right-click in the gray section above the grid in the Select Query window. Select SQL View. Now enter the following expression exactly as it appears here:

```
SELECT TwoItemBasket.FirstItem,
   TwoItemBasket.SecondItem, Count(*)
   AS SupportCount
FROM TwoItemBasket
GROUP BY TwoItemBasket.FirstItem,
   TwoItemBasket.SecondItem
```

Correct any typing mistakes and, once it works, save the query using the name SupportCount.

e. Examine the results of the second query and verify that the two query statements have correctly calculated the number of times that two items have appeared together. Explain further calculations you need to make to compute support.

f. Explain the calculations you need to make to compute lift. Although you can make those calculations using SQL, you need more SQL knowledge to do it and we will skip that here.

g. Explain, in your own words, what the query in part c seems to be doing. What does the query in part d seem to be doing? Again, you will need to take a database class to learn how to code such expressions, but this exercise should give you a sense of the kinds of calculations that are possible with SQL.

Career Assignments

25. Use your favorite search engine and search the Web for the term *data warehouse job opportunities*. Investigate several of the sites that you find to answer the following questions:

   a. Describe the two jobs in the search results that you find most interesting.
   b. Describe the educational requirements for each of these jobs.
   c. Describe internships and other experience that you could gain to better prepare you for each of these jobs.
   d. Using both Web resources and your own experience, describe the employment outlook for these jobs.

26. Same as question 25, but search for the term *data mining job opportunities*.

27. Same as question 25, but search for the term *knowledge management job opportunities*. You may have to click on some of the articles that you find and read them to obtain ideas on related job titles for which you can also search.

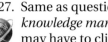

Case Study 9-1

Laguna Tools

Laguna Tools is a privately held reseller of high-end woodworking equipment. Based in Irvine, California, Laguna imports table saws, lathes, planers, jointers, and combination machines from top-quality European manufacturers. It resells those machines in the United States and Canada. Laguna is especially known for the comprehensive line of band saws that are constructed to its own specifications by factories in Italy and Poland.

Laguna's competitive strategy is to provide the highest-quality tools for woodworking professionals, including cabinet makers, artists, and wood fabricators. It also sells to high-end, "carriage trade" amateur woodworkers. With prices ranging from $2,000 to $20,000 per machine, Laguna's machines are among the most expensive woodworking equipment sold.

Most woodworking shops have a need for multiple machines. A common shop has table saw, band saw, jointer, planer, shaper, lathe, and mortise machines. Accordingly, once a customer orders one machine from Laguna, they become a particularly valuable asset. The machines are of such quality that a company or individual who buys one is quite likely to buy a second.

Laguna advertises in popular woodworking magazines, and it uses its Web site at *lagunatools.com* to gather leads. The company follows up on all leads with phone conversations and promotional literature. (So, out of courtesy to the company, do not fill out the customer information form on its Web site unless you are in the market for very high-quality machinery.)

Questions

1. What information should Laguna keep in its database of prospective customers?

2. What information should Laguna keep about customers who order?

3. When a salesperson is talking with a potential or actual customer, what data should he have available during the conversation?

4. Describe how Laguna could use an RFM analysis. What should it do with a [1, 1, 1] customer? What should it do with a [2, 2, 5] customer? What should it do with a [5, 1, 1] customer?

5. Explain how Laguna could use a market-basket analysis. What information must Laguna have to effectively use a market-basket analysis?

6. Explain how Laguna could use an OLAP analysis. Identify possible measures, dimensions, and cubes. What information would the company obtain from the OLAP analysis?

7. Examine your answers to the questions above and specify whether you think RFM, market-basket, or OLAP analysis would be the most useful to Laguna.

Case Study 9-2

3M Safety System

3M Company develops and manufactures diversified products for many industries, including industrial, consumer and leisure, safety, office, electronics, healthcare, and transportation. In 2004, its revenues exceeded $20 billion, with a net income of $2.99 billion. That same year, 3M employed 67,000 employees.

3M is a global company with different business divisions that focus on different industry segments. It is known for strong interdivision cooperation. It sells through many channels, including distributors, dealers, jobbers, and retailers; some products are even sold directly to consumers. 3M has 12 sales offices in the United States and 185 more offices internationally.

Sources: 3m.com (accessed January 2005); *finance.yahoo.com* (accessed January 2005).

Questions

1. To gain an appreciation of the complexity of this company, visit its Web site at *3m.com*. Assume that you are a U.S. customer. Access the 3M site and locate the Material Safety Data Sheet (MSDS) for the product 62-1838-5430-6. What is this product? What is the purpose of the MSDS?

2. Access a 3M site for any country other than the United States. Is the product in question 1 sold in the country you visited? If so, is there an MSDS for that product in that country?

3. Access the 3M site for "United States Manufacturing & Industry, Abrasives." Visit the sections of the site for applications, products, and purchase. Summarize how 3M could use OLAP analysis. Specify measures, dimensions, and cubes. What information would 3M obtain from this analysis? What value does the dynamic aspect of an OLAP analysis add?

4. Do you think the Abrasives division could effectively use an RFM analysis? If so, specify how it could perform such an analysis. If not, explain why not.

5. Do you think the Abrasives division could effectively use a market-basket analysis? If so, what would it do with the information? If not, why not?

6. Suppose that you want to learn which 3M product is the best for gluing fiberglass to teak (wood). Teak is particularly oily and is difficult to glue. Access the 3M site and attempt to determine which 3M adhesive is best suited for this task. Describe your experience.

7. Repeat question 6, but use Google instead. Describe your experience.

8. Somewhere in 3M there is a person who knows, off the top of his head, what product(s) to use to glue teak to fiberglass. Is there any way to find out who that person is? Does 3M know who that person is?

9. The 3M site is oriented around divisions and products. If you know the product you want, you can learn all about that product. But it is poorly organized with regards to problems and needs. 3M is a very successful company. Why do you think the site is constructed in this manner?

PART IV

Managing Information Systems Resources

The two chapters in this part conclude this text by describing how organizations manage information systems resources today. We begin in Chapter 10 by discussing the role, purpose, and organization of the IS department. You will learn about two key jobs: the chief information officer (CIO) and the chief technology officer (CTO). We will also discuss the benefits, costs, and risks of outsourcing of IS management functions. Chapter 10 concludes by describing the users' rights and responsibilities when using information systems.

Chapter 11 describes information systems security. You may wonder why we have a whole chapter on IS security when we have addressed security issues in the Security Guide of each chapter. Unlike the guides, Chapter 11 addresses IS security using a broad organization-wide perspective. You will learn about security threats and understand management's responsibility for developing an organizational security program. You will also learn safeguards that are used to protect against security threats.

By the time you finish the two chapters in this part, you will have gained a broad, comprehensive introduction to management information systems and how best to use them in the organizations for which you work.

Information Systems Management

Learning Objectives

✳ Understand the relationship of the CIO and CTO to other senior executives.

✳ Know the IS department's responsibilities for planning the use of IT/IS, managing infrastructure, developing systems, and protecting information assets.

✳ Understand the purpose and advantages of outsourcing.

✳ Understand the risks of outsourcing.

✳ Know users' rights and responsibilities with regard to the IS organization.

Guides

ETHICS GUIDE
Using the Corporate Computer

SECURITY GUIDE
Secure Development

OPPOSING FORCES GUIDE
Is Outsourcing Fool's Gold?

PROBLEM SOLVING GUIDE
What If You Just Don't Know?

REFLECTIONS GUIDE
Jumping Aboard the Bulldozer

Chapter Preview

As you learned in Chapters 7 through 9, information systems are a critical component of organizational success. But as you also learned in Chapters 2 through 6, they are complex. Considerable work is required to transform raw information technology into effective information systems that allow organizations to accomplish their goals and objectives.

This chapter surveys the means by which organizations manage this delicate combination of criticality and complexity. We begin with a survey of the major functions of the IS department and the relationship of the IS department to the enterprise. Then we will consider each of the major functions in greater detail: planning the use of IT/IS, creating and managing the computing infrastructure, creating and managing enterprise IS, and protecting organizational information assets.

Outsourcing is the process of hiring outside vendors to provide business services and related products. For information systems, outsourcing refers to hiring outside vendors to provide information systems, products, and applications. Outsourcing has been generating news and controversy in the United States, because it is causing the movement of white-collar, intellectual jobs from the United States to overseas sources. However, not all outsourcing is off shore; many outsourcing agreements exist between companies within the United States. We will examine the pros and cons of outsourcing and describe some of its risks. Finally, we will conclude this chapter by discussing the relationship of users to the IS department. In this last section, you will learn both your own and the IS department's rights and responsibilities.

The purpose of this chapter is not to teach you how to manage information systems. Such management is a huge and complicated task and, in truth, requires many years of experience. Instead, the goal of this chapter is to give you an appreciation for the scale and complexity of the information systems management task and to help you become an effective consumer of IS services.

Davidson Distribution

Suppose you are a department manager, say in purchasing or customer support, and one day one of your employees walks into your office very frustrated. Sitting down, he begins:

"I don't get it. I just don't get it. When we want new computers, the IS department selects the computer for us. Well, no, in truth it forces those computers down our throats. We have to take the computer and the related paraphernalia that they choose. I guess that's OK, in principle, but do you know what they're charging us? Mega-bucks! My budget was charged $1,700 for a computer I know I can buy from Dell for $750. It's ridiculous. And, I'll bet Dell could get it to me faster.

"Also, our choices are so narrow. Sure, we can pick how much memory we want, how fast a CPU, and how much storage, but always within the limits they set. And *they* pick the software. If I want to use WordPerfect, I'm out of luck because they don't support WordPerfect. Or

what if I want to use a Macintosh? Forget it! No way are they gonna let me use anything that isn't on their list!

"I wish they would just let us to buy the computers that we want to buy and negotiate our own deals. After all, it's coming out of our budget. I could get a better deal than they do, and be able to pick the software I want on top of it. Why don't we just start ordering from Dell? What do you think?"

As a manager, how do you respond? Why does the IS department require users to acquire computers from them? Just to protect their turf? Or is there some other reason? Does it make sense to propose that your department buy from Dell? Is it worthwhile for your employee to prepare a presentation detailing the money that you could save? To whom would you present such a proposal? How will the IS department respond? What is your best response to this employee?

▮ The Information Systems Department

The major functions of the information systems department are as follows:

- Plan the use of IT to accomplish organizational goals and strategy.
- Develop, operate, and maintain the organization's computing infrastructure.
- Develop, operate, and maintain enterprise applications.
- Protect information assets.
- Manage outsourcing relationships.

We will consider each of these functions in greater detail in the next sections of this chapter.

Figure 10-1 shows typical top-level reporting relationships. As you will learn in your management classes, organizational structure varies depending on the organization's size, culture, competitive environment, industry, and other factors. Larger organizations with independent divisions will have a group of senior executives like those

Davidson Distribution

(page 306)

GOALS

* Teach students about the need for organizational information systems standards.

* Discuss possible responses to a difficult management challenge.

WAYS TO STIMULATE STUDENT INVOLVEMENT

This employee's complaint is a common one. Many employees watch for sales of computers, software, and related gear. Sometimes, they are more up-to-date than IS personnel are.

The IS department has duties and obligations that complicate its job in many ways. We will describe and discuss many of those duties and obligations in this chapter. Consider some of the problems the IS department may face:

➤ **Suppose that half of the company uses Word and the other half uses WordPerfect. What complications do you foresee?**

➤ **What problems do you foresee if employees pick their own software?**

➤ **What problems do you foresee if employees pick their own computer equipment?**

➤ **If no one establishes hardware and software standards, what will happen in the organization?**

➤ **Who should be responsible for setting such standards?**

- **Consider, as an example, the responsibilities the IS department has for keeping the network up and running.**

- **In order to gain economies of scale, it needs to support common computer configurations. If some employees have a Mac with one set of communications protocols and others have Windows machines with other communications protocols, network administration becomes difficult and expensive.**

- **Heterogeneous computer environments can be supported, but they cause additional expense. The organization needs to decide whether the benefit of heterogeneous computers justifies the additional expense.**

➤ **If the network fails, who will be held responsible?**

➤ **If the network fails on a regular basis, who will be held responsible?**

➤ **Do your answers to the previous two questions justify strong standards for the computing environment?**

We can use this case to discuss a management challenge:

➤ **Suppose you agree with your employee. Suppose you believe that the computers are too expensive and that you should be able to buy them from your own sources. How do you respond?**

You can say you'll look into it and get back to the employee. Then, talk with the IS department to determine why they have these limits and why the prices are so high. There are probably factors involved that you do not know. If so, you can explain what you have learned to your employee.

If the policy still makes no sense, you can take it to your management. In no case, however, does it make sense to criticize your management or the IS department to your employee. That may raise your popularity in your department, at least in the short run, but it is highly unprofessional. That kind of behavior doesn't wear well over the long term.

➤ **In general, what do you do when you disagree with a policy of your management? If you tell your employee that you agree, you're being disloyal to the management team above you. If you state the management line, you are being dishonest to your own principles. What do you do?**

Try to understand the posture of your management. There may be factors that you do not understand. Talk to your manager. If you still disagree, attempt to initiate some change to the policy. If the policy is sufficiently important and management is unwilling to change it, you are in for some difficult times. For more important issues, such differences may cause you to change jobs.

➤ **Can you think of other examples, possibly not involving MIS, in which managers' beliefs may conflict with those of management?**

➤ **What should managers do in such situations?**

➤ **Does it ever make sense to side with the employees? Why or why not?**

Seldom does it make sense to side with your employees, even if you agree with them. You generate a culture of conspiracy within your group; ultimately that culture turns foul, and it may turn on you, too.

WRAP UP

➤ We'll consider the primary duties and responsibilities for IS management in this chapter. Once you've learned of these challenges, we'll return to this example. The knowledge you gain will help you respond to employee queries like this one.

➤ There will be times when you will be caught between your beliefs and management policy. Likely you will be caught by surprise—you won't be expecting the employee's question. It helps to think ahead of time about how you want to respond to such situations.

➤ This management challenge is a good topic for you to discuss among yourselves outside of class.

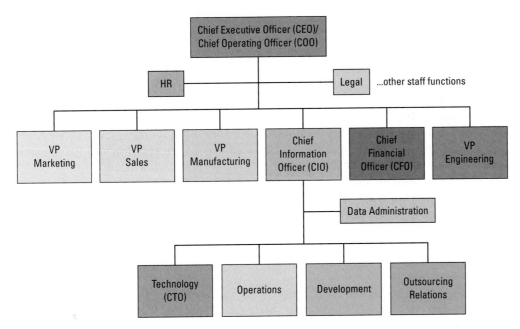

Figure 10-1
Typical Senior-Level
Reporting Relationships

shown here for each division. Smaller companies may combine some of these departments. Consider the structure in Figure 10-1 as a typical example.

The title of the principal manager of the IS department varies from organization to organization. A common title is **chief information officer**, or **CIO**. Other common titles are *vice president of information services, director of information services,* and, less commonly, *director of computer services.*

In Figure 10-1, the CIO, like other senior executives, reports to the chief executive officer (CEO), though sometimes these executives report to the chief operating officer (COO), who in turn reports to the CEO. In some companies, the CIO reports to the chief financial officer (CFO). That reporting arrangement may make sense if the primary information systems support accounting and finance activities. In organizations such as manufacturers that operate significant nonaccounting information systems, the arrangement shown in Figure 10-1 is more common and effective.

The structure of the IS department also varies among organizations. Figure 10-1 shows a typical IS department with four groups and a data administration staff function.

Most IS departments include a *technology* office that investigates new information systems technologies and determines how the organization can benefit from them. For example, today many organizations are investigating Web services technology and planning on how they can best use that technology to accomplish their goals and objectives. An individual called the **chief technology officer**, or **CTO**, often heads the technology group. The CTO sorts through new ideas and products to identify those that are most relevant to the organization. The CTO's job requires deep knowledge of information technology and the ability to envision how new IT will affect the organization over time.

The next group in Figure 10-1, *operations,* manages the computing infrastructure, including individual computers, computer centers, networks, and communications media. This group includes system and network administrators. As you will learn, an important function for this group is to monitor user experience and respond to user problems.

The third group in the IS department in Figure 10-1 is *development.* This group manages the process of creating new information systems as well as maintaining existing information systems. (Recall from Chapter 6 that in the context of information systems, maintenance means either removing problems or adapting existing information systems to support new features and functions.)

The size and structure of the development group depends on whether programs are developed in-house. If not, this department will be staffed primarily by systems analysts who work with users, operations, and vendors to acquire and install licensed software and to set up the system components around that software. If the organization develops programs in-house, then this department will include programmers, test engineers, technical writers, and other development personnel.

The last IS department group in Figure 10-1 is *outsourcing relations*. This group exists in organizations that have negotiated outsourcing agreements with other companies to provide equipment, applications, or other services. You will learn more about outsourcing later in this chapter.

Figure 10-1 also includes a *data administration* staff function. The purpose of this group is to protect data and information assets by establishing data standards and data management practices and policies.

There are many variations on the structure of the IS department shown in Figure 10-1. In larger organizations, the operations group may itself consist of several different departments. Sometimes, there is a separate group for data warehousing and data marts.

As you examine Figure 10-1, keep the distinction between IS and IT in mind. Information systems (IS) exist to help the organization achieve its goals and objectives. Information systems have the five components we have discussed throughout this text. Information technology (IT) is just technology. It concerns the products, techniques, procedures, and designs of computer-based technology. IT must be placed into the structure of an IS before an organization can use it.

In the next few sections, we will consider in greater detail each of the functions in Figure 10-1. Before we do that, however, consider the computer-use issues discussed in the *Ethics Guide* on page 309a.

■ Planning the Use of IT

We begin our discussion of IS functions with planning. Figure 10-2 lists the major IS planning functions.

Align Information Systems with Organizational Strategy

The first point in Figure 10-2 is obvious: Information systems must be aligned with organizational strategy. After all, the purpose of an information system is to help the organization accomplish its goals and objectives. No information system can do so without being aligned with the organization's strategy.

Think back, however, to the manager at Universal Electronics at the start of Chapter 7. He wanted to develop an information system to provide better purchase advice and assistance to customers. He wanted to do this because he saw that it could be done, and from his perspective, it seemed like a good idea. However, the competitive strategy of that organization was to be a cost leader, across the industry. As the COO pointed out, such a system would not have been consistent with the organization's strategy. "I'd be afraid someone might actually use it," was his statement.

Recall from Chapter 7 that according to Porter's competitive strategy model an organization can be a cost leader either across an industry or within an industry seg-

Figure 10-2
Planning the Use of IS/IT

- Align information systems with organizational strategy; maintain alignment as organization changes.
- Communicate IS/IT issues to executive group.
- Develop/enforce IS priorities within the IS department.
- Sponsor steering committee.

ment. Alternatively, an organization can differentiate its products or services either across the industry or within a segment. Whatever the organizational strategy, the CIO and the IS department must constantly be vigilant to align IS with it.

Maintaining alignment between IS direction and organizational strategy is a continuing process. As strategies change, as the organization merges with other organizations, as divisions are sold, IS must evolve along with the organization. *MIS in Use 10-1* details how the CIO of Cingular Wireless shepherded his organization through several realignments.

Unfortunately, however, IS infrastructure is not malleable. Changing a network requires time and resources. Integrating disparate information systems applications is even slower and more expensive. This fact is often not appreciated in the executive suite. Without a persuasive CIO, IS can be perceived as a drag on the organization's opportunities.

Communicate IS Issues to the Executive Group

This last observation leads to the second IS planning function in Figure 10-2. The CIO is the representative for IS and IT issues within the executive staff. She provides the IS perspective during discussions of problem solutions, proposals, and new initiatives.

MIS in Use 10-1

Cingular Wireless CIO Plans for Successes

SBC Communications and BellSouth merged in 2000 to form Cingular Wireless. In 2004, Cingular purchased AT&T Wireless, creating the largest U.S. wireless carrier, with more than 49 million customers and revenues in excess of $15.4 billion. A key player in the success of the activities was F. Thaddeus Arroyo, Cingular's CIO.

The CIO's first major challenge was blending the 1,400 different information systems and 60 separate call centers that existed when Cingular was born. For example, there were 11 different and separated billing systems. Since then, Cingular has consolidated those 11 systems into 1 and has replaced the 60 call centers with 20 new ones.

Cross-functional teams composed of both users and IT personnel played key roles in the consolidation. According to Arroyo, the IT professionals did not choose the computer systems for the users, but instead consulted with the cross-functional teams to make decisions. Of course, business didn't stop during this integration; in fact the wireless industry was expanding tremendously. Arroyo says, "During the growth period, we were rushing to keep the shelves stocked . . . It exasperated the complex infrastructure we had to support" (*cingular.com*, 2005).

To add complexity, in 2003 while the integration projects were underway, the Federal Communications Commission (FCC) created new regulations requiring the top 100 wireless companies to allow customers to keep their phone numbers when they changed carriers. The new regulation required Cingular to make major modifications to its billing and customer service applications—and to do so on short notice.

Even before the dust settled on that project, Cingular bought AT&T Wireless. Arroyo, as CIO, participated in months of merger preplanning involving more than 100 different and complex projects. For example, according to Arroyo, "the day after the deal was closed, over 70,000 employees were merged into one e-mail directory. Also, we had to merge our corporate intranets within 24 hours of closing" (Phillips, 2005). The company needed to accomplish dozens of other, similar projects as well.

In light of his accomplishments, Arroyo has earned numerous industry awards. In 2004, the magazine *Business 2.0* selected him as a member of its "Dream Team." His keys to success in managing all these programs are to build strong teams, to work hard, and "to plan, plan, plan."

Sources: cingular.com/download/business_solutions_cio.pdf (accessed March 2005); Bruce E. Phillips, "Thaddeus Arroyo, Chief Information Officer, Cingular Wireless," January 13, 2005, *hispanicengineer.com* (accessed July 2005).

ETHICS
GUIDE

Using the Corporate Computer

Suppose you work at a company that has the following computer use policy:

Computers, email, and the Internet are to be used primarily for official company business. Small amounts of personal email can be exchanged with friends and family, and occasional usage of the Internet is permitted, but such usage should be limited and never interfere with your work.

Suppose you are a manager and you learn that one of your employees has been engaged in the following activities:

1. Playing computer games during work hours
2. Playing computer games on the company computer before and after work hours
3. Responding to emails from an ill parent
4. Watching DVDs during lunch and other breaks
5. Sending emails to plan a party that involves mostly people from work
6. Sending emails to plan a party that involves no one from work
7. Searching the Web for a new car
8. Reading the news on CNN.com
9. Checking the stock market over the Internet

10. Bidding on items for personal use on eBay
11. Selling personal items on eBay
12. Paying personal bills online
13. Paying personal bills online when traveling on company business
14. Buying an airplane ticket for an ill parent over the Internet
15. Changing the content of a personal Web site
16. Changing the content of a personal business Web site
17. Buying an airplane ticket for a personal vacation over the Internet

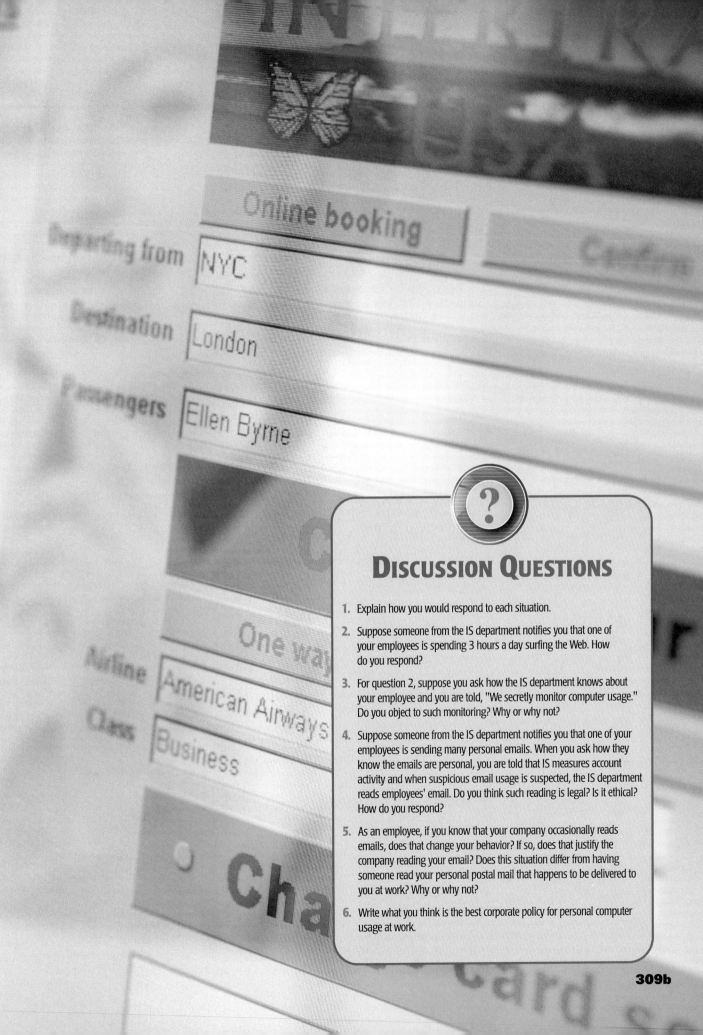

DISCUSSION QUESTIONS

1. Explain how you would respond to each situation.

2. Suppose someone from the IS department notifies you that one of your employees is spending 3 hours a day surfing the Web. How do you respond?

3. For question 2, suppose you ask how the IS department knows about your employee and you are told, "We secretly monitor computer usage." Do you object to such monitoring? Why or why not?

4. Suppose someone from the IS department notifies you that one of your employees is sending many personal emails. When you ask how they know the emails are personal, you are told that IS measures account activity and when suspicious email usage is suspected, the IS department reads employees' email. Do you think such reading is legal? Is it ethical? How do you respond?

5. As an employee, if you know that your company occasionally reads emails, does that change your behavior? If so, does that justify the company reading your email? Does this situation differ from having someone read your personal postal mail that happens to be delivered to you at work? Why or why not?

6. Write what you think is the best corporate policy for personal computer usage at work.

For example, when considering a merger, it is important that the company consider integration of information systems in the merged entities. This consideration needs to be addressed during the evaluation of the merger opportunity. Too often, such issues are not considered until after the deal has been signed. Such delayed consideration is a mistake, because the costs of the integration need to be factored into the economics of the purchase. Involving the CIO in high-level discussions is the best way to avoid such problems.

Develop Priorities and Enforce Within the IS Department

The next two IS planning functions in Figure 10-2 are related to each other. The CIO must ensure that priorities consistent with the overall organizational strategy are developed and communicated to the IS department. At the same time, she must also ensure that the department evaluates proposals and projects for using new technology in light of those communicated priorities.

Technology is seductive, particularly to IS professionals. The CTO may enthusiastically claim, "With XML Web services we can do this and this and this." Although true, the question that the CIO must continually ask is whether those new possibilities are consistent with the organization's strategy and direction.

Thus, the CIO must not only establish and communicate such priorities, but enforce them as well. The department must evaluate every proposal, at the earliest stage possible, as to whether it is consistent with the goals of the organization and aligned with its strategy.

Furthermore, no organization can afford to implement every good idea. Even projects that are aligned with the organization's strategy must be prioritized. The objective of everyone in the IS department must be to develop the most appropriate systems possible, given constraints on time and money. Well thought out and clearly communicated priorities are essential.

Sponsor the Steering Committee

The final planning function in Figure 10-2 is to sponsor the steering committee. A **steering committee** is a group of senior managers from the major business functions that works with the CIO to set the IS priorities and decide among major IS projects and alternatives.

The steering committee serves an important communication function between IS and the users. In the steering committee, information systems personnel can discuss potential IS initiatives and directions with the user community. At the same time, the steering committee provides a forum for users to express their needs, frustrations, and other issues they have with the IS department.

Typically, the IS department sets up the steering committee's schedule and agenda and conducts the meetings. The CEO and other members of the executive staff determine the membership of the steering committee.

▮ Managing the Computing Infrastructure

Managing the computing infrastructure is the most visible of all of the IS department's functions. In fact, the only interaction most employees have with the IS department is when they receive a computer or when they have problems using it. To many employees, the IS department is the "computer department"; they have little idea of the other important jobs the IS department performs behind the scenes.

This section focuses on the major tasks for this management function. We begin with another alignment issue. This issue, however, does not concern alignment with strategic direction, but rather alignment with infrastructure design.

Using the Ethics Guide

(page 309a)

GOALS

* Evaluate the ethics of employee activities in terms of a particular computer-use policy.

* Forewarn student that employers have the right to monitor computer usage, and many do.

* Develop techniques for managing employees' computer use.

BACKGROUND AND PRESENTATION STRATEGIES

This subject is a follow-on to the Ethics Guide in Chapter 5. This discussion differs from that one because it considers a specific computer-use policy. It also focuses on the student's role as a manager rather than as a computer user.

Many students use their computers in the classroom for email, Web surfing, and instant messaging. If that is the case in your classroom, you might consider the *following hoax:*

➤ **Did you know that the university monitors your use of its network? In fact, I receive a report after each class period on the emails you've sent, the Web sites you've visited, and the number of minutes you've spent in IM chat.**

➤ **Frankly, I'm a little shocked. The content of some of your emails is, well, embarrassing. . . . What is this world coming to, anyway?**

Pause. Let those statements settle in . . .

➤ **OK, those statements *are not true*, but they *could be at your job*. What do you think about that?**

  • **If you choose to spend your time in class surfing the Web or chatting with friends, that's your choice. You're wasting your time and money, but that's your choice.**

  • **However, if I were paying you to be here, if you were my employees, I'd want to know that you are actually engaged in accomplishing your job and not gossiping about your fellow employees with your sister-in-law across the state.**

➤ **How intrusive do you think an employer should be in making assessments about computer use?**

➤ **Suppose you manage a department and you suspect your employees are wasting time on their computers at work. What would you do?**

➤ **What do you think causes employees to waste time on their computers at work? Would they be wasting time staring out the window, if they did not have a computer?**

By the way, I disagree with that last justification. The Web, IM, email, and computer games are attractive, even addictive, in ways that staring out the window is not.

➤ **In theory at least, if employees have been given appropriate assignments, and if there is regular follow-up on employee progress on those assignments, then employees ought not to have time to waste on their computers. They should be so busy doing their work that there isn't time to surf or chat.**

➤ **This may be naïve, but excessive personal computer use is a symptom of poorly directed or poorly motivated employees. Get everyone in the right job, get them excited about what they're doing, follow up on their progress on a regular basis, and excessive personal computer use will not be a problem.**

➤ **Some senior managers will agree with that statement, too. So, if your department is known to have many employees excessively using their computers for personal work, that fact will reflect negatively on your management ability.**

On August 11, 2005, the blogger Michelle Malkin received a series of abusive, racist, and sexist emails in response to one of her blog entries. One of those exceedingly offensive emails was generated by a legal secretary from his desk at a law office in Los Angeles. The email system automatically generated a trailer that included the name of the law firm. Ms. Malkin posted the abusive email in its entirety, including the trailer with the firm's name, on her Web site. The law firm was inundated with criticism for its employee's behavior. The employee was promptly fired, but the public relations scandal continued to plague the firm for weeks.

➤ **If you managed that law firm, how would you have responded to this situation?**

⑦ SUGGESTED RESPONSES FOR DISCUSSION QUESTIONS

1. This is a long list of situations. One approach is to ask the students to group the situations into categories

according to the severity of the violation. Three possible categories are: *OK, Questionable,* and *Definitely Wrong.* I'd put the following in the *Definitely Wrong* category: situations a, f, g, k, l, and p. In the *OK* category, I'd put situations c, e, and m. I'd place all of the others in the *Questionable* category.

It will be interesting to see how your students respond to this!

2. If I was told that an employee was spending 3 hours a day on the Web, I'd evaluate that employee's recent performance. I'd find out what jobs the employee was supposed to have been doing and find out how well those jobs were done. Clearly, something's wrong. I'd talk with the employee. Perhaps this person is ready for new responsibilities; perhaps the employee has lost interest in work. I'd try to get to the root of the problem and make a change.

3. I personally find secret monitoring of employees computer use a bit creepy, but the employer *is* paying for the employees' time and for the equipment. I grant an employer's right to perform such monitoring. I think that the monitoring ought to be done in such a way, however, so as to minimize the intrusion on the employees' privacy. If someone is using the Web for personal business, neither I nor the company needs to know what sites were visited. Similarly, the company may monitor email, but the intrusion should be limited to the minimum possible needed to accomplish the company's goals.

4. It is certainly legal for companies to read employees' emails, and because the employer is paying for the employees' time and the computer and network equipment, I think it's ethical. When employees use their employer's equipment for personal use, I believe they give up any right to privacy. But, see the limitations stated for question 3.

5. I personally dislike a style of management that relies on the hammer of discovery to limit employees' misuse of computers. I'd prefer to manage by giving people work they want to do, by creating tight but not impossible schedules, by following up with them on progress, and by focusing on what they *should be* doing rather than on what the *ought not* to be doing.

But, my management experience is limited to managing highly skilled, motivated, ambitious employees in the software business. When employees must spend hours performing dreary, repetitive work, the motivational situation is entirely different. I can see how the hammer might need to be used in those circumstances.

I think the postal mail situation is different. For one, postal mail uses few company resources. Also, an employee reading a single letter is different from an employee sending out hundreds of emails.

6. I like the policy at the start of the guide. One could say it should be more specific, but the problem with that is that employees will be able to say about some behavior, "Well, that's not on the list." I think the key phrase is *never interfere with your work.* One could strengthen that statement by specifically excluding the use of the computer for personal business. Some of the wording depends on other HR policies as well.

WRAP UP

➤ **As a future employee, be forewarned that employers have the right, both legally and ethically, to monitor your computer use. Many do.**

➤ **As a future manager, consider how you will deal with employees who are misusing their computer resources. Know the organization's official policy.**

➤ **Understand, too, that excessive personal computer use by your employees reflects negatively on your management ability.**

➤ **If possible, manage positively. Give the employees sufficient work that they will not have time to misuse computer resources. Follow up with schedules and deadlines. Make sure that missed schedules are not caused by computer misuse.**

Align Infrastructure Design with Organizational Structure

The structure of the IS infrastructure must mirror the structure of the organization. A highly controlled and centralized organization needs highly controlled and centralized information systems. A decentralized organization with autonomous operating units requires decentralized information systems that facilitate autonomous activity.

To understand this further, consider Figure 10-3, which shows a distributed printing company that grew through a process of acquisition. This company expanded to new geographic locations by acquiring printers in different cities. As each entity was acquired, the company kept it as an independent operating center. The company held plant managers accountable for the performance of their own facilities, and these managers had considerable operational independence.

Initially, the IS department attempted to develop a centralized order-management system for use by all plants in the organization. Figure 10-4 (page 312) shows this situation. The company developed a customer order database at a data center in Denver and required all of the independent plants to process their orders through the centralized order-management system.

Even though all of the printing plants had been producing essentially the same products, there were small but significant differences in the ways that each plant prioritized and processed its orders. However, with the centralized system, the plant managers were unable to implement their own production-scheduling processes. Dissatisfaction with the centralized system was rampant.

At first, the IS department attempted to remedy the problems, but within a few weeks it was clear that the autonomous managers were never going to be satisfied

Figure 10-3
Distributed Check-Printing Company

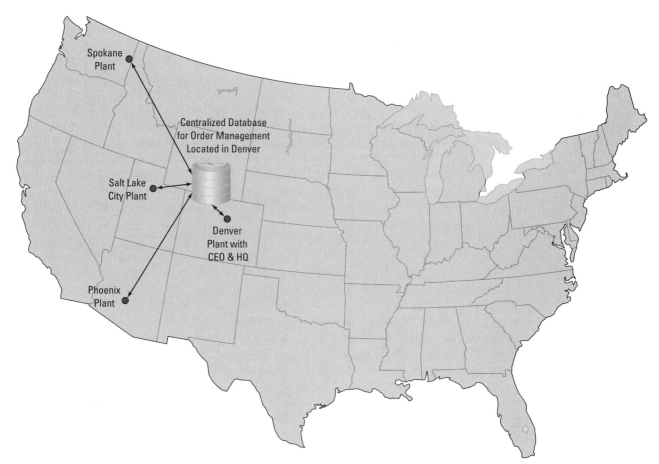

Figure 10-4
Problematic Centralized IS

with a centralized system. They wanted control over all aspects of the ordering and manufacturing process.

Accordingly, the IS department abandoned the concept of a single, centralized order entry system and instead developed a set of distributed order-management systems, as shown in Figure 10-5. Each of these systems was under the control of the local plant manager. The distributed systems did send order and production data to a centralized facility for the production of consolidated reports, but the control of the order entry, scheduling, and manufacturing remained with the local plant managers.

The system in Figure 10-5 was more successful than the centralized system because it was consistent with the underlying management style and philosophy of the organization. In fact, the system in Figure 10-4 should never have been developed. At the time it was envisioned, the IS department was buried deep in the accounting department, and it had little visibility to the rest of the company. After this problem developed, the company raised IS in the management hierarchy and instituted a steering committee. Close collaboration between the CIO and the steering committee prohibited the design of any future system that was so greatly misaligned with the organization.

Create, Operate, and Maintain Computing Infrastructure

Three more tasks in managing the computing infrastructure are to:

- Create and maintain infrastructure for end-user computing.
- Create, operate, and maintain networks.
- Create, operate, and maintain data centers, data warehouses, and data marts.

Those are *huge* tasks.

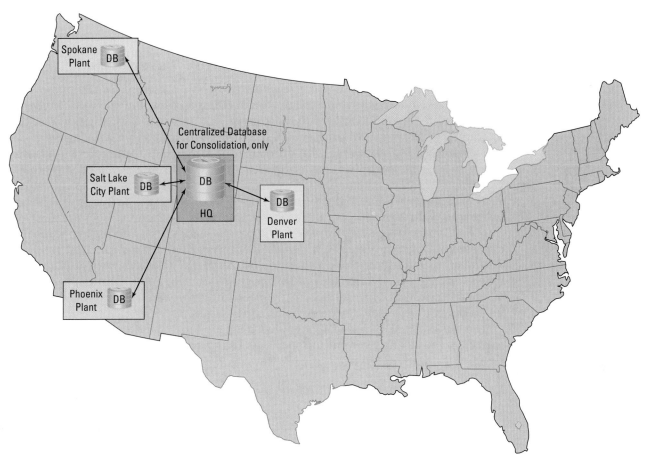

Figure 10-5
Decentralized Order-Management System

They are enormous jobs even for a mid-sized company like that shown in Figure 10-5. Consider just end-user computing. Almost every employee in that company has a computer. Each computer has a set of programs. From time to time, those computers need to be upgraded, and the software that resides on them needs to be upgraded as well. When Microsoft ships a new version of Windows or Office, the IS department immediately has user requests for the new version. (Also, it is likely to receive requests *not* to receive the new version.) How do you install a new version of Windows on 1,000 computers? On 5,000? Keep in mind that you have limited resources and cannot afford to send a trained technician to every user's computer.

Alternatively, suppose the steering committee decides the company needs to invest in a new XML-based supply chain management application. A different variation of your computer network protocol is required to support the new capability. This requirement means that you have to install a new version of your networking software on every computer, regardless of whether the computer will be involved in the SCM. How do you proceed?

Suppose you develop an automated process to upgrade all of the users' computers at night, when they are not in use. Your automated procedure works fine until it encounters a computer that has been modified by its user. She decided, secretly, to use Linux rather than Windows. Because of the difference, your automated upgrade program crashes. The IS department has to send a specialist to Phoenix to find out what went wrong with the install.

We will not address the management of the network and data centers here. The subject is too large and complicated and is not directly related to your future business career. Suffice it to say that when you see a diagram like that in Figure 9-18 (page 283), keep in mind that the IS department has to create, operate, and maintain the computers, software, and personnel in the data warehouse and all of the data marts.

Establish Technology and Product Standards

The failure of the network software upgrade points out the need for technology and product standards. The IS department cannot afford to allow every computer user to have her own personal configuration. Doing so not only would mean difficulties for upgrading computers and programs, but it also might mean that some users' computers become incompatible with others. For example, a document created using WordPerfect on a Macintosh may not be readable by a computer that uses Microsoft Word on a Windows machine. For this example, there is a way to import and export such documents, but the IS department has higher priorities for its budget than training users how to do it.

Users' computing needs vary according to the work they do. In response, most IS departments have developed a set of three or four different standard configurations. The most basic configuration might have just email and a Web browser. Another configuration might have Microsoft Office programs as well, and a third might have an extended version of Office, email, and some analysis software. A fourth configuration might be created for software development personnel.

No standard will please all of the users, all of the time. The IS department needs to work with the steering committee and other user groups to ensure the standards are effective for most of the users.

Track Problems and Monitor Resolutions

The IS department provides the computing infrastructure as a service to users. As in any service organization, a system must exist to record user problems and monitor their resolution. This system is no different from other customer service applications we have discussed.

In a well-run IS department, when a user reports a problem the department assigns a tracking number, and the problem enters a queue for service. Normally, problems are prioritized on the basis of how critical they are to the user's work. Higher-priority items are serviced first. When the item is placed in the queue, the user is told its priority and given an approximate date for resolution. When the problem is fixed, it is removed from the queue. If the problem is still not resolved, it reenters the queue at a higher priority.

The CIO and the manager of the computer operations group monitor the queue, the average length of time an item remains in the queue, the number of nonresolutions, and so forth. In the future, if you, as a user, encounter such a system, it may seem overly bureaucratic. In fact, it is a sign of good IS management.

Manage Computing Infrastructure Staff

Finally, the IS department also must manage the computing infrastructure staff. The department's employees must be organized, hired, trained, directed, evaluated, and promoted, just as with any other corporate function.

The organization of a typical operations department is shown in Figure 10-6. This generic chart has subdepartments for the network, computer center, data warehouse, and user support. In a large organization, these functions might be further divided as well. In particular, a separate department might staff the help-desk function. Sometimes operations groups have specialists for particular applications. There might be, for example, an ERP support group.

Typical job types are shown beneath each subgroup. As you can imagine, each of these specialists needs recurring training. The operations staff must constantly update its knowledge to keep up with upgrades in both hardware and software products. Consider the need for training, coupled with the need for 24/7 operations, coupled with the problems that can occur when a change is first made to, say, the

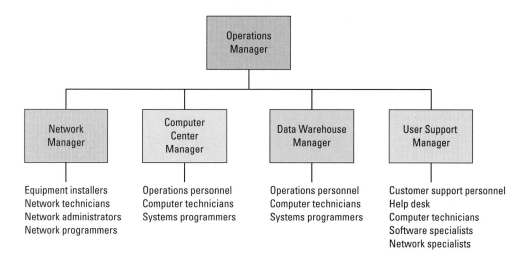

Figure 10-6
Organization of a Typical IS
Operations Group

network. Scheduling employees in such an environment is a complex task and a constant problem.

▓ Managing Enterprise Applications

In addition to managing the computing infrastructure, the IS department manages enterprise applications as well. The definition of what constitutes an enterprise application varies among organizations. In some organizations, the IS department manages every application, including individual and workgroup applications. In others, individuals and workgroups manage their own applications, with possible support from the IS department. In the latter case, the term *enterprise applications* is interpreted narrowly to mean applications that span more than one department, such as some functional applications as well as ERP, EAI, and SCM applications.

Develop New Applications

Figure 10-7 lists major application management functions. As shown, the IS department manages the development of new applications. The process of creating a new application begins when the IS department aligns its priorities with the organization's strategy. Using priorities that arise from that alignment, the IS department develops system plans and proposals and submits them to the steering committee (and possibly other executive groups) for approval. Once the company has selected and approved a system for development, it then initiates a development process.

We discussed application development processes in Chapter 6, and we will not repeat that discussion here. Realize, however, that all development processes are variations on the theme of *requirements, design, implementation*. The nature and amount of systems development work depends on the degree to which applications components are outsourced.

In all cases, however, the company will conduct the requirements phase in-house. Each organization has its own strategy, priorities, and direction, and those unique

- Manage development of new applications.
- Maintain legacy systems.
- Adapt systems to changing requirements.
- Track user problems and monitor fixes.
- Integrate applications.
- Manage development staff.

Figure 10-7
Managing Enterprise
Applications

requirements need to be developed and documented, even if major portions of the system will be outsourced.

The rest of the work to be done depends on the degree of reliance on outsource vendors. We discuss variations of outsource scope in the outsourcing section later in this chapter.

Maintain Systems

In addition to managing the development of new applications, the IS department has the responsibility for system maintenance. As stated in Chapter 6, *maintenance* means either to fix the system to do what it was supposed to do in the first place or to adapt the system to changed requirements. Either way, the IS department prioritizes maintenance work and implements changes in accordance with those priorities and budget. It may do the maintenance work in-house or outsource it.

Developing information systems is a service that is provided to the rest of the enterprise. Accordingly, the IS department must have a means to track user issues and problems, prioritize them, and record their resolution. Although such a tracking and monitoring system is similar to the same function provided for infrastructure management, the department usually uses different systems for these two functions. In fact, for larger organizations each major enterprise application has its own problem-tracking and resolution system. For example, ERP might have one system, SCM a second, and HR a third.

Companies need special maintenance activities to support legacy systems. A **legacy information system** is one that has outdated technologies and techniques but is still used, despite its age. Legacy systems arise because organizations cannot afford to replace an IS just because better technology has been developed.

Usually, legacy system maintenance entails adapting those systems to new tax laws, accounting procedures, or other requirements that must be implemented for the legacy system to be relevant and useful. Although the plan is always to replace legacy systems eventually, the question is how to keep them working until they are replaced.

Integrate Enterprise Applications

The third element in Figure 10-7 concerns enterprise application integration. As discussed at the end of Chapter 7, EAI requires developers to create intermediary layers of software, and possibly intermediary databases, to enable the integration of disparate systems. Because such work requires knowledge of many different systems, including legacy systems, companies usually conduct such work in-house rather than outsource it.

Manage Development Staff

The last management function in Figure 10-7 is to manage the development staff. Figure 10-8 shows the structure of a typical development group. Of course, this structure will be simpler for smaller organizations or for organizations that do little in-house development. As stated in Chapter 6, a computer programmer or developer typically is both a software designer as well as a programmer.

Sustaining-application developers work on existing applications. Typically, sustaining developers have fewer years of experience or less knowledge than new-application developers. Figure 10-8 shows sustaining developers and new-application developers as belonging to separate development teams. This arrangement varies considerably depending on the complexity of both sustaining and new development projects.

Product quality assurance (PQA) engineers specialize in the testing of software. In many cases, PQA engineers also are programmers who develop automated testing suites. Because applications must be thoroughly tested when they are modified, test automation is a great boon to productivity.

The final group in Figure 10-8 is technical writers who develop product installation instructions, help text, and other support documentation.

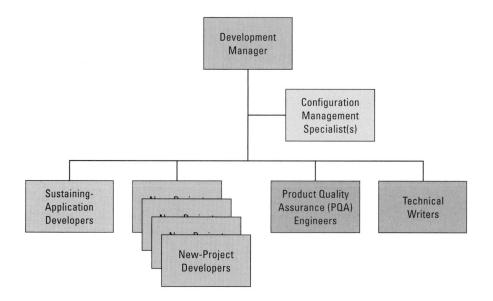

Figure 10-8
Organization of a Typical IS
Development Group

Development personnel such as programmers, test engineers, and writers can pose special security risks, as discussed in the *Security Guide* on page 317a.

Administer Data

Data and database administration functions sound similar, but actually are quite different. Typically, the term **data administration** describes a function that pertains to *all* of an organization's data assets. The term **database administration** describes a function that pertains to a *particular* database. A typical larger organization would have one data administrator and several database administrators—say, one for the ERP database, one for the SCM database, one for HR database, and possibly others as well.

The terminology *data administrator* and *database administrator* implies that there is a single person for each role. Normally, each data or database administrator has a staff of several employees. The manager of the group is called the *data administrator* or *database administrator,* and the staff members work in the office of data administration or database administration.

We discussed database administration in Chapter 4. Here we will address the organization-wide function of data administration. We will discuss the four primary responsibilities shown in Figure 10-9 next.

Define Data Standards

Data standards are definitions, or metadata, for data items shared across the organization. They describe the name, official definition, usage, relationship to other data items, processing restrictions, version, security code, format and other features of data items that are shared across the organization. Sometimes data standards include the *data owner*, which is a department within the organization that is most concerned with that data item and that controls changes to the definition of that data item.

On the surface, setting data standards may seem like an unnecessary clerical operation. It is not. In fact, the lack of documented and known data standards causes considerable duplication of effort, data inconsistency, wasted labor, and processing errors.

Enterprise-wide function to:
- Define data standards.
- Maintain data dictionary.
- Define data policies.
- Establish disaster-recovery plan.

Figure 10-9
Data Administration

Secure Development

A self-validating *number* has one or more digits that verify the accuracy of the other digits. For example, consider a part number with four digits. That part number can be made into a self-validating number by summing the four digits and appending the sum to the account number. Thus, the account number 1234 would become 123410, because 10 is the sum of $1 + 2 + 3 + 4$. If anyone ever enters the part number 123411, we immediately know there is an error because $1 + 2 + 3 + 4$ does not equal 11. Most self-validating digits are more complex than this scheme, but you get the idea.

Vendors frequently use self-validating numbers to limit usage of products or electronic services. When you install Microsoft Windows, for example, you supply a serial number, which is a self-validating number. The install program knows the algorithm for checking the number, and if you enter any invalid sequence, it will be able to determine that. (Of course, you might get lucky and accidentally enter a valid number, but the odds of doing so are minor, given the complex algorithms Microsoft uses.) Such numbers are also used to limit access to Web sites.

DISCUSSION QUESTIONS

1. Suppose you work for a financial institution that uses a self-validating account number scheme. Consider the following threats.

   Situation A: Someone steals your scheme and posts it on a publicly accessible Web site.

   Situation B: Someone steals your scheme and uses it to steal money from your clients' accounts.

   How will you find out about situation A? How will you find out about situation B? How will your respond to each? Which is the greater threat?

2. Suppose an investigation into the theft in question 1 reveals that the self-validating number scheme was stolen and publicly released by one of your development personnel (a programmer, test engineer, or technical writer). What actions do you take?

3. Suppose the self-validating program was developed using the SDLC development methodology discussed in Chapter 6. What characteristics of that process make tight security problematic when developing such programs? What can be done to reduce that risk?

4. Does your vulnerability change if you choose an independent software vendor to create the program for creating self-validating numbers? Does it matter if the vendor is located in a foreign country? How do you respond to these risks?

5. What general conclusions can you draw from your answers to these questions?

SELF
DESTRUCT
:05

To understand why, consider a data item as simple as *sku_description*. *SKU* stands for stock-keeping unit, and *sku_description* is a data item for holding the description of each part. But what is it? Without a data standard, one application might include component parts in the description, whereas another might place the component parts in a different data item. Without a standard definition, two different applications will refer to the same item with different names. For example, is a *sku_description* the same as *sku_item_desc*? Assume you are a sustaining developer and you encounter a data item named *sku_desc_2002*. How does that data item relate to the data item *current_sku_description*? Without a data standard, developers will waste considerable time trying to reconcile these differences.

Maintain the Data Dictionary

To resolve problems like those for the SKU descriptions, almost every organization maintains a data dictionary. A **data dictionary** is a file or database that contains data definitions. It contains an entry for each standard data item. Typically, the entries include the item's name, a description, the standard data format, remarks, and possibly examples, as shown in Figure 10-10.

As noted many times before, information systems evolve as business requirements change. The data administrator must maintain the data dictionary to keep it current. Obsolete entries must be removed, new items inserted, and changes recorded. Without maintenance, the data dictionary, an essential tool, loses its value. Notice, for example, the two versions of *sku_description* in Figure 10-10.

Define Data Policies

Data administration is also concerned with the creation and dissemination of data policies. Such policies vary in scope. Examples of broad policies are:

- "We will not share identifying customer data with another organization."
- "We will not share nonidentifying customer data with another organization without the approval of the legal department."
- "Employee data are never to be released to anyone other than the employee without the approval of the human resources department."

Narrower data policies pertain to particular data items. An example is: "We will maintain data about past employees for at least 7 years after their last day of work."

Of course, the data administrator does not create data policy on his own, out of the blue. Instead, the data administrator works with senior executives, the legal department, functional department managers, and others to determine them. Once the company has created data policies, the data administrator then communicates

Data Item Name	Data Item Description	Standard Data Format	Remarks	Example
sku_description	A description of a stock-keeping unit.	Character; length 1,000	Does not include component parts.	3/16-inch flathead screw, 20 tpi, stainless steel
sku_desc_2002	A description of a stock-keeping unit prior to the parts reorganization in August 2002.	Character; length 500	No longer used. All descriptions should have been converted to the current_sku_description.	
current_sku_description	A description of a stock-keeping unit after the parts reorganization in August 2002.	Character; length 1,000	Does not include component parts.	3/16-inch flathead screw, 20 tpi, stainless steel

Note: Other fields are common. Some data dictionaries record the data owner, aliases for the data item, security requirements, and additional data.

Figure 10-10
Example of Data Dictionary Fields

You Be the Guide

Using the Security Guide
(page 317a)

GOAL

✳ Introduce students to the need for security management for software development.

BACKGROUND AND PRESENTATION STRATEGIES

This guide uses self-checking numbers as an example of proprietary knowledge that must be embedded in program code. Use it as a means to set up the need for special measures when developing sensitive program code.

In the days before licensed software, when companies developed their own payroll, accounts receivable, accounts payable, and other software that directly managed the negotiable assets, protecting the source code was an important and challenging task. There was always the possibility that someone could change the code for personal financial gain. One of the common tasks during an audit of the software was to ensure that the source and object code matched. If not, it was possible that unknown changes had been made to the object code. Organizations that are not using licensed software still need to perform such checks on a periodic basis.

One of the advantages of licensing packaged software is that these considerations lose importance. Of course, they have become even more important for vendors of licensed software, who must ensure that none of their released products contain unauthorized changes.

Security can also be a reason to outsource business functions like payroll. If payroll checks are prepared in-house, there is always the chance for unauthorized changes or for computer operations personnel to conspire with other employees for mutual gain. By outsourcing payroll, a company can avoid many such problems.

The open nature of modern systems development conflicts with the need for secure development of proprietary features and functions. Open requirements meetings, user reviews, design and code reviews, and substantial testing activities require the involvement of many employees. However, involving many employees increases the risk of loss of the proprietary scheme. See question 3.

In light of this conflict, the development of proprietary aspects of information systems requires special development strategies and careful management.

SUGGESTED RESPONSES FOR DISCUSSION QUESTIONS

1. You'll find out about situation A when someone notifies you that the scheme is publicly available on the Web. For situation B, you'll find out when one of your customers reports a theft and you perform an investigation to determine how the theft occurred.

Your response depends on how the software is designed. You might begin by asking the students for general ideas:

➤ **In general what are the chief requirements when such a theft occurs?**

I think the general requirements, in order of priority, are:

• Shut down systems or take other action to limit future losses.

• Repair systems to restore capability.

• Determine the full extend of the loss and contact customers as required.

• Determine how the theft occurred and change development procedures to prevent further, similar losses.

Particular responses depend on how the scheme is implemented and used. For example, the software may be designed so that no software changes need to be made; a new scheme can be implemented by changing system data that is input to the programs. Or, it may be necessary to make program code changes. The latter will take time and require careful control.

It is difficult to say which threat is greater. If thousands upon thousands of people used the data on the Web site, the loss could be substantial. But, at least you would know about it. In the second situation, someone may have been stealing from your clients for a long time, unknown to you. The damage might be less in monetary amounts, but more serious in terms of your reputation.

2. If department staff personnel were involved, call your corporate legal department and human resources. Do nothing about the employee until you have formulated a plan with those professionals. Your organization may decide to bring in outside law enforcement or outside investigative consultants.

After dealing with the employee, determine how the event occurred and change development processes, as necessary, to prevent future occurrences.

3. Problematic SDLC characteristics: open requirements; user review of open requirements; possibly many people involved in design, programming, and testing. Overcome these characteristics by isolating the development of sensitive portions of the code. The general development community need know nothing more than that there is a self-validating number module. Keep the development of that module to as few people as possible. Isolate testing as well as program design and development.

4. Yes, if you choose an independent software vendor to create the program for creating self-validating numbers, the vulnerability changes. You have less control, but also less responsibility. A key element is to describe these risks and attendant responsibilities in your contract and to be certain that your vendor has sufficient resources to cover its financial obligations in the event of a loss caused by it. Involving a foreign company raises the risk, but this is a good question for the students, especially if you have foreign students in your class:

➤ **How does involving a company in a foreign country change the situation for a U.S. company?**

I can think of three possible consequences: the company's rights may be limited by foreign law; the consequences of the loss will be harder to manage; and the event may be more difficult to investigate.

5. Development of software and systems that involve proprietary knowledge or that require security for other reasons is difficult and risky. The company may need to change the systems development process. The company may need to develop sensitive aspects of the software system in isolation. The risks vary depending on whether program code is developed in-house or outsourced. Either way, however, there is risk that needs to be managed. When developing secure systems, it might be worth checking with human resources and legal about the need for specially written employment contracts. Special addendums to organizational insurance may be needed, as well.

WRAP UP

➤ **We have discussed the example of the development and loss of a self-checking number scheme. Consider this scheme as an example of proprietary and sensitive data that are sometimes required in software and systems.**

➤ **The development of such sensitive software may require a special development process.**

➤ **To those of you in accounting, when such software and systems are developed, the controls on their development and use may require special attention during either internal or external audits.**

them to appropriate departments and employees. Data policies also are dynamic; they need to be changed as new corporate policies and new systems are developed and as new laws are created.

Plan for Disaster Recovery

Disaster-recovery planning is the creation of systems for recovering data and systems in the event of a catastrophe such as an earthquake, flood, terrorist event, or other significant processing disruption. We will address this function further in the next chapter when we discuss computer security.

As you can tell from the preceding discussion, managing information systems is a broad and complicated task. Some organizations choose to outsource one or more IS functions. We will consider that alternative in the next section.

Outsourcing

Outsourcing is the process of hiring another organization to perform a service. Outsourcing is done to save costs, to gain expertise, and to free up management time.

The father of modern management, Peter Drucker, is reputed to have said, "Your back room is someone else's front room." For instance, the employee cafeteria is a back room; in most companies, running the cafeteria is not an essential function for business success. Universal Electronics (Chapters 7 and 8), for example, wants to be the cost leader in electronics sales. It does not want to run a cafeteria. Using Drucker's sentiment, Universal is better off hiring another company, one that specializes in food services, to run the cafeteria.

Because food service is some company's front room, that company will be better able to provide a quality product at a fair price. Hiring that company will also free Universal's management from attention on the cafeteria. Food quality, chef scheduling, plastic fork acquisition, waste disposal, and so on, will all be another company's concern. Universal can focus on cost leadership in electronics.

Video

Outsourcing Information Systems

Many companies today have chosen to outsource portions of their information systems activities. Figure 10-11 lists popular reasons for doing so. Consider each major group of reasons.

Management Advantages

First, outsourcing can be an easy way to gain expertise. Suppose, for example, that an organization wants to upgrade its thousands of user computers on a cost-effective basis. To do so, the organization would need to develop expertise in automated software installation, unattended installations, remote support, and other measures that can be

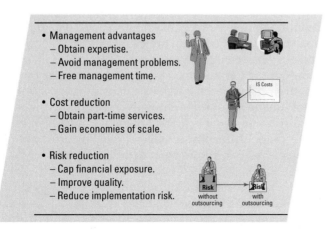

Figure 10-11
Popular Reasons for
Outsourcing IS Services

used to improve the efficiency of software management. Developing such expertise is expensive, and it is not in the company's strategic direction. Efficient installation of software to thousands of computers is not in the "front room." Consequently, the organization might choose to hire a specialist company to perform this service.

Another reason for outsourcing is to avoid management problems. Suppose Universal wants to develop Web services so as to share its inventory data with its suppliers. How can Universal hire the appropriate staff? It doesn't even know if it needs a C++ programmer or an HTML programmer. Even if the company could find and hire the right staff, how would it manage them? How does Universal create a good work environment for a C++ programmer, when it doesn't even know what such a person does? Consequently, Universal may hire an outside firm to develop and maintain the Web service just to avoid having to address such management problems.

Similarly, some companies choose to outsource to save management time and attention. Suppose Universal does substantial business over the Web and needs a large Web farm to process the workload. Even if the company knows how to manage a Web farm, acquiring the appropriate computers, installing the necessary software, tuning the software for better performance, and hiring and managing the staff will all require significant management time.

Note, too, that the management time required is not just that of the direct manager of the activity. It is also time from more senior managers who approve the purchase and hiring requisitions for that activity. And, those senior managers will need to devote the time necessary to understand enough about Web farms to approve or reject the requisitions. Outsourcing saves both direct and indirect management time.

Cost Reduction

Other common reasons for choosing to outsource concern cost reductions. With outsourcing, organizations can obtain part-time services. An office of 25 attorneys does not need a full-time network administrator. It does need network administration, but only in small amounts. By outsourcing that function, the office of attorneys can obtain network administration in the small amounts needed.

Another benefit of outsourcing is to gain economies of scale. If 25 organizations develop their own payroll applications in-house, then when the tax law changes, 25 different groups will have to learn the new law, change their software to meet the law, test the changes, and write the documentation explaining the changes. However, if those same 25 organizations outsource to the same payroll vendor, then that vendor can make all of the adjustments once, and the cost of the change can be amortized over all of them (thus lowering the cost that the vendor can charge).

Risk Reduction

Another reason for outsourcing is to reduce risk. First, outsourcing can cap financial risk. In a typical outsourcing contract, the outsource vendor will agree to provide, say, computer workstations with certain software connected via a particular network. Typically, each new workstation will have a fixed cost, say, $3,500 per station. The company's management team may believe that there is a good chance that they can provide workstations at a lower unit cost, but there is also the chance that they'll get in over their heads and have a disaster. If so, the cost per computer could be much higher than $3,500. Outsourcing caps that financial risk and leads to greater budgetary stability.

Second, outsourcing can reduce risk by ensuring a certain level of quality, or avoiding the risk of having substandard quality. A company that specializes in food service knows what to do to provide a certain level of quality. It has the expertise to ensure, for example, that only healthy food is served. So, too, a company that specializes in, say, Web-server hosting, knows what to do to provide a certain level of service for a given workload.

Note that there is no guarantee that outsourcing will provide a certain level of quality or quality better than could be achieved in-house. Universal might get lucky and hire a great chef. So, too, it might get lucky and hire the world's best Web farm manager. But, in general, a professional outsourcing firm knows what to do to avoid giving everyone food poisoning or to avoid 2 days of downtime on the Web servers. And, if that minimum level of quality is not provided, it is easier to hire another vendor than it is to fire and rehire internal staff.

Finally, organizations choose to outsource IS in order to reduce implementation risk. Hiring an outside vendor reduces the risk of picking the wrong hardware or the wrong software, using the wrong network protocol, or implementing tax law changes incorrectly. Outsourcing gathers all of these risks into the risk of choosing the right vendor. Once the company has chosen the vendor, further risk management is up to that vendor. *MIS in Use 10-2* illustrates the services of one particular outsource vendor, Hewitt Associates.

However, not everyone agrees on the desirability of outsourcing, as described in the *Opposing Forces Guide* on page 321a.

International Outsourcing

Many firms headquartered in the United States have chosen to outsource overseas. Microsoft and Dell, for example, have outsourced major portions of their customer support activities to companies outside the United States. India is a popular source

---

MIS in Use 10-2

Hewitt Associates, Inc.

Hewitt Associates is an Illinois-based company that provides outsourcing services, primarily for human resources (HR). The company, founded in 1940, initially provided employee benefits administration. Over the years it expanded to offer products and services for HR administration, healthcare, payroll, and retirement programs. Hewitt employs more than 19,000 people in 35 countries, and revenues in 2004 exceeded $2.2 billion.

Most of Hewitt's customers are large. According to Steve Unterberger, HR Outsourcing Technology Leader at Hewitt, "We focus, specialize, on large employer markets, which we define to be 15,000 to 20,000 employees and higher, all the way up to 150,000, 250,000 employees." Unterberger claims these companies choose Hewitt because it can provide HR systems at less cost and with a higher level of service than companies can do for themselves. Further, outsourcing requires no capital investment.

The demand for HR outsourcing grew dramatically in the last half of 2004. Unterberger believes demand accelerated due to Hewitt's growing reputation: "There are enough success stories for the really early adopter clients, so those who typically sit on the sidelines have talked to those folks, have gotten success stories and are now ready to engage, not as bleeding edge but more of the mainstream and leading edge."

The typical sales cycle is from 3 to 12 months, and during that period, Unterberger says prospective customers need to be reassured on three key factors. First, they want a commitment for a significant percentage reduction in current costs. Prospects need to know that they will not be "nickel-and-dimed or surprised." Second, they need to believe that Hewitt can provide HR services that will be effective within their particular company culture. Large clients like Hewitt's are unique, and they need to understand how Hewitt's HR services will work for them. Third, prospective customers want to know that outsourcing will provide new expertise and improved service. According to Unterberger, "You don't just put new shirts on the same old people."

One major challenge is that the people who contract with Hewitt are the very people whose jobs will be most changed. Says Unterberger, "It's a very complicated chain of interaction to get the full benefit of these services deployed. It takes a while. It takes some persistence. It takes some good communication skills and good communication programs."

When interviewed in January 2005, Unterberger projected a bright future: "We'll see more fence-sitters getting into the market. The trend we have now—which I call surf's up—will continue. The waves are going to ride pretty high for the next 12 to 18 months. I don't think this is an abnormal spike. More and more people in the mainstream are getting into this."

Source: Originally published at *www.EcommerceTimes.com/sotry/39468. html.* Reproduced with permission of E-Commerce Times ® and ECT News Network. Copyright 2005 ECT News Network. All rights reserved.

Is Outsourcing Fool's Gold?

People are kidding themselves. It sounds so good—just pay a fixed, known amount to some vendor, and all your problems go away. Everyone has the computers they need, the network never goes down, and you never have to endure another horrible meeting about network protocols, HTTPs, and the latest worm. You're off into information systems nirvana. . . .

"Except it doesn't work that way. You trade one set of problems for another. Consider the outsourcing of computer infrastructure. What's the first thing the outsource vendor does? It hires all of the employees who were doing the work for you. Remember that lazy, incompetent network administrator that the company had—the one who never seemed to get anything done? Well, he's baaaaak, as an employee of your outsource company. Only this time he has an excuse, 'Company policy won't allow me to do it that way.'

"So the outsourcers get their first-level employees by hiring the ones you had. Of course, the outsourcer says it will provide management oversight, and if the employees don't work out, they'll be gone. What you're really outsourcing is middle-level management of the same IT personnel you had. But there's no way of knowing whether the managers they supply are any better than the ones you had.

"Also, you think you had bureaucratic problems before? Every vendor has a set of forms, procedures, committees, reports, and other management 'tools.' They will tell you that you have to do things according to the standard blueprint. They have to say that because if they allowed every company to be different, they'd never be able to gain any leverage themselves, and they'd never be profitable.

"So now you're paying a premium for the services of your former employees, who are now managed by strangers who are paid by the outsource vendor, who evaluates those managers on how well they follow the outsource vendor's profit-generating procedures. How quickly can they turn your operation into a clone of all their other clients? Do you really want to do that?

"Suppose you figure all this out and decide to get out of it. Now what? How do you undo an outsource agreement? All the critical knowledge is in the minds of the outsource vendor's employees, who have no incentive to work for you. In fact, their employment contract probably prohibits it. So now you have to take an existing operation within your own company, hire employees to staff that function, and relearn everything you ought to have learned in the first place.

"Gimme a break. Outsourcing is fool's gold, an expensive leap away from responsibility. It's like saying, 'We can't figure out how to manage an important function in our company, so you do it!' You can't get away from IS problems by hiring someone else to manage them for you. At least you care about *your* bottom line."

DISCUSSION QUESTIONS

1. Hiring an organization's existing IS staff is common practice when starting a new outsourcing arrangement. What are the advantages of this practice to the outsource vendor? What are the advantages to the organization?

2. Suppose you work for an outsource vendor. How do you respond to the charge that your managers care only about how they appear to their employer (the outsource vendor), not how they actually perform for the organization?

3. Consider the statement, "We can't figure out how to manage an important function in our company, so you do it!" Do you agree with the sentiment of this statement? If this is true, is it necessarily bad? Why or why not?

4. Explain how it is possible for an outsource vendor to achieve economies of scale that are not possible for the hiring organization. Does this phenomenon justify outsourcing? Why or why not?

5. In what ways is outsourcing IS infrastructure like outsourcing the company cafeteria? In what ways is it different? What general conclusions can you make about infrastructure outsourcing?

because it has a large, well-educated, English-speaking population that will work for 20 to 30 percent of the labor cost in the United States. Other countries are used as well. In fact, with modern telephone technology and Internet-enabled service databases, a single service call can be initiated in the United States, partially processed in India, then Singapore, and finalized by an employee in England. The customer knows only that he has been put on hold for brief periods of time.

International outsourcing is particularly advantageous for customer support and other functions that must be operational 24/7. Amazon.com, for example, operates customer service centers in the United States, India, and Ireland. During the evening hours in the United States, customer service reps in India, where it is daytime, handle the calls. When night falls in India, customer service reps in Ireland handle the early morning calls from the east coast of the United States. In this way, companies can provide 24/7 service without requiring employees to work night shifts.

International IS/IT outsourcing is not without controversy, however. It is one thing to shift a job of making a tennis shoe to Singapore, or even to hire customer support representatives in India. But there was consternation and wringing of hands when IBM stated that it was shifting nearly 5,000 computer-programming jobs to India. Some perceive the moving of such high-tech, high-skill jobs overseas as a threat to U.S. technology leadership. Others say it is just economic factors guiding jobs to places where they are most efficiently performed.

Outsourcing Alternatives

Organizations have found hundreds of different ways to outsource information systems and portions of information systems. Figure 10-12 organizes the major categories of alternatives according to information systems components.

Some organizations outsource the acquisition and operation of computer hardware. Electronic Data Systems (EDS) has been successful for more than 20 years as an outsource vendor of hardware infrastructure. Figure 10-12 shows another alternative, outsourcing the computers in a Web farm.

Acquiring licensed software, as discussed in Chapters 3 and 6, is a form of outsourcing. Rather than develop the software in-house, an organization licenses it from another vendor. Such licensing allows the software vendor to amortize the cost of software maintenance over all of the users, thus reducing that cost for all users.

Another outsourcing alternative is to outsource an entire system. PeopleSoft attained prominence by outsourcing the entire payroll function. In such a solution, as the arrow in Figure 10-12 implies, the vendor provides hardware, software, data, and some procedures. The company need provide only employee and work information; the payroll outsource vendor does the rest.

A Web storefront is another form of application outsourcing. Amazon.com, for example, provides a Web storefront for product vendors and distributors who choose not to develop their own Web presence. In this case, rather than pay a fixed fee for the storefront service, the product vendors and distributors pay Amazon.com a portion of

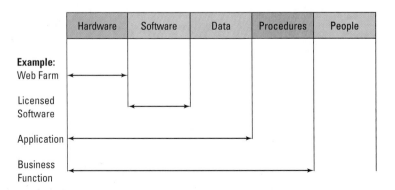

Figure 10-12
IS/IT Outsourcing
Alternatives

Using the Opposing Forces Guide *(page 321a)*

GOAL

* Investigate advantages and disadvantages of computer infrastructure outsourcing.

BACKGROUND AND PRESENTATION STRATEGIES

Here is a real-world case that you might use as an opening narrative:

When I worked for Wall Data in the mid-1990s, senior management gave up managing the firm's computing infrastructure and hired EDS to take over the IS function. From my perspective (a business-unit manager for an off-site development group), I didn't think the service was much better—but it wasn't worse—and senior management of the company no longer needed to devote so much of its time and attention to infrastructure management.

Prior to the change to EDS, our group, which was remote from headquarters, was supported by an individual who never seemed to be able to get anything done. Whenever I had a problem, it seemed to me that he had an excuse, but no fix. I'll never forget my shock and dismay when, after the switch to EDS, I rounded the corner in the hallway one morning, only to run into that same person, wearing an EDS shirt!

In fairness to the employee, and in fairness to EDS, his performance did improve. He wasn't much better at fixing problems on the spot, but the EDS reporting systems required him to keep better track of open problems, and eventually someone from his new management team would insist that he find a solution. Problem reports did not disappear into a black hole as they had prior to EDS involvement.

As an aside, I can't imagine a worse client for an outsourcing vendor than a company of professional software developers! Developers aren't prone to keeping their machines in the "standard configuration." They add all sorts of bells and whistles to their machines, and they're good at hiding it, too. Making additions to their computers tends to make the developers happy, and a happy developer is a more productive developer, so I'd look the other way unless the changes were particularly egregious.

I wasn't involved in the contract negotiation or the justification of the switch to EDS. I suspect it was quite expensive—certainly more expensive than the prior internal IS had been. But if you compute the opportunity cost of lost labor from the regular network failures that we'd had, and if you consider the savings in management time that resulted, it may have been more than worth it.

The contrarian makes an excellent point about conflicting management goals. During crunch time, we stressed our computing infrastructure just when we needed the highest reliability. The development team commonly put in 80-hour work weeks. It was a management challenge when we watched the outsourcing vendor's employees leave in the middle of a problem because they were not authorized to work overtime. We were exhausted from our long hours, the network was inhibiting our progress, and we needed a solution. Such events were rare, but they are memorable. They also made it difficult to convince developers of the need to keep their machines in the "standard configuration."

From this anecdotal experience from a single data point, I'd say that outsourcing computer infrastructure removes the highs and the lows from internal support. Although we didn't have heroic support during crunch time, we stopped having infrastructure disasters, too. The support provided by EDS middle management gave us reliability, if not immediate solutions.

By the way, an outsourcing vendor has an advantage that an in-house staff never has. *The outsource vendor can say no.* It is difficult for in-house staff to say no, especially to senior management. So the in-house staff finds itself supporting all sorts of "special situations" that an outsource vendor avoids. "It's not in the contract. Would you like to negotiate an out-of-scope change?" puts a severe damper on special requests.

 SUGGESTED RESPONSES FOR DISCUSSION QUESTIONS

1. Advantages to the vendor: reduced recruitment costs; quicker staffing; and reduced training time, because existing employees know much of the computing infrastructure. Advantages to the customer: no downtime while vendor hires personnel, working relationships already established, less customer time for training new personnel.

2. Good question for the students:

   ➤ **If you worked for EDS, how would your respond to a customer's complaint, "You care only about the EDS bottom line!"?**

I think the response has to be that the vendor's bottom line and the customer's bottom line are inextricably related. In the long run, the vendor succeeds only if the customer succeeds. Also, part of the evaluation of vendor employees' performance is customer satisfaction.

3. This statement need not be true. It could be that the company knows how to manage the infrastructure but finds the management opportunity cost to be too high. But, it probably is true for many outsourcing situations. It doesn't seem necessarily bad—if you say it about the company cafeteria, it seems innocuous enough, and, at bottom, how is outsourcing the cafeteria fundamentally different from outsourcing the computer infrastructure? See question 5.

4. Economies of scale are the key for outsourcing vendors' success. When an outsourcing vendor develops a system for problem recording, tracking, and resolution, it can amortize the cost of that system over all of its clients. A single company must pay for the development of such a system by itself.

Consider, too, the use of new technology. An outsourcing vendor can dedicate personnel to learning new technology and developing the means of utilizing the technology for its customers. It then amortizes the cost of that technology assessment and development over all of its clients.

An outsourcing vendor can also afford to train specialists in particular problems and to make those specialists available on an as-needed basis to all of its clients. An outsourcing vendor can afford to pay someone to know, for example, all of the dials and knobs and options on a Cisco router of a particular type and to understand how that router works with certain types of ACLs in particular firewalls. Such specialized knowledge is not available to a single company. Again, the cost of that specialized expertise is amortized over all clients.

5. I think the cafeteria is more separable than the computing infrastructure. It would be relatively easy to change the cafeteria vendor—just move one group out and another one in. Also, in most cases, the cafeteria could be closed for a period of time, if necessary. Employees can eat elsewhere.

The computing infrastructure is akin to the nervous system of the organization. Outsourcing personnel are integrated into the organization, removing them will be more problematic than removing cafeteria personnel. Also, the computing infrastructure is required—the organization cannot close it down for a period of time while it's being repaired.

Because of the difficulty and expense of recovering from a mistaken vendor choice, I believe there is considerably more risk when choosing a computer infrastructure outsource firm than when considering someone to run the cafeteria.

WRAP UP

➤ **Outsourcing computer infrastructure has both advantages and disadvantages.**

➤ **What are two advantages?**

(Figure 10-12 has a list of possibilities.)

➤ **What are two disadvantages?**

(Figure 10-14 has a list of possibilities.)

➤ **Suppose you're working as a department manager and you learn that your company has decided to outsource its computing infrastructure. In a weekly meeting, one of your employees asks you what you think about that. How do you respond?**

The answer depends on what I know: If I've been informed about the reasons for the change, then I explain those reasons. If this is a surprise to me, I would say I don't know anything about it, but will learn more and pass along information as I obtain it. I'd also say something positive about the company.

the revenue generated. Such Web-service hosting has become a major profit center for Amazon.com.

Finally, some organizations choose to outsource an entire business function. For years, many companies have outsourced to travel agencies the function of arranging for employee travel. Some of these outsource vendors even operate offices within the company facilities. More recently, companies have been outsourcing even larger and more important functions. In 2005, for example, **Marriott International** chose Hewitt Associates to handle its human resources needs for the next 7 years. Such agreements are much broader than outsourcing IS, but information systems are key components of the applications that are outsourced.

Choosing to outsource is a difficult decision. In fact, the correct decision may not be clear, but time and events may force the company to decide. Sometimes you just don't know the right decision but must choose one course of action. The *Problem-Solving Guide* on page 323a considers some of those situations.

The Risks of Outsourcing

With so many advantages and with so many different outsourcing alternatives, you may wonder why any company has any in-house IS/IT functions. In fact, outsourcing presents significant risks, as listed in Figure 10-13.

Loss of Control

The first risk of outsourcing is a loss of control. Outsourcing puts the vendor in the driver's seat. Each outsource vendor has methods and procedures for its service. The organization and its employees will have to conform to those procedures. For example, a hardware infrastructure vendor will have standard forms and procedures for requesting a computer, for recording and processing a computer problem, or for providing routine maintenance on computers. Once the vendor is in charge, employees must conform.

When outsourcing the cafeteria, employees have only those food choices that the vendor cooks. Similarly, when obtaining computer hardware and services, the employees will need to take what the vendor supports. Employees who want equipment that is not on the vendor's list will be out of luck.

The outsource vendor chooses the technology that it wants to implement. If the vendor, for some reason, is slow to pick up on a significant new technology, then the hiring organization will be slow to attain benefits from that technology. An organization can find itself at a competitive disadvantage because it cannot offer the same IS services as its competitors.

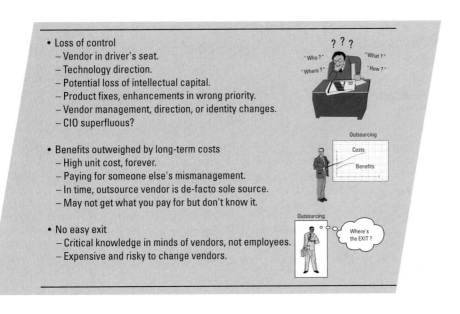

Figure 10-13
Outsourcing Risks

What If You Just Don't Know?

What if you have to make a decision and you just don't know which way to go? For complex issues like outsourcing, it can be difficult to know what the right decision is. In many cases, more analysis won't necessarily reduce the uncertainty.

Consider outsourcing as a typical, complex, real-life decision problem. The question is, will outsourcing save your organization money? Will the cap on financial exposure be worth the loss of control? Or, is your organization avoiding managing the IS function because you would just like to have the whole IS mess out of your hair?

Suppose the CIO is adamantly opposed to the outsourcing of computer infrastructure. Why is that? He is obviously biased, because such outsourcing will mean a huge cut in his department and a big loss of control for him. It might even mean he loses his job. But is that all there is to it? Or does he have a point? Are the projected savings real? Or are they the result of a paper analysis that misses many of the intangibles? For that matter, does that analysis miss some of the tangibles?

You could do another study; you could commission an independent consultant to examine this situation and make a recommendation. However, is that avoiding the issue, yet again? Further, what if there is no time? The network is down for 2 days for the third time this quarter, and you've got to act. You've got to do something. But what? Take it to the board of directors? No, they don't know. That's just another way of avoiding a tough decision. You've got to decide.

In some ways, higher education does you a disservice. In school, you're taught that a bit more study, another report, or a little more analysis will help you find a better answer. But many decisions don't work that way. There may not be the time or money for another study or another study may just cloud the issue more. Or maybe it's just not possible to know. What will be the price of IBM stock on January 1, 2010? You just don't know.

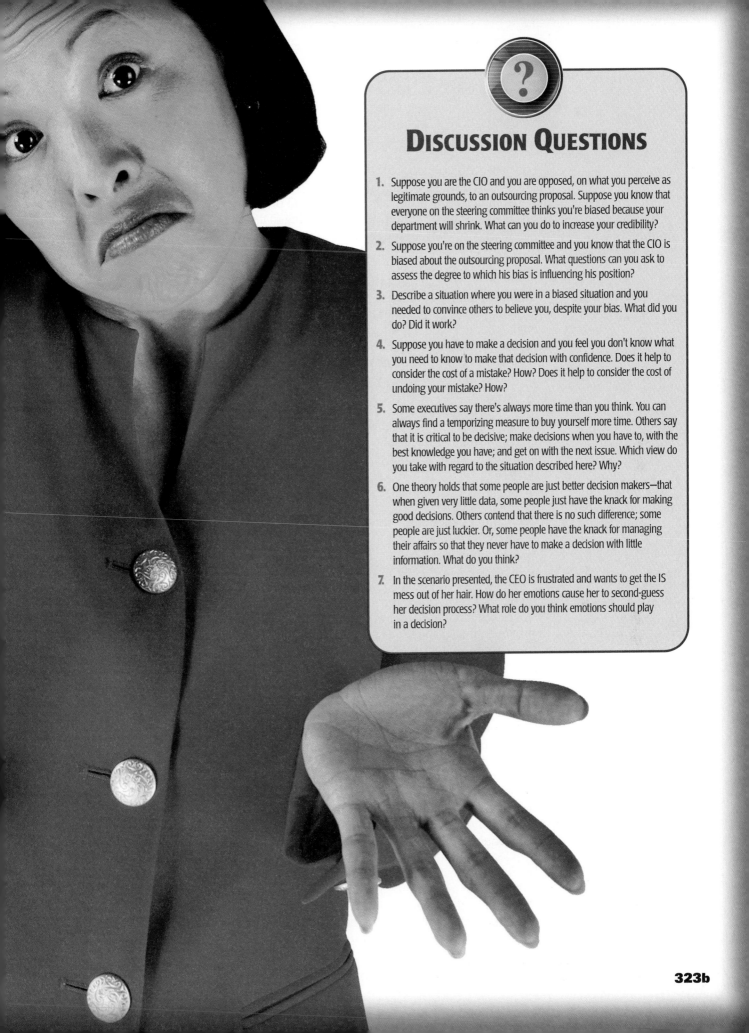

DISCUSSION QUESTIONS

1. Suppose you are the CIO and you are opposed, on what you perceive as legitimate grounds, to an outsourcing proposal. Suppose you know that everyone on the steering committee thinks you're biased because your department will shrink. What can you do to increase your credibility?

2. Suppose you're on the steering committee and you know that the CIO is biased about the outsourcing proposal. What questions can you ask to assess the degree to which his bias is influencing his position?

3. Describe a situation where you were in a biased situation and you needed to convince others to believe you, despite your bias. What did you do? Did it work?

4. Suppose you have to make a decision and you feel you don't know what you need to know to make that decision with confidence. Does it help to consider the cost of a mistake? How? Does it help to consider the cost of undoing your mistake? How?

5. Some executives say there's always more time than you think. You can always find a temporizing measure to buy yourself more time. Others say that it is critical to be decisive; make decisions when you have to, with the best knowledge you have; and get on with the next issue. Which view do you take with regard to the situation described here? Why?

6. One theory holds that some people are just better decision makers—that when given very little data, some people just have the knack for making good decisions. Others contend that there is no such difference; some people are just luckier. Or, some people have the knack for managing their affairs so that they never have to make a decision with little information. What do you think?

7. In the scenario presented, the CEO is frustrated and wants to get the IS mess out of her hair. How do her emotions cause her to second-guess her decision process? What role do you think emotions should play in a decision?

Another concern is a potential loss of intellectual capital. The company may need to reveal proprietary trade secrets, methods, or procedures to the outsource vendor's employees. As part of its normal operations, that vendor may move employees to competing organizations, and the company may lose intellectual capital as that happens. The loss need not be intellectual theft; it may simply be that the vendor's employees learned to work in a new and better way at your company, and then they take that learning to your competitor.

Similarly, all software has failures and problems. Quality vendors track those failures and problems and fix them according to a set of priorities. When a company outsources a system, it no longer has control over prioritizing those fixes. Such control belongs to the vendor. A fix that may be critical to an organization may be of low priority to the outsource vendor.

Other problems are that the outsource vendor may change management, adopt a different strategic direction, or be acquired. When any of those changes occur, priorities may change, and an outsource vendor that was a good choice at one time may be a bad fit after it changes direction. It can be difficult and expensive to change an outsource vendor when this occurs.

The final loss-of-control risk is that the company's CIO can become superfluous. When users need a critical service that is outsourced, the CIO must turn to the vendor for a response. In time, users learn that it is quicker to deal directly with the outsource vendor, and soon the CIO is out of the communication loop. At that point, the vendor has essentially replaced the CIO, who has become a figurehead. However, employees of the outsource vendor work for a different company, with a bias toward their employer. Critical managers will thus not share the same goals and objectives as the rest of the management team. Biased, bad decisions can result.

Benefits Outweighed by Long-Term Costs

The initial benefits of outsourcing can appear huge. A cap on financial exposure, a reduction of management time and attention, and the release of many management and staffing problems are all possible. (Most likely, outsource vendors promise these very benefits.) Outsourcing can appear too good to be true.

In fact, it *can* be too good to be true. For one, although a fixed cost does indeed cap exposure, it also removes the benefits of economies of scale. If the Web storefront takes off, and suddenly the organization needs 200 servers instead of 20, the using organization will pay 200 times the fixed cost of supporting one server. It is likely, however, that because of economies of scale, the costs of supporting 200 servers are far less than 10 times the costs of supporting 20 servers.

Also, the outsource vendor may change its pricing strategy over time. Initially, an organization obtains a competitive bid from several outsource vendors. However, as the winning vendor learns more about the business and as relationships develop between the organization's employees and those of the vendor, it becomes difficult for other firms to compete for subsequent contracts. The vendor becomes the *de facto* sole source and, with little competitive pressure, may increase its prices.

Another problem is that an organization can find itself paying for another organization's mismanagement, with little recourse. Over time, if the outsource vendor is mismanaged or suffers setbacks in other arenas, costs will increase. When this occurs, an outsourcing arrangement that initially made sense no longer makes sense. But the cost and risk of switching to another vendor are high.

Don Gray, a specialist in off-shore software development, warns that a common problem is the off-shore vendor's lack of management expertise: "If you contracted for 200 hours of programmer time, you will probably get that time. What you may not get, however, is the expertise required to manage that time well."[1] By choosing to employ an outsource vendor, the organization loses all visibility into the management effectiveness of the outsource vendor. The organization contracting with the outsource

---

[1]Don Gray, conversation with author, May 2003.

Using the Problem Solving Guide (page 323a)

GOALS

* Sensitize students to problems that cannot be solved by quantitative analysis.

* Discuss the impact of bias and emotions in such decisions.

BACKGROUND AND PRESENTATION STRATEGIES

One of the joys of working in business is the tremendous variety of problems that one encounters and the many different solution strategies that those problems require. Consider some examples:

➤ If you want to know the financial impact of a 2 percent raise in loan interest rate on the 5-year cost of purchasing an item of equipment, do a financial analysis. The quantitative techniques you are learning in your accounting and finance classes will serve you well.

➤ But *what about less quantitative decisions?* Or what about decisions for which there is no agreed-on procedure? Marketing is replete with examples of such decisions. For example:

➤ How do you select a product name? Say you have created a new XML data store software product. (See the Reflections Guide in Chapter 8.) Suppose you hire a name-development consultant who creates a list of the following alternative names: Baton, SmoothSail, and Kenya. How do you *decide which is the best name?*

➤ Or, consider strategic marketing. To whom do you sell your new XML data store? To the people who are using relational DBMS products? They will be *invested in the old, relational technology.* Or, do you sell it to people who are exchanging XML documents? They will not be aware of the *need for secure, reliable storage* and won't appreciate your product's features. Which market should you choose?

➤ Although you can commission analytical studies, convene focus groups, conduct surveys, and so on, these measures may not appreciably improve the quality of your decision. And often you don't have time.

➤ So you must make a subjective decision. But suppose the person who knows the most about the situation has a bias, as in the scenario in this guide.

The person who knows the most about the IS infrastructure is the person whose budget and responsibilities will be dramatically reduced—maybe even eliminated.

➤ How do you use the input from such a source when making a subjective decision?

Some business decisions, like the interest rate computation, are quantitative in nature. Others are very subjective—like choosing the best advertising campaign. (I know you can try them on focus groups, but still, ultimately, it's a subjective decision.) *Outsourcing* is a decision between these two extremes: Parts of the decision are quantitative, but other parts are subjective. The management decision team's decision-making capability is greatly hampered by the clear bias of the person who knows the most about the organization's IS infrastructure.

❓ SUGGESTED RESPONSES FOR DISCUSSION QUESTIONS

1. First, raise the objection! Tell everyone you know you're biased; tell everyone that you are, of course, concerned about the reduction in your budget and responsibilities. Then, having made your bias clear, make as fact based a quantitative analysis as you can. Do not be emotional. State the facts in a calm professional manner.

   If you cannot make a solid analysis against the outsourcing proposal, don't try. Be a professional, take your hit, and move on. You may end up with a job with the outsourcing vendor, or you may have to find another company. Or, you may find that you don't mind managing the outsourcing vendor's contract instead of managing IS. But, be a professional about it. Guard your reputation as a businessperson with high integrity; you need it for the long run.

2. In the case of the CIO's bias, look at the quality of the analysis. Is it solidly based on facts, or is it full of difficult-to-prove subjective judgments? Does the CIO appear to be defensive or balanced? This is tough—on everyone. It may be that you just have to discount the CIO's input.

3. The students should have good examples to share. You could start the discussion by asking for examples from academia. Though I have to be careful bringing it up, lest I have a line of students outside my door after the next exam, one example is the student who's arguing for 10 extra points on an exam score.

4. The circumstances are such that you may make a bad decision. You can use the best process available to you and still not have a solid basis for the decision. In this case, do consider the cost of the wrong decision. If the cost is likely to be catastrophic, seek more input; find out what you need to know; strive to find another way to analyze the situation. Use your professional network; talk to others. If the cost of a mistake is modest, it may make sense just to make the decision and move on, preparing as best you can for dealing with a mistake. If the cost of undoing the decision is not great, just make the decision. Or, try to alter the situation so that the cost of undoing it will not be great.

➤ **By the way, it is important to distinguish between a bad decision and a bad result. You can use a superb decision-making process and be unlucky. If so, you'll have a good decision but a bad result. That happens, but it's important to know, for future use, that your decision making was not defective.**

5. My answer to these opinions is that both may be right—it just depends. Usually, there is more time than you think. Usually, you don't have to decide right now, and usually you can take the time for further consideration, more points of view, or additional analysis. But not always!

At the same time, in some situations any decision, even a bad one, will be better than further temporizing. This occurs when the organization is "holding its breath," waiting for a signal about which way to go. In my experience, such situations in business are, thankfully, rare.

With regard to outsourcing, I think the steering committee should listen to the CIO, review the proposals from the outsourcing vendors, do its homework investigating the performance of the outsourcing vendors at other companies that are similar, and make a decision. The only reason I'd wait would be if there is a suspicion, based on the analysis of the vendors' reputations, that none of the vendors is particularly good.

6. To my mind, there is no question that some people are better decision makers with limited data than others. Some people just seem to make a long string of good decisions. Bill Gates is one of them. There were many, perhaps dozens, of young men like Gates who had successful early products and companies. Philippe Kahn (Borland) and Mitch Kapor (Lotus) are two examples. Neither of these two, nor the others, seemed to be able to thread the complexities of the early PC world as well as Gates. Recall that Gates out-finagled IBM when IBM was *the* powerhouse of the industry. Famous stock pickers like Peter Lynch are another example. Lynch would say that he just did his homework, but so did everyone else in that business, and no one had the success he had at Magellan.

I think part of it is that some people have an excellent sense of timing for their decisions. They delay a risky decision until the situation has clarified itself, and then they make the decision. For example, in the late 1980s, Microsoft supported both DOS/Windows and IBM's OS/2. Gates went out on the road, touting OS/2 along with IBM. He pushed both operating systems until the point when it was clear that DOS/Windows would be the winner. Then, when Windows was clearly the winner, he broke from IBM with Windows 95. (Of course, Microsoft heavily influenced that result. Microsoft Office ran only on Windows. OS/2 had few desktop applications, so no one wanted to use it. There was no way that Microsoft was going to put Office on OS/2 unless OS/2 started gaining market share. Had that occurred, Microsoft would have inundated the market with Office for OS/2, which, of course, it never had to do.)

7. She'll be concerned that her desire to be rid of the problem will overcome sound business judgment. Regarding the proper role of emotions, I'd say be guided, be informed, by one's emotions. They're pointing you in some direction. But, make the decision on as rational a basis as you can.

WRAP UP

➤ **Not every decision can be analyzed quantitatively. Some require subjective judgment.**

➤ **We've identified a few ways of dealing with difficult decisions. Keep thinking about them. For an exercise, consider this subjective decision:**

➤ **Cast out every thought you've ever had about what job you want. From that blank slate, what job do you want?**

vendor may be paying for gross inefficiency, and may not know it. Ultimately, such a situation will result in a competitive disadvantage with organizations that are not subsidizing such inefficiency.

No Easy Exit

The final category of outsourcing risk concerns ending the agreement. There is no easy exit. For one, the outsource vendor's employees have gained significant knowledge of the company. They know the server requirements in customer support, they know the patterns of usage, and they know the best procedures for downloading operational data into the data warehouse. Consequently, lack of knowledge will make it difficult to bring the outsourced service back in-house.

Also, because the vendor has become so tightly integrated into the business, parting company can be exceedingly risky. Closing down the employee cafeteria for a few weeks while finding another food vendor would be unpopular, but employees would survive. Shutting down the enterprise network for a few weeks would be impossible; the business would not survive. Because of such risk, the company must invest considerable work, duplication of effort, management time, and expense to change to another vendor. In truth, choosing an outsource vendor can be a one-way street.

Despite the risks, the movement toward outsourcing and toward organizational specialization is likely to continue. Where will it end? Consider the possibilities discussed in the *Reflections Guide* on page 325a.

User Rights and Responsibilities

We conclude this chapter with a summary of your rights and responsibilities with regard to the IS department. The items in Figure 10-14 lists what you are entitled to receive and indicate what you are expected to contribute.

Your Rights

You have a right to have the computing resources you need to perform your work as proficiently as you want. You have a right to the computer hardware and programs that you need. If you process huge files for data-mining applications, you have a right to the huge disks and the fast processor that you need. However, if you merely receive email and consult the corporate Web portal, then your right is for more modest requirements (leaving the more powerful resources for those in the organization who need them).

You have a right to:	You have a responsibility to:
– Computer hardware and programs that allow you to perform your job proficiently	– Learn basic computer skills
– Reliable network and Internet connections	– Learn standard techniques and procedures for the applications you use
– A secure computing environment	– Follow security and backup procedures
– Protection from viruses, worms, and other threats	– Protect your password(s)
– Contribute to requirements for new system features and functions	– Use computer resources according to your employer's computer use policy
– Reliable systems development and maintenance	– Make no unauthorized hardware modifications
– Prompt attention to problems, concerns, and complaints	– Install only authorized programs
– Properly prioritized problem fixes and resolutions	– Apply software patches and fixes when directed to do so
– Effective training	– When asked, devote the time required to respond carefully and completely to requests for requirements for new system features and functions
	– Avoid reporting trivial problems

Figure 10-14
User Information Systems Rights and Responsibilities

Jumping Aboard the Bulldozer

A recent popular theme in the media is how overseas outsourcing is destroying the U.S. labor market. The "jobless recovery" is how it's headlined. However, a closer look reveals that overseas outsourcing is not the culprit. First, Brainard and Litan cite research that indicates that organizations will move about 250,000 jobs per year overseas between now and 2015.[2] Although that may sound like a lot, in the context of the 137 million U.S. workers, and in the context of the 15 million Americans who lose their jobs due to other factors, 250,000 jobs overseas is not much.

The culprit—if culprit is the right word—is not overseas outsourcing; it is productivity. Because of information technology, Moore's Law, and all the information systems that you have learned about in this book, worker productivity continues to increase, and it is possible to have an economic recovery without a binge of new hiring.

The Austrian economist Joseph Schumpeter called such processes "creative destruction" and said that they are the cleansers of the free market.[3] Economic processes operate to remove unneeded jobs, companies, and even industries, and thereby keep the economy growing and prospering. In fact, the lack of such processes hindered the growth of Japan and some European nations in the 1990s.

(By the way, there's a historical irony here because creative destruction gave rise to one of the first information systems. This system consisted of a group of human "calculators" who were employed by the French in the 1790s to compute scientific tables for the then-new metric system. According to Ken Alder, the human calculators were wigmakers, made unemployed by the French Revolution.[4] The guillotine not only reduced the size of the market for wigs, but also made aristocratic hairstyles less popular. And so wigmakers became human calculators.)

This idea of creative destruction is all well and good for an economic theory, but what do you, as a student in the first decade of the twenty-first century, do? How do you respond to the dynamics of shifting work and job movements? You can take a lesson from the railroads in the 1930s. They were blindsided by air transportation. In a now-classic marketing blunder, the railroads perceived themselves as purveyors of railroad transportation instead of purveyors of transportation more generally. The railroads were well positioned to take advantage of air transportation, but they did nothing and were overtaken by the new airline companies.

How does this apply to you? As you have learned, MIS is the development and use of information systems that enable organizations to achieve their goals and objectives. When you work with information systems, you are not a professional of a particular

[2]Lial Brainard and Robert Litan, "Services Offshoring Bane or Bone and What to Do?" *CESifo Forum*, Summer 2004, Vol. 5, Issue 2, p. 307.
[3]Joseph Schumpeter, *Capitalism, Socialism, and Democracy* (New York: Harper, 1975), pp. 82–85.

[4]Ken Alder, *The Measure of All Things* (New York: The Free Press, 2002), p. 142.

system or technology; rather, you are a developer or user of a system that helps your organization achieve its goals and objectives.

Suppose, for example, you work with an EDI-based purchasing information system. If you view yourself as an expert in EDI, then you are doomed, because EDI will be supplanted by XML, as you learned in Chapter 8. Are you better off to define yourself as an expert in XML? No, because XML will someday be replaced with something else. Writing XML schemas is work that can easily be moved offshore. Instead, define yourself more generally as someone who specializes in the use of EDI or XML or Gizmo 3.0 to help your business achieve its goals and objectives.

From this perspective, the technology you learned in this class can help you start your career. If IS-based productivity is the bulldozer that is mowing down traditional jobs, then use what you have learned here to jump aboard that bulldozer. Not as a technologist, but as a business professional who can determine how best to use that bulldozer to enhance your career.

In the case of purchasing, learn something about XML and apply that knowledge to gain employment in a company that uses XML to accomplish its goals and objectives. But realize that XML only helps you get that job; it just gets you started. Your long-term success depends not on your knowledge of XML, but rather on your ability to think, to solve problems, and to use technology and information systems to help your organization achieve its goals and objectives.

Discussion Questions

1. Describe five ways that the overseas outsourcing problem is overstated.

2. Summarize the argument that the "culprit" is not overseas outsourcing, but rather productivity.

3. Why is it incorrect to consider productivity as a culprit?

4. Explain the phenomenon of creative destruction.

5. Why are your career prospects doomed if you define yourself as an expert in EDI? In XML? How should you define yourself?

6. Apply the line of reasoning you used in your answer to question 5 to some other technology or system. Use IPv6 (Chapter 4), CRM (Chapter 7), SCM (Chapter 8), decision trees (Chapter 9), or some other technology.

7. Explain how you can use one of the technologies in question 6 to help you start your career. To be successful, what perspective must you then maintain?

You have a right to reliable network and Internet services. Reliable means that you can process without problems almost all of the time. It means that you never go to work wondering, "Will the network be available today?" Network problems should be a rare occurrence.

You also have a right to a secure computing environment. The organization should protect your computer and its files, and you should not normally even need to think about security. From time to time, the organization may ask you to take particular actions to protect your computer and files, and you should take those actions. But such requests should be rare and related to specific outside threats.

You have a right to participate in requirements meetings for new applications that you will use and for major changes to applications that you currently use. You may choose to delegate this right to others, or your department may delegate that right for you, but if so, you have a right to contribute your thoughts through that delegate.

You have a right to reliable systems development and maintenance. Although schedule slippages of a month or two are common in many development projects, you should not have to endure schedule slippages of 6 months or more. Such slippages are evidence of incompetent systems development.

Additionally, you have a right to receive prompt attention to your problems, concerns, and complaints about information services. You have a right to have a means to report problems, and you have a right to know that your problem has been received and at least registered with the IS department. You have a right to have your problem resolved, consistent with established priorities. This means that an annoying problem that allows you to conduct your work will be prioritized below another's problem that interferes with his ability to do his job.

Finally, you have a right to effective training. It should be training that you can understand and that enables you to use systems to perform your particular job. The organization should provide training in a format and on a schedule that is convenient to you.

Your Responsibilities

You also have responsibilities toward the IS department and your organization. Specifically, you have a responsibility to learn basic computer skills and to learn the basic techniques and procedures for the applications you use. You should not expect hand-holding for basic operations. Nor should you expect to receive repetitive training and support for the same issue.

You have a responsibility to follow security and backup procedures. This is especially important because actions that you fail to take may cause problems for your fellow employees and your organization as well as for you. In particular, you are responsible for protecting your password(s). In the next chapter, you will learn that this is important not only to protect your computer, but, because of intersystem authentication, it is important to protect your organization's networks and databases as well.

You have a responsibility for using your computer resources in a manner that is consistent with your employer's policy. Many employers allow limited email for critical family matters while at work, but discourage frequent and long casual email. You have a responsibility to know your employer's policy and to follow it.

You also have a responsibility to make no unauthorized hardware modifications to your computer and to install only authorized programs. As described earlier in this chapter, one reason for this policy is that your IS department constructs automated maintenance programs for upgrading your computer. Unauthorized hardware and programs may interfere with these programs. Additionally, the installation of unauthorized hardware or programs can cause you problems that the IS department will have to fix.

You have a responsibility to install computer patches and fixes when asked to do so. This is particularly important for patches that concern security and backup and recovery. When asked for input to requirements for new and adapted systems, you have a

You Be the Guide

Using the Reflections Guide
(page 325a)

GOAL

✳ Motivate students to use knowledge of IS and IT to create and *sustain* competitive professional advantage.

BACKGROUND AND PRESENTATION STRATEGIES

This guide is among the most important guides in the textbook. In fact, it may be *the* most important guide.

I like to emphasize the following two points in this guide:

➤ **Knowledge of information systems and information technology can provide a competitive professional advantage—to all businesspeople, not just IS majors. This advantage accrues to those who know how to apply IS in innovative ways in the organizations in which they work.**

But:

➤ **That competitive advantage is sustainable only if the students learn how to efficiently learn *new technology* and learn *new ways to apply that new technology* to emerging opportunities. What you know now will open the door, but what you learn in the future will keep that door, in fact the whole building, open to you.**

The seventeenth-century philosopher Baruch Spinoza wrote that happiness does not occur by living on a high level of existence (wealth, health, family, etc.), but rather it occurs by *moving from one level of existence to one that is perceived to be higher*. Similarly, sorrow is not life on a low level of existence, but movement from one level to another that is perceived to be lower. According to this theory, people with $50 million in net worth can be miserable if they believe their life is degrading; likewise, people with $100,000 in net worth can be exceedingly happy if they believe their life is improving.

Thus, Spinoza defined happiness as *movement*—in math terms, as the derivative—in an upward direction. He defined sorrow as movement, the derivative, in a downward direction.

Now, what does this have to do with information systems? A particular level of IS knowledge gives a business professional a certain level of competency.

That level is *sustainable, however, only to the extent that the businessperson continues to learn, to think, to imagine* new applications and new opportunities. It is the derivative in one's knowledge that matters most. Without continuously learning, and continuously increasing one's ability to apply IS to new opportunities, the competitive advantage will erode. The true competitive advantage is thus not any particular level of knowledge, but an ability to increase one's level of knowledge. It is the movement, the derivative, in a positive direction.

In 1971, I was an expert, a true guru, on IBM Job Control Language (JCL):

```
//DD1 DD DSN=MYFILE,DISP=(NEW,KEEP),
  UNIT=2314,SPACE=(CYL,(2,3,10))
```

What good is that knowledge today? Or knowledge of the shortcut keys for the Wang word processor I once used? Or the knowledge I once had of Total, a popular DBMS product in 1975? It's *worthless* for solving any business problem today.

The great news, the *fantastic news,* is that the continual change in technology constantly *opens new opportunities.* The playing field is continually being releveled. The huge competitive advantage that Lotus once had in the spreadsheet market was wiped out by the emergence of GUI systems like the Macintosh. The huge competitive advantage that Microsoft Access had for Windows applications was wiped out by the emergence of the Web, which opened the door for languages like PHP and DBMS products like MySQL. Without technology change, IBM would still dominate the computer business; Bill Gates would be an aging systems engineer in an IBM office; Michael Dell would be watering golf courses; and thousands of incredibly bored clerks would punch computer cards.

Technological change is every ambitious person's friend. It is the *great equalizer,* the *marvelous opportunity creator,* the ultimate door opener. But this is true only for those who, to use the analogy of this guide, learn to jump aboard that bulldozer and use it creatively throughout their careers!

 SUGGESTED RESPONSES FOR DISCUSSION QUESTIONS

1. It's overstated because the 250,000 jobs lost per year is a small percentage of the 137 million U.S. workers.

2. Outsourcing does not impact a high percentage of U.S. jobs. Rather, it is increased productivity that

enables fewer people to accomplish more. The same level of output can be achieved with fewer people. The Web and email enable people to communicate not just faster and more conveniently, but it also reduces the amount of physical paper that needs to be produced, printed, and transported. More ideas are exchanged with fewer resources.

3. Productivity is not a "culprit"; rather, it enhances the material quality of everyone's life. It enables society to do more with less. Productivity makes existing means of operation obsolete; organizations must adapt to more efficient processes, or Schumpeter's creative destruction will clean them up and out.

4. Creative destruction occurs when economic factors remove organizations that have become inefficient. For example, Dell's direct-marketing model drove IBM to sell its personal computer business to Lenovo Group, Limited, a Chinese company. That acquisition will eliminate inefficient competitors in China, or if the acquisition was unwise, creative destruction will reduce or remove the Lenovo Group. However, creative destruction will occur only if the Chinese government allows capitalistic market forces to operate in China. If not, China will compete at a disadvantage on the world's markets, ultimately to its own disadvantage.

5. You should not define yourself in terms of a particular technology, because those technologies will be replaced by others. Define yourself as someone who can use the latest interorganizational communications technology (whether that's EDI, XML, or Gizmo 3.0) to help your business achieve its goals and objectives. Find innovative ways to use that technology for supply chain management, for e-commerce, or for some other interorganizational communication problem. If your organization is a cost leader, find innovative ways to save costs with that technology. If your organization has a differentiation strategy, find innovative ways to differentiate your product or service with those technologies.

6. The principle is the same for each of these systems and technologies. Knowledge of the system or technology will open the door, but that door will stay open only as long as the business professional continues to learn new systems and technology and new applications of those systems and technology. Or, as one pundit put it, "In this business, you are never finished until you're finished."

7. I use the example of IPv6 from this list because most students think they'd have to be a real techie to use it to get an interesting job. Not so!

➤ **How could you use knowledge of IPv6 to obtain a job? Write a great paper on why IPv6 is going to be the greatest thing since sliced bread. Or, write a great paper on why IPv6 is not going to be the greatest thing since sliced bread.**

(Take the data communications class to learn more. Negotiate credit for the paper with the data communications professor, thus killing two birds with one stone.)

➤ **Google the Web and identify interesting vendors and companies that have a vested interest in IPv6. While writing the paper, email as many people in those companies as possible, claiming status as a student who's writing a paper and who has a few questions. Build your contact list. Write the paper. While writing it, think of opportunities in marketing, sales, customer support, training, installation, or other personal interest. Slant the paper toward those opportunities. Send the finished paper to every contact you've made while writing it. Follow up with email querying the people about what they thought of it. Be sure to talk about the paper in every job interview.**

(By the way, this is a good place to remind the students of the advantages of never plagiarizing *anything* from any source. The people to whom they send this report will be widely read in the literature. Any attempt at plagiarism will be quickly detected. This is a good habit to have in all cases, but especially here.)

I would be exceedingly surprised if students who seriously embarked upon this course of action did not have more job opportunities than they would ever imagine.

WRAP UP

➤ **If you have enjoyed any aspect of this class, you owe it to yourself to take more IS classes. The future belongs to people who can apply information systems to business in innovative ways!**

➤ **Even if you don't want to become an IS major, think about combining IS knowledge with your major. Take a few of our classes, and while you're taking them, keep thinking about innovative ways to apply what you're learning to your major area of study. Ask the professor for help with that agenda. See if you can do projects for credit that apply what you're learning in those classes to your major field of interest.**

➤ **And, most important, learn how to learn ways of applying IS to your business interests! And keep on learning!**

responsibility to take the time necessary to provide thoughtful and complete responses. If you do not have that time, you should delegate your input to someone else.

Finally, you have a responsibility to treat information systems professionals professionally. Everyone works for the same company, everyone wants to succeed, and professionalism and courtesy will go a long way on all sides. One form of professional behavior is to learn basic skills so that you avoid reporting trivial problems.

Davidson Distribution (continued)

Suppose you are the manager of the employee who complains about the cost of computers and the limitations placed on employees by the IS department. How do you respond?

One approach is to take the side of the IS department and to explain why its standards are important and why, ultimately, the organization saves money by working within the guidelines set out by the IS department. Another approach is to have your employee develop a proposal for a different scheme—perhaps one that recognizes the need for standardization but that allows employees more leeway to acquire computers on their own. Yet a third approach would be to discuss this matter with the IS department and ask someone there to respond to your employee. Any of these actions is possible. You'll have a chance to formulate your own ideas in question 29 at the end of the chapter.

SUMMARY

- The major functions of the IS department are to plan the use of IT so as to accomplish the organization's goals and objectives; to manage the organization's computing infrastructure; to develop, operate, and maintain enterprise applications; to protect the organization's information assets; and to manage outsourcing relationships.

- The principal manager of the IS department is the chief information officer (CIO). In most companies, the CIO reports to the CEO and is a member of the senior management team. The CIO communicates IS/IT issues to executive staff, communicates and enforces priorities within the IS department, assesses emerging technology in light of those priorities, and sponsors the steering committee.

- Figure 10-2 shows the organizational structure of a typical IS department. The chief technology officer (CTO) identifies new IT products and ideas that will be relevant to the organization.

- IS and IT differ. Information systems consist of the five components and exist to help the organization achieve its goals and objectives. IT is just technology. IT underlies IS.

- The IS department has various planning functions. It must help align an organization's information systems with organizational strategy and keep systems aligned with the strategy as the organization changes.

- The IS department manages the computing infrastructure by aligning it with the organization's structure and dynamics; by creating and maintaining facilities for end-user computing; and by creating, operating, and maintaining the computer network, computing centers, data warehouses, and data marts. To accomplish that function, the IS department establishes standards, tracks user problems and monitors fixes, and manages the infrastructure staff.

■ To develop, operate, and maintain enterprise applications, the IS department manages development processes for new applications like those described in Chapter 6. It also maintains legacy applications and provides the connective tissue for EAI applications. Part of this process is to adapt IS to changing requirements, to track problems and monitor fixes, and to manage the development staff.

■ Data administration and database administration are functions in the IS department that protect the organization's information assets. Data administration serves the entire organization. It establishes and publishes data standards and data policies and creates a disaster-recovery plan. Database administration exists for a particular database and determines user data rights and responsibilities, establishes database security programs, and creates database backup and recovery plans.

■ Outsourcing is the process of hiring another organization to perform a function or service. Companies outsource hardware, programs, applications, and even entire business functions. The major reasons for outsourcing are to obtain expertise, avoid management problems, save costs, and reduce risk. Major problems with outsourcing are a loss of control, high long-term costs, and the lack of an easy exit from an outsourcing agreement.

■ As a future user of information systems, facilities, and services, you have the rights and responsibilities listed in Figure 10-14. In summary, you have a right to the computer equipment and computing environment you need to do your job. You have a responsibility to use IS professionally and in such a way as to protect the entire community of IS users.

KEY TERMS AND CONCEPTS

Chief information officer (CIO) **307**

Chief technology officer (CTO) **307**

Data administration **317**

Data dictionary **318**

Data standards **317**

Database administration **317**

Legacy information system **316**

Outsourcing **319**

Steering committee **310**

ASSIGNMENT MATERIAL

Review Questions

1. List the major functions of the IS department.
2. To whom does the CIO typically report?
3. Draw an organizational chart for a typical IS department.
4. Explain the difference between IS and IT.
5. Give an example of a situation in which IS is not aligned with organizational strategy.
6. Why are priorities important in controlling the seductive nature of technology?
7. List the major functions of the IS department in managing the computing infrastructure.
8. Why are standards important for managing the computing infrastructure?
9. Explain how problems are tracked and monitored in a well-run IS department.
10. Sketch an organizational chart for a typical operations department.
11. List the major functions of the IS department in managing enterprise applications.
12. Differentiate between the role of the IS department for developing new applications and for managing legacy applications.
13. What does the term *maintenance* mean in the context of information systems?
14. Sketch an organizational chart for a typical development group.
15. What is a data policy? Give an example other than one in this chapter.
16. What is outsourcing?
17. Why do companies choose to outsource?
18. What does the statement "Your back room is someone else's front room" mean?

You Be the Guide

Davidson Distribution
(continued) (page 327)

The text intentionally presents little in the way of a wrap-up for this case. This is the next-to-last chapter, and I wanted to ask the students to apply, the knowledge they've gained on their own. The text provides hints for three possible solution approaches and recommends the student answer question 27.

If you want to provide more guidance to the students or use this case for class discussion, consider the following approach.

RESPONDING TO THE CHALLENGE

► Let's suppose that you decide that the computers do seem overly expensive and that employees should have additional latitude for selecting the computers they use.

► Suppose you decide, as a first measure, that you want to request that the IS department involve a few users, such as the employees in your department, when it selects the computer equipment that it will support (and require). You decide to prepare a one-page memo to make this request.

► By the way, if you were the manager at Davidson, you might ask your employee to write this memo or work with him or her to write it.

► Do you recall, way back in Chapter 3, our discussion about empathetic thinking? What is the principle of empathetic thinking?

► Let's see if we can apply empathetic thinking to this situation. First, let's make a list of every responsibility of the IS department. Think through what you've read and what we've talked about, and let's list all of the IS department's functions. What are those functions?

► Make a list on the board or other display device. Keep listing all of the IS functions—this is a good review exercise apart from the Davidson case.

(Possible list: Plan the use of IT to accomplish organizational goals and strategy; develop, operate, and maintain computing infrastructure; develop, operate, and maintain enterprise applications; protect information assets; manage outsourcing relationships.)

► Let's look through this list and pick out those that would be more difficult to accomplish if employees could choose their own computers.

Check those that relate to computer standards. When you're done, erase those that are not checked.

For the next series of questions, you may want to group the students into small groups.

► Using the concept of empathetic thinking, write a paragraph or two that explains that you understand the importance of computer standards and their necessity for IS management.

(Pause for a few minutes of group work . . .)

► OK, read some of your paragraphs to the class.

► Assume that you start your memo with one of those statements. Now, write a paragraph or two explaining what you want (user involvement in choosing, more latitude in selection, whatever reasonable request you have).

► OK, let's hear what some of you wrote.

► What do you think? Is this a reasonable, responsible, and professional way to proceed?

WRAP UP

► The knowledge you've gained about IS management has already made you a better consumer of IS products and services.

► Look at the memo we just wrote. We've applied our knowledge using empathetic thinking and stated our request in a responsible, professional manner. We are likely to cause a change in the computer-selection process. We've also helped motivate at least one of our employees.

► What happens next will be up to the IS department. We, however, have done what we can to change the situation in a positive way. That's all we can do!

19. Compare outsourcing computing infrastructure to outsourcing the cafeteria. How are they the same? How do they differ?

20. Explain the advantages of outsourcing as they pertain to management, cost, and risk.

21. Explain the meaning of the four arrows in Figure 10-12.

22. Summarize the risks of outsourcing as they pertain to loss of control, long-term costs, and exit strategy.

23. Summarize the rights that you have as a user of information systems and services.

24. Summarize the responsibilities that you have as a user of information systems and services.

Applying Your Knowledge

25. According to this chapter, information systems, products, and technology are not malleable; they are difficult to change, alter, or bend. How do you think senior executives other than the CIO view this lack of malleability? For example, how do you think IS appears during a corporate merger?

26. Suppose you represent an investor group that is acquiring hospitals across the nation and integrating them into a unified system. List five potential problems and risks concerning information systems. How do you think IS-related risks compare to other risks in such an acquisition program?

27. What happens to IS when corporate direction changes rapidly? How will IS appear to other departments? What happens to IS when the corporate strategy changes frequently? Do you think such frequent changes are a greater problem to IS than to other business functions? Why or why not?

28. Consider the following statement: "In many ways, choosing an outsource vendor is a one-way street." Explain what this statement means. Do you agree with it? Why or why not?

29. Describe how you would respond to the employee at Davison Distribution who objects to how employees are forced to obtain computers. Consider the factors on page 327 in your response, but do not restrict yourself to these options.

Application Exercises

30. Suppose you work for a small manufacturer of industrial-handling equipment, such as conveyor belts, wheeled carts, dollies, and so on. Assume your company employs 80 people in standard functions such as product design, manufacturing, sales, and marketing. You work in accounting and have been asked to recommend three outsource vendors to manage the employees' 401(k) retirement plans. Use the Web to answer the following questions.

  a. Explain what a 401(k) retirement plan is.
  b. List three vendors that outsource such plans.
  c. Summarize the product offerings from each of the vendors in your answer to part b.
  d. Compare the costs of each of the products in your answer to part c.
  e. Based on the data you have, summarize the advantages and disadvantages of each of the alternatives in your answer to part d. Make and state assumptions, if necessary.

31. Assume you work in the IS department for the company described in question 30. Your department wants to license a software product to keep track of computer equipment and programs. Use the Web to answer the following questions.

  a. Identify three companies that license the needed software.
  b. Describe the products offered by each company.
  c. Compare the cost of each alternative in your answer to part b.
  d. Based on the data you have, summarize the advantages and disadvantages of each of the alternatives in your answer to part c. Make and state assumptions, if necessary.

32. Suppose you manage a department of 20 employees and you wish to build an information system to track their computers, the software that resides on those computers, and the licenses for each software product. Assume that employees can have more than one computer and that each computer has multiple software products. Each product has a single license. The license can be either a *site license* (meaning your organization paid for everyone in the company to be able to use that program) or the license is a purchase order number and date for the order that paid for the license.

  a. Design a spreadsheet for keeping track of the employees, computers, and licenses. Insert sample data for three employees and at least five computers with typical software.
  b. Design a database for keeping track of the employees, computers, and licenses. Assume your database has an EMPLOYEE table, a COMPUTER table, and a SOFTWARE_LICENSE table. Place appropriate columns in these tables and construct the relationship. Insert sample

data for three employees, five computers, and multiple software licenses per computer.

c. Compare the spreadsheet and database solutions to this problem. Which is easier to set up? Which is easier to maintain?

d. Use whichever of your solutions you prefer for producing the following two reports:
   - A list of employees and their computers, sorted by employee.
   - A list of software products, the computers on which they reside, and the employees assigned those computers, sorted by software product name.

Career Assignments

33. Search the Web for the term *outsourcing administration.*

   a. Summarize the nature of organizations involved in this activity.
   b. Go to interesting Web sites revealed by your search and look for employment opportunities. Describe the opportunities you find.
   c. What education, skills, and experience would you need to succeed at one of these jobs?

d. What courses, internships, and other activities could you take to prepare you for one of these jobs?

34. Search the Web for the term *IT employment trends.* Visit some of the sites that your search reveals. Also, the site *roberthalftechnology.com* often has recent survey data, as does *cio.com.* Use the information you find to answer the following questions.

   a. What is the outlook for IT/IS employment in the next 3 years? In the next 10 years?
   b. What jobs are projected to have the highest demand?
   c. Identify a job in which you might be interested. What is the projected demand for that job?
   d. Are there differences in job prospects in different geographic regions? Describe how you could improve your job prospects by moving.
   e. Are there differences in job prospects in different industries? Which industries are projected to have the most growth in IT/IS jobs? Which will have the least?

Case Study 10-1

Marriott International, Inc.

Marriott International, Inc., operates and franchises hotels and lodging facilities throughout the world. Its 2004 revenue was just over $10.1 billion. Marriott groups its business into segments according to lodging facility. Major business segments are full-service lodging, select-service lodging, extended-stay lodging, and timeshare properties. Marriott states that its three top corporate priorities are profitability, preference, and growth.

In the mid-1980s, the airlines developed the concept of *revenue management*, which adjusts prices in accordance with demand. The idea gained prominence in the airline industry, because an unoccupied seat represents revenue that is forever lost. Unlike a part in inventory, an unoccupied seat on today's flight cannot be sold tomorrow. Similarly, in the lodging industry, today's unoccupied hotel room cannot be sold tomorrow. So, for hotels, revenue management translates to raising prices on Monday when a convention is in town and lowering them on Saturday in the dead of winter when few travelers are in sight.

Marriott had developed two different revenue-management systems, one for its premium hotels and a second one for its lower-priced properties. It developed both of these systems using pre-Internet technology; systems upgrades required installing updates locally. The local updates were expensive and problematic. Also, the two systems required two separate interfaces for entering prices into the centralized reservation system.

In the late-1990s, Marriott embarked on a project to create a single revenue-management system that could be used by all of its properties. The new system, called OneSystem, was custom developed in-house, using a process similar to those you learned about in Chapter 6. The IT professionals understood the importance of user involvement, and they formed a joint IT–business user team that developed the business case for the new system and jointly managed its development. The team was careful to provide constant communication to the system's future users, and it used prototypes to identify problem areas early. Training is a continuing activity for all Marriott employees, and the company integrated training facilities into the new system.

OneSystem recommends prices for each room, given the day, date, current reservation levels, and history. Each hotel property has a revenue manager who can override these recommendations. Either way, the prices are communicated directly to the centralized reservation system. OneSystem uses Internet technology so that when the company makes upgrades to the system, it makes them only at the Web servers, not at the individual hotels. This strategy saves considerable maintenance cost, activity, and frustration.

OneSystem computes the theoretical maximum revenue for each property and compares actual results to that maximum. Using OneSystem, the company has increased the ratio of actual to theoretical revenue from 83 percent to 91 percent. That increase of 8 percentage points has translated into a substantial increase in revenues.

Source: Reprinted through the courtesy of CIO. Copyright 2005 CXO Media Inc.

Questions

1. How does OneSystem contribute to Marriott's objectives?

2. What are the advantages of having one revenue-management system instead of two? Consider both users and the IS department in your answer.

3. At the same time it was developing OneSystem in-house, Marriott chose to outsource its human relations information system. Why would it choose to develop one system in-house but outsource the other? Consider the following factors in your answer.
   • Marriott's objectives
   • The nature of the systems
   • The uniqueness of each system to Marriott
   • Marriott's in-house expertise

4. How did outsourcing HR contribute to the success of OneSystem?

5. Summarize the reasons why a company would choose to outsource rather than develop a system in-house.

Case Study 10-2

Starbucks, Inc.

Starbucks, Inc., roasts and sells coffee and related products. It buys coffee beans worldwide, roasts the beans, and sells coffee through multiple channels. Starbucks is widely known for the retail stores it operates worldwide, but it also sells coffee in grocery stores and large club warehouses and to food-service organizations. The company's

2004 revenue was $3.1 billion; 85 percent of that was from U.S. operations and 15 percent was from international operations. Starbucks employs more than 97,000 people.

Starbucks' growth has been phenomenal. From 1993 to 2003, the number of world-wide retail outlets (including some licensed but not operated by Starbucks) grew from 165 to 7,225. Starbucks stores are usually located in high-traffic, high-visibility properties, and the company varies the size and format of each store to match the local setting. Some stores are set up for "rush-in, grab your coffee, and go," whereas others provide lounge chairs and comfortable seating for leisurely sipping.

In addition to its popular retail stores, Starbucks sells coffee products to more than 19,500 grocery stores and food clubs. It sells coffee and related products to more than 12,800 organizations that provide food services. The company also operates three coffee-roasting plants in Kent, Washington; York, Pennsylvania; and Carson Valley, Nevada. The company continually innovates its product to reach new market segments. It has a partnership with PepsiCo, Inc. to produce the Frappuccino line and another with Dryer's Grand Ice Cream, Inc. to produce coffee-flavored ice cream. In 2005, Starbucks announced the creation of a new coffee liqueur that it will distribute to bars and restaurants.

Sources: businessmajors.about.com/cs/casestudyhelp/a/Starbucks.htm; finance.yahoo.com/q/pr?s=SBUX; and starbucks.com (all accessed April 2005).

Questions

1. Starbucks' operations pose three major challenges to the development and use of information systems: growth, complexity in sales channels, and multinational operations. Summarize the ways in which these challenges impact information systems management.

2. Read Case Study 10-1 about Marriott International. Marriott chose to develop an information system in-house while at the same time outsourcing the HR function. Considering the fundamental business systems described in Chapters 7 and 8 and then respond to the following.
   a. Name two business functions or processes that you think Starbucks could outsource. Describe the advantages and disadvantages of outsourcing for each.
   b. Name a business function or process for which you think Starbucks must develop in-house systems. Describe potential problems for such a development project.
   c. Name a business function or process for which you think Starbucks could acquire software and adapt it. Describe potential problems for such a development project.

3. How can Starbucks structure its IS department to support multinational operations? Adapt the organizational chart in Figure 10-2 in your answer.

4. Describe ways in which information systems can contribute to Starbucks's growth. Describe ways in which information systems might impede its growth.

5. If you were a CIO, would you want to be the CIO at Starbucks? Explain why or why not.

Information Security Management

Learning Objectives

- Know the sources of security threats.
- Understand management's role for developing a security program.
- Understand the importance and elements of an organizational security policy.
- Understand the purpose and operation of technical safeguards.
- Understand the purpose and operation of data safeguards.
- Understand the purpose and operation of human safeguards.
- Learn techniques for disaster preparedness.
- Recognize the need for a security incidence-response plan.

Guides

ETHICS GUIDE
Securing Privacy

OPPOSING FORCES GUIDE
Security Assurance, Hah!

PROBLEM SOLVING GUIDE
Testing Security

SECURITY GUIDE
Metasecurity

REFLECTIONS GUIDE
The Final, Final Word

Chapter Preview

This chapter describes the common sources of security threats and explains management's role in addressing those threats. It also defines the major elements of an organizational security policy. Given that management background, it then presents the most common types of technical, data, and human security safeguards. It also describes disaster preparedness techniques and explains the components of a security incidence-response plan.

The discussion in this chapter augments the Security Guides in the preceding 10 chapters. Those guides addressed security elements in isolation; here, we address information systems security systematically, from an organizational perspective.

Southwest Video Training

Suppose that you are the manager of telesales for Southwest Video Training, a company that produces, distributes, and sells video-training programs. Your company has programs on customer support, leadership, sales training, motivation, and other training topics. Southwest's competitive strategy is to differentiate its product on the basis of quality, and it has succeeded. The company's programs are perceived not only as the highest quality, but also as the most entertaining and effective.

You manage the telesales department. Your salespeople make "warm calls"; that is, they call existing customers or potential customers who have evidenced a strong interest in your programs. Your company uses a licensing model; rather than sell the videos outright, it sells a license to use them. Larger customers buy site licenses that authorize them to copy videos. Otherwise, customers are not allowed to make copies.

One day you're thinking about how useful your database is when it occurs to you how vulnerable you are. A loss of your database would hamper sales for months! You know that someone at the company backs up the database each week, but you don't know where the backup is stored. Are the backups in your building, and, if so, what would happen if your building caught fire and the backups were lost? Lately, you've been

reading about incidents in which data utilities lost data to thieves (page 354). What protection do you have against that possibility?

Two partners privately own Southwest, and you approach one of them and raise these issues. He states he hasn't thought about it, saying, "I rely on Ben [an employee who manages the Web storefront] to take care of it." Without criticizing Ben, you ask whether anyone knows how well-protected the data are. "No, not really," says the partner. "Why don't you look into it? I mean, don't do Ben's job for him, but tell him about your concerns and see what you learn. Maybe the two of you can work together on it and get back to me."

Your assignment seems clear enough. How will you proceed? You want to ask good questions of Ben and not sound like a technology know-nothing.

■ Security Threats

We begin by describing security threats. We will first summarize the sources of threats and then describe specific problems that arise from each source.

Sources of Threats

Three sources of security problems are human error and mistakes, malicious human activity, and natural events and disasters.

Human errors and mistakes include accidental problems caused by both employees and nonemployees. An example is an employee who misunderstands operating procedures and accidentally deletes customer records. Another example is an employee who, in the course of backing up a database, inadvertently installs an old database on top of the current one. This category also includes poorly written application programs and poorly designed procedures. Finally, human errors and mistakes include physical accidents like driving a forklift through the wall of a computer room.

The second source of security problems is *malicious human activity*. This category includes employees and former employees who intentionally destroy data or other system components. It also includes hackers who break into a system and virus and worm writers who infect computer systems. Malicious human activity also includes outside criminals who break into a system to steal for financial gain; it also includes terrorism.

Natural events and disasters are the third source of security problems. This category includes fires, floods, hurricanes, earthquakes, tsunamis, avalanches, and other acts of nature. Problems in this category include not only the initial loss of capability and service, but also losses stemming from actions to recover from the initial problem.

You Be the Guide

Southwest Video Training (page 335)

GOALS

* Motivate students to learn about organizational security requirements.

* Learn about management's security responsibility, common security threats, and safeguards from those threats.

WAYS TO STIMULATE STUDENT INVOLVEMENT

I like to use the Southwest case for a course review. Southwest's business is simple enough to understand in a short period of time, yet it touches on most of the class topics. Southwest operates a LAN, which connects to the Internet, and Southwest supports its own Web site. The company has a customer database that runs a simple CRM. It has a finished-goods inventory of expensive goods, and it needs to keep careful track of that inventory. Although not discussed in the case, the company claims to perform data mining, but it could be doing much more than it is.

To understand Southwest's business, then, the student needs to apply concepts from Chapter 4 (databases), Chapter 5 (data communications), Chapter 7 (CRM and inventory), Chapter 8 (e-commerce), and Chapter 9 (data mining). The informal nature of IS operations at Southwest indicates that the company needs a better understanding of IS management (Chapter 10), and it could definitely benefit from more knowledge of systems development (Chapter 6).

In other words, the student needs every topic from this class to truly understand this business.

➤ **What you have learned in this class puts you in a great position to understand information systems at this business. If you were a manager here, you would not only be able to help with the security question, but you would also be able to use, modify, and participate in the development of new information systems for all aspects of this company's business.**

Background: Southwest Video has won numerous awards, and its programs are both informative and hilarious. Southwest's programs literally sell one another; a company that has used one of its programs is likely to buy another.

Southwest sells high value at a high price. The price for a single license to use one of its programs is in the range of $550 to $650. Most of it market is medium to large corporations.

Given the likelihood that customers who have purchased a license for one program will purchase a license for two or more, and given their high price, Southwest can afford to invest telesales time calling existing customers.

All of this explains the importance and value of Southwest's customer database. The salespeople need to know who has purchased a program, which programs they have purchased, when they last purchased, and so forth.

Southwest is doing almost nothing in the way of data mining this data. When I mentioned it to them, managers said, "We're already doing that." However, they were not doing an RFM analysis, they were not doing market-basket analysis, and they were not looking for product purchase patterns. An example of the latter would be to determine that a company that has purchased the leadership program is more likely to purchase the motivation program than the customer support program. All of these data-mining analyses could make Southwest's telesales much more effective. All of that lost potential just drove me nuts! Southwest could do so much more with the database.

Southwest fosters an artsy company culture, and part of that culture is their location in a wonderful old building in a formerly industrial part of the city. Southwest's offices are full of movie and theater antiques, art, and posters. The building is wooden and was constructed long before modern building codes were enforced. At a glance, it appears that the company has greater-than-normal risk of fire or building collapse from earthquakes.

As a small business, one that carefully manages its costs, Southwest is unlikely to spend much in the way of disaster preparedness or security. The partners are optimistic, forward-looking, and cheerful, and they don't like to dwell on threats and disasters. It is difficult to get them to think about these problems. (I suppose life insurance salespeople encounter the same attitude.)

Southwest runs a LAN connected to a router to the Internet. The company supports its own Web site, using its own computing infrastructure. The partners have little understanding of their firewall, its type, or its effectiveness. They know they should know more, but something else always has a higher priority for their attention.

There are thousands of businesses like this one throughout North America, and undoubtedly throughout the world. From the standpoint of someone who cares about information security, the number of such businesses is incredibly depressing. From the standpoint of a student who might like to become a computer security specialist or consultant, the number of such businesses is incredibly exciting—what an opportunity!!!

WRAP UP

➤ This case should make you feel good about the investment you've made in MIS knowledge. In it, you can see the utility of almost everything we have discussed in this class. Even if you never work in IS security or never have to address a security question for a business like this, what you have learned in this class will help you to understand the basic operations and drivers of the information systems for this business.

➤ For example, suppose you manage telesales. When someone says, "We use a LAN with a wireless AP," you'll know what they mean, and you'll know to ask if it is protected.

➤ If they say, "We have a *CRM* database" you'll know what *CRM* means and what *database* means. You'll also know that most applications and databases have strong support for users, user groups, and permissions, and if you don't see such a system in use, you'll know to inquire about using those features.

➤ If the manager of operations says, "We developed our inventory management system ourselves, and it's so bad that we need to replace it with someone else's package," you'll know how to apply the systems development process (for building the system that incorporates the new package), or at least you'll know there is such a process that should be applied.

➤ Again, read this case and think about how you can apply the knowledge you've gained in this class. This case should make you feel great about the work you've invested!!!

Problem Types

Figure 11-1 summarizes threats by type of problem and source. Five types of security problems are listed: unauthorized data disclosure, incorrect data modification, faulty service, denial of service, and loss of infrastructure. We will consider each type.

Unauthorized Data Disclosure

Unauthorized data disclosure can occur by human error when someone inadvertently releases data in violation of policy. An example at a university would be a new department administrator who posts student names, numbers, and grades in a public place, when the releasing of names and grades violates state law. Another example is employees who unknowingly or carelessly release proprietary data to competitors or to the media.

The popularity and efficacy of search engines has created another source of inadvertent disclosure. Employees who place restricted data on Web sites that can be reached by search engines may mistakenly publish proprietary or restricted data over the Web.

Of course, proprietary and personal data can also be released maliciously. **Pretexting** occurs when someone deceives by pretending to be someone else. A common scam involves a telephone caller who pretends to be from a credit card company and claims to be checking the validity of credit card numbers: "I'm checking your MasterCard number; it begins 5491. Can you verify the rest of the number?" All MasterCard numbers start with 5491; the caller is attempting to steal a valid number.

Phishing is a similar technique for obtaining unauthorized data that uses pretexting via email. The *phisher* pretends to be a legitimate company and sends an email requesting confidential data, such as account numbers, Social Security numbers, account passwords, and so forth. Phishing compromises legitimate brands and trademarks. *MIS in Use 11-1* (page 338) looks in more detail at some examples of phishing.

Spoofing is another term for someone pretending to be someone else. If you pretend to be your professor, you are spoofing your professor. **IP spoofing** occurs when an intruder uses another site's IP address as if it were that other site. **Email spoofing** is a synonym for phishing.

		Source		
		Human Error	**Malicious Activity**	**Natural Disasters**
Problem	**Unauthorized data disclosure**	Procedural mistakes	Pretexting Phishing Spoofing Sniffing Computer crime	Disclosure during recovery
	Incorrect data modification	Procedural mistakes Incorrect procedures Ineffective accounting controls System errors	Hacking Computer crime	Incorrect data recovery
	Faulty service	Procedural mistakes Development and installation errors	Computer crime Usurpation	Service improperly restored
	Denial of service	Accidents	DOS attacks	Service interruption
	Loss of infrastructure	Accidents	Theft Terrorist activity	Property loss

Figure 11-1
Security Problems and Sources

Phishing for Credit Card Accounts

Before you read further, realize that the graphics in this case are *fake*. They were not produced by a legitimate business, but were generated by a phisher. A *phisher* is an operation that spoofs legitimate companies in an attempt to illegally capture credit card numbers, email accounts, driver's license numbers, and other data. Some phishers even install malicious program code on users' computers.

Phishing is usually initiated via an email. Go to *http://www.fraudwatchinternational.com/internet/phishing.shtml* and page down two screens. You will see an example that appears to be an email message from PayPal. It fact, that message is a fake. To see even more examples, follow the five-step tour displayed on that site.

The most common phishing attack is initiated with a bogus email. For example, you might receive the following email:

Your Order ID: "17152492"
Order Date: "09/07/05"
Product Purchased: "Two First Class Tickets to Cozumel"
Your card type: "CREDIT"
Total Price: "$349.00"

Hello, when you purchased your tickets you provided an incorrect mailing address.
See more details here
Please follow the link and modify your mailing address or cancel your order. If you have questions, feel free to cortact with us
account@usefulbill.com

Figure 1
Fake Phishing Email

This bogus email is designed to cause you to click on the "See more details here" link. When you do so, you will be connected to a site that will ask you for personal data such as credit card numbers, card expiration dates, driver's license number, Social Security number, or other data. In this particular case, you will be taken to a screen that asks for your credit card number (see Figure 2).

This Web page is produced by a nonexistent company and is entirely fake, including the link "Inform us about fraud." The only purpose of this site is to illegally capture your card number. It might also install spyware, adware, or other malware (see page 350) on your computer.

If you were to get this far, you should immediately close your browser and restart your computer. You should also run anti-malware scans on your computer to determine if the phisher has installed pro-

Figure 2
Fake Phishing Screen

gram code on your computer. If so, use the anti-malware software to remove that code.

How can you defend yourself from such attacks? First, you know that you did not purchase two first class tickets to Cozumel. (Had you by odd circumstance just purchased airline tickets to Cozumel, you should contact the legitimate vendor's site *directly* to determine if there had been some mix up.) Because you have not purchased such tickets, suspect a phisher.

Second, notice the implausibility of the email. It is exceedingly unlikely that you can buy two first-class tickets to any foreign country for $349. Additionally, note the misspelled word in the last line and the poor grammar ("contact with us"). All of these facts should alert you to the bogus nature of this email.

Third, do not be misled by legitimate-looking graphics. Phishers are criminals; they do not bother to respect international agreements on legitimate use of trademarks. The phisher might use names of legitimate companies like Visa, MasterCard, Discover, and AmericanExpress on the Web page, and the presence of those names might lull you into thinking this is legitimate. The phisher is illegally using those names. In other instances, the phisher will copy the entire look and feel of a legitimate company's Web site.

Phishing is a serious problem. To protect yourself, be wary of unsolicited email, even if the email appears to be from a legitimate business. If you have questions about an email, contact the company directly (*not* using the addresses provided by the phisher!) and ask about the email. And above all, never give confidential data such as account numbers, Social Security numbers, driver's license numbers, or credit card numbers in response to any *unsolicited* email.

The discussion of phishing is continued in Case Study 11-1, page 365.

Sniffing is a technique for intercepting computer communications. With wired networks, sniffing requires a physical connection to the network. With wireless networks, no such connection is required: **Drive-by sniffers** simply take computers with wireless connections through an area and search for unprotected wireless networks. They can monitor and intercept wireless traffic at will. Even protected wireless networks are vulnerable, as you will learn. Spyware and adware are two other sniffing techniques discussed later in this chapter.

Other forms of computer crime include breaking into networks to steal data such as customer lists, product inventory data, employee data, and other proprietary and confidential data.

Finally, people may inadvertently disclose data during recovery from a natural disaster. Usually, during a recovery, everyone is so focused on restoring system capability that they ignore normal security safeguards. A request like "I need a copy of the customer database backup" will receive far less scrutiny during disaster recovery than at other times.

Incorrect Data Modification

The second problem category in Figure 11-1 is *incorrect data modification*. Examples include incorrectly increasing a customer's discount or incorrectly modifying an employee's salary, earned days of vacation, or annual bonus. Other examples include placing incorrect information, such as incorrect price changes, on the company's Web site or company portal.

Incorrect data modification can occur through human error when employees follow procedures incorrectly or when procedures have been incorrectly designed. For proper internal control on systems that process financial data or that control inventories of assets like products and equipment, companies should ensure separation of duties and authorities and have multiple checks and balances in place.

A final type of incorrect data modification caused by human error includes *system errors*. An example is the lost-update problem discussed in Chapter 4 (pages 96–97).

Hacking occurs when a person gains unauthorized access to a computer system. Although some people hack for the sheer joy of doing it, other hackers invade systems for the malicious purpose of stealing or modifying data. Computer criminals invade computer networks to obtain critical data or to manipulate the system for financial gain. Examples are reducing account balances or causing the shipment of goods to unauthorized locations and customers.

Finally, faulty recovery actions after a disaster can result in incorrect data changes. The faulty actions can be unintentional or malicious.

Faulty Service

The third problem category, *faulty service*, includes problems that result because of incorrect system operation. Faulty service could include incorrect data modification, as just described. It also could include systems that work incorrectly by sending the wrong goods to the customer or the ordered goods to the wrong customer, incorrectly billing customers, or sending the wrong information to employees. Humans can inadvertently cause faulty service by making procedural mistakes. System developers can write programs incorrectly or make errors during the installation of hardware, software programs, and data.

Usurpation occurs when unauthorized programs invade a computer system and replace legitimate programs. Such unauthorized programs typically shut down the legitimate system and substitute their own processing. Faulty service can also result from mistakes made during the recovery from natural disasters.

Denial of Service

Human error in following procedures or a lack of procedures can result in **denial of service**. For example, humans can inadvertently shut down a Web server or corporate gateway router by starting a computationally intensive application. An OLAP application that uses the operational DBMS can consume so many DBMS resources that order entry transactions cannot get through.

Denial-of-service attacks can be launched maliciously. A malicious hacker can flood a Web server, for example, with millions of bogus service requests that so occupy the server that it cannot service legitimate requests. As you learned in Chapter 3 (page 53a), computer worms can infiltrate a network with so much artificial traffic that legitimate traffic cannot get through. Finally, natural disasters may cause systems to fail, resulting in denial of service.

Loss of Infrastructure

Human accidents can cause *loss of infrastructure*. Examples are a bulldozer cutting a conduit of fiber-optic cables and the floor buffer crashing into a rack of Web servers.

Theft and terrorist events also cause loss of infrastructure. A disgruntled, terminated employee can walk off with corporate data servers, routers, or other crucial equipment. Terrorist events can also cause the loss of physical plants and equipment.

Natural disasters present the largest risk for infrastructure loss. A fire, flood, earthquake, or similar event can destroy data centers and all they contain. The devastation of the Indian Ocean tsunami in December 2004 and of Hurricanes Katrina and Rita in the fall of 2005 are potent examples of the risks to infrastructure from natural causes.

You may be wondering why Figure 11-1 does not include viruses, worms, and Trojan horses. The answer is that viruses, worms, and Trojan horses are *techniques* for causing some of the problems in the figure. They can cause a denial-of-service attack, or they can be used to cause malicious, unauthorized data access, or data loss.

The Security Program

All of the problems listed in Figure 11-1 are real and as serious as they sound. Accordingly, organizations must address security in a systematic way. A security program[1] has three components: senior management involvement, safeguards of various kinds, and incident response.

The first component, senior management, has two critical security functions: First, senior management must establish the security policy. This policy sets the stage for the organization's response to security threats. However, because no security program is perfect, there is always risk. Management's second function, therefore, is to manage risk by balancing the costs and benefits of the security program.

Safeguards are protections against security threats. A good way to view safeguards is in terms of the five components of an information system, as shown in Figure 11-2. Some of the safeguards involve computer hardware and software. Some involve data; others involve procedures and people. In addition to these safeguards, organizations must also consider disaster recovery safeguards. An effective security program consists of a balance of safeguards of all these types.

The final component of a security program consists of the organization's planned response to security incidents. Clearly, the time to think about what to do is not when the computers are crashing all around the organization. We will discuss incident response in the last section of this chapter.

The balance of this chapter discusses these three information security components. We begin with the responsibility of senior management.

Senior Management's Security Role

Management has a crucial role in information systems security. Management sets the policy, and only management can balance the costs of a security system against the risk of security threats. The National Institute of Standards and Technology (NIST)

---

[1]Note the word *program* is used here in the sense of a management program that includes objectives, policies, procedures, directives, and so forth. Do not confuse this term with a computer program.

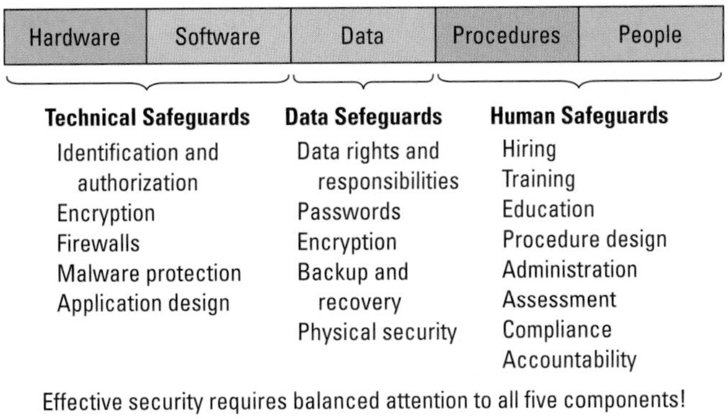

Hardware	Software	Data	Procedures	People

Technical Safeguards
Identification and
authorization
Encryption
Firewalls
Malware protection
Application design

Data Safeguards
Data rights and
responsibilities
Passwords
Encryption
Backup and
recovery
Physical security

Human Safeguards
Hiring
Training
Education
Procedure design
Administration
Assessment
Compliance
Accountability

Effective security requires balanced attention to all five components!

Figure 11-2
Security Safeguards
as They Relate to the Five
Components

published an excellent security handbook that addresses management's responsibility. It is available online at *csrc.nist.gov/publications/nistpubs/800-12/handbook.pdf.* We will follow its discussion in this section.

The *NIST Handbook* of Security Elements

Figure 11-3 lists elements of computer security described in the *NIST Handbook*. First, computer security must support the organization's mission. There is no "one size fits all" solution to security problems. Security systems for a diamond mine and security systems for a wheat farm will differ.

According to the second point in Figure 11-3, when you manage a department, you have a responsibility for information security in that department, even if no one tells you that you do. Do appropriate safeguards exist? Are your employees properly trained? Will your department know how to respond when the computer system fails? If these issues are not addressed in your department, raise the issue to higher levels of management.

Security can be expensive. Therefore, as shown in the third principle of Figure 11-3, computer security should have an appropriate cost-benefit ratio. Costs can be direct, such a labor costs, and they can be intangible, such as employee or customer frustration.

According to the fourth principle in Figure 11-3, security responsibilities and accountabilities must be explicit. General statements like "everyone in the department must adequately safeguard company assets" are worthless. Instead, managers should assign specific tasks to specific people or specific job functions.

Because information systems integrate the processing of many departments, security problems originating in your department can have far-reaching consequences. If one of your employees neglects procedures and enters product prices incorrectly on your Web storefront, the consequences will extend to other departments,

1. Computer security should support the mission of the organization.
2. Computer security is an integral element of sound management.
3. Computer security should be cost-effective.
4. Computer security responsibilities and accountability should be made explicit.
5. System owners have computer security responsibilities outside their own organizations.
6. Computer security requires a comprehensive and integrated approach.
7. Computer security should be periodically reassessed.
8. Computer security is constrained by societal factors.

Figure 11-3
Elements of Computer
Security

Source: National Institute of
Standards and Technology,
*Introduction to Computer Security:
The NIST Handbook*, Publication
800-12, p. 9.

other companies, and your customers. Understanding that computer system owners have security responsibilities outside their own departments and organizations is the fifth principle of computer security.

As the sixth principle in Figure 11-3 implies, there is no magic bullet for security. No single safeguard, such as a firewall or a virus protection program, or increased employee training, will provide effective security. The problems described in Figure 11-1 require an integrated security program.

Once a security program is in place, the company cannot simply forget about it. As the seventh principle in Figure 11-3 indicates, security is a continuing need, and every company must periodically evaluate its security program.

Finally, social factors put some limits on security programs. Employees resent physical searches when arriving at and departing from work. Customers do not want to have their retinas scanned before they can place an order. Computer security conflicts with personal privacy, and a balance may be hard to achieve.

Security Policy

As stated, senior management has two overarching security tasks: defining a security policy and managing computer-security risk. Although management may delegate the specific tasks, it maintains the responsibility for the organization's security and must approve and endorse all such work.

A **security policy** has three elements: The first is a general statement of the organization's *security program*. This statement becomes the foundation for more specific security measures throughout the organization. In this statement, management specifies the goals of the security program and the assets to be protected. This statement also designates a department for managing the organization's security program and documents, in general terms, *how* the organization will ensure enforcement of security programs and policies.

The second security policy element is *issue-specific policy*. For example, management might formulate a policy on personal use of computers at work and email privacy. The organization has the legal right to limit personal use of its computer systems and to inspect personal email for compliance. Employees have a right to know such policies. For another example, management sets security policies to ensure compliance with security law as discussed in the *Ethics Guide* on page 343a.

The third security policy element is *system-specific policy*, which concerns specific information systems. For example, what customer data from the order entry system will be sold or shared with other organizations? Or, what policies govern the design and operation of systems that process employee data? Companies should address such policies as part of the standard systems development process.

Risk Management

Management's second overarching security task is risk management. **Risk** is the likelihood of an adverse occurrence. Management cannot manage threats directly, but it *can* manage the likelihood that threats will be successful. Thus, management cannot keep hurricanes from happening, but it can limit the security consequences of a hurricane by creating a backup processing facility at a remote location.

Companies can reduce risks, but always at a cost. It is management's responsibility to decide how much to spend, or stated differently, how much risk to assume.

Unfortunately, risk management takes place in a sea of uncertainty. Uncertainty is different from risk. Risk refers to threats and consequences that we know about. **Uncertainty** refers to the things we don't know that we don't know. For example, an earthquake could devastate a corporate data center on a fault that no one knew about. An employee may have found a way to steal inventory using a hole in the corporate Web site that no expert knew existed. Because of uncertainty, risk management is always approximate.

1. Assets	5. Consequences
2. Threats	6. Likelihood
3. Safeguards	7. Probable loss
4. Vulnerability	

Figure 11-4
Risk Assessment

Risk Assessment

The first step in risk management is to assess what the threats are, how likely they are to occur, and what the consequences are if they occur. Figure 11-4 lists factors to consider. First, what are the assets that are to be protected? Examples are computer facilities, programs, and sensitive data. Other assets are less obvious. Phishing threatens an organization's customers as well its trademark and brand. Employee privacy is another asset that can be at risk.

Given the list of assets to be protected, the next action is to assess the threats to which they are exposed. The company should consider all of the threats in Figure 11-1; there may be other threats as well.

The third factor in risk assessment is to determine what safeguards are in place to protect company assets from the identified threats. According to the *NIST Handbook*, a **safeguard** is any action, device, procedure, technique, or other measure that reduces a system's vulnerability to a threat.[2] No safeguard is ironclad; there is always a *residual risk* that the safeguard will not protect the assets in all circumstances.

A **vulnerability** is an opening or a weakness in the security system. Some vulnerabilities exist because there are no safeguards or because the existing safeguards are ineffective. Because of residual risk, there is always some residual vulnerability even to assets that are protected by effective safeguards.

Consequences, the fifth factor listed in Figure 11-4, are the damages that occur when an asset is compromised. Consequences can be tangible or intangible. *Tangible* consequences are those whose financial impact can be measured. The costs of *intangible* consequences, such as the loss of customer goodwill due to an outage, cannot be measured. Normally, when analyzing consequences, companies estimate the costs of tangible consequences and simply list intangible consequences.

The final two factors in risk assessment are likelihood and probable loss. *Likelihood* is the probability that a given asset will be compromised by a given threat, despite the safeguards. *Probable loss* is the "bottom line" of risk assessment. To obtain a measure of probable loss, companies multiply likelihood by the cost of the consequences. Probable loss also includes a statement of intangible consequences.

Risk-Management Decisions

Given the probable loss from the risk assessment just described, senior management must decide what to do. In some cases, the decision is easy. Companies can protect some assets by use of inexpensive and easily implemented safeguards. Installing virus protection software is an example. However, some vulnerability is expensive to eliminate, and management must determine if the costs of the safeguard are worth the benefit of probable loss reduction. Such risk-management decisions are difficult because the true effectiveness of the safeguard is seldom known, and the probable loss is subject to uncertainty.

Uncertainty, however, does not absolve management from security responsibility. Management has a fiduciary responsibility to the organization's owners, and senior managers must make reasonable and prudent decisions in light of available information. They must consider the factors listed in Figure 11-4 and take cost-effective action to reduce probable losses, despite the uncertainty.

The next sections discuss safeguards. We begin with technical safeguards, then data safeguards, then human safeguards, and, finally, safeguards against natural disasters.

---

[2] *NIST Handbook, csrc.nist.gov/publications/nistpubs/800-12/handbook.pdf*, p. 61 (accessed July 2005).

Security
Privacy

Some organizations have legal requirements to protect the customer data they collect and store, but the laws may be more limited than you think. The GGramm-Leach-Bliley (GLB) Act, passed by Congress in 1999, protects consumer financial data stored by financial institutions, which are defined as banks, securities firms, insurance companies, and organizations that provide financial advice, prepare tax returns, and provide similar financial services.

The **Privacy Act of 1974** provides protections to individuals regarding records maintained by the U.S. government, and the privacy provisions of the **Health Insurance Portability and Accountability Act (HIPAA)** of 1996 gives individuals the right to access health data created by doctors and other health-care providers. HIPAA also sets rules and limits on who can read and receive your health information.

The law is stronger in other countries. In Australia, for example, the Privacy Principles of the Australian Privacy Act of 1988 govern not only government and health care data, but also records maintained by businesses with revenues in excess of AU$3 million.

To understand the importance of the limitations, consider online retailers that routinely store customer credit card data. Do Dell, Amazon.com, the airlines, and other e-commerce businesses have a legal requirement to protect their customers' credit card data? Apparently not—at least not in the United States. The activities of such organizations are not governed by the GLB, the Privacy Act of 1974, or HIPAA.

Most consumers would say, however, that online retailers have an ethical requirement to protect a customer's credit card and other data, and most online retailers would agree. Or at least the retailers would agree that they have a strong business reason to protect those data. A substantial loss of credit card data by any large online retailer would have detrimental effects on both sales and brand reputation.

Let's bring the discussion closer to home. What requirements does your university have on the data it maintains about you? State law or university policy may govern those records, but no federal law does. Most universities consider it their responsibility to provide public access to graduation records. Anyone can determine when you graduated, your degree, and your major. (Keep this service in mind when you write your resume.)

Most professors endeavor to publish grades by student number and not by name, and there may be state law that requires that separation. But what about your work? What about the papers you write, the answers you give on exams? What about the emails you send to your professor? The data are not protected by federal law, and they are probably not protected by state law. If your professor chooses to cite your work in research, she will be subject to copyright law, but not privacy law. What you write is no longer your personal data; it belongs to the academic community. You can ask your professor what she intends to do with your coursework, emails, and office conversations, but none of those data are protected by law.

The bottom line: Be careful with your personal data. Large, reputable organizations are likely to endorse ethical privacy policy and to have strong and effective safeguards to effectuate that policy. But individuals and small organizations may not. If in doubt, ask.

DISCUSSION QUESTIONS

1. As stated, when you order from an online retailer, the data you provide is not protected by U.S. privacy law. Does this fact cause you to reconsider setting up an account with a stored credit card number? What is the advantage of storing the credit card number? Do you think the advantage is worth the risk? Are you more willing to take the risk with some companies than with others? Why or why not?

2. Suppose you are the treasurer of a student club, and you store records of club members' payments in a database. In the past, members have disputed payment amounts; therefore, when you receive a payment, you scan an image of the check or credit card invoice and store the scanned image in a database.

   One day, you are using your computer in a local wireless coffee shop and a malicious student breaks into your computer over the wireless network and steals the club database. You know nothing about this until the next day, when a club member complains that a popular student Web site has published the names, bank names, and bank account numbers for everyone who has given you a check.

   What liability do you have in this matter? Could you be classified as a financial institution because you are taking students' money? (You can find the GLB at *ftc.gov/privacy/glbact*.) If so, what liability do you have? If not, do you have any other liability? Does the coffee shop have a liability?

3. Suppose you are asked to fill out a study questionnaire that requires you to enter identifying data as well as answers to personal questions. You hesitate to provide the data, but the top part of the questionnaire states, "All responses will be strictly confidential." So, you fill out the questionnaire.

   Unfortunately, the person who is conducting the study visits the same wireless coffee shop that you visited (in question 2), and the same malicious student breaks in and steals the study results. Your name and all of your responses appear on that same student Web site. Did the person conducting the study violate a law? Does the confidentiality assurance on the form increase that person's requirement to protect your data? Does your answer change if the person conducting the study is (a) a student, (b) a professor of music, or (c) a professor of computer security?

4. In truth, only a very talented and motivated hacker could steal databases from computers using a public wireless network. Such losses, although possible, are unlikely. However, any email you send or files you download can readily be sniffed at a public wireless facility. Knowing this, describe good practice for computer use at public wireless facilities.

5. Considering your answers to the above questions, state three to five general principles to guide your actions as you disseminate and store data.

Technical Safeguards

We have already addressed many security safeguards in the *Security Guides* in each chapter. You may wish to review some of those discussions before proceeding here. (See pages ii and iii, at the front of the book, for a quick overview of the *Security Guides*.) The discussion on passwords in Chapter 1 (page 5a) and the discussion of encryption in Chapter 5 (page 133a) are particularly relevant.

Technical safeguards involve the hardware and software components of an information system. Figure 11-5 lists primary technical safeguards. We have discussed all of these in prior chapters. Here we will just supplement those prior discussions.

Identification and Authentication

Every information system today should require users to sign on with a user name and password. The user name *identifies* the user (the process of **identification**), and the password *authenticates* that user (the process of **authentication**). Review the material on strong passwords and password etiquette in Chapter 1 (page 5a) if you have forgotten that discussion.

Passwords have important weaknesses. For one, users tend to be careless in their use. Despite repeated warnings to the contrary, yellow sticky notes holding written passwords adorn many computers. In addition, users tend to be free in sharing their passwords with others. Finally, many users choose ineffective, simple passwords. With such passwords, intrusion systems can very effectively guess passwords.

These deficiencies can be reduced or eliminated using smart cards and biometric authentication.

Smart Cards

A **smart card** is a plastic card similar to a credit card. Unlike credit, debit, and ATM cards, which have a magnetic strip, smart cards have a microchip. The microchip, which holds far more data than a magnetic strip, is loaded with identifying data. Users of smart-cards are required to enter a **personal identification number (PIN)** to be authenticated.

Biometric Authentication

Biometric authentication uses personal physical characteristics such as fingerprints, facial features, and retinal scans to authenticate users. Biometric authentication provides strong authentication, but the required equipment is expensive. Often, too, users resist biometric identification because they feel it is invasive.

Biometric authentication is in the early stages of adoption. Because of its strength, it likely will see increased usage in the future. It is also likely that legislators will pass laws governing the use, storage, and protection requirements for biometric data. For more on biometrics, see *searchsecurity.techtarget.com/originalContent/0,289142, sid14_gci884803,00.html.*

Note that authentication methods fall into three categories: what you know (password or PIN), what you have (smart card), and what you are (biometric).

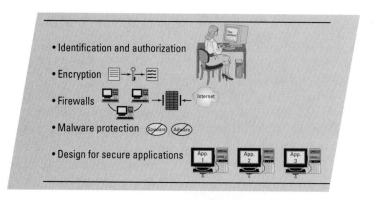

Figure 11-5
Technical Safeguards

Using the Ethics Guide

(page 343a)

GOALS

* Understand the legal requirements, ethical considerations, and business consequences of data acquisition, storage, and dissemination.

* Help students formulate personal principles with regard to data acquisition, storage, and dissemination.

BACKGROUND AND PRESENTATION STRATEGIES

Throughout this text, we've discussed three categories of criteria for evaluating business actions and employee behavior:

• Legal

• Ethical

• Good business practice

We can clearly see the differences in these criteria with regard to data security. A doctor's office that does not create systems to comply with HIPAA is violating the law. An e-commerce business that collects customer data and sells it to spammers is behaving unethically (at least according to the accepted principles of behavior of most business professionals). An e-commerce business that is lackadaisical about securing its customer data is engaging in poor business practices.

Business professionals need to be worried, much more so than they are, about unsecured wireless networks. Depending on the business, not securing a wireless network could be illegal, unethical, and poor business practice!

Recently, while stopped in a bad traffic jam in my car, I turned on my notebook computer to obtain a phone number. I was on the freeway in the middle of a residential neighborhood, and my laptop found three wireless networks, only one of which was secure. Later that week, while parked in a small tourist town on vacation, I turned on my notebook and found four wireless networks, *none* of which was protected! I'm wondering, "Why does anyone even bother to buy Internet access anymore?" One could just set up shop in their car!

Wireless security is changing rapidly; but as of this writing, one effective (not ironclad, but effective)

technique for securing a wireless network is MAC address filtering. It's simple to do: Access the management firmware of the wireless access point (the product documentation always shows how to do this). Check MAC address filtering, and enter the MAC address of every device that is allowed to connect to the LAN. Any device that is not in the list will not be able to connect to the access point.

Careful, here, though! Make sure to enter those addresses correctly—otherwise you won't be able to reconnect to the access point, and you'll have to call the vendor's help desk to learn how to recover.

On Windows, to obtain the computer's MAC address, open a command window (Click *Start, Run, cmd*), and execute the program *getmac*. It will return your computer's MAC address. For printer drivers and other devices, the product's documentation should include the MAC address.

➤ **MAC address filtering is easy to do. Not doing it is poor business practice, possibly unethical, and maybe even illegal!**

Two guidelines that apply the principle, "The best way to solve a problem is not to have it" are:

➤ **Resist providing sensitive data.**

➤ **Don't collect data you don't need.**

I have become very aggressive in not divulging personal data. At least 95 percent of the time, when I challenge someone as to why they need some piece of personal data, they respond, "Oh, don't bother—we don't have to have it." I recommend a similar strategy to my students.

When someone says, "All answers are strictly confidential," consider the source. If that statement comes from the university computer security staff, I believe they understand what they are claiming to provide and will take every professional effort to comply with that statement. If it is made by a team of undergraduates with majors that predispose me to believe they know little of computer security, then I suspect they may not know what they are claiming to provide. Furthermore, in the event of a security system failure, the university has a deep enough pocket to provide compensation for damages. It would be difficult to obtain compensation from a group of undergraduates.

➤ **Don't provide data to sources with questionable data security!**

SUGGESTED RESPONSES FOR DISCUSSION QUESTIONS

1. The advantage of an account is you don't have to enter credit card data every time you buy. The problem is that your credit card data is stored on at least one of their disks, and hence it is vulnerable to theft. (The order entry software may also store your credit card data for a one-time purchase, but that storage should be temporary.)

   I recommend four general principles:

   ➤ **Never set up an account with a vendor unless you know that vendor has substantial financial assets (Amazon.com versus Mom-and-Pop Plant Sales).**

   ➤ **Set up accounts only with companies with which you do enough business that the time-savings benefits of the account justify the risk of a security problem.**

   ➤ **Send credit card data only to organizations that are using SSL/TLS (https).**

   ➤ **Never send your Social Security number, driver's license number, or any password to anyone.**

   (Caveat: Maybe it would be OK to send your SSN to the IRS? The alternative is paying by mail, but is that any more secure? The IRS stores your SSN, regardless of how you pay. A good question.)

2. You probably do have some liability in this instance, but unless you have substantial personal assets, it's probably not worth anyone's time to sue you. Your club or university may have liability, however. I doubt anyone could claim that you are a financial institution, but there may be other liability. The possible liability of the coffee shop is interesting. I suspect there is some language somewhere that limits its liability. These are questions to explore with a business law professor, because the relevant case law is evolving.

   As a practical matter, whenever you collect any sort of confidential computer-sensible data, don't store it on the notebook computer you carry around campus or use for wireless access. Store it on a memory stick and when you're not using that data lock the memory stick up at home—or at the club offices. Take the memory stick out only when you need the data for a meeting, and don't sign on to a wireless network while you're using it.

3. Use the three categories of criteria: Collecting sensitive data and not protecting it is *poor business practice,* even if you provide no confidentiality statement. Collecting data and not protecting becomes *unethical* if you do provide a confidentiality statement.

As to the *legality,* I am not an attorney, but I don't believe this event violates any commonly enacted law. However, you may have violated an implied contract between you and the responder. If your statement does constitute a contract, you are expected to do what a reasonable and prudent person would do to protect that data. If you do not take such precautions, you are in violation of the contract and could be held financially accountable.

The three different backgrounds alter what the reasonable and prudent person would be expected to do. The student would have the least responsibility, because of his or her assumed immaturity and inexperience. The professor of music would have greater responsibilities, because his or her position as a professor would imply greater experience and world knowledge. The professor of computer security would have a very high level of expectation of behavior for protecting that data.

4. I think the following is the very best guideline for email:

   ➤ **Never send an email, from anywhere, unless you would be pleased to see it published on the front page of the *New York Times* or your local newspaper the next day. If you'd be embarrassed, likely to be sued, or likely to go to jail were that email published, don't send it. Don't write it, either.**

5. One possible list of general principles for storing and disseminating data:

   ➤ **Don't disseminate data when you can avoid it.**

   ➤ **Don't collect data when you can avoid it.**

   ➤ **When you do collect sensitive data, keep it on removable devices and minimize the exposure of those devices to security threats. (This guideline is appropriate for an individual; obviously a business has other requirements.)**

   ➤ **Never generate an email that you'd regret seeing on the front page of the *New York Times*.**

   ➤ **Secure your personal/home/SOHO wireless networks.**

WRAP UP

➤ **As a business professional, you have the responsibility to consider the legality, the ethics, and the wisdom when you request, store, or disseminate data. The more knowledge and experience you have, the greater that responsibility is.**

➤ **Think about this and develop your own code of behavior. Then, follow that code. Prevent problems before they occur!**

Single Sign-on for Multiple Systems

Information systems often require multiple sources of authentication. For example, when you sign on to your personal computer, you need to be authenticated. When you access the LAN in your department, you need to be authenticated again. When you traverse your organization's WAN, you will need to be authenticated to even more networks. Also, if your request requires database data, the DBMS server that manages that database will authenticate you yet again.

It would be annoying to enter a name and password for every one of these resources. You might have to use and remember five or six different passwords just to access the data you need to perform your job. It would be equally undesirable to send your password across all of these networks. The further your password travels, the greater the risk it can be compromised.

Instead, today's operating systems have the capability to authenticate you to networks and other servers. You sign on to your local computer and provide authentication data; from that point on, your operating system authenticates you to another network or server, which can authenticate you to yet another network and server, and so forth.

A system called **Kerberos** authenticates users without sending their passwords across the computer network. Developed by the Massachusetts Institute of Technology (MIT), Kerberos uses a complicated system of "tickets" to enable users to obtain services from networks and other servers. Windows, Linux, Unix, and other operating systems employ Kerberos and thus can authenticate user requests across networks of computers using a mixture of these operating systems.

This discussion indicates another reason why you must protect your user name and password. Once you have authenticated yourself on your local system, your operating system will authenticate you to networks and other servers. Someone who obtains your name and password will gain access not only to your computer, but via intersystem authentication, to many other computers and servers as well. The bottom line: Protect your passwords!

However, despite all that we know about the need for protecting passwords, compliance with password-protection guidelines is still lacking, as the *Opposing Forces Guide* on page 345a demonstrates.

Wireless Access

For a wired network, a potential intruder must obtain physical access to the network. For a wireless network, however, no direct connection is needed. Drive-by sniffers can walk or drive around business or residential neighborhoods with a wireless computer and locate dozens, or even hundreds, of wireless networks. The wireless network will broadcast whether it is protected. If not, the sniffer can use it to obtain free access to the Internet or to connect to LANs that are connected to the access point.

In 2004, in a short ride through the Back Bay section of Boston, Massachusetts, a security consultant found 2,676 wireless connections, most of which were residential. Of those, almost half were unprotected.[3] Anyone with a wireless device could have connected to those unprotected access points and tapped into the Internet for free or taken more disruptive actions.

It is possible to protect wireless networks. Businesses with sophisticated communications equipment use elaborate techniques—techniques that require the support of highly trained communications specialists. Common protections use VPNs and special security servers.

For the less sophisticated SOHO market, wireless networks are less secure. The IEEE 802.11 Committee, the group that develops and maintains wireless standards, first developed a wireless security standard called **Wired Equivalent Privacy (WEP)**.

---

[3]Bruce Mohl, "Tap into Neighbors' Wi-Fi? Why Not, Some Say," *The Boston Globe*, July 4, 2004, *boston.com/business/technology/articles/2004/07/04/tap_into_neighbors_wifi_why_not_some_say?pg=1* (accessed July 2005).

OPPOSINGFORCES
GUIDE

Security Assurance, Hah!

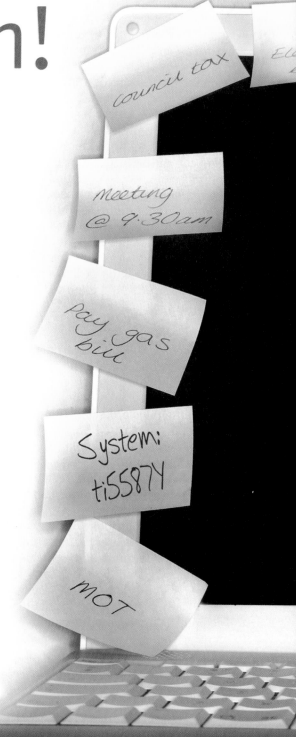

I f I have to go to one more employee meeting about security policy, I'm going to scream. The managers talk about threats, and safeguards, and risk, and uncertainty, and all the things they want us to do to improve security. Has any manager ever watched people work in this department?

"Walk through the cubicles here and watch what is happening. I'll bet half the employees are using the password they were assigned the day they started work. I'll bet they've never changed their password, ever! And for the people who have changed their passwords, I'll bet they've changed them to some simpleton word like 'Sesame' or 'MyDogSpot' or something equally absurd.

"Or, open the top drawer of any of my coworkers' desks and guess what you'll find? A little yellow sticky with entries like OrderEntry: 748QPt#7ml, Compensation: RXL87MB, System: ti5587Y. What do you suppose those entries are? Do you think anyone who worked here on a weekend wouldn't know what to do with them? And the only reason they're in the desk drawers is that Martha (our manager) threw a fit when she saw a yellow sticky like that on Terri's monitor.

"I've mentioned all this to Martha several times, but nothing happens. What we need is a good scare. We need somebody to break into the system using one of those passwords and do some damage. Wait—if you enter a system with a readily available password, is that even breaking in? Or is it more like opening a door with a key you were given? Anyway, we need someone to steal something, delete some files, or erase customer balances. Then maybe the idiotic management here would stop talking about security risk assurance and start talking about real security, here on the ground floor!"

Notes on screen:

OrderEntry: 748QPt#7ml

Rubbish

Phone mum

Road Tax

Pay TV licence

Compensation: RXL87MB

Doctors @ 4pm

Insurance

? DISCUSSION QUESTIONS

1. Summarize the point that this contrarian is making.

2. What do you think Martha should do about the points he makes? Surmise why nothing has been done to this point.

3. Explain three ways that our contrarian could make his point more effectively

4. We've now heard from eleven contrarians. What do you think about them? What are the advantages of having a contrarian in a group or meeting? What are the disadvantages?

5. Contrarians can be amusing, and they often make excellent points, but they become tiresome. Using your answers to question 4, explain why that is. What would drive you to the point of becoming a contrarian? What other strategy could you employ?

Unfortunately, WEP was insufficiently tested before it was deployed, and it has serious flaws. In response, the IEEE 802.11 committee developed improved wireless security standards known as **WPA (Wi-Fi Protected Access)** and a newer, better version, called **WPA2.** Unfortunately, only newer wireless devices can use these techniques.

Wireless security technology is changing rapidly. By the time you read this, even newer security standards will have been developed. Search the Internet for the term *wireless network security* to learn about the latest standards. In the meantime, on any wireless network you use, take the time to enable the highest level of security that you can and be aware that, at present, especially on SOHO networks, wireless networks are not nearly as secure as wired networks.

Encryption

The second technical safeguard in Figure 11-5 is **encryption**. We described some encryption techniques in Chapter 5 (page 133a). To review, senders use a key to encrypt a plaintext message and then send the encrypted message to a recipient, who then uses a key to decrypt the message. Figure 11-6 lists five basic encryption techniques (the first three were covered in Chapter 5).

With **symmetric encryption**, both parties use the same key. With **asymmetric encryption**, the parties use two keys, one that is public and one that is private. A message encoded with one of the keys can be decoded with the other key. Asymmetric encryption is slower than symmetric encryption, but it is easier to implement over a network.

Secure Socket Layer (SSL) is a protocol that uses both asymmetric and symmetric encryption. SSL is a protocol layer that works between Levels 4 (transport) and 5 (application) of the TCP–OSI protocol architecture. With SSL, asymmetric encryption transmits a symmetric key. Both parties then use that key for symmetric encryption for the balance of that session. Because SSL lies between Levels 4 and 5, most Internet applications, including HTTP, FTP, and email programs, can use it.

Technique	How it works	Characteristics
Symmetric	Sender and receiver transmit message using the same key.	Fast, but difficult to get the same key to both parties.
Asymmetric	Sender and receiver transmit message using two keys, one public and one private. Message encrypted with one of the keys can be decrypted with the other.	Public key can be openly transmitted, but needs certificate authority (see below). Slower than symmetric.
SSL/TLS	Works between Levels 4 and 5 of the TCP-OSI architecture. Sender uses public/private key to transmit symmetric key, which both parties use for symmetric encryption--for a limited, brief period.	Used by most Internet applications. A useful and workable hybrid of symmetric and asymmetric.
Digital signatures	Sender hashes message, and uses private key to "sign" a message digest, creating digital signature; sender transmits plaintext message and digital signature. Receiver rehashes the plaintext message and decrypts the digital signature with the public key. If the message digests match, receiver knows that message has not been altered.	Ingenious technique for ensuring plaintext has not been altered.
Digital certificates	A trusted third party, the certificate authority (CA), supplies the public key and a digital certificate. Receiver decrypts message with public key (from CA), signed with CA's digital signature.	Eliminates spoofing of public keys. Requires browser to have CA's public key.

Figure 11-6
Basic Encryption Techniques

Using the Opposing Forces Guide (page 345a)

GOALS

* Remind the students, one more time, to protect their passwords and to manage their employees to protect passwords as well.

* Discuss the differences between a *contrarian position* and a *contrarian,* and assess the proper role for each.

BACKGROUND AND PRESENTATION STRATEGIES

These contrarians are becoming tedious! They always do. Although we have learned much from the contrarians in these Opposing Forces Guides, they begin to seem like whiners.

➤ **What's the difference between a *contrarian position* and a *contrarian*?**

A *contrarian position* is a posture on an idea, a concept, a strategy, or a tactic that runs counter to the accepted perception, belief, or line of thinking. When the child in Hans Christian Anderson's *The Emperor's New Clothes* says, "But he has nothing on at all," in reference to the emperor's nakedness, the child was taking a contrarian position.

Were someone to say, "Wireless network security in unimportant," that person would be taking a contrarian position.

Contrarian positions can be right (the emperor was naked), or wrong (wireless security is very important). Often the value of a contrarian position is not so much in whether it is right or wrong, but rather because it causes people to reevaluate their thinking on some topic. When the late Seattle newspaper columnist Emmett Watson ran his *lesser Seattle* campaign with the slogan, "Keep the bastards out!" he forced citizens and the city to reconsider its population growth objectives.

A *contrarian* is someone who always takes the opposing position. Contrarians take a particular joy in conflict and opposition. They are predictable because they will choose whatever side no one else seems to be on. Although contrarians make great newspaper columnists, cartoonists, and bloggers, they seldom achieve notable success in business. They become a nuisance and tiresome. It's as if they enjoy butting their heads against the wall, often seeming to rejoice in what they perceive as the "stupidity" of coworkers, their managers, the company, their industry, whatever.

I think the contrarian in this chapter has crossed into nuisance territory. His protests are adding little value. He's made his security opinion known, and both his manager and his fellow employees have taken some action. He's probably right that not much else will happen until a disaster occurs, and, having made as much contribution as he can, further expostulations won't create a solution.

The inappropriate password behavior he cites is not really his problem; it's his manager's and his company's problem. Having said what he has, he should let it go.

Advice to the future business professional:

➤ **Although taking a contrarian position from time to time on important issues can be an effective behavior that leads to a successful business career, becoming a contrarian can limit your career.**

➤ **Contrarians are fundamentally destructive; they only say what's wrong. The bulk of their words are critical rather than constructive. When a business looks for leaders and managers, it needs to find people who can construct and build, not people who constantly complain. Contrarians are usually relegated to a corner, but seldom to the corner office.**

➤ **What's the point of this contrarian?**

His point is that sophisticated security management will never be possible without proper password management. That statement is obviously true.

➤ **Does that mean that security management and planning ought not to be done?**

No, of course not. So, make your point and move on!

 SUGGESTED RESPONSES FOR DISCUSSION QUESTIONS

1. The contrarian's point is that effective security cannot occur unless employees appropriately protect their passwords. He doesn't want to think about larger security issues when he knows that his fellow employees are reckless with their passwords. He's frustrated that his manager hasn't taken more action than she has.

2. Martha should listen to him, and consistent with her own priorities and those of the department (meaning she should make this a high priority, but not to the exclusion of other important tasks that need to be done), she should instigate a program to improve password use in her department.

If she thinks that she and her employees can handle it, she should consider putting the contrarian in charge of the new password management program. She could also enlist the help of her IS department. There may be ways that they can require employees to regularly change their passwords to strong passwords and to ensure that they are not reusing prior passwords too frequently.

Why hasn't Martha done more? Possibly she's busy with other problems, possibly she doesn't understand the importance of good password use, possibly she thinks the contrarian is a crank and dismisses most of what he says. Maybe she's avoiding the problem because she just hates to meet with him!

3. Three ways for the contrarian to make his point more effectively:

- Use empathic thinking—consider the perspectives of fellow employees and Martha.

- Write a memo suggesting, specifically, how the department could develop better password management. Perform all of the staff work needed for Martha to implement the plan.

- Prepare a PowerPoint or other presentation that shows employees easy ways to generate and remember strong passwords. (See the Security Guide in Chapter 1.)

4. See commentary in the Guidelines. Contrarians identify problems, and usually they are important problems. Contrarians don't "wear well" in organizations, though; over time, they become a nuisance.

5. See comments in the Guidelines.

It would be tempting to become a contrarian if a person believed, even knew, that he or she had excellent ideas but those ideas were continually and consistently ignored. In some ways, contrarians have turned bitterness into words.

➤ **If you are communicating on some issue, and your communications seems to have no effect, change tactics. Don't keep blasting the same horn. Either find another way to make your case or give up. Is it really your job to force change on this issue? Or, are you frustrated about something else?**

➤ **If you don't have the power to force a change, if no one seems open to that change, and if the issue is very important, you may have to change jobs. Blasting the same horn is tiresome for you and for everyone else.**

WRAP UP

➤ **We've considered 11 different contrarians and contrarian positions in this text. We've learned a lot from these opposing forces; they've helped us focus our thinking.**

➤ **I do not, however, want to leave you with the impression that becoming a contrarian is a good pathway to a successful career. An occasional *contrarian position* on an important matter can be effective and useful. Seldom, however, do perpetual contrarians go far.**

➤ **If you're prone to critical commentary, give these warnings some thought!**

Netscape originally developed SSL. After a brief skirmish in the marketplace, Microsoft endorsed its use and included it in Internet Explorer and other products. SSL version 1.0 had problems, most of which were removed in version 3.0, which is the version Microsoft endorsed. A later version, with more problems fixed, was renamed **Transport Layer Security (TLS)**.

By either name, SSL or TLS, this is the protocol used whenever you see *https://* in your browser's address bar. As stated in Chapter 5, never send any sensitive data over the Internet unless you see the *s* after *http*.

Using SSL/TLS, the client verifies that it is communicating with the true Web site, and not with a site that is spoofing the true Web site. However, to ease the burden on users, the opposite is not done. Web sites seldom verify the true identity of users. Hence, programs can spoof legitimate users and fool Web sites. Because the consequences affect the Web site and not the client, such spoofing has no effect on the consumer. It is a problem that Web sites must address, however.

Digital Signatures

Because encryption slows processing, most messages are sent over the Internet as plaintext. By default, email is sent as plaintext. This means, by the way, that you ought not to send your Social Security number, credit card numbers, or any other such numbers in email.

Because email is plaintext, it is possible that someone can intercept your email and change the message unbeknownst to you. For example, suppose a purchasing agent sends an email to one of its vendors with the message, "Please deliver shipment 1000 to our Oakdale facility." It is possible for a third party to intercept the email, remove the words *our Oakdale facility*, substitute its own address, and send the message on to its destination.

Digital signatures ensure that plaintext messages are received without alterations. Figure 11-7 (page 348) summarizes their use. The plaintext message is first *hashed*. **Hashing** is a method of mathematically manipulating the message to create a string of bits that characterize the message. The bit string, called the **message digest**, has a specified, fixed length, regardless of the length of the plaintext. According to one popular standard, message digests are 160 bits long.

Hashing is a one-way process. Any message can be hashed to produce a message digest, but the message digest cannot be unhashed to produce the original message.

Hashing techniques are designed so that if someone changes any part of a message, rehashing the changed message will create a different message digest. For example, the email message with the words "our Oakdale facility" and the same message but with the interceptor's address will generate two different message digests.

Authentication programs use message digests to ensure that plaintext messages have not been altered. The idea is to create a message digest for the original message and to send the message and the message digest to the receiver. The receiver hashes the message it received and compares the resulting message digest to the message digest that was sent with the message. If the two message digests are the same, then the receiver knows that the message was not altered. If they are different, then the message was altered.

For this technique to work, the original message digest must be protected when it is transmitted. Accordingly, as Figure 11-7 shows, the message digest (MD in this figure) is encrypted using the sender's private key. The result is called the message's digital signature. Applying one's private key to the message digest is called *signing* the message. As shown in step 4 of Figure 11-7, the system sends the signed message to the receiver.

The receiver hashes the plaintext message that arrived to produce a message digest for the received message. It then decrypts the digital signature with the sender's public key (called the *true party's* public key, in this figure) and compares the message digest for the received message with the original message digest. If they are the same, then the message was not altered. If the message digests differ, then the receiver knows that someone altered the message somewhere along the line.

Only one problem remains: How does the receiver obtain the true party's public key? The receiver cannot ask the sender for its public key, because the sender could be

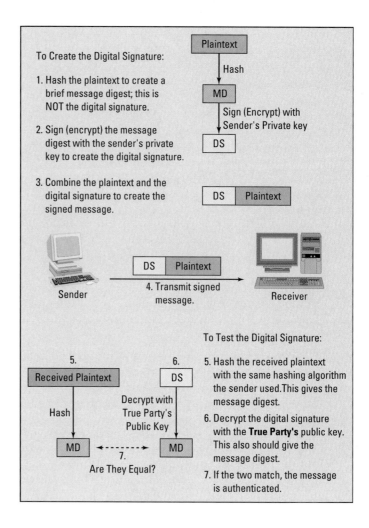

Figure 11-7
Digital Signatures for
Message Authentication

Source: Ray Panko, *Corporate
Computer and Network Security*, 1st
Edition, © 2004. Reprinted by
permission of Pearson Education,
Inc., Upper Saddle River, NJ.

spoofing. For example, if someone is spoofing Bank of America, the spoofer will send the spoofer's public key while claiming that it is sending the public key for Bank of America. The receiver cannot know the received public key is not the true Bank of America public key. Digital certificates prevent such spoofing.

Digital Certificates

When using public keys, a message recipient must know that it has the true party's public key. As just explained, a program that asks a sender to transmit its public key could be fooled. To solve this problem, trusted, independent third-party companies, called **certificate authorities (CAs)**, supply public keys.

Thus, for your browser to obtain the public key for Bank of America, either to conduct a secure session using SSL/TLS or to authenticate a digital signature, your browser will obtain Bank of America's public key from a certificate authority. The CA will respond to the request with a **digital certificate** that contains, among other data, the name Bank of America and Bank of America's public key. Your browser will verify the name and then use that public key.

By the way, the CA is in no way verifying that Bank of America is a legitimate concern, that it is law abiding, that it has paid its taxes, that its accounting standards are high, or anything else. The CA is simplify verifying that a company known as Bank of America has the public key that it sent to your browser.

The digital certificate is sent as plaintext, so there is still the possibility that an entity can intercept the digital certificate sent by the CA and substitute its own public key. To prevent that possibility, the CA signs the digital certificate with its digital signature.

Before continuing, let's review. Suppose you want to transfer money from one account to another at Bank of America. When you access the bank's Web server, it initiates an SSL/TLS session with your browser. Your browser needs the public key for Bank of America to participate, so it contacts a CA and asks for the digital certificate for Bank of America.

The certificate arrives with the CA's digital signature. Your browser hashes the certificate to obtain the message digest for the certificate it received. It then uses the CA's public key to decrypt the signature and obtain the message digest for the certificate that the CA transmitted. If the two message digests match, your browser can rely on the fact that it has the true public key for Bank of America.

Except . . . See if you can find the flaw in what we have described so far before you continue reading.

The flaw is that your browser needs the CA's public key to authenticate the digital certificate. Your browser cannot ask for that public key from the CA because someone could be spoofing the CA. Your browser could obtain the CA's public key by requesting a digital certificate for the first CA from a second CA, but the problem still remains. Your browser would then need to contact a third CA to obtain a digital certificate for the second CA. And so it goes. Meanwhile, you're thinking it would be easier to walk down to the bank.

The infinite regress halts because browsers contain the public keys for the common CAs in their program code. As long as you receive your browser from a reputable source, you can rely on the public keys it uses when authenticating digital certificates from the CAs it uses.

Firewalls

Firewalls are the third technical safeguard listed in Figure 11-5. A **firewall** is a computing device that prevents unauthorized network access. A firewall can be a special-purpose computer or it can be a program on a general-purpose computer or on a router.

Organizations normally use multiple firewalls. A **perimeter firewall** sits outside the organizational network; it is the first device that Internet traffic encounters. In addition to perimeter firewalls, some organizations employ **internal firewalls** inside the organizational network. Figure 11-8 shows the use of a perimeter firewall that protects all of an organization's computers and a second internal firewall that protects a LAN.

A **packet-filtering firewall** examines each packet and determines whether to let the packet pass. To make this decision, it examines the source address, the destination addresses, and other data.

Packet-filtering firewalls can prohibit outsiders from starting a session with any user behind the firewall. They can also disallow traffic from particular sites, such as known hacker addresses. They also can prohibit traffic from legitimate, but unwanted

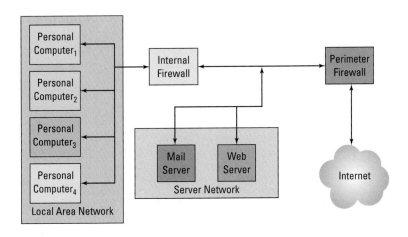

Figure 11-8
Use of Multiple Firewalls

addresses, such as competitors' computers. Firewalls can filter outbound traffic as well. They can keep employees from accessing specific sites, such as competitors' sites, sites with pornographic material, or popular news sites.

A firewall has an **access control list (ACL)**, which encodes the rules stating which packets are to be allowed and which are to be prohibited. As a future manager, if you have particular sites with which you do not want your employees to communicate, you can ask your IS department to establish rules to enforce your policy in the ACL for the routers that protect your network. Most likely, your IS organization has a procedure for making such requests.

Packet-filtering firewalls are the simplest type of firewall. Other firewalls filter on a more sophisticated basis. If you take a data communications class, you will learn about them. For now, just understand that firewalls help to protect organizational computers from unauthorized network access.

No computer should connect to the Internet without firewall protection. Many ISPs provide firewalls for their customers. By nature, these firewalls are generic. Large organizations supplement such generic firewalls with their own. Most SOHO routers include firewalls, and Windows XP has a built-in firewall as well. Third parties also license firewall products.

How do you know if your firewall works? In fact, how do you know if your security program is tight or has major holes? See the *Problem Solving Guide* on page 351a for ideas on testing security.

Malware Protection

The next technical safeguard in our list in Figure 11-5 is malware. The term **malware** has several definitions. Here we will use the broadest one: *malware* is viruses, worms, Trojan horses, spyware, and adware. We discussed viruses, worms, and Trojan horses in Chapter 3 (page 53a); you should review that material now if you have forgotten their definitions.

Spyware and Adware

Spyware programs are installed on the user's computer without the user's knowledge or permission. Spyware resides in the background and, unknown to the user, observes the user's actions and keystrokes, monitors computer activity, and reports the user's activities to sponsoring organizations. Some malicious spyware captures keystrokes to obtain user names, passwords, account numbers, and other sensitive information. Other spyware supports marketing analyses, observing what users do, Web sites visited, products examined and purchased, and so forth.

Adware is similar to spyware in that it is installed without the user's permission and that it resides in the background and observes user behavior. Most adware is benign in that it does not perform malicious acts or steal data. It does, however, watch user activity and produce pop-up ads. Adware can also change the user's default window or modify search results and switch the user's search engine. For the most part, it is just annoying, but users should be concerned any time they have unknown programs on their computers that perform unknown functions.

Figure 11-9 lists some of the symptoms of adware and spyware. Sometimes these symptoms develop slowly over time as more and more malware components are

- Slow system start up
- Sluggish system performance
- Many pop-up advertisements
- Suspicious browser homepage changes
- Suspicious changes to the taskbar and other system interfaces
- Unusual hard-disk activity

Figure 11-9
Spyware and Adware Symptoms

installed. Should these symptoms occur on your computer, remove the spyware or adware using anti-malware programs.

Malware Safeguards

Fortunately, it is possible to avoid most malware using the following malware safeguards:

1. *Install antivirus and antispyware programs on your computer.* Your IS department will have a list of recommended (perhaps required) programs for this purpose. If you choose a program for yourself, choose one from a reputable vendor. Check reviews of anti-malware software on the Web before purchasing.
2. *Set up your anti-malware programs to scan your computer frequently.* You should scan your computer at least once a week and possibly more. When you detect malware code, use the anti-malware software to remove them. If the code cannot be removed, contact your IS department or anti-malware vendor.
3. *Update malware definitions.* **Malware definitions**—patterns that exist in malware code—should be downloaded frequently. Anti-malware vendors update these definitions continuously, and you should install these updates as they become available.
4. *Open email attachments only from known sources.* Also, even when opening attachments from known sources, do so with great care. According to professor and security expert Ray Panko, about 90 percent of all viruses are spread by email attachments.[4] This statistic is not surprising, because most organizations are protected by firewalls. With a properly configured firewall, email is the only outside-initiated traffic that can reach user computers.

   Most anti-malware programs check email attachments for malware code. However, all users should form the habit of *never* opening an email attachment from an unknown source. Also, if you receive an unexpected email from a known source or an email from a known source that has a suspicious subject, odd spelling, or poor grammar, do not open the attachment without first verifying with the known source that the attachment is legitimate.
5. *Promptly install software updates from legitimate sources.* Unfortunately, all programs are chock full of security holes; vendors are fixing them as rapidly as they are discovered, but the practice is inexact. Install patches to the operating system and application programs promptly.
6. *Browse only in reputable Internet neighborhoods.* It is possible for some malware to install itself when you do nothing more than open a Web page. Don't go there!

Malware Is a Serious Problem

America Online (AOL) and the National Cyber Security Alliance conducted a malware study using Internet users in 2004. They asked the users a series of questions and then, with the users' permission, they scanned the users' computers to determine how accurately the users understood malware problems on their own computers. This fascinating study can be found online at *staysafeonline.info/news/safety_study_v04.pdf*.

Figure 11-10 (page 352) shows a few important results from this study. Among the users, 6 percent thought they had a virus, but 18 percent actually did. Further, half of those surveyed did not know if they had a virus. Of those computers having viruses, an average of 2.4 viruses were found, and the maximum number of viruses found on a single computer was 213!

When asked how often they update their antivirus definitions, 71 percent of the users reported that they had done so within the last week. Actually, only one-third of the users had updated their definitions that recently.

Figure 11-10 shows similar results for spyware. The average user computer had 93 spyware components. The maximum number found on a computer was 1,059. Note that only 5 percent of the users had given permission for the spyware to be installed.

---

[4]Ray Panko, *Corporate Computer and Network Security* (Prentice Hall, 2004), p. 165.

ProblemSolving
GUIDE

Testing Security

When highly motivated employees work together intensely for a period of time, they begin to believe the whole world thinks as they do. The team begins with assumptions and hopes, and, over time, their minds transform those assumptions and hopes into accepted truths and facts. This process is not intentional deception, it's a natural characteristic of intense group work. One senior executive explained the failure of a carefully planned and orchestrated marketing plan with the statement, "We started believing our own hype."

So it is with security. A group of bright, highly motivated people work with sophisticated tools to develop the perfect configuration of firewalls with ACLs so well thought out and tested by the group that they believe that the network is truly a fortress! And, as the days go by, the group's thinking transforms ideas that began as hopes and goals into facts.

Unfortunately, that bias toward believing one's own hype is compounded by another factor. Employees like systems analysts who have advanced their careers by playing by the rules cannot empathize with a hacker or a computer criminal. The worldview of a systems analyst and a hacker are too different for the systems analyst to anticipate what the hacker might do.

The combination of bias and dissimilar worldviews means that security systems cannot be tested by the people who built the system—or at least not only by the people who built the system.

Therefore, many companies hire outsiders to test the security of their systems. **White-hat hackers** are people who break into networks for the purpose of helping the organization that operates the network. White-hat hackers report the problems they find and suggest solutions. Or at least they are supposed to. What if the white-hat hacker doesn't reveal all that he learns?

Clearly, companies must be exceedingly careful when hiring such consultants. Some companies hire only reputable, larger consulting firms, supposing that those firms will have performed background screening on their employees. They also ensure those firms have liability insurance to cover potential problems caused by their employees.

A second problem concerns the results: "Never ask a question for which you don't want the answer." What will a company do with the white-hat's results? If the problems found are severe and widespread, they may be too expensive to fix. Or, they may require more attention than management is able to supply. Knowing about weaknesses that it cannot fix exposes management to a liability—a liability that does not exist if management does not know about the problems.

Discussion Questions

1. Explain the downside of strong belief in an idea, program, or project. Have you seen this phenomenon is your own life? How?

2. Describe the limits of empathetic thinking (page 33a). How do those limits apply to security systems?

3. Describe the dangers of using a white-hat hacker. Explain ways of overcoming those dangers; do not restrict your thinking to ideas presented here.

4. Explain the sentiment of the statement, "Never ask a question for which you do not want the answer." How does this sentiment apply to computer security testing? How does it apply to your life, in general?

5. If you worked at Southwest Video Training, how would you recommend that the partnership test the security of its Web site?

Question	User Response	Scan Results
Do you have a virus on your computer?	Yes: 6%	Yes: 19%
	No: 44%	No: 81%
	Don't know: 50%	
Average (maximum) number of viruses on infected computer		2.4 (213)
How often do you update your antivirus software?	Last week: 71%	Last week: 33%
	Last month: 12%	Last month: 34%
	Last 6 months: 5%	Last 6 months: 6%
	Longer than 6 months: 12%	Longer than 6 months: 12%
Do you think you have spyware or adware on your computer?	Yes: 53%	Yes: 80%
	No: 47%	No: 20%
Average (maximum) number of spyware/adware components on computer		93 (1,059)
Did you give permission to someone to install these components on your computer?	Yes: 5% No: 95%	

Figure 11-10
Malware Survey Results

Source: AOL/NCSA Online Safety Study, October 2004, *staysafeonline.info/news/safety_ study_v04.pdf* (accessed March 2005).

Although the problem of malware will never be eradicated, you can reduce its size by following the six safeguards listed on page 351. You should take these actions as a habit, and you should ensure that employees you manage take them as well.

Design Secure Applications

The final technical safeguard in Figure 11-5 concerns the design of applications. As a future IS user, you will not design programs yourself. However, you should ensure that any information system developed for you and your department includes security as one of the application requirements.

Data Safeguards

Data safeguards are measures used to protect databases and other organizational data. We discussed database security in Chapter 4 (starting on page 85a), and you may wish to review that discussion.

Figure 11-11 summarizes some important data safeguards. First, the organization should specify user data rights and responsibilities. Second, those rights should be enforced by user accounts that are authenticated at least by passwords.

The organization should protect sensitive data by storing it in encrypted form. Such encryption uses one or more keys in ways similar to that described for data communication encryption. One potential problem with stored data, however, is that the key might be lost or that disgruntled or terminated employees might destroy it. Because of this possibility, when data are encrypted, a trusted party should have a copy of the encryption key. This safety procedure is sometimes called **key escrow**.

Another data safeguard is to periodically create backup copies of database contents. The organization should store at least some of these backups off premises, possibly in a remote location. Additionally, IT personnel should periodically practice recov-

Using the Problem Solving Guide (page 351a)

GOALS

✱ Discuss the dangers of a group believing its own hype.

✱ Consider the proper role of outside testing.

BACKGROUND AND PRESENTATION STRATEGIES

This guide presents several principles:

• The dangers of believing one's own hype

• The difficulty of empathetic thinking when backgrounds and experiences vary widely

• The need for out-of-house testing for security systems

• Asking questions for which you do not want the answers

Workgroups tend to make their own reality. Working side-by-side intensely for an extended period of time, people will transform assumptions into facts, hopes into realities, hypotheses into accepted dogma.

Accordingly, it is so important to involve external feedback and to *pay attention to that feedback*. Sometimes, the group's reality has become so strong that the group even will disdain or disregard the opinions of outside experts.

Ironically, the better the communications skills of the group, the faster the group reality develops and the more deeply embedded it becomes. I've seen this phenomenon most frequently in strategic marketing. Generally, senior marketing people communicate exceptionally well, and it's difficult to maintain a degree of healthy skepticism in the face of their strong and effective arguments. Two or three times I've watched substantial investments in marketing programs that an outside review would have indicated were foolish or wasteful.

Then, too, the supporting cast for a new marketing program has a serious conflict of interest. New strategic programs require graphic design firms, ad agencies, public relations firms, video production companies, and similar supporting companies. None of those people have an incentive to throw cold water on the new program; they just keep talking about "how great it's going to be."

Then, too, most groups have a collective blind spot or spots. I recall this most vividly when, during a strategy session to develop new products, the CEO looked at the results of our analysis and said, "Funny how we're always projecting that we'll make the most money in the business we know the least about."

All of these comments pertain to security testing. The group that develops the security system has, of course, a professional responsibility to test that system themselves. However, the process of building that system will predispose the developers to certain avenues of thought. That predisposition will inhibit truly effective testing. Testing by people uninvolved with the project is essential!

Software vendors avoid that predisposition via beta programs. They expose their products to computer users who have had nothing to do with the product's development. In that way, they obtain feedback from many people who cannot have been influenced by the group's thinking.

Using beta testing as an example, one way to pose the problem is to ask:

➤ **"How do you find a beta tester for a security system?"**

This is a tough question. You cannot advertise in the newspaper; you have to be very careful about whom you invite to find holes in your security system. White-hat hackers are one solution, but see the Security Guide in this chapter for problems related to that alternative.

Note: Two guides in this chapter refer to white-hat hackers. This guide refers to the need for an outside white-hat *consultant*. The Security Guide discusses the need for and problems with white-hat hacker *employees*.

The most controversial statement in this guide is to never ask a question for which you do not want the answer. Although I think there are times when that principle is appropriate (when the cost of answering the question is high and/or when the answer doesn't help you alter your course of action), I'm not sure computer security is the proper domain for that attitude. Some questions for the class:

➤ **Do you agree that you should never ask a question for which you do not want the answer?**

➤ **Are there instances in either your personal or professional life in which you think that principle is wise?**

➤ **Is it a wise principle to apply to computer security?**

➤ **Suppose that you cannot afford to fix your security holes, but learning of those holes exposes you to liability you would not otherwise have. Is *not asking the question* (a) wise? (b) cowardly?**

See question 24 for an assignment that concerns the appropriate use of a white-hat hacker at Southwest Video.

 ## SUGGESTED RESPONSES FOR DISCUSSION QUESTIONS

1. The downside of strong belief is that you confuse hope with reality. You start "counting your chickens before they hatch," and you become blind to possible threats and dangers.

2. Empathetic thinking requires that we consider an issue from the standpoint of another person. People who have made their careers by practicing good ethics and following sound business practices will have difficulty empathizing with a computer criminal.

   In most cases, when one is far removed from another person's experience, they can ask for information. "How do you see the situation?" is a common query. This query is obviously not possible with an actual computer criminal; hence the need for white-hat hackers or other professionals who better understand the mind-set and techniques of a computer criminal.

3. The danger of using white-hats is that you don't know if they have revealed all; you don't know whether they have kept the analysis confidential; and you don't know whether they will use that knowledge against you.

   To overcome these dangers, the guide suggests hiring large firms that have done background checks on their employees and that have liability insurance. Other considerations are hiring those with sterling reputations; hiring those that are running a successful business and hence have an incentive to protect their reputation; asking for references from prior clients; or performing your own background investigation.

4. The sentiment behind the question is, "If you can't do anything with the answer, why ask the question?" This is especially true if the cost of answering the question is high. An appropriate application of this principle is that if you cannot do anything to improve employee parking, why ask the employees what they think of their parking situation. You'll just draw their attention to an unavoidable irritation.

   Applying that analogy, if you can't do anything to improve your security, why ask about it? You'll just draw someone's attention to an unavoidable weakness and possibly create professional liability for yourself.

   ➤ **I disagree about applying this principle to security. However, I do think there's an important corollary: Before you test your security system, *be prepared to deal with the results*. You may not like what you find!**

5. The partners at Southwest Video will tend to trivialize this situation. They're optimistic and creative, and they'll resent spending money on security testing. Their attitude will be, "Ah, heck, we'll deal with that when we have to." They'll probably ask the Web site manager what he thinks, but they won't do much about it.

   If they lose their Web site, they can always rebuild it. If, however, they lose data from their customer database, they will be in deep trouble. So, to get their attention, I'd ask them about threats to that asset. They might agree to "looking into how vulnerable their customer data is."

WRAP UP

➤ **Beware of the tendency of groups to turn assumptions into facts and hopes into realities. This is true not just for computer security, but for every business endeavor.**

➤ **When you are incapable of engaging in empathetic thinking on some matter, consider hiring someone who is capable of it.**

➤ **Independent security testing is important!**

- Data rights and responsibilities
- Rights enforced by user accounts authenticated by passwords
- Data encryption
- Backup and recovery procedures
- Physical security

Figure 11-11
Data Safeguards

ery, to ensure that the backups are valid and that effective recovery procedures exist. Do not assume that just because a backup is made, the database is protected.

Physical security is another data safeguard. The computers that run the DBMS and all devices that store database data should reside in locked, controlled-access facilities. If not, they are subject not only to theft, but also to damage. For better security, the organization should keep a log showing who entered the facility, when, and for what purpose.

In some cases, organizations contract with other companies to manage their databases. If so, all of the safeguards in Figure 11-11 should be part of the service contract. Also, the contract should give the owners of the data permission to inspect the premises of the database operator and to interview its personnel on a reasonable schedule.

MIS in Use 11-2 (page 354) describes one company's major loss of sensitive data. Read about it and decide where they went wrong, if they did go wrong.

Human Safeguards

Human safeguards involve the people and procedure components of information systems. In general, human safeguards result when authorized users follow appropriate procedures for system use and recovery. Restricting access to authorized users requires effective authentication methods and careful user account management. In addition, appropriate security procedures must be designed as part of every information system, and users should be trained on the importance and use of those procedures. In this section, we will consider the development of human safeguards first for employees and then for nonemployee personnel.

Human Safeguards for Employees

Figure 11-12 (page 355) lists security considerations for employees. The first is position definitions.

Position Definitions

Effective human safeguards begin with definitions of job tasks and responsibilities. In general, job descriptions should provide a separation of duties and authorities. For example, no single individual should be allowed both to approve expenses and write checks. Instead, one person should approve expenses and another person pay them. Similarly, in inventory, no single person should be allowed to authorize an inventory withdrawal and also to remove the items from inventory.

Given appropriate job descriptions, user accounts should be defined to give users the least possible privilege needed to perform their jobs. For example, users whose job description does not include modifying data should be given accounts with read-only privilege. Similarly, user accounts should prohibit users from accessing data their job description does not require. Because of the problem of semantic security (Chapter 9, page 275a), even access to seemingly innocuous data may need to be limited.

Finally, the security sensitivity should be documented for each position. Some jobs involve highly sensitive data (e.g., employee compensation, salesperson quotas, and proprietary marketing or technical data). Other positions involve no sensitive data. Documenting *position sensitivity* enables security personnel to prioritize their activities in accordance with the possible risk and loss.

The ChoicePoint Attack

ChoicePoint, a Georgia-based corporation, provides risk-management and fraud-prevention data. Traditionally, ChoicePoint provided motor vehicle reports, claims histories, and similar data to the automobile insurance industry; in recent years, it broadened its customer base to include general business and government agencies. Today, it also offers data for volunteer and job-applicant screening and data to assist in the location of missing children. ChoicePoint has over 4,000 employees, and its 2004 revenue was $918 million.

In the fall of 2004, ChoicePoint was the victim of a fraudulent spoofing attack in which unauthorized individuals posed as legitimate customers and obtained personal data on more than 145,000 individuals. According to the company's Web site:

> These criminals were able to pass our customer authentication due diligence processes by using stolen identities to create and produce the documents needed to appear legitimate. As small business customers of ChoicePoint, these fraudsters accessed products that contained basic telephone directory-type data (name and address information) as well as a combination of Social Security numbers and/or driver's license numbers and, at times, abbreviated credit reports. They were also able to obtain other public record information including, but not limited to bankruptcies, liens, and judgments; professional licenses; and real property data.

ChoicePoint became aware of the problem in November 2004, when it noticed unusual processing activity on some accounts in Los Angeles. Accordingly, the company contacted the Los Angeles Police Department, which requested that ChoicePoint not reveal the activity until the department could conduct an investigation. In January, the LAPD notified ChoicePoint that it could contact the customers whose data had been compromised.

This crime is an example of a failure of authentication and not a network break-in. ChoicePoint's firewalls and other safeguards were not overcome. Instead, the criminals spoofed legitimate businesses. The infiltrators obtained valid California business licenses, and until their unusual processing activity was detected, appeared to be legitimate users.

In response to this problem, ChoicePoint established a hotline for customers whose data were compromised to call for assistance. They also purchased a credit report for each of these people and paid for a one-year credit-report-monitoring service. In February 2005, attorneys initiated a class-action lawsuit for all 145,000 customers with an initial loss claim of $75,000 each. At the same time, the U.S. Senate announced that it would conduct an investigation.

Ironically, ChoicePoint exposed itself to a public relations nightmare, considerable expense, a class-action lawsuit, a Senate investigation, and a 20 percent drop in its share price because it contacted the police and cooperated in the attempt to apprehend the criminals. When ChoicePoint noticed the unusual account activity, had it simply shut down data access for the illegitimate businesses, no one would have known. Of course, the 145,000 customers whose identities had been compromised would have unknowingly been subject to identity theft, but it is unlikely that such thefts could have been tracked back to ChoicePoint.

This case continues as Case Study 11-2 on page 366.

Source: *choicepoint.com/news/statement_0205_1.html#sub1* (accessed February 2005). Used with permission of Choice.Point.com.

Hiring and Screening

Security considerations should be part of the hiring process. Of course, if the position involves no sensitive data and no access to information systems, then screening for information systems security purposes will be minimal. When hiring for high-sensitivity positions, however, extensive interviews, references, and background investigations are appropriate. Note, too, that security screening applies not only to new employees, but also to employees who are promoted into sensitive positions.

Dissemination and Enforcement

Employees cannot be expected to follow security policies and procedures that they do not know about. Therefore, employees need to be made aware of the security policies, procedures, and responsibilities they will have.

- Position definition
  - Separate duties and authorities.
  - Determine least privilege.
  - Document position sensitivity.

  "OK to pay this"

- Hiring and screening

  "Where did you last work?"

- Dissemination and enforcement (responsibility, accountability, compliance)

  "Lets talk security..."

- Termination
  - Friendly

  "Congratulations on your new job"

  - Unfriendly

  "We've closed your accounts. Goodbye"

Figure 11-12
Security Policy for In-House Staff

Employee security training begins during new-employee training, with the explanation of general security policies and procedures. That general training must be amplified in accordance with the position's sensitivity and responsibilities. Promoted employees should receive security training that is appropriate to their new positions. The company should not provide user accounts and passwords until employees have completed required security training.

Enforcement consists of three interdependent factors: responsibility, accountability, and compliance. First, the company should clearly define the security *responsibilities* of each position. The design of the security program should be such that employees can be held *accountable* for security violations. Procedures should exist so that when critical data are lost, it is possible to determine how the loss occurred and who is accountable. Finally, the security program should encourage security *compliance*. Employee activities should regularly be monitored for compliance, and management should specify disciplinary action to be taken in light of noncompliance.

Management attitude is crucial: Employee compliance is greater when management demonstrates, both in word and deed, a serious concern for security. If managers write passwords on staff bulletin boards, shout passwords down hallways, or ignore physical security procedures, then employee security attitudes and employee security compliance will suffer. Note, too, that effective security is a continuing management responsibility. Regular reminders about security are essential.

Termination

Companies also must establish security policies and procedures for the termination of employees. Most employee terminations are friendly, and occur as the result of promotion, retirement, or when the employee resigns to take another position. Standard human resources policies should ensure that system administrators receive notification in advance of the employee's last day, so that they can remove accounts and passwords. The need to recover keys for encrypted data and any other special security requirements should be part of the employee's out-processing.

Unfriendly termination is more difficult because employees may be tempted to take malicious or harmful actions. In such a case, system administrators may need to remove user accounts and passwords prior to notifying the employee of her termination. Other actions may be needed to protect the company's information assets. A terminated sales employee, for example, may attempt to take the company's confidential customer and sales-prospect data for future use at another company. The terminating employer should take steps to protect those data prior to the termination.

The human resources department should be aware of the importance of giving IS administrators early notification of employee termination. No blanket policy exists; the information systems department must assess each case on an individual basis.

Human safeguards are even more important for employees who manage the security system, as discussed in the *Security Guide* on page 357a.

Human Safeguards for Nonemployee Personnel

Business requirements may necessitate opening information systems to nonemployee personnel—temporary personnel, vendors, partner personnel (employees of business partners), and the public. Although temporary personnel can be screened, to reduce costs, the screening will be abbreviated from that for employees. In most cases, companies cannot screen either vendor or partner personnel. Of course, public users cannot be screened at all. Similar limitations pertain to security training and compliance testing.

In the case of temporary, vendor, and partner personnel, the contracts that govern the activity should call for security measures appropriate to the sensitivity of the data and IS resources involved. Companies should require vendors and partners to perform appropriate screening and security training. The contract should also mention specific security responsibilities that are particular to the work to be performed. Companies should provide accounts and passwords with least privilege and remove those accounts as soon as possible.

The situation differs with public users of Web sites and other openly accessible information systems. It is exceedingly difficult and expensive to hold public users accountable for security violations. In general, the best safeguard from threats from public users is to *harden* the Web site or other facility against attack as much as possible. **Hardening** a site means to take extraordinary measures to reduce a system's vulnerability. Hardened sites use special versions of the operating system, and they lock down or eliminate operating systems features and functions that are not required by the application. Hardening is actually a technical safeguard, but we mention it here as the most important safeguard against public users.

Finally, note that the business relationship with the public, and with some partners, differs from that with temporary personnel and vendors. The public and some partners use the information system to receive a benefit. Consequently, safeguards need to protect such users from internal company security problems. A disgruntled employee who maliciously changes prices on a Web site potentially damages both public users and business partners. As one IT manager put it, "Rather than protecting ourselves from them, we need to protect them from us." This is an extension of the fifth principle in Figure 11-3.

Account Administration

The third human safeguard is account administration. The administration of user accounts, passwords, and help-desk policies and procedures are important components of the security system.

Account Management

Account management concerns the creation of new user accounts, the modification of existing account permissions, and the removal of unneeded accounts. Information system administrators perform all of these tasks, but account users have the responsibility to notify the administrators of the need for these actions. The IS department should create standard procedures for this purpose. As a future user, you can improve your relationship with IS personnel by providing early and timely notification of the need for account changes.

The existence of accounts that are no longer necessary is a serious security threat. IS administrators cannot know when an account should be removed; it is up to users and managers to give such notification.

Password Management

Passwords are the primary means of authentication. They are important not just for access to the user's computer, but also for authentication to other networks and servers to which the user may have access. Because of the importance of passwords, NIST recommends that employees be required to sign statements similar to that shown in Figure 11-13.

When an account is created, users should immediately change the password they are given to a password of their own. In fact, well-constructed systems require the user to change the password on first use.

Additionally, users should change passwords frequently thereafter. Some systems will require a password change every 3 months or perhaps more frequently. Users grumble at the nuisance of making such changes, but frequent password changes reduce not only the risk of password loss, but also the extent of damage if an existing password is compromised.

Some users create two passwords and switch back and forth between those two. This strategy results in poor security, and some password systems do not allow the user to reuse recently used passwords. Again, users may view this policy as a nuisance, but it is important.

Help-Desk Policies

In the past, help desks have been a serious security risk. A user who had forgotten his password would call the help desk and plead for the help-desk representative to tell him his password or to reset the password to something else. "I can't get this report out without it!" was (and is) a common lament.

The problem for help-desk representatives is, of course, that they have no way of determining that they are talking with the true user and not someone spoofing a true user. But, they are in a bind: If they do not help in some way, the help desk is perceived to be the "unhelpful desk."

To resolve such problems, many systems give the help-desk representative a means of authenticating the user. Typically, the help-desk information system has

I hereby acknowledge personal receipt of the system password(s) associated with the user IDs listed below. I understand that I am responsible for protecting the password(s), will comply with all applicable system security standards, and will not divulge my password(s) to any person. I further understand that I must report to the Information Systems Security Officer any problem I encounter in the use of the password(s) or when I have reason to believe that the private nature of my password(s) has been compromised.

Figure 11-13
Sample Account Acknowledgment Form

Source: National Institute of Standards and Technology, *Introduction to Computer Security: The NIST Handbook*, Publication 800-12, p. 114.

Metasecurity

Recall from Chapter 4 that metadata is data about data. In a similar vein, metasecurity is security about security. In other words, it asks the question, "How do we secure the security system?"

Consider an obvious problem: What is a secure way to store a file of accounts and passwords? Such files must exist, otherwise operating systems would be unable to authenticate users. But, how should one store such a file? It cannot be stored as plaintext, because anyone who reads the file gains unlimited access to the computer, the network, and other assets. So, it must be stored in encrypted form, but how? And who should know the encryption key?

Consider another problem. Suppose you work at the help desk at Vanguard Funds, and part of your job is to reset user passwords when users forget them. Clearly, this is an essential job that needs to be done, but what keeps you from resetting the passwords of accounts held by elderly people who never look at their statements? What keeps you from accessing those accounts with your reset password and moving funds to the accounts of your friends?

The accounting profession has dealt with some of these problems for decades and has developed a set of procedures and standards known as **accounting controls**. In general, these controls involve procedures that provide checks and balances, independent reviews of activity logs, control of critical assets, and so forth. Properly designed and implemented, such controls will catch the help-desk representative performing unauthorized account transfers. But many computer network threats are new, proper safeguards are under development, and some threats are not yet known.

The safeguards for some problems have unexpected consequences. For example, suppose you give one of your employees the task of finding security flaws in your network and financial applications. (See the discussion of white-hat hacking in the Problem Solving Guide on page 351a.) Assume that your employee finds ways to crack into your system and, say, schedule undetectable, unauthorized shipments of goods from inventory to any address she wants. Your employee reports the flaws, and you fix them. Except, how do you know she reported all the flaws she found?

Further, when she's finished, what do you do with your in-house white-hat hacker? You are afraid to fire her, because if she's disgruntled, you have no idea what she'll do with the information she has. But what job can she safely perform now that she knows the holes in your security system? Do you want her, ever again, to have an account and password in your corporate computer network? Even if you fix all the problems she reports, which is doubtful, you suspect that she can always find more.

Or, consider Microsoft's problem. If you were a computer criminal, where is the ultimate place to lodge

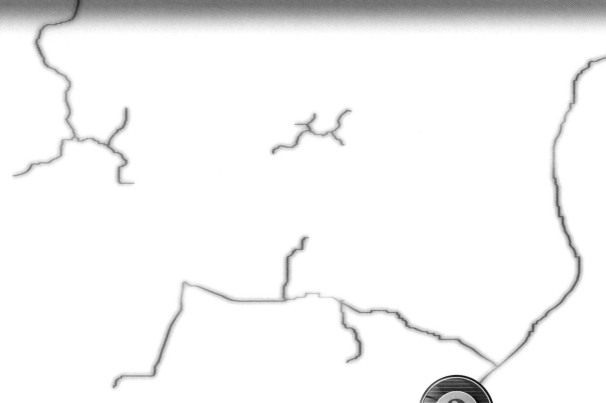

a Trojan horse or trapdoor? In Windows code. Microsoft hires hundreds of people to write its operating system; people who work all over the world. Of course Microsoft performs background screening on everyone it can, but did it get a complete and accurate background report on every Windows programmer in India, France, Ireland, China, the United States, and so on? Microsoft uses careful procedures for controlling what code gets into its products, but even still, somebody at Microsoft must lose sleep over the possibilities.

Ironically, the answers for many metasecurity problems lie in openness. Encryption experts generally agree that any encryption algorithm that relies on secrecy is ultimately doomed, because the secret will get out. Secrecy with encryption must lie only with the (temporary) keys that are used, and not with a secret method. Thus, encryption algorithms are published openly, and anyone with a mathematical bent is encouraged to find (and report) flaws. An algorithm is safe to deploy only when thousands of people have tested and retested it. WEP was unwisely deployed before it was tested, and thousands upon thousands of wireless networks are vulnerable as a result.

Clearly, hardware and software are only part of the problem. Metasecurity extends to the data, procedures, and people components as well. It's a fascinating field, one that is continually developing, and one of great importance. It would make an interesting career choice—but be careful what you learn!

DISCUSSION QUESTIONS

1. Explain the term metasecurity. Describe two metasecurity problems not mentioned in this guide.

2. Explain the control problem that exists when personnel can reset customer passwords. Describe a way to reduce this threat using an audit log and at least two independent employees.

3. Describe the dilemma posed by an in-house white-hat hacker. Describe the problem of using an outside company for white-hat hacking. If you were asked to manage a project to test your computer network security, would you use in-house or outsourced personnel? Why?

4. A typical corporate computer has software from Microsoft, SAP, Siebel, Oracle, and possibly dozens of smaller vendors. How do users know that none of the software from these companies contains a Trojan horse?

5. Explain why part of the security solution lies in openness. Describe how openness applies to accounting controls like the one you designed in your answer to question 2. Explain the danger of procedural controls that rely on secrecy.

answers to questions that only the true user would know, such as the user's birthplace, mother's maiden name, or last four digits of an important account number. Often, too, the method by which the new password can be obtained is sent to the user in an email. Email, as you learned, is sent as plaintext, however, so the new password itself ought not to be emailed. If you ever receive notification that your password was reset when you did not request such a reset, immediately contact IS security. Someone has compromised your account.

All such help-desk measures reduce the strength of the security system, and, if the employee's position is sufficiently sensitive, they may create too large a vulnerability. In such a case, the user may just be out of luck. The account will be deleted, and the user must repeat the account-application process.

Systems Procedures

Figure 11-14 shows a grid of procedure types—normal operation, backup, and recovery. Procedures of each type should exist for each information system. For example, the order entry system will have procedures of each of these types, as will the Web storefront, the inventory system, and so forth. The definition and use of standardized procedures reduces the likelihood of computer crime and other malicious activity by insiders. It also ensures that the system's security policy is enforced.

Procedures exist for both users and operations personnel. For each type of user, the company should develop procedures for normal, backup, and recovery operations. As a future user, you will be primarily concerned with user procedures. Normal-use procedures should provide safeguards appropriate to the sensitivity of the information system.

Backup procedures concern the creation of backup data to be used in the event of failure. Whereas operations personnel have the responsibility for backing up system databases and other systems data, departmental personnel have the need to back up data on their own computers. Good questions to ponder are, "What would happen if I lost my computer (or PDA) tomorrow?" "What would happen if someone dropped my computer during an airport security inspection?" "What would happen if my computer were stolen?" Employees should ensure that they back up critical business data on their computers. The IS department may help in this effort by designing backup procedures and making backup facilities available.

Finally, systems analysts should develop procedures for system recovery. First, how will the department manage its affairs when a critical system is unavailable? Customers will want to order, and manufacturing will want to remove items from inventory even though a critical information system is unavailable. How will the department respond? Once the system is returned to service, how will records of business activities during the outage be entered into the system? How will service be resumed? The system developers should ask and answer these questions and others like them and develop procedures accordingly.

	System users	Operations personnel
Normal operation	Use the system to perform job tasks, with security appropriate to sensitivity.	Operate data center equipment, manage networks, run Web servers, and related operational tasks.
Backup	Prepare for loss of system functionality.	Back up Web site resources, databases, administrative data, account and password data, and other data.
Recovery	Accomplish job tasks during failure. Know tasks to do during system recovery.	Recover systems from backed up data. Role of help desk during recovery.

Figure 11-14
System Procedures

Using the Security Guide
(page 357a)

GOALS

* Sensitize students to problems of securing security.

* Emphasize the importance of managers' responsibilities for controls over the security system.

BACKGROUND AND PRESENTATION STRATEGIES

This is the *Security Guide* in the *security chapter,* and so it makes sense to discuss securing security, or *metasecurity.*

The problem of storing passwords is a technical security problem and is presented only to introduce the idea of metasecurity; it is not the concern of future business managers. The remaining three issues in this guide are relevant to future managers, however.

First, considering accounting controls, most such controls have a strong procedural component. The payables system, for example, is set up so that one person authorizes a payment and a second person generates the check (or uses an information system that causes the check to be created). That separation of duties and authorities is crucial to effective control.

Future managers need to understand the reason and validity of such procedural controls, and they need to manage accordingly. Ultimately, the security of such systems lies in the hands of the managers on the front line.

This knowledge is especially true for managers who work at help desks that have privileges to reset or override passwords or that provide other computer account services. Typically, security administration systems create logs that show summary data, such as how many passwords were reset, which accounts were reset, whether an appropriate notification was sent to the customer, and so forth. If the control requires that the help-desk manager review or reconcile these totals against other data, the manager should take such reconciliation very seriously.

We introduced the need for a white-hat hacker consultant in the Problem Solving Guide. Here, we consider the management of a white-hat hacker employee. The two crucial questions about managing such an employee are: How do you know you learned all of the problems, and what do you do with that person next?

Unlike a consultant, an employee has a continuing need for an account and password in your organization's network. But that person is situated to take advantage of any problems that she did not reveal. As the guide points out, given that person's expertise, do you want her to have access to your network?

I think the guide overdraws this issue in a way that we can use for class discussion:

➤ **All major software vendors, including Microsoft, Oracle, SAP, Siebel, and others, are obvious targets for security attacks. Every one of those companies has a staff of in-house hackers and other security experts who have the knowledge and access to create havoc in their networks. What do you think these companies do to prevent this?**

➤ **What extra precautions can you take when you hire and manage employees like white-hat hackers?**

Some possibilities: Perform substantial background checks; require such employees to sign specially written employee contacts; regularly investigate the employees' lifestyle and spending habits; require periodic lie-detector tests; perform unannounced security audits of the employees' computers and accounts.

➤ **Those measures are fine for sophisticated software companies. But what about a company like Southwest Video? It won't have the expertise, employees, or resources to perform, for example, an unannounced computer and account audit.**

Southwest may be too small to have an employee dedicated to white-hat testing, but it may have one or two employees who have knowledge to steal data and create other problems. The company should perform extensive background checks on such employees and perhaps have the employee sign a specially worded employee contract. It's a trade-off, however. A heavy-handed security policy with underlying assumptions of suspicion conflicts with Southwest's open, creative, and artsy culture. For good or ill, Southwest is unlikely to do much about this issue.

The students may not understand how openness can improve security. One good example concerns the separation of duties and authorities. If everyone is trained that managers review logs of their activity, if everyone knows that random checks are made by calling persons whose accounts have been modified, if everyone is trained on such procedures and understands the need for them, security will improve. By the way, when such procedures are presented as standard business practice for a well-managed company, then no one needs to feel that they are under suspicion or that they aren't trusted.

In a related vein, if employees understand all of the capabilities that their passwords give them, they will be more likely to safeguard it. If, for example, the employee's account and password provide unlimited access to the employee's salary, benefit, and other personal data, and if every employee is aware of that fact, password management will improve.

? SUGGESTED RESPONSES FOR DISCUSSION QUESTIONS

1. Metasecurity is security about security. Two additional examples:

   a. Where and how do you store the list of known holes in your security system? Who can contribute to this list? Who has access to this list?

   b. Where and how do you store the procedures for conducting a security audit of the computer files and user accounts of in-house security personnel? Who has access to these procedures? Who writes these procedures? Who performs the computer audit of the person who manages computer audits? Who performs the computer audit of that person?

2. Personnel can grant themselves unauthorized access to customer accounts. To reduce this threat: Use software that automatically generates a log of all password changes. Assign responsibility for reviewing that log to a manager. Assign responsibility for reviewing the managers' review to a manager outside of the help-desk's management chain.

3. (Note: This answer requires knowledge from the Problem Solving Guide as well as from this guide.) Using an outside white-hat hacker involves a stranger and a strange organization, but it eliminates the problem of managing the in-house person. Using an inside white-hat hacker involves a known employee, but that employee will require special management due to his or her knowledge. The hiring decision depends, in large measure, on how large the organization is. For all but the largest, hire the outside person, but be very careful! Large organizations will have a large IS department to address this issue.

   An interesting side question:

   ➤ **Who provides security testing when the computer infrastructure has been outsourced?**

   ➤ **What special security considerations apply to outsourcing?**

4. No one knows, not even the vendors, whether their software contains a Trojan horse. This possibility reinforces the need to apply patches to vendor software when they are announced. Vendors seldom announce all of the problems they've fixed in a patch. It could be that the patch involves removing some suspicious code. In general, the larger the installed base, the more likely that security problems have been identified and fixed. Systems with only a few users are vulnerable to unknown internal problems.

5. See the comments on openness in the Guidelines. In short, if everyone knows what should be happening, it will be harder for exceptions to security procedures to go unnoticed. Procedural controls that rely on secrecy assume that the secret will be kept secret; such controls lose their effectiveness if the secret is lost. As Benjamin Franklin wrote in *Poor Richard's Almanac*, "Three people can keep a secret, as long as two of them are dead."

WRAP UP

➤ **As a manager, you may have control responsibilities for the security system. If so, take those responsibilities seriously. They are important!**

➤ **Securing security is a challenging, interesting, difficult, and important problem. It could make a great career!**

Security Monitoring

Security monitoring is the last of the human safeguards we will consider. Important monitoring functions are activity log analyses, security testing, and investigating and learning from security incidents.

Many information system programs produce *activity logs*. Firewalls produce logs of their activities, including lists of all dropped packets, infiltration attempts, and unauthorized access attempts from within the firewall. DBMS products produce logs of successful and failed log-ins. Web servers produce voluminous logs of Web activities. The operating systems in personal computers can produce logs of log-ins and firewall activities.

None of these logs adds any value to an organization unless someone looks at them. Accordingly, an important security function is to analyze these logs for threat patterns, successful and unsuccessful attacks, and evidence of security vulnerabilities.

Additionally, companies should test their security programs. Both in-house personnel and outside security consultants should conduct such testing. See the information on white-hat testing on page 351a.

Another important monitoring function is to investigate security incidents. How did the problem occur? Have safeguards been created to prevent a recurrence of such problems? Does the incident indicate vulnerabilities in other portions of the security system? What else can be learned from the incident?

Security systems reside in a dynamic environment. Organization structures change. Companies are acquired or sold; mergers occur. New systems require new security measures. New technology changes the security landscape, and new threats arise. Security personnel must constantly monitor the situation and determine if the existing security policy and safeguards are adequate. If changes are needed, security personnel need to take appropriate action.

Security, like quality, is an ongoing process. There is no final state that represents a secure system or company. Instead, companies must monitor security on a continuing basis.

Disaster Preparedness

A disaster is a substantial loss of computing infrastructure caused by acts of nature, crime, or terrorist activity. As stated several times, the best way to solve a problem is not to have it. The best safeguard against a disaster is appropriate location. If possible, place computing centers, Web farms, and other computer facilities in locations not prone to floods, earthquakes, hurricanes, tornados, or avalanches. Even in those locations, place infrastructure in unobtrusive buildings, basements, backrooms, and similar locations well within the physical perimeter of the organization. Also, locate computing infrastructure in fire-resistant buildings designed to house expensive and critical equipment.

However, sometimes business requirements necessitate locating the computing infrastructure in undesirable locations. Also, even at a good location, disasters do occur. Therefore, some businesses prepare backup processing centers in locations geographically removed from the primary processing site.

Figure 11-15 (page 360) lists major disaster preparedness tasks. After choosing a safe location for the computing infrastructure, the organization should identify all mission-critical applications. These are applications without which the organization cannot carry on and which, if lost for any period of time, could cause the organization's failure. The next step is to identify all resources necessary to run those systems. Such resources include computers, operating systems, application programs, databases, administrative data, procedure documentation, and trained personnel.

Next, the organization creates backups for the critical resources at the remote processing center. So-called **hot sites** are remote processing centers run by commercial disaster-recovery services. For a monthly fee, they provide all the equipment needed to

Figure 11-15
Disaster Preparedness

- Locate infrastructure in safe location.
- Identify mission-critical systems.
- Identify resources needed to run those systems.
- Prepare remote backup facilities.
- Train and rehearse.

continue operations following a disaster. **Cold sites**, in contrast, provide office space, but customers themselves provide and install the equipment needed to continue operations.

Once the organization has backups in place, it must train and rehearse cutover of operations from the primary center to the backup. Periodic refresher rehearsals are mandatory.

Preparing a backup facility is very expensive; however, the costs of establishing and maintaining that facility are a form of insurance. Senior management must make the decision to prepare such a facility, by balancing the risks, benefits, and costs.

Incident Response

The last component of a security plan that we will consider is incident response. Figure 11-16 lists the major factors. First, every organization should have an incident-response plan as part of the security program. No organization should wait until some asset has been lost or compromised before deciding what to do. The plan should include how employees are to respond to security problems, whom they should contact, the reports they should make, and steps they can take to reduce further loss.

Consider, for example, a virus. An incident-response plan will stipulate what an employee should do when he notices the virus. It should specify whom to contact and what to do. It may stipulate that the employee should turn off his computer and physically disconnect from the network. The plan should also indicate what users with wireless computers should do.

The plan should provide centralized reporting of all security incidents. Such reporting will enable an organization to determine if it is under systematic attack or whether an incident is isolated. Centralized reporting also allows the organization to learn about security threats, take consistent actions in response, and apply specialized expertise to all security problems.

When an incident does occur, speed is of the essence. Viruses and worms can spread very quickly across an organization's networks, and a fast response will help to mitigate the consequences. Because of the need for speed, preparation pays. The incident-response plan should identify critical personnel and their off-hours contact information. These personnel should be trained on where to go and what to do when they get there. Without adequate preparation, there is substantial risk that the actions of well-meaning people will make the problem worse. Also, the rumor mill will be alive with all sorts of nutty ideas about what to do. A cadre of well-informed, trained personnel will serve to dampen such rumors.

- Have plan in place
- Centralized reporting
- Specific responses
  - Speed
  - Preparation pays
  - Don't make problem worse
- Practice!

Figure 11-16
Factors in Incident Response

Finally, organizations should periodically practice incident response. Without such practice, personnel will be poorly informed on the response plan, and the plan itself may have flaws that only become apparent during a drill.

Southwest Video Training (continued)

As you think about your task, you realize that you can use Figure 11-1 to summarize the threats to which Southwest Video is vulnerable. As you document these threats, you are amazed at how many there are and how severe they could be.

Southwest is a small company, however, and the partners are careful with their time and with the partnership's money. You're certain that a proposal to create a broad and comprehensive security plan will seem like overkill to the partners, at least initially. So, you decide to focus on the three biggest needs you see: improved firewalls, protection from malware, and backup and off premise storage of the customer database. You also suggest employee training.

Currently, Southwest has a single firewall in front of the Web server. You do not know the rules in the access control list, but you explain how critical those rules are, and without openly criticizing the current Web manager, you suggest a review of those rules by a firewall specialist consultant. In addition, you suggest the installation of a second, internal firewall to protect the network and computers behind the Web server.

Second, you know from your own department that the company runs anti-malware on its computers on a sporadic basis, at best. Accordingly, you recommend that Southwest purchase antivirus and antispyware software for every computer. Additionally, you recommend that the company develop a policy to ensure that employees regularly update the malware defi-nitions and that they conduct malware scans at least once a week.

Third, you are concerned about the possibility of fire in the wonderful old building that your offices occupy. Accordingly, you recommend that the IS department back up all critical application software and store it at a remote location. You also recommend that the company back up the customer database once a week and store it with a vendor that specializes in off-premise backup storage.

You know that Southwest should have a security policy and that the partnership should take an active role in developing that policy and in analyzing risk. However, you decide to proceed slowly on those measures because you believe that the partners will be overwhelmed with the cost of the work to be done and therefore do nothing. Instead, you suggest that the partners think seriously about security and the risk they are taking and then present their security interest and concern to the staff. After that, you recommend that you and the Web programmer conduct security training for the company.

When you make that presentation. . . . Well, we don't know what happened. In reality, it will soon be up to you—it will be your career and your presentation, and your successes or failures. See exercises 23 and 24 to make your own speculations on how this turned out.

That's it! You've reached the end of this text. Take a moment to reflect on how you will use what you will learn, as described in the *Reflections Guide* on page 361a.

The Final, Final Word

Congratulations! You've made it through the entire book. With this knowledge you are well prepared to be an effective user of information systems. And with work and imagination, you can be much more than that. Many interesting opportunities are available to those who can apply information in innovative ways. Your professor has done what she can do, and the rest, as they say, is up to you.

I believe that, today, computer communications and data storage are free—or so close to free that the cost is not worth mentioning. What are the consequences? I do not know, and my nearly 40 years in the IT business make me wary of predictions that extend beyond next year. But I know that free communication and data storage will cause fundamental changes in the business environment. When a company like Getty Images (page 258) can produce its product at zero marginal cost, something's fundamentally different. Further, Getty Images is not the only business with this opportunity.

I suspect the rate of technology development will slow in the next five years. Businesses are still digesting the technology that already exists. According to Harry Dent, technology waves always occur in pairs.[4] The first phase is wild exuberance, in which new technology is invented, its capabilities flushed out, and its characteristics understood. That first phase always results in overbuilding, but it sets the stage for the second phase in which surviving companies and entrepreneurs purchase the overbuilt

infrastructure for pennies on the dollar and use it for new business purposes.

The automotive industry, for example, proceeded in two stages. The irrational exuberance phase culminated in a technology crash; General Motors' stock fell 75 percent from 1919 to 1921. However, that exuberance led to the development of the highway system, the development of the petroleum industry, and a complete change in the conduct of commerce in the United States. Every one of those consequences created opportunities for business people alert to the changing business environment.

I believe we are poised today to see a similar second stage in the adoption of information technology. Businesses are configuring themselves to take advantage of the new opportunities. Dell builds computers to order and pays for the components days after the customer has paid Dell for the equipment. I use my new computer before Dell pays the supplier for the monitor.

Fiber-optic cable will come to my home (and yours) when telecom companies buy today's dark fiber for pennies on the dollar and light it up. With fiber-optic cable to my house, goodbye video store! Hello DK Enterprises—Internet broadcaster of my music library and sailing photos.

In 2005, bloggers stunned the mainstream media (MSM) with their commentary that contributed to the Rathergate and Eason affairs. A new age is coming to news as bloggers demolish the MSM monopoly and obliterate MSM news control. The readership of newspapers has fallen consistently for more than a

[4]Harry Dent, *The Next Great Bubble Boom* (New York: The Free Press, 2004), pp. 40 ff.

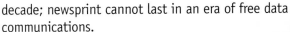

decade; newsprint cannot last in an era of free data communications.

So, as you finish your business degree, stay alert for new technology-based opportunities. Watch for the second wave and catch it. If you found this course interesting, take more IS classes. Enroll in a database class or a systems development class, even if you don't want to be an IS major. If you're technically oriented, take a data communications class or a security class. If you enjoy this material, become an IS major. If you want to program a computer, great, but if you do not, then don't. There are tremendous opportunities for nonprogrammers in the IS industry. Look for novel applications of IS technology to the emerging business environment. Hundreds of them abound! Find them and have fun!

DISCUSSION QUESTION

How will you further your career with what you've learned in this class? Give that question serious thought, and write a memo to yourself to read from time to time as your career progresses.

SUMMARY

- Computer threats come from human errors and mistakes, malicious human activity, and natural disaster. Five types of security problems are unauthorized data disclosure, incorrect data modification, faulty service, denial of service, and loss of infrastructure. Figure 11-1 lists specific sources of threats.

- Management has two critical security functions: establishing a security policy and managing security risk. A security policy consists of a program policy statement (why, what, who, and how), an issue-specific policy, and a systems-specific policy.

- Risk is the likelihood of an adverse occurrence. Uncertainty refers to the things we don't know we don't know. Management must assess assets, threats, safeguards, vulnerability, consequences, likelihood, and probable loss to decide what security safeguards to implement. In this assessment, management decides how much risk to accept.

- Safeguards are classified into technical, data, and human categories. Technical safeguards include identification and authentication, encryption, firewalls, malware protection, and application design. Data safeguards include data rights and responsibilities, user accounts and passwords, encryption, backup and recovery, and physical security. Human safeguards include safeguards for both employee and nonemployee personnel, as well as account administration, systems procedures, and security monitoring.

- Disaster preparedness safeguards include asset location, identification of mission-critical systems, and the preparation of remote backup facilities. Organizations should prepare for security incidents ahead of time by developing a plan, ensuring centralized reporting, defining responses to specific threats, and practicing the plan.

KEY TERMS AND CONCEPTS

Access control list (ACL)   **350**
Accounting controls   **357a**
Adware   **350**
Asymmetric encryption   **346**
Authentication   **344**
Biometric authentication   **344**
Certificate authority (CA)   **348**
Cold site   **360**
Denial of service   **339**
Digital certificate   **348**
Digital signatures   **347**
Drive-by sniffer   **339**
Email spoofing   **337**
Encryption   **346**
Firewall   **349**
Gramm-Leach-Bliley (GLB) Act   **343a**
Hacking   **339**
Hardening   **356**
Hashing   **347**

Health Insurance Portability and Accountability Act (HIPAA)   **343a**
Hot site   **359**
Identification   **344**
Internal firewall   **349**
IP spoofing   **337**
Kerberos   **345**
Key escrow   **352**
Malware   **350**
Malware definitions   **351**
Message digest   **347**
Packet-filtering firewall   **349**
Perimeter firewall   **349**
Personal identification number (PIN)   **344**
Phishing   **337**
Pretexting   **337**
Privacy Act of 1974   **343a**
Risk   **342**

Safeguard   **343**
Secure Socket Layer (SSL)   **346**
Security policy   **342**
Security program   **342**
Smart card   **344**
Sniffing   **339**
Spoofing   **337**
Spyware   **350**
Symmetric encryption   **346**
Technical safeguard   **344**
Transport Layer Security (TLS)   **347**
Uncertainty   **342**
Usurpation   **339**
Vulnerability   **343**
White-hat hacker   **351a**
Wi-Fi Protected Access (WPA, WPA2)   **346**
Wired Equivalent Privacy (WEP)   **345**

You Be the Guide

Southwest Video (continued)
(page 361)

The text presents a detailed summary of the protagonist's plan. Normally, this late in the class, I would not provide so many details but would ask the students to do most of the work—as was done in Chapter 10. Here, however, when I leave the students to their own devices, they concoct an amazingly complicated response that will be infeasible at a company as small and laid-back as Southwest Video.

Although the plan that the sales manager recommends leaves many security issues unaddressed, this plan represents a good first start. As stated in the text (in the discussion of Figure 11-3), there is no one-size-fits-all solution for computer security.

If you want the students to work more of the problem on their own, one possibility is to change the setting from a partnership to a wholly owned subsidiary of, say, a major motion picture company. See the following suggestion.

RESPONDING TO THE CHALLENGE

There's lots of detail in the wrap-up of this case. If you want to discuss those details, questions 22 and 23 are helpful.

For question 22:

a. Use the threats in Figure 11-1 to guide the discussion. Ask the students to specify a safeguard for each threat. Some of those safeguards are not addressed in the wrap-up.

b. It will be tempting for the partners to say, "We must have worked on the wrong solution." If they're more evolved, or more generous, they may say, "Well, we made a good decision, but had a bad result." The protagonist can hedge his or her bets a bit by indicating that not all threats are covered by the recommended plan.

c. I think it's appropriate and probably appreciated. The sales manager needs to tell the partners that he or she did that, however, and offer to review the limitations and their rationale.

d. I think the protagonist did a good job, considering the constraints at Southwest.

For question 23:

a. Use Figure 11-1 as a guide. The biggest threats are loss or compromise of customer data; loss of inventory data (or loss of inventory); and loss of the Web site.

b. WPA is better, but it runs only on new equipment. Southwest Video may need to buy a new wireless access point.

c. At least use MAC filtering—it runs on WEP or WPA.

One way to extend this case to a larger organization:

➤ **Let's suppose that Southwest is part of a larger corporation, say, part of a major motion picture company.**

➤ **Using Figure 11-1 as a guide, what threats seem particularly serious to Southwest as part of that company?**

➤ **If you are the sales manager, how would you proceed? Assume you report to a vice president of sales at the home office in a distant city.**

➤ **Would you contact your boss, the headquarters IS staff, or an independent consultant for help with your security concerns?**

I think the sales manager should contact the boss and, with the concurrence from the boss, the IS department. I wouldn't contact the consultant unless the IS department is completely unresponsive and then only with the full support of the boss.

➤ **Review the list of recommendations that the sales manager made for Southwest as a small partnership. Would your recommendations change for the firewall, the malware protection, and the backup storage?**

No, not really, but the IS department will have their own, more comprehensive plan that addresses more security threats.

Here's another thought for extending this case:

➤ **Suppose that a major motion picture company decides to acquire Southwest Video. Suppose that you are a member of a temporary team involved in constructing the merger of Southwest into the parent organization.**

➤ **Assume you have been asked to assess Southwest's computer security situation (from a management, not a technical, perspective). What would you say in your response?**

WRAP UP

➤ **The key to security, from an organizational perspective, is to understand the threats to which you** are exposed (Figure 11-1) and the safeguards that are available (Figure 11-2).

➤ Also, notice the fifth point in Figure 11-3. As a manager, your security responsibilities extend outside your organization. Not fulfilling your security responsibilities can cause problems to the rest of the organization, to your customers, and to your suppliers.

➤ So, learn your security responsibilities and take them seriously!

➤ If no one is thinking about security (as in the Southwest Video case), talk to your manager and think about positive steps you might take to rectify the situation.

Using the Reflections Guide

(page 361a)

GOAL

Inspire the students to use what they have learned to find, create, and manage innovative applications of IS technology.

BACKGROUND AND PRESENTATION STRATEGIES

The best is yet to come!

It's tempting to look at Microsoft and Bill Gates, Oracle and Larry Ellison, or Dell and Michael Dell and think, "All the good opportunities are gone." But, the great news is, *it's not true*. Rather, the *great* opportunities are in front of us.

Although I'm sure that many fortunes are yet to be made by companies that develop, market, and sell technology products, I think most of the great opportunities involve innovative applications of the technology that already exists or that others will develop.

The second-wave phenomenon identified by Harry Dent makes sense to me. Although his predictions of a 30,000 Dow-Jones average by 2010 seem over the top (not cited in the guide, but see his book referenced in the footnote), his analysis about the second wave, the application of technology use, seems sensible to me.

Getty Images (GYI) is an excellent example of success through innovative application of IS and IT. The company has harnessed database technology to create a system that produces images at near zero marginal cost. I learned about GYI in September 2004, when its stock was trading at $53 or so. I thought, "This is interesting. I should buy some of their stock." Did I? No. And their stock? Today, a year later, GYI is trading at $81, a 50-some percent increase in less than a year.

GYI is not the last company to find innovative applications of technology. Many, many more such opportunities exist, and our students are positioned to take advantage of them.

Even students who are uninterested in entrepreneurial opportunities can apply their knowledge to find innovative ways to accomplish the organization's competitive advantage.

➤ **Recall the Universal Electronics case (Chapters 7 and 8)? How did the protagonist of that case use IS for career advancement?**

➤ **What did the protagonist learn?**

Applications of IS, no how matter how clever or how innovative, must reinforce the organization's competitive strategy.

I do not think we can overemphasize the importance of the opportunities for nearly free data storage and data communications. Here are some consequences:

➤ **Numerous cities are sponsoring projects to provide fiber-optic cable to the home.**

➤ **Wireless networks are everywhere—city parks, public buildings, coffee shops, etc.**

➤ **The entertainment, computer, and data communications industries are reinforcing one another.**

➤ **Blogs have revolutionized mainstream media and, in the process, are changing the dynamics of politics.**

➤ **Podcasting provides a podium for everyone and enables listeners to consume the products on their own time and in their own, very flexible space.**

➤ **Cheap storage and data communications, along with standards like XML, will have a major, possibly revolutionary, impact on interorganizational activities like supply chain management.**

➤ **What do you think are some consequences of these changes?**

➤ **What are some opportunities for innovation within a company?**

➤ **Even those of you who aren't interested in innovative applications of IS and IT can think about innovative ways of NOT using IS and IT. For example, wireless, podcasting, and cell phones make it impossible to get off the grid.**

➤ **What opportunities does that fact create for recreation? For travel? For tourism? For employee counseling? Other?**

 SUGGESTED RESPONSES FOR DISCUSSION QUESTION

I think this is a very important exercise and I assign it for substantial credit.

This exercise asks students to:

• Take business seriously.

• Take their goal of becoming a business professional seriously.

- Take the knowledge they have learned from this class seriously.
- Merge those interests together into a document that can be useful to them during the early years of their careers.

I caution the students to write this memo using as specific language as they can. They should write it expecting that they will evaluate themselves on it in a few years. The more specific the memo is, the easier it will be to perform the evaluation.

I have the students email me their memos, and I take a lot of time grading it. If the student is seriously engaged in the assignment, I sometimes ask for several revisions and amplifications.

In many ways, this question, this memo, is our bottom line. What have the students learned from the class that will help them further their careers as business professionals?

There are so many possibilities—and that's the beauty of teaching this class. This exercise can be useful to anyone who takes their goal of becoming a business professional seriously.

WRAP UP

➤ **The best is yet to come!**

➤ **What that best is, what happens next, will be in large measure up to you!**

➤ **Prosper, do good work, and have fun!**

ASSIGNMENT MATERIAL

Review Questions

1. Summarize threats due to human errors and mistakes.
2. Summarize threats due to malicious human behavior.
3. Summarize threats due to natural disasters.
4. Describe the three major components of a security program.
5. Explain how elements 2, 4, and 5 in Figure 11-3 pertain to you as a future manager.
6. Describe the three major elements of a security policy.
7. Describe the risk-assessment process.
8. Explain how the five components relate to safeguards.
9. Describe, in your own words, how digital signatures work.
10. Describe, in your own words, how digital certificates work. What stops the infinite regress involving certificate authorities?
11. List the symptoms of spyware and adware.
12. Describe malware safeguards.
13. Summarize data safeguards.
14. Summarize safeguards for in-house personnel.
15. How do safeguards for nonemployees differ from those for employees?
16. Explain essential components of account administration.
17. Describe six types of systems procedures.
18. What are the major elements of security monitoring?
19. How should organizations prepare for disaster?
20. What constitutes an incident-response plan?

Applying Your Knowledge

21. Search online to find the cheapest way possible to purchase your own credit report. Several sources to check are *equifax.com*, *experion.com*, and *transunion.com*. Assume you can afford to purchase that report (and, if you can, do purchase it).

    a. You should review your credit report for obvious errors. However, other checks are appropriate. Search the Web for guidance on how best to review your credit records. Summarize what you learn.
    b. What actions should you take if you find errors in your credit report?
    c. Define *identity theft*. Search the Web and determine the best course of action if someone thinks he has been the victim of identity theft.

22. Reread the Southwest Video scenario on pages 335 and 361.

    a. The sales manager in this scenario chose to limit the recommendations to three safeguards. What threats does Southwest have that are not addressed by these three safeguards? If you need to make assumptions, make reasonable ones and state them.
    b. Suppose the partners implement the three safeguards and suffer a loss due to one of the unaddressed threats in your answer to part a. What will happen?
    c. In limiting the recommendations, the sales manager essentially performed a risk assessment in an attempt to save the partners' time. Is it appropriate for a subordinate to do that? Why or why not?
    d. If you were the sales manager, what would you have done in this situation?

23. Suppose that you have been asked to install a wireless network at Southwest Video. Use the material in this text to answer the following questions, but also search the Web for recent news and information about wireless security that relates to these issues.

    a. Describe the importance of securing your network. Describe the vulnerabilities that will exist if the network is not secure.
    b. Search the Web for the terms WEP and WPA. Explain the advantages and disadvantages of each.
    c. Given your answer to question b, how would you recommend securing your wireless network?

24. Assume you work for Southwest Video and Ben, the Webmaster, tells you that he has thoroughly tested the firewalls.

    a. Suppose you tell him that you've read that having independent testing is important. If he disagrees, what do you do?

b. Write a brief statement of the importance and use of white-hat hackers. In your statement explain both the advantages and the risks.

c. Visit the Web, and identify three potential white-hat hackers that you would consider appropriate for Southwest.

d. Suppose that one of the partners asks you and Ben to discuss the use of outside testers for your firewalls. How will you argue?

e. If one of the partners asks you how Southwest can protect itself from damages caused by a white-hat hacker who turns black, how will you answer?

f. Explain how the adage, "Never ask a question for which you do not want the answer" pertains in this situation.

Application Exercises

25. Develop a spreadsheet model of the cost of a virus attack in an organization that has three types of computers: employee workstations, data servers, and Web servers. Assume the number of computers affected by the virus depends on the severity of the virus. For the purposes of your model, assume that there are three levels of virus severity: Low-severity incidents affect fewer than 30 percent of the user workstations and none of the data or Web servers. Medium-severity incidents affect up to 70 percent of the user workstations, up to half of the Web servers, and none of the data servers. High-severity incidents can affect all organizational computers.

Assume 50 percent of the incidents are low severity, 30 percent are medium severity, and 20 percent are high severity.

Assume employees can remove viruses from workstations themselves, but that specially trained technicians are required to repair the servers. The time to eliminate a virus from an infected computer depends on the computer type. Let the time to remove the virus from each type be inputs to your model. Assume that when users eliminate the virus themselves, they are unproductive for twice the time required for the removal. Let the average employee hourly labor cost be an input to your model. Let the average cost of a technician also an input to your model. Finally, let the total number of user computers, data servers, and Web servers be inputs to your model.

Run your simulation 10 times. Use the same inputs for each run, but draw a random number (assume a uniform distribution for all random numbers) to determine the severity type. Then, draw random numbers to determine the percentage of computers of each type affected, using the constraints stated above. For example,

if the attack is of medium severity, draw a random number between 0 and 70 to indicate the percentage of infected user workstations, and a random number between 0 and 50 to indicate the percentage of infected Web servers.

For each run, calculate the total of lost employee hours, the total dollar cost of lost employee labor hours, the total hours of technicians to fix the servers, and the total cost of technician labor. Finally, compute the total overall cost. Show the results of each run. Show the average costs and hours for the 10 runs.

26. Suppose that you have been asked to develop a database to facilitate the creation of access control lists for your organization's firewall. Assume that managers submit all blocking requests and that each request is reviewed by a data communications specialist.

Your database is to keep track of managers, their requests for blocking IP addresses, and each specialist review of the request. For each request, track the date of the request, the IP address to be blocked, and whether the block applies to incoming, outgoing, or both types of access.

Assume that your database is to track the name and email of the manager who made each request. Assume that a manager can make many requests, but that a particular blocking request is made by one manager. Finally, assume that all requests are reviewed by data communications specialists. After a review, the specialist grants the block, refuses the block, or places the block into a pending status (waiting for more information). Your database is to track the name and email of the specialist who made the review. A specialist can review many requests, but each request is reviewed by at most one specialist.

Create appropriate tables and fill them with data. Create a data entry form to enter requests and a second data entry form to enter reviews. Create the following reports:

- All data for all requests sorted by IP address
- All data for all requests sorted by request date
- All pending requests
- All requests for a particular specialist, sorted by request date
- All requests for a particular manager, sorted by request date

Career Assignments

27. The Web site iNFOSYSSEC (*infosyssec.net/infosyssec/jobsec1.htm*) is an Internet security resource for IS security professionals. Search that site for security management jobs in the United States. Find five different jobs that are currently available.

a. Describe, in general terms, the responsibilities of security management jobs.

b. Describe qualifications that you think successful candidates would need for these jobs.

c. What courses could you take at your university to prepare yourself for one of these jobs?

d. Describe internships or other activities in which you could engage to prepare yourself for one of these jobs.

28. The Information Systems Audit and Control Association maintains a Web site at *isaca.org*. Visit this site and answer the following questions.

a. What is the purpose of this organization?

b. What are the CISA and CISM examinations? Why would an auditor or accountant or other non-IS professional seek one of these certificates? What value would such a certificate add?

c. Click on the Students and Educators tab on this site. What benefit would you gain from joining this organization?

d. What courses does this organization recommend for systems auditing and systems management?

e. Navigate this site, both the Students and Educators section as well as the overall site. Based on the information presented, what skills and abilities does someone need to become an effective information systems auditor? An effective information systems manager?

f. Search the Web for job opportunities for CISA- or CISM-qualified professionals. Characterize the employment prospects for such professionals.

29. Search the Web for the term *security jobs white-hat hacking*.

a. What qualifications does someone need to become a white-hat hacker?

b. What courses or other experience does someone need to become a white-hat hacker?

c. Characterize the employment prospects for white-hat hackers.

d. Would you want to be a white-hat hacker? Why or why not? What are the risks of such a job, as described in this chapter and also as described in articles you find on the Web?

Case Study 11-1

Antiphishing Tactics at More Than 50 Companies

Read about phishing in MIS in Use 11-1 (page 338), if you have not done so already.

In February 2005, Fraudwatch International posted phishing examples for over 50 companies on its Web site at *fraudwatchinternational.com/internetfraud/phishing/examples*. This list is a who's who of major, legitimate financial institutions, e-commerce retailers, and software companies. It includes Amazon.com, eBay, Microsoft/MSN, Yahoo!, Wells Fargo, Washington Mutual, and many other large firms, worldwide. All of these companies have suffered phishing attacks, and the list is by no means complete.

Several characteristics of phishing make it difficult to eliminate. First, attacks often are indirect. Organizations do not know that their name, brand, and graphics are being used to deceive their own customers until someone reports the attack. Second, it is difficult to gauge the size of the attack, and thus it is difficult to calibrate a response. Notifying every customer will alarm the customer base and create a negative brand impression. If the attack is limited, such a warning may not be justified, but who knows if the worst of the attack is yet to come?

Third, according to the Financial Services Technology Consortium, phishing is seldom perpetrated by a single individual, but is perpetrated by organized criminal enterprises. These crime organizations hire technical specialist contractors to phish, but these contractors give the results to the organization, which quickly disseminates them to criminals throughout the world.

Phishing is an attack on an organization's brand, which can be worth millions, even billions, of dollars. The phishing attack is clothed in the brand image, using the brand's familiar graphics. After the attack, in the mind of the customer the brand may be paired with deception, problems, and financial loss. These are not the emotions that any marketer wants paired with its brand.

Additionally, the financial consequence of each incident may be small to the spoofed organization, and so the organization may not be moved to respond. It is only in the aggregate that the tangible and intangible costs mount. Consequently, the cost/benefit ratio of helping a single customer is high. Yet, there does not seem to be any way to resolve the problem except one by one.

Finally, enforcement and punishment of phishers is exceedingly difficult. It is easy for phishers to operate in countries where such activity is tolerated. Also, the victims of a given attack potentially are spread worldwide. Who is available to punish the phishers?

Questions

1. Suppose that you work for Barclays, PayPal, Visa, or any other major organization that is vulnerable to phishing. (It will be easier to answer this question if you choose an organization for which you are a customer.) Using the information in this chapter, write a single-page memo that describes the phishing threat to your company and explains why the threat is difficult for the company to address.

2. List possible actions, if any, that your company can take to eliminate the phishing threat.

3. List possible actions that your company can take to mitigate the consequences of the phishing threat.

4. Phishing is an industry-wide problem. How can organizations better solve the problem or mitigate its consequences by working together?

5. Write a specific policy that you think your organization should take concerning phishing. (Include a program policy, an issue-specific policy, and a system-specific policy in your recommendation.)

6. Suppose you manage a customer help desk. Describe a procedure for the help-desk employees to take when a customer reports a phishing attack.

7. Describe the elements of a phishing incident-reporting system for your company.

Case Study 11-2

ChoicePoint

Read the ChoicePoint case in MIS in Use 11-2 (page 354), if you have not done so already.

ChoicePoint offers a wide array of data products for industries, businesses, and consumers. ChoicePoint's homepage states, "ChoicePoint is the nation's leading provider of identification and credential verification services." Figure 1 shows just the Consumer Solutions from ChoicePoint's Web site at *choicepoint.com* as of February 2005. ChoicePoint provides some of these services directly; partners and data providers offer other of these services by links at the ChoicePoint site.

For example, a user who clicks on Certified Birth Certificate in Figure 1 will be asked to provide a state. ChoicePoint then links to other data providers to process the request. Figure 2 shows the link activated for obtaining the birth certificate for someone in Denver, Colorado.

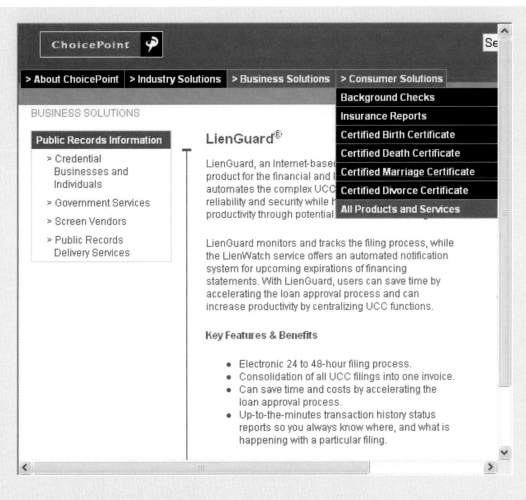

Figure 1
ChoicePoint Consumer
Services

Source: Used with permission of
ChoicePoint.com.

Figure 2
Ordering a Birth Certificate
via a ChoicePoint Partner

Source: Used with permission of
ChoicePoint.com.

Notice the red type in the form in Figure 2. Apparently, Colorado law restricts access to birth certificates to those who have a "direct and tangible" interest. It would seem unlikely that this Web site enforces this law. The law and this language possibly exist to provide a basis for legal action when fraudulent use of a birth certificate occurs.

As a data utility, ChoicePoint maintains relationships with many different entities. It obtains its data from both public and private sources. It then sells access to this data to its customers. Much of the data, by the way, can be obtained directly from the data vendor. ChoicePoint adds value by providing a centralized access point for many data needs. In addition to data sources and customers, ChoicePoint maintains relationships with partners like the City of Denver Vital Records shown in Figure 2. Finally, ChoicePoint also has relationships to the subjects on which it maintains data.

Questions

1. As discussed in *MIS in Use 11-2*, ChoicePoint exposed itself to considerable expense, many problems, and a possible loss of brand confidence because it notified the Los Angeles Police Department, cooperated in the investigation, and notified the individuals whose records had been compromised. It could have buried the theft and possibly avoided any responsibility. Comment on the ethical issues and ChoicePoint's response. Did ChoicePoint choose wisely? Consider that question from the viewpoint of customers, law enforcement personnel, investors, and management.

2. Given ChoicePoint's experience, what is the likely action of similar companies whose records are compromised in this way? Given your answer, do you think federal regulation and additional laws are required? What other steps could be taken to ensure that data vendors notify people harmed by data theft?

 3. Visit *choicepoint.com*. Summarize the products that ChoicePoint provides. What seems to be the central theme of this business?

4. Review the security policy material in this chapter and reflect on an appropriate program policy for ChoicePoint. Describe why ChoicePoint needs a security policy and who and what should be governed by such a policy. Consider not only employees, but also data subjects, customers, data sources, and partners.

5. Suppose that ChoicePoint decides to establish a formal security policy on the issue of inappropriate release of personal data. Summarize the issues that ChoicePoint should address.

10/100/1000 Ethernet A type of Ethernet that conforms to the IEEE 802.3 protocol and allows for transmission at a rate of 10, 100, or 1,000 Mbps (megabits per second). 124

Access A popular personal and small workgroup DBMS product from Microsoft. 82

Access control list (ACL) A list that encodes the rules stating which packets are to be allowed through a firewall and which are to be prohibited. 350

Access devices Devices, typically special-purpose computers, that connect network sites. The particular device required depends on the line used and other factors. Sometimes switches and routers are employed, but other types of equipment are needed as well. 130

Access point A point in a wireless network that facilitates communication among wireless devices and serves as a point of interconnection between wireless and wired networks. The AP must be able to process messages according to both the 802.3 and 802.11 standards, because it sends and receives wireless traffic using the 802.11 protocol and communicates with wired networks using the 802.3 protocol. 125

Accounting controls A set of procedures and standards developed by the accounting profession that provide checks and balances, independent reviews of activity logs, control of critical assets, and so forth. 357a

Accurate information Information that is based on correct and complete data and that has been processed correctly as expected. 12

Adware Programs installed on the user's computer without the user's knowledge or permission that reside in the background and, unknown to the user, observe the user's actions and keystrokes, modify computer activity, and report the user's activities to sponsoring organizations. Most adware is benign in that it does not perform malicious acts or steal data. It does, however, watch user activity and produce pop-up ads. 350

Analog signal A wavy signal. A modem converts the computer's digital data into analog signals that can be transmitted over dial-up Internet connections. 126

Analysis paralysis When too much time is spent documenting project requirements. 171

Antivirus programs Software that detects and possibly eliminates viruses. 53b

Application software Programs that perform a business function. Some application programs are general purpose, such as Excel or Word. Other application programs are specific to a business function such as accounts payable. 62

Asymmetric digital subscriber lines (ADSL) DSL lines that have different upload and download speeds. 129

Asymmetric encryption An encryption method whereby different keys are used to encode and to decode the message; one key encodes the message, and the other key decodes the message. Symmetric encryption is simpler and much faster than asymmetric encryption. 133a, 346

Asynchronous transfer mode (ATM) A protocol that divides data into uniformly sized cells, eliminates the need for protocol conversion, and can process speeds from 1 to 156 Mbps. ATM can support both voice and data communication. 131

ATA-100 Within a computer, a standard type of channel connecting the CPU to main memory. The number 100 indicates that the maximum transfer rate is 100MB per second. 58

Attribute (1) A variable that provides properties for an HTML tag. Each attribute has a standard name. For example, the attribute for a hyperlink is *href*, and its value indicates which Web page is to be displayed when the user clicks the link. (2) Characteristics of an entity. Example attributes of *Order* would be *OrderNumber*, *OrderDate*, *SubTotal*, *Tax*, *Total*, and so forth. Example attributes of *Salesperson* would be *SalespersonName*, *Email*, *Phone*, and so forth. 89, 236

Auctions Applications that match buyers and sellers by using an e-commerce version of a standard auction. This e-commerce application enables the auction company to offer goods for sale and to support a competitive bidding process. 232

Augmentation information system An information system in which humans do the bulk of the work but are assisted by the information system. 35

Automated information system An information system in which in which the hardware and software components do most of the work. 35

Beta testing The process of allowing future system users to try out the new system on their own. Used to locate program failures just prior to program shipment. 168

Bill of materials (BOM) A list of the materials that comprise a product. 202

Binary digits The means by which computers represent data; also called *bits*. A binary digit is either a zero or a one. 49

Biometric authentication The use of personal physical characteristics, such as fingerprints, facial features, and retinal scans, to authenticate users. 344

Bits The means by which computers represent data; also called *binary digits*. A bit is either a zero or a one. 49

Broadband Internet communication lines that have speeds in excess of 256 kbps. DSL and cable modems provide broadband access. 129

Brooks's Law   The famous adage that states: *Adding more people to a late project makes the project later*. Brooks's Law is true not only because a larger staff requires increased coordination, but also because new people need training. The only people who can train the new employees are the existing team members, who are thus taken off productive tasks. The costs of training new people can overwhelm the benefit of their contribution.   159

Browser   A program that processes the HTTP protocol; receives, displays, and processes HTML documents; and transmits responses.   236

Bullwhip effect   Phenomenon in which the variability in the size and timing of orders increases at each stage up the supply chain, from customer to supplier.   243

Bus   Means by which the CPU reads instructions and data from main memory and writes data to main memory.   53

Business intelligence (BI) system   A system that provides the right information, to the right user, at the right time. A tool produces the information, but the system ensures that the right information is delivered to the right user at the right time.   268

Business intelligence (BI) tools   Tools for creating information from data by searching, processing, and reporting.   268

Business process design   The creation of new, usually cross-departmental business practices during information systems development. With process design, organizations do not create new information systems to automate existing business practices. Rather, they use technology to enable new, more efficient business processes.   209

Business-to-business (B2B)   E-commerce sales between companies.   50, 231

Business-to-consumer (B2C)   E-commerce sales between a supplier and a retail customer (the consumer).   231

Business-to-government (B2G)   E-commerce sales between companies and governmental organizations.   232

Byte   (1) A character of data; (2) An 8-bit chunk.   51, 78

Cable modem   A type of modem that provides high-speed data transmission using cable television lines. The cable company installs a fast, high-capacity optical fiber cable to a distribution center in each neighborhood that it serves. At the distribution center, the optical fiber cable connects to regular cable-television cables that run to subscribers' homes or businesses. Cable modems modulate in such a way that their signals do not interfere with TV signals. Like DSL lines, they are always on.   129

Cache   A file on a domain name resolver that stores domain names and IP addresses that have been resolved. Then, when someone else needs to resolve that same domain name, there is no need to go through the entire resolution process. Instead, the resolver can supply the IP address from the local file.   143

Cache memory   A small amount of very fast computer memory that holds the most frequently used data. Typically, the CPU stores intermediate results and the most frequently used computer instructions in the cache. Cache can be thought of as a local, dedicated memory for the CPU and as "elbow room" for processing.   55

Calculation systems   The very first information systems. The goal of such systems was to relieve workers of tedious, repetitive calculations. These systems were labor-saving devices that produced little information.   197

CASE   An acronym for *computer-assisted software engineering* or *computer-assisted systems engineering*. The first meaning focuses on program development; the second focuses on development of systems having the five components. For either meaning, the basic idea is to use a computer application, called a CASE tool, to help develop computer programs or systems.   174

CASE tool   A tool used to help develop computer programs or systems. CASE tools vary in their features and functions. Some such tools address the entire systems development process from requirements to maintenance; others address just the design and implementation phases.   174

CD-R   An optical disk that can record data once.   58

CD-ROM   A read-only optical disk.   58

CD-RW   A rewritable optical disk.   58

Central processing unit (CPU)   The CPU selects instructions, processes them, performs arithmetic and logical comparisons, and stores results of operations in memory.   48

Certificate authorities (CAs)   Trusted, independent third-party companies that supply public keys for encryption.   348

Chief information officer (CIO)   The title of the principal manager of the IS department. Other common titles are *vice president of information services, director of information services,* and, less commonly, *director of computer services.*   307

Chief technology officer (CTO)   The head of the technology group. The CTO sorts through new ideas and products to identify those that are most relevant to the organization. The CTO's job requires deep knowledge of information technology and the ability to envision how new IT will affect the organization over time.   307

Clearinghouses   Entities that provide goods and services at a stated price, price and arrange for the delivery of the goods, but never take title to the goods.   232

Clickstream data   E-commerce data that describes a customer's clicking behavior. Such data includes everything the customer does at the Web site.   282

Clock speed   The speed of the CPU; it is measured in cycles per second, or hertz. A fast, modern computer has a clock speed of 3.0 gigahertz (abbreviated GHz), or 3 billion cycles per second. Clock speed determines the rate computations are accomplished. In general, the faster the clock speed, the faster work will be done.   55

Cluster analysis   An unsupervised data mining technique whereby statistical techniques are used to identify groups of entities that have similar characteristics. A common use for cluster analysis is to find groups of similar customers in data about customer orders and customer demographics.   284

Code generators   Programs that generate application code for commonly performed tasks. The idea is to improve developer productivity by having the tool generate as much code as possible. The developer can then add code for application-specific features.   174

Columns   Also called *fields*, or groups of bytes. A database table has multiple columns that are used to represent the attributes of an entity. Examples are PartNumber, EmployeeName, and SalesDate.   78

Commerce server   A computer that operates Web-based programs that display products, support online ordering, record and process payments, and interface with inventory-management applications.   235

Communication hardware   Hardware devices that support inter-computer communication. Examples are switches, routers, and access points.   48

Communications protocol   A means for coordinating activity between two or more communicating computers. Two machines must agree on the protocol to use, and they must follow that protocol as they send messages back and forth. Because there is so much to do, communications tasks are broken up into levels, or layers of protocols.   119

Competitive advantage   Gaining an edge over other businesses that seek the same customers.   26

Computer hardware   One of the five fundamental components of an information system.   4

Computer-assisted software engineering (CASE)   A style of program development that uses a tool, called a CASE tool, to help develop computer programs.   174

Computer-assisted systems engineering   A style of program development that uses a tool, called a CASE tool, to help develop computer systems.   174

Computer-based information system   An information system that includes a computer.   5

Confidence   In market-basket terminology, the probability estimate that two items will be purchased together.   286

Content management systems   Information systems that track organizational documents, Web pages, graphics, and related materials.   290

Cost feasibility   One of four dimensions of feasibility.   162

Cross-departmental systems   The third era of computing systems. In this era, systems are designed not to facilitate the work of a single department or function, but rather to integrate the activities of a complete business process.   197

Cross-functional systems   Synonym for *Cross-departmental systems*.   197

Crow's foot   A line on an entity-relationship diagram that indicates a 1:N relationship between two entities.   91

Crow's-foot version   A type of entity-relationship diagram that uses a crow's foot symbol to designate a 1:N relationship.   91

CRT monitors   A type of video display monitor that uses *cathode ray tubes*, the same devices used in traditional TV screens. Because they use a large tube, CRTs are big and bulky, and about as deep as they are wide.   58

Curse of dimensionality   The more attributes there are, the easier it is to build a data model that fits the sample data but that is worthless as a predictor.   282

Custom software   Tailor-made software.   62

Customer relationship management (CRM)   The set of business processes for attracting, selling, managing, and supporting customers.   31, 213

Customer relationship management (CRM) system   An information system that maintains data about customers and all of their interactions with the organization.   31, 213

Data   Recorded facts or figures. One of the five fundamental components of an information system.   4

Data administration   A staff function that pertains to *all* of an organization's data assets. Typical data administration tasks are setting data standards, developing data policies, and providing for data security.   317

Data channel   Means by which the CPU reads instructions and data from main memory and writes data to main memory.   53

Data dictionary   A file or database that contains data definitions.   318

Data integrity problem   In a database, the situation that exists when data items disagree with one another. An example is two different names for the same customer.   92

Data marts   Facilities that prepare, store, and manage data for reporting and data mining for specific business functions.   279

Data mining   The application of statistical techniques to find patterns and relationships among data and to classify and predict.   283

Data model   A logical representation of the data in a database that describes the data and relationships that will be stored in the database. Akin to a blueprint.   88

Data standards   Definitions, or metadata, for data items shared across the organization. They describe the name, official definition, usage, relationship to other data items, processing restrictions, version, security code, format, and other features of data items that are shared across the organization.   317

Data warehouses   Facilities that prepare, store, and manage data specifically for reporting and data mining.   279

Database   A self-describing collection of integrated records.   78

Database administration   The management, development, operation, and maintenance of the database so as to achieve the organization's objectives. This staff function requires balancing conflicting goals: protecting the database while maximizing its availability for authorized use. In smaller organizations, this function usually is served by a single person. Larger organizations assign several people to an office of database administration.   97, 317

Database application   A collection of forms, reports, queries, and application programs that process a database.   84

Database application system   Applications, having the standard five components, that make database data more accessible and useful. Users employ a database application that consists of forms, formatted reports, queries, and application programs. Each of these, in turn, calls on the database management system (DBMS) to process the database tables.   81

Database management system (DBMS)   A program used to create, process, and administer a database.   81

Database tier   In the three-tier architecture, the tier that runs the DBMS and receives and processes SQL requests to retrieve and store data.   237

Data-mining tools   Tools that use statistical techniques, many of which are sophisticated and mathematically complex, to process data to look for hidden patterns.   268

DB2   A popular, enterprise-class DBMS product from IBM.   82

DBA   Either the *database administrator* or the *office of database administration.*   97

Decision tree   A hierarchical arrangement of criteria for classifying customers, items, and other business objects.   287

Device access router   A generic term for a communications device that includes an access point, a switch, and a router. Normally the device access router provides DHCP and NAT services.   141

Dial-up modem   A modem that performs the conversion between analog and digital in such a way that the signal can be carried on a regular telephone line.   128

Digital certificate   A document supplied by a certificate authority (CA) that contains, among other data, an entity's name and public key.   348

Digital dashboard   An electronic display that is customized for a particular user.   271

Digital subscriber line (DSL)   DSL uses voice telephone lines with a DSL modem; it operates so that the signals do not interfere with voice telephone service. DSL provides much faster data transmission speeds than dial-up connections. Additionally, DSL is an always-on connection, so there is no need to dial in.   128

Dimension   A characteristic of an OLAP measure. Purchase date, customer type, customer location, and sales region are examples of dimensions.   276

Direct installation   Sometimes called plunge installation, a type of system conversion in which the organization shuts off the old system and starts the new system. If the new system fails, the organization is in trouble: Nothing can be done until either the new system is fixed or the old system is reinstalled. Because of the risk, organizations should avoid this conversion style if possible.   169

Dirty data   Problematic data. Examples are a value of *B* for customer gender and a value of *213* for customer age. Other examples are a value of *999-999-9999* for a U.S. phone number, a part color of *green*, and an email address of WhyMe@GuessWhoIAM-Hah-Hah.org. All of these values are problematic when data-mining.   281

Discussion groups   A form of organizational knowledge management. They allow employees or customers to post questions and queries seeking solutions to problems they have.   293

Disintermediation   Elimination of one or more middle layers in the supply chain.   232

Distributed computing   The process of a program on one computer invoking programs on a second computer.   250

Domain name   The registered, human-friendly valid name in the domain name system (DNS). The process of changing a name into its IP address is called *resolving the domain name.*   142

Domain name resolution   The process of converting a domain name into a public IP address.   142

Domain name resolvers   Computers that facilitate domain name resolution by storing the correspondence of domain names and IP addresses.   143

Domain name system (DNS)   A system that converts user-friendly names into their IP addresses. Any registered, valid name is called a domain name.   142

Dot pitch   The distance between pixels on a CRT monitor; the smaller the dot pitch, the sharper and brighter the screen image will be.   58

Drill down   With an OLAP report, to further divide the data into more detail.   276

Drive-by sniffers   People who take computers with wireless connections through an area and search for unprotected wireless networks in an attempt to gain free Internet access or to gather unauthorized data.   339

DSL modem   A type of modem. DSL modems operate on the same lines as voice telephones and dial-up modems, but they operate so that their signals do not interfere with voice telephone service. DSL modems provide much faster data transmission speeds than dial-up modems. Additionally, DSL modems always maintain a connection, so there is no need to dial in; the Internet connection is available immediately.   128

DVD-R   A digital versatile disk that can record data once.   58

DVD-ROM   A read-only digital versatile disk.   58

DVD-RW   A rewritable digital versatile disk.   58

Dynamic Host Configuration Protocol (DHCP)   A service provided by some communications devices that allocates and de-allocates a pool of IP addresses. A device that hosts the DHCP service is called a DHCP server. On request, a DHCP server loans a temporary IP address to a network device like a computer or printer. When the device disconnects, the IP address becomes available, and the DHCP server will reuse it when needed.   135

Dynamic reports   Reports that are generated at the time of request; the reporting system reads the most current data and generates the report using that fresh data. A report on sales today and a report on current stock prices are both dynamic reports.   270

E-commerce   The buying and selling of goods and services over public and private computer networks.   231

EDI X12 standard   An EDI standard that formally describes hundreds of documents that are commonly exchanged among businesses.   248

EDIFACT standard   An EDI standard that formally describes hundreds of documents that are commonly exchanged among businesses. Used internationally.   249

Electronic Data Interchange (EDI)   A standard for exchanging documents from machine to machine, electronically. In the past, EDI was used over point-to-point or value-added networks. Recently, EDI systems have been developed that use the Internet as well.   247

Electronic exchanges   Sites that facilitate the matching of buyers and sellers; the business process is similar to that of a stock exchange. Sellers offer goods at a given price through the electronic exchange, and buyers make offers to purchase over the same exchange. Price matches result in transactions from which the exchange takes a commission.   232

Email spoofing   A synonym for phishing. A technique for obtaining unauthorized data that uses pretexting via email. The *phisher* pretends to be a legitimate company and sends email requests for confidential data, such as account numbers, Social Security numbers, account passwords, and so forth. Phishers direct traffic to their sites under the guise of a legitimate business.   337

Encryption   The process of transforming clear text into coded, unintelligible text for secure storage or communication.   133a

Encryption algorithms   Algorithms used to transform clear text into coded, unintelligible text for secure storage or communication. Commonly used methods are DES, 3DES, and AES.   133a

Enterprise application integration (EAI)   The integration of existing systems by providing layers of software that connect applications and their data together.   219

Enterprise DBMS   A product that processes large organizational and workgroup databases. These products support many users, perhaps thousands, and many different database applications. Such DBMS products support 24/7 operations and can manage databases that span dozens of different magnetic disks with hundreds of gigabytes or more of data. IBM's DB2, Microsoft's SQL Server, and Oracle's Oracle are examples of enterprise DBMS products.   87

Enterprise resource planning (ERP)   The integration of all of the organization's principal processes. ERP is an outgrowth of MRP II manufacturing systems, and most ERP users are manufacturing companies.   215

Entity   In the E-R data model, a representation of some thing that users want to track. Some entities represent a physical object; others represent a logical construct or transaction.   89

Entity-relationship (E-R) data model   The most popular technique for creating a data model. Developers describe the content of a database by defining the things (*entities*) that will be stored in the database and the *relationships* among those entities.   88

Entity-relationship (E-R) diagrams   A type of diagram used by database designers to document entities and their relationships to each other.   89

Ethernet   Another name for the IEEE 802.3 protocol, Ethernet is a network protocol that operates at Layers 1 and 2 of the TCP/IP–OSI architecture. Ethernet, the world's most popular LAN protocol, is used on WANs as well.   124

Executive information system (EIS)   An information system that supports strategic decision making.   34

Expert systems   Knowledge-sharing systems that are created by interviewing experts in a given business domain and codifying the rules used by those experts.   294

eXtensible Markup Language (XML)   A very important document standard that separates document content, structure, and presentation; eliminates problems in HTML; and offers advantages over EDI. Most believe XML will eventually replace EDI.   250

Extreme programming (XP)   An emerging technique for developing computer programs. Programmers create only features and functions of the new program that they can complete in 2 weeks or less. If many programmers are working on the project, each person's work must be done in such a way that all of their work can be combined and assembled at the end of that period. Users and PQA professionals test the developed code continuously through the process. Three key XP characteristics are: It (1) it is customer centric, (2) it uses just-in-time design, and (3) it involves paired programming.   180

Feasibility   Whether a project is or is not possible. Feasibility has four dimensions: cost, schedule, technical, and organizational feasibility. The purpose of assessing feasibility is to eliminate any obviously infeasible systems as soon as possible.   162

Fields   Also called *columns*, groups of bytes in a database table. A database table has multiple columns that are used to represent the attributes of an entity. Examples are PartNumber, EmployeeName, and SalesDate.   78

File   A group of similar rows or records. In a database, sometimes called a *table*.   78

File Transfer Protocol (FTP)   A Layer-5 protocol used to copy files from one computer to another.   120

Firewall   A computing device located between a firm's internal and external networks that prevents unauthorized access to or from the internal network. A firewall can be a special-purpose computer or it can be a program on a general-purpose computer or on a router.   85a, 349

Firmware   Computer software that is installed into devices like printers, print services, and various types of communication devices. The software is coded just like other software, but it is installed into special, programmable memory of the printer or other device.   63

Five component framework   The five fundamental components of an information system—computer hardware, software, data, procedures, and people—that are present in every information system, from the simplest to the most complex.   4

Foreign keys   A column or group of columns used to represent relationships. Values of the foreign key match values of the primary key in a different (foreign) table.   80

Form   Data entry forms are used to read, insert, modify, and delete database data.   85

Frame Relay   A protocol that can process traffic in the range of 56 kbps to 40 Mbps by packaging data into frames.   131

Frames   The containers used at Layers 1 and 2 of the TCP/IP–OSI model. A program implementing a Layer-2 protocol packages data into frames.   121

Frequently asked questions (FAQs) A form of knowledge sharing in which the organization edits, prioritizes, and summarizes questions generated from discussion groups. 293

Functional systems The second era of information systems. The goal of such systems was to facilitate the work of a single department or function. Over time, in each functional area, companies added features and functions to encompass more activities and to provide more value and assistance. 196

General-purpose computers Computers that can run different programs to perform different functions. 48

Gigabyte (GB) 1,024MB. 51

Gramm-Leach-Bliley (GLB) Act Passed by Congress in 1999, this act protects consumer financial data stored by financial institutions, which are defined as banks, securities firms, insurance companies, and organizations that provide financial advice, prepare tax returns, and provide similar financial services. 343a

Granularity The level of detail in data. Customer name and account balance is large granularity data. Customer name, balance, and the order details and payment history of every customer order is smaller granularity. 282

Hacking Occurs when a person gains unauthorized access to a computer system. Although some people hack for the sheer joy of doing it, other hackers invade systems for the malicious purpose of stealing or modifying data. 339

Hardening The process of taking extraordinary measures to reduce a system's vulnerability. Hardened sites use special versions of the operating system, and they lock down or eliminate operating systems features and functions that are not required by the application. Hardening is a technical safeguard. 356

Hardware Electronic components and related gadgetry that input, process, output, store, and communicate data according to instructions encoded in computer programs or software. 48

Health Insurance Portability and Accountability Act (HIPAA) The privacy provisions of this 1996 act give individuals the right to access health data created by doctors and other health-care providers. HIPAA also sets rules and limits on who can read and receive a person's health information. 343a

HIPAA standard An EDI standard that is used for medical records. 249

Horizontal-market application software Software that provides capabilities common across all organizations and industries; examples include word processors, graphics programs, spreadsheets, and presentation programs. 62

https:// An indication that a Web browser is using the SSL/TLS protocol to ensure secure communications. 133

Hyperlinks A pointer on a Web page to another Web page. A hyperlink contains the URL of the Web page to access when the user clicks the hyperlink. The URL can reference a page on the Web server that generated the page containing the hyperlink, or it can reference a page on another server. 236

Hypertext Markup Language (HTML) A language that defines the structure and layout of Web page content. An HTML tag is a notation used to define a data element for display or other purposes. 235

Hypertext Transfer Protocol (HTTP) A Layer-5 protocol used to process Web pages. 119

Identifier An attribute (or group of attributes) whose value is associated with one and only one entity instance. 89

IEEE 802.3 protocol This standard, also called *Ethernet*, is a network protocol that operates at Layers 1 and 2 of the TCP/IP–OSI architecture. Ethernet, the world's most popular LAN protocol, is used on WANs as well. 124

If ... then ... Format for rules derived from a decision tree (data mining) or by interviewing a human expert (expert systems). 288, 294

Incremental development A development process whereby developers design, implement, and fix portions of an application, one-by-one, until the entire program has been developed in pieces. This method reduces development challenges by using a divide-and-conquer strategy. 172

Information (1) Knowledge derived from data, where *data* is defined as recorded facts or figures; (2) Data presented in a meaningful context; (3) Data processed by summing, ordering, averaging, grouping, comparing, or other similar operations; (4) A difference that makes a difference. 9a, 10

Information system (IS) A group of components that interact to produce information. 4

Information technology (IT) The products, methods, inventions, and standards that are used for the purpose of producing information. 13

Inherent processes The procedures that must be followed to effectively use licensed software. For example, the processes inherent in MRP systems assume that certain users will take specified actions in a particular order. In most cases, the organization must conform to the processes inherent in the software. 209

Input hardware Hardware devices that attach to a computer; includes keyboards, mouse, document scanners, and bar-code (Universal Product Code) scanners. 48

Instruction set The collection of instructions that a computer can process. 50

Internal firewalls A firewall that sits inside the organizational network. 349

International Organization for Standardization (ISO) An international organization that sets worldwide standards. ISO developed a seven layer protocol architecture called Open Systems Interconnection (OSI). Portions of that protocol architecture are incorporated into the TCP/IP–OSI hybrid protocol architecture. 119

Internet When spelled with a small i, as in internet, a private network of networks. When spelled with a capital I, as in Internet, the public internet known as the Internet. 117

Internet Corporation for Assigned Names and Numbers (ICANN) The organization responsible for managing the assignment of public IP addresses and domain names for use on the Internet. Each public IP address is unique across all computers on the Internet.   135

Internet Engineering Task Force (IETF)   An organization that specifies standards for use on the Internet. Developed a four-layer scheme called the TCP/IP (Transmission Control Program/Internet Protocol) architecture. TCP/IP is part of the TCP/IP–OSI protocol architecture that is used on the Internet and most internets today.   119

Internet Protocol (IP)   A Layer-3 protocol. As the name implies, IP is used on the Internet, but it is used on many other internets as well. The chief purpose of IP is to route packets across an internet.   121

Internet service provider (ISP)   An ISP provides users with Internet access. An ISP provides a user with a legitimate Internet address; it serves as the user's gateway to the Internet; and it passes communications back and forth between the user and the Internet. ISPs also pay for the Internet. They collect money from their customers and pay access fees and other charges on the users' behalf.   125

IP addresses   A series of dotted decimals in a format like 192.168.2.28 that identifies a unique device on a network or internet. With the IPv4 standard, IP addresses have 32 bits. With the IPv6 standard, IP addresses have 128 bits. Today, IPv4 is more common but will likely be supplanted by IPv6 in the future. With IPv4, the decimal between the dots can never exceed 255.   135

IP spoofing   A type of spoofing whereby an intruder uses another site's IP address as if it were that other site.   337

IPv4   An IP addressing scheme that constructs addresses having 32 bits. The bits are divided into four groups of 8 bits, and a decimal number represents each group. The decimal number can never exceed 255.   144

IPv6   A new IP addressing scheme that uses 128 bits for IP addresses. Currently, both IPv4 and IPv6 addresses are used on the Internet. Over the coming years, however, IPv6 will likely replace IPv4.   144

Islands of automation   The structure that results when functional applications work independently in isolation from one another. Usually problematic because data is duplicated, integration is difficult, and results can be inconsistent.   196

Joint application design (JAD)   A key element of rapid application design. A team of users, developers, and PQA personnel conducts design activities during JAD sessions. JAD came about because developers wanted to incorporate feedback and testing earlier in the development process. Ultimately, developers decided that the best place to get feedback was during design creation.   174

Just-barely-sufficient information   Information that meets the purpose for which it is generated, but just barely so.   13

Just-in-time (JIT) inventory policy   A policy that seeks to have production inputs (both raw materials and work-in-process) delivered to the manufacturing site just as they are needed. By scheduling delivery of inputs in this way, companies are able to reduce inventories to a minimum.   202

Kanban   A Japanese word that means "card"; it refers to a signal to build something. Manufacturing processes that respond to kanbans must be more flexible than those that are MPS based. A process based on such signals is sometimes called a *pull manufacturing process*, because the products are pulled through manufacturing by demand.   204

Kerberos   A system that authenticates users without sending their passwords across the computer network. Kerberos uses a complicated system of "tickets" to enable users to obtain services from networks and other servers.   345

Key   (1) A column or group of columns that identifies a unique row in a table. (2) A number used to encrypt data. The encryption algorithm applies the key to the original message to produce the coded message. Decoding (decrypting) a message is similar; a key is applied to the coded message to recover the original text.   79, 133a, 352

Key escrow   A control procedure whereby a trusted party is given a copy of a key used to encrypt database data.   252

Kilobyte (K)   A collection of 1,024 bytes.   51

Knowledge management (KM)   The process of creating value from intellectual capital and sharing that knowledge with employees, managers, suppliers, customers, and others who need that capital.   289

Knowledge management system (KMS)   An information system for storing and retrieving organizational knowledge, whether that knowledge is in the form of data, documents, or employee know-how.   32

Layered protocol   A communications architecture in which work is allocated to protocols in layers. This arrangement allows communications tasks to be divided into manageable chunks. The layered protocol used on the internet is the TCP/IP–OSI protocol architecture.   119

LCD monitors   A type of video display monitor that uses a technology called *liquid crystal display*. LCD monitors are flat and require much less space than CRT monitors.   58

Legacy information system   An older system based on outdated technologies and techniques that is still used, despite its age. Legacy systems arise because organizations cannot afford to replace an IS just because better technology has been developed. Some legacy systems give value and service for many years.   316

License agreement   Stipulates how a program can be used. Most specify the number of computers on which the program can be installed and sometimes the number of users that can connect to and use the program remotely. Such agreements also stipulate limitations on the liability of the software vendor for the consequences of errors in the software.   61a

Lift   In market-basket terminology, the ratio of confidence to the base probability of buying an item. Lift shows how much the base probability changes when other products are purchased. If the lift is greater than 1, the change is positive; if it is less than 1, the change is negative.   286

Linkages Process interactions across value chains. Linkages are important sources of efficiencies and are readily supported by information systems. 208

Linux A version of Unix that was developed by the open-source community. The open-source community owns Linux, and there is no fee to use it. Linux is a popular operating system for Web servers. 61

Local area network (LAN) A network that connects computers that reside in a single geographic location on the premises of the company that operates the LAN. The number of connected computers can range from two to several hundred. 117

Logical addresses Also called *IP addresses*, a series of dotted decimals in a format like 192.168.2.28 that identifies a unique device on a network or internet. With the IPv4 standard, IP addresses have 32 bits. IP addresses are called logical addresses because they can be reassigned from one device to another. 135

MAC address Also called *physical address.* A permanent address given to each network interface card (NIC) at the factory. This address enables the device to access the network via a Level 2 protocol. By agreement among computer manufacturers, MAC addresses are assigned in such a way that no two NIC devices will ever have the same MAC address. 122

Mac OS An operating system developed by Apple Computer, Inc. for the Macintosh. The current version is Mac OS X. Macintosh computers are used primarily by graphic artists and workers in the arts community. Mac OS was developed for the PowerPC, but as of 2006 will run on Intel processors as well. 61

Macro viruses Viruses that attach themselves to a Word, Excel, PowerPoint, or other type of document. When the infected document is opened, the virus places itself in the startup files of the application. After that, the virus infects every file that the application creates or processes. 53a

Main memory A set of cells in which each cell holds a byte of data or instruction; each cell has an address, and the CPU uses the addresses to identify particular data items. 49

Maintenance In the context of information systems, (1) to fix the system to do what it was supposed to do in the first place or (2) to adapt the system to a change in requirements. 158

Malware Viruses, worms, Trojan horses, spyware, and adware. 350

Malware definitions Patterns that exist in malware code. Antimalware vendors update these definitions continuously and incorporate them into their products in order to better fight against malware. 351

Management information systems (MIS) The development and use of information systems that help businesses achieve their goals and objectives. 4, 34

Managerial decisions Decisions that concern the allocation and use of resources. 34

Manufacturing information system An information system that supports one or more aspects of manufacturing processes, including planning, scheduling, integration with inventory, quality control, and related processes. 201

Manufacturing resource planning (MRP II) A follow-on to MRP that includes the planning of materials, personnel, and machinery. It supports many linkages across the organization, including linkages with sales and marketing via the development of a master production schedule. It also includes the capability to perform what-if analyses on variances in schedules, raw materials availabilities, personnel, and other resources. 204

Many-to-many (N:M) relationship Relationships involving two entity types in which an instance of one type can relate to many instances of the second type, and an instance of the second type can relate to many instances of the first. For example, the relationship between Student and Class is N:M. One student may enroll in many classes and one class may have many students. Contrast with one-to-many relationships. 91

Margin The difference between value and cost. 207

Market-basket analysis A data-mining technique for determining sales patterns. A market-basket analysis shows the products that customers tend to buy together. 285

Master production schedule (MPS) A plan for producing products. To create the MPS, the company analyzes past sales levels and makes estimates of future sales. This process is sometimes called a *push manufacturing process*, because the company pushes the products into sales (and customers) according to the MPS. 203

Materials requirements planning (MRP) An information system that plans the need for materials and inventories of materials used in the manufacturing process. Unlike MRP II, MRP does not include the planning of personnel, equipment, or facilities requirements. 204

Maximum cardinality The maximum number of entities that can be involved in a relationship. Common examples of maximum cardinality are 1:N, N:M, and 1:1. 91

Measure The data item of interest on an OLAP report. It is the item that is to be summed, averaged, or otherwise processed in the OLAP cube. Total sales, average sales, and average cost are examples of measures. 276

Media access control (MAC) address Also called *physical address.* A permanent address given to each network interface card (NIC) at the factory. This address enables the device to access the network via a Level 2 protocol. By agreement among computer manufacturers, MAC addresses are assigned in such a way that no two NIC devices will ever have the same MAC address. 122

Megabyte (MB) 1,024KB. 51

Memory swapping The movement of programs and data into and out of memory. If a computer has insufficient memory for its workload, such swapping will degrade system performance. 54

Merchant companies In e-commerce, companies that take title to the goods they sell. They buy goods and resell them. 231

Metadata Data that describe data. 80

Minimum cardinality The minimum number of entities that must be involved in a relationship. 91

Modem   Short for *modulator/demodulator,* a modem converts the computer's digital data into signals that can be transmitted over telephone or cable lines.   126

Moore's Law   A law, created by Gordon Moore, stating that the number of transistors per square inch on an integrated chip doubles every 18 months. Moore's prediction has proved generally accurate in the 40 years since it was made. Sometimes this law is stated that the performance of a computer doubles every 18 months. While not strictly true, this version gives the gist of the idea.   13

Motherboard   A circuit board upon which the CPU processing components are mounted and/or connected.   53

Multi-user processing   When multiple users process the database at the same time.   86

MySQL   A popular open-source DBMS product that is license free for most applications.   82

Narrowband   Internet communication lines that have transmission speeds of 56 kbps or less. A dial-up modem provides narrowband access.   129

Network   A collection of computers that communicate with one another over transmission lines.   117

Network Address Translation (NAT)   The process of changing public IP addresses into private network IP addresses, and the reverse.   139

Network interface card (NIC)   A hardware component on each device on a network (computer, printer, etc.) that connects the device's circuitry to the communications line. The NIC works together with programs in each device to implement Layers 1 and 2 of the TCP/IP–OSI hybrid protocol.   122

Network of leased lines   A WAN connection alternative. Communication lines are leased from telecommunications companies and connected into a network. The lines connect geographically distant sites.   129

Neural networks   A popular supervised data-mining technique used to predict values and make classifications such as "good prospect" or "poor prospect."   285

Nonmerchant companies   E-commerce companies that arrange for the purchase and sale of goods without ever owning or taking title to those goods.   231

Nonvolatile memory   Memory that preserves data contents even when not powered (e.g., magnetic and optical disks). With such devices, you can turn the computer off and back on, and the contents will be unchanged.   53

Normal forms   A classification of tables according to their characteristics and the kinds of problems they have.   93

Normalization   The process of converting poorly structured tables into two or more well-structured tables.   92

Object-oriented development (OOD)   A systems development methodology that arose from the discipline of object-oriented programming. OOD develops programs using the object-oriented programming (OOP) techniques. Programs developed using OOP are easier to maintain than those developed using traditional techniques.   176

Object-oriented programming (OOP)   A discipline for designing and writing computer programs. Programs developed using OOP are easier and cheaper to maintain than those developed using traditional techniques.   176

Object-relational database   A type of database that stores both OOP objects and relational data. Rarely used in commercial applications.   80n

Off-the-shelf software   Software that can be used without having to make any changes.   62

OLAP cube   A presentation of an OLAP measure with associated dimensions. The reason for this term is that some products show these displays using three axes, like a cube in geometry. Same as OLAP report.   276

OLAP servers   Computer servers running software that performs OLAP analyses. An OLAP server reads data from an operational database, performs preliminary calculations, and stores the results of those calculations in an OLAP database.   279

Onboard NIC   An NIC built into the motherboard.   122

One-to-many (1:N) relationship   Relationships involving two entity types in which an instance of one type can relate to many instances of the second type, but an instance of the second type can relate to at most one instance of the first. For example, the relationship between Department and Employee is 1:N. A department may relate to many employees, but an employee relates to at most one department.   91

Online analytical processing (OLAP)   A dynamic type of reporting system that provides the ability to sum, count, average, and perform other simple arithmetic operations on groups of data. Such reports are dynamic because users can change the format of the reports while viewing them.   276

Open-source community   A loosely coupled group of programmers who mostly volunteer their time to contribute code to develop and maintain common software. Linux and MySQL are two prominent products developed by such a community.   61

Operating system (OS)   A computer program that controls the computer's resources: It manages the contents of main memory, processes keystrokes and mouse movements, sends signals to the display monitor, reads and writes disk files, and controls the processing of other programs.   54

Operational decisions   Decisions that concern the day-to-day activities of an organization.   34

Optical fiber cables   A type of cable used to connect the computers, printers, switches, and other devices on a LAN. The signals on such cables are light rays, and they are reflected inside the glass core of the optical fiber cable. The core is surrounded by a *cladding* to contain the light signals, and the cladding, in turn, is wrapped with an outer layer to protect it.   123

Optimal resolution   The size of the pixel grid (e.g., 1,024 × 768) on a video display monitor that will give the best sharpness and clarity. This optimal resolution depends on the size of the screen, the dot or pixel pitch, and other factors.   59

Oracle   A popular, enterprise-class DBMS product from Oracle Corporation.   82

Organizational feasibility. One of four dimensions of feasibility. 162, 163

Original equipment manufacturers (OEM) A company that produces a computer or other computing device and sells that product to others who add additional features and functions (hardware or software) before selling it to the eventual user. 50

Output hardware Hardware that displays the results of the computer's processing. Consists of video displays, printers, audio speakers, overhead projectors, and other special-purpose devices, such as large flatbed plotters. 48

Outsourcing The process of hiring another organization to perform a service. Outsourcing is done to save costs, to gain expertise, and to free up management time. 319

Packet-filtering firewall A firewall that examines each packet and determines whether to let the packet pass. To make this decision, it examines the source address, the destination addresses, and other data. 349

Paired programming The most unconventional characteristic of XP. With it, two programmers work together, side by side, on the very same computer. They look over each other's shoulders, and they continuously communicate as they program on that single machine. According to XP proponents, studies show that two programmers working in this way can do at least as much work as two programmers working separately, and the resulting program code has fewer errors and is more easily maintained. 180

Parallel installation A type of system conversion in which the new system runs in parallel with the old one for a while. Parallel installation is expensive because the organization incurs the costs of running both systems. 169

Patch A group of fixes for high-priority failures that can be applied to existing copies of a particular product. Software vendors supply patches to fix security and other critical problems. 53a, 170

Payload The program code of a virus that causes unwanted or hurtful actions, such as deleting programs or data, or even worse, modifying data in ways that are undetected by the user. 53a

Perimeter firewall A firewall that sits outside the organizational network. It is the first device that Internet traffic encounters. 349

Personal DBMS DBMS products designed for smaller, simpler database applications. Such products are used for personal or small workgroup applications that involve fewer than a 100 users, and normally fewer than 15. Today, Microsoft Access is the only prominent personal DBMS. 87

Personal identification number (PIN) A form of authentication whereby the user supplies a number that only he or she knows. 344

Phased installation A type of system conversion in which the new system is installed in pieces across the organization(s). Once a given piece works, then the organization installs and tests another piece of the system, until the entire system has been installed. 168

Phisher An operation that uses email to spoof legitimate companies in an attempt to illegally capture credit card numbers, email accounts, driver's license numbers, and other sensitive data. 338

Phishing A technique for obtaining unauthorized data that uses pretexting via email. The *phisher* pretends to be a legitimate company and sends an email requesting confidential data, such as account numbers, Social Security numbers, account passwords, and so forth. 337

Physical address Also called *MAC address*. A permanent address given to each network interface card (NIC) at the factory. This address enables the device to access the network via a Level 2 protocol. By agreement among computer manufacturers, physical addresses are assigned in such a way that no two NIC devices will ever have the same address. 135

Pilot installation A type of system conversion in which the organization implements the entire system on a limited portion of the business. The advantage of pilot implementation is that if the system fails, the failure is contained within a limited boundary. This reduces exposure of the business and also protects the new system from developing a negative reputation throughout the organization(s). 168

Pixel pitch The distance between pixels on the screen of a LCD monitor; the smaller the pixel pitch, the sharper and brighter the image will be. 58

Pixels Small spots on the screen of a video display monitor arranged in a rectangular grid. The number of pixels displayed depends not only on the size of the monitor, but also on the design of the computer's video card. 58

Plunge installation Sometimes called direct installation, a type of system conversion in which the organization shuts off the old system and starts the new system. If the new system fails, the organization is in trouble: Nothing can be done until either the new system is fixed or the old system is reinstalled. Because of the risk, organizations should avoid this conversion style if possible. 169

Point of presence (POP) The location at which a line connects to a PSDN network. Think of the POP as the phone number that one dials to connect to the PSDN. Once a site has connected to the PSDN POP, the site obtains access to all other sites connected to the PSDN. 131

Point-to-Point Protocol (PPP) A Layer-2 protocol used for networks that involve just two computers, hence the term *point-to-point*. PPP is used between a modem and an ISP as well as on some networks of leased lines. 128

Porter's five competitive forces model A model developed by Porter that states that five competitive forces determine industry profitability: bargaining power of suppliers, bargaining power of customers, new entrants to the market, rivalry among firms in the market, and the threat of substitutions for an organization's products or services. 230

Pretexting A technique for gathering unauthorized information in which someone pretends to be someone else. A common scam involves a telephone caller who pretends to be from a credit card company and claims to be checking the validity of credit card numbers. Phishing is also a form of pretexting. 337

Price elasticity   A measure of the sensitivity in demand to changes in price. It is the ratio of the percentage change in quantity divided by the percentage change in price.   234

Privacy Act of 1974   Federal law that provides protections to individuals regarding records maintained by the U.S. government.   343a

Private IP addresses   A type of IP address used within private networks and internets. Private IP addresses are assigned and managed by the company that operates the private network or internet.   135

Problem   A perceived difference between what is and what ought to be.   31

Procedures   Instructions for humans. One of the five fundamental components of an information system.   4

Process blueprint   In an ERP product, a comprehensive set of inherent processes for organizational activities.   215

Process-based systems   The third era of computing systems. In this era, systems are designed not to facilitate the work of a single department or function, but rather to integrate the activities in an entire business process.   197

Processing hardware   In a computer, the CPU and main memory.   48

Product quality assurance (PQA)   The testing of a system. PQA personnel usually construct a test plan with the advice and assistance of users. PQA test engineers themselves perform testing, and they also supervise user-test activity. Many PQA professionals are themselves programmers who write automated test programs.   168

Protocol   A standardized means for coordinating an activity between two or more entities.   118

Prototype   A mock-up of an aspect of a new system; it could be a mock-up of a form, report, query, or other element of the user interface.   172

Public IP addresses   IP addresses used on the Internet. Such IP addresses are assigned to major institutions in blocks by the Internet Corporation for Assigned Names and Numbers (ICANN). Each IP address is unique across all computers on the Internet.   135

Public key/private key   A special version of asymmetric encryption that is popular on the Internet. With this method, each site has a public key for encoding messages and a private key for decoding them.   133a

Public switched data network (PSDN)   A WAN connection alternative. A network of computers and leased lines is developed and maintained by a vendor that leases time on the network to other organizations.   131

Pull manufacturing process   A manufacturing process whereby products are pulled through manufacturing by demand. Items are manufactured in response to signals from customers or other production processes that products or components are needed.   204

Pull report   A report that the user must request. To obtain a pull report, a user goes to a Web portal or digital dashboard and clicks a link or button to cause the reporting system to produce and deliver the report.   272

Push manufacturing process   A plan for producing products whereby the company analyzes past sales levels, makes estimates of future sales, and creates a master production schedule. Products are produced according to that schedule and pushed into sales (and customers).   203

Push report   Reports sent to users according to a preset schedule. Users receive the report without any activity on their part.   272

Query   A request for data from a database.   85

Query reports   Reports prepared in response to data entered by users.   270

Radio frequency identification tags (RFIDs)   A computer chip that transmits data about the container or product to which it is attached. RFID data include not just product numbers, but also data about where the product was made, what the components are, special handling requirements, and, for perishable products, when the contents will expire. RFIDs facilitate inventory tracking by signaling their presence to scanners as they are moved throughout the manufacturing facility.   201

RAM memory   Stands for *random access memory*. Computer memory consisting of cells that hold data or instructions. Each cell has an address that the CPU uses to read or write data. Memory locations can be read or written in any order, hence the term *random access*. RAM memory is almost always volatile.   53

Rapid application development (RAD)   A type of application development pioneered by James Martin. The basic idea is to break up the design and implementation phases of the SDLC into smaller chunks and to design and implement those chunks using as much computer assistance as possible.   172

Records   Also called *rows*, groups of columns in a database table.   78

Reference Model for Open Systems Interconnection (OSI)   A protocol architecture created by ISO that has seven layers. Portions of the OSI model are incorporated into the TCP/IP–OSI hybrid architecture that is used on the Internet and most internets.   119

Regression analysis   A type of supervised data mining that estimates the values of parameters in a linear equation. Used to determine the relative influence of variables on an outcome and also to predict future values of that outcome.   285

Relation   The more formal name for a database table.   80

Relational databases   Databases that carry their data in the form of tables and that represent relationships using foreign keys.   80

Relationship   An association among entities or entity instances in an E-R model or an association among rows of a table in a relational database.   90

Relevant information   Information that is appropriate to both the context and the subject.   12

Remote computing   The process of a program on one computer invoking programs on a second computer.   250

Report   A presentation of data in a structured, or meaningful context.   85

Reporting system A system that creates information from disparate data sources and delivers that information to the proper users on a timely basis. 269

Reporting tools Programs that read data from a variety of sources, process that data, produce formatted reports, and deliver those reports to the users who need them. 268

Repository A CASE tool database that contains documents, data, prototypes, and program code for the software or system under development. 174

RFM analysis A way of analyzing and ranking customers according to the recency, frequency, and monetary value of their purchases. 275

Risk The likelihood of an adverse occurrence. 342

Root servers Special computers that are distributed around the world that maintain a list of IP addresses of servers that resolve each type of TLD. 142

Rotational delay On a disk, the time it takes the data to rotate under the read/write head. The faster the disk spins, the shorter the rotational delay. 57

Routing table A table of data used by a router to determine where to send a packet that it receives. 137

Rows Also called *records,* groups of columns in a database table. 78

Safeguard Any action, device, procedure, technique, or other measure that reduces a system's vulnerability to a threat. 343

Schedule One of four dimensions of feasibility. 162

Secure Socket Layer (SSL) A protocol that uses both asymmetric and symmetric encryption. SSL is a protocol layer that works between Levels 4 (transport) and 5 (application) of the TCP–OSI protocol architecture. When SSL is in use, the browser address will begin with https://. The most recent version of SSI is called TLS. 133a, 346

Seek time On a disk, the time it takes the read/write arm to position the head over the correct circle. Seek time is determined by the make and model of the disk device. 57

Segments The containers that a TCP uses to carry messages. The TCP program places identifying data at the front and end of each segment that are akin to the To and From addresses that you would put on a letter for the postal mail. 120

Semantic security Concerns the unintended release of protected information through the release of a combination of reports or documents that are independently not protected. 275a

Server tier In the three-tier architecture, the tier that consists of computers that run Web servers to generate Web pages and other data in response to requests from browsers. Web servers also process application programs. 236

Service description With Web services, an XML file that details what programs exist on another computer and how to communicate with those programs. 252

Service packs A large group of fixes that solve low-priority software problems. Users apply service packs in much the same way that they apply patches, except that service packs typically involve fixes to hundreds or thousands of problems. 170

Simple Mail Transfer Protocol (SMTP) A Layer-5 architecture used to send email. Normally used in conjunction with other Layer 5 protocols (POP3, IMAP) for receiving email. 119

Smart card A plastic card similar to a credit card that has a microchip. The microchip, which holds much more data than a magnetic strip, is loaded with identifying data. Normally requires a PIN. 344

Sniffing A technique for intercepting computer communications. With wired networks, sniffing requires a physical connection to the network. With wireless networks, no such connection is required. 339

Software Instructions for computers. One of the five fundamental components of an information system. 4

Software piracy When programs are used in violation of the license agreement. Piracy occurs on a large scale when a company illegally copies a program and sells it on the black market. Also occurs on a small scale when one user allows another user to load the program on his or her computer in violation of the license agreement. 61a

SOHO (small office, home office) An acronym for the small office/home office market. 141

Special function cards Cards that can be added to the computer to augment the computer's basic capabilities. 49

Special-purpose computers Computers that are designed to perform one and only one function. The logic for that function may be designed into hardware or it may be written as computer programs and installed as firmware. 48

Spoofing When someone pretends to be someone else with the intent of obtaining unauthorized data. If you pretend to be your professor, you are spoofing your professor. 337

Spyware Programs installed on the user's computer without the user's knowledge or permission that reside in the background and, unknown to the user, observe the user's actions and keystrokes, modify computer activity, and report the user's activities to sponsoring organizations. Malicious spyware captures keystrokes to obtain user names, passwords, account numbers, and other sensitive information. Other spyware is used for marketing analyses, observing what users do, Web sites visited, products examined and purchased, and so forth. 350

SQL Server A popular enterprise-class DBMS product from Microsoft. 82

Static reports Reports that are prepared once from the underlying data, and they do not change. A report of the past year's sales, for example, is a static report. 270

Steering committee A group of senior managers from the major business functions that works with the CIO to set the IS priorities and decide among major IS projects and alternatives. 310

Storage hardware Hardware that saves data and programs. Magnetic disk is by far the most common storage device, although optical disks such as CDs and DVDs also are popular. 48

Strategic decisions   Decisions that concern broader-scope, organizational issues.   34

Strong password   A password with the following characteristics: seven or more characters; does not contain the user's user name, real name, or company name; does not contain a complete dictionary word, in any language; is different from the user's previous passwords; and contains both upper- and lowercase letters, numbers, and special characters.   5a

Structured decision   A type of decision for which there is a formalized and accepted method for making the decision.   34

Structured Query Language (SQL)   An international standard language for processing database data.   82

Supervised data mining   A form of data mining in which data miners develop a model prior to the analysis and apply statistical techniques to data to estimate values of the parameters of the model.   284

Supplier relationship management (SRM)   A business process for managing all contacts between an organization and its suppliers.   245

Supply chain   A network of organizations and facilities that transforms raw materials into products delivered to customers.   239

Supply chain profitability   The difference between the sum of the revenue generated by the supply chain and the sum of the costs that all organizations in the supply chain incur to obtain that revenue.   243

Support   In market-basket terminology, the probability that two items will be purchased together.   286

Sustainable   How likely an organization will be able to maintain a competitive advantage. For example, when an organization adds value to its product and obtains an increase in price, it may not be able to maintain that price. Suppliers upstream may demand a portion of the value added by raising their prices. Similarly, depending on how competitive an industry is, other firms may copy the value added by the firm.   231

Switch   A special-purpose computer that receives and transmits data across a network.   122

Switch table   A table of data used by switch to determine where to send frames that it receives.   137

Switching costs   Organizations can lock in customers by making it difficult or expensive for customers to switch to another product.   27

Symmetric encryption   An encryption method whereby the same key is used to encode and to decode the message.   133a, 346

Symmetrical digital subscriber lines (SDSL)   DSL lines that have the same upload and download speeds.   129

System   A group of components that interact to achieve some purpose.   4

Systems analysts   IS professionals who understand both business and technology. They are active throughout the systems development process and play a key role in moving the project from conception to conversion and, ulti-mately, maintenance. Systems analysts integrate the work of the programmers, testers, and users.   163

System conversion   The process of *converting* business activity from the old system to the new.   168

Systems analysis and design   The process of creating and maintaining information systems. It is sometimes called systems development.   157

Systems development   The process of creating and maintaining information systems. It is sometimes called *systems analysis and design*.   157

Systems development life cycle (SDLC)   The classical process used to develop information systems. These basic tasks of systems development are combined into the following phases: system definition, requirements analysis, component design, implementation, and system mainte-nance (fix or enhance).   160

Table   Also called a *file*, a group of similar rows or records in a database.   78

Tags   In markup languages such as HTML and XML, nota-tion used to define a data element for display or other pur-poses.   235

TCG/NGSCB   A joint project launched by Microsoft, Intel, and other companies to control the copying of files and programs. *TCG* stands for Trusted Computing Group and refers to an organization of computer and software vendors created to develop standards for the project. *NGSCB* stands for Next Generation Secure Computing Base.   61a

TCP/IP (Transmission Control Program/Internet Protocol) architecture   A protocol architecture having four layers that was developed by IETF. It is used as part of the TCP/IP–OSI architecture.   119

TCP/IP–OSI architecture   A protocol architecture having five layers that evolved as a hybrid of the TCP/IP and the OSI architecture. This architecture is used on the Internet and on most internets.   119

Technical feasibility   One of four dimensions of feasibil-ity.   162, 163

Technical safeguards   Safeguards that involve the hard-ware and software components of an information sys-tem.   344

Terabyte (TB)   1,024GB.   51

Test plan   Groups of sequences of actions that users will take when using the new system.   168

Three-tier architecture   Architecture used by most e-commerce server applications. The tiers refer to three different classes of computers. The user tier consists of users' computers that have browsers that request and process Web pages. The server tier consists of computers that run Web servers and in the process generate Web pages and other data in response to requests from browsers. Web servers also process application programs. The third tier is the database tier, which runs the DBMS that processes the database.   236

Timely information   Information that is produced in time for its intended use.   12

Top-level domain (TLD)   The last letters in any domain name. For example, in the domain name *www.icann.org* the top-level domain is *.org*. Similarly, in the domain name *www.ibm.com*, *.com* is the top-level domain. For non-U.S. domain names, the top-level domain is often a two-letter abbreviation for the country in which the service resides.   142

Transaction processing system (TPS)   An information system that supports operational decision making.   34

Transmission Control Program (TCP)   TCP operates at Layer 4 of the TCP/IP–OSI architecture. TCP is used in two ways: as the name of a Layer 4 *protocol* and as part of the name of the TCP/IP–OSI protocol architecture. In fact, the architecture gets its name because it usually includes the TCP protocol. TCP receives messages from Layer 5 protocols (like http) and breaks those messages up into segments that it sends to a Layer 3 protocol (like IP).   120

Transport Layer Security (TLS)   A protocol, using both asymmetric and symmetric encryption, that works between Levels 4 (transport) and 5 (application) of the TCP–OSI protocol architecture. TLS is new name for a later version of SSL.   347

Trojan horses   Viruses that masquerade as useful programs or files. The name refers to the gigantic mock-up of a horse that was filled with soldiers and moved into Troy during the Peloponnesian Wars. A typical Trojan horse appears to be a computer game, an MP3 music file, or some other useful, innocuous program.   53a

Tunnel   A virtual, private pathway over a public or shared network from the VPN client to the VPN server.   132

Uncertainty   Those things we don't know that we don't know.   342

Unified Modeling Language (UML)   A series of diagramming techniques that facilitates OOP development. UML has dozens of different diagrams for all phases of system development. UML does not require or promote any particular development process.   89, 176

Unified process (UP)   A methodology designed for use with the Unified Modeling Language (UML) that uses use cases that describe the application of a new system.   177

Uniform resource locator (URL)   A document's address on the Web. URLs begin on the right with a top level domain, and, moving left, include a domain name and then are followed by optional data that locates a document within that domain.   142

Unix   An operating system developed at Bell Labs in the 1970s. It has been the workhorse of the scientific and engineering communities since then.   61

Unshielded twisted pair (UTP) cable   A type of cable used to connect the computers, printers, switches, and other devices on a LAN. A UTP cable has four pairs of twisted wire. A device called an RJ-45 connector is used to connect the UTP cable into NIC devices.   122

Unstructured decision   A type of decision for which there is no agreed-on decision-making method.   34

Unsupervised data mining   A form of data mining whereby the analysts do not create a model or hypothesis before running the analysis. Instead, they apply the data-mining technique to the data and observe the results. With this method, analysts create hypotheses after the analysis to explain the patterns found.   284

Use case   A description of an application of a new system that is used with the Unified Modeling Language (UML) and the Unified Process (UP).   177

User accounts   A security feature of network and DBMS accounts whereby each user is assigned specific permissions and roles. Normally, users are authenticated to accounts using passwords. When assigned a role, the user inherits all permissions for that role.   85a

User role   A named set of permissions used as a security feature of networks and DBMS products. When users are assigned to the role, they inherit that set of permissions. User roles simplify network and database security administration.   85a

User tier   In the three-tier architecture, the tier that consists of computers that have browsers that request and process Web pages.   236

Usurpation   Occurs when unauthorized programs invade a computer system and replace legitimate programs. Such unauthorized programs typically shut down the legitimate system and substitute their own processing.   339

Value   The total revenue that a customer is willing to spend for a product or service.   207

Value chain   A network of value-creating activities.   207

Value-added resellers   Generally small, local companies that analyze customer needs, determine computer requirements, buy the hardware, and then set up and maintain the computer systems.   50

Vertical-market application   Software that serves the needs of a specific industry. Examples of such programs are those used by dental offices to schedule appointments and bill patients, those used by auto mechanics to keep track of customer data and customers' automobile repairs, and those used by parts warehouses to track inventory, purchases, and sales.   62

Virtual private network (VPN)   A WAN connection alternative that uses the Internet or a private internet to create the appearance of private point-to-point connections. In the IT world, the term *virtual* means something that appears to exist that does not exist in fact. Here, a VPN uses the public Internet to create the appearance of a private connection.   131

Visual development tools   Tools used in RAD projects to improve developer productivity. An example is Microsoft's Visual Studio.Net.   175

Volatile memory   Data that will be lost when the computer or device is not powered.   53

Vulnerability   An opening or a weakness in a security system. Some vulnerabilities exist because there are no safeguards or because the existing safeguards are ineffective.   343

Waterfall   The fiction that one phase of the SDLC can be completed in its entirety and the project can progress, without any backtracking, to the next phase of the SDLC.

Projects seldom are that simple; backtracking is normally required.   171

Web farm   A facility that runs multiple Web servers. Work is distributed among the computers in a Web farm so as to maximize throughput.   237

Web pages   Documents encoded in HTML that are created, transmitted, and consumed using the World Wide Web.   235

Web server   A program that processes the HTTP protocol and transmits Web pages on demand. Web servers also process application programs.   236

Web storefront   In e-commerce, a Web-based application that enables customers to enter and manage their orders.   231

White-hat hackers   People who break into networks for the purpose of helping the organization that operates the network to identify security weaknesses.   351a

Wide area network (WANs)   A network that connects computers located at different geographic locations.   117

Windows   An operating system designed and sold by Microsoft. It is the most widely used operating system.   60

Wired Equivalent Privacy (WEP)   A wireless security standard developed the IEEE 802.11 committee that was insufficiently tested before it was deployed in communications equipment. It has serious flaws.   345

Wireless NIC (WNIC)   Devices that enable wireless networks by communicating with wireless access points. Such devices can be cards that slide into the PCMA slot or they can be built-in, onboard devices. WNICs operate according to the 802.11 protocol.   124

World Wide Web Consortium (W3C)   A body that sponsors the development and dissemination of Web standards.   250

Worm   A virus that propagates itself using the Internet or some other computer network. Worm code is written specifically to infect another computer as quickly as possible.   53a

Worth-its-cost information   When an appropriate relationship exists between the cost of information and its value.   13

WPA (Wi-Fi Protected Access)   An improved wireless security standard developed by the IEEE 802.11 committee to fix the flaws of the Wired Equivalent Privacy (WEP) standard. Only newer wireless hardware uses this technique.   346

WPA2   An improved version of WPA.   346

XML schema   An XML document that specifies the structure of other XML documents. An XML schema is metadata for other XML documents. For example, a SalesOrder XML schema specifies the structure of SalesOrder documents.   250

XML Web services   Sometimes called *Web services*; a set of standards that facilitate distributed computing using Internet technology. The goal of Web services is to provide a standardized way for programs to access one another remotely, without the need to develop proprietary solutions.   252

NOTE: Page numbers in italics refer to illustrations; page numbers followed by n refer to footnotes